S0-BYR-266

READER'S DIGEST

THE
MAKE IT
YOURSELF
GIFT
BOOK

GIFTS TO MAKE AT HOME FOR ALL
YOUR FAMILY AND FRIENDS

Adapted from *The Make-It-Yourself Gift Book*,
published in Australia in 1995.
Copyright © 1995 The Reader's Digest (Australia) Pty Limited

Copyright © 1997 The Reader's Digest Association (Canada) Ltd.
Copyright © 1997 The Reader's Digest Association, Inc.
Copyright © 1996 Reader's Digest Association Far East Limited
Philippines copyright © 1996 Reader's Digest Association Far East Limited

All rights reserved. Unauthorized reproduction, in any manner, is prohibited.
Reader's Digest and the Pegasus logo are registered trademarks of The Reader's Digest Association, Inc.
Printed in Canada.
For information on this and other Reader's Digest products or to request a catalogue, please call our 24-hour
Customer Service hotline at 1-800-465-0780.
You can also visit us on the World Wide Web at http://www.readersdigest.ca

Canadian Cataloguing in Publication Data
Main entry under title: The make it yourself gift book: gifts to make at
home for all your family and friends
Includes index.
ISBN 0-88850-605-8
1. Handicraft.   2. Gifts.
TT157.M34 1997   745.5   C97-900563-9

97 98 99 / 5 4 3 2 1

READER'S DIGEST

THE
MAKE IT
YOURSELF
GIFT
BOOK

GIFTS TO MAKE AT HOME FOR ALL
YOUR FAMILY AND FRIENDS

PUBLISHED BY THE READER'S DIGEST ASSOCIATION (CANADA) LTD. MONTREAL

CONTENTS

Sweethearts, brides & grooms

Parents

Homemakers, hosts & hostesses

Edible gifts

Techniques

Indexes

Acknowledgments

U.K./AUSTRALIAN STAFF

EDITORS
Janet Healey, Rosemary Wilkinson

PICTURE RESEARCH EDITOR
Martin Smith

DESIGNERS
Kate Finnie, Mike Spiller

CRAFT CONSULTANTS
Sally Milner, Hilary More, Tonia Todman

CRAFT ADVISERS
Robyn Baker & Margaret Broun (Hornsby College of TAFE),
Laurine Croasdale, Maureen Holmes, Barbara Lennon
(Coats Patons Crafts), Marilyn McCann, Effie Mitrofanis (DMC),
Lucia Ruffo, Phillip Searle, David Thompson, David Zaikowski

EDITORIAL ASSISTANTS
Maggie Aldhamland, Tom Cabot

ILLUSTRATORS
Gerry Blake, Stephen Dew, Kalliopi Papageorgiou,
Colin Seton, Mike Spiller

STYLISTS
Mary-Anne Danaher, Louise Owens

PHOTOGRAPHERS
Andrew Elton, Mark Gatehouse

PATTERN MAKER
Lesley Griffith

CANADIAN STAFF

PROJECT EDITOR
Anita Winterberg

ART DIRECTOR
John McGuffie

DESIGNER
Cécile Germain

PROOFREADERS
Gilles Humbert,
Joseph Marchetti,
Judy Yelon

RESEARCHERS
Kathy Giangaspero,
Melanie Kindrachuk

PRODUCTION MANAGER
Holger Lorenzen

PRODUCTION ASSISTANT
Susan Wong

EDITORIAL ADMINISTRATOR
Elizabeth Eastman

The publishers would also like to thank Dover Publications,
Mineola, NY, for permission to use the images on the printed
T-shirts (pages 100-1).

ABOUT THIS BOOK

Throughout history and in every culture, gifts have always been a traditional way of expressing love, thanks and good wishes, and of celebrating life's many happy occasions. Giving a gift means giving part of yourself.

In this busy modern world, buying gifts can be a boring chore, but with this book you'll put the joy back into giving by making your own gifts for every occasion. And you'll rediscover the great pleasure that even the simplest handmade gift can bestow on both giver and receiver.

How often have you spent hours trudging around stores shopping in vain for just the right gift? Now you can spend that time much more enjoyably and profitably in making your own gifts at home. At the same time, you'll be honing the craft skills you already have and learning new ones. And you'll have the satisfaction of putting your creativity to work, because making the gifts in this book will give you lots of ideas for designing and making your own unique and original gifts.

The projects in the *Make-It-Yourself Gift Book* cover a range of crafts that you can do easily at home – needlecraft, yarn crafts, woodwork, découpage, papier-mâché, stenciling, folk art . . . and many more. If you've done only basic sewing, you'll find simple gifts to make, either by hand or with a sewing machine, and you'll be learning more about sewing at the same time. And if you're a more experienced sewer, you can extend your skills even further by finding out how to make exquisite heirloom-style garments and luxury items such as the patchwork evening bag.

USING THE BOOK
Each chapter contains gifts specially designed to suit a particular kind of recipient. There are gifts for children, young people, partners, parents, friends, homemakers, hosts and hostesses, and more. Each chapter has gifts suitable for various occasions, and each includes some "quick and easy" gifts and some that are more difficult to make, so you can choose a gift according to your skills and the time you have to spare. And, of course, many of these gifts can be made for people other than the recipients described by the chapter title.

CHOOSING WHAT TO MAKE
To find the perfect gift to make for that special person in your life, look through the relevant chapter. Are you looking for something to give an extra special infant? How about a handmade christening gown, modeled on a Victorian design and made of delicate lace and batiste. Or for a beloved Dad, you could make a wine rack to hold his favorite vintages.

A special feature of the book is the range of "quick and easy" gifts. These are gifts that a beginner can tackle with confidence, and that can be made in three hours or less – just the thing for a free afternoon or evening. Most of these gifts need little equipment and can be made in the comfort of an armchair or a garden seat. Find the quick and easy gifts by looking for the symbol ● at the top of the page and in the contents and index listings.

MAKING THE GIFTS
Read all the instructions carefully, including the hints and notes, before you begin to make your gift. This is important because you need to understand exactly how the gift is made and how long it will take you. Think how frustrating it would be to start a découpage project for a birthday present in a week's time, only to discover that you need weeks to apply all the layers of varnish.

The instructions for making the gifts are written so that they are easy to follow and will give you the best possible result. The tinted boxes contain hints to make the work easier, and variations on the gifts illustrated – use these to spark your imagination and create your own craft works.

A list of **what you need** is the first information you will come to, so that you will know what equipment and materials you already have and what you need to buy. In some projects we have listed trade names and specific colors for paints or yarns. These were the materials used to make the gifts illustrated. However, the colors of paints and yarns change from time to time, so you may not be able to find the exact ones specified. Craft shops and other suppliers have color charts for the major manufacturers and will be able to advise you how to choose a suitable substitute.

All **paper sizes** listed in the book follow standards established by the International Organization for Standardization (ISO). Refer to the following list of ISO paper sizes when purchasing paper for a project: A0 paper (841 mm x 1189 mm); A1 paper (594 mm x 841 mm); A2 paper (420 mm x 594 mm); A3 paper (297 mm x 420 mm); A4 paper (210 mm x 297 mm); and A5 paper (148 mm x 210 mm).

For most projects, the list of what you need is followed by a reference to the **technique pages** at the back of the book. These contain basic instructions for the major crafts you need to make the gifts. If you have not attempted a particular craft before, or are not completely confident about your skills, read the relevant techniques section before beginning to make the item.

Then come the **instructions** for making the gift. These are divided into sections, each containing a numbered sequence of steps. There are also step-by-step diagrams illustrating the procedures to follow.

The first section is usually to do with the **preparation** of your materials. Preparation is key to making any craft project. If you try to save time or money by taking shortcuts or using inferior materials, you may be disappointed with the final product, so be as careful with the preparation as you are when you are making and finishing the project.

After preparing the materials, you are ready for the exciting part – **making the gift**. For simple projects, this part may consist of only one section, but for more complex projects there may be several sections. Just follow the numbered sequence of steps and the diagrams.

Finally, there's a section on giving your gift **a truly professional finish**. Again, follow the numbered sequence of steps and you can't go wrong.

USING THE INDEXES

There are three indexes: a gifts and crafts index, a techniques index and a general index. The gifts and crafts index lists all the projects in alphabetical order and shows which crafts you need to make them and whether there is a master pattern. The techniques index provides a quick reference to the techniques section in case you need to look up a particular stitch or folk art stroke. The general index divides the gifts into categories of use – for example, "kitchen gifts" has the subcategories "equipment," "furniture," and "picture," so that you can quickly find a gift for a dedicated cook.

USING THE MASTER PATTERNS

Supplied with this book are five sheets of master patterns, printed on both sides. The instructions for each gift tell you whether you need a master pattern and what its number is. Identify the pattern pieces on the sheet and trace them carefully to make an individual pattern that you can keep in case you want to use it again. On page 351 you'll find a key to the master pattern pieces, so that you can be sure you have found all the pieces of the pattern.

GENERAL HINTS

Just as important as the preparation of the materials for making a specific item is the organization of your working time, space and equipment. Follow a few simple rules and achieve good results every time.

Allow **time** to do the job properly. For needlecraft and woodwork, leave enough time to mark and cut pieces accurately. Many crafts require you to wait while glue, paint or varnish dries before you can proceed to the next step – and don't forget that high humidity can slow down the drying process. If you are in too much of a hurry, you risk wasting the time you have already put in and having to start again.

Your **working space** needs to be well organized too. If possible, dedicate a room – or even part of a room if space is a problem – to the craft you are currently working on, so that you don't have to clear everything out of the way each time you stop work. Remember too that it is important that the area where you do craft work is free of dust, well lit but protected from strong sunlight, and well ventilated.

Buy the **best-quality equipment** you can afford, especially if you plan to do a lot of craft work – it will save you money in the end. Scissors, craft knives, pins and needles, and saws, chisels and hammers should be kept sharp and rust-free. Make sure you have the right equipment for the job; craft and hardware stores are very helpful in finding the right equipment or suggesting suitable substitutes.

If you are trying out a new craft, **practice the techniques** using scraps until you are satisfied that you have mastered them. You will be quicker and more proficient when you come to make the gift itself.

The *Make-It-Yourself Gift Book* is more than a source of great ideas for gifts; you can also use it to improve your craft skills and learn new ones. And everyone in the family will find something that they can enjoy making and giving. With some adult supervision, children can make many of the simpler projects – an excellent way of introducing them to the delights of making items that are beautiful as well as useful, which is what craft is all about.

BABIES

We all want to express our joy when a new baby is born. In this chapter you'll find a great selection of gifts that you can make to welcome a new arrival and to delight the baby's parents.

Classic christening gown

What parent could resist this beautifully crafted heirloom, which will certainly be handed down for generations to come? The design is adapted from a Victorian christening gown.

Master pattern A3(a–e) • 1.5 m batiste, 115 cm wide • Swiss or suitable fabric laces: 12 m beading with entredeux, 10 mm wide, 5.6 m fabric insertion lace, 30–40 mm wide, 2.8 m fagoting, 5–10 mm wide, 9 m edging lace, 40 mm wide • 13 m satin ribbon, 2 mm wide (for beading insertion) • 3 small pearl buttons • fine machine thread • colored basting thread • needles: fine sharp, fine machine • lace pins • tracing paper • pencil • scissors • sewing machine
● *Technique pages 292–301, 303–4, 343–4*

❶ CUTTING OUT THE FABRIC

1 Using tracing paper and a pencil, trace all the pattern pieces from the master pattern and cut them out. Make sure you transfer all markings.
2 Pull a thread at each raw edge of the batiste to find the straight grain. Following the cutting guide, pin all pattern pieces except the front panel to the fabric and cut them out.
3 Cut a 12.5 cm strip the width of the fabric and a 12.5 cm strip half the width of the fabric. Join these strips selvage to selvage with a small flat seam to make a strip 12.5 cm by 1.7 m (this will be used to make the tucked insert for the heirloom fabric). The

rest of the fabric is used for bias and straight grain strips for the neck binding and the placket.

❷ MAKING THE LACE FABRIC

See the box "Heirloom sewing techniques" (page 14) for the methods of assembling the heirloom fabric.

Tucked insert

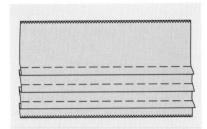

1 From one long edge of the 1.7 m strip of batiste, measure three intervals 2.5 cm apart. Pull a thread the whole width of the fabric at each interval. (This is to ensure that the tucks are stitched on the straight grain.)
2 Press folds along the pulled threads and machine 5 mm from the folds. Roll and whip the top and bottom edges of the tucked inserts, using heirloom sewing method 1.

Lace inserts

1 Cut four pieces of beading with entredeux 2.8 m long, two pieces of insertion lace 2.8 m long, and a piece of edging lace 4.8 m long.

2 Gather the edging lace until it measures 2.8 m, using heirloom sewing method 4.
3 Following steps A to H below, and using the appropriate heirloom sewing method, assemble a composite lace fabric about 2.8 m long by joining: **A** beading (method 2) to **B** insertion lace (method 2) to **C** beading (method 3) to **D** fagoting (method 3) to **E** beading (method 2) to **F** insertion lace (method 2) to **G** beading (method 2) to **H** gathered edging lace.

Adjusting the skirt length

Having made the lace fabric, you can adjust the length of the skirt.
1 Measure the finished width of the lace fabric. If you are making a skirt with tucks and lace edging, subtract 3.4 cm (this allows for three 5 mm tucks and a 4 mm seam allowance to roll and whip). Cut this amount from the hem of the skirt.
2 For a skirt with lace edging only, subtract 4 mm (this allows a 4 mm seam allowance to roll and whip). Cut this amount from the hem of the skirt.

❸ MAKING THE FRONT PANEL

1 From both the lace fabric and the tucked fabric, cut the following pieces: one 40 cm wide, one 35 cm wide, one 29 cm wide, one 23 cm wide, and one 18 cm wide. (The rest of the lace fabric is for the hem of the skirt.)
2 Using heirloom sewing method 2, join the pieces of lace fabric and tucked fabric of equal width to each other. Find the vertical centers of all five pieces of heirloom fabric and mark them using a needle and colored basting thread.

Cutting guide

Pin all the pattern pieces except the center front panel to the folded batiste as shown, and cut them out. From the remaining fabric, cut one strip 12.5 cm x 115 cm, and one strip 12.5 cm x 57.5 cm; these strips will be joined and pin-tucked to make the tucked inserts for the heirloom fabric. Use the fabric left over to cut the strip for the placket and the bias strip for the neck. Cut out the center front panel from the assembled heirloom fabric.

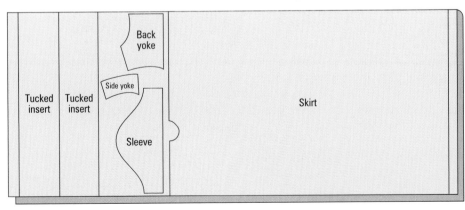

Tucked insert | Tucked insert | Back yoke | Side yoke | Sleeve | Skirt

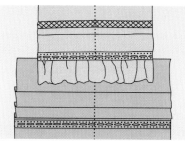

3 Starting with the widest piece and keeping the tucked part uppermost, match the basted center lines and join all pieces together with the edging

lace overlapping, using method 2. Press the edging lace down.
4 Place the center front of the front panel pattern piece on the basted center line of the heirloom fabric. Pin the pattern piece to the fabric and cut out.
5 Thread the ribbon through all the beading. Trim 6 mm of the 1 cm seam allowance from both sides of the front panel and roll and whip down each edge (heirloom sewing method 1), ensuring that the ends of the ribbon are caught in the stitching.

6 Cut two pieces of edging lace one-and-three-quarter times the length of the front panel (about 1.75 m). Roll and whip one short end of each piece.

7 Roll, whip and gather the two pieces of edging lace, using heirloom sewing method 4, and then stitch them to the long edges of the front panel with the rolled and whipped short ends at the hem, using heirloom sewing method 2.

HINT
Use flat mother-of-pearl buttons that will not stick into delicate skin and cause discomfort.

HEIRLOOM SEWING TECHNIQUES

To create the heirloom fabric, you will need four basic machine sewing techniques. These are referred to in the instructions as heirloom sewing methods 1, 2, 3 and 4. If you have not attempted heirloom sewing before, practice these techniques on scraps of fabric and lace before starting to make the christening gown.

All the techniques use the sewing machine's zigzag function, and the aim is to join the components of the heirloom fabric together with as little bulk as possible. Set the stitch length short enough to hold the fabrics together securely, but not so short as to form a closed satin stitch.

To make laces easier to handle when machine stitching, spray them with a commercial fabric stiffener or starch.

1 Roll and whip: Place the cut edge of the fabric about 2 mm to the right of the center of the machine foot. Set the zigzag width at 3–5 mm so that the needle will come down on either side of the cut edge, thus forming the fabric into a fine roll.

2 Joining beading with entredeux to

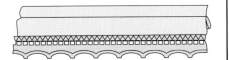

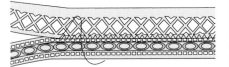

fabric or fabric insertion lace: With the right sides together, machine zigzag a fine seam along the raw edges.

3 Joining two straight edges (for example, beading with entredeux to fagoting): Trim the edges of the laces and butt them together. Do not overlap them. Set the zigzag width to catch both laces and machine with the right sides facing up.

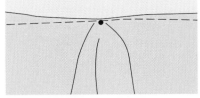

4 Roll, whip and gather (for example, gathering lace): Proceed as for roll and whip, but place a strong thread – buttonhole twist or quilting thread – under the center of the machine foot. Guide the thread through the center of the zigzag as you work. Pull the thread up to gather the lace to the required length.

4 ASSEMBLING THE GOWN

When you are assembling the christening gown, use a 1 cm seam allowance for all standard seams.

Skirt placket

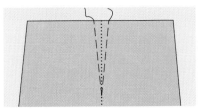

1 Make the placket by machine stitching about 4 mm down either side of the center back to the point, taking one stitch across to turn at the point. Cut between the lines of stitching.

2 Cut a strip of batiste 22 cm x 3 cm along the straight grain. Open the placket right out so that the stitching is in a straight line. With the right side of the strip to the wrong side of the skirt, machine along the previous line of stitching. When you reach the point, leave the needle down, raise the presser foot and push the excess fabric back out of the way. Lower the presser foot and finish the stitching.

3 Press down 5 mm along the raw edge of the strip. Fold the strip over to the right side of the skirt, place the pressed edge over the machine stitching, and machine topstitch as close to the edge as possible.

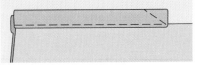

4 Machine stitch the end of the placket diagonally to reinforce it, and press the placket into place.

Skirt hem

1 If you are making tucks at the lower edge of the skirt, sew three tucks following the steps for tucked inserts in "Making the lace fabric."

2 Join the remaining piece of lace fabric to the hem of the skirt, using heirloom sewing method 2.

Skirt to yokes

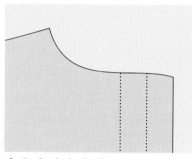

1 On both the back yoke pieces, press creases along the fold line of the self-interfacing and the fold line of the button extension.
2 Machine two rows of large gathering stitches along the top edges of the front and back skirt. With right sides together, match the dots on the four yoke pieces and the skirt piece. Align the placket edge with the fold line of the button extension. Adjust the gathers and machine stitch the seams.

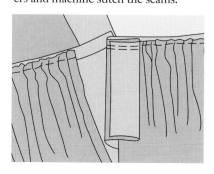

3 Press the self-interfacing to the wrong side along the fold line. Fold the back yoke over the skirt along the button extension line and stitch the skirt to the yokes through all layers along the seam line.
4 Neaten the edges with a fine zigzag stitch and press the seams toward the yokes. The finished seam will be about 4 mm wide.

Front panel to garment

1 Trim the front seam allowances of the side panels to 4 mm.
2 With right sides together, attach the front panel to the garment, using heirloom sewing method 2. Widen the zigzag to catch all three layers.

Shoulder seams and neck binding

1 With right sides together, machine stitch the shoulder seams. Neaten the edges with a narrow zigzag.
2 Cut a bias strip of batiste 4 cm wide and about 35 cm long. Press it in half lengthwise, wrong sides together.

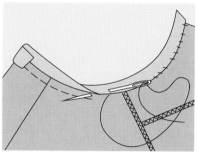

3 Trim a 1 cm seam allowance from the neck and machine stitch the bias strip to the right side of the garment using a 5 mm seam. Wrap about 1 cm of binding around to the wrong side at either side of the back opening. Fold the binding over to the wrong side and slipstitch it into place.

Sleeves

1 Using heirloom sewing method 2, join 70 cm of beading with entredeux to 70 cm of edging lace. (Do not gather the edging lace.) Cut the piece in half and attach one piece to each sleeve hem, using heirloom sewing method 2.
2 Sew two rows of gathering stitches around the shoulder line of the sleeves between the dots.

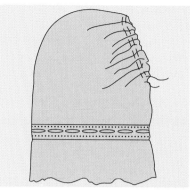

3 With right sides together and the lace edging aligned, machine stitch the underarm seams and neaten them with a fine zigzag stitch. The finished seams will be about 4 mm wide.

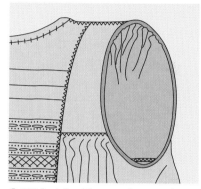

4 With right sides together, set the sleeves into the armholes, matching the dots and notches and adjusting the gathers evenly. Machine stitch the seams and zigzag to neaten.

5 FINISHING THE GOWN

1 Machine three horizontal buttonholes in one back yoke buttonhole extension, in the positions marked on the master pattern. Sew the buttons to the other back yoke on the center back line, in positions to correspond with the buttonholes.
2 Cut the remainder of the ribbon in half and thread the pieces through the beading on the sleeves. Use the threaded ribbons to gather the sleeves slightly, and tie the ribbons in a bow.

NOTE
If the laces you choose are wider or narrower than those specified, work out a plan for sewing the laces together that will give you a piece of lace fabric about 10 cm wide.

Jingle bears

The bright colors, contrasting stitching and jingling bells of this string of soft bears are sure to hold a baby's attention and will not drive mom crazy!

`--` Backstitch	• French knot
▲ Satin stitch	✿ Spider's web stitch
⅄ Fly stitch	◊ Lazy daisy stitch

WHAT YOU NEED

Master pattern **A7(a)** • 2 m each of red, yellow and blue cording • 3 pieces of different colored fabric, each 15 cm x 20 cm • polyester stuffing, 50 g • small quantities of stranded embroidery cotton: green, yellow, blue, brown, black • sewing thread to match the fabric • 1 m red embroidery ribbon, 4 mm wide • 50 cm blue embroidery ribbon, 4 mm wide • strong sewing thread • needles: size 8 crewel, size 20 tapestry • 4 bells (enclosed safety variety) • tracing paper • pencil • scissors

● *Technique pages 292–301, 307–14, 343–4*

❶ BRAIDING THE CORDS

1 Place the three cords side by side. Knot them together 4 cm from one end and knot them again a further 4 cm along. This forms a loop for attaching the toy to the carriage.
2 Braid the three cords together to make a length as wide as the carriage and tie off the cords. (Two meters of cord will make just over a meter of braid.) Tie off the cord to form another loop. Trim surplus cord.

❷ CUTTING OUT THE BEARS

1 Trace the design from the master pattern, including the dots that indicate the turning holes.
2 Fold the fabric in half, pin the pattern to the fabric and cut out to make two identical bear shapes. Repeat for each piece of fabric.

❸ EMBROIDERING THE BEARS

1 Using two strands of embroidery cotton and following the stitch guide, embroider the bears' eyes in black and their mouths and noses in brown.
2 Following the stitch guide, embroider the tummies of the bears with the ribbon and embroidery cotton. Work the tummy design on the blue bear and the yellow bear with red ribbon in spider's web stitch, and on the third bear work the tummy design in lazy daisy stitch using blue ribbon.
3 Embroider the stems of the small flowers in fly stitch using two strands of green cotton. Form the flowers with French knots, using two strands of yellow embroidery cotton for two of the bears and two strands of blue embroidery cotton for the third.

Stitch guide

Silk ribbon is best for ribbon embroidery, as it sits and folds more smoothly and is easier to manage than synthetic ribbon.

❹ FINISHING

1 Using thread to match the fabrics and with right sides facing, stitch around each bear to join the backs to the fronts, leaving the sections between the dots open.
2 Trim and clip the curves and turn the work right side out.
3 Fill the bears with polyester stuffing. Close the opening with ladder stitch and then sew across the ears, close to the head, using running stitch.
4 Position the bears along the cord and sew each paw to it. Sew the bells to the cord between the bears. Use strong sewing thread and attach the bells and bears very firmly.

VARIATION

To adapt this toy for a crib, lengthen the braided cord to match the width of the crib and add extra bears as required. For each additional bear you will need 15 cm x 20 cm of colored fabric and a bell, plus a small quantity of filling.

New baby sampler

The birth of a baby is a very special time for parents, and what better way to mark the occasion than with this cross-stitch sampler? Mounted in a suitable frame, it makes a unique and lasting gift.

WHAT YOU NEED

Master pattern J68(a–b) • 50 cm x 45 cm 14 gauge aida cloth • stranded cotton: Anchor colors 1 (white), 11 (red), 24 (pink), 216 (green), 293 (yellow), 313 (orange), 355 (light brown), 382 (dark brown), 9159 (blue) • colored basting thread • needle: size 24 tapestry • embroidery hoop • picture frame with an inside measurement of 41 cm x 36.5 cm • acid-free white backing board • acid-free mounting board • linen carpet thread or fine, strong string (for mounting) • craft knife • steel ruler • tracing paper • scissors • pencil • tape measure • spray glue

● *Technique pages 309, 343–4*

❶ MAKING THE SAMPLER

1 Iron the aida cloth and hand oversew or machine zigzag the raw edges.
2 Mark the vertical and horizontal center lines with basting stitches.
3 Following the stitch and color guide on the master pattern, work the border design. This becomes a reference point for the rest of the design.
4 Complete the design, working one small area at a time and following the stitch and color guide carefully.

❷ PERSONALIZING THE SAMPLER

1 On tracing paper, rule a straight line to act as a guide. From the master pattern for cross-stitch letters, trace the letters of the baby's name and the date of birth. Leave a space the width of two cross-stitches between letters and a space equivalent to four cross-stitches between words. You will not

be able to fit more than 12 characters across the sampler, so use only the child's given name if necessary. Mark the mid-point of your tracings.
2 Match the mid-point of the name to the center point of the design in the space provided at the top of the sampler. Embroider the letters using colors of your choice, starting from the middle and working outward.
3 Repeat step 2 for the date of the baby's birth, embroidering in the space provided at the base of the sampler. You may need to shorten the name of the month.

❸ FRAMING THE SAMPLER

1 Press the sampler on the wrong side through a damp cloth, being very careful not to stretch the fabric or the stitching.
2 To frame the sampler, follow the steps described in "Wedding day sampler" (pages 194–5).

NOTE

For some tips on counted cross-stitch, turn to "Wedding day sampler" (pages 194–5).

When you are embroidering the baby's name and date of birth, begin at the mid-point of the line of text and work outward to the sides of the sampler.

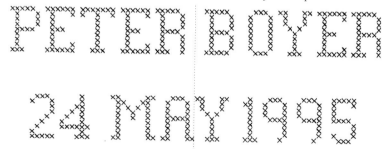

Benjamin Bear

Every young child loves a teddy bear as a friend. This appealing mohair bear is fully jointed and stands 27 cm tall. A colorful neck bow is the perfect finishing touch.

WHAT YOU NEED

Master pattern C23(a–j) • 65 cm x 30 cm mohair fabric • two 8 mm safety eyes • joint set: two 30 mm wooden disks, eight 25 mm wooden disks, five M5 x 25 mm machine screws, five M5 locknuts, 10 small washers • 15 cm x 15 cm felt • sewing thread to match mohair fabric • black and brown embroidery cotton • coarse thread or waxed dental floss • polyester stuffing, about 300 g • needles: general sewing, size 22 chenille (for embroidery), size 18 tapestry (for closing seams) • dressmaking pins • 50 cm ribbon, 25 mm wide • tracing paper • pencil • fabric marker • sewing machine • fine-pointed scissors • socket wrench (for locknuts) • screwdriver • chopstick
● *Technique pages 292–301, 343–4*

Cutting guide
Cut the body pieces from mohair fabric and the paws and foot pads from felt.

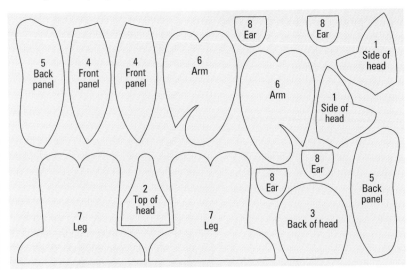

❶ TRACING THE PATTERN

1 Trace the pattern pieces from the master pattern onto tracing paper, tracing reverse pattern pieces where indicated. Transfer all the arrows, markings, lettered points and symbols.
2 Cut carefully around the outline of each piece.

❷ CUTTING OUT

1 Establish the direction of the pile of the mohair fabric by running your hand over it. It will feel smooth when your hand is moving in the direction of the pile. Lay all the pattern pieces in the same direction as the pile.

NOTE

A 6 mm seam allowance is included in the pattern. As you pin the pieces of fabric together, push the pile away from the cut edge. You can sew the bear with a sewing machine (except for the last stages) or by hand, using backstitch and strong thread.

2 With the wrong side of the mohair fabric facing up, pin each pair of pattern pieces 1 to 8 onto the fabric, following the cutting guide in the panel on page 18. Make sure the arrows marked on the pattern pieces follow the direction of the pile.

3 Trace around each pattern piece with the fabric marker. Transfer all markings, including the positions of joints and eyes.

4 Cut out the mohair pieces with the fine-pointed scissors, taking care not to cut through the pile of the mohair.

5 Pin pairs of pattern pieces 9 and 10 to the felt, trace around them with the fabric marker and cut out.

❸ SEWING
Head and ears

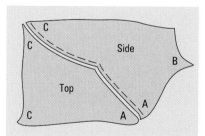

1 With the right sides of the fabric together, pin and stitch the center front seam under the chin from A to B and the top of the head to the sides of the head from A to C.

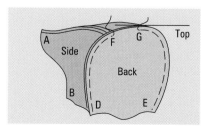

2 Pin and sew the back of the head to the front and side head piece, sewing

from D to F and E to G. Pin across the opening FG at the top of the head, but do not stitch.

3 Using a strong thread, run a gathering stitch by hand around the base of the neck. Draw up the ends of the thread tightly and secure.

4 Turn the work right side out and make small holes with pointed scissors at the positions marked for the eyes. Push the shafts of the safety eyes through the holes and click the safety disks onto the shafts on the wrong side of the fabric.

5 With right sides facing, pin ear pieces together in pairs. Sew around the curved edge of each ear, but not along the base. Turn right side out.

6 At the base of each ear, fold the raw edges approximately 5 mm to the inside and oversew by hand. Put the ears aside for later use.

Arms and legs

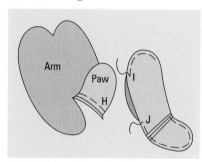

1 Matching H on the felt paw pad to H on the arm, and with right sides of the fabrics together, pin and sew the paw to the inner arm.

2 Fold the arm in half lengthwise, so that the right sides of fabric are facing. Pin and sew around the top of the arm and down around the felt paw pad, leaving an opening between I and J. Turn the work to the right side.

3 Repeat steps 1 and 2 to sew a paw pad to the other arm.

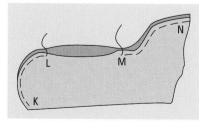

4 Fold the leg in half lengthwise, so that right sides of the fabric are facing.

Pin and sew from K to L and M to N leaving an opening between L and M.

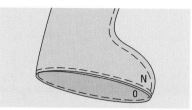

5 Match the foot pad center O to the center seam of the leg (N). Ease the foot pad to fit the leg snugly, and sew. Turn the work to the right side.

6 Repeat steps 3 and 4 to sew the pad to the other leg.

Body

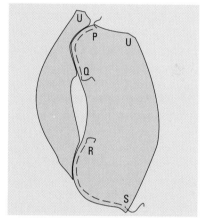

1 With right sides of fabric facing, pin and sew the back panels together from P to Q and R to S, leaving an opening between Q and R.

2 With right sides of fabric facing, pin and sew the front panels together from T to S.

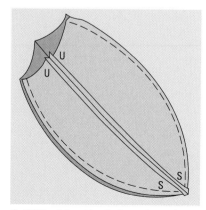

3 With right sides facing, pin and sew the front body piece to the back body piece, matching the points at U on both sides and also matching the seams at the crotch (S).

BEAR PERSONALITY

When you embroider the face onto your bear, give some thought to the expression you want to achieve. Try sketching the face on paper first, experimenting with the shape and position of the nose and mouth. Keep the shapes simple and when you are happy with your face, start embroidering from the center of the nose, following your sketch.

4 With a strong, coarse thread, run a gathering stitch by hand around the top of neck. Draw up the ends tightly and secure with a knot. Turn the work to the right side.

❹ ASSEMBLING THE BEAR

1 Onto a screw, put a washer and then a 30 mm wooden disk and a ring of felt cut a little larger than the disk. The felt will prevent the disk from rubbing and weakening the fabric.
2 Place the screw into the head through the opening at the top. Push the shaft through the gathered edge of the neck so that the end of the screw protrudes from the base of the head. Then push the protruding screw through the gathered neck opening at the top of the body.
3 Reaching through the back body

opening, place on the screw another piece of felt, a 30 mm wooden disk, a washer and a locknut.
4 Finger-tighten the locknut. Using a single socket wrench, continue to tighten the locknut until it feels snug. Use a screwdriver, through the opening at the top of the head, to prevent the machine screw from turning.
5 Using fine-pointed scissors, carefully make holes through the fabric at the joint marks on the inner arms and legs and on the body.
6 Follow steps 1 to 4 above to make the arm joints. Use the smaller wooden disks and position the joints by working through the openings in the limbs and back. Make sure that the joints are screwed firmly together, otherwise the arms and legs will soon begin to flop.

You can buy a joint set from specialist craft stores. The set consists of five joints, used to make the neck, arm and leg joints rigid. Assemble the joints as shown in the diagram. Make sure the bottom nuts are firmly screwed home, or the limbs will tend to flop.

❺ FINISHING

1 Using the chopstick, stuff the arms and legs firmly, making sure that the polyester filling is pushed well down into the paws and feet. Be careful not to push the stuffing tool through the felt paw pads.
2 Close all seam openings in the limbs with ladder stitch, using coarse thread or waxed dental floss. Embroider black claws on the paws with straight stitch, securing the thread with tiny backstitches.
3 Stuff the body firmly, being careful to push plenty of stuffing around the neck, arm and leg joints. Close the opening in the back in the same way as for the limbs.
4 Stuff the head firmly, molding it into shape as you go. Close the opening on top of the head.
5 Work the nose with brown embroidery cotton. Secure the thread with a knot in the center of the nose area. Using closely spaced satin stitch, go over and over the same area until the nose is built up. To finish, fasten off the thread by running the needle back and forth underneath the satin stitches to catch the material.
6 Pin the ears into position and ladder stitch them to the head. Remember that different positions for the eyes and ears can completely change the look of the bear.
7 Tie the ribbon in a bow round the bear's neck. Choose ribbon in a bright color or a bold pattern, such as tartan or Paisley.

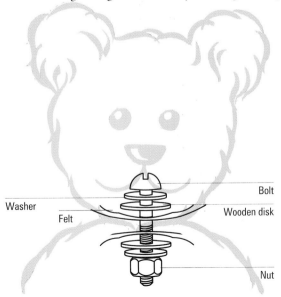

Bolt

Washer

Felt

Wooden disk

Nut

Embroidered baby's T-shirts

Buy inexpensive cotton T-shirts and transform them into a beautiful, personalized present for a small baby by working simple designs on the T-shirts using colored cottons and a few easy stitches.

WHAT YOU NEED

Baby's T-shirts, short-sleeved and long-sleeved • stranded embroidery cotton: DMC colors white (blanc), color or colors of your choice • embroidery marking pen • needles: size 7 crewel, size 7 straw or milliner's
● *Technique pages 307–12, 343–4*

When you are working the embroidery, use the straw needle for the bullion knots and the crewel needle for all other stitches.

❶ BUNNY T-SHIRTS
Embroidering the armholes
1 Fold the T-shirt in half to find the center. Using the embroidery marking pen, mark positions for the French knots so that they are evenly spaced around the armholes. Avoid the armpit area, as the embroidery may irritate the baby's skin.
2 With three strands of embroidery cotton in your chosen color, work French knots at the marked positions, running the thread behind the fabric and onto the next stitch.

Embroidering the bunnies
1 Find the center front point of the neck. Using an embroidery marking pen, mark the positions of the bunnies. Place the center bunny slightly lower than the other two.
2 Using three strands of embroidery cotton in your chosen color, work the bodies with four bullion knots, turning the thread around the needle 10 times. Make the necks with two bullion knots, turning the thread six times. Make one bullion knot for each ear, turning the thread five times.
3 Work the tail using three strands of white embroidery cotton and straight stitch.

❷ LONG-SLEEVED T-SHIRT
Embroidering the neckline
Using two strands of embroidery cotton in your chosen color, work chain stitch around the neckline.

Embroidering the sleeves
1 Mark the positions of the seven bullion rosebuds so that they are evenly spaced around the wrists.
2 Embroider the rosebuds in the colors of your choice, turning the thread

Stitch guide
To work the designs, trace and transfer the diagrams above. The bunny is made up of eight bullion stitches and two straight stitches. Follow the stitch key below for the flower bouquet.

🪶 Padded satin stitch		🌀 Bullion rose	
Satin stitch flower		Lazy daisy stitch	
French knot flower		Backstitch	
Bullion rosebud		● French knot	

five times round the needle for the center bullion knots and seven times for the two outer bullion knots.

Embroidering the body
1 Following the stitch guide, and using colors of your choice, work the design on the body of the T-shirt.
2 To make the bow, backstitch the outline with two strands and work the center in padded satin stitch using three strands. Make the surrounding French knots using three strands.
3 Work the roses in bullion knots, turning the thread around the needle six times for the centers and 12 times for the outside petals.
4 Work the half-open roses with three bullion knots.
5 Make the French knot flowers with three strands. Start by working a central knot, and then make five or six knots around the edge.
6 To make the lazy daisy flower petals, use two strands. Repeat for the other three petals. The bud is one French knot using three strands.
7 To make the satin stitch buds, work a central French knot using three strands of embroidery cotton. Work the four surrounding petals in satin stitch using two strands.
8 Work the individual French knots using three strands.

"B is for Baby" quilt

This quilt, measuring 90 cm x 125 cm, is embroidered in traditional cream on cream using simple embroidery stitches. It is an ideal gift for either a girl or a boy.

HINT
Use an embroidery hoop to work the embroidery on the square blocks of fabric. You will not need an embroidery hoop for the border panels, since only a few colonial knots are worked there.

WHAT YOU NEED

Master pattern **A2**(a–h) • 2.5 m quilter's muslin, 150 cm wide • 7 m heavy, double-edged, cream cotton lace, 60 mm wide • Coton à broder (the same color as the fabric) • 100 cm x 150 cm batting • cream quilting thread • cream machine sewing thread • needle: chenille size 22 • dress-making pins • large embroidery hoop • tracing paper • black felt-tipped pen • water-erasable fabric marking pen • scissors • sewing thread to match muslin and lace • sewing machine
● *Technique pages 292–301, 307–12, 343–4*

❶ PREPARING THE FABRIC

1 Fold the quilter's muslin in half lengthwise, selvage to selvage, and cut out the following pieces, as shown in the diagram *Cutting out the fabric:*
A one 100 cm x 150 cm piece

(backing); **B** six 36 cm squares (embroidery blocks); **C** two 92 cm x 13 cm strips (end borders); **D** two 104 cm x 13 cm strips (side borders); **E** two 95 cm x 9 cm strips (end bindings); **F** two 128 cm x 9 cm strips (side bindings).
2 Fold and quarter the embroidery blocks and borders to find the centers, and mark the center of each piece.

❷ EMBROIDERING THE FABRIC

1 Using tracing paper and the black felt-tipped pen, trace a working design from the master pattern.
2 Match the center of each embroidery block and border with the center of the appropriate working design and pin them together with the fabric on top. Note that the bunny, bear and bluebird look best if they face into the center of the quilt.
3 Place the fabric and design on a light box or tape it firmly to a window. Using the fabric marking pen, trace the design on to the fabric.
4 Embroider the designs, following the stitch guides given on the master pattern pieces.
5 When the embroidery is complete, wash out any transfer marks. Dry the work flat and press the pieces from the back on a towel.

❸ ASSEMBLING THE EMBROIDERED FABRIC

1 Arrange the blocks in position. With right sides facing, stitch the blocks together in pairs, then join the pairs, matching the seam lines.
2 With right sides facing, sew the side border strips to the center panel. Then sew the top and bottom borders to the center panel and side borders. Trim if necessary.
3 Place the work face down on a towel and press from the back.

❹ ATTACHING THE LACE

1 Wash and press the lace to preshrink it. From the 7 m length of double-edged lace, cut two 70 cm strips and one 104 cm strip.
2 Fold under 5 mm at each end of the lace strips. Using a medium zig-zag stitch, machine down the center of the lace in the least obvious place, attaching the two shorter strips along the horizontal seam lines of the center panel and the long strip down the vertical seam of the center panel. The folded ends of the lace, which will extend beyond the edges of the center panel, will be secured in step 3.

CUTTING OUT THE FABRIC

Pattern pieces include a 1 cm seam allowance. The sizes given are those you need to construct the quilt. You can cut the fabric blocks larger for easy handling in a large embroidery hoop, then trim them to the correct size after rinsing and pressing. Cut the border strips a little longer to allow a safety margin, and trim them to size after sewing each pair of strips to the blocks.

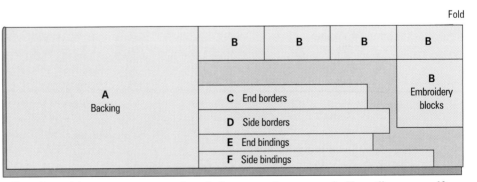

Allow plenty of time to measure, cut and mark the pattern pieces accurately. You will save yourself time and frustration later on, and the result will be a professional finish that will delight you.

The six motifs are worked on separate blocks of fabric that are stitched together. The whole panel is framed with long strips of fabric and then the embroidered blocks are bordered with lace.

3 Use the remainder of the lace to stitch a border around the center panel, securing the ends of the other lace strips in the process and mitering the raw edges neatly.

4 Carefully press the finished piece from the back over a towel.

⑤ ASSEMBLING THE QUILT

1 Lay the backing piece out flat with the wrong side facing up. Tape or pin the batting onto it and then lay the embroidered fabric over the top, right side facing up. Pin all the layers together, matching the centers. Note that the backing and the batting are larger than the top fabric. Baste all three layers together by hand.

2 Using a small running stitch, hand quilt around the outlines of the motifs.

3 Hand quilt around each block, securing the lace edges as you go. Handstitch any remaining loose edges of lace to the top layer.

4 Fold all the binding strips in half lengthwise, wrong sides facing, and press, then open the pieces out again.

5 Working first with a short piece of binding, pin the binding to the top edge of the quilt, right sides facing, and machine stitch through all layers, allowing a 1.5 cm seam.

6 Repeat step 5 to attach the binding to the bottom edge of the quilt. Trim the batting and the backing fabric at the top and bottom edges of the quilt and fold the bindings to the back.

7 Turn under a 1.5 cm hem and slipstitch the back of the binding strips into place along the row of machine stitching. Trim the ends of the binding level with the edges of the quilt.

8 Repeat steps 5 to 7 to attach the long pieces of binding to the sides of the quilt, trimming the ends of the binding so that they extend about 1.5 cm beyond the edge.

9 Fold the ends back into the binding and slipstitch them neatly into place, keeping the stitching at the back of the quilt and the corners square.

Soft animal toys

The soft and simple animal toys in this project are designed to stimulate a baby's senses. You can make them as clutch toys for tiny babies or rattle toys for older babies, or as flat bath toys. Be sure to secure the bell or rattle to prevent it from coming loose.

WHAT YOU NEED

Master pattern **B13**(a–f)
Clutch toys
Scraps of closely woven fabric • fabric scraps: seersucker, taffeta, satin or heavily napped fabric • sewing thread • polyester stuffing • fabric paints or black embroidery cotton • needles: size 6 sharp, size 7 crewel • dressmaking pins • scissors • blunt implement (e.g. chopstick) • tracing paper • pencil • sewing machine • small ball-shaped bell and piece of 6 mm foam sheeting 3 cm **x** 6 cm (for a bell), or small plastic screw-on lid 3–4 cm in diameter, small flat button and piece of interfacing or firmly woven fabric (for a rattle)
Bath toys
60 cm **x** 30 cm terry cloth or 2 washcloths, 30 cm **x** 30 cm • 6 mm foam sheeting, 30 cm **x** 30 cm • needles: size 6 sharp, size 7 crewel • sewing thread • embroidery threads • tracing paper • pencil • scissors • dressmaking pins • sewing machine
● *Technique pages 292–301, 307–12, 343–4*

These toys are an ideal gift for a new baby. They are portable, washable, and inexpensive to make using scraps from the ragbag or the remnant bin.

Clutch toys

❶ MAKING THE TOY

1 Using tracing paper and scissors, trace and cut the shape you have selected from the master pattern.
2 Cut a pair of shapes from the fabric, making sure that the straight grain runs the same way for both shapes.
3 Using fabric paints or embroidery thread, add facial details or decorative features to the right side of the fabric. Remember that the larger the area covered by paint, the more difficult the shape will be to turn right side out. Do not paint within the 5 mm seam allowance. Let the paint dry.

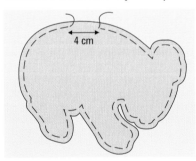

4 With right sides of the fabric facing, pin the shapes together, leaving a 4 cm opening on a straight, gently

> ### VARIATION
> *The simple shapes that make up this set of toys can be part of a whole range of matching gifts. They can be used as motifs for quilts, pillowcases and curtains, or as stencils for furniture, to give a baby's room that totally coordinated look.*

curving section. Machine stitch along the seam line, 5 mm from the edges. Stitch again for strength.
5 Clip the curves and notch the seam allowance in the tight corners, taking care not to cut the stitching. Tie and cut off the loose threads.

❷ MAKING THE BELL OR RATTLE
The bell
Firmly secure the bell in a pillow of foam sheeting so that the toy will be safe for the baby to play with.

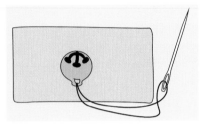

1 Using a needle, attach a double thread to the bell. Place the bell on the foam and fold the foam over so that the bell and the thread are enclosed in the fold.

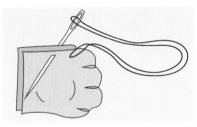

2 Securely handstitch the edges of the foam together to form a little pillow containing the bell.

The rattle
1 Cut a circle of fabric or interfacing 5 mm larger in diameter than the container lid and another circle 5 mm larger in diameter than the first.

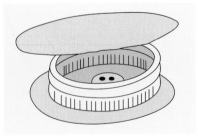

2 Place the lid on the smaller circle of fabric, put a button in the lid, and cover with the larger circle.

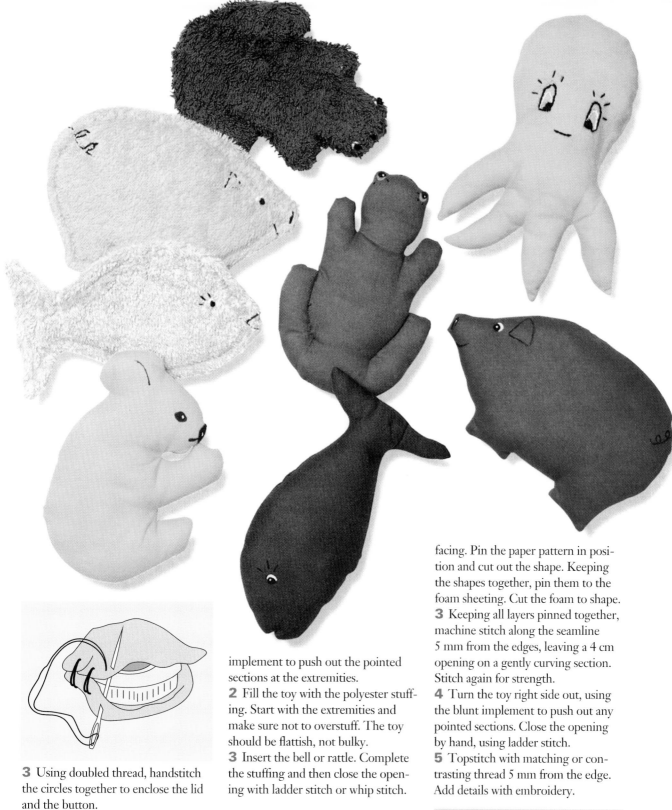

3 Using doubled thread, handstitch the circles together to enclose the lid and the button.

4 Sew around the circles again to make the fabric fit tightly against the lid. If the fabric is not pulled tight, the stuffing will push into the lid and the rattle will not work.

❸ FINISHING THE TOY

1 Turn the fabric shape right side out. You will need to use the blunt implement to push out the pointed sections at the extremities.

2 Fill the toy with the polyester stuffing. Start with the extremities and make sure not to overstuff. The toy should be flattish, not bulky.

3 Insert the bell or rattle. Complete the stuffing and then close the opening with ladder stitch or whip stitch.

Bath toys

❶ MAKING THE BATH TOY

1 Using the tracing paper and scissors, trace and cut a broad, simple shape from the master pattern.

2 Place two washcloths or pieces of terry cloth together, right sides facing. Pin the paper pattern in position and cut out the shape. Keeping the shapes together, pin them to the foam sheeting. Cut the foam to shape.

3 Keeping all layers pinned together, machine stitch along the seamline 5 mm from the edges, leaving a 4 cm opening on a gently curving section. Stitch again for strength.

4 Turn the toy right side out, using the blunt implement to push out any pointed sections. Close the opening by hand, using ladder stitch.

5 Topstitch with matching or contrasting thread 5 mm from the edge. Add details with embroidery.

> **HINT**
> *A terry cloth bath toy (without a bell or rattle) can be used as a teething aid. Simply dampen the fabric and chill the toy in the refrigerator to make a safe, soothing object for a teething baby to suck on.*

Rocking horse overalls

Designed for an energetic one-year-old, these overalls are a practical and attractive gift to make for a busy baby.

WHAT YOU NEED

Master pattern A4(a–e) • 1.5 m light to medium weight fabric, 115 cm wide • 15 cm x 40 cm even-weave linen for cross-stitch (26 threads to 2.5 cm) • 30 cm lightweight iron-on interfacing • 2.5 m fine piping cord • 2.5 m bias binding, to complement the main fabric • 2 buttons (15 mm), to match bias binding • Anchor stranded embroidery thread: 376 (beige), 380 (brown), 109 (mauve), 928 (duck egg blue) (or a color scheme of your choice) • sewing thread to match fabric • needles: tapestry, general sewing • embroidery frame (optional) • scissors • tracing paper • pencil • dressmaker's pencil • sewing machine • dressmaking pins
● *Technique pages 292–301, 309, 343–4*

❶ CUTTING OUT THE FABRIC

1 Using tracing paper, pencil and scissors, trace all the pattern pieces from the master pattern. Make sure that all markings are transferred.
2 Pin the pattern pieces onto the main fabric, following the cutting guide, and cut them out. Do not cut the linen for the front panel piece.
3 From the interfacing, cut out one front yoke, one back yoke and two leg bands.

❷ MAKING THE FRONT PANEL

1 To center the cross-stitch design, measure and mark the horizontal and vertical center lines of the linen with colored basting thread. The intersection of the lines is the center point.
2 Using two strands of embroidery thread, follow the stitch and color guide to work the rocking horse.
3 When you have finished the cross-stitch, place the work face down, cover it with a damp cloth and press it carefully with a warm iron.
4 Center the pattern piece for the cross-stitched panel on the cross-stitched linen by matching the center front of the pattern piece with the vertical basted line. Pin the pattern piece to the linen and cut out the panel. Remove the basting threads.
5 Cover the piping cord with bias binding, using the machine zipper foot and machining close to the cord. On the right side of the neck edge of the embroidered panel, lay the piping along the seam allowance line. Using the zipper foot, machine the piping to the panel.
6 Fold and press the seam allowance to the back so that the piping lies along the edge of the fold.

> **NOTES**
> ● *Seam allowances are 1 cm.*
> ● *Finish all seams with over-locking or zigzag.*

❸ SEWING THE YOKE

1 Fuse the yoke interfacings to the wrong sides of one main fabric front yoke and one main fabric back yoke.

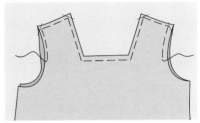

2 With the right sides of the two main fabric front yokes together, start machining the armhole 5 cm below the shoulder. Sew up to the shoulder, along the shoulder, around the neckline and along the other shoulder, finishing at the same point on the other armhole. Notch and clip the seam.
3 Turn the front yoke right side out and press. Ensuring that the front yoke piece is sitting free of the interfaced front yoke and that the neck turnings are pressed down, baste the cross-stitched panel to the right side of the front yoke piece just below the horizontal edge of the neckline so that the piping sits up over the

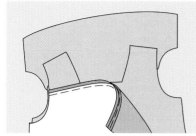

finished edge. Topstitch the cross-stitched panel into place across the front yoke from armhole to armhole.
4 Turn the front yoke inside out as far as necessary. With right sides facing, sew the front of the yoke to the back along the side seams. Repeat for the yoke facings. Press seams open.

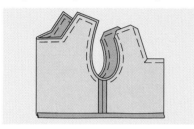

5 Machine the remainder of the yoke to the facing in one continuous seam, blending the seam into the previous stitching at the upper front armholes. Press the lower edge of the yoke facing up 1 cm. Attach piping around the lower edge of the right side of the main yoke along the seam line, as for the embroidered panel in step 3.
6 Clip and notch the armhole and neckline turnings. Turn the work right side out and press.

④ SEWING THE PANTS
1 With right sides together, machine the front and back inside leg and side seams. Zigzag to finish, and press the seams toward the back.
2 With right sides together, place one leg inside the other and stitch the crotch seam from the center front to the center back. Zigzag to finish, and press to one side.
3 Machine two rows of gathering stitches around the upper edge and the calf edges of the pants.

⑤ SEWING THE YOKE TO THE PANTS
1 With right sides facing, pin the lower edge of the outside yoke to

STITCH AND COLOR GUIDE
Embroider the linen panel before sewing it onto the front yoke of the overalls. Find the center of the panel by basting the horizontal and vertical center lines, and then follow the color and stitch guide below.

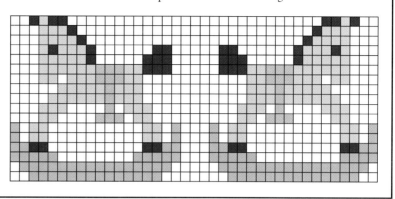

the top edge of the pants, matching center points and side seams. Pull up the gathering and adjust the gathers evenly. The piping will be sandwiched in the seam. Using the zipper foot, stitch around the seam. Trim the seam and press it up into the yoke.
2 Slipstitch the pressed edge of the interfaced yoke over the seam.

⑥ LEG BANDS
1 Iron the leg band interfacings to the wrong sides of two of the leg bands. With right sides facing, stitch all four leg band seams. Press open.
2 Pin and stitch covered piping cord to the right sides of the long edges of the outside leg bands (not interfaced), using the zipper foot.
3 With right sides together, and using the zipper foot, machine the

interfaced leg bands to the lower edges of the piped leg bands. Press down a 1 cm hem along the other edges of the interfaced leg bands.
4 Around the calf edges, match the inner leg seams of the pants to the leg band seams, with right sides together and raw edges aligned. Pull up the gathers and adjust evenly. Using the zipper foot, stitch the leg bands to the legs in the same way as you stitched the yoke to the top of the pants.
5 Slipstitch the pressed edges of the interfaced leg bands to the wrong sides over the seam line.

⑦ FINISHING
Machine stitch vertical buttonholes in the back shoulder straps. Sew the buttons to the front shoulder straps, aligning them with the buttonholes.

Cutting guide
Cut two of each piece from the main fabric. To cut the yokes, trace around the pattern pieces onto the fabric with the dressmaker's pencil and then flip the pattern pieces, as shown by the dotted lines. For the embroidered panel, use a piece of linen 25 cm x 40 cm and work the cross-stitch embroidery before cutting out the pattern.

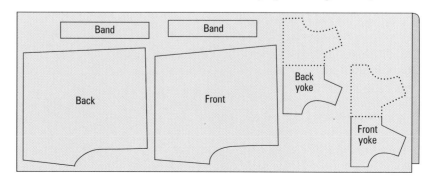

Crib blanket

Made by embroidering crocheted panels, this attractive little blanket will keep baby warm during those first months and then will become a treasured "cover-up" for naps. It measures about 75 cm x 110 cm.

WHAT YOU NEED

Yarn: 19 balls Patons 4 ply Fairytale (50 g balls) • Anchor stranded embroidery cotton: 8 skeins 336 (apricot), 3 skeins 976 (pale blue), 3 skeins 978 (dark blue), 1 skein 338 (terra-cotta), 1 skein 403 (black) • crochet hook: 3.50 mm (no. 9) • needle: size 20 chenille • dressmaker's pencil
● *Technique pages 307–12, 320–2, 327*

CHECKING THE TENSION

Before you begin, check your tension for both plain and lace crochet so that the measurements of the finished article will be as close as possible to the specified size. Using a 3.50 mm crochet hook, you should have 24 double crochets and 27 rows to a 10 cm square of plain crochet and 11 patterns and 12 rows to a 10 cm square of lace crochet. If you have fewer stitches, use a smaller hook; if you have more, use a bigger hook. The

SPECIAL TERMS

Cluster: ★ yo, draw up a loop in next 2 ch sp, yo and draw through first 2 loops on hook, rep from ★ twice in same 2 ch sp, yo and draw through all 4 loops on hook.
Crab stitch: Crab stitch is like double crochet, except that it is worked from left to right instead of right to left, so that the stitches are worked backward.

STITCH AND COLOR GUIDE

Find the center of the square you intend to work in and match it with the center of the motif on the grid below. Starting from the center point, cross-stitch the motif in the colors specified by matching the stitches in your crocheted square to the squares on the grid below.

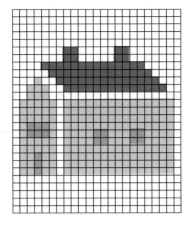
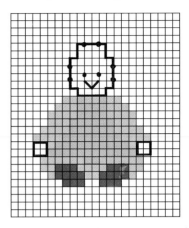
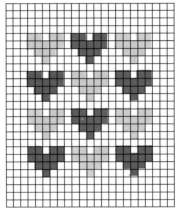

blanket has been designed to be worked on a bigger hook at a looser tension than is usually recommended.

CROCHETING THE PANELS

The blanket is made up of seven panels, each consisting of 10 alternating squares of plain and lace crochet. The first panel begins with a plain square and the second begins with a lace square. Make four of the first panel and three of the second.

❶ FIRST PANEL

Plain square
Loosely work 24 ch.
1st row: Miss 1 ch, 1 dc in each ch to end to make 23 dc.
2nd row: ★★ 1 ch, 1 dc in each dc to end.
Rep 2nd row 25 times.

Lace square
1st row: 2 ch, 1 htr in each of first 2 dc, ★ 2 ch, miss 1 dc, 1 htr in next dc, rep from ★ to last dc, 1 htr in last dc to make 10 sps.
2nd row: (1 dc, 1 ch) in first htr, 1 tr in next htr, cluster in first 2 ch sp, ★ 1 ch, miss 1 htr, cluster in next 2 ch sp, rep from ★ to last 2 htr, 1 tr in each of last 2 htr.
3rd row: 2 ch, 1 htr in each of first 2 tr, 2 ch, miss cluster, ★ 1 htr in next 1 ch sp, 2 ch, miss cluster, rep from ★ to last 2 sts, 1 htr in next tr, 1 htr in top of turning ch.
Rep 2nd and 3rd rows 5 times. †

Plain square
1st row: 1 ch, 1 dc in each of first 2 htr, ★ 1 dc in 2 ch sp, 1 dc in next htr, rep from ★ to last htr, 1 dc in

4 EMBROIDERING THE DESIGNS

1 Find the center of each of the squares to be embroidered by using the dressmaker's pencil to mark the point where the diagonals cross. Match these center points to the center points of the embroidery designs and work the embroidery, treating the rows and stitches on the square as the cross-stitch grid.
2 Following the stitch and color guide, and using the diagram below for the position of each motif, work the cross-stitch designs on the plain squares in the four first panels.
3 Using the black stranded cotton, outline the hands and faces in back-stitch and French knots, as shown on the stitch and color guide.

5 FINISHING OFF

With the right side of the work facing, work three rounds of double crochet and then one round of crab stitch around the outside edge of the blanket to make a border. Increase or decrease as necessary to keep the work flat.

The blanket consists of seven panels, with 10 squares in each panel. Alternate panels start with a plain square or a lace square. Embroider the motifs on the blanket after sewing the panels together.

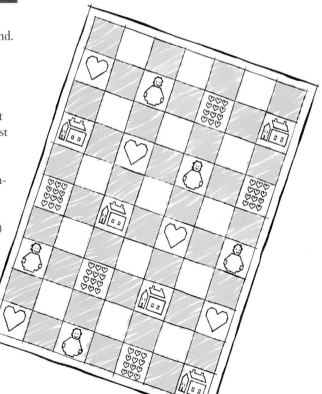

last htr to make 23 dc. ★★
Rep from ★★ to ★★ 4 times, finishing at † at end of last rep.
Fasten off.
(Make 4 of these panels altogether.)

2 SECOND PANEL

Lace square
Loosely work 25 ch.
1st row: Miss 2 ch, 1 htr in each of next 2 ch, ★ 2 ch, miss 1 ch, 1 htr in next ch, rep from ★ to last ch, 1 htr in last ch to make 10 sps.
2nd and 3rd rows: ★★★ Work as for 2nd and 3rd rows of lace square in 1st panel 6 times.

Plain square
1st row: 1 ch, 1 dc in each of first 2 htr, ★ 1 dc in 2 ch sp, 1 dc in next htr, rep from ★ to last htr, 1 dc in last htr

to make 23 dc.
2nd row: 1 ch, 1 dc in each dc to end. Rep 2nd row 25 times. ††

Lace square
1st row: 2 ch, 1 htr in each of first 2 dc, ★ 2 ch, miss 1 dc, 1 htr in next dc, rep from ★ to last dc, 1 htr in last dc to make 10 sps. ★★★

Rep from ★★★ to ★★★ 4 times, finishing at †† at end of last rep.
Fasten off.
(Make 3 of these panels altogether.)

3 MAKING UP

1 Arrange the seven panels, alternating first and second panels as shown. Do not press.
2 Join the panels using a flat seam and matching yarn.

Daisy & bee baby's outfit

A bright bee and delicate daisy motif attracts the eye immediately on this dainty dress and bonnet. The embroidery design is worked mainly in shadow stitch. The outfit consists of a plain dress of batiste and a bonnet and an embroidered sheer collar trimmed with lace. It is designed to fit an average one-year-old.

WHAT YOU NEED

Master pattern **A1(a–i)** • fine sewing machine thread • stranded embroidery cotton: 3 shades green, 2 shades pink, yellow, orange black, pale gray • embroidery hoop • 20 cm **x** 40 cm non-woven interfacing (to protect fabric) • fine embroidery needles • dressmaking pins • water-soluble marker pen • tracing paper • scissors • pencil • tape measure • sewing machine
Dress
1.2 m batiste, 115 cm wide • 30 cm pure cotton organdy or pure silk organza, 115 cm wide (for the collar) • 1 m woven cotton edging lace, 9 mm wide • 2 mother-of-pearl shank buttons (for the collar), 6 mm diameter • 3 flat mother-of-pearl buttons (for the yoke), 6 mm diameter
Bonnet
18 cm **x** 36 cm pure cotton organdy or pure silk organza (for the brim) • 30 cm batiste, 115 cm wide (for the crown) • 1.6 m woven cotton edging lace, 9 mm wide (to match the collar lace) • 50 cm narrow entredeux • 1.5 m double-faced satin ribbon, 5 mm wide • 1.3 m double-faced satin ribbon, 7 mm wide
● *Technique pages 292–301, 307–12, 343–4*

❶ PREPARING THE COLLAR
1 Using the tracing paper and pencil trace a working pattern for the collar from the master pattern. Trace all markings, including the embroidery design. Do not cut out the pattern.
2 Pin a rectangle of organdy, 25 cm **x** 15 cm, over the traced pattern, pinning around the edges of the fabric so that the pin marks will not show on the finished collar.

3 Using the water-soluble marker, trace the front collar pattern onto the organdy. Then lightly trace the embroidery design onto the organdy.
4 Remove the traced paper pattern. To allow for the fabric to be held in the embroidery hoop, do not cut out the collar piece yet. If you are using silk organza, overcast the edges of the rectangle to minimize fraying.

❷ EMBROIDERING THE COLLAR
Work the whole design with two strands of embroidery cotton. The leaves are worked in three shades of green and the daisies are worked in two shades of pink.

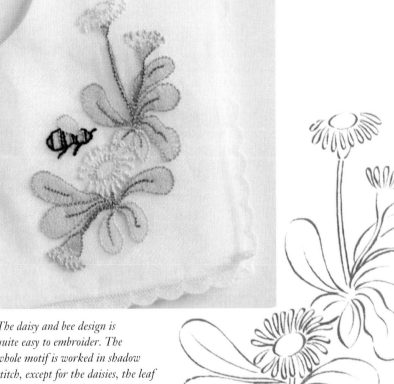

The daisy and bee design is quite easy to embroider. The whole motif is worked in shadow stitch, except for the daisies, the leaf veins and stems and the bee's body. The daisies are worked in pistil stitch in two shades of pink, and the bee's outline, legs and antenna are worked in backstitch.

1 Place the organdy in the embroidery hoop, making sure that the fabric is protected by the interfacing circles and the design is centered in the hoop. (See page 32 for a note on working with sheer fabrics in a hoop.)

Daisies

1 Choose a pale pink for open flowers and mid pink for closed flowers and use a 50 cm long thread to complete a whole flower.
2 Work the daisy centers in shadow stitch using yellow thread. Work the petals in pistil stitch. Begin from the center of the blossom on the right side of the fabric. Follow only one line of

the petal at a time.

3 Work one or two tiny backstitches, and then take the thread down to the wrong side, bringing it up again a few stitches from the tip of the petal.

4 Backstitch on the right side of the fabric to the tip, ending with a two-turn French knot. Your needle and thread are now on the wrong side. Bring them up at the start of the next

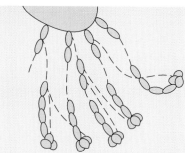

petal, and repeat the process.

Stems and leaves

1 Work flower stems in backstitch using the darkest shade of green. At the same time, shadow stitch the calyx at the top of each stem using the same green. Work two rows of backstitch to complete each stem.

2 Shadow stitch the leaves, working from the tips to the bases. Use pale

WORKING SHADOW STITCH

Shadow stitch is worked like herringbone stitch, but from the back of the fabric, producing a

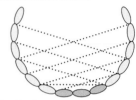

subtle and charming effect. Turn to page 311 for details of how to work shadow stitch.

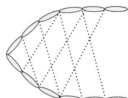

On the leaves, start with several backstitches before beginning to work the shadow stitch.

On the bee's wing, start at the pointed end and make sure the cross-over stitches are even.

NOTE

When working on fine fabric in an embroidery hoop, protect the fabric from damage by placing two rings of non-woven interfacing between the fabric and the hoops. The outer circumference of each interfacing ring should be 5 cm larger in diameter than the hoop and the inner circumference 4 cm smaller.

green for the smaller leaves and mid green for the larger leaves.

3 Work the leaf veins in backstitch using the darkest shade of green. Start stitching at the stalk end and work toward the tip.

Bee

1 Work the wing in shadow stitch using pale gray cotton.

2 Shadow stitch the body in alternate vertical stripes of orange and black. Outline the body and work the legs and antenna with backstitch using black thread.

❸ MAKING THE COLLAR

1 Cut out the embroidered front collar to the size of the pattern. Then cut one plain front collar (for the lining) and four back collar pieces (two for the lining) from the organdy.

2 Using small French seams, stitch the front and a left and right back together at the shoulders. Do the same with the lining pieces.

3 Pin the lace to the outside edge of the collar on the right side, with the lace heading on the seamline and the scalloped edge toward the center. When pinning, follow the outer

perimeter of the collar, allowing extra fullness at the corners so that the collar will sit properly when it is turned right side out. Do not run the lace up the center backs, as the collar will overlap here. Baste the lace in place.

4 Place the collar lining on top of the collar, right sides together. Starting near the center of one of the back overlaps, and stitching through all layers, sew around the entire collar, including the neck edge and back, to 5 cm from the starting point. (This opening will be used to turn the collar through to the right side.)

5 Machine sew a fine line of zigzag stitching beside the seam before trimming the seam closely and turning the collar to the right side.

6 Neatly sew up the opening with a few handstitches.

7 Make two horizontal buttonholes in the left back in the positions marked on the pattern. Sew the two mother-of-pearl shank buttons in the corresponding positions on the right back so that the back edges overlap.

④ MAKING THE DRESS

1 Using the tracing paper and pencil, trace a working pattern for the dress from the master pattern and cut out the various pieces.
2 Fold the batiste in half widthwise. Pin the pattern on, matching fold lines, and cut out the fabric. Cut two skirt pieces, and yoke self-linings.

Yoke

Using narrow French seams, stitch the front yoke to the back yokes at the shoulders. Repeat to join the yoke lining pieces.

Skirt

1 Make a cut 8 cm long in the center of the skirt back for the back placket.
2 Roll 6 mm of fabric under on each edge of the cut on the wrong side, tapering toward the bottom of the cut, and stitch in place by hand, using running stitch.
3 Fold the fabric under again and sew on each side with tiny hemstitches.

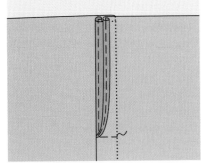

4 Fold the right side of the opening under 1.5 cm and overlap it onto the left side by the same amount, making a pleat. Pin the pleat into place and secure it by stitching firmly across the width of the pleat at the bottom.
5 Using a 1 cm seam allowance, sew two rows of gathering stitches, 3 mm apart, along the top of the skirt front and the skirt back on either side of the placket, stopping short of the placket. Pull up the gathering threads until the skirt front fits the yoke front, with the centers matched, and the skirt back fits the yoke backs on each side.

HINT
When choosing your fabrics, remember that the intensity of the colors in the embroidery will depend on the type of fabric. A sheer organdy barely diminishes the colors, while much softer hues are produced with batiste, silk or fine linen. The embroidered collar is just as effective on a dress made from mint green, peach or pink batiste as it is on white fabric.

Sleeves

1 Sew one row of gathering stitches along the tops of the sleeves and one along the lower edges, between the dots marked on the pattern.
2 Using a narrow French seam, stitch the underarm seams.
3 With right sides facing, stitch together the short ends of one of the bias-cut sleeve bindings.
4 Pull up the gathers on the lower sleeve edge (cuff), adjusting them to fit the sleeve binding.
5 Pin and then stitch the right side of the sleeve binding to the right side of the gathered lower sleeve edge, aligning the raw edges.
6 Turn under 6 mm on the raw edge of the sleeve binding and handstitch it to the inside of the sleeve at the machine stitching line.
7 Gather the shoulder section of the upper sleeve, taking care not to gather the areas near the underarm seam.
8 Repeat steps 3 to 7 to make the other sleeve.

Assembling the dress

1 With right sides together, stitch the gathered skirt front to the yoke front.
2 Do the same with the gathered skirt back and the yoke backs, extending the center edges of the yoke backs 6 mm past the edges of the placket to create a seam allowance when joining the yoke and the lining.
3 Place the yoke lining over the yoke with right sides together, and machine stitch around the center back edges and neckline.

4 Clip the neck edge and turn the work right side out.
5 Turn under the raw edge of the lining and hemstitch it by hand to the skirt gathering line.
6 Using narrow French seams, stitch the side seams of the skirt.

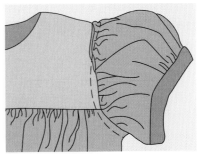

7 Set the sleeves into the armholes with narrow French seams, matching the underarm seams to the skirt side seams and the sleeve centers to the yoke shoulder seams.

Finishing

1 Along the lower edge of the skirt, turn under a 6 mm hem and press with a warm iron. Fold under a further 10 cm, making a deep hem. Press the hem again and then handsew it in place with invisible hemstitching.
2 Make three horizontal buttonholes in the left back yoke, in the positions marked on the pattern, and then sew the three flat mother-of-pearl buttons to the right back yoke in the corresponding positions.

⑤ MAKING THE BONNET

The bonnet is adjustable and fully lined, and has an ungathered lace trim. The lace in the bonnet illustrated was attached by enclosing it in the seams as the bonnet was assembled. However, if you prefer, you could stitch the lace on by hand after completing the bonnet.

1 Using the tracing paper and pencil, trace a working pattern for the bonnet from the master pattern and cut it out.
2 Fold the batiste and cut out two crown pieces. Fold the organdy and cut out two brim pieces.

Crown

1 Pin the edging lace all around the right side of one crown piece,

except along the straight front edge, with the lace heading on the seamline and the scalloped edge facing toward the center of the bonnet. Ease the lace around the corners so that there will be enough fullness.

2 Baste the edging lace in place along the lace heading, using stitches of medium length.

3 With right sides together, machine stitch the crown lining to the crown along the line of basting stitches, stitching through all layers.

4 Clip the curves, turn the crown right side out and press gently.

Brim

1 Pin the edging lace to the right side of the front edge of one brim piece, with the lace heading on the seam line and the scalloped edge lying toward the center. Ease the lace to fit.

2 Baste the edging lace in place along the lace heading.

3 Trim one batiste edge of the entredeux to 6 mm and clip it to allow for curvature. With raw edges aligned,

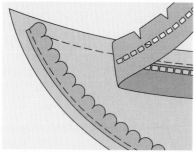

pin the entredeux to the right side of the other edge of the brim along the seamline and baste it in place.

4 With right sides together, lay the second organdy brim piece over the first, sandwiching the edging lace and the entredeux between the two

pieces. Stitch around all seam lines, taking care at the points and leaving a 3 cm opening in the crown edge for turning.

5 Machine sew a line of fine zigzag stitching beside the seam and trim the seam allowance carefully and evenly to prevent any uneven or jagged edges that will show through the organdy.

6 Turn the work to the right side through the opening and close the opening by hand with slipstitch.

Joining the brim to the crown

1 Trim the other batiste edge of the entredeux to 6 mm. With right sides together and raw edges aligned, lay the entredeux edge of the brim over the straight, unstitched edge of the crown. Stitch the entredeux to the outer layer of the crown only.

2 Turn the brim over, fold the raw edge of the crown lining under and handsew it to the entredeux with invisible hemstitching.

Finishing

1 Cut the narrow ribbon into one 60 cm length and two 35 cm lengths.

2 Machine stitch along the casing lines, as marked on the master pattern, and unpick the seams between the line of stitching and the lower edges of the bonnet to thread the ribbon through.

3 Thread the 60 cm length of ribbon through the casing at the back of the bonnet and secure the ribbon in place with a few handstitches at the edges and the center back. Thread the 35 cm lengths of ribbon through the casings at each side, threading from the front to the back, and pull the ribbon through until the end is level with the opening of the casing at the front. Use a few backstitches to secure the end of the ribbon to the bonnet, 6 mm from the end of the casing.

4 Finish off the ends of the casings by hand with a few slipstitches.

5 Cut the wide ribbon in half. At one end of each piece, fold the ribbon to form two small loops.

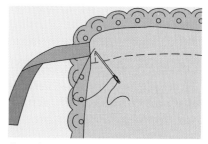

6 Make a small gathered pleat at the base of the loops and secure it with a few handstitches.

7 Stitch the folded and pleated ends of the wide ribbons to either side of the bonnet, at the point where the brim joins the crown.

8 Embroider the free ends of all the ribbons with daisies, following the embroidery instructions below. If the ribbon is likely to fray, leave enough ribbon below the embroidery to fold back a hem to cover the back of the embroidery.

9 Fold hems at the ends of all ribbons and slipstitch them in place, ensuring that the hems cover the embroidery.

Embroidering the wide ribbons

Use one strand of cotton throughout. Choose one of the pink embroidery cottons that you used for the daisies on the collar. Starting all stitches from the center point, work the petals by making loose straight stitches and securing them with a tiny stitch at the outer end. Overlay this small end stitch with a two-turn French knot, finishing on the wrong side of the work. Return to the center to begin each new stitch, varying the lengths. Using green cotton, make the calyx by working a straight stitch across the base of the tendrils and a fly stitch underneath. Work small straight stitches for the stem.

Embroidering the narrow ribbons

Work in the same way as for the wide ribbon and with the same colors, but use smaller stitches and work only five pistil stitches for the daisy.

Embroidering the ribbons

The petals are worked with long, loose straight stitches, secured at the end with a tiny stitch and finished with two-turn French knots. To make the calyx (the green base), sew a straight stitch under the stems and a fly stitch below that. Use small straight stitches for the stem.

Soft rattles for a baby

These unusual rattles will please both parents and baby. Made from fabric and felt, they will capture a baby's attention with their bright colors and decoration, yet are soft to handle. Because they have bells inside to make the rattling sound, all stitching must be very firm and the bells securely attached.

WHAT YOU NEED

Master pattern B14(a–b) • 15 cm x 60 cm colored fabric • 2 or 3 felt scraps in different colors • dress-making pins • strong sewing threads to match fabric and felt • stranded embroidery cotton: green, various colors for the flowers • embroidery needle • 6 bells • toy filling • scissors • sewing needle • ribbon • tracing paper • pencil • sewing machine
● *Technique pages 292–301, 307–12, 343–4*

HINT

For a stylish rattle ball, use a fabric with a broad patterned stripe. Cut out the segments carefully so that the stripes will match up, as in the photograph.

5 Join the last seam, leaving a 5 cm opening, and carefully turn the work to the right side through the opening.
6 Stuff the ball with toy filling until it is firm, and then handstitch the opening to close.

Stitch guide

Use two strands of green cotton for the stem stitch. To work the flowers, choose colors that contrast with the segments of felt.

- ○ French knot
- ∫ Stem stitch
- ◊ Lazy daisy stitch

where the segments converge and leaving an opening for turning.
8 Turn the work to the right side and stuff the ball firmly with toy filling, and then stitch up the opening securely by hand.
9 Mask the point where the handle joins the ball with a band of ribbon stitched firmly into place.

Rattle ball

1 With tracing paper and pencil, trace a working pattern from the master pattern and cut it out.
2 Using the pattern, cut out seven segments from the colored fabric.
3 With right sides facing, pin the segments together. Taking a 1 cm seam allowance, join all the seams except the last one.
4 Using strong thread, firmly hand-stitch three bells to the seams on the wrong side of the fabric.

Hand rattle

1 Using the tracing paper, pencil and scissors, trace and cut a working pattern from the master pattern.
2 From the felt, cut out two handle pieces and six segments, using all the colors.
3 Join three of the segments with a fine seam, alternating the colors. Join the other three segments in the same way and put the pieces aside.
4 Join the handle pieces together, leaving the small end open. Turn the handle right side out and stuff it firmly with toy filling.
5 Following the stitch guide, use two strands of embroidery cotton, in green and another color, to embroider the flower sprays on each of the segments.
6 Handstitch the three bells firmly to the seams on the wrong side of the work.
7 Sew the two sets of seg-ments and the handle together, stitching the handle in at one end

VARIATION

Decorate the rattles with ribbon bows. Make the bows small enough to ensure that baby's hands don't become entangled in the ribbon, and stitch them very firmly to the rattles. Attach a ribbon loop to the rattle ball so that it can be suspended from the framework of a crib or carriage.

Balloon cardigan & striped sweater

Knitted in soft pastels or bright primary colors, these basic patterns can be varied to suit both boys and girls. They can be given separately or as a pair. The balloons are embroidered onto the cardigan after the garment has been made up.

WHAT YOU NEED

Sizes	A	B	C	D
Age (months)	3	6	12	18
Fits chest (cm)	40	45	50	53
Sweater measures (cm)				
Chest	43	49	54	57
Length	20	23	26	29
Sleeves	13	16	19	21
Cardigan measures (cm)				
Chest	44	50	55	58
Length	22	25	28	31
Sleeves	13	16	19	21

The yarn used in this project is 4 ply baby yarn (25 g balls) and the colors are: main color (mc), (white); 1st contrast color (cc1), (mint); 2nd contrast color (cc2), (buttermilk); 3rd contrast color (cc3), (lemon).

Sweater				
mc	2	3	3	3
cc1	1	1	1	1
cc2	1	1	1	1
cc3	1	1	1	1
Cardigan				
mc	3	4	5	6

You will also need a small quantity of the three contrasting colors to work the embroidery.

Knitting needles: 3.25 mm (no. 10) and 2.75 mm (no. 12) • circular needle 2.75 mm (no. 12) – optional, for front band of cardigan • 3 stitch holders and 2 buttons for the sweater • 1 stitch holder and 4 buttons for the cardigan • needles: wool sewing, large crewel • small quantity of black stranded embroidery cotton

● *Technique pages 312, 323–7*

CHECKING THE GAUGE

Check your gauge to ensure that the measurements of the finished garments will be as close as possible to the size specified. You should have 29 stitches to a 10 cm width over stockinette stitch, using 3.25 mm knitting needles. If you have fewer stitches, use smaller needles; if more stitches, use bigger needles.

Sweater

❶ BACK

Using 2.75 mm needles and mc, cast on 62 (70-78-82) sts.
1st row: K2, ★ P2, K2, rep from ★ to the end.
2nd row: P2, ★ K2, P2, rep from ★ to the end.
Rep 1st and 2nd rows 6 (7-7-8) times, inc 3 sts evenly across last row...65 (73-81-85) sts, 14 (16-16-18) rows of rib in all.
Change to 3.25 mm needles.
Work stst in stripes throughout, 2 rows each mc, cc1, mc, cc2, mc and cc3, until work measures 9 (11-13-15.5) cm from beg, ending with a purl row.
Tie a colored thread at each end of last row to mark beg of armholes, as there is no armhole shaping. ★★
Work 22 (26-30-32) rows stst, continuing the striped pattern.

Dividing for back opening

1st row: K35 (39-43-45), turn and cont on these sts.
2nd row: K5, purl to end.
3rd row: Knit.
Rep 2nd and 3rd rows 5 times, then 2nd row once.
15th row: Knit to last 3 sts, yfwd, K2 tog (this is the buttonhole), K1.
Keeping garter st border correct, work 3 rows stst.

Shaping the shoulder

Cast off 7 (8-9-10) sts at beg of next row and foll alt row, then 7 (9-10-10) sts at beg of foll alt row. Work 1 row. Leave rem 14 (14-15-15) sts on a stitch holder.

Completing the back

Join yarn to rem sts on needle, cast on 5 sts for underlap and work other side to correspond, omitting buttonhole and "Work 1 row."

❷ FRONT

Work as for back to ★★. Keeping stripes correct, work 26 (30-32-34) rows of stst.

Dividing for neck

1st row: K26 (30-34-36), turn and cont on these sts.
Dec at neck edge in alt rows until 21 (25-28-30) sts rem.
Work 3 rows stst.

Shaping the shoulder

Cast off 7 (8-9-10) sts at beg of next row and foll alt row.
Work 1 row. Cast off.
Slip next 13 sts on to stitch holder.
Join yarn to rem sts on needle and work other side to correspond.

❸ SLEEVES

Using 2.75 mm needles and mc, cast on 34 (34-38-38) sts. Work 11 (13-13-15) rows of rib as given for back.
Next row: Rib 4 (2-4-2), ★ inc in next st, rib 1, rep from ★ to the last 4 (2-4-2) sts, rib 4 (2-4-2), giving a total of 47 (49-53-55) sts.
Change to 3.25 mm needles.
Working in stripes as for back, inc at each end of 5th and foll 4th rows until there are 63 (69-67-65) sts.
Sizes C and D: Inc at each end of foll 6th rows until there are (75-77) sts.
For all sizes: Continue until work measures 13 (16-19-21) cm from beg, ending with a purl row.
Cast off loosely.

4 NECKBAND

Using backstitch, join the shoulder seams together.

With right side facing, using 2.75 mm needles and mc, knit up 73 (73-79-79) sts evenly around neck, incl sts from stitch holders.

1st row: K5, ★ P1, K1, rep from ★ to last 4 sts, K4.

2nd row: K6, ★ P1, K1, rep from ★ to last 5 sts, K5.

Rep 1st and 2nd rows 3 (3-4-4) times, then 1st row once, working a buttonhole (as before) in 4th row. Cast off loosely in rib.

5 MAKING UP THE SWEATER

Do not press. Using the wool sewing needle and backstitch, join sleeve and side seams to colored threads. Sew in sleeves. Sew underlap in position. Sew on buttons.

Cardigan

1 BACK

Using 2.75 mm needles and mc, cast on 70 (78-86-90) sts.
Work 14 (16-16-18) rows rib as for back of sweater, dec 2 sts evenly across

last row…68 (76-84-88) sts.
Change to 3.25 mm needles.
Work in stst until work measures 10 (12-14-16.5) cm from beg, ending with a purl row.
Tie a colored thread at each end of last row to mark beg of armholes, as there is no armhole shaping.
Work 44 (48-52-54) rows stst.

Shaping the shoulders

Cast off 7 (9-10-10) sts at beg of next 4 rows, then 8 (8-9-11) sts at beg of foll 2 rows. Leave rem 24 (24-26-26) sts on stitch holder until required.

❷ FRONTS

Left front

Using 2.75 mm needles cast on 34 (38-42-42) sts.

Work 14 (16-16-18) rows rib as for back, inc 0 (0-0-2) sts in last row...34 (38-42-44) sts.

Change to 3.25 mm needles.

Work in stst until work measures same as back to colored threads, ending with a purl row. ★★

Tie a colored thread at end of last row to assist with making up.

Shaping front edge

Dec at end of next and foll alt rows until 31 (36-40-42) sts rem, then in foll 4th rows until 22 (26-29-31) sts rem.

Work 3 (5-5-7) rows stst.

Shaping the shoulder

Cast off 7 (9-10-10) sts at beg of next

STITCH AND COLOR GUIDE

Embroider the balloons and their strings using the photograph as a guide for the position. Work the balloons in duplicate stitch using the three contrasting colors. Work the strings in stem stitch using three strands of the black stranded embroidery cotton.

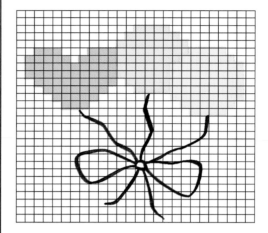
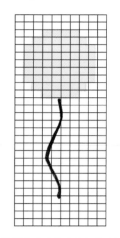

row and foll alt row. Work 1 row.
Cast off loosely.

Right front

Work to correspond with left front, reversing shaping.

❸ SLEEVES

Using 2.75 mm needles, cast on 42 (42-46-46) sts.

Work 11 (13-13-15) rows rib, as given for back.

Next row: Rib 4 (0-3-8), ★ inc in next st, rib 2 (2-2-1), rep from ★ to last 2 (0-1-6) st/s, rib to end...54 (56-60-62) sts.

Change to 3.25 mm needles.

Working in stst, inc at each end of 5th and foll 4th rows until there are 64 (70-70-74) sts, then in foll 6th rows until there are 68 (74-80-84) sts.

Cont without shaping until work measures 13 (16-19-21) cm from beg, ending with a purl row.

Cast off loosely.

❹ FRONT BAND

Using backstitch, join shoulder seams. With right side facing and using 2.75 mm needles, knit up 37 (45-52-62) sts evenly along right front edge to beg of shaping, then 46 (50-54-56) sts evenly along shaped edge to shoulder seam, then knit 24 (24-26-26) sts from back

neck stitch holder, then knit up 46 (50-54-56) sts evenly along shaped edge to end of shaping, then 37 (45-52-62) sts to lower edge, giving a total of 190 (214-238-262) sts.

(If this number of stitches will not fit comfortably on a needle, try using a circular needle.)

Work 3 rows rib as for back, beg with a 2nd row.

4th row: Rib 4, ★ cast off 1 st, rib 9 (12-14-17), rep from ★ 3 times; rib to the end.

5th row: Rib to last 31 (40-46-51) sts, ★ turn, cast on 1 st, turn, rib 9 (12-14-17), rep from ★ twice, turn, cast on 1 st, turn, rib 4 – this makes a total of 4 buttonholes.

Work 4 (4-6-6) rows rib.
Cast off loosely in rib.

❺ MAKING UP THE CARDIGAN

Do not press. Using wool sewing needle and backstitch, join sleeve and side seams up to colored threads. Sew in sleeves. Sew on buttons.

❻ WORKING THE BALLOONS

Work the balloons in duplicate stitch in the three contrasting colors and the balloon strings in black cotton stem stitch. Follow the stitch and color guide, and use the photograph to help you position the balloons.

Folk art frames for baby photos

Using simple designs and different-colored backgrounds, someone with little experience in folk art painting can produce these attractive picture frames with ease and confidence.

2 plain wood photograph frames • craft paints: white, and colors of your choice • pencil • stylus (from a craft supply shop) or metal skewer • clear varnish • paintbrush: no. 1 or no. 2 round • large flat brush or sponge brush • container for water • paper towels • fine-grade sandpaper and brown paper • plastic wrap • plate or ice-cream carton lid (for palette) • masking tape
● *Technique pages 334–5*

① PAINTING THE PINK FRAME

1 If necessary, lightly sand the wooden frame with fine sandpaper. Apply two or three coats of paint in the base color with a large flat brush or a sponge brush. If it is still a little rough between coats, rub it back lightly with brown paper. Allow the paint to dry thoroughly.

2 The ragging is two shades lighter than the the base color, so mix white paint with the base color to give the desired shade. Screw a piece of plastic wrap into a loose ball, dab it into the paint (using a few sheets of paper towel to blot off the excess), and lightly dab the frame until you have achieved the effect you want.

3 Mark out the flowers lightly in pencil. Select a color and, using the tip of the round brush, paint an oval petal in two strokes, the first curving slightly to the left and the second curving slightly to the right. The more pressure you apply, the thicker the stroke will be. Repeat until there are five petals in each large flower.

4 Choose a color for the flower centers and, with the end of the brush handle, dot a spot of color into each center. Reload the end of the brush with paint for every spot.

5 Paint the stems with the very tip of the brush, applying the lightest pressure possible to make a fine line in an elongated S-shape.

6 To paint the leaves, place the brush tip on the edge of the stem and press down lightly to create a small oval shape in one stroke.

7 Using the stylus or the pointed tip of a skewer, dot small three-petaled flowers to fill the spaces between the larger flowers. Allow to dry.

8 Apply two or three coats of varnish using the large flat brush or sponge brush. Allow each coat to dry thoroughly before applying the next.

② PAINTING THE BLUE FRAME

1 Proceed as for step 1 in "Painting the pink frame."

2 Cover three-quarters of the frame front with masking tape, leaving a narrow edge on the inside of the frame. Paint this with two coats of paint, using a different color to the base. When the paint is dry, remove the

tape and touch up any small spots if necessary. This makes the border on the inside edge of the frame.

3 Choose the colors for the flowers and make a large dot flower in each corner of the frame. To do this, use the end of the brush handle to paint five spots in a circle and a different-colored spot in the center.

4 Make smaller dot flowers using the same method with the stylus or skewer. If you are not confident about placing the flowers evenly around the frame, use a ruler and pencil to lightly mark their positions.

5 Join up the flowers with a stem, as in the pink frame, and, if you like, add some leaves.

6 When the paint is dry, apply two or three coats of varnish, allowing each coat to dry before adding the next.

NOTE
Make sure that the paint is completely dry before starting each new step. Wash your brush out after using each color and use kitchen paper to blot up excess paint and water.

Baby's bootees in soft leather

These luxurious, soft-as-silk bootees will keep a small baby's feet warm and snug.

WHAT YOU NEED

Master pattern **A6**(a–c) • soft leather (such as chamois), about 30 cm **x** 21 cm • strong cream sewing thread • 50 cm red ribbon, 4 mm wide • tracing paper • pencil • scissors • dressmaking pins • craft knife • sewing machine
● *Technique pages 295-8, 343-4*

❶ CUTTING OUT THE LEATHER

1 Trace each pattern piece twice from the master pattern onto tracing paper. Make sure you mark the center points and the ribbon-lacing slits. Cut out the pattern pieces and pin them to the leather.
2 Cut the leather out. Where indicated, mark the front and back centers with a pencil and cut small slits in the bootee fronts and back/side pieces with the craft knife.

Cutting guide
Cut two of each pattern piece. Transfer all markings and cut small ribbon-lacing slits, as shown on the master pattern.

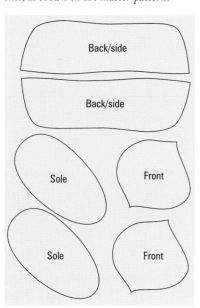

❷ SEWING THE BOOTEES

1 Consult your sewing machine manual to set stitch tension and foot pressure correctly, and select an appropriate needle.

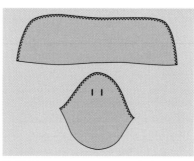

2 Taking care not to stretch the cut-out pieces as you work, machine zigzag over the upper edge of each back/side piece and each front piece.

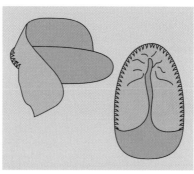

3 With the wrong sides together, place the back/side piece onto the sole, matching the center backs. Secure the edges together by machine zigzagging around the sole.
4 With the wrong sides together, place the front piece onto the sole, matching the center fronts. Machine

CAUTION
Do not give these bootees to a baby who is beginning to stand, because the soles are slippery and the bootees are not thick enough to protect and support the baby's feet.

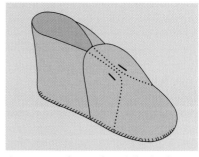

zigzag over these edges. The back/side piece and the front should overlap at the sides, with the slits aligned.

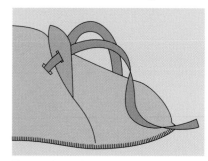

5 Cut the ribbon into two 25 cm lengths and thread each length from the inside through the slits in the sides and up through the pairs of slits in the fronts of the bootees. Tie the ends of the ribbons into bows.

TODDLERS & PRE-SCHOOLERS

Toddlers are kept busy

exploring their environment

and joyfully discovering

its secrets. Here's a range

of gifts for them to play with

and dress up in, and

to stimulate their senses

and imagination.

Fairy wings & wand

Encourage fantasy with these fairy accessories. Be sure to supervise the use of the wand.

WHAT YOU NEED

Wings: 2 wire coat-hangers • opaque white tights • white sewing thread • 1.5 m silver braid • 2.5 m silver grosgrain ribbon, 40 mm wide • 1.5 m ribbon or elastic, 40 mm wide, for harness • metallic silver stars • wire cutters • hammer • needle • craft glue
Wand: Balsa wood dowel, at least 45 cm long • stiff cardboard • pencil • ruler • gold paint • craft glue • 1 m ribbon, 40 mm wide • craft knife
● *Technique pages 292–5*

❶ MAKING THE WINGS

1 Using the wire cutters, cut the hooks from the coat-hangers 5 cm from the base of the twist.
2 Pull and bend the hangers into wing shapes, using a hammer to smooth out any persistent bumps.
3 Pull one leg of the tights over one of the wing shapes until you reach the toe. Stretch the tights evenly so that there are as few wrinkles as possible.
4 Gather the tights leg firmly around the stem of the hook piece. Wind the thread around the fabric and the stem about 20 times, then tie off.
5 Cut through the tights at least 2 cm away from the wound thread.
6 Repeat steps 3 to 5 to make the other wing.

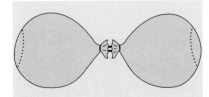

7 Overlap the two coat-hanger stems, and fasten them together by winding thread around both stems, up and down the length of the stem. When the wings are firm, tie off the cotton.

❷ DECORATING THE WINGS

1 Sew the silver braid around the wings, taking the needle down through the inside edge of the wire, around the outside edge and over the braid. Leave 2 cm of braid at the wing stems; these will be concealed under the center ribbon to give a neat finish.
2 Wind the ribbon several times around the overlapped stems, covering the cut ends of the tights and the braid. Cut the ribbon and secure it by sewing at the back.
3 Thread the rest of the ribbon through the top layer of wound ribbon and tie a bow. Trim the tails of the bow so that they are long enough to flow down the fairy's back.
4 Glue the silver stars randomly over the fronts and backs of the wings.

❸ MAKING THE HARNESS

1 Measure and cut two strips of elastic or ribbon long enough to fit loosely around the child's arms. Stitch both ends of each strip to the wing stem to form loops.

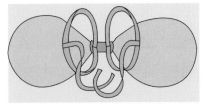

2 Stitch long ribbons to the front of the loops, level with the armpits. These ribbons are tied at the front in another flowing bow to dress up the fairy and hold the wings firm.

❹ MAKING THE WAND

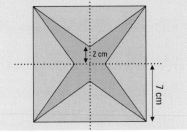

1 With a pencil and ruler, mark a 14 cm square on the cardboard. Rule lines joining the mid-points of opposite sides of the square. Along each line, mark points 2 cm away from the center. Rule a four-pointed star by ruling lines from these points to the corners of the square. Draw another 14 cm square, and make another four-pointed star by repeating the steps above, but this time mark points 3 cm away from the center.
2 Cut out the stars with the craft knife, and glue them together so that the points of one of the stars are positioned between the spokes of the other to make a star with eight points.
3 Using the craft knife, carefully cut a straight notch into one end of the balsa wood dowel. The notch should be about 15 mm deep and the same width as the cardboard.
4 Apply glue to both sides of one of the star points and push this into the cut in the dowel. Wind cotton around the join to make it completely secure.
5 Paint the star gold. Leave to dry. Tie the ribbon into a bow around the join and leave the ribbon trailing.

Mommy's little helper's apron

Ideal for a little girl who loves to help with those messy chores, this apron looks cute over most outfits and keeps clothes spotless at both the front and the back.

WHAT YOU NEED

Master pattern **C20(a–b)** • 70 cm plain or patterned cotton fabric, 115 cm wide • 1.5 m each of 3 contrasting colors of bias binding (colors A, B, C) • sewing thread to match fabric and binding • tracing paper • pencil • tape measure • scissors • dressmaking pins • sewing needle • sewing machine
● *Technique pages 292–301, 343–4*

❶ CUTTING OUT THE FABRIC

1 Fold a piece of tracing paper in half and match the fold of the tracing paper with the center line of the master pattern. Trace a working pattern for the main apron piece. Keeping the tracing paper folded, cut around the outline and open it out to produce a complete apron front and back.
2 Trace and cut out a working pattern for the shoulder frills.
3 Fold the fabric in half and cut out as shown in the cutting guide.
4 From the remaining fabric, cut four 6 cm x 38 cm strips for the ties.

❷ SEWING THE APRON

1 With the right sides together and the raw edges aligned, join the front

CUTTING GUIDE

Fold the fabric selvage to selvage and cut two of each piece.

Fold

Ties | Ties | Shoulder frills | Front and back

VARIATION
Adapt the apron for a little boy by choosing a plain bright fabric, or one with a large print, and omitting the shoulder frills.

of the apron to the back at one shoulder, with a 1 cm flat seam.
2 With right sides together, pin and sew one raw edge of bias binding A around the neck edge.
3 With right sides together, join the front to the back at the second shoulder. Include the bias binding in the seam.
4 Turn the binding over the neck edge and slipstitch it into place.

❸ ATTACHING THE FRILLS

1 With right sides together, sew one edge of bias binding A to the straight edge of the armhole frill. Fold the binding over to the wrong side and slipstitch it into place.
2 Run two rows of gathering stitches along the curved edge of the frill.
3 Pull up the gathering threads until the frill fits between the armhole dots marked on the pattern front and back.
4 With the wrong sides together, pin and then stitch the gathered frill to the armhole, taking a 6 mm seam allowance. The armhole edge will be trimmed with bias binding later.
5 Repeat steps 1 to 4 to stitch the frill to the second armhole.

❹ ATTACHING THE TIES

1 Fold the four straight strips in half lengthwise, right sides together.
2 Taking a 1 cm seam allowance, stitch the long side and one short side of each tie. Turn the tie right side out and press.
3 Sew the ties to the wrong sides of the front and back where indicated on the master pattern,

---

taking a 6 mm seam allowance. The ties should lie back against the fabric, because the seams will be bound with bias binding to encase all the raw seams (see "Finishing").

❺ FINISHING

1 Join bias binding B to bias binding C and align the join with the center of the front bottom edge of the apron.

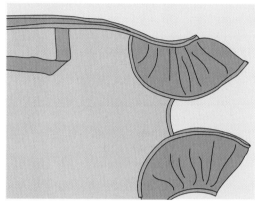

2 Stitch the bias binding around the outer edge of the apron, encasing the ends of the ties and the raw armhole seams. Join the two colors neatly at the center of the back edge.
3 Trim the edges, fold the bias binding over and slipstitch it into place.

Cuddly rag doll

The construction of this rag doll is so simple that you can hand over parts of the project to an older child who can help you make the doll for a younger friend or relation.

WHAT YOU NEED

Tracing paper • pencil • scissors •
dressmaking pins • tape measure •
dressmaker's carbon paper • sewing
machine • needle: general sewing
Doll: Master pattern **B8(a–e)** •
90 cm **x** 60 cm plain or patterned
cotton fabric (for the body, arms
and legs) • 30 cm **x** 20 cm plain
fabric (for the head and face) •
1.5 m ribbon, 12 mm wide (for the
pigtails) • 60 cm ribbon, 6 mm wide
(for the neck bow) • 50 g ball 8 ply
black wool (for the hair) • embroidery cottons (for embroidering the
features) • sewing thread to match
the fabric • soft toy filling • stiff
cardboard, 35 cm **x** 35 cm • needles:
darning, embroidery
Petticoat: 23 cm **x** 80 cm net fabric •
90 cm edging lace, 20 mm wide •
60 cm elastic, 8 mm wide
Dress: Master pattern **B9(a–b)** •
60 cm **x** 80 cm cotton fabric • 40 cm
edging lace, 20 mm wide (same as
for petticoat) • 30 cm elastic, 6 mm
wide • 60 cm cotton tape, 12 mm
wide • sewing thread to match
the fabric • bodkin • 6 mm snap •
25 cm ribbon, 35 mm wide (for
the sash)
● *Technique pages 292–301, 343–4*

Doll

❶ CUTTING THE FABRIC

1 Using tracing paper, pencil and
scissors, trace and cut out a working
pattern from the master pattern.
2 Fold the fabric for the body in half
widthwise. Pin the pattern pieces to
the fabric, making sure that the front
and back body pieces are pinned along
the fold, and cut out the pieces.
3 Fold the fabric for the head in half
and pin the pattern piece for the head
to it. Cut around the pattern to produce a back and front head piece.

NOTE
*There is a seam allowance of
6 mm for all seams on the doll.*

DOLL FEATURES
Careful choice of facial features will give
your doll its own personality. Define lips
with a single line of stem stitch, or make
fuller lips with two rows of satin stitch to
form a top and bottom lip. Make nostrils
with two French knots. Embroider eyes,
lashes and brows in appropriate colors. You
can also sew on beads or buttons for eyes,
or buy safety eyes from a craft shop. An
alternative is to draw the features in with
waterproof markers. Finally, experiment
with different hair styles and colors.

*To try out different expressions, draw faces on
tracing paper and pin them to your doll's face.*

4 Using the dressmaker's carbon
paper, mark the facial features on the
right side of one of the head pieces.

❷ SEWING THE BODY AND HEAD
1 With right sides facing, sew the
body together along the side, shoulder
and crotch seams. Turn the body
right side out, fold the remaining raw
edges 6 mm to the inside and press.

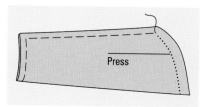

Press

2 Fold the leg pieces in half lengthwise, right sides together. Sew down
the leg seams and across the foot.
Turn the leg right side out, fold the
remaining raw edges 6 mm to the
inside and press.
3 Repeat step 2 to sew the arms.
4 With right sides together, stitch
around the head, leaving the neck
edge open. Turn the head right side
out, fold the raw edges at the neck
6 mm to the inside and press.
5 Stuff each piece lightly with soft
toy filling. So that the doll will be soft
and cuddly, do not overfill.
6 Using slipstitch, neatly sew the
arms, legs and head to the body.

7 To make the hands and feet,
thread a needle with a double length
of sewing thread. Fasten the thread
firmly to the fabric 3 cm from the
end of each limb, wrap the thread two
or three times around the limb and
pull it tight. Fasten the thread
securely and finish off.

❸ EMBROIDERING THE FACE
1 Using two strands of embroidery
cotton, embroider the eyebrows and
nose with two rows of stem stitch.
2 Fill in the eyes with stem stitch
and add single straight stitches around
them to make eyebrows.
3 Using a single embroidery thread,
work the mouth in a single row of
stem stitch.

❹ ADDING THE HAIR
1 Wind the black wool around
the 35 cm square of cardboard about
125 times, so that the strands are
wound side by side in one layer.
2 Using the scissors, carefully cut
through the strands along one edge
of the cardboard.
3 Lay the doll face down and drape
the strands of wool over the back
and crown of the head, matching the
center of the strands to the center
of the head.
4 Using the darning needle and black
wool, backstitch the wool to the head

along the center line, catching two or three strands at a time.

5 Slipstitch the wool to the fabric along the forehead and the sides of the face to create a hairline.

6 Making sure that the strands of wool are flat against the head and that the fabric beneath is not showing, catch the wool here and there down to about ear level for the first 2 cm back from the forehead.

7 Smoothing the wool over the crown and back of the head, divide the ends into three even bundles at each side. Plait the bundles into pigtails, leaving the last 3 cm or so free.

8 Cut the 12 mm ribbon in half and tie a bow on the end of each pigtail.

9 Tie the 6 mm ribbon around the neck and secure it with a few stitches so that it will not unravel.

Petticoat

1 With right sides facing, sew the two short sides of the 23 cm x 80 cm piece of net fabric together.

2 Using a zigzag stitch to overlock the raw edge of the fabric, sew the edging lace to the right side of the net fabric along the lower edge.

3 At the waistline edge, fold the net fabric 3 mm to the wrong side and press. Fold and then stitch a 1 cm hem to the inside, leaving a small opening to insert the elastic.

4 Thread the elastic through the casing and oversew the ends to secure. Close the opening with slipstitch.

Dress

1 CUTTING THE FABRIC

1 Using tracing paper, pencil and scissors, trace and cut a working pattern from the master pattern. Transfer the dots and the position of the waist casing onto the working pattern.

2 Fold the fabric in half lengthwise and pin the dress pattern to the fabric, placing the dress center front on a fold. Cut out the pieces and mark the positions of the dots and waist casing with dressmaker's carbon paper. From the remaining fabric, cut out a 25 cm x 18 mm bias strip.

2 SEWING THE DRESS

1 With right sides together and using a 1 cm seam allowance, machine stitch the front of the dress to the backs at the shoulder seams. Press the seams open and neaten to prevent fraying.

2 Before sewing the back seam, turn and stitch the raw edges of the fabric under 5 mm. With the right sides together, and using a 1.5 cm seam allowance, sew the back seam between the dots. Press the seam open. Fold back the seam allowance along the unstitched part of the seam and press.

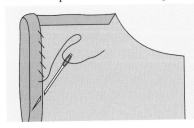

3 Before sewing the side seams, turn and machine stitch the raw edges of the fabric under 5 mm. With right sides facing, and using a 1.5 cm seam allowance, machine stitch the front to the back at the side seams between the dots. Press the seam open. Fold under the seam allowance around the armhole edges and press. Catch the turned edge of the fabric around the armhole with small slipstitches.

3 SEWING THE NECK

1 Gather the lace to fit around the neckline by working a row of running stitches along top edge of lace. Pull up to fit neck edge. Tuck the raw ends under 5 mm, and then pin the lace to the right side of the neckline. Baste it in place along the edge.

2 Turn and press the bias strip under 3 mm to the wrong side along both edges. Fold the ends 5 mm to the wrong side and press.

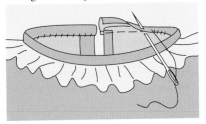

3 With right sides together, machine stitch the raw edge of the bias strip to the neckline, making sure you catch the edge of the lace as you go. Turn the folded edge of the bias strip over to the inside of the neck and slipstitch it into place along the previous line of machine stitching.

4 MAKING THE WAIST

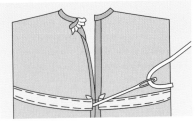

1 Turn the tape under 5 mm at both ends. Starting at the back seam, pin the tape around the waistline on the wrong side of the fabric in the position marked for the waist casing on the pattern. Stitch along both sides, leaving the ends unsewn to form an opening for threading the elastic.

2 With a bodkin, thread the elastic through the opening and around the casing. Sew the ends of the elastic together securely and then close the opening in the casing with slipstitch.

5 FINISHING

1 Turn up the lower hem and straight machine stitch in place.

2 Overlap the back opening at the neck and sew on snap.

3 Put the dress on the doll and tie the sash ribbon at the waist, so that it covers the casing stitching.

Sporty clothespin players

Easy and inexpensive to make, these pin dolls are painted in the colors of sports teams. For added interest, use the colors of the recipient's local team. A sporty pin player would be the perfect gift for a child to make for a friend or sibling.

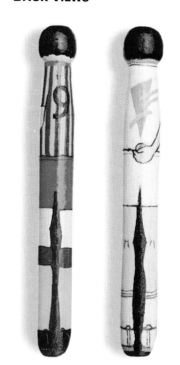

BACK VIEWS

Don't neglect the backs of the sporty clothespin players. You can draw a number on the back of the shirt, or paint some of the pins with their hands behind their backs. Any humorous detail you can add will delight a youngster.

WHAT YOU NEED

Wooden clothespins • artist's acrylic paints: skin tone, colors of a favorite sports team, black • clear gloss varnish • paintbrushes: no. 6 or 8 flat, no. 00 liner • pencil • very fine black drafting pen (optional)
● *Technique pages 334–5*

❶ MIXING THE PAINT

Make skin-colored paint by mixing white paint with tiny quantities of scarlet and yellow; you can mix darker skin tones by adding a very small amount of blue. Experiment with these colors to find the right blend. If children are to paint the pins, they will probably need adult help to mix the skin-colored paint, as only very small quantities of scarlet, yellow and blue need to be added.

If you want to make a darker skin tone, add only a very small amount of blue at a time. Remember that it is very much easier to apply darker coats of paint over a light-colored first coat than to lighten a first coat that is too dark.

❷ PAINTING THE PINS

1 Using a no. 6 or no. 8 flat brush, apply an undercoat of skin-colored paint to the pins. Allow them to dry.
2 Using the illustration as a guide, or making up your own designs,

> **NOTE**
> *Clothespins can be bought at craft stores or from hardware stores, where they are usually sold in packets.*

paint the pins in the colors you have chosen. You could use generic colors, such as white for tennis players, or paint the pins in the colors of a local team's uniform. Leave the pins to dry.
3 Use the drafting pen, the pencil or the liner brush and black paint to add details such as the outlines of jackets, sweaters and pants, buttons, hands, facial features and hairline, and sports equipment. Don't forget to add interesting details to the backs. Leave the pins to dry thoroughly.

❸ FINISHING

Using a no. 6 or no. 8 flat brush, apply two coats of clear gloss varnish, leaving the pins to dry for at least 24 hours between coats.

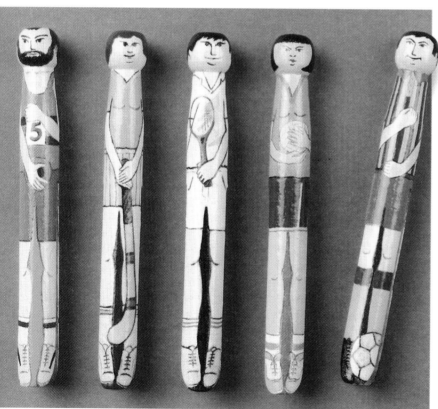

Kindergarten carry bags

A pre-schooler will love these colorful potato-printed muslin bags for carrying books and bits and pieces to nursery school or child care. To make the smaller bag, use a smaller piece of muslin and follow the instructions for the large bag.

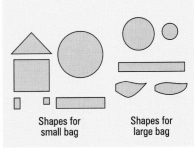

Shapes for
small bag

Shapes for
large bag

2 Cut into the potato to a depth of about 1.5 cm around the outline of the shape, then cut away the surrounding areas to a depth of 1 cm. The cut-away area is the part that will not print. To make a circle, push a circular cookie cutter into the potato to a depth of about 1.5 cm and cut away the surrounding area.

3 Go on carving potato stamps until you have made all the components of your design.

4 Place several layers of paper towels inside the bag, behind the area on which you wish to print, to prevent the paint from seeping through to the fabric at the back.

5 Pour each paint color into a separate flat container. Dip the cut side of the potato into the paint so that the shape you want to print is completely coated. Test the print on a piece of scrap paper and cut away any irregularities.

6 When you are happy with the printed shape, dip the potato into the paint again and press it firmly onto the fabric. Be careful not to move the potato when it touches the fabric, or the design will smudge.

7 To print the same design in a different color, wash the potato clean and wipe the surface with a damp rag to remove any residue before you dip the potato into the new color.

WHAT YOU NEED

45 cm x 64 cm unbleached muslin •
1 m twisted cord, 4 mm diameter •
2–3 large potatoes • fabric paints
in 4–5 primary colors • 4–5 flat
containers (e.g. lids of ice-cream
containers), for paint palettes •
sewing thread • scissors • bodkin
or safety pin • tape measure • black
felt-tipped pen • paper towels •
sharp vegetable knife • circular
cookie cutter • sewing machine
● *Technique pages 292–301*

HINT
*If you carve the potato stamps
for them, even toddlers can
create their own designs on bags
that they can make as gifts for
their own friends.*

Strengthen the edges of the gap with
a double row of machine stitching.
3 To make it easier to apply the
fabric paints, wash the bag to remove
any fabric treatments. Press.

❷ PRINTING THE DESIGN
Keep potato prints simple, and cut
each component shape from a separate piece of potato. Study the bags
illustrated and copy them, or create
a design of your own.
1 Cut a potato cleanly in half with
the vegetable knife. Draw the design
component on the cut surface with
a water-soluble felt-tipped pen.

❶ MAKING THE BAG
1 Fold the fabric in half widthwise
and machine stitch the side seams
of the bag using 1 cm French seams.
2 To make the casing for the drawstring, turn under a 1 cm hem at the
top edge of the bag, and then fold
over another 2.5 cm. Machine stitch
along the lower edge of the hem,
leaving a 2 cm gap at the center front.

❸ FINISHING
1 When the printing is complete,
follow the directions given by the
paint manufacturer to set the paint
and make it washable.
2 Thread the cord through the casing
using a bodkin or a safety pin and then
knot the ends of the cord.

Rock-a-bye doll's cradle

Delight a youngster with this easy-to-make rocking cradle. Fit it with mini bed linen made with fabric scraps and it's ready for a favorite toy.

WHAT YOU NEED

Master pattern **C21(a–c)** • plywood: **800 mm x 420 mm x 18 mm** (for the head and foot); **700 mm x 520 mm x 10 mm** (for the sides and base) • 2 lengths of scrap wood, **310 mm x 10 mm x 10 mm** (for the base supports) • white glue • 30 mm finishing nails • sandpaper: medium, fine • 2 paintbrushes, 13 mm • wood primer • gloss paint • tracing paper • pencil • masking tape • scissors • hand plane • drill and 6 mm drill bit • jigsaw • hammer
● *Technique pages 338–42, 343–4*

❶ PREPARING THE PLYWOOD

1 Carefully trace all the pattern pieces from the master pattern onto the tracing paper.
2 Cut out the pattern pieces. Cut the heart-shaped holes from the pieces for the head and foot.

Cutting guide
Place your traced pattern pieces on the sheets of plywood as shown below: 18 mm plywood (top), 10 mm plywood (bottom).

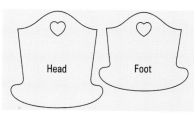

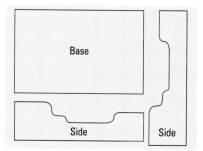

3 Lay the pieces on the plywood as shown in the cutting guide, and secure them with masking tape. Mark a base piece 500 mm x 305 mm on the 10 mm plywood.
4 Trace around the pattern pieces with pencil and then remove them from the wood. Cut out all the pieces with a jigsaw.
5 Inside the heart shapes, drill holes large enough to take the jigsaw blade. Insert the blade and cut out the heart-shaped holes. Sand the cut edges with medium-grade sandpaper.

❷ MAKING THE CRADLE

1 Plane the outside of the lower edges of the sides so that the angle between the sides and the base will be slightly greater than 90°.
2 Glue and nail the sides of the cradle to the head, driving four or five nails straight down through the end into the sides. Support the sides in a vise.
3 Turn the cradle onto its head and glue and nail the foot down onto the sides. Use three or four nails for each join. Let the glue set completely before proceeding to the next step.
4 Turn the cradle upside down and glue the lower edges of the sides. Position the base and hammer in four or five nails on each side, spacing them evenly and allowing for the angle of the sides to the base.

CRADLE CONSTRUCTION

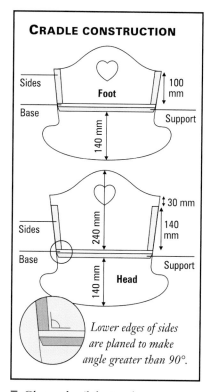

Lower edges of sides are planed to make angle greater than 90°.

5 Glue and nail the two base supports onto the end pieces as shown on the plan. Leave the glue to set.

❸ FINISHING

1 Sand all surfaces thoroughly with fine-grade sandpaper.
2 Ensure that all surfaces are clean and free of dust, and apply undercoat.
3 When dry, apply gloss paint in a color of your choosing.

Dollhouse

Dollhouses are a perennial source of delight and entertainment for children over 3 years old. This house should keep a small child happily and creatively absorbed for hours. You can furnish the house with the dollhouse furniture on pages 54–5, or children can create their own.

WHAT YOU NEED

Medium density fiberboard (MDF): 565 mm x 370 mm x 18 mm, 605 mm x 600 mm x 9 mm, 1145 mm x 505 mm x 6 mm, 980 mm x 600 mm x 3 mm • white woodworking glue • plastic wood • flathead wood screws: eight 6 gauge (30 mm), two 6 gauge (20 mm) • acrylic paints • paintbrush • panel saw • jigsaw • drill, 3 mm drill bit, countersink drill bit • router • medium- and fine-grade sandpaper • screwdriver • pencil • ruler • square • 60 cm broderie anglaise, 50 mm wide
● *Technique pages 338–42, 343–4*

❶ CUTTING THE FIBERBOARD

Use a pencil, ruler and square to measure and mark all pieces, following the cutting guide. Mark the pieces clearly, using a light pencil so that the labels will not show through the paint.

1 Cut out and label the following pieces from the 18 mm MDF:

A one base, 560 mm x 300 mm; **L** two battens, 560 mm x 18 mm; **M** one door runner, 200 mm x 18 mm.
2 Cut out and label the following pieces from the 9 mm MDF:
B/C two sides, 540 mm x 300 mm; **G** one balcony, 570 mm x 55 mm.
3 Cut out and label the following pieces from the 6 mm MDF:
D one front, 570 mm x 450 mm; **E** one floor, 570 mm x 220 mm; **F** one divider, 380 mm x 200 mm; **J** one front door, 150 mm x 100 mm; **H** one railing, 565 mm x 50 mm.

> **NOTE**
> *It is important to paint the door its final color before you slide it into place. Do not paint the bottom edge, and make sure that the paint is completely dry before slotting the door into the runners, otherwise the paint will stick and the door will not slide back and forth smoothly.*

4 From the 3 mm MDF, cut out and label the following:
K one roof, 600 mm x 340 mm; **I** eight tile lengths, 600 mm x 60 mm; **N** one ridge cap, 600 mm x 20 mm; **O** 14 shutters, 100 mm x 35 mm.

❷ PREPARING THE PIECES OF FIBERBOARD
Base (A)

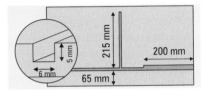

1 Using the router, cut a groove 6 mm wide and 5 mm deep along the full width of the base, 65 mm from the front edge and parallel to it.

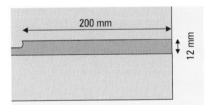

CUTTING GUIDE

Four thicknesses of MDF are used in this project. With the diagram (right) as a guide, measure and mark the pieces listed in "Cutting the fiberboard" on the appropriate boards, and cut the pieces out with a panel saw. Label each piece lightly in pencil, so that the marks will be concealed when you paint the house. The base and side walls are grooved and the room divider and upper floor are slotted so the pieces slide easily together.

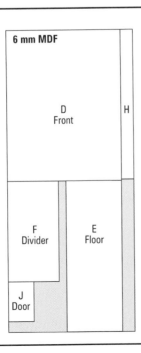

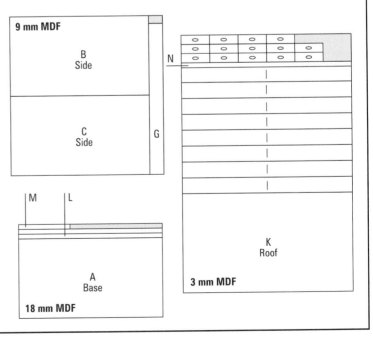

2 To accommodate the sliding door, widen the right-hand 200 mm of the groove to 12 mm by cutting another groove immediately behind the first.
3 Cut a second groove 6 mm wide and 5 mm deep at right angles to the first groove, starting at the center point of the first groove and stopping 20 mm from the rear edge.

Sides (B and C)

The wall in the diagram (right) is for the left-hand side, and steps 2 and 3 below refer to the left-hand wall. Make the right-hand wall as a mirror reflection of the left-hand wall.
1 Clamp B and C together. Mark the angle of the roof on one piece and, with the panel saw, cut through both boards along this line. Unclamp pieces and mark them "left" and "right."

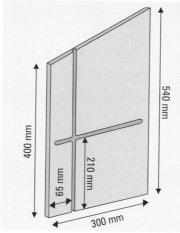

540 mm

400 mm

65 mm

210 mm

300 mm

2 On the inside face of each side, 65 mm parallel to the front edge, use the router to cut a full-length vertical groove 6 mm wide and 5 mm deep.
3 On each side, 210 mm parallel to the lower edge, starting 10 mm in

HINT

Instead of painting the interior, you could use wallpaper with a small motif and place carpet or linoleum scraps on the floor.

from the front edge and finishing 10 mm from the rear edge, use the router to cut a horizontal groove 6 mm wide and 5 mm deep.

Front (D)

1 Using a ruler and pencil, draw the doors and windows on the front and side panels, following the measurements in the diagram "Cutting the windows and door" (page 52).
2 Cut out the door and the windows with a jigsaw. Sand all edges smooth.

Assembling the dollhouse

Measure, cut and prepare the fiberboard with care, and the dollhouse will be easy to assemble. Four flathead wood screws secure the side walls to the base, and then the balcony, the front and the interior walls are slotted in. Finally, the roof is secured with four more flathead wood screws.

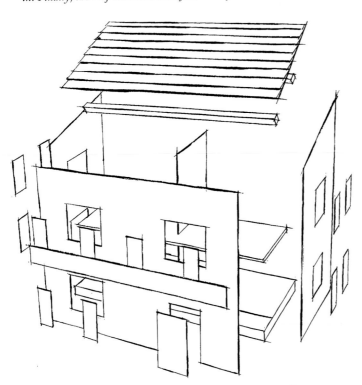

CUTTING THE WINDOWS AND DOOR

To cut the windows, drill holes in the window spaces large enough to take the jigsaw blade, and then work from the drilled holes to cut out the windows.

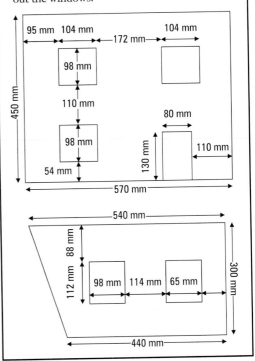

Floor (E)

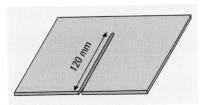

Starting at the center of one of the long edges and using the router, cut a slot 120 mm long and 6 mm wide, at right angles to the edge.

Room divider (F)

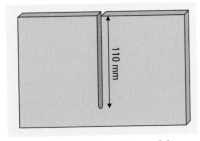

Starting at the center of one of the long edges, use the router to cut a slot 110 mm long and 6 mm wide, at right angles to the edge.

Balcony (G)

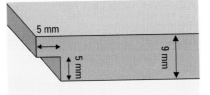

Using the router, cut rabbets 5 mm wide and 5 mm deep at both ends.

Balcony railing (H) and door (J)

Using the medium-grade sandpaper, sand all edges smooth.

Door runner (M)

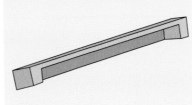

Beginning and finishing 10 mm from each end, use the router to cut a rabbet 7 mm wide and 7 mm deep.

Roof (K), roof tiles (I) and ridge cap (N)

1 Glue the two roof battens to the underside of the roof, 30 mm from the top and bottom edges and 20 mm in from the sides. Sand all edges.

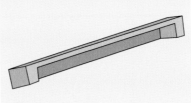

2 Glue the eight roof tile sections to the main roof piece, beginning at the lower edge and lapping each section 20 mm onto the previous section – i.e., leaving 40 mm of each roof tile section exposed. Glue the ridge cap to the uppermost edge of the top roof tile section.

3 Plug the gaps between the main roof piece and the roof tile sections with plastic wood.

❸ ASSEMBLING THE DOLLHOUSE

1 Using the drill and the 3 mm drill bit, make a pilot hole at each corner of the side walls (B and C), 30 mm from the front and back edges and 9 mm from the top and bottom edges.

2 Use the countersink bit to enlarge the drill holes on the outer surfaces so that the screws can be countersunk.

3 Screw the side walls (B and C) to the base (A) through the lower pilot holes, using four 30 mm 6 gauge screws. Make sure that the corners are perfectly aligned.

4 Position the rabbeted edges of the balcony (G) in the horizontal grooves on the side walls and slide the balcony to the front of the house.

5 Slide the front wall (D) down the vertical grooves cut into the side walls, making sure that the doorway is positioned at the right-hand side.

6 Turn the house onto its front on a horizontal surface. Position the door (J) in the door groove in the house base, just inside the door frame. Hold the rabbeted runner over the top of

the door and against the inside of the front wall, so that the door is held upright but can slide freely. The end of the runner should be 20 mm from the corner. Check that the door fills the door frame when closed and clears it when open, and mark the position of the runner with the pencil. Fix the runner to the wall with the two 20 mm 6 gauge screws.

7 Join the room divider (F) to the floor (E) by meshing the two slots at right angles until they lock into position. Ease the bottom edge of the room divider into the center groove on the base, at the same time carefully working the side edges of the floor into the horizontal grooves in the side walls (B and C).

8 Place the roof (K) in position. Attach the roof to the walls through the upper pairs of drilled and counter-sunk holes using four 30 mm 6 gauge screws. The screws should enter the ends of the roof battens.

9 Glue the balcony railing (H) and the window shutters (O) in position.

❹ FINISHING

1 Sand all surfaces well and paint and decorate the house. Choose good strong colors for the roof and the doors and shutters and paler colors for the interior. Place miniature trees and shrubs on the verandas.

2 Glue the length of broderie anglaise to the balcony railing to simulate wrought iron work.

HOME BEAUTIFUL

The gift of a dollhouse can be an inspiration for other gifts – there are so many things you can make or buy to add to the house as the years go by. Try the following ideas.

• Make a chimney with a piece of wood measuring 50 mm x 50 mm x 60 mm. Cut one 50 mm x 50 mm face at an angle so that the piece will sit on the roof tile sections. Sand it, and paint it to match the door and shutters. Attach with glue.

• Buy stylish little wooden trees and animals from a good toy store – or design and make them yourself.

• Make the set of doll furniture (pages 54–5), and look in toy stores and gift shops for miniature kitchen and bathroom equipment, musical instruments, and a host of other home improvers and beautifiers.

• Provide the proud homeowner with a car, a bicycle, a wheelbarrow, and even a garden shed.

Miniature furniture

Add a touch of elegance to a youngster's dollhouse with these home-crafted furnishings that you can make a room at a time as gifts for different occasions. All you need is imagination, scraps of wood, and odds and ends from the sewing basket.

WHAT YOU NEED

Scraps: wood, plywood, fabric, lace, ribbon, aluminum foil, small images (for pictures) • acrylic paint • small paintbrushes • tiny brass screws • small transfers • pencil • ruler • white glue • medium- and fine-grade sandpaper • fretsaw • small chisel • drill, fine drill bits
● *Technique pages 338–42*

❶ THE KITCHEN
Sink

1 Using a fretsaw, cut a block of wood 90 mm x 45 mm x 35 mm. From 3 mm thick plywood, cut one piece 45 mm x 30 mm and two pieces 45 mm x 25 mm.
2 To make the cupboard doors, glue the plywood strips to the wood block.

3 Make handles by gluing three small scraps of wood to the doors or by screwing small brass screws to them.
4 On the top of the sink unit, in the center third, use a drill and a small chisel to scoop out a depression for the sink. It should be no larger than 25 mm x 20 mm.

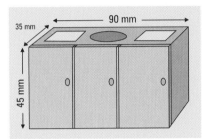

5 For the drain boards, cut two pieces of very thin plywood, 25 mm x 20 mm. Glue these pieces on either side of the sink.

6 Make the tap spindle from a scrap of wood and glue it to the back edge of the sink. Screw brass screws on either side of this for the tap handles.
7 Sand the surfaces smooth. Using acrylic paints and a small paintbrush, paint the sink and the drain boards silver. Paint the unit and doors in colors of your choice.

Refrigerator

1 Using a fretsaw, cut a block of wood 90 mm x 35 mm x 35 mm.
2 Sand all sides and then apply two coats of white acrylic paint, sanding gently between coats.
3 Glue on a small scrap of black-painted wood for a handle.

Table and chairs

1 Use a fretsaw to cut a table top measuring 90 mm x 52 mm from 3 mm thick plywood.

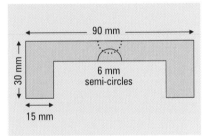

2 For the legs, cut two plywood rectangles measuring 90 mm x 35 mm, and from these cut out rectangles 60 mm x 25 mm. Discard the smaller rectangles. Each remaining shape forms two legs and a cross-piece. At the mid-points, cut out a 6 mm semi-circle from the upper edge of one piece and a 6 mm semi-circle from the lower edge of the other piece.

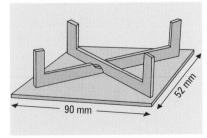

3 If you wish, use the fretsaw to shape the legs and the table top, as shown in the photograph at the left. Glue the legs to the table top.
4 For each chair, use a fretsaw to cut,

from 3 mm thick plywood, one back 60 mm x 25 mm, one seat 25 mm x 25 mm, and one front leg 25 mm x 20 mm. Use the fretsaw to cut a small rectangular section from the top of the back piece.

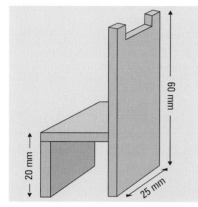

5 Glue the seat and the leg together at right angles and let the glue dry. Then glue the seat to the back, making sure that the back and the leg will sit evenly on the floor.

6 Sand the surfaces smooth. Using acrylic paint and a small paintbrush, paint the table and chairs in a color of your choice.

② THE LIVING ROOM
Lounge suite

1 From 9 mm thick plywood, use the fretsaw to cut one base 100 mm x 36 mm, one back 100 mm x 35 mm and two arms 45 mm x 40 mm. Round off one corner of each arm with sandpaper.

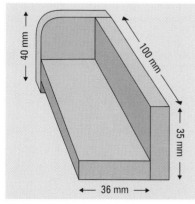

2 Glue the back and the base together at right angles, and let the glue dry. Glue the arms to the base and back, aligning the top edges of all pieces. The arms should extend 5 mm below the base to form the legs.

3 For each armchair, cut one base 40 mm x 36 mm, one back 40 mm x 35 mm, and two arms 45 mm x 40 mm. Make up as for the sofa.

4 Sand the surfaces smooth. Using acrylic paint and a small paintbrush, paint the lounge suite in a color or colors of your choice.

③ THE BEDROOMS
Wardrobes

1 To make the small wardrobe, use the fretsaw to cut a block of wood 125 mm x 75 mm x 35 mm. Then, from 3 mm plywood, cut two strips measuring 125 mm x 36 mm for the wardrobe doors.

2 Glue the doors to the front, leaving a 3 mm gap between them.

3 For the door handles, glue a small scrap of wood to the center edge of each door, about 55 mm from the top edge.

4 For the large wardrobe, cut a wood block 170 mm x 105 mm x 30 mm and, from 3 mm thick plywood, three pieces 105 mm x 55 mm for the doors and the center panel. Assemble the wardrobe following steps 2 and 3 above. The gaps on either side of the center panel should be 3 mm.

5 Sand the surfaces smooth. Using acrylic paint and a small paintbrush, paint the wardrobes in a color or colors of your choice.

Beds

1 To make the small bed, use a fretsaw to cut from 5 mm thick plywood one bed head 45 mm x 40 mm and one bed foot 45 mm x 20 mm. From 9 mm thick plywood, cut one base 105 mm x 45 mm.

2 Glue the bed head and foot to the base, allowing the foot and head to extend 3 mm below the base.

3 For the large bed, cut a block of timber 130 mm x 80 mm x 20 mm for the base and from 3 mm plywood cut two rectangles, one 90 mm x 55 mm (head) and one 80 mm x 40 mm (foot). To assemble, repeat step 2.

4 Sand the surfaces smooth. Using acrylic paint and a small paintbrush, paint the beds in colors to match or complement the wardrobes.

MORE THINGS TO MAKE OR BUY

• Once you have made these pieces of furniture for the dollhouse, it will be easy to work out how to make other pieces, such as a stove, dressing tables, sideboard, or television set. Remember to keep the sizes in proportion.

• You can buy miniature toys, musical instruments, cooking equipment and crockery, even bathroom fittings, from toy shops, gift shops and novelty shops. Exterior items such as trees, plants, animals, cars and farm equipment are also readily available.

④ THE FINISHING TOUCHES

1 Decorate some of the furniture by applying small decorative transfers, or paint designs by hand. For the furniture illustrated, we used a design of fruit and flowers for the fridge and a classic bow design for the center panel of the large wardrobe.

2 Using very thin plywood and a fretsaw, cut out little motifs and glue them to wardrobes and beds before painting. We used a simple heart motif on the blue bedroom furniture.

3 Make rugs, cushions, bed linen and a table runner from scraps of printed fabric. Use aluminum foil pasted on thin plywood for mirrors and cut images from postcards for pictures.

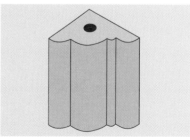

4 Make planter boxes by drilling small holes in pieces of wooden molding 25–30 mm long. Paint the molding if desired, and insert a tiny sprig of dried flowers in the hole.

Edward Bear suit

Great for a fancy dress or special party, this outfit has mittens and a large opening for ease of dressing. The suit is 95 cm from the back neck to the toes and 80 cm from the underarm to the toes. To complete the costume, purchase a mask.

WHAT YOU NEED

Master pattern **B12(a–h)** • **1.6 m fake fur, 140 cm wide** • **contrasting felt, fleecy fabric or vinyl (for soles and mittens)** • **small quantity of ribbing (for mitten welts)** • **35 cm zipper** • **sewing thread to match fur fabric** • **sewing needle** • **dressmaking pins** • **tracing paper** • **pencil** • **dress-making scissors** • **sewing machine**
● *Technique pages 292–301, 343–4*

SEWING FAKE FUR

Fake fur is awkward to sew, as the pile tends to slip against itself. To minimize problems, use the following techniques.

• This project involves curved seams, so do not choose a fabric with a thick, heavy pile – these fabrics are very prone to slipping.

• Cut fur fabric with extreme care, making sure that the pile does not cause the fabric base to move and distort the shape of the pattern piece.

• Baste all seams firmly before machining them; pinning alone is not adequate to prevent the fabric from moving.

• As far as possible, stitch in the direction of the pile.

• Use the eye end of a heavy, blunt needle to release pile caught in the stitching.

---

❶ CUTTING OUT THE FABRIC

1 Trace all the pattern pieces from the master pattern onto tracing paper and cut them out. Ensure that you also transfer all markings.

2 Pin the pattern pieces to the fur fabric, following the cutting guide. Make sure that all the pattern pieces are running in the same direction (the direction of the pile).

3 Cut out the ears, mittens and paws from the contrasting material, as shown on the cutting guide.

❷ ASSEMBLING THE BODY

1 Using the sewing machine, staystitch around the front and back neckline 1 cm from the neck edge to

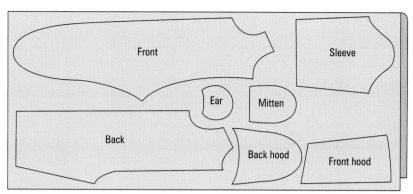

Cutting guide

From the fur fabric, cut one back hood piece and two of all the other pattern pieces. If you prefer, you can cut all four ear pieces from the fur fabric. Ensure that the

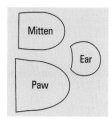

fur pieces are all cut in the same direction, so that the pile on the suit will lie from head to shoulder, from shoulder to ankle and from shoulder to wrist. All seam allowances are 1.5 cm.

prevent the fabric from stretching while you are working with it.

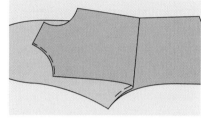

2 To fit the zipper, place the right sides of the front together and machine the center front seam from the dot toward the inside leg seam for a short distance. Backstitch to reinforce the stitching at the dot.

3 Press down the seam allowances along the center front zipper opening and lay the zipper face down along the seam line over the pressed seam allowances. Using the zipper foot, machine stitch the entire length of the zipper on both sides, stitching as close as possible to the zipper teeth.

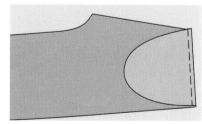

4 Baste the contrasting paw pads to the lower legs of the two back pieces with right sides together, and machine stitch the seams.

5 With right sides together and raw edges aligned, baste and machine stitch the shoulder seams. Press open.

6 Matching the dots, baste and machine stitch the sleeves to the armholes, with right sides together and raw edges aligned. Press the seams toward the sleeves.

7 Place the front piece and the back piece right sides together and machine stitch from the inside leg seam at the crotch around the leg and foot to the wrist in one continuous seam. Repeat for the other side of the suit.

8 With right sides together, place one body piece within the other and baste and machine the seam from the center back neckline to the crotch. Carry the seam on up the remainder of the front crotch seam to the zipper.

❸ ASSEMBLING THE HOOD

1 To sew the ears, match a fur with a fabric piece and place right sides together. Baste and machine around the ears, leaving the bottom edges open. Trim and clip the seams.

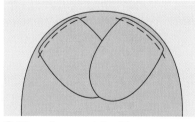

2 Turn the ears right side out and press. Baste the open edges of the ears to the edge of the right side of the back hood piece, at the top of the curved edge. Stitch 1 cm from the edge of the fabric.

3 Baste the right sides of the front hood together at the top, stitch and press open. With right sides together, baste the joined front hood piece to the back hood, matching centers and dots. Sew in place. (The ears will be sandwiched in the seam.)

4 Baste and machine the hood to the front and back necklines, matching shoulder seams to head seams. Press the hood face opening and the ends

of the zipper opening to the wrong side along the seam line. Topstitch around the pressed area.

❹ SEWING THE MITTENS

1 With right sides together, baste and machine the two fabric mitten pieces to the two fur mitten pieces, leaving the wrist edges open. Trim and clip the seams.

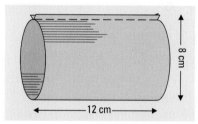

2 From the ribbing, cut two strips measuring 12 cm in the direction of the rib and 16 cm in the opposite direction. Machine in the direction of the rib to sew each strip into a tube.

3 Fold both of the tubes in half, wrong sides matching, to make double-thickness tubes 6 cm long. Divide each tube equally into four, marking the quarter points with pins.

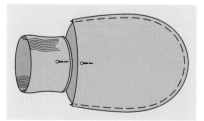

4 Mark the center points between the mitten seams with pins and match the four pins in the ribbing to the seams and the pins in the mittens. Use a zigzag or overlock stitch to machine the ribs to the mittens, stretching the ribbed fabric so that the marked points will meet.

A very special Christmas stocking

For young children, the thrill of hanging up a Christmas stocking is matched only by the excitement of opening it on Christmas morning. Delight a toddler with this stocking, which is sure to become an indispensable part of the family's festive decorations for years to come.

WHAT YOU NEED

Master pattern C16(a–c) • 1 m red fabric, 90 cm wide • 40 cm x 30 cm fabric with Christmas print • 30 cm x 20 cm green print fabric (for tree appliqué) • Christmas print fabric scraps (for present appliqués) • 2 pieces polyester batting, 40 cm x 30 cm • sewing thread: red, green, gold lamé • 50 cm ribbon, 10 mm wide • pencil • tracing paper • scissors • sewing machine
● *Technique pages 292–301, 302, 343–4*

① CUTTING OUT

1 Trace the pattern pieces for the stocking and the stocking collar from the master pattern onto tracing paper and cut them out. Trace the tree pattern onto another piece of tracing paper and cut that out.
2 Fold the red fabric in four. Pin the stocking pattern piece to the folded fabric and cut out four stocking shapes. Put one pair aside for the lining and work on the other pair to make the outer stocking.
3 Cut a collar piece 40 cm x 30 cm from the Christmas print fabric.
4 Cut the Christmas tree from the green fabric and the shapes of the presents from scraps of suitable Christmas print fabric.
5 Pin the main stocking pattern piece (not the collar) to the batting and cut out two stocking shapes.

② SEWING THE APPLIQUÉ

1 Using the master pattern as a position guide, baste the appliqué shapes in place on the right side of one outer stocking piece.

2 Stitch the shapes in place with machine satin stitch (closed zigzag), using the green thread for the tree and the red for the presents.
3 Thread the sewing machine with gold lamé thread and use a long, straight machine stitch to add such details as Christmas tree decorations and ribbon ties to the appliqués.

③ MAKING UP THE STOCKING

1 Pin the cut-out batting stocking pieces to the wrong sides of both outer stocking pieces.
2 With right sides facing and allowing a 1.5 cm seam, sew the back and front stocking pieces and the batting together, leaving the top open. Trim and clip the seams and press flat. Turn the work to the right side and press.
3 Repeat step 2 to sew the inner stocking pieces (the lining) together.
4 With wrong sides together, slip the lining inside the outer stocking. Baste the lining to the outer stocking along the upper edge.
5 With right sides facing, stitch the short ends of the collar together to form a cylinder. Press the seam open.

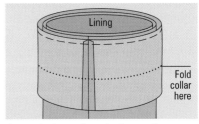

Lining

Fold collar here

6 With the right side facing the outside of the stocking, match the seam of the collar to the back seam of the stocking. Pin and baste the collar to the upper edge of the stocking and machine stitch it in place.
7 On the unsewn edge of the collar, press down a 1.5 cm double hem. Fold the collar over to the inside of the stocking and slipstitch it into place, covering the line of stitching on the inside of the stocking. Turn the collar down to the outside to form the stocking top and press.
8 Make a loop for hanging the stocking up by oversewing the ends of the ribbon to the back seam on the inside of the top of the stocking.

Party pinafore dress

With some simple embroidery stitches and a little lace, you can transform a plain pinafore dress into a party outfit. Choose a dress made of plain-colored fabric to set off the embroidery.

WHAT YOU NEED

Plain pinafore dress • stranded embroidery cottons: DMC colors 3053 (pale green), ecru (cream), 814 (rose red), 815 (mid-red) • needles: size 7 crewel, size 7 straw or milliner's • embroidery marking pen • small drinking glass • dressmaking pins • sewing machine • stretchy self-gathered lace
● *Technique pages 292–5, 307–12*

1 EMBROIDERING THE DESIGN

1 To mark out the design, fold the front of the dress in half to find the center. Place a small drinking glass over the crease and mark out a circle by drawing around the glass using the embroidery marking pen.
2 Work the rosebuds in bullion knots, using the crewel needle. For the center of every second rosebud, use three strands of rose red cotton and wind around the needle seven times. Work the alternate centers in the same way with mid-red.
3 Use three strands of cream cotton and wind nine times around the needle to make the outer petals.
4 With two strands of green cotton and the straw needle, work the bud cases in straight stitch, the stems joining the rosebuds in stem stitch, and the leaves on either side of the stems in lazy daisy stitch.

⟨ Bullion rosebud
⌐ Stem stitch
𝒞 Lazy daisy stitch

Stitch guide
The circle of rosebuds is formed by bullion knots. The rosebud centers are stitched alternately in rose red and mid-red, and the outer petals in cream. The leaves and bud cases are worked in lazy daisy stitch.

2 FINISHING
Sew stretchy self-gathered lace by hand around the armholes.

Toddler's table & chairs

Some lucky child will have hours of fun with this practical gift. The table and chairs are sturdy enough for all those toddler activities – tea parties, arts and craft projects and meetings with friends over milk and cookies.

WHAT YOU NEED

Master pattern **C15(a–g)** • plywood or MDF, 2400 mm x 1200 mm x 18 mm • 8 gauge wood screws: 32 mm, 38 mm • 30 mm finishing nails • white woodworking glue • masking tape • wood filler • wood primer • gloss paint: yellow, blue • small stencil • tracing paper • transfer paper • jigsaw • wood rasp • scissors • pencil • hammer • nail punch • drill, drill bits • paintbrush • medium-grade sandpaper
● *Technique pages 337, 338–42, 343–4*

❶ PREPARING THE PLYWOOD

1 Trace the pattern pieces from the master pattern onto the tracing paper, including all markings. Cut out the pattern pieces.
2 Lay out all the pattern pieces on the plywood, as shown in the cutting guide, and secure them in place with the masking tape.
3 Trace around all the pattern pieces with a pencil, and then remove the pattern pieces from the plywood.
4 Cut out the pieces with a jigsaw and round off the edges and corners with a wood rasp.

5 From the leftover plywood, cut a strip 120 mm long x 18 mm wide x 18 mm thick. Cut this strip into four pieces 30 mm long. (These are the glue blocks.)

❷ MAKING THE CHAIRS

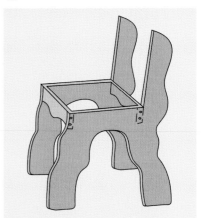

1 Glue and screw the cross bar supports to the leg pieces with two

CAUTION
Because this project is for small children, all surfaces must be finished smoothly so that there is no danger of splinters or rough edges hurting small hands.

38 mm screws at each join in the positions shown on the master pattern.
2 Stand the assembled leg and cross bar unit the right way up, and then glue and screw the seat into position. Use two screws through the seat into the top of each leg and cross bar support (eight screws per seat).

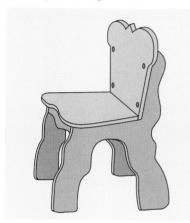

3 Glue and screw the back into position, using two screws on each side.
4 Repeat steps 1 to 3 to make the second chair.

❸ MAKING THE TABLE

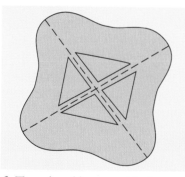

1 Turn the table top upside down. With a pencil, mark the positions of the legs and triangular leg supports.

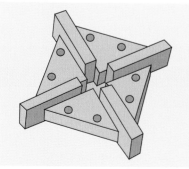

2 Place plywood offcuts in the channels between the penciled positions for the supports – these will help you

---

CUTTING GUIDE

Trace the pattern pieces from the master pattern onto tracing paper, cut them out and lay them on the plywood as shown in the diagram. Attach the pattern pieces with masking tape and trace around them. Cut out the pieces with a jigsaw.

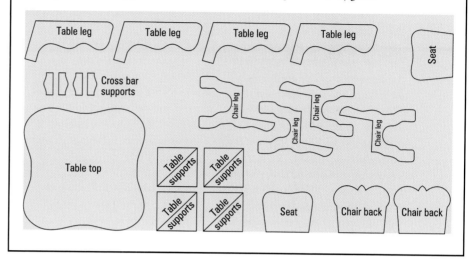

---

to space the supports correctly. Push four of the leg supports up against the spacers and glue and screw them in place with the 32 mm screws.
3 Glue and nail the other four leg supports directly on top of the first four leg supports.
4 Glue the tops of the table legs. Knock out the spacers and slide the legs into the channels, making sure that the curved edges of the legs face in toward the center. While the glue is drying, hold all the pieces in place with masking tape. Since the leg pieces do not touch one another, there should be a small square space left at the middle of the table.

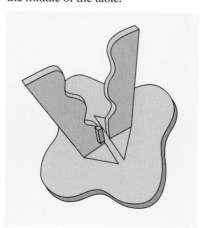

5 Glue and nail the four 30 mm glue blocks (cut from the leftover pieces) to the inside corners created

by the meeting of the table legs. With the table still upside down, the blocks rest on the built-up table leg supports.

❹ FINISHING

1 Fill in any holes and rough spots with wood filler, sand all surfaces and wipe them clean. If necessary, round off the edges further with a rasp.
2 Apply the wood primer and allow it to dry completely, and then paint the table and chairs with several coats of the yellow gloss paint.
3 Stencil your chosen shape on each corner of the table and each side of the chair backs, using the blue paint.

NOTE
Assemble the table and chairs with 8 gauge 38 mm and 32 mm wood screws. Drill a 2.5 mm pilot hole through the top piece into the section to which it will be fastened, and then enlarge the hole through the top piece with a 4 mm bit to make a clearance hole, which is then countersunk.

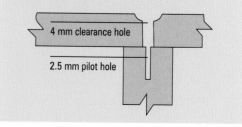

Balloon shorts

In these colorful shorts, your favorite young person will be the best-dressed toddler at the party or the beach. The basket of the largest balloon forms a small pocket for keeping little treasures safe.

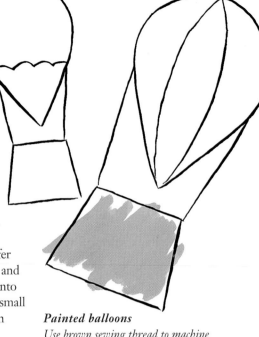

WHAT YOU NEED

Master pattern **C22(a)** • **50 cm white, medium-weight fabric, 115 cm wide** (for the shorts) • **20 cm x 15 cm white fabric** (for the large balloon) • **10 cm x 12 cm fawn fabric** (for the basket) • **20 cm x 15 cm lightweight batting** (for the large balloon) • **25 cm x 25 cm tear-off backing** (for the small balloons) • **1.5 m fawn braid, 2 mm wide** • **6 novelty buttons** (e.g. cars, planes) • **55 cm non-roll elastic, 15 mm wide** • **sewing thread to match the fabrics** • **dark brown sewing thread** (for outlining the small balloons) • **fabric paints: red, brown, yellow, green, blue** • **paintbrushes** • **tracing paper** • **dressmaker's carbon paper** • **pencil** • **scissors** • **dressmaking pins** • **safety pin** • **sewing needle** • **sewing machine**
● *Technique pages 292–301, 302, 343–4*

The pattern fits an average four-year-old (waist 53 cm, outside leg 38 cm, inside leg 11 cm).

❶ MAKING THE PATTERNS

1 Using tracing paper, pencil and scissors, trace and cut out a working pattern for the shorts from the master pattern, including all markings.
2 Trace and cut out working patterns for the large balloon and its basket (drawn in a solid line on the master pattern), adding an extra 1.5 cm seam allowance all round the basket.

❷ PREPARING THE FABRIC

1 Wash, dry and iron all fabric – this removes fabric conditioners so that the paint will fix more satisfactorily.
2 Fold the fabric for the shorts in half, selvage to selvage. Pin the shorts pattern piece to the folded fabric, with

the straight grain parallel to the selvage, and cut the shorts out. You will have two identical sides that will be joined at the center front and back and the inside leg.
3 Separate the pieces and, using dressmaker's carbon paper, transfer the patterns for the large balloon and its basket (drawn in a solid line) onto the left-hand piece. Transfer the small balloon patterns (drawn in broken lines) onto the right-hand piece.
4 Pin the patterns for the large balloon and its basket to the appropriate fabrics and cut them out. Then pin the large balloon pattern to the batting and cut it out, allowing an extra 5 mm around the edge.
5 For each of the three small balloons, cut a piece of tear-off backing slightly larger than the whole motif, including the basket and ropes.

❸ MAKING THE BALLOONS

1 On the fabric piece for the large balloon, use the red, green, yellow and blue paints to make each of the four panels a different color.
2 Working directly onto the shorts fabric, paint the tiny balloon green, the slightly larger balloon yellow and the remaining balloon red. Paint all three baskets brown.
3 Set the fabric paints according to the manufacturer's instructions.
4 Pin or baste the pieces of tear-off backing to the wrong side of the fabric behind the painted shapes of the three small balloons.
5 Either by hand or by machine, use brown thread to stitch around the painted balloons, down the ropes and around the baskets. Still using the brown thread, stitch a row of scallops across the center of the yellow balloon. Stitch vertical curves on the red balloon to form panels, and stitch a basket weave pattern on its basket.

Painted balloons
Use brown sewing thread to machine stitch along all design lines.

6 Remove the pins (or basting stitches) and carefully tear away the backing from the back.

❹ APPLIQUÉING THE LARGE BALLOON

1 Pin the batting for the large balloon to the wrong side of the previously painted fabric. Machine or handstitch the layers together, 5 mm from the edge.

HINTS
● *Look for the type of tear-off backing that can be stitched onto the fabric and torn off later. Do not use non-woven iron-on interfacing or batting as these will wash badly and may irritate delicate skin.*
● *The three small balloons on the shorts illustrated are painted directly onto the white shorts fabric. If you want to use colored fabric for the shorts instead of white, you will need to paint these balloons onto pieces of white fabric and then cut them out and appliqué them to the colored fabric, using the method described for appliquéing the large balloon.*

1 With right sides together, pin and sew the two pieces of the shorts together at the crotch seams, and then pin and sew the inside leg seam. Finish the seams and press.
2 Turn the raw edges of the legs under 6 mm to the wrong side, making sure that you also turn the lower edge of the appliquéd balloon basket. Sew with straight stitch. Turn under a further 1.5 cm and sew the hem, either by hand using slipstitch or by machine using topstitch.
3 To make the waist casing, fold down the raw edge of the waist 6 mm to the wrong side and press. Fold the waist over a further 4 cm and press.
4 Topstitch the waist casing in place, leaving a 3 cm gap near a seam to thread the elastic through.

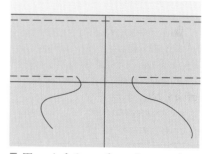

5 Topstitch 2 mm from the top edge, using a large machine stitch or back-stitching by hand.

⑦ FINISHING
1 Using a large safety pin, thread the non-roll elastic through the waistband. Pull the ends of the elastic together and stitch them securely, first ensuring that the elastic is not twisted Close the opening with small slipstitches.
2 Stitch the novelty buttons at random on the shorts, the cars near the bottom of the shorts and the planes near the top, as though flying around the balloons.

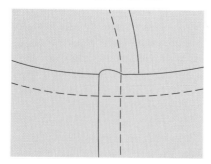

Appliqué balloon
Paint the panels and stitch narrow fawn braid along all the design lines except the top and bottom of the basket.

2 Trim away the excess batting. Fold the raw edge of the fabric to the wrong side and pin or baste it down.
3 Place the padded balloon motif on the right side of the shorts fabric, in the position marked, and pin it in place. Topstitch around the outer edge of the balloon.
4 Finish the edges of the fabric for the large basket with zigzag stitch to prevent fraying. Turn under a 1.5 cm hem along the top and side edges and press it into place. Topstitch the top edge 2 mm and 8 mm from the fold – this will be the pocket opening. Pin and baste the basket to the fabric, aligning the raw edge at the bottom of the basket with the raw edge at the bottom of the shorts fabric.
5 Topstitch the basket in place along the sides only, leaving the top and bottom open. (The bottom edge will be caught in the leg hem later.) Reinforce the sides with a second row of stitching, 6 mm from the first.

⑤ ATTACHING THE BRAID
1 Using straight stitch, sew single rows of braid between the panels and around the edge of the large balloon.
2 Starting at a lower corner of the basket, stitch a single row of braid up the side of the basket to a point midway up the side of the balloon. Loop the braid in shallow scallops across the middle of the balloon, then stitch down to the bottom corner of the basket, opposite where you started.

⑥ SEWING THE SHORTS
The seam allowance is 1.5 cm.

Push-along duck

This amusing toy makes a very satisfying noise as it is wheeled along. Children love to toddle along after the toy which delights them with its novel walking action.

WHAT YOU NEED

Master pattern B10(a–d) • plywood, 500 mm x 500 mm x 15 mm • 570 mm dowel, 12 mm diameter (for handle shaft) • 130 mm dowel, 25 mm diameter (for handle grip) • 60 mm dowel, 12 mm diameter (for axle) • heavy duty rubber gloves (for feet) • white glue • epoxy glue • sandpaper • primer • gloss paint in your chosen colors • tracing paper • transfer paper • pencil • scissors • jigsaw or coping saw • clamps • drill and drill bits
● *Technique pages 338–42, 343–4*

❶ PREPARING THE PLYWOOD

1 Trace and transfer the pattern pieces from the master pattern onto the plywood, being careful to transfer all details. Note that you need to cut two body pieces.
2 Using a jigsaw or coping saw, cut the shapes from the plywood and sand them smooth. Make sure the slits in the wheels are the right size for the thickness of the feet.

DUCK CHARACTER

Toy ducks are traditionally colored plain bright yellow, which appeals to very small children. For a slightly older child you may like to base your paint colors on a real duck. Shown below are color schemes based on the mallard (right), which has a dark emerald head and a white collar, and the chestnut teal (left), with its green-black head and black tail.

HINT
You can use scraps of leather or felt instead of rubber to make the duck's feet.

❷ MAKING THE DUCK

1 Glue the two body pieces together, making sure that all edges are aligned exactly. Clamp them together until they are dry. Sand the edges to remove any irregularities.
2 In the position indicated on the plan, drill a hole in the duck's back, 12 mm in diameter and 40 mm deep, to take the handle shaft. Push the pre-glued dowel end into the hole and allow to dry.
3 Round off the ends of the handle grip with sandpaper and drill a 12 mm diameter hole in the center; this hole should not be more than 12 mm deep. Glue the end of the handle shaft into the hole. Allow to dry.
4 Glue the wings to the body in the position shown on the master pattern.
5 Cut open the rubber gloves and trace and transfer the duck foot from the master pattern to the rubber six times. Transfer three foot shapes, flip the tracing and transfer the next three reversed. Squeeze a small amount of epoxy glue into the slits cut in the wheels and insert the rubber feet.

6 Using a 13 mm or 14 mm drill bit, drill the axle hole through the duck's body at the position marked.
7 Using a 12 mm drill bit, drill a hole in the center of each wheel.
8 Push a pre-glued axle end into one of the wheels, pass it through the body, and glue the other end into the other wheel. Do not butt the wheels right up to the body – leave enough play for the wheels to move freely.

❸ FINISHING

1 When the glue is thoroughly dry, sand, prime and paint the duck in acrylic gloss paint.
2 Decorate the duck's neck with a bright ribbon tied in a bow and sewn securely together.

Cutting guide
Cut two body pieces and glue them together. The wing piece fits into the square notch behind the head.

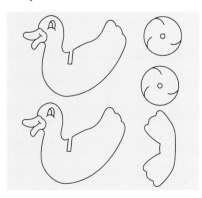

CHILDREN &
YOUNG ADULTS

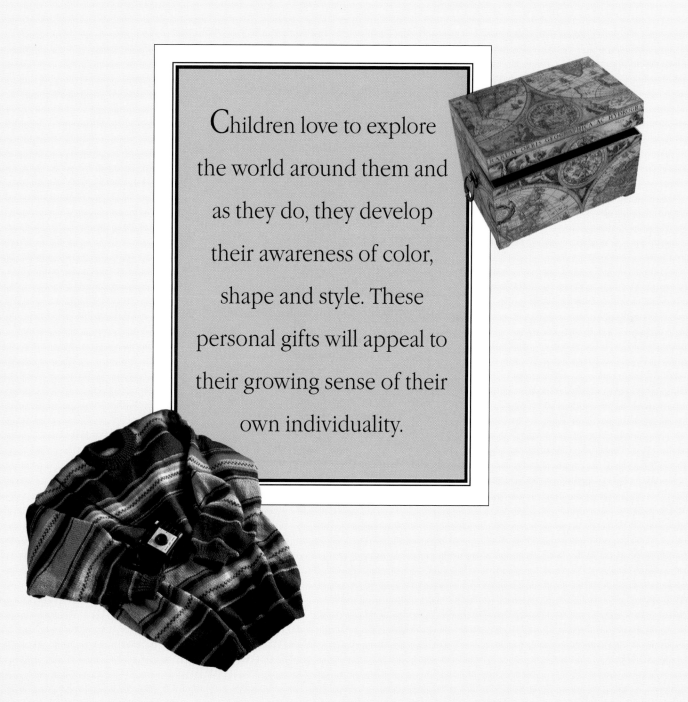

Children love to explore the world around them and as they do, they develop their awareness of color, shape and style. These personal gifts will appeal to their growing sense of their own individuality.

Cuddly cow sweatshirt

A plain sweatshirt becomes an eye-catching and novel garment with this simple appliqué and embroidery design.

WHAT YOU NEED

Master pattern C18(a) • sweatshirt • lightweight iron-on interfacing, 40 cm x 35 cm • non-woven tear-off backing, 35 cm x 25 cm • white fabric, 28 cm x 18 cm • black fabric, 25 cm x 10 cm • pink fabric (for the udder, nose and ears), 10 cm x 10 cm • sewing thread: black, pink • stranded embroidery cotton: black, green, bright pink, lemon, blue, gold, white • cardboard, 3 cm x 2 cm • needle: medium crewel • tracing paper • dressmaker's carbon paper • hard pencil • dressmaking pins • scissors • sewing machine
● *Technique pages 302, 307–12, 343–4*

❶ PREPARING THE COW

1 Trace the cow outline from the master pattern onto the tracing paper. Trace the black patches and pink features onto a separate piece of paper.
2 Using dressmaker's carbon paper and a pencil, transfer all the shapes to the shiny side of the interfacing.
3 Cut out all the shapes, making sure that you separate the shapes that will be cut from black fabric from those to be cut from pink fabric.
4 Place the interfacing shape for the complete cow silhouette, shiny side down, on the wrong side of the white fabric. Fuse the shape to the fabric with a hot iron and cut out.
5 Place the interfacing shapes for the black patches, shiny sides down, on the wrong side of the black fabric. Fuse them to the fabric with a hot iron and cut them out.
6 Fuse the udder, nose and ear shapes onto the pink fabric with the iron and cut out these shapes too.

CREATING YOUR OWN MOTIF

You can use any animal shape for the appliqué motif, as long as it is fairly rounded and has no thin, protruding pieces that would be hard to cut and sew. This cat shape is perfect, as all details except one or two of the whiskers are within the silhouette. Embroider the whiskers in straight stitch after you have appliquéd the cat shape to the sweatshirt.

❷ APPLIQUÉING THE COW

1 Position the pieces for the nose, udder, ears and black patches on the cow and baste them in place.
2 With a machine satin stitch (closed zigzag), sew the pieces onto the cow. Remove the basting thread.
3 Using the master pattern as a guide, straight machine stitch any elements that need to be defined – for example, the line between the legs and the side of the face. At this stage, do not stitch any of the outline; this will be worked when you appliqué the cow to the sweatshirt.
4 Embroider the facial features, using satin stitch for the pupils and nostrils and straight stitch for the eye outlines and eyelashes.

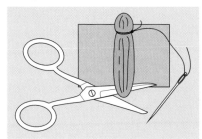

5 To make the end of the tail, cut out a piece of cardboard 3 cm x 4 cm. Wind black and white stranded cotton round the cardboard about 30 times, and then cut through one end. Bunch up the threads in the middle of the bundle and tightly wind a piece of black stranded cotton a few times

HINTS

For appliqué work, choose smooth fabrics of light or medium weight. Very bulky fabrics or fabrics with a loose weave are not suitable. It is important to iron fabrics flat before you begin working.

around the bundle. Thread the end of the cotton onto a needle and push it through the end of the tail on the appliqué. Stitch through the interfacing several times to secure. The tail will be sewn on more securely when you attach the cow to the sweatshirt.

❸ ATTACHING THE COW

1 Decide where to place the cow appliqué on the sweatshirt. Mark the top, bottom and side positions with pins. Using the pins as guides, lightly baste the non-woven tear-off backing to the wrong side of the sweatshirt, covering the place where the cow will

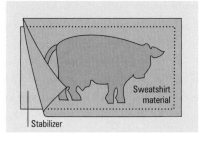

Sweatshirt material

Stabilizer

be attached. This will stabilize the knit fabric while you sew the appliqué, and will be removed later. Baste the cow into position on the right side of the sweatshirt, making sure that the tear-off backing is behind the appliqué cow.

2 Using a machine satin stitch, sew around the outline of the cow, making sure that the cotton threads at the end of the tail are securely sewn onto the fabric. Cut and peel the backing from the back of the shirt.

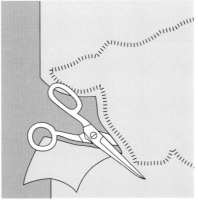

Stitch guide
Use the diagram above and the key at the right as guides when you are embroidering the flowers.

○	French knot
/	Straight stitch
⊘	Lazy daisy stitch

3 Referring to the stitch guide above and the photograph below, embroider the flowers around the cow's feet. Embroider the flowers in lazy daisy stitch and put a French knot in the center of each flower. Work the stems in straight stitch.

Delectable lace collar

Made from fine crochet cotton, this lacework collar would please any little girl. It is designed to sit around the neckline without sewing, so it can be worn over several outfits.

WHAT YOU NEED

1 ball crochet cotton no. 50 • no. 3 darning needle • 1 m satin ribbon, 3 mm wide
● *Technique page 328*

❶ MAKING THE COLLAR

Work 64 basic loops over a double strand of cotton. Turn.
2nd row: Work a basic loop into each loop. Turn.

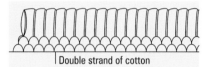
Double strand of cotton

3rd row: Work a small turning loop and a long closed loop into the first loop. Work a long closed loop into each loop to the end of the row. Turn.
4th row: On top of the large loops work a foundation row in a multiple of three-plus-one basic loops. Turn.
5th row: Work a turning loop into the first basic loop and work a basic loop into each loop to the end of the row. Turn and repeat this row twice. (Ribbon-threading edge made.) Turn.

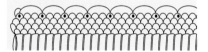

8th row: Work a turning loop into the first loop. Make a large loop by missing two loops and working into the next loop. Repeat to the end of the row. Turn.

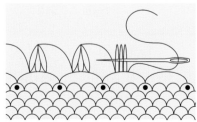

9th row: Work a large turning loop and three long picots into the first large loop. Insert the needle through the three picots and join them together with a closed loop knot. (In this way, you have made joined picots.) ★ Work a large loop and three joined picots into the next large loop. ★ Repeat from ★ to ★ until the end of the row. (The last large loop is worked into the turning loop of the previous row.) Turn.

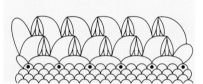

10th row: Work a large turning loop and three joined picots into the first large loop. Work another row of joined picots.

11th row: Turn and work a large turning loop into the first large loop. Work large loops into each large loop to the end of the row. Turn.
12th row: Work a foundation row of basic loops in a multiple of three-plus-one basic loops onto the large loops.

Repeat 5th row five times.
Repeat 7th row through to 12th row once.
Repeat 5th row five times.
Repeat 7th row through to 12th row once. Pull the last knot very tight and trim the thread close to the knot.

❷ WORKING THE EDGING FOUNDATION

1st row: With the wrong side of the lacework facing, join thread into the first loop on the neck edge and work basic loops in a multiple of seven-plus-six loops to the corner. Work a corner loop, then work basic loops in

a multiple of seven-plus-three loops onto the large loops. Work a corner loop. Work basic loops in a multiple of seven-plus-six loops to the neck edge. Turn.

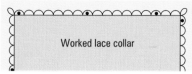
Worked lace collar

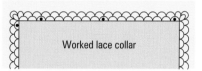
Worked lace collar

2nd row: Work a turning loop into the first loop and a basic loop into each basic loop, increasing in both corner loops. Turn.
Repeat 2nd row twice.

❸ WORKING THE EDGING

Worked edging foundation

1st row: Work a small turning loop into the first loop and a basic loop into the next six basic loops. ★ Make a large loop by missing one loop and working into the next loop. Work five basic loops. ★ Repeat from ★ to ★ to the end of the row. Work one basic loop and turn.

Worked edging foundation

2nd row: Work a small turning loop into the first loop and a basic loop into the next five basic loops. ★ Make a

---

ORDER OF WORKING
The first three rows make up the neckline of the collar, through which the ribbon will be threaded. Then the main part of the collar is worked as a long, straight piece. Finally, the edging is worked around the three outer sides of the collar; the fourth side is the neck edge, where the ribbon is to go.

bridging loop and four long picots into the large loop. Bridge into the next loop then work four basic loops. ★ Repeat from ★ to ★ to the end of the row. Work one basic loop. Turn.

3rd row: Work a small turning loop into the first loop and a basic loop into the next four basic loops. ★ Make a large loop by missing the bridging loop and then working into the first long picot. Join the next three long picots with basic loops. Miss the bridging loop and work a large loop into the next loop. Work three more basic loops. ★ Repeat from ★ to ★ to the end of the row. Work one basic loop and turn.

4th row: Work a small turning loop into the first loop and a basic loop into the next three basic loops. ★ Miss the large loop and work into the next basic loop. Work two basic loops. ★ Repeat from ★ to ★ to the end of the row. Work one basic loop and turn.

5th row: Work a small turning loop into the first loop and a basic loop into the next two loops. ★ Miss the large loop and work one large loop into the next basic loop. Work one

basic loop. ★ Repeat from ★ to ★ end of row. Work one basic loop and turn.

6th row: Work a small turning loop into the first loop and a basic loop into the next basic loop. ★ Bridge into the first large loop and work five small picots. Into the basic loop on top of the motif, work a bridging loop and three long picots. Bridge into the next long loop and work five small picots. Work a bridging loop and two small picots into the next basic loop. ★ Repeat from ★ to ★ to the last two loops. Bridge into the second last loop. Make a basic loop into the last loop, pull knot tight and trim thread. Thread ribbon through neck edge.

Flower seeds in homemade packets

This is a gift that will delight youngsters who are keen to try their hand at growing flowers. Children can make the paper packets to give to their friends.

WHAT YOU NEED

Brown paper • artist's acrylic paints • paintbrushes • clear craft glue • flower seeds • paper punch • ribbon, 5 mm wide • scissors • pencil • ruler
● *Technique pages 334–5*

❶ MAKING THE PACKETS

1 From brown paper, cut rectangles measuring 36 cm x 13 cm.
2 Fold the rectangles in half width-wise and make firm creases along the fold lines. Unfold the rectangles.
3 Fold 1 cm strips down the two long sides of each rectangle.

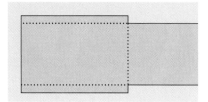

4 Cut halfway down each side crease and cut away the 18 cm x 1 cm strips.

5 Refold the rectangles in half along the original folds, and then glue the 1 cm flaps over the cut edges.
6 At the tops of the packets, fold down 5 cm flaps to the back.
7 Use the hole punch to make two holes through all thicknesses, about 2 cm from the tops of the packets.

❷ FINISHING THE PACKETS

1 On the fronts of the packets, paint flowers to identify the seeds inside. Experiment on scrap paper, keeping the designs simple. Alternatively, you can trace the designs reproduced on this page (bottom left) and transfer them to the fronts of the packets. Then paint over the designs in one or two colors of your choice and write the names of the seeds beneath.
2 Place the appropriate seeds in the packets, fold the tops of the bags over and secure them with a dab of glue.

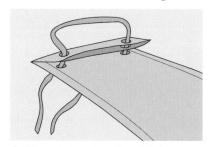

3 Thread short lengths of ribbon through the holes and tie them in bows at the fronts of the packets.

VARIATION

Decorate the fronts of your homemade packets with the illustrations from bought packets of seeds, or with pictures cut from magazines – this is an excellent quick and easy way for small children to make this gift with little help.

Flower designs
If you do not feel confident about drawing the flower yourself, trace and transfer one of the generic designs above onto the packet, paint it, and write the name of the seeds below.

Basic window box

Using inexpensive wood, or even wood scraps, you can make this small window box in less than an hour. Present the window box with seeds or plants in small pots already in place.

HINT
Instead of sowing the seeds, you could give the recipient packets of seeds to plant at the appropriate times of the year. For a really personal touch, place the seeds in homemade packets (see opposite page). Don't forget to include instructions for growing.

WHAT YOU NEED

Wood (e.g. pine), 530 mm **x** 100 mm **x** 12 mm • plain lath or door strapping, about 1280 mm **x** 30 mm **x** 12 mm • 12 finishing nails, 25 mm long • clear varnish or paint in a color of your choice • pencil • ruler • medium-grade sandpaper • masking tape • drill and 2 mm drill bit • hammer • handsaw
● *Technique pages 338–42*

❶ CUTTING THE WOOD

1 Using the pencil, ruler and handsaw, cut the 100 mm **x** 12 mm wood into one 300 mm length (for the base) and two 115 mm lengths (for the ends). Then cut the lath into four 320 mm strips.
2 Sand all the pieces, paying particular attention to the edges and corners.

❷ CONSTRUCTING THE BOX

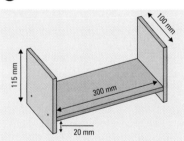

1 Drill two holes in each of the end pieces, 20 mm up from the bottom and 10 mm in from each side. Nail the ends to the base, nailing one end on at a time. The end pieces should protrude below the base piece to form the legs of the window box.

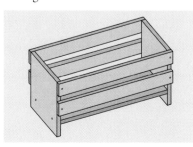

2 Position a strip of lath on each side of the box, level with the tops of the ends. Drill a hole at each end of the strips, and then hammer in the nails to attach the strips to the end pieces.
3 Repeat step 2 to nail the other strips below the first strips, leaving a gap of about 15 mm between them.

❸ FINISHING

1 Sand the window box all over with medium-grade sandpaper.
2 Seal with two coats of clear varnish or with paint in your chosen color.

❹ FILLING THE WINDOW BOX

1 Look for small plant pots that will fit into the window box. You should be able to fit three or four in. Make sure that the pots have saucers and that these will also fit into the box.
2 Put a few small pebbles or pieces of broken pottery in the bottoms of the pots to assist drainage, and fill the pots with soil. If you are using good-quality potting mix, you will not need to add the pebbles.
3 Plant the pots with seeds from dwarf varieties of herbs or flowers. For the best results, use plants that require similar growing conditions.

Personalized name plates

Make a child feel special with this richly painted name plate. Stylized heavenly bodies are picked out in gold and silver against a midnight blue background.

WHAT YOU NEED

Master patterns **C19(a)** (the design), **E35(a)** (the letters) • wooden plaque, at least 27 cm long and 12 cm high • Jo Sonja's (or Liquitex): silver, pale gold, rich gold • Jo Sonja's (or Liquitex) artist's color: gold oxide • Matisse background color: Ritz blue • sealer • water-based clear flat varnish • paintbrushes: 25 mm decorating, no. 3 round, no. 00 liner • paint stripper (if you are recycling an old board) • small picture hook (for the back of the board) • fine sandpaper • lint-free cloth • tracing paper • transfer paper • pencil • hard pencil (or empty ballpoint pen) • ruler • masking tape • soft artist's eraser
● *Technique pages 334–5, 343–4*

FINDING THE PLAQUE
New plaques are available ready shaped from craft stores. Alternatively, you may be able to find suitable boards in second-hand stores.

❶ PREPARING THE PLAQUE
1 If you are using an old board that is already painted or varnished, you will need to remove the paint or varnish with a commercial stripper and then sand it smooth. If the board is new and untreated, sand it lightly with fine sandpaper and wipe it clean with a lint-free cloth.
2 Using the decorating brush, apply two coats of Ritz blue, mixed with sealer, to all surfaces of the board (back and front), sanding lightly between coats. Put it aside to dry.

HINT
When you are positioning the letters of the child's name, remember that the center point of the name is not necessarily the middle letter or space. To center the name exactly in relation to the sun, measure the whole name and mark the center point, and then align that point with the center of the sun.

3 Using tracing paper and pencil, trace the main design (the sun, the stars, and the cherubs for the girl's name plate) from the master pattern.
4 On a separate piece of tracing paper, rule a line. From the master pattern, trace onto the line the letters that you need for the child's name, spacing the letters evenly.
5 Place the traced name over the design to find out whether it fits comfortably into the space. If necessary, you can use a photocopier to reduce or enlarge the letters. (Remember that a longer name will need to be reduced and a shorter one enlarged.)
6 Center the traced main design on the board, secure it with masking tape and transfer the design.
7 Transfer the traced name to the board in the same way, making sure that the center point of the name is aligned with the center of the sun.

❷ PAINTING THE DESIGN
1 Load the liner brush with silver paint and stroke in the letters of the name. You may need two coats to obtain good coverage.
2 When the letters are dry, use the liner brush loaded with gold oxide to

paint shadow lines on the left-hand side of each main downstroke.
3 Base-coat the sun (and the cherubs for the girl's name plate), using the round brush loaded with pale gold.
4 Following the color guide, paint the remaining pale gold areas of the design. Allow the paint to dry.

"Tom"
To make a name plate for a boy, buy a board with squarer molding. Use the same colors and design elements as for "Carol," but arrange them differently.

5 If necessary, re-transfer the details of the elements of the main design. Load the liner brush with gold oxide to fill in the shaded areas of the sun and stars, and to complete the cherubs for the girl's name plate.
6 Following the appropriate color guide, paint the rest of the gold oxide areas. Paint the rest of the design in rich gold and silver, using the liner brush for the finer work.

❸ FINISHING
1 If the board has a molded edge, paint the molding silver and then float Ritz blue around the inside edge of the front of the board.

"Carol"
This plaque has rounded edges, and the focus is the pair of nestling cherubs. The use of three different shades of gold adds interest to a basically simple design.

2 Allow all the paint to dry completely before erasing any visible transfer lines with an artist's eraser.
3 Using the decorating brush, apply at least two coats of clear varnish, sanding very lightly between coats.
4 Fix a small hook to the back of the board for hanging.

Treasure chest

Use gift-wrapping paper with an interesting motif to turn a plain box into a delightful chest for a youngster's special treasures and trinkets.

WHAT YOU NEED

Small wooden box with hinged lid •
2 matching sheets of attractive gift-wrapping paper • wallpaper paste •
white glue • wood filler • artist's
acrylic gloss medium (sealer) • gold
paint • polyurethane gloss varnish •
3 small paintbrushes (for sealing,
gluing and painting) • 25 mm
imitation sable brush (for
varnishing) • medium-grade, wet-and-dry sandpaper nos. 80 and 120
• rubber sanding block • rubber
roller • scalpel or craft knife •
small pieces of kitchen sponge •
lint-free cloth
● *Technique pages 329–31*

If you are unfamiliar with découpage techniques, study the craft techniques section for découpage before starting this project.

❶ PREPARING THE BOX

1 Remove the handles and any exterior hinges from the box and store them carefully.
2 Fill any cracks or nail holes in the box with the wood filler, following the manufacturer's directions.
3 Lightly sand all outside surfaces with medium-grade dry abrasive paper and wipe them completely clean with the lint-free cloth. Paint both the inside and the outside of the box with the sealer and allow to dry.

❷ SEALING AND CUTTING THE PAPER

1 Coat the wrapping paper on both sides with the sealer, allowing the paper to dry between applications.
2 Place the lid of the box upside down on the wrong side of one of the sheets of wrapping paper and trace around the outside of the top. Remove the lid and use the scalpel to cut the paper exactly to size. (The paper may stretch slightly when you glue it to the box, but the excess can be trimmed away when the glue is dry.) If the paper has a large design, you may wish to center the design on the lid.
3 Put the lid on the box and wrap a full sheet of paper around all four sides of the box, adjusting the position of the paper on the box to show off the design. Cut the paper to the exact size – it should not overlap at the ends or extend under the box.

❸ PAPERING THE BOX

1 Mix three parts wallpaper paste and one part white glue to a smooth paste, making sure that no lumps remain.
2 Apply a generous coat of glue to the top of the lid. Press the trimmed paper for the lid top into position.

6 Use the scalpel or craft knife to carefully separate the lid of the box from the base, starting from one of the corners. Trim excess paper from the edges and corners so that the paper is as flat as possible, with no ridges or bumps. If any paper lifts or tears as you work, apply a little more glue and gently massage the paper back onto the surface of the box.

④ VARNISHING THE BOX

1 Work in a well-ventilated area, as varnish fumes can be toxic. Apply about 10 coats of varnish to the paper on the box, making sure that each coat is thoroughly dry before applying the next (at least 24 hours).
2 Using no. 80 wet-and-dry sandpaper wrapped around the sanding block and a little water, very lightly sand the box, paying attention to the corners and the join in the paper, where the varnish may have built up. Wipe the box with a lint-free cloth and apply another coat of varnish.

3 Apply another four or five coats of varnish, and then repeat step 2. The idea is to sand back the varnish where it is building up in the corners or seams and to build up the varnish elsewhere, until eventually the entire box feels smooth and seamless.
4 Repeat steps 2 and 3 until you are satisfied that the surface of the box is absolutely flat and smooth.
5 Apply three more coats of varnish, polishing the surface with no. 120 wet-and-dry sandpaper between applications to achieve a very smooth, dull finish.

⑤ FINISHING

1 Paint the rims of the box and the lid with gold paint, and paint the inside gold or a color of your choice.
2 When the paint is dry, attach the hinges and handles.
3 For a shiny, lasting finish, wax the box, following the instructions given in the techniques section for découpage.

3 Using the rubber roller and working from the center outward, smooth the surface, squeezing out air bubbles and excess glue. Wipe off any excess glue with a damp sponge.
4 When the glue is dry, use a scalpel or craft knife to trim the edges of the paper to fit the lid top exactly.
5 With the lid in position, and working on one side at a time, repeat steps 2 to 4 to stick the paper to the sides of the box.

COVERING THE BOX

It is best to use the type of wrapping paper that is sold in rolled sheets. If you use a folded paper, do not use any part that has fold creases in it, as they will show through the finish. Seal the paper on both sides with acrylic gloss medium before you begin.

Decide where on the box you want the design elements to appear: for example, the paper used on the box illustrated features old maps of the world and includes a lettered border, which looks very effective around the upper edge of the lid.

Covering the lid
Cut a sheet of paper to the exact size of the top of the lid. If the paper stretches when it is glued, you can trim away the excess later.

Covering the sides
Put the lid on the box and wrap the paper around the sides. Position the design to your satisfaction, and trim the paper to cover the sides exactly; it should not overlap or extend over the edge of the box. Place the join inconspicuously on a corner or at the back of the box. When the glue is dry, carefully run a scalpel between the box and the lid to separate them.

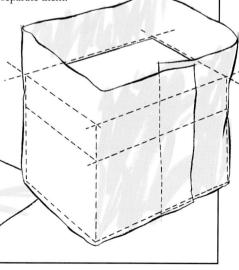

Child's hat & scarf

Your favorite niece or nephew will be as warm as toast on chilly winter days in this wool crepe hat and scarf. Make them in colors that complement the child's sweater or jacket.

WHAT YOU NEED

Size	A	B
Age (years)	4–8	10–14
Hat fits (cm)	52–54	56
Scarf length (cm)	100	120

The yarn used in this project is 4 ply (50 g balls). The colors for both garments are: main color (mc), cream; 1st contrast (cc1), cornflower; 2nd contrast (cc2), light blue; 3rd contrast (cc3), pink.

Hat

Main (mc)	2	2
1st contrast (cc1)	1	1
2nd contrast (cc2)	1	1
3rd contrast (cc3)	1	1

Scarf

Main (mc)	4	5
1st contrast (cc1)	1	1
2nd contrast (cc2)	1	1
3rd contrast (cc3)	1	1

Knitting needles: 4.00 mm (no. 8), 3.75 mm (no. 9), 3.25 mm (no. 10)• wool sewing needle
● *Technique pages 323–7*

CHECKING THE GAUGE

Before you begin, check your gauge so that the measurements of the finished garment will be as close as possible to the size specified. You should have 27.5 stitches and 28 rows to a 10 cm square over Fair Isle using 4.00 mm needles, and 26.5 stitches to a 10 cm width over stockinette stitch using 3.75 mm needles. If you have fewer stitches, use smaller needles; if more, use bigger needles.

❶ KNITTING THE HAT
Using 3.25 mm needles and mc, cast on 161 (169) sts.

NOTE

Do not weave colors in Fair Isle knitting. Instead, carry colors not in use loosely across on the wrong side of your work. Always carry colors to ends of rows, and always carry the main color above the contrast colors.

1st row: K2, ★ P1, K1, rep from ★ to last st, K1.
2nd row: K1, ★ P1, K1, rep from ★ to end.
Rep 1st and 2nd rows 4 times, inc once in last row...162 (170) sts, making 10 rows rib in all.

Change to 4.00 mm needles.
Work 19 rows of pat from graph A.
Change to 3.75 mm needles and work 3 rows in mc, dec 6 (0) sts evenly across last row...156 (170) sts.
★★ Change to 4.00 mm needles and work 5 rows of pat from graph B, dec 4 (0) sts evenly across last row...152 (170) sts.
Work 5 rows from graph C, inc 2 (0) sts evenly across the last row...154 (170) sts.
Work 5 rows from graph D, inc 2 (0) sts evenly across the last row...156 (170) sts. ★★

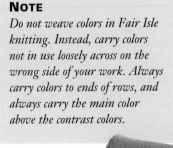

Work 5 rows from graph B, dec 2 (0) sts evenly across the last row...154 (170) sts. Change to 3.75 mm needles and work 0 (2) rows in mc.

Shaping the top
Working in mc only:
1st row: K1, ★ K2 tog, K2, rep from ★ to last st, K1...116 (128) sts.
2nd and alt rows: Purl.
3rd row: K1, ★ K2 tog, K1, rep from ★ to last st, K1...78 (86) sts.
5th row: K1, ★ K2 tog, rep from ★ to last st, K1...40 (44) sts.
7th row: ★ K2 tog, rep from ★ to end...20 (22) sts.
Break off yarn, carefully run end through rem sts, draw up tightly and fasten off securely.

❷ MAKING UP THE HAT
1 Press lightly with a warm iron through a slightly damp cloth.
2 Using wool sewing needle and backstitch, join the two edges together. Press seam.
3 Using mc, make a pompom and sew it to the top of the hat.

❸ KNITTING THE SCARF
Using 3.75 mm needles and mc, cast on 22 (23) sts.
1st row: K1, ★ inc in next st, rep from ★ to last st, K1...42 (44) sts.
2nd and 4th rows: Purl.
3rd row: K1, ★ inc in next st, K1, rep from ★ to last st, K1...62 (65) sts.
5th row: K1, ★ inc in next st, K2, rep from ★ to last st, K1...82 (86) sts.
6th row: Purl.
Change to 4.00 mm needles.
Work 19 rows of pat from graph A.
Change to 3.75 mm needles and work 3 rows in mc, inc 4 (0) sts evenly across last row...86 sts.
Work as for hat from ★★ to ★★, omitting inc and dec.
Change to 3.75 mm needles and work in stst until scarf measures 84 (104) cm from beg, ending with a purl row.
Change to 4.00 mm needles and work 5 rows of pat from graph D.
Work 5 rows of pat from graph C.
Work 5 rows of pat from graph B.
Change to 3.75 mm needles and work 2 rows in mc, dec 4 (0) sts evenly

KNITTING GRAPHS
Reading knit rows from right to left and purl rows from left to right, work from the graph. Strand the colors loosely across the back of the work to the end of the row.

Graph A

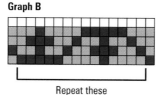

work these 40 stitches four times for hat
work these 40 stitches twice for scarf

work these 42 stitches four times for hat
work these 42 stitches twice for scarf

Graph B

Repeat these 14 stitches

Graph C

Repeat these 6 stitches

Graph D

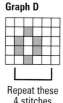

Repeat these 4 stitches

across last row...82 (86) sts.
Change to 4.00 mm needles.
Work 19 rows of pat from graph A.
Change to 3.75 mm needles.
Working in mc only, shape the end:
1st row: K1, ★ K2 tog, K2, rep from ★ to last st, K1.
2nd and 4th rows: Purl.
3rd row: K1, ★ K2 tog, K1, rep from ★ to last st, K1.
5th row: K1, ★ K2 tog, rep from ★ to last st, K1...22 (23) sts.
Break off yarn, carefully run end through rem sts, draw up tightly and fasten off securely.

❹ MAKING UP THE SCARF
1 With a slightly damp cloth and warm iron, press lightly.
2 With wrong side outside, back-stitch the side seam to form a tube. Turn the scarf to the right side and gather the cast-on edge, pulling it up

tightly. Fasten off the ends securely.
3 Make two pompoms and sew one to each end of the scarf. Press the seam through a damp cloth.

VARIATION
A plain scarf makes an excellent introduction to knitting for a child who would like to make a gift for a special friend.
Use five (six) balls of yarn and needles as specified in the pattern. Cast on and work the first five rows as given in the pattern. Continue working in stockinette stitch (beginning with a purl row) until the work measures 98 (118) cm from the beginning, ending with a purl row. Work the last five rows and finish off as in the pattern.

Sculpted floral hair comb

Decorate a plain plastic hair comb and create a colorful accessory for a little girl. Older children could make this pretty floral hair comb themselves for a special friend.

and carefully follow the directions for making the dough. If you find the dough is too crumbly to manipulate easily, add more glue, or, if it is too sloppy, add more breadcrumbs. Before you begin the project, you may need to practice making and rolling

WHAT YOU NEED

Hair comb • 6 slices white bread (a few days old, with the crusts removed) • white glue • artist's acrylic paints: white, green, and 2 or 3 colors of your choice for the flowers • 4 cake-decorating flower stamens • water-based clear flat varnish • plastic food wrap • sticky tape or Blu Tack • piece of A4 paper • electric blender or hand grater • bowl • small wooden stick (for mixing the dough) • smooth laminated board • scissors • knife • pencil • paint palette • 2 small paintbrushes (for varnishing and gluing) • piece of dowel about 8 cm long (for a rolling pin) • selection of small cake-decorating cutters in the shapes of stars, leaves and flowers

White breadcrumbs kneaded with white glue form a wonderfully elastic and pliable modeling dough. The dough, which requires no baking, can be tinted with acrylic paints to create stunning jewelry and knickknacks.

To achieve the best results, use the ingredients in the quantities specified

Cutting the shapes

Any small cake-decorating cutters can be used for cutting the shapes from the dough. To make this project, the cutters illustrated below were used. They are shown to exact size.

the dough and cutting shapes from it until you are happy with the result.

❶ MAKING THE DOUGH

1 Using a blender, a grater or a food processor, reduce the bread to very fine crumbs.

NOTE

It is important to add white acrylic paint to the basic dough mixture – otherwise, the dough will become transparent and will crack when it dries. The paint also helps to improve the texture of the dough for easy working.

2 Place the breadcrumbs in a bowl with 60 ml of white glue and mix with a wooden stick.
3 Place the dough on the laminated board and knead it with your hands, working the dough until it is smooth and quite free of lumps. The dough will become softer and smoother as you knead it.
4 Add a small amount of white paint and knead this through the mixture, adding more paint if necessary until the dough is an even white color.
5 Wrap the dough in plastic food wrap until you are ready to use it so that it does not dry out. The dough should be used within 12 days.

❷ PLANNING THE DESIGN

1 Using a pencil, trace the shapes of your cutters onto a piece of paper. Cut out at least two of each shape. Draw a template the size and shape of the part of the hair comb where the design is to be placed.

2 Arrange the paper cut-outs on the template until you are happy with the design. Fix them in place on the template with sticky tape or Blu Tack.
3 Decide what color each shape is to be. (You can create more colors by mixing the paints on the palette before adding them to the dough.)

❸ CREATING THE DESIGN

It is important to press all the dough shapes onto the comb before the dough hardens, in order to allow for greater manipulation of the elements in the design.

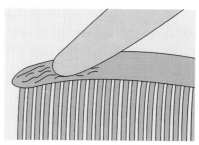

1 Using a knife, scratch all over the top surface of the hair comb. This will roughen the surface so that the dough will stick to it.
2 Break off a piece of dough large enough to cover the top of the hair comb. Knead some green paint into it until the color is evenly spread through the dough.
3 Using the dowel, roll out a flattish sausage of dough large enough to cover the top of the comb. Fix the green dough base to the comb with a little white glue, and score the dough at either end with a knife or pencil to create leaf shapes.
4 Break off enough dough to cut out all the shapes of one color. Knead in paint of the chosen color, and then roll out the dough thinly. Use the cutters to cut out the shapes.
5 Repeat step 4 until you have colored and cut out all the shapes.
6 Cut the artificial stamens into short lengths (about 1 cm) and press them into the centers of the two largest flowers. In the middle of the other flowers, press little balls of dough in contrasting colors to make inner petals. Flatten the balls into petals with the end of a pencil.
7 Glue the flower shapes into place following the design of your paper plan.

❹ FINISHING

Leave the comb in a warm place (not in direct sunlight) to dry for two or three days. When it is completely dry, coat it with clear varnish using a small paintbrush.

Mouse bookends

Sturdily made with long base plates, these novel bookends will brighten up a child's shelves and keep books tidy.

WHAT YOU NEED

Master pattern **C17(a–e)** • plywood: 290 mm **x** 250 mm **x** 18 mm; 250 mm **x** 250 mm **x** 4 mm • two milled wood blocks, 120 mm **x** 70 mm **x** 70 mm (for the cheese) • eight 20 mm finishing nails • six 35 mm finishing nails • wood primer • gloss paint: color to suit decor, yellow (for cheese) • 40 cm **x** 25 cm soft kid leather or suede • 8 small toy eyes • 4 small beads • large bath sponge • 25 cm nylon fishing line • compass • handsaw or jigsaw • hammer • drill and drill bits of various sizes (5 mm to 15 mm) • medium-grade sandpaper • white glue • clear craft glue • paintbrush • steel ruler • scissors • craft knife • darning needle • clothespins • pencil
● *Technique pages 338–42, 343–4*

CUTTING THE BASES

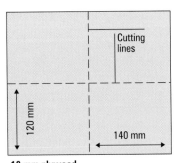

120 mm

140 mm

18 mm plywood

Cutting lines

120 mm

Cutting line

250 mm

4 mm plywood

❶ MAKING THE BOOKENDS

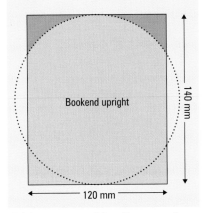

Bookend upright

140 mm

120 mm

1 Trace an arc with a diameter of about 140 mm at one end of two of the rectangles of 18 mm plywood, using a pencil and a compass or a guide such as the rim of a saucer.
2 Using a handsaw or a jigsaw, cut around the tops of the circles to make the arched uprights of the bookends. The other two 18 mm thick rectangles form the bases for the bookends.
3 With medium-grade sandpaper, sand the edges and surfaces of the uprights, bases and base plates (the two rectangles of 4 mm plywood).

VARIATION
You can vary the mice by using leather or felt scraps of different colors or textures, by making them bigger or smaller, or by changing the shape of their ears or the set of their eyes.

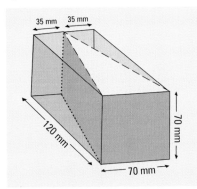

4 Using white glue and four nails, glue and nail the base to the base plate for each bookend. Using three 35 mm nails at each join, glue and nail the upright to the base and base plate for each bookend.

❷ MAKING THE CHEESE

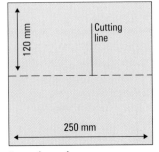

35 mm   35 mm

120 mm

70 mm

70 mm

1 Mark up and cut the two wood blocks as shown.

2 One at a time, clamp the wood wedges firmly in a vise, and carefully drill holes at random through the wedges, using a variety of drill sizes and angles of approach.
3 Sand all surfaces smooth and wipe them clean and free of dust.

❸ MAKING THE MICE

1 Trace the pattern pieces and all markings on them from the master pattern onto tracing paper and cut them out. Place the pattern pieces on the leather, and mark and cut out four sets of all pattern pieces.

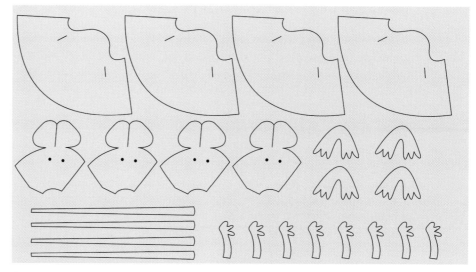

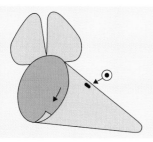

2 Roll the head piece into a cone shape to form the nose. Apply clear craft glue where indicated and clamp the leather with a clothespin until dry. Glue the eyes to the head.

3 Cut small slits in the body with a craft knife, where indicated on the pattern piece. Insert the ends of the arms into the slits, adjust them to the desired length, and glue.

4 Form the body shape by gluing the straight sides together with a 5 mm overlap. Glue the head to the body. Clamp the join firmly with a clothespin until the glue dries.
5 Using the darning needle, make a hole right through the snout, just

Cutting guide
Cut eight arms and four of all other pieces, remembering to transfer markings. To make bigger or smaller mice, enlarge or reduce the master pattern on a photocopier.

behind the nose. Push two 3 cm lengths of fishing line through the hole to make the whiskers. Glue a bead at the end of the nose cone.

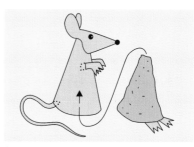

6 Glue the base of the tail in place inside the body. With a craft knife, cut a cone from the sponge to fit inside the body. Glue the feet to the base of the foam cone so that the toes are visible, and then glue the sponge cone inside the mouse's body.
7 Repeat steps 2 to 6 three times to make three more mice.

❹ FINISHING

1 Apply the wood primer to the bookends and the cheese and leave all the pieces to dry.
2 Paint the cheese yellow and the bookends in a color of your choice. Allow to dry thoroughly.
3 Glue the cheese wedges in place on the bookends. Glue the mice to the cheese and the bookends as illustrated.

Beginner's flower press

Encourage a child's interest in botany by making this attractive flower press as a gift, perhaps accompanied by a little book on wildflowers. Pressed flower arrangements are ideal for craft projects such as cards or bookmarks.

WHAT YOU NEED

Plywood, 400 mm x 200 mm x 12 mm • wood, 200 mm x 200 mm x 9 mm (for the base plate) • 2 pieces felt, 200 mm x 200 mm • 4 bolts, 6 mm diameter, about 200 mm long, with matching washers and wing nuts • 15 mm finishing nails • white woodworking glue • clear craft glue • medium- and fine-grade sandpaper • FolkArt acrylic paints: wicker white, poetry green • wrapping paper (for cut-out flower motifs) • 2 small paintbrushes • varnish • drill and drill bits • scrap wood • clamp • hammer • nail scissors • handsaw
● *Technique pages 338–42*

❶ PREPARING THE WOOD

1 Cut the plywood into two pieces, each measuring 200 mm x 200 mm.
2 Sand smooth the cut edges of the plywood and the wood with medium-grade sandpaper.

❷ MAKING THE PRESS

1 Clamp together one of the 200 mm x 200 mm pieces of plywood (this will be the lid) and the wood base plate.
2 About 10 mm in from each corner, and with a drill bit to suit the diameter of the bolts, drill four bolt access holes right through the plywood and the base plate into a piece of scrap wood. Unclamp the wood.
3 Using a drill bit with a larger diameter, enlarge the bolt access holes on one side of the base plate so that the bolt heads can be recessed into the base plate.
4 Insert the bolts through the holes drilled in the base plate. Using the white glue and finishing nails, glue and nail the undrilled piece of plywood to the bottom of the base plate, trapping the bolt heads.
5 Sand the corners of the press with medium-grade sandpaper until they are gently curved.
6 Using fine sandpaper, sand all surfaces smooth, including the lid (the plywood with the holes drilled in it).

❸ FINISHING THE PRESS

1 Using a small decorating brush, paint all surfaces with a base coat of wicker white and then two coats of poetry green. Allow each coat to dry thoroughly before applying the next.
2 Cut out suitable flower motifs from the wrapping paper with nail scissors, cutting neatly around the outlines.
3 Glue the paper motifs to the flower press lid, using the clear craft glue. Allow the glue to dry.
4 Apply a coat of varnish, allow to dry thoroughly, and then apply a second coat. Allow to dry.
5 Using the nail scissors, trim the corners of the two pieces of felt to match the rounded corners of the press. Cut a hole at each corner to accommodate the bolts.
6 Sandwich the two pieces of felt between the top plate and the base plate of the flower press.

NOTE

The flowers are pressed between sheets of blotting paper enclosed between sheets of cardboard. With the gift, include a supply of blotting paper and cardboard, cut to about 150 mm square.

Beach tote bag & towel

This coordinated beach bag and towel set is an ideal gift for a young person who enjoys standing out from the crowd, even on the beach.

WHAT YOU NEED

Master pattern **D28(a–d)** • stencil film or treated manila cardboard • fabric paints: sea-green, jade, peach, lapis blue, crimson • paintbrushes: 2 large stenciling, 3 medium stenciling • spray adhesive • tracing paper • transfer paper • hard pencil (or empty ballpoint pen) • pencil • permanent marker pen • craft knife • cutting mat or board • sewing thread • tape measure • dressmaking pins • scissors • sewing machine
Bag: 1.2 m cotton canvas, 150 cm wide • 21 m cotton cord, 3 mm diameter • 30 cm x 30 cm heavy plastic (for the base) • 2 cotton tassels • assorted seashells • paintbrushes: 13 mm decorating, no. 4 round • masking tape • ruler • compass • bulldog clip • drill and 5 mm masonry drill bit
Towel: large white towel • cotton twill (see "Buying the twill," page 85) • 12 cotton tassels
● *Technique pages 292–301, 337, 343–4*

MAKING THE STENCILS

1 If you are using cardboard, trace and transfer the stencil designs from the master pattern onto the cardboard. For stencil plastic, trace the design straight onto the plastic, using a fine permanent marker pen.

2 Cut out the stencils with a craft knife on a cutting mat or board, being particularly careful when you are cutting the fine, inner lines.
3 With a compass, mark on the stencil material a circle 13 cm in diameter, and carefully cut it out.

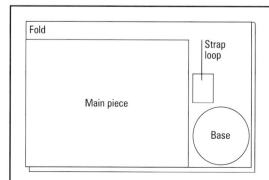

CUTTING GUIDE

Cut five pieces of canvas to make the beach bag – two rectangular pieces 66 cm x 87 cm (main piece), two circles 30 cm in diameter (base), and one strip 5 cm x 11 cm for the strap loop.

Beach bag

❶ CUTTING OUT THE BAG

1 Wash the canvas to shrink it and remove any fabric conditioners.
2 For the main section and lining, cut two pieces of canvas 87 cm x 66 cm.
3 Using the compass, mark and cut two circles of canvas 30 cm in diameter for the base and the lining.
4 Cut a strip of fabric 5 cm wide and 11 cm long for the shoulder loop.
5 Mark a 27 cm diameter circle on the heavy plastic with the compass, and cut it out with the craft knife. This is to keep the base rigid.

❷ STENCILING THE BAG

1 Fold one main section of fabric in quarters to find the center. Unfold the fabric and mark the center.

2 Spray the backs of the shell stencils with adhesive and place the large shell on the fabric along the center fold, near the bottom of the fabric. Place the medium shell over the marked center point and then place the small shell near the top of the fabric, in line with the other two shells.

3 Using a medium stencil brush, stencil each shell all over with the peach paint and then shade here and there with crimson.

4 Repeat steps 2 and 3 to place two more columns of shells toward the outer edges of the fabric.

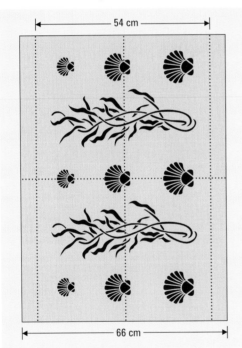

5 Spray the large seaweed stencil with adhesive and place it between the columns of shells. Using a large stencil brush and the sea-green paint, brush the color lightly all over the seaweed stencil. Change to a smaller brush and darken some areas by adding more sea-green on top of the base coat. Using a medium stencil brush and jade paint, add shading at random. Paint over the top of some of this shading with lapis blue. Finally, lightly stencil the edges here and there with crimson. Repeat this procedure to stencil a seaweed frond on the other

side of the central column of shells.

6 Measure and rule lightly in pencil a line 6 cm from the edges of the top and bottom of the fabric (along the two long sides). Run masking tape along the inside of these lines to give you a straight edge guide for the paint. Using the decorating brush, paint a strip of jade along the top and bottom edges of the canvas. Add an occasional lapis blue stroke with a medium stenciling brush to create a watery effect. Carefully remove the masking tape.

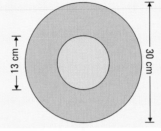

7 Apply spray adhesive to one side of the 13 cm circle of stencil material and press it firmly onto the center of one of the fabric circles. Paint the area between the outside edge of the fabric and the edge of the plastic with jade. Allow to dry.

8 Remove the plastic circle. Spray the large shell stencil with adhesive and place it in the center of the fabric. Stencil the shape with peach and then shade it in places with crimson.

9 When all the fabric paint is dry, set the paint by pressing the painted and stenciled areas back and front with a dry iron, following the manu-facturer's instructions.

❸ SEWING THE BAG

1 With right sides facing, stitch together the short sides of the unsten-ciled main section (the lining) to form a tube, using a 1.5 cm seam allowance.

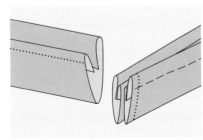

2 To make the small loop for the shoulder strap, fold and press a 5 mm

hem along one 11 cm side of the fab-ric strip and a 1 cm hem along the opposite 11 cm side. Machine stitch the folded edges together, wrong sides facing. Machine stitch the short ends together to form a loop.

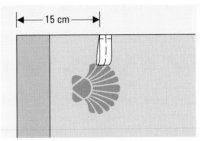

3 Lay out the stenciled main section, right side up, and place the loop against the left-hand, short side, 15 cm from the bottom. Baste it in place along the edge.

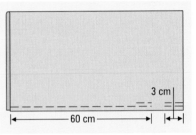

4 With right sides facing, fold the stenciled main piece in half widthwise. Starting from the bottom edge, sew a 1.5 cm seam up 60 cm along the side edge, reinforcing the last 5 cm by sewing the seam twice. Leave a 3 cm

gap for the shoulder strap to be threaded through, and then double-sew the remaining 3 cm of the seam to the top edge of the folded canvas.

5 Open out the seams and press them flat. Turn and press a 1 cm hem along the top edge of both the stenciled main piece and the lining canvas.

6 With right sides facing, sew the stenciled main section to the stenciled base section using a 1.5 cm seam allowance. Ease the bag gently onto the base as you go.

7 Repeat step 6 with the lining and the lining base.

8 Turn the stenciled bag right side out. Push the plastic base cut-out firmly down into the base of the stenciled bag, then put the lining bag inside the stenciled bag so that the wrong sides of each bag are facing.

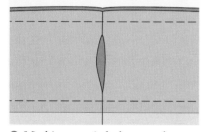

9 Machine topstitch the outer bag to the lining along the turned hem edges. Sew another row of stitching, parallel to this stitch line and 6 cm from the top edge, to make a channel for the shoulder strap.

❹ MAKING THE STRAP

1 Cut the cord into six equal lengths of 3.5 m, and knot them together 50 cm from one end. Secure the cords to a table top with a bulldog clip and plait them into a three-strand braid, using two cords per strand. Tie off with a knot 50 cm from the other end.

HINT

When making the towel, stencil the twill strips before you sew them in place so that if you make a mistake you do not have to waste time unpicking the strip – you need only cut out a new strip and stencil it.

2 Thread the braided cord through the opening of the bag channel, around the channel and back out, adjusting the ends until both are even. Thread one end of the braid through the loop at the bottom of the bag and tie the ends of the braid together with a large knot.

3 Using the drill and 5 mm masonry bit, drill holes in the base of the shells. Tie a knot 10 cm from the end of one of the cords used to make the braid. Thread a shell onto the cord and push it up to the knot. Tie another knot to secure the shell. Trim off excess cord. Do the same with the other shells, tying them at various lengths. Knot the ends of the remaining cords to prevent fraying.

4 Attach the cotton tassels by tying them to the large knot in the braid.

Beach towel

❶ PREPARING THE TOWEL

1 Wash the towel and the twill to allow for shrinkage and remove any fabric conditioners.

2 When dry, iron the twill and towel flat. Measure the towel and cut four strips of twill 22 cm wide and 2 cm longer than the sides of the towel.

3 Turn and press a 1.5 cm hem along both sides of each twill strip. Spread the towel on a flat surface and arrange the strips on the towel, about 1.5 cm from the outer edge of the towel.

4 At each corner, make a miter by folding the twill at an angle of 45°. Pin these folds into place, press them firmly and remove the pins. Trim excess twill to leave 1.5 cm hems at the miters. Remove the twill strips from the towel.

❷ STENCILING THE TOWEL

1 Fold each twill strip in half width-wise and mark its center.

2 Spray the back of the clam stencil with adhesive and place it in the center of one strip with the bubbles flowing to the center. Stencil the clam and bubbles with peach paint, and shade here and there with crimson. Repeat on the other three strips of twill.

BUYING THE TWILL
To make the twill strips to trim the towel, buy a piece of cotton twill 90 cm wide and 2 cm longer than the towel.

3 On each strip, stencil the smaller seaweed frond on both sides of the clam, positioning the fronds to look as if they are growing away from the miter. Position the base of the frond about 12 cm from the miter. Employ the method and colors that you used to stencil the large seaweed fronds onto the bag (see step 5 of "Stenciling the bag").

4 Allow the stencils to dry, then sew the mitered corners of the twill together and press them flat.

5 At each corner, over the mitered seams, stencil one large shell and then stencil a medium shell underneath it. Stencil a small shell on either side of the medium shell.

6 When the corner stencils are dry, set the paint by pressing the twill back and front with a dry iron, following the manufacturer's instructions.

7 Pin the twill rectangle onto the towel and machine stitch along the folded edges. Sew three cotton tassels to each corner of the towel.

Découpage pencil box

A pencil box ornamented with a lively découpage design is an ideal gift for a young person, especially one who loves writing or drawing. Choose images to suit the recipient's taste – pop stars or movie stars would be an up-to-date choice.

WHAT YOU NEED

Wooden pencil box with sliding lid • printed images • artist's gesso • artist's acrylic gloss medium (sealer) • artist's acrylic paint: gold, a dark background color for the images • polyurethane gloss varnish • 3 small paintbrushes (for sealing, gluing and painting) • 25 mm imitation sable brush (for varnishing) • wet-and-dry sandpaper: nos. 60, 80 and 120 • rubber sanding block • wallpaper paste • white glue • rubber roller • clear beeswax • cabinetmaker's or French furniture polish • lint-free cloth • pieces of thick kitchen sponge • Blu Tack • fine curved scissors • scalpel

● *Technique pages 329–31*

❶ PREPARATION

1 Using no. 60 sandpaper, sand all the surfaces of the box and the lid until they are completely smooth. (If there is paint or varnish on the box, use paint stripper to remove it before sanding.)
2 Wipe the box with a lint-free cloth to remove any dust.
3 If necessary, apply two coats of artist's gesso to ensure a smooth, non-porous surface, allowing the gesso to dry thoroughly between coats. Sand the surfaces lightly.
4 Paint the box and the lid, using artist's acrylic paint in your chosen background color. (If the paint does not contain sealer, mix one part paint and one part sealer for this step.) You may need to apply several coats of paint to achieve good coverage, particularly with a very dark color. Allow the paint to dry thoroughly between coats.
5 Load a dry brush with gold paint and then wipe most of the paint off the brush. Stroke and pounce gold

paint lightly and randomly onto the box and the lid, working always in the same direction. The background color should show through the strokes of gold paint.
6 Cut out the images, leaving plenty of background at this stage. This will give you something to hold on to while you are trimming the images later, and it will also allow you to retain some of the background if the design requires it.
7 Seal the images with artist's acrylic gloss medium. Apply the medium sparingly to the backs of the images and allow it to dry, then repeat this step on the fronts of the images.

❷ FIXING THE IMAGES

1 Position the sealed images on the box and the lid with small pieces of

---

CHOOSING IMAGES

It is important to select your images carefully. The images you choose should make up a harmonious design when they are placed together. Creating découpage will be easier if you use images printed on papers of similar quality and weight and with consistent depth of color. Cut your images from thin paper, such as the pages of a magazine – if you use thick paper, it will be very difficult to cover the cut edges. Art books are a good source of images, and so are wrapping papers. Note, however, that you should not use folded wrapping papers, as the creases will show. Color photocopies can be used, but they need special treatment because the color bleeds easily. Textured, metallic and very glossy papers are not recommended.

NOTE

Instead of using beeswax and cabinetmaker's or French furniture polish to give the pencil box its soft, glowing finish, you can use a micromesh kit. Micromeshing is an excellent alternative finish for a découpage gift since, unlike the waxed finish, it does not need to be reapplied every few months. If you decide to use the beeswax and cabinetmaker's polish to finish the pencil box, it is a good idea to include with your gift the equipment needed to renew the finish and instructions on how to use it and how often.

Blu Tack, rearranging them until you are satisfied with the design. Make a paper template of each facet of the box, indicating the top of each facet. Mark the positions of all the images on the templates.
2 At this point, decide exactly where you want to trim the images and whether you need to leave any background. Carefully trim the images, using fine, sharp, curved scissors and allowing the paper to curl through the blades, rather than cutting with a chopping motion of the scissors – this should give a smooth, sharp edge to the images. Use a scalpel to cut any straight edges.
3 Mix together three parts wallpaper paste and one part white glue. Working on one surface and one image at a time, apply the glue mixture generously to the box. Place the image in position and apply a small amount of glue to the right side.
4 With your fingers, gently massage the image into the surface to press out any lumps of glue or air bubbles. Flatten the image perfectly onto the surface with the rubber roller, using light pressure and working in one direction from the center of the image toward the edges.
5 Gently remove any excess glue from the surface of the image with a wet piece of kitchen sponge.

6 Repeat steps 3 to 5 until you have stuck down all the images. Allow the glue to dry thoroughly.

7 Apply two coats of artist's acrylic medium (sealer) to the découpaged surfaces. Allow the sealer to dry for one hour between coats and before starting to apply the varnish.

❸ VARNISHING AND SANDING

1 Using the imitation sable brush, apply 5 to 10 coats of varnish to all the découpaged surfaces. It is important to work carefully and to let the varnish dry for at least 24 hours between coats, otherwise lumps and drips of varnish will form.

2 When you are sure that the images are well protected with varnish, begin sanding between each third coat, using no. 80 wet-and-dry sandpaper wrapped around a rubber sanding block and moistened with a little water. Sand lightly in one direction, and aim to allow the varnish on the background to build up to the level of the images. Before applying a new coat of varnish, use a lint-free cloth to remove any dust.

3 Continue varnishing and sanding until the découpaged surface is completely smooth and flat and you cannot feel the edges of the images – they should appear to be submerged in the layers of varnish. You may need as many as 30 coats of varnish to achieve the desired effect, although on a flat surface 10 coats may be enough.

4 Apply three more coats of varnish, sanding the surface between coats with no. 120 wet-and-dry sandpaper. This will give the box a very smooth, dull finish.

❹ FINISHING

1 Leave the pencil box to stand for two weeks to allow the varnish to harden and cure completely.

2 Make a mixture of equal parts of clear beeswax and cabinetmaker's polish and warm it slightly. Working on a small area at a time, rub the mixture evenly into the découpaged surfaces with a soft, lint-free cloth. Wipe the waxed area vigorously with a damp cloth and then polish it with a soft, dry cloth.

3 Repeat steps 2 and 3 if necessary.

CAUTION

Because the many layers of varnish used in découpage will increase the thickness of the lid, it is important to sand the lid right back so that it slides easily and very loosely in the grooves. For the same reason, do not paint or varnish in the grooves, and do not attempt to fit the finished lid into the box until you are satisfied that the varnish on both the box and the lid is completely dry and cured.

Stylish soft knapsack

Smart enough for any outing and strong enough to carry quite a load, this quilted knapsack will please the fussiest of teenagers. Made from two contrasting fabrics, it is easy to make up using a standard sewing machine.

WHAT YOU NEED

Master pattern D27(a–c) • 1 m main fabric, 115 cm wide • 50 cm contrasting fabric, 90 cm wide • 50 cm lining fabric, 115 cm wide • 75 cm craft batting, 115 cm wide • sewing thread • sewing needle • 2 buttons • 10 large eyelets • dressmaking pins • tracing paper • pencil • dressmaker's pencil • scissors • tape measure • sewing machine
● *Technique pages 292–301, 305–6, 343–4*

❶ CUTTING OUT THE KNAPSACK

1 Using the tracing paper and pencil, trace the pattern pieces for the base, the bag flap, and the pocket flap. Cut the pattern pieces out.
2 Cut out the fabrics as follows.

Main fabric

One main piece, 87 cm x 44 cm; two straps, 8 cm x 75 cm; one reinforcing strip, 5.5 cm x 25 cm; one handle, 8 cm x 24 cm; one base (from master pattern); one bag flap (from master pattern); one pocket flap bias strip, 4 cm x 38 cm; one bag flap bias strip, 4 cm x 70 cm.

Contrasting fabric

One pocket, 32 cm x 32 cm; one bottom band, 5.5 cm x 87 cm; one cord, 90 cm x 3.5 cm; two pocket flaps (from master pattern); one bag flap (from master pattern).

Lining fabric

One main piece, 87 cm x 36 cm; one base (from master pattern).

Batting

One main piece, 90 cm x 48 cm; one base (from master pattern) – cut this piece 1 cm larger all around; one bag flap and one pocket flap (from master pattern); two straps, 8 cm x 75 cm; one handle, 8 cm x 24 cm.

❷ QUILTING THE PIECES

Use iron-on or regular craft batting.

1 Iron or baste the batting to the wrong side of the main piece cut from the main fabric, and machine-quilt them together in a 7 cm grid pattern. Trim away the excess batting.
2 Repeat step 1 to quilt the base piece cut from the main fabric.
3 Iron or baste the batting to the wrong side of one of the pocket flaps cut from the contrasting fabric. Lay

VARIATION

Instead of making the knapsack with contrasting prints, you could use plain fabrics in either complementary or contrasting colors – for example, purple and pink or black and white. You could also buy the cord rather than making it.

the other pocket flap over the batting, right side up, and baste the three layers together. Machine-quilt the pocket flap in the same grid pattern as before.

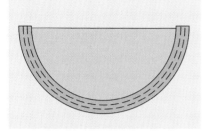

4 With right sides together and raw edges aligned, and taking a 1 cm seam allowance, stitch the shorter bias strip around the curve of the pocket flap, easing the fabric to fit. Fold the binding to the other side of the flap and turn the raw edge under. Topstitch close to the fold, and then make

another row of stitching about 6 mm away from the edge.
5 Repeat steps 3 and 4 to make the bag flap. The contrasting fabric will become the outer side of this flap, so stitch the binding to the main fabric first, and then turn it over and top-stitch it to the contrasting fabric.

❸ MAKING THE STRAPS AND THE HANDLE

1 Iron or baste together the strap pieces of main fabric and batting.
2 Fold the straps in half lengthwise, with right sides facing, and stitch the long sides together, using a 1 cm seam allowance. Turn the straps right side out. Topstitch the straps close to the edges and then again 6 mm further in.
3 Repeat steps 1 and 2 to make the handle from the 8 cm x 24 cm pieces of main fabric and batting.

❹ ATTACHING THE POCKET

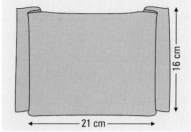

1 Fold the fabric for the pocket in half, with right sides together. Using a 1 cm seam allowance, stitch the seams at the two short ends. Turn the pocket right side out and press. Make a pleat on each side of the pocket, bringing the pocket down to about 21 cm wide. Press the pleats.
2 Pin the pocket to the right side of the main piece, in the center, with the raw edge of the pocket 4 cm from the bottom edge of the main piece.

CUTTING GUIDE

Trace the pattern pieces for the base and the flaps from the master pattern. Use a tape measure and a dressmaker's pencil to measure and mark all the other pieces to the dimensions given in "Cutting out the knapsack." For the flap bindings, ensure that you cut on the bias.

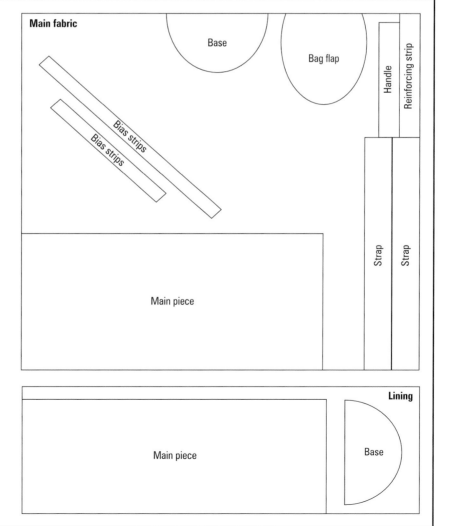
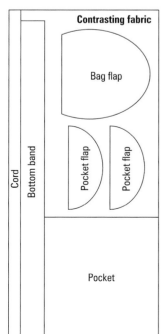

Keeping the pleat folds out of the way, attach the pocket to the main piece by topstitching the sides close to the edges and then topstitching again 6 mm further in.

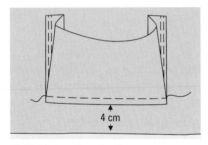

3 Fold the pleats back over, press them again, and then baste the raw bottom edge to the main piece.
4 Press a 1 cm hem along one long side of the bottom band.

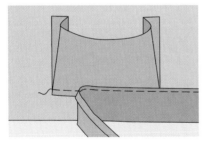

5 With the wrong side of the band facing the right side of the main piece, align the raw edge of the band with the bottom raw edge of the main piece, making sure that the folded edge covers the raw bottom edge of the pocket. Baste the band into place.
6 Topstitch close to the folded edge and then topstitch again, 6 mm away.
7 With the front of the pocket flap facing the right side of the main piece, place the pocket flap upside down, 1.5 cm above the pocket, and align

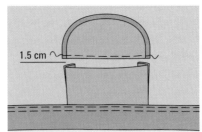

the sides of the pocket flap with the sides of the pocket. Sew the flap in place 5 mm from the raw edge.
8 Turn the pocket flap down and press. Topstitch close to the folded edge and then topstitch again 6 mm from the fold.

⑤ ASSEMBLING THE PIECES OF THE KNAPSACK
1 With right sides together and using a 1.25 cm seam allowance, stitch the center back seam of the main piece to form a cylinder. Press the seam open and topstitch on either side, with the rows of topstitching 6 mm apart.
2 Position the ends of the straps on the bottom band, 7 cm either side of the center back seam, with the raw edges of the straps aligned with the raw edges of the band. Topstitch the straps to the band with a rectangle of stitching. Reinforce by sewing across the diagonals of the rectangles.
3 With right sides together, sew the base to the lower edge of the main piece, using a 1.25 cm seam allowance. Work carefully, easing the cylindrical main piece on to the base.

⑥ ATTACHING THE BAG FLAP AND THE STRAPS
1 At the top of the knapsack, press down a 6 cm hem to the inside to make a facing. Topstitch close to the fold. (The facing will be finished after the straps have been sewn on.)
2 With the contrast fabric uppermost and the bound edge of the flap overlapping the folded edge of the main piece, center the bag flap over the back seam, with the raw edge 6.5 cm below the top fold. Stitch the flap to the main piece along the raw edge.
3 With raw edges aligned, baste the handle over the bag flap, positioning the ends 2 cm either side of the main

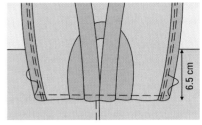

piece seam. The handle will lie on the bag flap in a curve, with the top of the curve folded down.

4 Bring the strap ends up and position them between the ends of the handle, overlapping them slightly to fit. Align all the raw edges and baste them down.
5 Turn under and press a 1 cm hem around all sides of the 5.5 cm x 25 cm reinforcing strip. Center it over the raw edges of the bag flap, the handle and the straps, and baste it into place.
6 Topstitch the reinforcing strip close to the turned edges and then 6 mm further in, being careful not to catch up the facing at the back.

⑦ FITTING THE LINING
1 With right sides together and using a 1.25 cm seam allowance, stitch the center back seam of the lining to make a cylinder 36 cm deep. With right sides together, baste and then sew the lining base to the lining main piece.
2 With wrong sides together, insert the lining in the bag. Turn the raw edge of the top facing under 1 cm.
3 Catching the lining under the facing, topstitch the facing down with two rows of stitching 6 mm apart.

⑧ FINISHING
1 Fix 10 eyelets at 10 cm intervals around the top facing, following the manufacturer's instructions.
2 With right sides facing and using a 6 mm seam allowance, stitch together the long sides of the fabric for the cord. Turn the cord right side out, thread it through the eyelets and tie a neat knot at each end.
3 Make vertical buttonholes in the top flap and the pocket flap in the positions marked on the pattern. Sew the buttons onto the knapsack and the pocket in positions to correspond with the buttonholes.

Snappy sneakers

Turn plain canvas shoes and sneakers into designer footwear with a few deft strokes of a paintbrush. The quick-drying acrylic paint is so easy to use that children can create and paint individually designed shoes to give to their friends.

WHAT YOU NEED

Canvas shoes or sneakers • artist's gesso • artist's acrylic paints in a selection of colors • paintbrushes: medium round and liner • pencil • newspaper • fabric waterproofing spray

● *Technique pages 334–5*

❶ PREPARING THE SHOES

1 Remove the shoelaces and make sure the canvas is clean and free from dust. If the shoes are not new, or are marked in any way, you may wish to coat the fabric with artist's gesso, which will give a smooth, clean surface for painting.

2 Stuff the shoes with newspaper so that they will keep their shape while you are painting the design.

❷ PAINTING THE SHOES

1 On paper, sketch out the design you want to use on the shoes, or copy the design on the shoes in the photo-graph. When sketching your design, consider the shape of the shoes and make your design appropriate for the contours of the shoes.

2 Lightly pencil the main features of the design onto the canvas.

3 Paint the main design features first, and then the background. If the canvas shoes have rubber toe pieces, paint them in solid colors.

4 When the paint is dry, use a liner brush to add details.

❸ FINISHING THE SHOES

1 Allow the paint to dry thoroughly.

2 Spray the canvas shoes with fabric waterproofing to protect them from both dirt and water.

3 Remove the newspaper when waterproofing spray is completely dry.

4 Rethread the shoelaces.

HINT
Buy colored or patterned shoelaces to match your design colors.

OVER THE RAINBOW

Even if you are not particularly creative, you can achieve a colorful design by painting the shoes with simple patterns such as rainbows or stick people.

Another fun idea is to transfer one of the recipient's own draw-ings onto the shoes.

1 Trace the drawing onto a sheet of tracing paper. You may need to separate some ele-ments of the drawing so that they fit around the shoes.

2 Using carbon paper, transfer your tracing onto the shoes.

3 Fill in the transferred lines with acrylic paints in the colors of the child's original drawing, and buy laces to match the colors you have used.

Summer top & hat

Any teenage girl would love this cool cotton top and hat. The hat is crocheted and the top is knitted, with a wide crocheted midriff band.

WHAT YOU NEED

Size	8	10	12	14	16	18
Chest (cm)	75	80	85	90	95	100
Top measures (cm)						
Chest		84	89	94	99	104	109
Length		43	44	45	47	49	51

Hat fits a 56 cm circumference

The yarns used in this project are: Sirdar Optimum DK cactus green (50 g balls), for the top and soft rose petal (50 g balls), for the band and the hat.

Top

top	3	3	4	4	4	4
band	1	1	2	2	2	2

Hat (one size only)

cc1	2

Knitting needles: 3.75 mm (no. 9) • crochet hooks: 3.50 mm (no. 9), 4.00 mm (no. 8) • wool sewing needle
● *Technique pages 320–2, 323–7*

CHECKING THE GAUGE

Check your gauge before you begin. *Knitting:* 22 stitches to a 10 cm width over seed stitch, using Stonewash cotton. *Crochet:* each motif measures 4 cm across, working with Gem cotton and a 3.50 mm hook.

The knitting is worked on smaller needles at a tighter gauge than is usually recommended. If you have

SPECIAL TERMS

Picot 2: 2 ch, slst in the last dc.
Picot 3: 3 ch, slst in the last tr.

fewer stitches, use smaller needles; if you have more, use bigger needles.

Work from two balls when using Stonewash cotton. Work two rows from the first ball, two rows from the second, then two rows from the first. Do not carry the yarn too tightly along the side of the work.

❶ KNITTING THE BACK

Using 3.75 mm knitting needles and Stonewash cotton, cast on 95 (99-105-111-117-121) sts.
1st row: K1, ★ P1, K1, rep from ★ to the end.
Rep 1st row until work measures 14 (14-15-16-18-19) cm from beg, working last row on wrong side.

Shaping the armholes

Keeping pat correct, cast off 9 (9-10-10-12-12) sts at beg of next 2 rows. Dec at each end of next and alt rows until 61 (63-67-69-71-73) sts rem. ★★ Work 47 (47-47-45-45-47) rows pat.

Shaping the neck

Next row: Pat 18 (19-21-22-23-24) sts, cast off 25 sts, work in pat to the end.
Cont on last 18 (19-21-22-23-24) sts. Dec at neck edge in every row until 10 (11-13-14-15-14) sts rem, then in alt rows until 8 (8-10-10-11-11) sts rem. Work 1 row. Cast off.
Join yarn to rem sts and work other side to correspond.

❷ KNITTING THE FRONT

Work as for back to ★★.
Work 21 (21-21-19-19-19) rows pat.

Shaping the neck

Next row: Pat 19 (20-22-22-23-24)
sts, cast off 23 (23-23-25-25-25) sts,
work in pat to end.
Cont on last 19 (20-22-22-23-24) sts.
Dec at neck edge in alt rows until
13 (13-15-16-17-17) sts rem, then in
every foll 4th row until 8 (8-10-10-11-
11) sts rem.
Work 7 rows. Cast off.
Join yarn to rem sts and work other
side to correspond.

❸ CROCHETING THE BAND

First motif

Using 3.50 mm crochet hook and
Gem cotton, work 8 ch, join with
a slst to form a ring.
1st round: 3 ch, 1 tr in ring, (Picot
3, 2 tr in ring) 11 times, Picot 3, slst
in 3rd ch at beg.
Fasten off.

Second motif

Using 3.50 mm crochet hook and
Gem cotton, work 8 ch, join with
a slst to form a ring.
1st round: 3 ch, 1 tr in ring, ★ 2 ch,
drop loop from hook, insert hook in
any picot of 1st motif, draw dropped
loop through picot, 1 ch, slst in last
tr of 2nd motif (to complete the picot)
★, 2 tr in ring, rep from ★ to ★ once
in next picot of 1st motif, complete
as for 1st motif.
Fasten off.

Continue joining motifs in this way,
leaving 4 picots free before joining the
next motif, until there are 20 (21-22-
23-25-26) motifs.
Make 1 more motif, joining it (as
before) to the previous motif and
also to the first motif with the 7th
and 8th picots.
Make another 21 (22-23-24-26-27)
motifs, joining each (as before) to the
previous motif and also to a 1st round
motif with 4th and 5th picots. Join the
final motif to the previous motif, the
1st round motif and the 1st motif of
the 2nd round.

❹ FINISHING THE TOP

Using Stonewash cotton and wool
sewing needle, join side and shoulder
seams with backstitch. It is best not
to press this garment, because of its
textured pattern.

Waist

Using 3.50 mm crochet hook and
Gem cotton, work 1 rnd of dc evenly
around lower edge. Fasten off. Using
a flat seam, sew picots of midriff band
to dc rnd.

Neckline and armholes

1st round: Using 3.50 mm crochet
hook and Gem cotton, work 1 rnd dc
evenly around the neck edge, taking
care to keep work flat and working
an even number of sts.
2nd round: 1 ch, 1 dc in the first dc,
★ Picot 2, 1 dc in each of next 2 dc,
rep from ★ to last dc, Picot 2, 1 dc
in next dc, slst in first dc. Fasten off.
Work the same edging around the
armholes.

❺ CROCHETING THE HAT

Check your gauge before you begin.
You should have 24 dc and 28 rows to
10 cm over double crochet fabric,
using a 4.00 mm hook.
   This hat is designed to be worked
with a bigger hook at a looser gauge
than is usually recommended.

Using 4.00 mm crochet hook and
Gem cotton, work 4 ch, join with
slst to form a ring.
1st round: 1 ch, 12 dc in ring, slst
in first dc.

MOSS STITCH

Moss stitch is sometimes called
seed stitch. It produces a firm,
textured fabric that keeps its
shape. It can be used to make a
whole garment or as a contrast.

2nd round: 1 ch, 2 dc in same place as
slst, 2 dc in each dc to end, slst in first
dc...24 dc.
3rd round: 1 ch, 1 dc in
same place as slst, 1 dc in
each dc to end, slst in
first dc.
4th round: 1 ch, 1 dc
in same place as slst, 2 dc
in next dc, ★ 1 dc in next
dc, 2 dc in next dc, rep
from ★ to end, slst
in first dc...36 dc.
5th round: As for 3rd round.
6th round: 1 ch, 1 dc in same place as
slst, 1 dc in next dc, 2 dc in next dc, ★
1 dc in each of next 2 dc, 2 dc in next
dc, rep from ★ to end, slst in first
dc...48 dc.
7th round: As for 3rd round.
8th round: 1 ch, 1 dc in same place
as slst, 1 dc in each of next 2 dc, 2 dc
in next dc, ★ 1 dc in each of next 3 dc,
2 dc in next dc, rep from ★ to end, slst
in first dc...60 dc.
9th round: As for 3rd round.
10th round: 1 ch, 1 dc in same place
as slst, 1 dc in each of next 3 dc, 2 dc
in next dc, ★ 1 dc in each of next 4 dc,
2 dc in next dc, rep from ★ to end,
slst in first dc...72 dc.
Rep 3rd round twice.
13th round: 1 ch, 1 dc in same place
as slst, 1 dc in each of next 4 dc, 2 dc
in next dc, ★ 1 dc in each of next 5 dc,
2 dc in next dc, rep from ★ to end, slst
in first dc...84 dc.
Rep 3rd round twice.
16th round: 1 ch, 1 dc in same place
as slst, 1 dc in each of next 5 dc, 2 dc
in next dc, ★ 1 dc in each of next 6 dc,
2 dc in next dc, rep from ★ to end, slst
in first dc...96 dc.
Cont inc in this way (working 1 more
dc between inc each time) in each foll
3rd rnd, until there are 132 dc.
Rep 3rd rnd until work measures
17 cm from beginning. (The length
may be varied at this point to suit
individual requirements.)
Next round: 1 ch, 1 dc in same place
as slst, miss 2 dc, 5 tr in next dc, miss
2 dc, ★ 1 dc in next dc, miss 2 dc, 5 tr
in next dc, miss 2 dc, rep from ★ to
end, slst in first dc.
Fasten off.

Fabric hair accessories

Cover headbands, combs, and other hair accessories with pretty fabrics in colors to complement her favorite outfit – they're sure to be a hit with a fashion-conscious young woman.

NOTE

The fabric measurements for covering the headbands are approximate only. Measure each band before cutting the fabric, and adjust the width of the bias strip accordingly. For the narrow band, you will need a strip twice the width of the band plus 12 mm (for the seam allowance); for the ruffled band, you will need a strip twice the width of the band plus 2 cm (to allow for the ruffle) plus 12 mm (for the seam allowance).

WHAT YOU NEED

Strong sewing threads to match the fabrics • invisible thread • needle: fine sharp • sewing machine (optional) • scissors • tape measure • long knitting needle • craft glue

Scrunchie
Liberty-print or calico fabric strip, 12 cm x width of fabric • 30 cm narrow elastic

Ruffled clasp
Liberty-print or calico fabric strip, 15 cm x width of fabric • hair clasp

Narrow headband
Liberty-print or calico bias strip, 3 cm x 33 cm • plastic headband, about 10 mm wide, with no teeth or grips on the underside

Ruffled headband
Liberty-print or calico bias strip, 6 cm x 122 cm (join short bias strips as described in "Bias binding," page 299) • plastic headband, about 15 mm wide, with no teeth or grips on the underside • batting (enough to cover the headband)

Side comb
Liberty-print or calico bias strip, 3 cm x 50 cm • plastic side comb, with no teeth or grips on underside
● *Technique pages 292–5*

❶ MAKING THE SCRUNCHIE

1 Fold the fabric in half lengthwise, with right sides together.
2 Leaving 4 cm open at each end, sew the long sides together. Turn the tube right side out, using a long knitting needle to push the end through.

3 Place the two short ends together and, with right sides facing, sew them together so that the fabric forms a closed tube. Leave the opening on the long side unstitched at this stage.
4 Thread the elastic through the tube and sew the ends together with strong thread. Slipstitch the opening in the scrunchie with invisible thread.

❷ MAKING THE RUFFLED CLASP

1 Fold the fabric in half lengthwise, with right sides together, and sew along the entire length. Leave the ends open.
2 Turn the tube right side out and press it with an iron so that the seam lies flat in the middle of the tube.
3 Fold the corners into a triangular point at one end. Fold the point down to the middle of the base of the triangle formed by the previous folds and

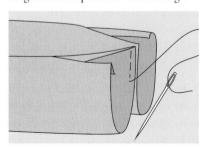

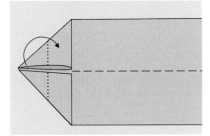

slipstitch the fold down at the point, using strong thread. Repeat this step at the other end of the tube.

4 Using strong thread, sew long gathering stitches along the entire length of the stitched seam, being careful not to catch the top layer of fabric with the needle.

5 Oversew one end of the fabric to one end of the clasp base at the point where you slipstitched the fold down. Sew through the holes in the clasp to keep the fabric in place.

6 Draw up the gathering stitches until the ruffle is the same length as the clasp. Arrange the gathers evenly. Oversew the free end of the ruffle to the end of the clasp, as in step 5.

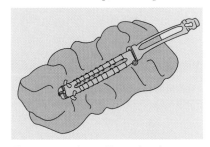

7 Oversew the ruffle to the clasp along the gathered seam, again being careful not to catch the top layer of fabric with the needle. Finish off securely, and arrange the ruffle evenly over the clasp.

❸ COVERING THE NARROW HEADBAND

1 Fold the strip of fabric in half lengthwise, with right sides together.

2 Sew the long sides together leaving a 5 mm seam allowance, so that the tube formed is slightly wider than the headband. (This will allow the headband to fit snugly inside the fabric.)

3 At one short end, sew the sides together. Trim the seams and turn the tube right side out, using a long knitting needle to push the fabric through.

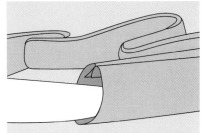

4 Feed the headband into the tube, smoothing the fabric over the band as you work. Trim any excess fabric from the open end.

5 Turn in the raw edges to fit snugly over the end of the headband. Close the headband cover using slipstitch and invisible thread.

❹ COVERING THE RUFFLED HEADBAND

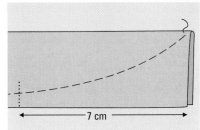

7 cm

1 Fold the bias strip in half lengthwise, with right sides together.

2 Begin stitching the long sides together with a curved, tapering seam, so that the tube is about 1 cm wide at the end and broadens to about 2.5 cm with a 5 mm seam allowance at a point 7 cm from the end. Then continue sewing a straight seam to 7 cm from the other end. Fasten off.

3 Trim the seam at the tapered end of the tube, and use a knitting needle to turn this end of the tube in on itself for about 15 mm.

> ### HINTS
> ● *To glamorize the narrow headband for evening wear, glue on ribbon roses or a matching bow, or wind and glue a satin ribbon around the band.*
> ● *When a favorite outfit becomes too old to wear, save fabric from the least worn areas to make these hair accessories.*

4 Spread a thin coat of glue evenly on the top surface of the headband and attach a layer of batting. Trim the batting to the shape of the band.

5 Spread a thin layer of glue on the last 5 cm of the underside of one end of the headband and push this end into the tapered end of the fabric tube, pulling the fabric smooth. Push all the fabric on to the band, turning it right side out along its entire length as you work, and keeping the seam on the underside of the band.

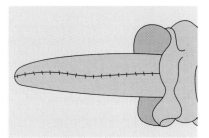

6 Scrunch the fabric into an even ruffle along the wide part of the band.

7 Fit the open end of the fabric tube to the band by overlapping the edges of the fabric very tightly and using the invisible thread to sew them together with fine stitches. This end must be stitched very firmly to hold the ruffled band cover in place.

❺ DECORATING THE SIDE COMB

1 With wrong sides together, fold the two long edges of the fabric strip in 5 mm and press the folds. Again with wrong sides together, fold the strip in half lengthwise and press.

2 Apply a small amount of glue to one end of the underside of the bar of the comb, and glue one end of the bias strip to the comb. Allow the glue to dry completely.

3 Hold the comb in your left hand and, from the glued end, wind the bias strip over the bar and through to the right side of the comb. Keeping the fabric taut, wind the bias strip neatly between each tooth of the comb and around the bar until you reach the other end.

4 Trim away any excess fabric and glue the raw end to the inside of the bar.

Rainbow sweater

Delight a young person by knitting them this vibrant striped sweater, which appeals equally to both girls and boys.

WHAT YOU NEED

Size	A	B	C
Chest (cm)	75	85	95
Sweater measures (cm)			
Chest	100	110	120
Length	68	69	70
Sleeves	43	43	43

The yarn used in this project is Patons DK (weight 50 g balls) and the colors are: main color (mc), slate; 1st contrast color (cc1), natural; and 1 ball each cherry, ever green, medium green, pale green, pale grey, pale pink, medium pink, rose pink, plum, navy blue, medium blue, pale blue, orange red, maroon, purple, mauve, lemon, tan, yellow.

mc	6	7	7
cc1	3	3	3

Knitting needles: 4.00 mm (no. 8), 3.25 mm (no. 10) • wool sewing needle • 2 stitch holders
● *Technique pages 323–7*

CHECKING THE GAUGE

Before you begin knitting the sweater, make a sample square to check the gauge of your knitting so that the measurements of the finished garment will be as close as possible to the size specified in the pattern.

You should have 22.5 stitches to a 10 cm width over stockinette stitch, using 4.00 mm knitting needles. Check very carefully. If you have fewer stitches, use smaller needles; if more stitches, use bigger needles.

COLOR SCHEMES

Colors can look very different, depending on the colors that appear in combination with them.

In a harmonious color scheme, all the colors come from the same part of the color wheel. Each color tones down the impact of the others, which produces a sophisticated effect of understated richness.

In a contrasting color scheme, the colors come from opposite segments of the color wheel. This heightens and intensifies each color and creates a striking and dramatic effect.

Try this alternative color scheme as a variation on the sweater shown in the photograph.

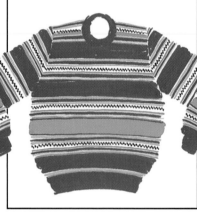

❶ BACK

Using 3.25 mm needles and mc, cast on 113 (125-137) sts.
1st row: K2, ★ P1, K1, rep from ★ to last st, K1.
2nd row: P1, ★ K1, P1, rep from ★ to end.
Rep 1st and 2nd rows 5 times…12 rows rib in all.
Change to 4.00 mm needles.
Work in stst in stripes as foll:
3 rows mc, 1 row cherry, 1 row natural, 1 row ever green, 15 rows mc, 1 row ever green, 1 row natural, 1 row cherry, 3 rows mc, 2 rows ever green, 2 rows medium green, 2 rows pale green, 2 rows pale grey.
36th row: P1 natural, ★ P1 mc, P1 natural, rep from ★ to end.

37th row: K1 mc, ★ K1 natural, K1 mc, rep from ★ to end.
Cont in stripes as foll: 2 rows pale pink, 2 rows medium pink, 2 rows rose pink, 2 rows plum, 3 rows mc, 1 row cherry, 1 row natural, 1 row ever green, 16 rows natural, 1 row ever green, 1 row natural, 1 row cherry, 3 rows mc, 2 rows navy blue, 2 rows medium blue, 2 rows pale blue.
80th row: Rep 36th row.
81st row: Rep 37th row.
Cont in stripes as foll: 2 rows natural, 2 rows orange red, 2 rows cherry, 2 rows maroon, 3 rows mc, 1 row natural, 1 row ever green, 1 row cherry, 15 rows mc, 1 row cherry, 1 row ever green, 1 row natural, 3 rows mc, 2 rows purple, 2 rows mauve, 2 rows pale pink.
123rd row: Rep 37th row.
124th row: Rep 36th row.
Cont in stripes as foll: 2 rows lemon, 2 rows tan, 2 rows yellow.
Last 130 rows form pat.
Cont in pat until work measures 65 (66-67) cm from beg, ending with a purl row.

Shaping the shoulder

Keeping pat correct, cast off 10 (12-13) sts at beg of next 6 rows, then 12 (11-13) sts at beg of foll 2 rows. Transfer rem 29 (31-33) sts on to a stitch holder.

❷ FRONT

Work as for back until there are 22 (24-26) rows fewer than there are in the back to shoulder shaping, ending with a purl row.

Shaping the neck

Next row: Keeping pat correct, pat 49 (54-60), then turn and cont on these sts.
Dec at neck edge in alt rows until 42 (47-52) sts rem.
Work 7 (9-9) rows.

Shaping the shoulder

Cast off 10 (12-13) sts at beg of next and alt rows 3 times in all.
Work 1 row. Cast off.
Slip next 15 (17-17) sts on to stitch holder and leave.

Join yarn to rem sts and work the neck and shoulder of the other side to correspond.

③ SLEEVES

Using 3.25 mm needles and mc, cast on 49 (49-51) sts.
Work 13 rows rib as for back.
14th row: Rib 6 (4-6), ★ inc in next st, rib 1, rep from ★ to last 7 (5-5) sts, rib to end...67 (69-71) sts.
Change to 4.00 mm needles.
Working in pat as for back, inc at each end of 5th and foll 6th (6th-4th) rows until there are 73 (73-105) sts, then in foll 4th (4th-alt) rows until there are 103 (107-113) sts.

Cont until work measures 43 cm from beg, ending with a purl row. Cast off loosely.

④ NECKBAND

Using backstitch, join right shoulder seam. With right side facing, and using 3.25 mm needles and mc, knit up 97 (105-109) sts evenly around the neck, incl sts from stitch holders.
Work 21 rows rib as for back, beg with a 2nd row.
Cast off loosely in rib.

⑤ MAKING UP

1 Press the garment pieces with a damp cloth and a warm iron.

2 Tie a colored thread at sides of back and front, 44 cm up from lower edge, to mark armhole positions.
3 Backstitch sleeve and side seams to the colored threads. Sew in sleeves.
4 Fold neckband in half to the wrong side, and slipstitch into place.
5 Press the seams.

> ### HINT
> *To add that extra special touch to this gift, knit a plain fringed scarf in one of the contrast colors. Or look for a pair of warm socks in a plain color to match one of the colors featured in the sweater.*

Painted mat

Rather than opting for a ready-made floor mat, you can brighten a teenager's room with a mat you have painted yourself. Teenagers may like to make this gift themselves to give to friends.

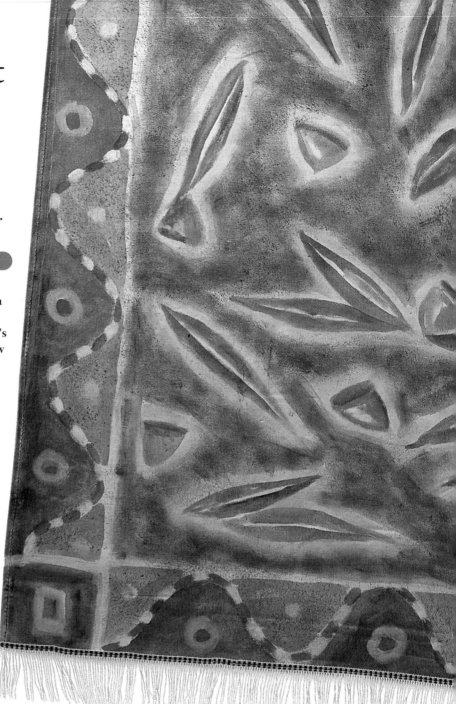

WHAT YOU NEED

1 m primed 10 oz canvas, 150 cm wide, hemmed around edges • 2 m fringing • white acrylic house paint, flat or semi-gloss • Jo Sonja's (or Liquitex) artist's colors: yellow light, green oxide, jade, raw sienna, gold oxide, ultramarine, dioxazine purple, titanium white, naphthol crimson • paintbrushes: 50 mm decorating, no. 12 round • toothbrush • metal spatula (or old table knife) • water-based clear flat varnish • white glue • soft pencil

● *Technique pages 334–5*

❶ PREPARING THE CANVAS

1 Apply two coats of white acrylic house paint to the canvas, allowing the paint to dry between coats.
2 Using a soft pencil, draw a 10 cm border around the edge of the mat. Sketch in the border design, following the painting guide or inventing your own pattern. The design looks most

MAKING A WALL HANGING

This design could also be used to make a wall hanging, either the same size as the mat or somewhat smaller – simply scale down the elements of the design to suit whatever size of hanging you want to make.

Follow the instructions for making the painted mat, omitting the fringing at one end and making the hem at that end large enough to take a piece of strong, flat dowelling about 10 cm longer than the width of the canvas. When the design is painted and finished, push the dowelling through the wide hem and attach a strong cord for hanging. Trim with tassels if desired.

2 Dry-brush over the leaves with jade paint. This will add dimension, depth and light.

Nuts
1 Paint the nuts with gold oxide, leaving patches of canvas unpainted to create highlights.
2 Dry-brush the nuts in raw sienna to define and shape them.

Background
1 Leaving a 1 cm border around the nuts and leaves, lightly cover the background with ultramarine and allow to dry.
2 Dry-brush over the same area with dioxazine purple. In some places allow the colors to blend into each other, and in other places allow single colors to stand out.
3 Paint around each leaf and nut in yellow light, allowing the edges to blend into the blue paints.

Border
1 Following the painting guide, paint the border design. Paint the background to the design in green oxide.
2 Using a toothbrush and a spatula, spatter blue paint over the mat by sliding the paint-loaded spatula across the mat and releasing the paint particles with light toothbrush strokes.

Painting guide
The design illustrated is based on the shapes and colors of nuts and leaves. The border motif is created from abstract motifs and designs.

However, this design and the colors specified are meant as suggestions only. The free style of painting used offers you plenty of scope for your own ideas. Before starting to paint the canvas, use wallpaper lining paper to experiment with color and design and develop your own style.

❸ FINISHING
1 When the paint has dried, apply two or three coats of clear varnish.
2 Coat the back of the mat with a mixture of one part white glue and one part water. Allow to dry.
3 If the fringing has not already been attached by the supplier of the canvas, stitch it to the ends of the mat.

> **HINT**
> *Ready-primed canvas bought from a sailmaker is the most economical material for this project. Heavy-duty canvas is difficult to sew, so ask the sailmaker to stitch the hems around the edges and attach the fringing to the short ends.*

effective if the border has a free appearance rather than a precise geometrical look.
3 In the center area of the mat, sketch in nuts and leaves.

❷ PAINTING THE CANVAS
Leaves
1 Paint the leaves in green oxide, leaving a thin unpainted strip down the center of each leaf to represent the vein of the leaf. Allow to dry.

Printed T-shirts

Personalize a T-shirt for a young friend with this simple method. You don't have to be an artist to create eye-catching designs – all you need is access to a photocopier and a good eye for suitable images.

¡qɔunl əəɹɟ ɐ sɐ ɓuᴉɥʇ ɥɔns oN

WHAT YOU NEED

T-shirts • images to photocopy • photocopy acetate • turpentine • fabric paints: red, blue, yellow, black • tablespoon • paintbrushes: medium round, small liner • adhesive tape • chopping board • old tea towel • old towel • iron • plate

❶ PREPARING THE IMAGES

1 Any illustration or photograph is suitable for printing on a T-shirt, so long as it photocopies well in black and white and the image is clear with good lines and shading.

2 Photocopy the image, enlarging or reducing until you have a size appropriate to the size of the T-shirt. It is best to make the copies fairly dark.

3 If you want to include text with the picture, you need to make a mirror image of the writing so that it prints the correct way on the fabric. To make a mirror image, photocopy the image on acetate film. Then place the sheet of acetate back to front on the photocopier glass and photocopy the reversed image onto a sheet of paper.

❷ FIXING THE IMAGES ONTO THE T-SHIRT

1 Lay the T-shirt on an old towel on a flat working surface. Have the turpentine, tablespoon, adhesive tape, photocopies and paintbrush within easy reach.

2 Wrap an old tea towel around a chopping board and secure it with some tape. Place the wrapped board inside the T-shirt, beneath where you plan to place the design. This provides a firm, slightly absorbent surface against which to apply the photo-

HINTS

• *For added interest, put smaller versions of the image onto the sleeves or back of the shirt.*

• *Center the image on the top two-thirds of the T-shirt so that it is shown to its best advantage. Remember that the bottom of a T-shirt is often tucked into jeans or a skirt.*

• *Practice on an old T-shirt or other fabric scrap first until you have perfected the technique.*

copied design, and prevents the dye running through to the other side of the shirt.

3 Cut around the photocopied image, leaving at least 2 cm of blank paper all around. Place the photocopy face down on the T-shirt and secure it with adhesive tape, taking care not to cover any of the design.

4 Paint turpentine over the back of the image until it is saturated. You should be able to see the image through the paper quite clearly, but there should be no pools of liquid on the surface.

5 Rub firmly all over the image area with the back of the spoon, holding the paper and T-shirt down securely as you go so that the image doesn't move around. Go over the whole area about three times. If the turpentine evaporates before you have finished, reapply and continue rubbing.

6 Lift one corner of the paper to see whether the image has transferred to the fabric. If you can see any areas that are missing, replace the corner and rub the entire image again. With experience you will be able to judge the correct degree of pressure, rubbing and saturation of turpentine to achieve the best effect.

7 Remove the paper carefully, starting from one corner and slowly peeling it back. Some makes of T-shirt are slightly fluffier than others; if any pieces of blackened fluff appear as you peel the paper back, pick them off the surface with your fingers or a brush. If fragments land on clean areas of the shirt, don't remove them until the turpentine has evaporated.

8 To fix the image, iron the shirt at a temperature suitable for the fabric.

Look for suitable images in art books and magazines. If you prefer, you can photocopy the images on this page. The text has already been reversed for you. Enlarge or reduce the images to fit the size of your T-shirt.

Stepping out

❸ APPLYING THE COLOR

1 Decide what colors to use on the images. Place the chopping board behind the images to protect the other side of the shirt.

2 Mix the fabric paints on a plate with a small amount of water. It is a good idea to experiment on scraps of fabric first until you have a good consistency. If the paint is too runny, the color will "bleed" over the edges of the image. If the paint is too dry, it will create a rough, caked-on effect.

3 Paint the images by filling in different areas with flat colors and outlining the image with a small liner brush. Alternatively, create more unusual effects. See folk art techniques (pages 334–5) for suggestions for creative brushstrokes and shading.

4 Follow the manufacturer's instructions for fixing the paints and washing.

VARIATION

This method of transferring images can be used to make unusual curtains, cushions or a bedspread for a teenager's room. You can repeat the same image across the fabric or print several different images at random.

Bead jewelry

Jewelry design is limited only by your imagination. With a selection of interesting beads and some basic equipment, you can make a gift that will delight any young person.

WHAT YOU NEED

Selection of decorative beads of your choice • wire cutters • pliers: long-nosed, round-nosed
Necklace or bracelet
nylon-coated wire (tiger tail), 5 cm longer than finished length of necklace or bracelet • 2 crimps for each item • barrel or ring clasp
Earrings
2 headpins for each pair of earrings • 2 eyepins for each pair of earrings (for double-section earrings) • screw-on or clip-on fittings, or pierced-ear wires

❶ MAKING THE NECKLACE OR BRACELET

1 First thread a crimp onto one end of the wire, positioning it about 2 cm from the end.
2 Take one half of the clasp and

thread the short end of the wire through the loop of the clasp and then back through the crimp.
3 Making sure that the crimp and clasp are fitted snugly together, squeeze the crimp with the pliers until it locks the wire securely.
4 Thread the beads of your choice on to the wire, leaving the last 3 cm of wire free.
5 Thread the free end of the wire through the second crimp, then through the other half of the clasp and back through the crimp. Do not squeeze the crimp shut yet.
6 Push the excess wire back through the last two or three beads. Pull the end of the wire as tightly as possible, so that there are no gaps between beads, crimp and clasp. Squeeze the crimp firmly with the pliers to lock the wire in place. Carefully snip off any excess wire.

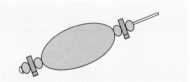

EXTRA LONG EARRINGS

• You can make really long earrings by adding a further eyepin threaded with one or more beads before you attach the earring fitting.
• Try adding several eyepins, each threaded with a single bead for a different effect.
• The wires may also be bent into interesting shapes to add variety to the designs.

❷ MAKING THE EARRINGS

1 Thread the selected beads onto the headpin, leaving the last 1 cm of wire bare. The headpin wire can be cut to any length, depending on how long you want the earrings to be.

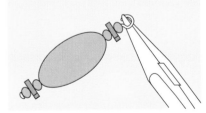

2 With the long-nosed pliers, bend the end of the wire to make a slightly open loop.

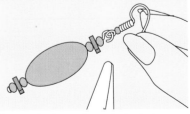

3 Pass the loop through the hole on the earring clips or wires and close with the round-nosed pliers.

BEST FRIENDS & RELATIONS

It's often hard to find just
the right thing for a
dear friend or close relative.
In this chapter there are
some delightful ideas for
gifts that you can make
to show a loved one how
much you care.

Herb-filled sleep pillow

The delicate heirloom-style fabric of the outer pillow allows the relaxing aroma of the herbs inside to slowly release during sleep.

WHAT YOU NEED

24 cm voile, 115 cm wide • 2.5 m insertion lace, about 20 mm wide • 4 m edging lace, 50 mm wide • loose-weave fabric for inner cushion, about 38 cm x 48 cm • 2 spools white sewing thread • sewing machine with double needle and zigzag setting • scissors • tape measure • aromatic herbs or an herb potpourri (see "Fragrant potpourri," pages 214–15)
● *Technique pages 292–301, 303–4*

❶ SEWING THE PILLOWCASE

1 To make the front, fold the fabric in half and cut six 12 cm squares of voile, as shown in the cutting guide. The rest of the fabric is for the back.
2 Using a double sewing machine needle, stitch each square in a pattern of diagonal lines.

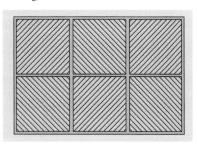

3 Press down a 1 cm hem all around each square. Using a medium zigzag setting and a fairly long stitch, join the squares together with insertion lace. Make two rows of three squares and then join the rows to form a rectangle. Edge the rectangle with insertion lace.
4 Measure the finished front piece. (It should measure 24 cm x 36 cm, but there may be some variation depending on the width of the insertion lace and how closely you have joined the squares.) From the voile, cut two pieces 24 cm wide and 27 cm long, or as long as the short edge of the front piece plus 3 cm (see cutting guide). These pieces will form a lapped back.
5 Turn under 1 cm on one 27 cm edge of each piece and machine hem. Turn under 1.5 cm on the remaining three sides of each back piece and press flat.
6 Lay one back piece on the front piece, wrong sides together, and then lay the second back piece right side up over the first, so that the hemmed edges overlap

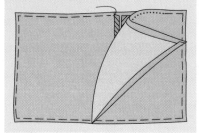

to form a flap at the back through which to insert the pillow.
7 Baste the three layers together, and then topstitch all around the pillowcase as close to the edges as possible.
8 Using a gathering stitch, sew along the inside edge of the edging lace. Gather the lace until it fits around the outside of the pillowcase. Use a medium zigzag stitch to attach the gathered lace around the insertion lace border.

❷ MAKING THE INTERIOR

1 Using any fine, loose-weave fabric, make an inner pillow slightly smaller than the cover (about 22 cm x 34 cm), leaving one end open.
2 Fill the pillow with a mixture of aromatic herbs or an herb potpourri, stitch up the open end, and insert the pillow in the lace cover.

CUTTING GUIDE

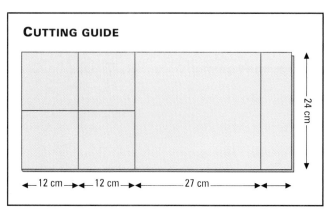

← 12 cm → ← 12 cm → ← 27 cm →

24 cm

Fabric necklace

Make this charming and unusual necklace to coordinate with a friend's or relative's favorite dress, or create it from a more neutral-colored fabric that will complement several outfits.

WHAT YOU NEED

Fine lawn or silk, 1 m x 8.5 cm • 18 round wooden beads about 1 cm in diameter • 19 ceramic beads with large holes, in a color suitable for the fabric • matching sewing thread • knitting needle • invisible thread • protective fabric spray • sewing machine • sewing needle: sharp size 12 • scissors
● *Technique pages 292–301*

❶ PREPARING THE FABRIC

1 With right sides facing, fold the fabric in half lengthwise. Beginning 10 cm from the end, cut both ends of the fabric at an angle to create a point.
2 With a 1 cm seam allowance, machine stitch around the open edges, leaving a 5 cm opening at one end of the long side for turning out.

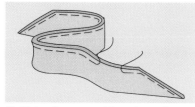

3 Trim the excess fabric from the tapered ends and turn the fabric to the right side, pushing the tapered points out neatly with a knitting needle.

❷ THREADING THE BEADS

1 Thread a ceramic bead onto the fabric tube, positioning it 15 cm from the end furthest from the opening.

NOTE
It is essential to choose a very fine, soft fabric that will thread easily through the ceramic beads and lie smoothly against the large wooden beads.

2 Push a wooden bead through the opening in the fabric tube and guide it down the fabric until it is butting up against the ceramic bead. Make sure that the hole in the wooden bead fits snugly against the ceramic bead. Manipulate the beads and the fabric so that the fabric covers the wooden bead as smoothly as possible.

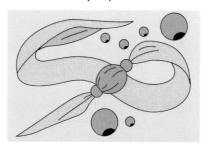

3 Thread on another ceramic bead, pushing it up against the wooden bead inside the tube. Again, adjust the fabric to lie as smoothly as possible.

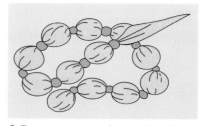

4 Repeat steps 2 and 3 until you have used all the beads. Finish with a ceramic bead, leaving a tail of about 15 cm of fabric without beads.

❸ FINISHING

1 Using invisible thread, close the opening in the tube with slipstitch.
2 Iron the fabric tails and treat all the fabric with a protective spray. Tie the tails together in a loose knot.

Raffia sunhat

A cloche-shaped raffia sunhat makes a thoughtful gift for a dear friend or relative who enjoys being out in the sun, but is careful about her skin.

WHAT YOU NEED

About 400 g raffia • 20 cm raw silk or similar fabric, 90 cm wide • 70 cm grosgrain ribbon, 20 mm wide (optional) • clear craft glue • small bunch of old-fashioned dried flowers (optional) • sewing thread to match silk and grosgrain ribbon • needles: very large-eyed tapestry, general sewing • small, sharp scissors

● *Technique pages 292–5*

❶ MAKING THE RAFFIA BRAID

It is important that the weaving pattern is the same as that shown in the diagram. Untangle the raffia strands as you work, and keep the braid the same width – about 2 cm. With practice you will be able to work with more than one strand at a time.

1 Untie and untwist the hank of raffia and draw out 20–25 strands. Bind and

NOTE

It is important to know or estimate the size of the recipient's head. If you want your gift to be a surprise, measure your own head size and then guess at any differences between your head and the recipient's, or look for someone who has a similar head size. The hat should sit just above the ears.

If you cannot estimate the size accurately, make the hat larger rather than smaller, and adjust the size by threading a strand of raffia through the crown in a running or gathering stitch. Draw up the thread and tie it in a bow, which will be covered with the silk band.

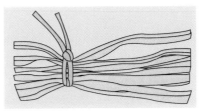

tie them together firmly at one end with another strand of raffia and attach the bundle to a stable, solid object, such as a door handle.

2 Divide the bundle of raffia strands into four equal sections. Take the left-hand strand (1) and pass it over the second strand (2), then under the third strand (3) and over the last strand (4). Start again on the left-hand strand (which is now strand 2), and weave over, under and over again.

3 Continue weaving until the braid starts to become thinner as some of the strands begin to run out. Weave in more strands of raffia to make a continuous braid, adding a few strands of raffia at a time. Take the thinning section to one side and overlap the new strands along its length, allowing the ends to protrude about 10 cm. Continue braiding.

4 Repeat steps 2 and 3 until you have about 8 meters of braiding, and then trim the ends of the raffia strands to the same length and bind them loosely so that they do not get in the way while you are working on the hat.

5 Untie the start of the braid and fix the ends together by applying craft glue across all strands. Allow the glue to dry and trim off the excess raffia. (The loose strands at the other end of the braid will be woven into the hat when you have finished making it.)

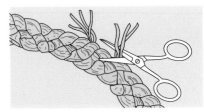

6 Carefully trim the excess raffia away from the points where you added new strands to the braid.

❷ TO MAKE THE HAT

If you are right-handed, the braid will run clockwise; if you are left-handed, it will run counterclockwise.

1 To make the crown of the hat, start in the middle by forming the raffia braid into a tight circle. Tuck the start of the braid under the first coil and stitch it firmly into place with a tapestry needle and a strong raffia strand.

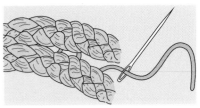

2 Still using the tapestry needle and a strong strand of raffia, begin stitching the braid to itself in a smooth, sloping coil. Take the needle straight across, making the stitches at such an angle that they hardly show. Stitch through one section only on each side. When the strand you are stitching with runs out, weave it back through the raffia braid and start another strand.

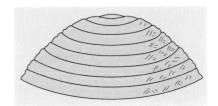

3 Keep stitching the raffia to itself in a coiled circle, and form the rounded top crown of the hat by leaning the braid over slightly to slope the coil. The top crown should measure about 24 cm across, which will take six or seven rounds of raffia braid.

4 Begin to slope the raffia coil a little more sharply to form the sides of the crown. The sides should measure about 7 cm – four or five rounds

of raffia braid. Adjust the angle of the braid to achieve the right size. Keep trying the hat on as you work, allowing for any difference in head size. It is preferable to undo a small amount of work and adjust it until the size is right than to finish the hat and find that it doesn't fit.

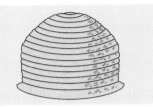

5 Begin to form the brim of the hat by angling the next round of raffia braid out from the side crown. Mold and shape the braid as you work.
6 Complete the brim by adding three or four more rounds of raffia braid,

HINTS
• *Raffia varies considerably in quality. Spend a little extra and choose a high-quality product – the result will be well worth it.*
• *When you are coiling the braid, keep the circle as round as possible. This is necessary because an oval shape will distort the overall shape of the hat.*
• *Loose stitching will result in a floppy hat, so stitch the braids together tightly.*

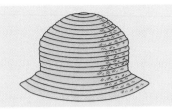

continuing to stitch the braid at a gentle angle. Trial and error will achieve the result you want.
7 To secure the end of the raffia braid, stitch the final coil to within about 10 cm of the center back of the hat. Cut the braid, beyond the 10 cm, and taper it down to half its width by cutting out some of the pieces of raffia and then threading each of the four strands back into the brim with the tapestry needle. Follow the weave of the raffia braid so that the finishing doesn't show.

❸ FINISHING THE HAT
1 To make the hat band, stitch the grosgrain ribbon around the inside of the crown, just where the hat will encircle the head. Stitch only the lower edge, leaving the upper edge lying free. Overlap the ends of the ribbon 1 cm at the back of the hat. To prevent fraying, turn the raw ends under and handstitch them together with hemming stitch, using a sewing thread that matches the ribbon. Alternatively, cut the ends of the ribbon at an angle. (It is not essential to insert this ribbon, but it does make the hat more comfortable to wear.)
2 Stitch a narrow hem along each long side of the silk and wrap the silk around the hat to measure the length you will require. With right sides facing, join the two short ends of the fabric to form a circle to fit the hat.
3 Turn the silk to the right side and press. Ruche the silk band around the base of the crown with the seam at the back. (If you are trimming the hat with dried flowers, position the seam where the flowers will be placed.)
4 Stitch the silk into place with a few backstitches in matching thread.
5 If you are using dried flowers, stitch them in place over the seam of the silk band with a strand of raffia.

RAFFIA HAT STYLES

Stripped from palm leaves grown in Madagascar, raffia has a rustic appeal and a variety of uses. It is a satisfying and versatile material to work with, as it will stay exactly where you have stitched it, yet it is easy to model and coax into shape as you work.

A raffia hat, being made of a natural fiber, is cool in summer and gives maximum protection from the sun.

The hat illustrated has a rustic, handmade look that suits raffia and is very attractive. However, you may prefer your hat to have a smoother, more even finish. To achieve this, steam iron the braid between damp cloths before you begin to make the hat. Another variation that you could try is to dye the raffia before you begin to make the braid. Any commercial fabric dye is suitable, or use natural dyes (see "Natural dyeing methods," page 118).

As you gain experience in working with raffia, you will want to make different shaped hats. You can modify the hat illustrated by giving it a flatter crown or a snap brim. For a flatter crown, make a flatter coil when you are working the top of the crown and increase the angle when you come to the sides. For a snap brim, bring the last three or four rounds up at a sharp angle.

Découpage picture frame

Use the art of découpage to decorate a wooden frame with images selected to set off a favorite family photograph.

WHAT YOU NEED

Wooden photo frame with large frame area • suitable printed images • artist's gesso • artist's acrylic paint in a color to tone with images • artist's acrylic gloss medium (sealer) • polyurethane gloss varnish • paintbrushes: 3 small (for sealing, gluing and painting), 25 mm imitation sable (for varnishing) • wet-and-dry sandpaper: nos. 80, 120, 600 • sanding block • wallpaper paste • white glue • gilding cream • clear beeswax • cabinetmaker's or French furniture polish • small natural sponge • lint-free cloth • Blu Tack • pieces of thick kitchen sponge • fine, curved scissors
● *Technique pages 329–31*

❶ PREPARATION

1 Cut out the images. Seal them with artist's acrylic gloss medium and allow them to dry.
2 Remove the backing and glass from the frame and sand the frame surface with no. 80 sandpaper, smoothing out rough spots and edges. Apply a coat of artist's gesso and allow to dry. Sand with no. 120 sandpaper, apply a coat of the sealer and allow to dry.
3 Sponge the acrylic paint onto the frame with a natural sponge to achieve a textured effect. Leave it to dry.
4 Apply the gilding cream along the inside and outside edges of the frame.

❷ FIXING THE IMAGES

1 Make a paper template of the shape of the frame and arrange the images on it, attaching them with Blu Tack and rearranging them until you are satisfied with the design.
2 Apply a mixture of three parts wallpaper paste and one part white

NOTE
If you are unfamiliar with découpage techniques, read the appropriate technique pages before starting this project.

glue to the surface of the frame where the first image is to go and a small amount to the right side of the image.
3 Massage and mold the image onto the frame, adding more glue if necessary. Repeat until all images are glued in place. Remove excess glue with a wet sponge and allow to dry.
4 Apply two coats of sealer to the surface, allowing each coat to dry thoroughly before applying the next.

❸ VARNISHING AND SANDING

1 Wipe the frame with a lint-free cloth and, allowing at least 24 hours between coats, apply as many coats of varnish as necessary – six to 10 coats – to make sure the images are protected from sanding damage.

2 Apply further coats of varnish, sanding with no. 80 wet-and-dry sandpaper between coats. Make sure the sandpaper is wet, and sand in one direction only. Wipe with a lint-free cloth. Always allow at least 24 hours between applications.
3 When you are satisfied that the varnish is evenly applied and the surface has no shiny patches, sand lightly with the no. 600 sandpaper and wipe with a lint-free cloth.
4 Apply three more coats of varnish, sanding with the no. 600 sandpaper between coats to achieve a very smooth, dull finish.

❹ FINISHING

1 Mix equal parts of beeswax and cabinetmaker's polish and warm the mixture. Apply the wax to the surface a little at a time.
2 Wipe over vigorously with a damp cloth, and polish with a soft, dry cloth.
3 Apply a light coat of gilding cream with a natural sponge, encroaching only slightly on the images.

Dried flower wreath

A floral wreath captures nature's beauty, and is a welcome gift for a friend or relation who loves flowers but has no garden. Flowers from your own garden make this gift extra special.

WHAT YOU NEED

Vine wreath base (available from florist's suppliers) • hot glue gun • maidenhair fern • line-establishing flowers: delphinium, larkspur, Hidcote lavender • filler flowers: daisies, Japanese anemones, straw flowers, white and blue statice, soft white daisies • focal-point flowers: dahlias, shasta daisies, gerberas, Canterbury bells

● *Technique pages 332–3*

① SELECTING THE FLOWERS
Plan your choice of flowers with regard to the range of hues and the strength of tones. Keep the colors balanced, and remember that warm, light colors – such as yellows and pinks – will come forward, while cool, dark colors – such as blues and violets – will recede.

Select flowers at different stages of growth so that you have buds as well as half-open and full blooms. Include different sizes, shapes and textures –

for example, flat, smooth leaves will counterpoint delicate, lacy flowers, and slender, pointed leaves will complement full-bodied flowers.

You could buy fresh flowers from a florist and supplement them with flowers from your own garden or with wild flowers.

② DRYING THE FLOWERS
Dry the plant material according to the methods outlined in "Flower and foliage drying." Note that drying methods vary according to the type of flower.

If you want to make this project at short notice, buy flowers and foliage already dried from a florist or florist's suppliers.

③ ASSEMBLING THE WREATH
1 Make small bundles of maidenhair fern, apply glue to the ends of the stems and attach them to the vine wreath base. Add ferns until the vine base and sides are completely covered. If the effect is too flat, give the wreath depth by adding individual leaves or small bunches here and there, in more upright positions.
2 Place the line-establishing flowers around the wreath, varying the length and direction of the stems in order to achieve a balanced, rounded effect. Do not glue the flowers down until you are happy with the arrangement.
3 Glue the ends of the stalks and press them into the layer of maidenhair fern. Hold the blooms in place until the glue hardens.
4 Turn the wreath constantly as you work and look at it from all angles to make sure that the arrangement is well balanced.
5 Being careful to keep within the established height and width of the

VARIATIONS
The flowers and foliage shown below are suggestions only; you can vary them to produce many different effects. For a harvest wreath, choose blooms in autumn tonings – orange and yellow tea roses, chrysanthemums and buttercups. Try leaving some parts of the vine wreath base uncovered. Or wire small sprays of flowers at intervals around the base, then wind matching ribbons in between.

NOTE
Remember to tell the recipient of this gift that the flowers are more likely to retain their natural colors if the wreath is displayed away from direct sunlight or fluorescent lighting.

wreath, position and glue filler flowers to fill in the outline. Push some of the filler flowers in among the maidenhair fern, so that they seem to be growing out of the foliage.

6 Position the focal-point flowers around the wreath, arranging them to face in various directions. Nestle some of them deeply among the fern fronds. Do not use too many focal-point flowers – just a few, strategically placed, will give the best effect. When you are satisfied with the arrangement, glue them in place.

7 Add a few filler stems of white and blue statice to lighten the overall effect, and glue into position. Position and glue bunches of daisies evenly around the wreath.

Starting the wreath

First the vine wreath base is covered completely with small bundles of maidenhair fern. Depth and fullness are achieved by placing some fern fronds in an upright position.

Crinolined lady lampshade

This stenciled lampshade, featuring ladies with crinolines and parasols strolling amid spring flowers, will brighten any bedroom. It would also be charming in a small sitting room.

WHAT YOU NEED

Master pattern **E74(a–d)** • stencil film or treated manila cardboard • plain lampshade in a truncated cone shape, about 34 cm across the base and 21 cm high • spray adhesive • fabric spray paints: pale blue, deep blue, deep red • artist's acrylic paints: deep green, bright yellow, ultramarine, burgundy • paint palette • paintbrushes: 4 small stenciling, no. 4 round • tracing paper • transfer paper • pencil • fine permanent marker pen • craft knife • cutting mat or board • lightweight cardboard (for masking) • masking tape • light-colored chalk • paper towels • spray-on fabric protector
● *Technique pages 337, 343–4*

➊ MAKING THE STENCILS

1 Trace and transfer the stencil designs from the master pattern onto the sheet of stencil material and cut them out using the craft knife and the cutting mat or board. If you are using stencil film, trace the design straight onto the film with a fine permanent marker pen.

2 Use masking tape to stick pieces of lightweight cardboard around the edges of the stencil. This is to protect the lampshade from paint drift while you are spraying.

➋ STENCILING THE CRINOLINED LADIES

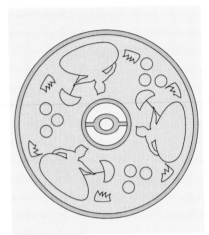

1 With chalk, mark the positions on the lampshade where you plan to place the crinolined lady motif. On a lampshade this size, you should be able to repeat the design three times.

The lamp base makes all the difference to the appearance of this gift – choose plain blond wood for a simple cottage style, or plastic in a clear primary color for an ultra-modern look.

CRINOLINED LADY COORDINATES

Stenciling is a popular home-decorating technique, and a coordinated set of furnishings using the crinolined lady stencil would be a very welcome gift. Find out what a friend's new color scheme will be, and choose the colors for the stencils accordingly.

As well as making the lampshade, you could stencil the motifs on sheets and pillowcases for a guest room, or on a pair of cushion covers for a sitting room. And, as a final touch, why not complete your gift with a pair of crinolined lady curtains?

Use a photocopier to enlarge or reduce the master stencil pattern to sizes suitable for the various items.

The crinolined lady stencil could even provide the perfect inspiration for someone who is looking for decorating ideas. The lampshade might suggest a color scheme, and the stencils could be used to create a wall frieze. Stencil the lampshade in colors to the recipient's taste, and present your gift along with the stencils, brushes and paints, and a set of instructions for stenciling. General stenciling techniques are described in the technique pages, and some stenciling tips are given in "Oak & acorn drawer liners" (pages 128–9).

2 Apply spray adhesive lightly to the back of the stencil. Place the stencil in position on the lampshade and press it firmly down. Shake the can of paint well before spraying and test it on a piece of scrap paper to make sure the nozzle is not clogged. Spray the stencil with pale blue paint, holding the can upright at an angle of 90° to the shade to prevent the paint from drifting under the edge of the stencil. Aim to achieve a soft, even tone.

HINT
It is not necessary for all the stenciled figures to be identical. Part of the charm of stenciling lies in the slight variations among basically similar motifs.

VARIATION
You could devise different color schemes to suit the recipient's taste. For example, imagine the effect of black stenciled motifs on a white ground, reminiscent of Victorian silhouette pictures. A simple lamp base in black wood or metal would provide a dramatic finishing touch.

3 Using the deep blue spray paint, add more color here and there.
4 Finally, spray small amounts of deep red very lightly on selected areas to create further shades of color.
5 Wipe the stencil clean before fixing it in the next position. Repeat steps 2 to 4 for the other crinolined ladies.

❸ STENCILING THE FLOWERS
1 Lightly mark the lampshade with colored chalk where you intend to place the daisies, forget-me-nots and grape hyacinths.
2 Apply spray adhesive lightly to the back of each flower stencil and place in position over the appropriate chalk marks. Work one flower at a time. Using the acrylic paints and the stenciling brushes, gently pounce on deep green for the leaves and yellow, ultra-

marine and burgundy for the flowers. Repeat each flower motif as desired.
3 To stencil the grass, mask the flowers on the grape hyacinth stencil with small pieces of masking tape. Use the remaining parts of the stencil to paint scattered tufts of deep green grass here and there.

❹ FINISHING
1 Place masking tape evenly around the top and bottom of the lampshade, 1.5 cm from the edge.

2 Using the masking tape as a guide, paint a 1.5 cm cuff around the top and bottom of the shade with the dark green paint and a no. 4 brush. Allow the paint to dry and remove the tape.
3 Spray the entire surface of the lampshade with fabric protector.

Crazy patchwork evening bag

Made from scraps of luxury fabric, this unusual bag is richly embroidered and trimmed. The bag measures 22 cm x 24 cm and is designed to be carried on the shoulder.

WHAT YOU NEED

Master pattern **D26(a)** • 30 cm x 30 cm main evening fabric (e.g. satin, shantung, taffeta) • 30 cm x 50 cm lining fabric • 90 cm satin bias binding in a shade to match the lining • 30 cm x 50 cm lightweight iron-on craft batting • 6 scraps evening fabrics, about 26 cm x 15 cm (for the patchwork) • 26 cm x 6 cm evening fabric (for the front binding) • 30 cm x 10 cm chiffon • 2.5 m gimp (furnishing braid) (for the strap) • 2 tassels • suggested trimmings: embroidery, ribbons, braids, decorative buttons, seed beads, metallic ornaments • sewing thread to tone with the color scheme • needles: sharps and crewels, in sizes to suit the fabrics and trimmings • craft glue • tracing paper • dressmaking pins • pencil • scissors • dressmaker's pencil • tape measure • sewing machine
● *Technique pages 292–301, 343–4*

❶ CUTTING OUT THE FABRICS

1 Using the tracing paper and pencil, trace a working pattern for the patchwork from the master pattern. Make sure you mark the numbers on each shape in the patchwork pattern. Do not cut out the individual pieces yet.
2 From the main fabric cut a rectangle 26 cm x 27 cm, and from both the lining fabric and the iron-on batting cut rectangles 26 cm x 44 cm.
3 Before you cut out the patchwork shapes from the scrap fabric, study the pattern and decide how you want to arrange the fabrics. Using the dress-

maker's pencil, number each fabric to correspond with the numbering on the pattern. Cut up the working pattern along the lines so that you have a pattern for each patchwork piece.
4 Pin the patchwork patterns onto the corresponding numbered fabrics and cut them out, adding a 1 cm seam allowance all round.
5 Near your work area, lay out the pieces as in the master pattern to avoid confusion when joining them.

> ### HINT
> *It is easy and fun to create your own crazy patchwork, and this bag would be an excellent beginner's project. Choose fabrics and trimmings that complement each other – they don't need to be of similar weight or weave but don't include too many prints.*

❷ SEWING THE BACK

1 Baste and then iron the batting to the wrong side of the lining.
2 With right sides together, sew the main fabric to the lining along one 26 cm edge. Press the seam toward the main fabric. Turn the work to the right side and topstitch through the main fabric and the seam allowance close to the seam line.

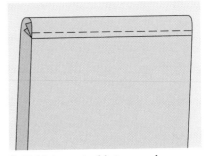

3 Fold the main fabric over the seam so that 1 cm of the main fabric is on the inside (the lining side) of the bag. Press down the fold.

VARIATION
The bag illustrated in the photograph was made from scraps of evening fabric in various shades of burgundy and deep rose. The trimmings were selected to blend with the fabrics, and some of the braids have a gold lamé finish to add sparkle to the bag. You can create your own design by changing the patchwork shapes and by using different fabrics, colors and trimmings.

3 SEWING AND TRIMMING THE PATCHWORK

1 With right sides facing, sew fabric 1 to fabric 2. Then sew joined fabrics 1 and 2 to fabric 3, fabric 3 to fabric 4, and fabric 5 to joined fabrics 1, 3 and 4. Finally, sew fabric 6 to joined fabrics 1 and 5. The basic patchwork is now complete.

2 Sew fabric 6 to the main fabric, and press the seams open.

3 With the wrong sides together, pin and then baste the lining to the joined patchwork and main fabric piece along the raw edges, making sure that the 1 cm of main fabric that was folded over previously is still on the lining side of the work.

4 Quilt the patchwork by machining your chosen ribbons and braids along the seam lines of the patchwork.

5 Sew on the chiffon overlay following the steps outlined in "Adding the chiffon overlay."

6 Decorate the bag as desired with embroidery, ribbon, braid, buttons and beads, and metallic ornaments attached with craft glue.

4 BINDING THE FRONT EDGE

1 With wrong sides facing, fold the 26 cm x 6 cm fabric strip in half lengthwise. Press. Placing all the raw edges together, stitch the binding strip to the right side of the patchwork, 1 cm down from the front edge.

2 Turn the folded edge of the strip over to the wrong side and slipstitch it to the lining along the row of machine stitching.

3 If you have trimmed the patchwork with seed beads, use a fine needle to sew a row of seed beads just below the binding at 1 cm intervals.

5 SEWING THE SIDE SEAMS

1 Fold the completed fabric piece in half widthwise, right sides together, ensuring that the top edges are even.

2 Starting at the top, and using a 2 cm seam allowance, sew a 10 cm seam down both sides. Backstitch to finish these seams and then complete the side seams with a 1 cm seam allowance. This method of joining the sides will form a pleat that will give the bag a slightly tapered shape.

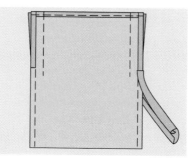

3 Turning the edge of the binding under at each end, bind the edges of the seams with satin bias binding. First bind the edges of the 2 cm side seams separately, and then bind the edges of the 1 cm seams together.

4 Press the large bound seams open and slipstitch them to the inside of the bag at the top.

5 Turn the bag right side out.

6 ATTACHING THE SHOULDER STRAP

1 Cut the gimp in half and sew the two lengths together, wrong sides facing, with a row of straight stitches along each edge.

2 Place one end of the strap along each side seam, about 8 cm from the top of the bag. Slipstitch around all the edges of the strap to attach it firmly to the bag.

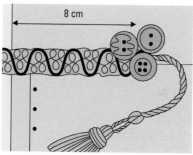

8 cm

3 Oversew the tassel cords to the sides of the bag, immediately below the strap ends, adjusting the length of the cords so that one tassel hangs lower than the other. Cover the joins by attaching braid or buttons to match the trimmings on the patchwork.

ADDING THE CHIFFON OVERLAY

When you are slipstitching the chiffon to the underlying fabric, ensure that the raw edges are turned under 1 cm.

1 Lay one 10 cm raw edge of the chiffon along the raw edge of patchwork fabric 1 and baste it into place along the seam allowance.

2 Slipstitch one 30 cm side along the seams joining fabric 1 to fabrics 2 and 3, and about 2 cm along the seam joining fabrics 5 and 3. Leave the rest of this side and the remaining 10 cm side free.

3 Starting at the bottom of the basted 10 cm raw edge, slipstitch the first 7 cm of the remaining 30 cm side to fabric 1 at an angle of 30° to the seam joining fabrics 1 and 6. Leave the next 9 cm of chiffon free.

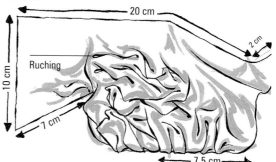

20 cm

2 cm

10 cm

Ruching

7 cm

7.5 cm

4 Slipstitch the remaining 16 cm of chiffon into place, bunching it loosely as you go to fit along the last 7.5 cm of the seam joining fabrics 1 and 6.

5 Loosely ruche the chiffon on to fabric 1, pleating and gathering it and then catching it here and there with small backstitches.

6 Ruche the rest of the chiffon to extend over the seam between fabrics 5 and 1.

Pastoral poppy tray

With its delicate poppy illustration – reminiscent of a medieval Italian herbal picture – this recycled wooden tray would be an ideal gift for someone who values traditional design.

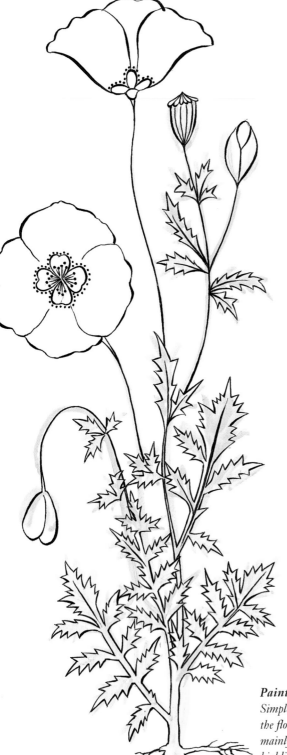

WHAT YOU NEED

Master pattern **D29(a)** • rectangular wooden tray, about 36 cm **x** 50 cm, preferably made of old wood • paint stripper (if necessary) • artist's acrylic paints: green, cadmium red medium, vermilion, raw sienna, black, white, burnt umber shades • Jo Sonja's artist's color: Turner's yellow (or Liquitex yellow) • clear sealer • water-based flat varnish • paint palette • paintbrushes: nos. 2 and 5 round, no. 000 liner, small decorating • fine-grade sandpaper • pencil • eraser • tracing paper • transfer paper • hard pencil (or empty ballpoint pen)

● *Technique pages 334–5, 343–4*

❶ PREPARING THE TRAY

1 Use the paint stripper to take off any old paint or varnish. Sand the tray well to create a good, smooth surface on which to paint the design.
2 Seal the tray with clear sealer mixed with water according to the manufacturer's instructions.

❷ TRANSFERRING THE DESIGN

1 Trace the design from the master pattern onto the tracing paper.
2 Transfer the design to the center of the inside surface of the tray, using the transfer paper and the hard pencil or ballpoint pen.

❸ PAINTING THE DESIGN

Stems and leaves

1 Using the medium round brush, paint the stems and leaves of the poppy in green. To vary the tone of the leaves, make some of them lighter

Painting guide
Simple and dramatic, this classic poppy design shows the flower in all its phases. The plant is painted mainly in dark green and shades of brilliant red, highlighted with yellow, umber and sienna.

by adding a touch of Turner's yellow to the green. Apply a second coat if necessary.
2 When the paint is dry, erase any carbon lines that show through.
3 Using the fine liner brush and black paint that has been watered down, outline the stems and leaves.

Roots

1 Using the small round brush and burnt umber, paint the roots.
2 Use the liner brush and raw sienna to add the fine roots and root hairs.

Open poppies

1 Load the medium round brush with cadmium red and take a heavy side-load of vermilion. Place the brush down next to the edge of the petal, with the vermilion side-load facing toward the outside. Wiggle the brush along the design line of each petal, pushing the side-load off the brush and onto the petal.
2 Reload with cadmium red. Place the brush down on the petal near the side-load and press on the brush to open it up like a fan. Gently drag the brush toward the center of the flower, using about three strokes to fill each petal. The fewer strokes you use, the better the effect. Leave to dry.
3 Using the small round brush loaded with black, paint the center of the petals on the open poppy. Use the liner brush to paint the stamens with Turner's yellow, then add tiny dots of white around the edge of the black.

A MODERN VERSION

The tray illustrated was made from old mortised wood paneling; the knots and nail holes and some of the original paint were left untreated, giving a delightfully rustic quality.

For a more modern look, buy or make a new tray. Sand it very smooth and paint it white or cream. When the tray is dry, transfer and paint the poppy design. Finish with several coats of high-gloss varnish.

4 Use the small round brush and thinned black paint for the calyx (the outer covering at the base of the petals) on the center (tallest) poppy, then paint small dots around the calyx.

Seed pods and buds

1 With the same mixture of Turner's yellow and green that you used on the leaves, paint the dry seed pod. Then use raw sienna to dry-brush the ridges on the pod.

2 Using green, paint textured commas on the top of the seed pod to form the "hat." Shade the pod with dry brushstrokes of raw sienna.

3 Paint the two unopened buds in green, then add some shading to the right-hand side with dry brushstrokes of raw sienna.

4 Paint the bud that is just beginning to open in the mixture of Turner's yellow and green, then add some shading by dry-brushing with green. Dry-brush highlights of raw sienna on the opposite side. Paint the petal that is just starting to show through in cadmium red.

HINT

The poppy design is intended for a tray that measures about 50 cm x 36 cm. If your tray is larger or smaller, use a photocopier to make the design the right size for your tray.

❹ FINISHING

When the tray is dry, varnish it. Use at least three coats of varnish if the tray is meant for practical use in the dining room, rather than simply for display.

Raffia bag

You can make this unusual bag as an accessory for either daytime or evening wear by choosing an appropriate fabric for the upper portion.

About 300 g raffia • fabric dye, in a color of your choice • 60 cm x 60 cm fabric, in a color to complement the dyed raffia • sewing thread to match the fabric • 60 cm fine, strong cord • dried flowers or silk flowers • needles: large-eyed tapestry, general sewing • dressmaking pins • sewing machine
● *Technique pages 292–301*

❶ MAKING THE RAFFIA BRAID

1 Dye the hank of raffia following the maker's instructions on the packet of dye. Put aside a small quantity of the dyed raffia to make the drawstrings.
2 Follow the instructions for "Making the raffia braid" ("Raffia sun hat," page 106) to make about 5 meters of raffia braid. Glue one end and bind the other, and trim away the excess raffia, as for the raffia hat.

❷ MAKING THE SIDES AND BASE

1 Starting at the center of the base, begin to form the braid into a tight, flat coil. Tuck the start of the braid under the coil and stitch it firmly, using the tapestry needle and a strand of raffia.

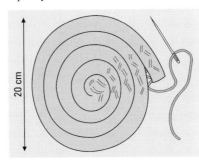

2 Keeping the coil as flat as possible, stitch rounds of raffia until you have made a circle with a diameter of 18–20 cm (about five rounds). Use a basic hemming or cross-stitch, taking the needle straight across so that the stitches go in at an angle, and sew the rounds together as firmly as possible so the base is flat and strong. Ease the raffia braid to keep the work flat.

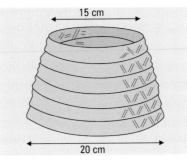

3 Sew the next round at right angles up from the base. Continue for six rounds, sloping the braid in slightly. When you have finished the sixth round, the work should look like a truncated cone with a diameter of 18–20 cm at the base and a diameter of about 15 cm at the top.

4 Finish the raffia part of the bag by tapering the braid and weaving it back into the last round.

❸ MAKING THE LINING

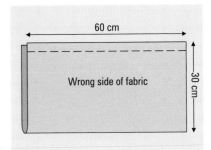

1 Fold the fabric in half, right sides together. Pin down the long edge to form a tube. Adjust the seam allowance so that the tube fits comfortably into the top circumference of the bag. Machine stitch the seam.

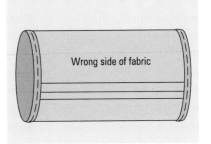

2 Press the seam open and zigzag the raw edges to prevent fraying. On the same side as the seam, turn down 1 cm hems at the top and bottom.

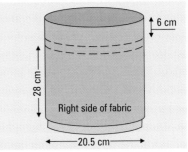

3 Fold the fabric tube in half, wrong sides facing, to make a double tube about 28 cm long. Press, and sew a line of stitching around the tube 6 cm from the top fold. Sew a parallel line of stitching 1.5 cm down from the first. (These two lines of stitching form the casing for the drawstrings.)
4 At the hem on the inside layer of the fabric tube, unpick a few stitches in the seam at the wrong side of the

---

NATURAL DYEING METHODS

Instead of using commercial dyes to color the raffia, you can make your own dyes from various plant materials – infusions of leaves, flowers, berries and tree barks can produce subtle and exciting colors. You will also have the satisfaction of knowing that you have made even the dye yourself.

You can use imported dyestuffs such as cochineal (the dried insect bodies, not the liquid food coloring) or brazilwood. Properly used, these dyestuffs yield good, strong colors – this is useful for dyeing

raffia, because vegetable fibers do not accept dyes as readily as animal fibers.

For the best results from natural dyeing, you need to treat the fibers with mordants (mineral solutions to help the colors to penetrate). Different mordants produce different colors from the same dyestuff.

It is important to remember that many of the materials used for natural dyeing are poisonous. Before you start using natural dyes, look for a reliable book that gives precautions, recipes and detailed instructions.

HINTS

• *The way you prepare the raffia will depend on the style of bag you want to make. For example, if you are making the bag as a daytime accessory, you may wish to dye the raffia after you have made the braid. The color will be uneven because the braid is thick, but this produces an interesting texture.*

• *If you are making the bag as an evening accessory, dye the raffia before braiding it to give a more even color, and steam iron the braid between damp cloths to make the raffia sleek and smooth.*

• *Use dried flowers or raffia flowers for a daytime bag, and silk flowers for an evening bag.*

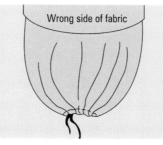

Wrong side of fabric

fabric and thread the cord through the hem. Draw the bottom of the lining together by pulling the cord tight on the wrong side of the fabric. Tie off the cord firmly.

5 To make the holes for the drawstrings, unpick the outer side seam only between the two rows of stitching that form the drawstring casing. Reinforce the seam with a few hand-stitches at the top and bottom of this gap. Exactly opposite the seam, cut a slit between the two rows of stitching in the outside fabric only. Work buttonhole stitch around the slit.

❹ MAKING THE DRAWSTRINGS

1 Take four single strands of raffia and make a narrow braid 3 meters long. Cut it into four equal lengths.
2 Twist two of the braids together tightly. Repeat this procedure with the other two braids.

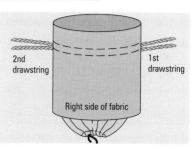

2nd drawstring

1st drawstring

Right side of fabric

3 Thread one of the twisted braids right around the drawstring casing through the opening on one side, and thread the other braid through the other opening and around the casing in the same way.
4 Tie the ends of the braids together on either side of the bag about 2 cm from the end of the braids. Unravel the braids beyond these ties and splay them out to make raffia tassels.

❺ FINISHING THE BAG

1 Find the end of the braid and, treating that point as the back of the raffia base, push the lining down into the base with the drawstrings at either side. Using the large-eyed tapestry needle and matching thread, slipstitch the outside layer of the lining to the raffia base around the top of the last round of braiding. Use small stitches that will not show on the raffia, being careful not to catch the inner layer of the lining.
2 Handstitch the silk or dried flowers to the front of the bag so that they sit just where the raffia base meets the silk lining. Pull the drawstrings tight.

Seagrass mat

The natural seagrass fibers of this mat are long-wearing as well as attractive. The mat is made by a quick and simple weaving technique and the colored strips can be dyed in any color you choose.

Sew eleven 60 cm strips of seagrass onto a 45 cm strip to form the base, and weave in alternate short strips of dyed and undyed seagrass to form the pattern.

WHAT YOU NEED

15.5 m seagrass braid, 35 mm wide • 30 strands (about 35 g) khaki raffia • scissors • needle: size 20 chenille • orange fabric dye

● *Technique pages 292–5*

❶ PREPARING THE SEAGRASS

1 Cut a 3.5 m strip of seagrass braid. Following the dye manufacturer's directions, dye the braid orange and hang it up to dry. Then cut it into five 45 cm strips and two 60 cm strips.
2 From the remaining undyed braid, cut six 45 cm strips, nine 60 cm strips and two 190 cm strips.

❷ LAYING THE BASE

1 Using the undyed seagrass, place a short (45 cm) strip and a long (60 cm) strip at right angles, with the short strip on top, overlapping the ends by 3 cm. With a strand of raffia and a chenille needle, stitch the overlapping braids together.

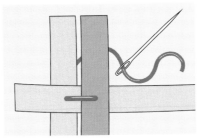

2 Place a long orange strip next to the long undyed strip, laying it over the short strip. Backstitch this orange strip firmly to the short strip.
3 Add seven more long strips of the undyed braid in a similar way, alternately placing them on top of and underneath the short strip. Backstitch each in turn on to the short strip.

4 Add another long orange strip and one more undyed strip in the same way. This completes the weaving base.

❸ WEAVING

1 Weave a short (45 cm) orange strip alongside the first short undyed strip and backstitch it in place.
2 Repeat step 1, alternating orange strips with undyed strips, until you have woven in, and securely backstitched, a total of 11 short strips. When you get to the end of each strand of raffia, take it through to the underside of the mat, tie it firmly into the back of the mat and neaten it off, then tie on a new strand.

❹ BINDING THE EDGES

1 Trim the edges of the mat to within a regular 3 cm of the weaving and cut the corners into a curve.
2 Place one of the 190 cm strips of seagrass braid underneath and the other on top of the raw edges at one end of the mat.

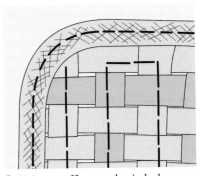

3 Using a raffia strand, stitch the binding strips together through the raw edges of the mat. As you work around the corners, gently ease and stretch the braid so that it lies flat.

Framed memories

Photographs keep memories alive, and a montage of photographs celebrating a dear one's life makes a special and personal gift for a family member or a close friend.

WHAT YOU NEED

Selection of photographs • large picture frame • mounting board, cut to fit the frame • scalpel or craft knife • ruler • square • jar lid or saucer, with a circumference large enough to frame several of the photographs • invisible or masking tape • sheet of rub-off decorative corners and borders • hard pencil (or empty ballpoint pen)

❶ CHOOSING THE PHOTOGRAPHS

1 Select a series of images that are related thematically. You will need one main photograph, such as a large portrait, as a focal point for the arrangement. For the montage illustrated here, the focal point is a favorite photograph of the recipient's grandfather; the other images reflect various aspects of his life – his wife, his daughter, his home and his first car.

2 Experiment with the positions of the photographs on the mounting board until you are happy with the arrangement. Remember that symmetrical arrangements are the most pleasing to the eye.

3 Decide which images you would like to place in a circular opening. (Circular openings make excellent frames for displaying portraits, especially old black-and-white or sepia portrait photographs.)

❷ CUTTING THE OPENINGS

1 Working on the back of the mounting board, mark the cutting lines for the frames with a pencil. Use a ruler and a square to mark the square-edged frames and an inverted jar lid or saucer of the appropriate size for the circular frames. You can cut each frame to display either the whole image or only part of it, but the frame must be smaller than the photograph so that the photograph will sit behind the mounting board. Start by marking the frame for the focal image, and measure the distances between images carefully to keep them uniform.

2 With the scalpel or craft knife, cut out the frames. Cut the square-edged frames first, using the steel ruler. To cut out the circular frames, take the lid or saucer that you used to trace the shape and place it over the tracing. Gently score around the shape with the craft knife, as you would with a pencil. Remove the lid or saucer and cut out the circle along the score line. Work slowly and carefully and do not press the scalpel too hard.

PICTURE FRAMES

Select a large picture frame so that there will be enough space to display the photographs to the best advantage. The frame shown here is made of recycled wood, which suits the subject perfectly.

You can buy picture frames with holes already cut in various shapes in the mounting boards.

NOTE
Work on a clean surface with clean hands. If a smudge occurs, remove with an ordinary pencil eraser; if this doesn't work, use the rub-on border to hide it.

❸ MOUNTING THE PHOTOGRAPHS

1 When you have cut out all the frames, carefully fix the photographs in position with invisible tape or masking tape. Use only one piece of tape along the top edge of each photograph – this allows the photographic paper to expand and shrink with the weather, which prevents the photographs from wrinkling.

2 With the hard pencil, transfer the rub-on borders onto the mounting board around the photographs. Place them to accentuate the focal image and embellish the secondary images.

❹ FINISHING

Make sure that the glass is clean, and carefully fit the mounting board with the photographs into the picture frame. Secure the back of the frame according to the manufacturer's or frame-maker's instructions.

Cream-on-cream cushion

This stylish muslin and lace cushion with self-color embroidery uses simple embroidery stitches and is made from inexpensive materials. It would be a delightful addition to any room.

❷ TRACING AND TRANSFERRING THE DESIGN

1 Trace the design from the master pattern with tracing paper and the black felt-tipped pen.
2 Match the center of the fabric with the center of the working design and pin them together with the fabric on top. Place the fabric and the design on a light box or tape it to a window. Using the fabric marking pen, trace the design on to the fabric.

❸ EMBROIDERING THE FRONT

Place the fabric with the marked design in the embroidery hoop, pulling it taut. Embroider the design following the stitch guide, completing one section at a time.

Large flowers

1 With a double strand of candlewick cotton, work the outlines of the petals in a double row of colonial knots. Work several colonial knots in the center of the flower.
2 Work the stamens in stem stitch, placing a single colonial knot at the end of each stamen.

Medium flowers

1 With a double strand of candlewick cotton, outline the petals with a single row of colonial knots.
2 Complete the centers of the flowers in the same way as the large flowers.
3 Work the small sprays of buds below the flowers in colonial knots, using a single strand of cotton.
4 Work the flat leaves below the sprays in chain stitch.

WHAT YOU NEED

Master pattern E32(a) • muslin, 75 m x 150 cm • 2 m cotton lace, about 40 mm wide • 40 cm x 40 cm cushion insert • candlewick cotton (same color as muslin) • needle: size 22 chenille • coton à broder • embroidery hoop • tracing paper • black felt-tipped pen • water-erasable fabric marking pen • scissors • sewing thread to match muslin and lace • sewing machine
● *Technique pages 292–301, 307–14*

❶ PREPARING THE FABRIC

1 Before cutting out the cushion, prewash and then iron the lace and the muslin.
2 From the muslin, cut out a 45 cm square for the front, two pieces 45 cm x 25 cm for the back, and two strips 15 cm x 150 cm for the frill.
3 Fold the 45 cm square in half and then in quarters to find the center. Using dark-colored thread, baste along the straight grain of the folds to mark the center horizontal and vertical lines.

HINT

You can work the embroidery in any order you prefer, but it is best to complete one section at a time so that you do not have to clamp the fabric in the embroidery hoop too often.

5 Place colonial knots on both sides of the lower lines of the heart.

Daisies and other small flowers

1 Work the daisies in straight stitch with a single strand of cotton, and place a single colonial knot in the center of each one.

2 Work the small petaled flowers, the foliage surrounding these flowers and the foliage around the daisies in lazy daisy stitch.

Foliage

Work the scrolled stems and the outlines of the leaves in stem stitch using a single strand of cotton. Work the veins of the leaves in feather stitch.

❹ FINISHING THE FRONT

1 Wash the fabric to remove all traces of the marking pen. Gently steam press from the wrong side.

2 Pin and baste the lace around the right side of the embroidered square, 1.5 cm from the outer edge and with the scalloped edge of the lace facing toward the embroidered heart. Miter the corners and sew the lace in place.

3 Sew another row of stitching just below the scalloped edge of the lace to keep the lace flat against the fabric.

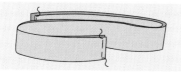

4 Join the two long frill pieces together to form a continuous band and press the seams open.

5 Press the band in half lengthwise with wrong sides facing.

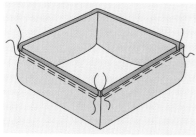

6 Divide the frill into quarters. In each quarter, sew two rows of gathering stitches through both sides, 5 mm from the raw edge, starting and finishing at quarter marks.

7 Pin the frill to the front of the cushion, outside the lace border. Match the quarter marks on the frill to the corners of the cushion. Pull up and adjust the gathers to fit.

8 Stitch the frill to the cushion front, leaving a 1.5 cm seam. Remove the gathering threads.

❺ MAKING UP THE CUSHION

1 Sew a double hem along one 45 cm side of each back piece.

2 Place the two back pieces on top of the embroidered front, right sides facing and with the hemmed edges of the back overlapping in the middle.

Stitch		Stitch	
Colonial knot		Straight stitch	
Stem stitch		Lazy daisy stitch	
Chain stitch		Feather stitch	

Stitch guide

The design is created with just a few basic stitches worked in cotton thread.

Pin, baste and stitch the cushion front to the back, leaving a 1.5 cm seam allowance all round.

3 Trim the seams, iron with a damp cloth, then turn the cushion through to the right side. Iron the right side with a damp cloth.

4 Insert the cushion pad and close the back opening with slipstitch. This can be opened for washing.

CUTTING GUIDE

Made of muslin and cotton lace, the cushion will wash and wear well. For the best results, buy good-quality muslin. Prewash both the fabric and the lace to allow for shrinkage, and be sure to cut along the straight grain.

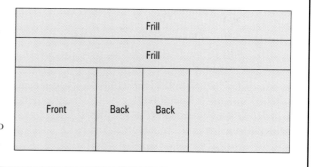

Handmade hatboxes

Hats are back in fashion, and these functional yet stylish fabric-covered boxes provide decorative storage for them.

WHAT YOU NEED

The measurements given first are for making the larger box, and those in brackets are for making the smaller box.

Heavy cardboard: A1 sheet • light cardboard: A1 sheet, A0 sheet • 50 cm (30 cm) lightweight, firmly woven cotton fabric, 115 cm wide • about 35 cm x 35 cm lightweight batting • 1.2 m (2 m) braid • 1.2 m cord, 10 mm diameter • white glue • pencil • ruler • compass • scissors • scalpel or craft knife • wide masking tape • spring clothespins

① CUTTING OUT THE CARDBOARD

1 Using the pencil, compass and scalpel, mark, label and cut the following shapes from the heavy cardboard: **A** one circle radius 153 mm (115 mm) for the lid; **B** one circle radius 150 mm (112 mm) for the base.

2 With the pencil, compass, ruler and scalpel, mark, label and cut the following shapes from the light cardboard: **C** one circle radius 153 mm (115 mm) for the lid liner; **D** two circles radius 146 mm (108 mm) for the base liners;

E two strips 1020 mm x 42 mm (750 mm x 40 mm) for the lid rims; **F** one strip 1020 mm x 38 mm (750 mm x 36 mm) for the lid rim liner; **G** one rectangle 990 mm x 180 mm (730 mm x 170 mm) for the base wall; **H** one strip 990 mm x 176 mm (730 mm x 166 mm) for the base wall liner.

② CONSTRUCTING THE LID

1 Apply a strip of masking tape along one edge of one lid rim (E), so that half the width of the tape overhangs the edge of the cardboard.

2 Cut V-shaped notches along the overhanging tape.

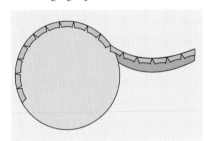

3 With the rim at right angles to the lid (A), roll the rim around the edge of the lid and attach it by pulling the notched masking tape onto the lid and pressing it firmly into place.

4 Overlap the ends of the rim and tape them together.

③ COVERING THE LID

1 Apply glue to the lid top and place it on the batting. Smooth out the batting and trim it to fit exactly.

2 Trace the outline of the lid onto the wrong side of the fabric, adding a 1.5 cm seam allowance. Cut the traced shape from the fabric and notch the seam allowance.

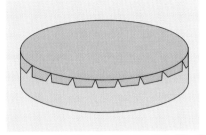

3 Glue the fabric and place it over the batting, pulling it taut as you work. Glue the notched seam allowance down onto the rim.

4 Trace the shape of the second lid rim (E) onto the wrong side of the fabric. Add a 1.5 cm seam allowance all around and cut out.

5 Glue the lid rim and place it on the wrong side of the fabric. Turn over and glue the seam allowance to the wrong side along one long edge only.

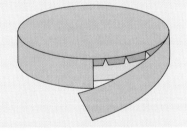

6 Glue the second rim over the first, with the glued-down seam allowance sitting over the notched lid cover. Trim one end so that the cardboard ends sit flush. Glue the remaining seam allowance over the join.

7 Glue the lower edge of the seam allowance to the inside of the rim. Clamp the fabric to the rim with clothespins until the glue has dried.

④ LINING THE LID

1 Place the lid rim liner (F) on the wrong side of the fabric and trace around it, adding a 1.5 cm seam allowance. Cut out the traced shape from the fabric.

2 Glue the lid rim liner and place it on the wrong side of the cut-out fabric. Glue the 1.5 cm seam allowance to the wrong side along both long

---

CUTTING THE CARDBOARD PIECES

Cut the fabric using the cardboard pieces as templates.

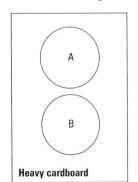

Heavy cardboard

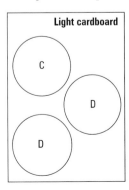

Light cardboard

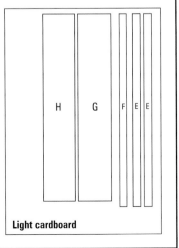

Light cardboard

lid rim to the lid. Overlap the ends of the wall and secure with masking tape.

3 Coat the base wall with glue and center it on the wrong side of the fabric. Roll the base wall along the fabric piece until it is covered, smoothing out any wrinkles as you go.

4 Glue the top seam allowance to the inside of the base wall.

5 Notch the seam allowance along the lower edge and glue it to the base.

6 ATTACHING THE CORD HANDLES

1 Using sharp scissors, pierce two holes in the base wall, opposite each other and about 5 cm from the top.

2 Measure and cut enough cord to form a handle running from hole to hole across the top of the box. Thread the ends of the cord through the holes from the outside and hold them in place by gluing and taping them flat to the inside of the box.

7 LINING THE BASE

1 Place the base liners (D) on the wrong side of the fabric and trace around them, adding a 1.5 cm seam allowance. Cut out the traced shapes from the fabric.

2 Working on one at a time, coat the base liners with glue and place them on the wrong sides of the fabric circles. Notch the seam allowances and glue them to the wrong sides of the cardboard liners.

3 Glue one of the covered base liners to the outside of the base of the box and the other to the inside.

4 Trace around the base wall liner (H) on the wrong side of the fabric, adding a 1.5 cm seam allowance, and cut the traced shape from the fabric.

5 Glue the base wall liner to the wrong side of the cut-out fabric. Turn and glue the seam allowance to the wrong side along the upper and lower edges. Trim off the seam allowance at one short end.

6 Glue the wrong side of the liner and fit it inside the box, pressing it into place. Lap the remaining seam allowance over the join. Hold the liner against the base wall with clothespins until the glue dries.

edges. Glue the covered lid rim liner to the inside of the lid rim, trimming one end to fit snugly and gluing the seam allowance over the join.

3 Trace around the lid liner (C) on the wrong side of the fabric, adding a 1.5 cm seam allowance. Cut out the traced shape from the fabric.

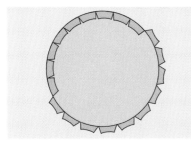

4 Glue the lid liner and place it on the wrong side of the cut-out fabric. Notch the seam allowance and glue it around the edge of the lid liner. Glue the liner to the inside of the lid.

5 Glue the braid around the outside edge of the rim. (The smaller hat box illustrated has two rows of braid.)

5 CONSTRUCTING AND COVERING THE BASE

1 Trace the shape of the base wall (G) onto the wrong side of the fabric, adding 1.5 cm all around for the seam allowance. Cut out the traced shape.

2 Join the base wall (G) to the base (B) in the same way as you joined the

Hand-covered photograph album

Most people have photographs lying around waiting to be mounted. Here is a simple method of converting an inexpensive, purchased photograph album into a distinctive and useful gift.

WHAT YOU NEED

Photograph album with spiral binding • craft batting, a little larger all round than the complete cover (back and front) of the album • fabric, 4 cm larger all round than the complete cover of the album • 1 m ribbon, 25 mm wide, to coordinate with fabric • wrapping paper to coordinate with fabric • sewing thread • sewing needle • tape measure • scissors • white glue • clean scrap paper
● *Technique pages 292–5*

❶ APPLYING THE BATTING

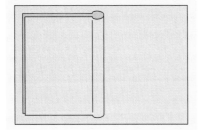

1 Evenly coat the outside of the front cover of the album, including the edges and the spine, with a thin layer of white glue.
2 Lay the piece of batting flat and position the glued front cover of the album on it, with the edges just inside the edges of the batting.
3 Repeat step 1 for the outside back cover of the album.
4 Bring the batting over the spine, keeping it taut and smooth, and press it down over the glued back cover.
5 If necessary, trim the batting so that it will just wrap around the edges of the cover. Clip the corners so that they will not be bulky, and press the batting down onto the glued edges. Allow the glue to dry.

❷ COVERING THE ALBUM

1 Cut the ribbon in half. With right sides facing, lay one piece of ribbon over the fabric with the end centered on one short edge of the fabric. Stitch a 2 cm x 3 cm rectangle to hold the ribbon flat and secure.

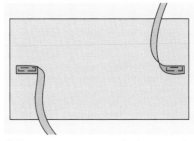

2 Repeat step 1 to attach the second piece of ribbon to the opposite edge of the fabric, and then trim the ribbon ends at an angle to prevent fraying.

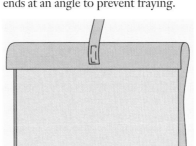

3 Open the album. On the inside cover, mark the center point of the vertical edge. Run glue along this edge from top to bottom. Press the wrong side of one short edge of the fabric onto the glued area, aligning the stitched end of the ribbon with center point. Let the glue dry.
4 Turn the album over and repeat step 3 on the other side, pulling the fabric firmly over the cover with the album as nearly closed as possible.

Close the album, placing sheets of clean paper between the cover and the pages in case of glue leakage. Let the glue dry thoroughly.

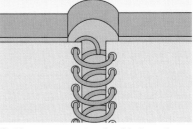

5 If necessary, trim the fabric at the spine so that it will tuck down flat behind the spiral binding. Glue the top and bottom of the inside of the spine and stick the fabric down.
6 Apply glue to the top and bottom edges of the inside front cover. Stick the fabric down, mitering the corners and ensuring that the fabric covers the outside of the album smoothly. Repeat this step on the inside back.

❸ FINISHING

1 To make endpapers, cut two pieces of wrapping paper 5 mm smaller all round than the inside dimensions of the cover. Glue the endpapers to the insides of the covers to conceal the raw edges of the fabric.
2 When the glue is dry, close the album and tie the ribbon in a bow.

Garden sculpture

Give this sculpture to a friend who has a shady garden nook. The painted faux finish on an ordinary plaster or concrete bust or statue will give it the appearance of weathered bronze and verdigris.

WHAT YOU NEED

Garden statue • artist's acrylic paints: deep brown, aqua blue, acid green • paint palette • paintbrushes: 25 mm decorating, large stencil • paper toweling • flat polyurethane varnish • coarse sandpaper
● *Technique pages 334–5*

❶ PREPARATION

1 Scrub the statue quite clean and allow it to dry thoroughly.
2 Gently sand it to remove any old paint, grime or surface irregularities, and wash it again. Allow it to dry.

❷ APPLYING THE FAUX FINISH

1 Using the 25 mm decorating brush, paint the entire surface of the statue with the brown acrylic paint. Add a little water to the paint, so that it flows well but retains its opacity.
2 Allow the paint to dry thoroughly, and then apply another coat of brown paint. Leave the statue to dry for at least 24 hours.
3 Squeeze a small amount of the aqua blue paint onto the palette and add water until the paint has a smooth, light, creamy consistency.
4 Dip the stencil brush lightly into the paint. Then tap the brush on

NOTE

For the example illustrated, a Roman-style cement head was bought from a second-hand store. Garden statues suitable for this treatment are also available from plant nurseries and garden stores.

paper toweling to remove any excess paint until there is only a small amount left in the brush.
5 Using an up-and-down pouncing motion, stipple the blue very lightly over the entire surface of the statue. Pay special attention to crevices or folds, which may need a little extra paint. Allow to dry for 24 hours.
6 Mix a small amount of acid green paint with water to make a mixture of light consistency, like the aqua blue mixture, and take a small amount of the paint on to the brush.
7 Stipple the entire surface very lightly – be exceptionally sparing with this color. If the color is too strong, pounce a small amount of the brown paint on the affected areas. Allow the statue to dry out for at least 24 hours.
8 Seal all surfaces with a coat of flat polyurethane varnish. This will give

the statue a dry, flat look, like that of weathered bronze, which is very attractive nestled among foliage.

PAINT COLORS

Any good quality artist's acrylic paint can be used for this project. Choose colors that match the color swatches below.

Deep brown

Aqua blue

Acid green

Oak & acorn shelf paper

The geometric design of bows and diamonds framing oak leaves and acorns adds a touch of class to shelf paper – a gift that would be a good housewarming present.

Master pattern G49(a–b) • 1 roll wallpaper lining paper • stencil film or treated manila cardboard • spray adhesive • artist's acrylic paints: gold, pale olive green, red violet • paint palette • paintbrushes: 2 small stenciling, 1 medium stenciling • yardstick • tracing paper • transfer paper • pencil • gold pen • fine, permanent marker pen • craft knife • cutting mat or board • paper towels • eraser • lint-free cloth
● *Technique pages 337, 343–4*

❶ MAKING THE STENCILS

1 Trace and transfer the stencil designs from the master pattern. For stencil film, trace the designs straight onto the film using a fine, permanent marker pen. For treated cardboard, trace the designs and

NOTE

Wallpaper lining paper was used for this project, but any heavy paper with a smooth finish would be suitable. Cream or off-white paper is the best.

transfer them to the cardboard using transfer paper. Cut the designs out using the craft knife and cutting mat.
2 Transfer the center lines from the master pattern onto the oak leaf stencil. These are used to help place the stencil accurately.

❷ PREPARING THE PAPER

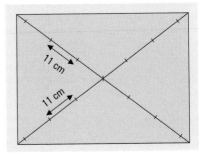

1 Cut pieces of wallpaper lining paper 60 cm wide and 42 cm deep, then draw a grid to help you position the stencils evenly. Using the pencil and the yardstick, lightly draw diagonal lines from corner to corner of each sheet of paper.

2 Starting from the center and working out toward the corners, mark the diagonals at 11 cm intervals. The marks furthest from the center will be 3 cm from the corners.

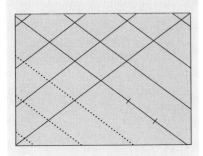

3 Using the pencil marks as guides, lightly draw in lines parallel to the two central diagonals to form a regular diamond-shaped lattice.

❸ STENCILING THE DESIGN

1 Lightly spray the back of the bow stencil with adhesive. Starting in a top corner, position the stencil on the intersection of the penciled lines

on the grid, placing the knot in the center of the bow over the intersection of the lines. Press down firmly. Using the gold paint and a small stenciling brush, stencil the bow. Gently remove the stencil from the paper and wipe it clean with a lint-free cloth.

2 Repeat step 1 until you have stenciled bows on all the intersecting lines. Allow the paint to dry.

HINT
Roll the shelf paper with the stenciled design facing outward and tie with a ribbon. Stencil the oak and acorn design onto a plain card to accompany the gift.

Stenciling guide
Pounce the three leaves in pale olive green, adding touches of red violet on two of them for the shading. Use red violet to paint the acorns and add highlights in gold.

3 Find the center of a diamond shape in a top corner of the grid by joining opposite corners of the diamond with a pencil. The point where the two lines intersect is the center of the diamond. Lightly spray

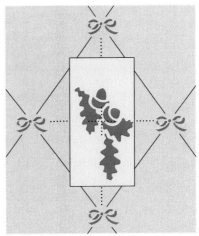

the oak and acorn stencil with adhesive and place the center of the stencil over the center of the diamond.

4 Using the medium stenciling brush and red violet paint, pounce paint evenly all over the acorns and their shells and over parts of the leaves as shown in the illustration. Next, using the pale olive green paint, pounce in the leaves to complete the shapes.

5 With the small stenciling brush and gold paint, pounce in the gold highlights on the acorns and shells. Remove the stencil and wipe it clean.

6 Repeat steps 3 to 5 until all the oak and acorn designs are stenciled.

❹ FINISHING

1 Using the gold pen and the yardstick, over-draw the penciled lines of the grid, stopping about 1 cm short of the stenciled bows.

2 When all the paint and ink is thoroughly dry, carefully remove any pencil lines that are still visible with the eraser.

STENCILING TIPS

• Before you start to cut out the stencil pattern, make sure that the stencil material (stencil plastic or treated manila cardboard) has no rough patches to catch under the knife blade and make accurate cutting difficult. Surface roughness can be smoothed off with fine sandpaper, but discard any piece of cardboard with a fibrous fault throughout its thickness.

• As a further aid to accurate cutting, fix the stencil material to the cutting board with masking tape to hold it firm and flat.

• Using special stencil plastic for your stencils will save time when you transfer the design. The plastic is transparent so you can trace your design straight on to it. Craft shops stock stencil plastic.

• For painting stenciled designs, the paint should be of a creamy consistency – if it is too thin, it will bleed under the edges of the stencil, giving a smudgy outline. Spray paints work well for stenciling, but they are quite messy to use, so all the working area needs to be well protected.

• Used stencils can be cleaned and kept for re-use. Wipe them with a cloth dampened with water or turpentine (depending on the type of paint used). Leave them until they are quite dry, and then place them between sheets of paper or in plastic envelopes. Store them flat.

• Pre-cut stencils are available from arts and crafts shops – or you can make your own, remembering that simple designs work best.

Garden tote box

Growing, preserving and eating your own fruit and vegetables is a source of great satisfaction. This tote box for bringing produce from the garden to the kitchen will double the pleasure of any keen gardener.

WHAT YOU NEED

Master pattern l65(a–b) • wooden tote box • Jo Sonja's (or Liquitex) artist's acrylic colors: teal green (for base coat), yellow oxide, warm white, naphthol crimson, burgundy, raw umber, burnt umber, green oxide, pine green, rich gold • water-based flat or gloss varnish • sealer • paintbrushes: 25 mm decorating, no. 5 round, no. 00 liner • fine sandpaper • lint-free cloth • tracing paper • transfer paper • masking tape • fine-tipped marker • hard pencil • artist's eraser
● *Technique pages 334–5, 343–4*

❶ PREPARING THE TOTE BOX

1 Lightly sand all surfaces of the box and wipe clean with the lint-free cloth.
2 Using a decorating brush, apply teal green mixed with equal parts of sealer. Allow to dry, then sand lightly and apply another coat.
3 Trace the designs from the master pattern using tracing paper and a fine marker. Center the large design on the side of the box and fix it in place

Painting guide
The strawberries are painted in several shades of red and highlighted with yellow oxide. The yellow and white flowers point up the rich, dark colors of the strawberries and leaves.

with masking tape. Slip the transfer paper under the design and, using the hard pencil, transfer the design to the box.
4 Fix the design to the other side of the box and transfer the design again.
5 Transfer the smaller design onto both sides of the divider.

❷ PAINTING THE DESIGN

Unless directed otherwise, use the round brush to paint the design.

Leaves

1 Base-coat the leaves with green oxide and allow to dry. Using pine green, dry-brush shading onto one side of the leaves.
2 Highlight the opposite sides of the leaves by dry-brushing with a mixture of green oxide and warm white.

3 Using a liner brush loaded with the same mixture of green oxide and warm white, outline the leaves and paint in the tendrils.
4 Load the liner brush with pine green paint and carefully mark in the veins of the leaves.

Strawberries

1 Base-coat the strawberries using a mixture of yellow oxide and warm white. Allow them to dry.
2 Paint over the base coat with several coats of naphthol crimson. Using burgundy paint, dry-brush shading along one side of each strawberry.
3 With the liner brush and raw umber, paint in the seeds.
4 On the side opposite the shading, use the liner brush to paint in a yellow oxide highlight beside the seeds.

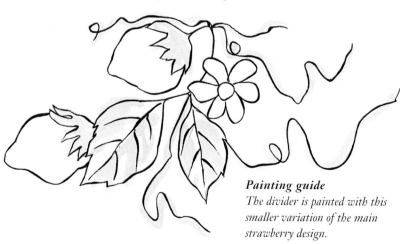

Painting guide
The divider is painted with this smaller variation of the main strawberry design.

HINT

Any type of twin-compartment, wooden tote box – a toolbox, a cleaning box or a shoe-shining caddy – is suitable for this project, as long it is at least 30 cm long and 10 cm high, so that the design will fit. Some boxes have dividers that are too low to take the smaller design; if this is the case, paint the small design on the ends of the box.

GIFT SET IDEAS

It is very easy to add items to the tote box
to make a marvelous composite gift.

• It would make an excellent companion gift
for the strawberry garden chair (page 207) or
the iris garden apron (pages 210–1), or you
could make all three as a gift for a special
anniversary or birthday.

• Include pruning shears or garden scissors
for cutting flowers, vegetables and fruit, garden twine or raffia for tying up bunches of
produce, and small cane baskets to protect soft
fruits and tomatoes.

• Decorate a cotton or linen sunhat with
the smaller strawberry design. Use fabric
paints, applied according to the manufacturer's directions.

VARIATION

*Base-coat the box in the recipi-
ent's favorite color or in a color
that suits their kitchen decor.
A strong color is best.*

5 Paint each calyx using green
oxide with a side-load of yellow oxide.
(The calyx is the green "cap" at the
stem end of the strawberry.)

Flowers

1 Fill the brush with yellow oxide
side-loaded with warm white, and use
a single stroke for each petal.

2 Paint the centers of the flowers
with burnt umber, and when dry
add small dots of yellow oxide.

❸ FINISHING

1 Rub rich gold paint along all the
top edges of the tote box and inside
the handle grip. Allow to dry.

2 Remove any remaining transfer
lines with the eraser. Apply two coats
of varnish, drying well between coats.

Wind chimes

The gentle tinkle of wind chimes is a welcome sound. The chimes in this project can be created by anyone with a few basic woodworking skills.

1400 mm copper piping, 12 mm diameter • conch-shaped shell, no longer than 6 cm • scallop-shaped shell • thick, soft wood, 120 mm x 120 mm x 10 mm • 2 wooden beads, about 20 mm diameter, with large holes • small wooden bead, about 10 mm diameter • 1.5 m fine nylon fishing line • 2 m white nylon cord • white sewing thread • exterior varnish • epoxy resin glue • paintbrush (for varnishing) • hacksaw • jigsaw • miter box • hand or electric drill • drill bits: 5 mm, 2.5 mm • 1 medium-sized nail • hammer • 2 clamps or a vise • fine sandpaper • fine-grade steel wool • lint-free cloth • compass • pencil
● *Technique pages 338–42*

❶ MAKING THE PIPES

1 Using the hacksaw, cut the copper piping into the following five lengths: 180 mm, 240 mm, 280 mm, 310 mm and 340 mm. Cut one end of each pipe straight, and cut the other end at an angle using the miter box. Measure the length of each pipe from the straight end to the longest point of the angled end.
2 Using the 5 mm bit, drill a hole

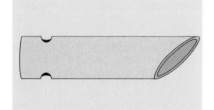

on either side of each length of pipe 10 mm from the straight end. To start the hole, hammer the nail into the pipe until there is a dent which is big enough for the head of the drill bit to rest in.

3 Smooth all the cut edges with the fine sandpaper and burnish each length of pipe with steel wool.

❷ MAKING THE WOODEN DISK

1 With the compass, draw a circle 100 mm in diameter on the piece of wood. Carefully cut around the circle with the jigsaw.
2 On the circle of wood, draw a concentric circle with a diameter of 80 mm. Mark five points evenly around this circle – each point will

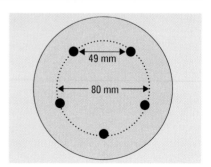

be about 49 mm from the next. Using the 5 mm bit, drill holes right through the wood at these five points.

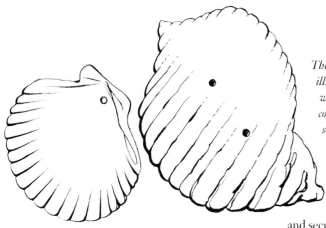

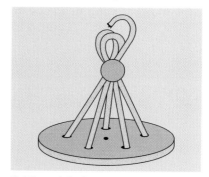

The wind chimes illustrated are decorated with two shells, one conch-shaped and one scallop-shaped. Instead of shells, you could use small bells, large beads, or even little mirror balls.

3 Using the 2.5 mm bit, drill a hole through the middle of the disk.
4 Sand the disk until it is smooth. Wipe it clean with a lint-free cloth.
5 Apply at least four coats of varnish to the disk, ensuring that each coat is fully dry before applying the next.

❸ PREPARING THE SHELLS

1 Using the 2.5 mm bit, carefully drill a hole through the scalloped shell, about 15 mm from the top.
2 Drill two holes in the back of the conch-shaped shell, 20 mm apart.

❹ ASSEMBLING THE CHIMES

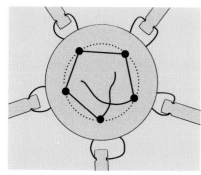

1 Cut 90 cm of fishing line. Leaving 5–10 cm of line sticking out of the top, thread one end through one hole in the disk, through the drilled holes in one of the pipes, and then back up through the same hole in the disk, suspending the pipe 1 cm beneath the disk. Take the end of the line over the top of the disk, thread it down the next hole, and secure another pipe in the same way as the first.
2 Continue weaving the line through the disk and pipes in this manner until all five pipes are evenly suspended. Tie the ends of the line together with a double knot.
3 Cut 60 cm of fishing line. Tie the scalloped shell to one end of the line

and secure it with a double knot. Thread the other end through one of the holes in the conch-shaped shell, out through the other hole, and then back through the first hole. Make sure that the shell is hanging horizontally. Adjust the position of this shell so it hangs about 30 cm above the scalloped shell.
4 Thread the free end of the fishing line through the middle hole of the wooden disk. Pull through sufficient line so that the conch-shaped shell is hanging level with the center of the shortest pipe. Knot the line several times until the knot is slightly bigger than the hole. Trim the end of the line and put a small quantity of glue on the knot to secure it inside the hole, just below the surface.
5 Trim the end of the line on the scalloped shell and secure it with glue.

❺ HANGING THE CHIMES

1 Knot one end of the white cord and thread the other end through one of the holes from the underside of the disk, pulling it all the way through.

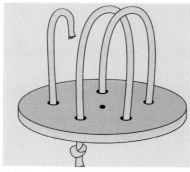

2 Carry the cord across and then down the next hole, leaving a 75 cm loop between the holes. Carry the cord across the underside of the disk and up through the next hole. Carry the cord down again through the next hole, once again leaving a 75 cm loop.

Carry the cord across the underside and up through the last hole. The free end of the cord will be a little longer than the doubled loops – about 50 cm.

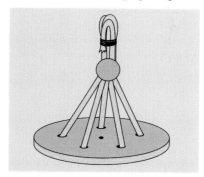

3 Thread the loops and the free end of the cord through one of the large wooden beads, positioning the bead about 8 cm above the wooden disk. Make sure the two loops are even and the chimes are hanging straight.

4 Fold the free end over so that there are three even loops. Bind this free end to the other cords with white sewing thread. Trim if necessary.
5 Push the ends of the loops through the remaining large bead, positioning it over the bound cords. Place a small quantity of glue around the top of the bead to secure it.

❻ FINISHING

1 Trim the end of the fishing line that is holding the chimes and push the knot down into the nearest hole, securing it with a little glue.
2 To finish off the middle hole, glue the small wooden bead over it.

NOTE
When cutting or drilling, use the clamps or the vise to hold the work steady.

Quilted oven cloth & mitt

Make this colorful gift for a friend and teach yourself to make quilted patchwork at the same time. Once you have worked out how to piece the patchwork, the project is easy to make.

WHAT YOU NEED

Master pattern **G48(a)** • colored fabric strips, 250 cm long, in varying widths (these will be joined to make a piece 250 cm **x** 20 cm) • 1 m backing fabric, 114 cm wide, in a toning or contrasting shade • 1 m batting, 90 cm wide • sewing thread to match the fabric • large wooden bead • tracing paper • pencil • scissors • tape measure • sewing machine
● *Technique pages 292–301, 305–6*

❶ MAKING THE FABRIC

1 Sew the strips of fabric together along their long edges to make a strip measuring 250 cm **x** 20 cm.

2 Trim the short ends of the strip so that they are straight and even.
3 Cut off a piece 160 cm long for the oven cloth. The remaining piece will make the mitt.

❷ CUTTING THE FABRIC BLOCKS FOR THE CLOTH

1 Measure and cut the 160 cm strip into eight 20 cm **x** 20 cm squares (step A in the diagram opposite).

NOTE
Use a 6 mm seam allowance, unless otherwise specified, and press the fabric and the seams as you go.

2 Cut each square into quarters diagonally and, following step B in the diagram, number the triangles on the wrong side of the fabric in the sequence shown. Make sure the stripes are running in the same direction as the stripes in the diagram.

❸ ASSEMBLING THE BLOCKS

1 Working with two squares' worth at a time, join the triangles together as follows to make four different blocks. The first block is shown in step C of the diagram. Join triangles 1 and 3, triangles 1 and 4, triangles 2 and 3, and triangles 2 and 4. With right sides facing, sew the quarters together.
2 Repeat step 1 with the other triangles, working with two squares' worth at a time. Stack together blocks of the same

COMBINING THE SQUARES

The pattern on the cloth is created by cutting eight identical 20 cm x 20 cm squares into triangles and then combining them as shown in step D. Combining the triangles in different ways will create other designs, and you may like to experiment. To make the design illustrated, make sure the stripes are running vertically (as in step B) before you number the triangles. If you divide the finished cloth into four squares, you will see that there are two distinct combinations of triangles.

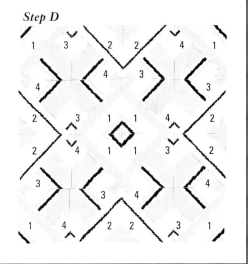

Step A   Step B   Step C

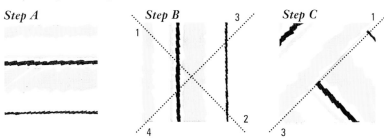

Step D

HINT

Do not use synthetic fabrics for this project, as they are not always heat or flame resistant. Use firmly woven cotton fabrics of about the same weight.

combination. You should end up with four blocks of each kind.

3 Following step D of the diagram, arrange your 16 blocks in the order shown, referring to the numbers you wrote on the back of each triangle.

4 With right sides facing, pin and sew the blocks together. Press all seams flat.

❹ QUILTING THE OVEN CLOTH

1 Cut pieces of backing fabric and batting a little larger than the assembled main fabric.

2 Lay out the backing wrong side up, then the batting, then the main fabric right side up. Baste the three layers together firmly along the outside edge.

3 With a long machine stitch, quilt along the seam lines joining the blocks, and along the diagonal seams joining the triangles. Trim all edges.

❺ FINISHING THE OVEN CLOTH

1 From the backing fabric, cut four strips 50 cm x 5 cm along the straight grain. These are for the binding.

2 With right sides facing, align one raw edge of one of the binding strips with the raw edge of the quilted cloth. Machine stitch through all layers 6 mm from the edge.

3 Turn the remaining raw edge of the binding strip to the back of the cloth, fold it under and slipstitch it into place along the line of machine stitching. Trim the ends of the binding level with the edges of the cloth.

4 Repeat steps 2 and 3 at the opposite edge of the cloth.

5 Bind the two remaining edges of the quilted cloth in the same way, tucking in the raw edges of the binding at the corners and neatening them with a few hand stitches.

❻ MAKING THE OVEN MITT

1 Using the master pattern and tracing paper, pencil and scissors, trace and cut out a working pattern for the oven mitt. Cut out one mitt shape from the main fabric strip and put it to one side.

2 From the backing fabric cut out three mitt shapes, and from the batting cut out two.

3 Take the main fabric mitt shape and the matching mitt shape cut from the backing fabric. Place these pieces together, with wrong sides facing. Place one of the batting shapes between them. Then pin or baste all three layers together.

4 Repeat step 3 with the two remaining mitt shapes.

5 With a long machine stitch, quilt diagonal lines across each of the layered shapes, with the rows of quilting stitches 2 cm apart.

6 With the right sides of the quilted pieces facing and using a 1 cm seam allowance, sew the two quilted shapes together around the outside of the mitt, leaving the wrist end open.

7 Trim the seam, clip the curves and turn the work to the right side.

8 Cut a strip of backing fabric 30 cm x 5 cm along the straight grain and use it to bind the raw wrist edge, following the same procedure as for binding the oven cloth.

❼ FINISHING THE OVEN MITT

1 From the backing fabric cut a strip 12 cm x 5 cm along the straight grain. Fold the long edges in 1 cm and press.

2 Fold the strip in half lengthwise with the wrong sides facing and top-stitch the folded edges together.

3 Thread on the wooden bead. Double the strip over to form a loop and stitch the raw ends to the inside of the thumb seam at the wrist.

NOTE

If the backing fabric has an obvious right side, make sure that two mitt shapes make up one complete pair and the third shape pairs with the mitt shape cut from the main fabric.

Elegant Victorian bows

Decorative bows can be mounted on a board for hanging on the wall or used to add a finishing touch to curtain tiebacks. One of these Victorian-style bows would give great pleasure to a friend who values the sumptuous elegance of an age that is past.

WHAT YOU NEED

Tape measure • scissors • sewing thread to match fabric • sewing needle • sewing machine
Wall-mounted bow
Suitable fabric: 1 strip 40 cm x 115 cm (for the bow), 1 strip 12 cm x 20 cm (for the hanging loop), 2 strips 14 cm x 43 cm (to cover the hanging board) • 2 pieces firm cardboard, 10 cm x 40 cm and 9.5 cm x 38.5 cm • 1 piece polyester batting, 10 cm x 40 cm • white glue • 3 decorative metal charms • 1 brass ring
Angel-trimmed bow
Suitable fabric: 1 strip 40 cm x 68 cm (for the loops), 1 strip 40 cm x 83 cm (for the tails), 2 strips 12 cm x 20 cm (for the knot) • small plastic, papier-mâché or wooden angel • artist's acrylic paints: gold, a color to match the fabric • small paintbrush • brass or plastic ring • white glue
● *Technique pages 292–301*

Wall bow

❶ MAKING THE BOW

If the fabric you have chosen is not suitable for making a tied bow, follow the instructions for making a picture bow instead (page 137).

1 With the right sides facing, fold the 40 cm x 115 cm fabric strip in half lengthwise.

2 Cut the fabric at each end of the strip at a slight angle to shape the tails of the bow.

3 Machine the long side and the two short sides together 1 cm from the raw edge, leaving an opening in the middle of the long side for turning.

4 Pull the fabric right side out through the opening. Press the fabric,

then close the opening by hand using slipstitch or by machine.

5 Tie the strip into a good, plump bow, making sure that both loops and ends are symmetrical.

❷ MAKING THE HANGING BOARD

1 To make the loop for hanging the bow, fold the 12 cm x 20 cm fabric strip in half lengthwise, right sides facing, then proceed as in steps 3 and 4 of "Making the bow."

2 Using white glue, attach the batting to one side of the 10 cm x 40 cm piece of cardboard.

3 Lay one 14 cm x 43 cm strip of fabric on a hard surface, wrong side facing up, and center the cardboard, batting side down, on top. Fold the edges of the fabric around the cardboard and glue them in place, mitering the corners if necessary to give a smooth appearance.

4 Cover the other piece of cardboard with the remaining fabric in the same way. (This piece of cardboard is not padded with batting.)

NOTE

The method of constructing a bow depends partly on personal preference and partly on the type of fabric you are using. Picture bows are especially suitable for very stiff fabrics that cannot easily be knotted or for crisp fabrics that may crease when knotted. The wall-mounted bow illustrated is a knotted bow and the angel-trimmed bow is a picture bow.

MAKING A PICTURE BOW

1 *Cutting out the fabric:* For the loops, cut a strip of fabric twice the width of the finished bow by twice

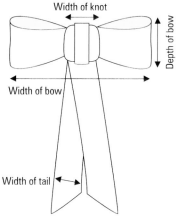

the depth, plus a seam allowance. For the tails, cut a strip twice the length of one tail by twice the width of the tail plus a seam allowance. For the knot, cut two strips about 30 cm long and twice the width of the finished knot plus a seam allowance.

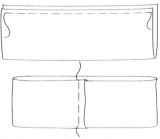

2 *Making the loops:* With right sides together, fold the fabric in half lengthwise. Machine stitch the long edges together. Turn the work to the right side and press. Fold a 1 cm hem into the inside of the fabric at one end and press it down. Slide this end over the other end and sew through all thicknesses, easing the inside fabric slightly to fit. This seam will be at the back of the bow.

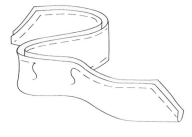

3 *Making the tails:* Fold the fabric for the tails in half lengthwise, right sides facing. Shape the tails of the bow by cutting the fabric at each end of the strip at a slight angle. Machine stitch around the raw edges, leaving an opening in the middle of the long side for turning. Pull the fabric right side out, through the opening. Press the fabric, then close the opening, by hand using slipstitch or by machine stitching.

4 *Making the knot:* With right sides facing, machine stitch the two strips of fabric for the knot together along the 30 cm edges. Turn the work to the right side and press.

Fold the strip you have made in half, seam edge to seam edge. Make a line of firm running stitches through all layers of fabric, parallel to the fold at half the width of the folded strip. Open out the strip and press the stitched section into a box pleat.

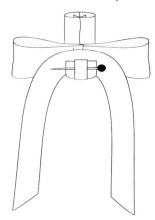

5 *Attaching the knot:* Lay the knot piece on a hard surface, box pleat downward, and lay the bow loop over the top with its center seam facing upward. Position the tail on top of the back seam of the loops. Fold the ends of the knot over the bow loops and tails, pulling the knot to bunch the loops and tails.

Pin the ends of the knot at the back, then pleat the loops and tails evenly under the knot. Trim the knot piece if necessary. Slipstitch the ends together at the back of the bow.

5 Thread the brass ring onto the fabric hanging loop. Glue the ends of the loop to the middle of the larger piece of cardboard on the wrong side (the side not covered with fabric).
6 With wrong sides facing, glue the pieces of covered cardboard together.
7 Center the bow at the top of the front of the hanging board (the side with the batting) and glue it in place.
8 Glue the metal charms onto the board, in a line under the bow.

Angel bow

1 Make a large picture bow with the fabric, following the instructions for "Making a picture bow."
2 Firmly stitch the brass ring to the center top of the knot so that the bow can be hung up.
3 Paint the angel the same color as the bow and allow the paint to dry.
4 Use the gold paint to add highlights to the angel.
5 When the paint has dried, glue the angel to the knot of the bow.

Luxury handkerchief bag

You can use remnants to make this quick and easy fabric bag for storing handkerchiefs, stockings, scarves or luxury soaps. Put a miniature bottle of perfume and some lace-edged handkerchiefs inside it to complete your gift.

VARIATIONS

● *Adapt the bag for storing soap, perfume or cosmetics by lining it with shower curtain fabric instead of silk.*

● *The bag can also contain an inner bag filled with potpourri, and can be hung in closets or from door handles or tucked in among cushions. Make a sachet of tulle to fit into the bag, leaving a small opening in one side. Turn the sachet right side out, fill it with potpourri, and close the opening with slipstitch. Place the sachet in the bag and tie the cord. Sew a fabric loop to the bag for hanging.*

❷ MAKING THE LINING

1 Using the lining fabric, proceed as for steps 1 and 2 of "Making the bag."
2 At the top, turn down a 1 cm double hem to the wrong side. Sew it down by machine or with slipstitch.

❸ ASSEMBLING THE BAG

1 Turn the bag right side out and leave the lining wrong side out.

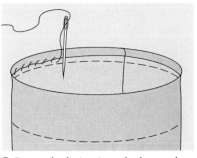

2 Insert the lining into the bag and baste it into place just below where the large hem folds over. Slipstitch the lining to the inside of the bag, easing it to fit if necessary. Remove the basting stitches.
3 Fold the upholstery cord in half and mark the mid-point. Measure about 9 cm down from the top of the bag along a side seam and stitch the mid-point of the cord to the side seam. Bring the cord to the other side of the bag and tie it in a bow.

WHAT YOU NEED

25 cm **x** 80 cm heavy upholstery fabric (chintz, tapestry or damask) ●
25 cm **x** 60 cm silk lining fabric ●
90 cm thick silk upholstery cord, in a shade to tone with the fabric ●
sewing thread to match the fabric ● tape measure ● dressmaking pins ● sewing needle ● sewing machine
● *Technique pages 292–301*

NOTE
It is important to neaten the raw edges by zigzagging or overlocking them because heavy upholstery fabric often has a complex weave that frays easily.

❶ MAKING THE BAG

1 Use the sewing machine to zigzag around the raw edges of the upholstery fabric to prevent fraying.
2 Fold the fabric in half widthwise with the right sides together, and straight machine stitch the sides together with a 1 cm seam allowance. Press the seams open.
3 To make a deep hem along the top edge, fold the top raw edge over 1 cm

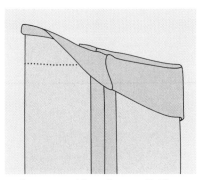

to the wrong side and press. Fold over a further 9 cm to the wrong side and slipstitch in place.

Easy mothball bags

A cluster of mothball bags is a great present. The bags are quick and easy to make, and are an excellent way of using up those odd scraps of cotton fabric that are too pretty to throw away.

WHAT YOU NEED

3 scraps printed cotton fabric, 20 cm x 20 cm • 2 m lace edging, 10 mm wide • 2.5 m ribbon, 3 mm wide • sewing thread to match the fabric • mothballs or naphthalene • scissors • pinking shears (optional) • sewing needle or sewing machine • tape measure
● *Technique pages 292–301*

❶ PREPARING THE FABRIC

1 Cut three 20 cm diameter circles from the fabric scraps.
2 To prevent the raw edges from fraying, neaten them by hand or by machine with zigzag stitch, or trim them with pinking shears.

❷ ATTACHING THE LACE

1 Cut the lace into lengths the measurement of the circumference of the circles plus 1 cm, and pin it around the circles so that it overlaps the edge of the fabric. Stitch it to the fabric.
2 Run small gathering stitches 2 cm in from the edge of each circle.

❸ ASSEMBLING THE BAGS

1 Place a little pile of mothballs (or naphthalene flakes) in the center of each circle, and then close the bags by carefully pulling the gathering threads. Tie the threads securely.
2 Tie a length of ribbon around the top of each bag to cover the gathering.
3 Tie the three bags together with ribbon and stitch the ends of the ribbon to make a loop for hanging.

NOTE

Mothballs (or naphthalene flakes) can be dangerous if swallowed. Fasten the bags securely so that the contents cannot fall out, and keep the bags out of reach of children.

Birdseed rings, cakes & bells

These environmentally friendly seedcake shapes will attract birds to a friend's garden where native plants and trees are not well enough established to provide food for birds. Seedcakes are also suitable for caged birds.

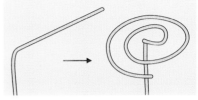

WHAT YOU NEED

Birdseed mixture (available from pet shops) • unprocessed bran • eggs • measuring cup • large mixing bowl • egg beater or whisk • cooking oil (for oiling the cooking containers) • aluminum foil • ovenproof container: ring mold, ramekin or terra-cotta flowerpot *For the cake and the bell* medium-gauge wire, at least 25 cm longer than the depth of the container • pliers

❶ PREPARING THE MIXTURE

To make one cup of the mixture, you will need three-quarters of a cup of birdseed and a quarter of a cup of bran mixed well together, and one egg. Multiply these amounts as required, according to the size of seedcake you are making. Make two cups of mixture for a small ramekin, and four cups for a 10 cm deep flowerpot or a 20 cm ring mold 3 cm deep.

1 Remove all the oven racks except one in the lower center, and preheat the oven to 160°C.
2 Oil the inside of your chosen container and line it with foil. Lightly oil the foil.
3 Lightly beat the eggs in a mixing bowl. Add the prepared seed-bran mixture and stir until well mixed.

❷ BAKING THE SEEDCAKES
Birdseed rings
1 Spoon the mixture into the oiled ring mold and press it down firmly using the back of a spoon.
2 Bake until the mixture is solid and sounds hollow when tapped. The baking time depends on size of mold used.
3 Transfer the container to a wire rack. Remove seedcake and foil when it is cool enough to touch.

Birdseed cakes and bells
1 Make a mount by using pliers to bend the wire at right angles about 15 cm (or less, if the container is very

small) from one end. Coil the bent end at right angles into a spiral.
2 *To make a flat cake:* Put a small amount of mixture into the bottom of the oiled ramekin. Place the wire coil on top of the mixture so that the shaft is upright and in the center and spoon remaining mixture into the container. Taking care not to move the wire mount, press the mixture down firmly, using the back of a spoon.
3 *To make a bell:* Spoon all of the mixture into the oiled flowerpot and press it down well. Push the uncoiled end of the wire through the center of the seed mixture and out through the hole in the bottom. Pull the wire until the coil is embedded below the surface of the seed mixture. Gently tamp the surface of the mixture until smooth.
4 Bake until the mixture is solid and sounds hollow when tapped. Baking time depends on size of container.
5 Transfer the container to a wire rack, taking care not to burn yourself on the wire. Remove the seedcake and foil when it is cool enough to touch.

❸ FINISHING

Thread a length of cord or ribbon through a seedcake ring to make a hanging loop. To hang flat cakes and bells, shape the free end of the wire mount into a hook with the pliers.

CAUTION
Use seedcakes only to attract birds to a new garden. Find out which birds are likely to visit the recipient's garden and use the appropriate birdseed mixture. Hang seedcakes out of reach of cats and other predators, and remove them if the garden is to be sprayed with chemicals.

Seagrass basket

Lined with calico, this handy braided seagrass basket can be used for shopping or picnics, or for storing craft materials.

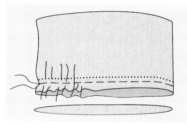

WHAT YOU NEED

10 m seagrass braid, 35 mm wide • oval basket base, 36 cm x 20 cm, with holes around the edge • raffia: 35 g natural, 10 g red, 10 g green, 10 g mauve • 1 m calico fabric • needle: size 20 chenille • sewing thread • dressmaking pins • sewing machine • fabric marking pen or pencil • scissors • hot glue gun (optional)

● *Technique pages 292–301, 309–10*

❶ MAKING THE BASKET

1 Cut two pieces of seagrass braid 60 cm long and put them to one side.
2 Thread the needle with a length of natural raffia. Sew the seagrass braid to the basket base by pushing the needle through each hole in the basket base and back through the seagrass braid.

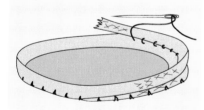

3 When you reach the starting point, begin the next round by placing the braid so that it slightly overlaps the previous row, forming a ridge up the side of the basket. Firmly stitch the braid where the rows overlap.
4 Continue adding rounds until the basket is about 15 cm deep.
5 Tuck the braid inside the rim of the basket directly above the starting position so that the top edge is even. Ensure that you have enough unused braid left to go around the circumference of the basket, and then cut off the braid and sew the end down firmly.
6 Thread the needle with red raffia and, using the photograph as a guide,

embroider three large daisies on one side of the basket. Embroider the centers in mauve and feather stitch the leaves in green.

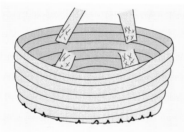

7 To make the handles, take the two 60 cm pieces of braid that were put aside. Cross them at the carrying point and place the ends 4 cm inside the rim of the basket and about 5 cm apart. Sew them in place with natural raffia. Stitch the handles together at the carrying point.

❷ LINING THE BASKET

1 For the side lining, cut out a rectangle of fabric 1 m long and 16 cm wide. With right sides facing, sew the short sides together, using a 1 cm seam. Run a gathering thread along one edge.
2 To make the base lining, place the basket on the fabric. Trace around the base with the pen or pencil and cut the shape from the fabric.

3 Draw up the side lining with the gathering thread until it fits the base lining. With right sides together, pin the base lining to the side lining, adjusting the gathers evenly. Stitch using a 1 cm seam.
4 With the wrong side of the lining against the inside of the basket, pin the lining in place around the rim. There is no need to turn the raw edge under. Fix in place either by sewing or with the hot glue gun.
5 To cover the raw edge and strengthen the basket, place the remaining length of braid inside the top rim and sew it to the outer braid along the edge using natural raffia.

HINT

For neatness and extra strength, when sewing the braids leave long ends of raffia that can be threaded back into the work.

Fragrant herbs in a terra-cotta pot

For a friend who likes to use fresh herbs, this pot planted with kitchen herbs is an ideal gift. The terra-cotta pot, painted in two colors, can be of any size, depending on which herbs you choose to plant and how many.

WHAT YOU NEED

Terra-cotta pot • herbs • potting soil • acrylic paints: 1 light shade and 1 dark • paintbrushes: 3 small decorating • polyurethane gloss or flat varnish
● *Technique pages 334–5*

① PAINTING THE POT

1 Using a small decorating brush, apply a coat of the lighter paint to the outside surface of the pot and the inside of the top rim. Allow to dry.
2 With another decorating brush, apply the darker paint in rings of varying thickness around the pot. Allow some of the first coat of paint to show through. Leave the paint to dry.
3 If the pot is to be placed outside, apply two coats of varnish to all painted surfaces. Allow the varnish to dry thoroughly between coats.

② PLANTING THE HERBS

If you are planting a variety of herbs in the same pot, be aware that they will grow much better if all the herbs you choose require the same conditions. Herbs such as rosemary, thyme, marjoram and sage love a very sunny position, whereas the mint family, chervil and chives prefer filtered sunlight and a more humid atmosphere.

NOTE

You will need to use a pot with a ring design on it if you wish to obtain the same results as in the photograph. The herbs can be grown from seeds or bought from a garden nursery.

CARE AND USE OF HERBS

● Most herbs are easy to grow in containers and need little maintenance, but it is still a good idea to include a note to the recipient of your gift explaining how to care for the herbs. If you grew the herbs from seed, include the seed packet, which often has instructions for caring for the plants. Similarly, herbs bought as seedlings from a nursery normally have instructions attached for caring for the plants.
● Herbs thrive in a stable temperature, free from drafts. Water them regularly, but err on the dry side. If in doubt, finger-test the soil – if it feels dry, it needs water. Always use tepid water (not cold), and spray with water if the weather is hot or the plants are inside. Turn pots regularly so that all parts of the plant receive equal light. During the growing season, apply liquid fertilizer every two weeks. During cold periods place delicate herbs under transparent cover in good light.
● Popular herbs suitable for pots include chervil, parsley, chives, sage, oregano, basil and thyme. Delicate herbs like lemongrass and lemon verbena grow well in pots because they can be brought indoors during cold snaps. Large plants like rosemary and bay are best grown in pots of their own, rather than planted in groups with other herbs.

Basil likes a very sunny spot that is well sheltered from the wind.
1 To ensure that drainage from the pot is sufficient, place a few stones, some pieces of broken pottery or a layer of gravel in the bottom of the pot to prevent waterlogging.
2 If you are growing herbs from seed, fill the pot with proprietary potting soil. Gently tamp the soil down with your fingertips. Plant the seeds as directed on the packet.
3 If you are potting the herbs up from nursery plants, put a little potting soil in the bottom of the pot, place the plant in the pot and pack soil around the root mass, tamping down gently.

SWEETHEARTS, BRIDES & GROOMS

For a partner,
we want to find a gift that
says "I love you." What
better way to express your
affection than to give
a little piece of yourself
by making your own
handcrafted gift?

Monogrammed linen handkerchief

Monogramming always adds a personal touch to a gift. This man's handkerchief, made from fine white linen, is monogrammed quite simply, using basic embroidery techniques.

WHAT YOU NEED

Master pattern **E35(a)** • white handkerchief linen, 40 cm x 40 cm • white no. 20 crochet cotton • fine white cotton sewing thread • needles: size 18 tapestry, size 7 crewel • tracing paper • dressmaker's carbon paper • pencil • dressmaking pins • scissors • sharp embroidery scissors • tape measure
● *Technique pages 292–301, 307–12*

❶ PREPARING THE FABRIC

1 Make sure that the fabric is square by pulling threads along each edge and trimming the fringe of counter threads as required.

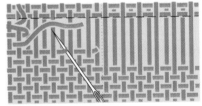

2 From the center of one edge, measure in 3 cm. Carefully cut two or three horizontal fabric threads and gently draw them out of the weave with the tip of a tapestry needle, to the left and right of the center, working toward the edges. If your fabric is very fine, you may need to pull four or five threads to make the draw threads noticeable. Stop drawing the threads 3.5 cm from the edge. Be very careful not to over-draw the threads.
3 Repeat step 2 along each edge. Carefully work lines of drawn threads toward each other, meeting at the corners of the inner square. If you

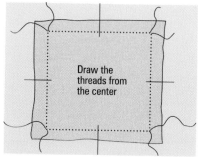

Draw the threads from the center

accidentally draw a thread too far, you can carefully weave it back in, but as this is a tedious job, it is best to work in very short sections as you approach the corners.

4 When the inner square of drawn threads is complete, weave the loose threads back into the wrong side of the fabric for about 2 cm. Trim off the ends of threads after weaving.

❷ MONOGRAMMING THE INITIAL

1 Trace and transfer the chosen letter from the master pattern onto one corner of the fabric. Before you start embroidering, study your chosen monogram. Some letters, for example "B," require two separate lines of embroidery. The letter "A" requires three lines.

2 Thread the tapestry needle with a piece of crochet cotton twice the length of the first design line to be stitched, plus an extra 25 cm.

3 Bring the crochet cotton up from the wrong side of the fabric at one end of the design line, leaving a tail of about 10 cm on the wrong side. Remove the needle.

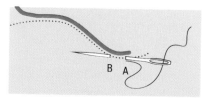

4 Using the crewel needle and fine sewing thread, take a small backstitch to secure the thread at point A. Work the first stitch from A to B, holding the crochet cotton in place on the design line with your other hand.

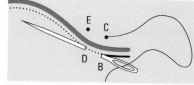

5 Stitch back from B to A and bring the needle out at C, which is just above the crochet cotton. Work the next stitch from C down to B, bringing the needle out at D.

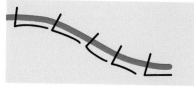

6 Stitch back from D to B and bring the needle out at E. Repeat this stitch sequence until the crochet cotton is anchored to the design line.

7 At the end of the design line, make a few anchoring stitches over the crochet cotton, then turn the crochet cotton and lay it back along the design line. Make a further anchoring stitch and continue as before, making sure that you stitch into the holes that were made on the first pass, so that a textured, hemstitched look is achieved.

8 When you have returned to the beginning of the stitching line, thread the crochet cotton into the tapestry needle again and take it back through to the wrong side of the fabric. Make several overcasting stitches with the fine cotton thread over the crochet cotton to anchor it, then take the fine cotton to the back also. Stitch into the back of the fabric to end off. Neatly clip the ends of the crochet cotton close to the fabric.

9 Repeat this procedure for the other design lines, as required.

❸ FINISHING THE DRAWN THREAD WORK

1 When the embroidery has been completed, rinse the fabric gently to remove any transfer lines. Dry flat and press well from the wrong side.

2 Press a double hem around the fabric so that the hem edge is one thread from the outer edge of the square of drawn threads. Miter the corners, tuck any loose threads into the hem and baste the hem in place.

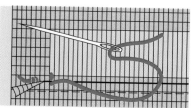

3 Working from the wrong side, start at the left edge and take a small vertical stitch just to the right of the drawn thread work, making sure you catch in the hem. Pass the needle around three or four threads and pull them together in a bundle.

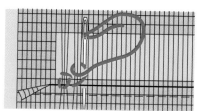

4 Take the needle through to the right side and pass it back to the wrong side so that it catches in the hem again.

5 Continue hemstitching in this manner along each edge.

6 Turn the work the other way around and, still working from the back, hemstitch the opposite edge, catching the same bundles of thread that you caught at the other side. This time there is no hem to catch in.

Before you begin embroidering, study the shape of your letter to decide how many lines you will need to form the letter, and which line you will stitch in place first.

Marble kitchen board

This attractive marble board has a multitude of uses – breadboard, cheese or fruit platter, or heat pad – and is a practical gift for a partner who enjoys cooking and entertaining.

WHAT YOU NEED

Marble tile, between 300 mm and 400 mm square • 2 m decorative wooden beading, the same depth as the combined thickness of the tile and the plywood • marine plywood, 400 mm x 400 mm x 18 mm • 4 rubber feet with screws • epoxy resin glue • cellulose or plastic-based filler • wood stain or varnish • paintbrush • pencil • miter box • handsaw • clamps • drill
● *Technique pages 338–42*

❶ MAKING THE BOARD

1 Put the marble tile on the plywood and draw around it with a pencil.

2 Trim the plywood to this traced size, and then glue the plywood to the tile with epoxy resin glue. Clamp together firmly and put aside until the glue has set thoroughly.

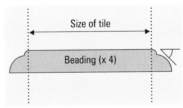

3 Measure the edges and use the miter box to cut four pieces from the wooden beading to the dimensions of the tile. Cut the ends at a 45° angle.

4 Glue the beading into position around the tile and plywood with the epoxy glue. Again, clamp together until the glue has set.

5 Fill in any gaps between the tile and the beading with cellulose or plastic-based filler.

6 Apply stain or varnish to the wooden beading, taking care not to coat the marble tile.

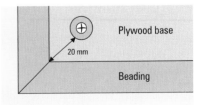

7 Drill a hole 20 mm from each corner of the plywood base and screw in the four rubber feet.

Trinket box

Transform a wooden box into a reminder of a wonderful time spent together at the beach. The box can be used to store buttons, paperclips or small trinkets and treasures.

WHAT YOU NEED

Small wooden box • shells of varying shapes, sizes and colors • artist's acrylic paints: aqua, yellow, white • paint palette • natural sea sponge or scrunched-up rag • hot glue gun and glue sticks • clear gloss varnish • small paintbrush
● *Technique pages 334–5*

❶ PREPARATION

1 Wash the shells thoroughly in a bucket of warm soapy water, rinse them well and allow them to dry.
2 Sort the shells into three sizes: small, medium and large.
3 On the paint palette, mix a small amount of aqua paint with a little white to make a mid-aqua shade. Take up a little of the paint on a damp sponge and apply it to the interior and the sides of the box. Sponging creates a soft, lightly textured effect.
4 When the first coat is dry, mix a lighter shade of aqua and apply a second, more sparing coat so that the mid-aqua is still visible. When this coat is dry, add a little white to the yellow to make a pale straw color, and apply delicate highlights here and there with the sponge.

❷ DECORATING THE LID

1 Arrange the large shells and the medium-sized shells on the lid of the box, placing the largest in the center and using contrasting shapes, forms

> **CAUTION**
> *Do not paint the rim of the box or lid where the two pieces fit together, as they will be liable to stick together in warm weather.*

and colors as secondary points of interest. Move the shells around until you are satisfied with the effect.

2 Heat the glue gun and glue the shells in place, working from the center of the lid toward the edges. To create a natural effect, the shells should be overlapped and butted together in an irregular fashion until the lid is covered.
3 Use the smaller shells to fill the crevices. You can also create interest by gluing groups of smaller shells onto larger ones.

❸ FINISHING

Coat the shells with clear gloss varnish to seal them and give a glossy finish.

Braided leather belt

Make this beautiful belt from good-quality leather, and it will last for years. The design is suitable for either a man or a woman, or the belt could be made for both to share.

WHAT YOU NEED

Strip of leather, 35 mm wide **x** about 150 cm long • matching strip of leather, 25 mm wide **x** 12 cm long • solid metal belt buckle, to fit belt 35 mm wide • black leather dye • small, stiff sponge brush • pencil • long steel ruler • craft knife or utility knife, suitable for cutting leather • access to shoemaker or leather worker (for assembling and stitching the belt)

❶ PREPARING THE LEATHER

1 Ensure that the edges of the long leather strip are perfectly straight and even. Trim them with the craft knife or utility knife if necessary.
2 On the wrong side of the leather, mark off 35 cm at each end. In the center of the strip, between the marks, carefully measure and mark six parallel lines 5 mm apart along the strip.
3 Use the craft knife or utility knife to cut along the lines. At one end, start the inner four cuts 2 cm in from the outer two (this will be the buckle end). At the other end, start the outer two cuts 3 cm in from the inner pair of cuts, and the cuts between 2 cm in from the inner two cuts (this will be the tongue end).

BUCKLING UP

Select a buckle heavy enough to match the belt and, as a general rule, choose a plain design if the belt is for a man and a more elaborate one for a woman. The buckle illustrated is of brass bound with a narrow strip of fine, soft leather, but plain metal would look equally good. The buckle must be made of solid, heavy metal – plastic or cheap, soft metal will not last.

4 Using the sponge brush, carefully apply black leather dye to all the cut edges of the leather strip. Allow the dye to dry thoroughly.

❷ MAKING THE BRAID

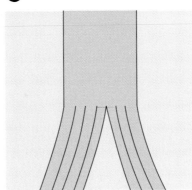

1 Working from the buckle end, divide the cut portion of the belt into four strips on the left and three strips on the right.

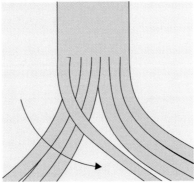

2 Draw the outer left-hand strip over the three other left-hand strips to the right-hand side.

3 Draw the outer right-hand strip over the two other right-hand strips and the strip that was originally on the outer left.
4 Repeat steps 2 and 3 until you have braided in all seven strips once, finishing with a step 2. Each time, you will draw the outer strip over three strips to the opposite side of the belt.

5 Thread the tongue end of the belt through the upper gap between the braided strips, from front to back. Then thread the tongue end of the belt through the lower gap between the strips, again from front to back.

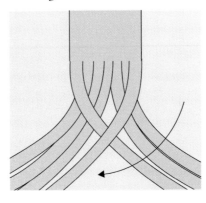

6 To braid the second sequence of seven strips, draw the outer right-hand strip over to the opposite side of the belt.

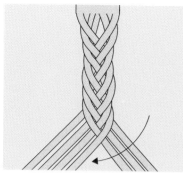

7 Proceed as for the first braiding sequence, drawing strips over alternately from side to side until you have braided in all seven strips. Repeat step 5 to complete the sequence.

8 Repeat the whole sequence until the complete braid is formed.

③ ASSEMBLING THE BELT

To put the belt together and add the finishing touches, you will need to find a shoemaker or leather worker who has the right equipment to punch the holes, attach the loop and buckle to the belt and add any decorative stitching that you require.

1 Using the craft knife or utility knife, taper the tongue end of the belt. At the buckle end, mark a point 20 cm from the braid and cut an oval hole 2 cm long for the prong of the buckle.

2 Using the black leather dye and the sponge brush, dye the cut edges of the hole, the cut edges of the tapered tongue end, and the cut edges of the 12 cm strip of leather.

3 Ask the shoemaker to stitch the 12 cm strip of leather into a loop that will fit the belt, trimming off any excess. Slide the loop over the buckle end of the belt.

4 Work the oval hole over the prong of the buckle and ask the shoemaker to stitch down the short end of leather to the wrong side to secure the buckle, trimming off any excess.

5 Ask the shoemaker to punch six holes 25 mm apart along the tongue end in the correct positions for the recipient's waist measurement.

6 If you want decorative stitching, get the shoemaker to stitch your desired pattern along the edges of the unbraided sections of the belt.

Man's luxury sweater

This richly patterned sweater is the perfect gift for that special person in your life. It has been designed to fit generously for a casual yet smart look.

WHAT YOU NEED

Size	12	14	16	18	20
Chest (cm)	90	95	100	105	110
Sweater measures (cm)					
Chest	111	115	119	123	127
Length	68	68	69	69	70
Sleeves	48	48	48	48	48

The yarn used in this project is Patons DK (50 g balls).
Colors are as follows:
main color (mc), cream;
1st contrast color (cc1), gosling;
2nd contrast color (cc2), iced green;
3rd contrast color (cc3), steel;
4th contrast color (cc4), dark navy.

mc	11	11	12	12	13
cc1	2	2	2	2	2
cc2	4	4	4	4	4
cc3	3	3	3	3	3
cc4	3	3	3	3	3

Knitting needles: 4.50 mm (no. 7), 3.25 mm (no. 10) • wool sewing needle
● *Technique pages 323–7*

CHECKING THE GAUGE

Before you begin knitting the sweater, check the gauge of your knitting. This is necessary in order to ensure that the measurements of the finished garment will be as close as possible to the size specified in the pattern.

Knit a sample square of the pattern, using 4.50 mm needles. You should have 23.5 stitches to a width of 10 cm. If you have fewer stitches, you should use smaller needles; if you have more stitches, use bigger needles.

❶ BACK

Using 3.25 mm needles and mc, cast on 122 (126-134-138-142) sts.
1st row: K2, ★ P2, K2, rep from ★ to the end.
2nd row: P2, ★ K2, P2, rep from ★ to the end.
Rep 1st and 2nd rows 10 times; inc 11 (11-9-9-9) sts evenly across the last row...133 (137-143-147-151) sts,

NOTE

Strand the colors loosely across the back; do not weave them in.

making 22 rows rib in all. Change to pair of 4.50 mm needles.
Work in pat from graph until the work measures 41 cm from beg, working last row on the wrong side. Tie a colored thread at each end of the last row to mark beg of armholes, as there is no armhole shaping. ★★
Work 62 (62-64-64-68) rows pat.

Shaping the shoulders

Keeping pat correct, cast off 11 (12-12-12-13) sts at beg of next 6 rows, then 12 (10-13-14-13) sts at beg of foll 2 rows. Cast off rem 43 (45-45-47-47) sts.

KNITTING GRAPH

Knit the Fair Isle pattern by following the stitches and colors as indicated on the graph. Odd rows are knit rows and even rows are purl.

In Fair Isle knitting, loop unused yarns quite loosely across the back of the work to the end of the row – otherwise the finished work will pucker.

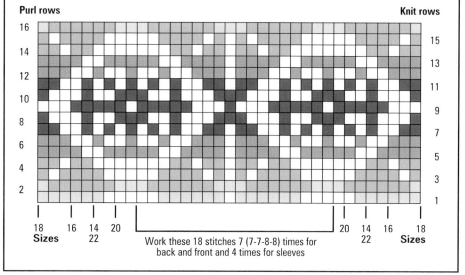

Purl rows

Knit rows

Sizes 18 16 14 20 / 22

Work these 18 stitches 7 (7-7-8-8) times for back and front and 4 times for sleeves

20 14 16 18 / 22 Sizes

❷ FRONT

Work as for back to ★★.
Work 4 (4-4-4-6) rows pat.

Shaping the neck

Work in pat 53 (55-58-60-62) sts, cast off 27 sts, pat to end.
Cont on last 53 (55-58-60-62) sts.
Keeping pat correct, dec at neck edge in every foll 6th (6th-6th-4th-4th) row until 48 (46-49-57-60) sts rem.
For sizes 14, 20 and 22 only: dec in every foll 8th (6th-6th) row until 45 (50-52) sts rem.
For all sizes: work 4 (4-6-6-6) rows, following the pat.

Shaping the shoulder

Cast off 11 (12-12-12-13) sts at beg of next and alt rows, 3 times in all, until 12 (10-13-14-13) sts rem.
Work 1 row.
Cast off.
Join yarn to rem 53 (55-58-60-62) sts and work other side to correspond, decreasing at the neck edge. Work 1 less row before starting to shape the shoulder.

❸ SLEEVES

Using 3.25 mm needles and mc, cast on 58 (58-62-62-62) sts.
Work 17 rows rib as for back.
18th row: Rib 8 (8-10-10-4), ★ inc in next st, rib 1, rep from ★ to last 8 (8-10-10-4) sts, rib to end...79 (79-83-83-89) sts in total.
Work in pat from graph as for size 14 (14-16-16-18), and, working extra sts into pat, inc at each end of 5th and then alt rows until there are 85 (85-89-89-93) sts. Then inc at each end of every foll 4th row until there are 123 (123-127-127-131) sts in total.
Cont without shaping until work measures 48 cm from beg, working last row on wrong side.
Cast off loosely.

HINT

If this large number of stitches will not fit comfortably on the needle, use a circular needle.

❹ COLLAR

Using 3.25 mm needles and mc, cast on 230 (234-242-246-254) sts.
Work 40 rows rib as for back.
Keeping rib correct, cast off 5 sts at beg of next 16 rows...150 (154-162-166-174) sts.
Next row: Cast off 5 sts, rib 29 (29-31-31-33), (work 2 tog) 41 (43-45-47-49) times, rib to end... 104 (106-112-114-120) sts.
Keeping both ribs correct, cast off 5 sts at beg of next 11 rows.
Cast off rem 49 (51-57-59-65) sts.

❺ MAKING UP

1 With a slightly damp cloth and warm iron, press lightly.
2 Using backstitch, join the shoulder seams, the sleeve seams and the side seams to the colored threads.
3 Sew in sleeves, and then sew collar in position, crossing left over right at the center front.
4 Press seams. Do not press ribbing.

Hanging flower basket

Suitable for hanging from a veranda or patio, or in a bathroom, this is a practical gift for a partner who loves potted plants. The wire basket can be flattened or elongated to suit the space it is to fill or to hold a favorite flowerpot.

WHAT YOU NEED

6 m galvanized wire, 3.15 mm diameter • 60 cm galvanized wire, 1.25 mm diameter • pliers • wire cutters • ruler • exterior metal paint

❶ PREPARING THE WIRE

1 Using the wire cutters, cut the 3.15 mm diameter wire into one piece 46 cm long (for the base) and nine pieces 61 cm long (eight pieces for the sides and one for the handle).

2 Cut the 1.25 mm diameter wire in half to make two 30 cm brace wires.

3 Using the pliers, make a hook 2 cm long at each end of the base wire. The hooks should be at right angles to one another so they will loop together.

4 Bend each end of the pieces for the side wires and the handle into 2 cm hooks so that the hooks are facing one another on the same plane.

❷ ASSEMBLING THE BASKET

The base

1 Form the base wire into a circle, hook the ends together and crimp them shut with the pliers.

2 Wind the end of one brace wire three or four times around the base wire near the joined hooks. Keeping

HINT

To prepare the basket for planting, line it with sphagnum moss and fill it with good quality potting mixture. Alternatively, buy and fill an attractive pot from a plant nursery and set it in the basket on a bed of sphagnum moss. If you are going to use a plant pot, select the pot before finishing the basket so that you can shape the basket accordingly.

the brace wire taut, wind the other end around the base wire directly opposite the first wound end.

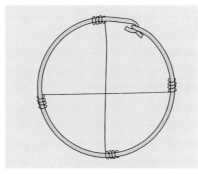

3 Using the same technique, wind the remaining brace wire at right angles to the first. The base circle should now be divided into four equal segments by the two brace wires.

The sides

1 Take one of the side wires, one end in each hand with the hooks facing inward, and draw the ends together until the distance separating the ends equals the diameter of the base circle.

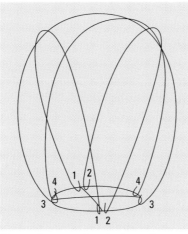

2 Hook one end to the base alongside one of the brace wires. Keeping on the same side of the brace wire, hook the other end of the side wire to the opposite side of the circle. Crimp both hooks shut with the pliers.

3 Take a second side wire. Following the same procedure and keeping to the other side of the brace wire, hook the ends over the base wire.

4 In the same way, hook wire 3 to the base wire alongside one end of the other brace wire (at 90° to wires 1 and 2). Hook the other end to the opposite side of the base, taking care to

keep wire 3 underneath wires 1 and 2. Attach wire 4 alongside wire 3 on the other side of the brace wire.

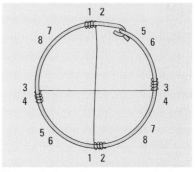

5 Attach the other two pairs of side wires (5 and 6, and 7 and 8) in the same way, filling the spaces between the first two pairs.

The handle

1 Before attaching the handle, you may want to compress the basket to make it more squat or squeeze it to make it longer and thinner.

2 When you are satisfied with the shape, draw the ends of the handle wire together as for the side wires.

3 Hook one end over the intersection of side wires 1 and 5 and the other over the intersection of side wires 2 and 6. Crimp both hooks shut to enclose the side wires.

❸ FINISHING THE BASKET

For a special finishing touch, paint the basket with exterior gloss metal paint in your partner's favorite color.

Sewing box

This very practical sewing box is a gift that any keen home dressmaker would be thrilled to receive. The lid of the box opens out to ensure that all sewing equipment is at the user's fingertips.

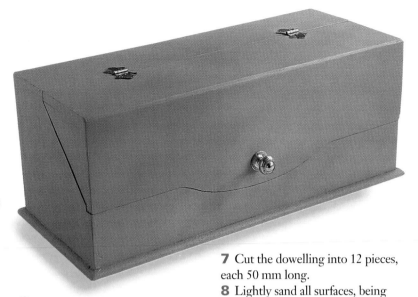

WHAT YOU NEED

Master pattern **G45(a–i)** • MDF or plywood, 1200 mm **x** 600 mm **x** 12 mm • 650 mm dowel, 6 mm diameter • 2 decorative 20 mm brass hinges, with screws no longer than 12 mm • brass knob, about 20 mm in diameter • 1500 mm length 6 mm quarter round molding • 12 rubber grommets (8 mm, with 5 mm diameter holes – they must fit tightly over the 6 mm dowelling) • 25 brads (25 mm) • 20 brads (12 mm) • white woodworking glue • paint, stain or clear varnish • paintbrushes • fabric, 12 cm **x** 15 cm • thick plastic foam, 11 cm **x** 7 cm • 4 decorative brass upholstery tacks • sewing thread • sewing machine • sewing needle: medium ball-point • handsaw or circular saw • jigsaw • hammer • ruler • drill and drill bits • miter box • screwdriver • medium- and fine-grade sandpaper • pencil • tracing paper • transfer paper
● *Technique pages 292–301, 338–42, 343–4*

❶ PREPARING THE PLYWOOD

1 Trace all the master pattern pieces onto the tracing paper.
2 Mark out all pattern pieces on the plywood as shown in the cutting guide, taking care to mark all dotted abutment and cutting lines.
3 To avoid confusion later, label all the pieces lightly in pencil.
4 Using the handsaw or the circular saw, cut out all pieces accurately.
5 Use the jigsaw to cut away the lid from the lower front along the curved dotted cutting line.
6 Cut away the triangular lid ends from the sides along the dotted lines.

Cutting guide

Before you begin to cut, ensure that you have marked all dotted abutment and cutting lines. You should also check all measurements and label each piece.

7 Cut the dowelling into 12 pieces, each 50 mm long.
8 Lightly sand all surfaces, being careful not to round joining edges.

❷ ASSEMBLING THE BOX

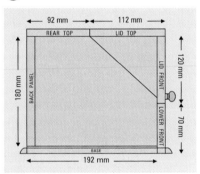

1 Glue and nail the main pieces in the following order with white wood-working glue and 25 mm brads:
● shelf front to shelf (shelf front should be at right angles to shelf);
● shelf to inner surface of dividers;
● dividers to base;
● side and back panels to top of base;
● lower front to front edges of base, sides and dividers;
● rear top panel to top of sides, back panel and dividers.
2 Measure and mark the quarter round molding to fit around the base and miter-cut it as required. Apply glue to the molding and nail it in place with 12 mm brads.

❸ ASSEMBLING THE LID

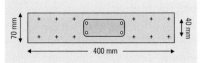

Cutting guide diagram labels: Spool holder • Base • Back panel • Lid front • Lower front • Lid top • Rear top • Shelf front • Shelf • Lid end • Side • Inside divider • Lid end • Side • Inside divider

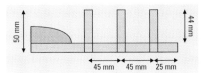

50 mm 44 mm 45 mm 45 mm 25 mm

1 With a 5 mm bit, drill 12 holes through the spool holder in the positions shown. These holes are for the 6 mm dowel for the spools.
2 Glue and nail the spool holder to the inside of the lid top, centered vertically and horizontally.
3 Glue and nail the triangular lid ends to the inside of the lid top.
4 Glue and nail the lid front to the lid top and to the triangular ends.
5 Glue the ends of the dowels and insert them in the holes drilled in the spool holder.

④ FINISHING

1 Sand all surfaces to a smooth finish. Paint, stain or varnish all surfaces.

2 Put the lid on top of the box in the closed position. Attach the lid to the rear top panel with the hinges, placing the hinges 100 mm from the ends.
3 Screw the brass knob to the lid front as marked on the pattern.
4 Push a grommet onto the top of each dowel to hold the spools on the dowels when the lid is closed.

⑤ PINCUSHION

1 Fold the fabric in half widthwise with right sides facing.
2 Machine stitch along the long side and one short side, leaving a 5 mm seam allowance, and then turn the work right side out.
3 Slide the foam into the fabric and close the opening with slipstitch.
4 Center the pincushion between the two sets of dowels on the spool holder and fix it in place with an upholstery tack at each corner.

NOTE
Check that you have transferred all the patterns to the wood correctly. The dimensions should be as shown below.
- *lid front/lower front, 192 mm (includes 2 mm to allow for clearance) x 500 mm*
- *lid top, 112 mm x 500 mm*
- *spool holder, 70 mm x 400 mm*
- *rear top, 92 mm x 500 mm*
- *back panel, 180 mm x 500 mm*
- *base, 192 mm x 500 mm*
- *sides/dividers, 180 mm x 180 mm*
- *shelf, 90 mm x 240 mm*
- *shelf front, 20 mm x 240 mm*

Romantic flowers in a pot

Flowers are a lovely way to say you care. Plant your sweetheart's favorite flower in this decorated pot, and your gift will be a charming reminder of your devotion.

WHAT YOU NEED

Terra-cotta flowerpot • small flowering plants • potting soil, enough to fill your pot • suitable images from wrapping paper, books or greeting cards • artist's gesso • white glue • wallpaper paste • artist's acrylic gloss medium (sealer) • polyurethane gloss varnish • Blu Tack • paintbrushes: 2 small (for gluing and sealing), 20 mm imitation sable (for varnishing) • wet-and-dry sandpaper: no. 80 • rubber sanding block • rubber roller • pieces of thick kitchen sponge • fine, curved scissors • pencil
● *Technique pages 329–31*

This project uses some découpage techniques. However, it does not require the application of a great many coats of varnish, so it will not have the porcelain-like finish that marks true découpage.

❶ PREPARATION

1 Sand all surfaces of the flowerpot lightly with sandpaper.
2 Apply a coat of artist's gesso to the outside of the pot. Allow the gesso to dry, then sandpaper the surface again. Seal the inside and outside surfaces with artist's acrylic medium.
3 Plan where you will put your images by fixing them to the pot with Blu Tack and rearranging them until you are satisfied with the design. Trim the images with sharp scissors if necessary. Remove the images and lightly mark their positions on the pot.
4 Seal the images on both sides with artist's acrylic medium. Be careful not to make the coat of sealer too heavy, as the images may then become less

NOTE
Remember to choose plants that are suitable for the conditions in which they will be grown.

pliable, so that it will be difficult to mold them around the pot. Allow the images to dry thoroughly.

❷ FIXING THE IMAGES

1 Taking one image at a time, apply a mixture of three parts wallpaper paste and one part white glue to the pot where the image is to go, and a small amount to the right side of the image.
2 Massage and mold the image into the surface, adding more glue if neces-

sary. Roll over the image with the rubber roller to get rid of any lumps of glue or air bubbles. Remove the excess glue with a wet sponge.
3 Repeat steps 1 and 2 until all the images are in place.
4 Apply two coats of artist's acrylic medium to the surface, allowing each coat to dry thoroughly before applying the next.

❸ FINISHING

1 Apply at least two coats of varnish, allowing the first coat to dry before applying the next. Leave the pot to dry thoroughly.
2 Fill the pot with potting soil and plant the flower according to the instructions supplied by the nursery.

Aromatic beeswax candles

Make these candles to set the mood for you and your partner on a special occasion. Beeswax is long-burning and does not drip, and when the candles are lit they will fill the room with the delicious scent of natural honey.

WHAT YOU NEED

Sheets of preformed beeswax • length of braided wick, 3 mm wide • ruler • large pair of scissors • hair dryer (in cold weather)

❶ MAKING THE CANDLES

1 Experiment with the shapes and sizes of the candles by cutting out sheets of thin, pliable cardboard and rolling them up in various ways.
2 When you are satisfied with the shape you have achieved, unroll and flatten the cardboard, place it on a beeswax sheet and cut carefully around it. To increase the thickness, add more sheets of wax.
3 Cut a piece of wick 2 cm longer than the finished candle will be.
4 Unless it is a fairly warm day, you may need to soften the beeswax slightly to make it pliable and to prevent the sheet from cracking as you roll. To soften the beeswax, wave a hair dryer over the sheet for about 10 seconds or leave the beeswax near a sunny window for about 10 minutes.

5 Lay the softened beeswax flat on a clean surface. Pinch off a small piece of the wax from the place where you will begin to roll and set it aside. Place the wick along the edge of the sheet and push it gently into the wax.
6 Turn the edge of the sheet over the wick to make a small fold and press lightly to encase the wick.
7 Using the palms of both hands, roll the wax away from you with a light but even pressure, making sure that the base of the candle is level so that it will sit flat when it is finished.

HINTS

When they are alight, beeswax candles give off a natural honey-like fragrance. However, if you would like to add a special scent to the candles, use an eye dropper to drop fragrant oil onto the wick before you roll the beeswax. A small candle requires three or four drops, and a large one between 10 and 20 drops.

CANDLE SHAPES

Tapered candles
To achieve an attractive tapered look, trim one side of the sheet diagonally and roll from the long end.

Square candles
To make a square candle, place a ruler close to the edge of the beeswax sheet and turn the wax around it. Repeat this step each time you turn the sheet.

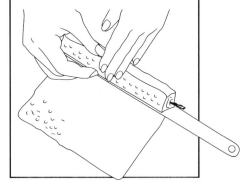

8 Continue rolling more sheets of beeswax around the first until the candle is the thickness you want. Press the outside edge of the wax against the candle to prevent it from unrolling.
9 If the shape has become a little distorted because of uneven pressure when rolling, you can make the candle perfectly cylindrical by rolling it briskly back and forth a few times.

❷ FINISHING

1 Trim the wick to 1.5 cm and pinch the piece of reserved wax around the base of the wick. This will help it to light more easily.
2 As a final touch to the gift, group a few candles of complementary shapes and include a box of luxury matches.

Man's summer nightshirt

Made from cool, pure cotton, this nightshirt will help to keep your man comfortable, even on the hottest nights.

WHAT YOU NEED

Master pattern **F38(a–e)** • 2.5 m lightweight cotton fabric, 150 cm wide • 80 cm iron-on interfacing • sewing thread to match fabric • 3 medium-sized buttons, 15 mm diameter • tracing paper • pencil • scissors • needle: general sewing • dressmaking pins • tape measure • sewing machine
● *Technique pages 292–301, 343–4*

❶ CUTTING THE PATTERN

1 Using the tracing paper, pencil and scissors, trace and cut out a working pattern from the master pattern. Transfer all markings.
2 Cut out the pattern pieces from the fabric. Use the collar and front facing pattern pieces to cut the interfacings.

❷ MAKING THE COLLAR

1 Staystitch the neckline of the nightshirt 1 cm from the raw edges. With right sides together, machine stitch the front and back shoulder seams.

Zigzag or overlock the edges together and press the seams toward the back.

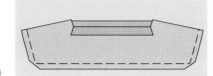

2 Iron the collar interfacing to the wrong side of one collar piece. Zigzag or overlock the outer edges. Place the right sides of the collar pieces together and machine around the unnotched edge, leaving the neck edge open. Trim the seam allowance and the corners. Clip the neck edge of the collar at the large dots to the seamline. Turn down the middle section of the interfaced side and press.

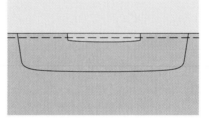

3 Turn the collar to the right side and press. With the right side of the non-interfaced side of the collar to the right side of the nightshirt, staystitch the collar to the neckline, matching the large dots.

NOTES
● *Consult technique pages 295–6 to find out how to match the stripes when you are cutting plaid or striped fabrics.*
● *All seam allowances are 1.5 cm and all seams are over-locked or zigzagged to finish.*

❸ ATTACHING THE FRONT FACINGS

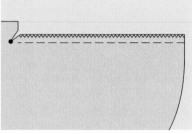

1 Starting at the hem, with the right sides of the center front seams together, machine stitch to the large dot and backstitch to reinforce. Clip diagonally to the large dot, overlock or zigzag the edges together, and press the seam toward one side.

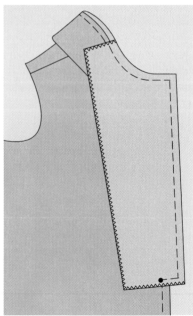

2 Iron the interfacings to the front facing pieces. Starting at the large dot on the center front seam, with right sides together, pin the facings along both sides of the center front opening and around the neck edges, overlapping the collar. From the large dot

---

CUTTING GUIDE

Fold the fabric in half lengthwise and lay out the pattern pieces as shown to cut two of each piece. Place the center backs of the back piece and the two collar pieces on the fold. For the interfacings, cut two front facing pieces and one complete collar piece from the iron-on interfacing.

To make the nightshirt with plaid or striped fabric, you will need extra fabric to match the stripes. If you cannot buy the fabric you want in the 150 cm width specified here, measure the pattern pieces to work out how much 115 cm wide or 90 cm wide fabric you will need to buy.

Fold

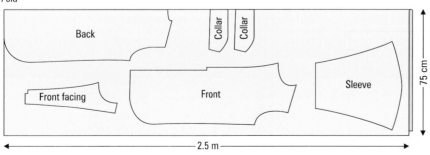

at the center front, stitching through all layers, machine stitch a continuous seam up the center front opening, around the front and back neck and down the other center front opening to the large dot. Pivot the needle at the corners, and backstitch to reinforce the beginning and end of the seam.

3 Trim the seams and corners and clip the neck edge so that the work will be smooth and neat when it is turned right side out.

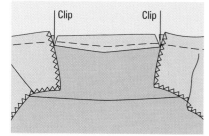

4 Clip diagonally through all layers of the neck seam at the shoulders, so that the exposed part of the seam at the back of the neck can be pressed up into the collar.

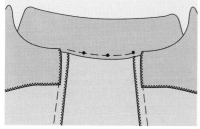

5 Turn the facings to the inside of the nightshirt and press. Press the exposed back neck seam up into the collar and bring the folded edge of the collar over the machine stitching at the back neck. Stitch the folded edge down by hand or machine, and secure the facings at the shoulder seams.

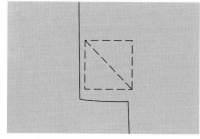

6 Reinforce the center front opening at the large dots by topstitching a square and then bisecting it with one diagonal line of stitching.

④ ASSEMBLING THE NIGHTSHIRT

1 With right sides together, pin and machine stitch the sleeves to the armholes. Neaten the raw edges and press the seams toward the sleeves. Neaten the wrist edges of the sleeves.

2 With right sides facing, pin the front and back side seams together, matching the dots and underarm seams. Machine from the dots on the side seams to the wrists. At the side seam openings, clip the front hem to the machine stitching.

3 Starting at one wrist, neaten the side seam and continue around the back hem to the opposite side, finishing at the other wrist. Then neaten the raw edge of the front hem.

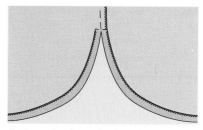

4 Press the front, back and sleeve hems to the inside and machine hem at the desired width from the edge.

⑤ FINISHING

1 Mark and machine three buttonholes on the left front in the positions marked on the master pattern.

2 Sew the buttons on the center line of the right front to match up with the buttonhole positions.

Elegant indoor planter box

This decorative planter box will delight your partner and add a touch of style to any home. The box is large and strong enough to hold a plant pot about 30 cm in diameter and 36 cm high.

WHAT YOU NEED

Exterior quality milled lumber: 70 mm x 12 mm (finished size), 2 lengths 4500 mm and 1 length 3300 mm; 50 mm x 50 mm (finished size), 1 length 5400 mm; 20 mm x 20 mm (finished size), 1 length 3600 mm • 4 decorative wooden knobs, about 60 mm diameter • galvanized finishing nails, 25 mm, 30 mm and 75 mm long • white woodworking glue • wood filler or putty • exterior paint or stain • paintbrush • medium-grade sandpaper • handsaw or power saw • miter box • combination square • hammer • drill and drill bits • nail punch • ruler • pencil
● *Technique pages 338–42*

❶ PREPARING THE WOOD

1 Using the handsaw or power saw, accurately cut the 70 mm boards into 24 lengths of 360 mm (for the side panels), and two lengths of 400 mm

NOTE
When ordering lumber, if the lengths itemized above are not available, be sure to specify pieces that will supply you with the multiple lengths listed in section 1, "Preparing the wood." Also, be sure to measure out all of your pieces before you cut any to length, in order to minimize waste.

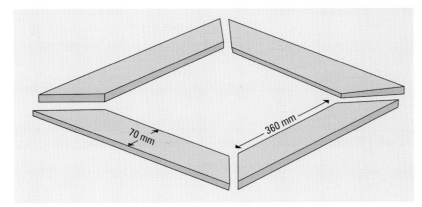

NOTE
If you are using lumber other than a very soft wood for this project, make sure that you drill guide holes for all the nails to prevent the wood from splitting. To drill the guide holes, use a drill bit with a diameter slightly smaller than the diameter of the nails.

(for the cross bars). From the remaining 70 mm wood, cut the four pieces for the top trim to the dimensions shown above, mitering them at 45°.

2 Using a handsaw or power saw, cut the 50 mm square lumber into four 600 mm lengths (for the legs) and eight 360 mm lengths (for the two top rails, the two bottom rails and the four cross rails).

3 Using a handsaw or power saw, cut the 20 mm square lumber (inside supports) into eight 420 mm lengths (or lengths equal to six times the width of the side panel boards).

4 If the wooden knobs have any protrusions from the back, saw them off so that the surfaces are completely level.

5 Sand all cut edges smooth.

❷ ASSEMBLING THE PLANTER

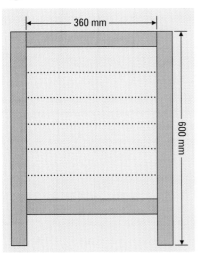

1 Using the glue and 75 mm nails, glue and nail one top and one bottom rail to two of the legs in the positions shown. Make sure that the inside distance between the top and bottom

rails corresponds to six times the actual width of the boards used for the side panels. Repeat this step with the other two legs.

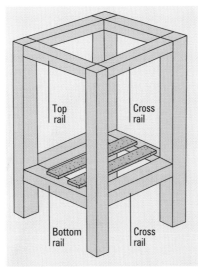

2 Using 75 mm nails, join the two leg units by nailing the legs to the top and bottom cross rails in the positions shown. Glue and nail the two 70 mm cross bar supports from one bottom rail to the other in the positions shown, using 25 mm nails.

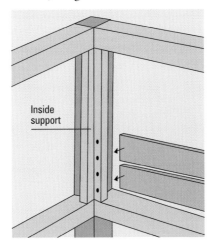

3 Attach one pair of inside supports to each leg with white glue and 30 mm nails, and then glue and nail the side panels to the inside supports, making sure that there are no gaps between the boards. The panels are recessed from the front edges of the legs and the top and bottom rails, they should fit snugly between the legs.

4 Fit the mitered 70 mm trim to the top of the planter and fix it in place with white glue and 30 mm nails.

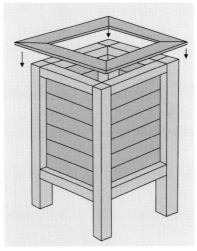

5 Glue a decorative wooden knob to each mitered corner of the top trim, centering the knobs carefully over the legs.

❸ FINISHING

1 Sink all nails and fill holes with putty or wood filler. Sand all surfaces until they are smooth.

2 Paint or stain all visible surfaces in a color to complement the decor of the area where the box will stand. If you decide to use stain, finish the planter box with two or three coats of flat polyurethane varnish.

Sweet-scented solutions

Pamper your partner with a gift of homemade fragrant bath oil, hand cream or cologne, presented in an attractive glass container with a decorative label. The ingredients are available from alternative health shops and pharmacies.

WHAT YOU NEED

Eye dropper (1 ml capacity) • measuring cup, graduated in milliliters • non-aluminum double boiler • stainless steel spoons • stainless steel or ceramic bowls • stainless steel whisk • fine muslin • coffee filter papers • sterilized, colored glass bottles and jars (for sterilizing directions see "Tips for making cosmetic preparations" in the box on this page).

Bath oil
30 ml sweet almond oil • 5 ml avocado oil • 5 ml wheatgerm oil • essential oils: 6 drops chamomile, 6 drops rose, 18 drops lavender

After-shower body oil
10 ml jojoba oil • 10 ml wheatgerm oil • 40 ml hazelnut oil • 40 ml apricot kernel oil • essential oils: 12 drops frankincense, 12 drops geranium, 6 drops jasmine, 24 drops lavender

Nourishing hand cream
10 g beeswax • 5 g anhydrous lanolin (wool fat) • 60 ml almond oil • 5 ml sweet wheatgerm oil • 20 ml distilled water • 20 ml aloe vera juice • essential oils: 10 drops carrot, 5 drops rose, 2 drops lemon, 2 drops frankincense, 1 drop geranium

Protective hand cream
Handful chopped lemongrass (*Cymbopogon citratus*) • 300 ml boiling water • 15 g anhydrous lanolin (wool fat) • 10 g beeswax • 70 ml almond oil • 5 ml wheatgerm oil • 20 ml aloe vera juice • 2 tsp strained lemon juice • 3 drops friar's balsam

Body cologne
140 ml vodka • essential oils: 3 ml bergamot, 3 ml lemon, 1.5 ml orange, 20 drops neroli, 10 drops rosemary • 60 ml distilled water

❶ BATH OIL
1 Pour the ingredients into a bottle and shake well until all the oils are thoroughly blended. Store the mixture away from heat and direct sunlight.
2 Ten drops will provide a deliciously fragrant bath. The mixture should be used within six months.
● Makes about 50 ml.

❷ AFTER-SHOWER BODY OIL
1 Pour the ingredients into a bottle and shake well until all the oils are thoroughly blended. Store the mixture away from heat and direct sunlight.

NOTE
Essential oils are quite expensive to buy – but once you have acquired a good selection of them, you will be able to make wonderful gifts for all your family and friends.

2 The oil is poured into the palm of the hand and smoothed all over the body when it is towel-dry after a bath or shower. The mixture should be used within six months.
● Makes about 150 ml.

❸ NOURISHING HAND CREAM
1 Melt the wax and the lanolin in a double boiler over a medium heat.
2 Keeping the double boiler over the heat, add all the remaining ingredients, except for the essential oils, and stir gently until the mixture is thoroughly blended.
3 Pour the mixture into a ceramic bowl and allow it to cool slightly.
4 Add the essential oils, and use a whisk to beat the mixture until it is creamy in texture.
5 Transfer the cream to the sterilized jar and label the jar.
6 The cream is rubbed into the hands when the skin feels dry. The mixture should be used within two months.
● Makes about 200 ml.

❹ PROTECTIVE HAND CREAM
1 Place the lemongrass in a ceramic bowl and cover it with the boiling water. Steep for two hours, and then strain the liquid through fine muslin into the other ceramic bowl.

TIPS FOR MAKING COSMETIC PREPARATIONS
For the best results, and to avoid contaminating the mixtures, observe the following rules.
● Measure all your ingredients as accurately as possible. When you are measuring essential oils, use good-quality graduated eye droppers, which are available from pharmacies. A standard dropper holds 1 ml and is graduated in tenths of a milliliter.
● Use only stainless steel, glass or enamel pans for warming and boiling (never use aluminum pans), and use stainless steel spoons for mixing.
● Keep all your equipment spotlessly clean, and use it only for making up cosmetic preparations.
● Always use distilled water – this is essential to prevent creams and

lotions from becoming rancid. Water from the tap contains chemicals and impurities that are likely to contaminate the other ingredients.
● For filtering the mixtures, use coffee filter papers (unbleached if possible), or sterilized fine muslin.
● Store creams and oils in colored glass jars – amber glass is best. It is essential to sterilize jars and lids properly before using them to store cosmetic preparations. Wash them thoroughly in warm, soapy water and then boil them for 10 minutes. Leave them upside down to dry.
● Label all preparations with their names, the ingredients used, the use-by date and, if applicable, how much to use and how often.

HINT
With your gift, include a card describing how to patch-test new cosmetics before using them to ensure that there is no allergic reaction to the ingredients. Tell the recipient to apply a small quantity of the preparation to the underside of the forearm – if the skin reddens, blisters, burns or becomes itchy, the person should not use the product without professional advice.

2 Put the lanolin, beeswax, almond oil and wheatgerm oil in the top part of a double boiler, and warm the mixture over a gentle heat until all the ingredients are melted.
3 Keeping the double boiler over the heat source, add the aloe vera juice and 20 ml of the strained lemongrass infusion. Stir until well blended.
4 Remove the mixture from the heat and pour it into a ceramic bowl. Allow the mixture to cool slightly.
5 Add the lemon juice and the friar's balsam, and beat the mixture with the whisk until it is cool and creamy.
6 Store the cream in the sterilized jar.
7 The protective cream is rubbed into the hands before using detergents or cleaners. The mixture should be used within two months.
● Makes about 400 ml.

❺ BODY COLOGNE
1 Pour the vodka into a sterilized glass jar and add the essential oils, stirring slowly until the oils are completely blended. Seal the jar and let the mixture stand for 48 hours.
2 Add the distilled water, stirring slowly to mix thoroughly.
3 Leave the mixture to steep in the jar for 48 hours to four weeks, depending on how strong you want the fragrance to be. If you feel that the fragrance is too strong, dilute the mixture with a little more distilled water.
4 When the scent has matured, drip the mixture through a coffee filter into a sterilized glass bottle; one with a ground glass stopper is ideal.
5 The cologne makes a refreshing pick-me-up when it is splashed on to the body. The mixture should be used within six months.
● Makes about 250 ml.

Man's scarf & hat

To keep the man in your life warm and cozy, make him this scarf and matching hat. The hat is shaped like a beanie and the scarf is finished off with tassels.

WHAT YOU NEED

Length of scarf	**160 cm**
Width of scarf	**22 cm**
Hat fits a 59 cm circumference	

The yarn used in this project is Patons DK (100 g balls), and the colors are:
main color (mc), college grey;
1st contrast color (cc1), berber;
2nd contrast color (cc2), charcoal.

Hat

Main (mc)	1
1st contrast (cc1)	1
2nd contrast (cc2)	1

Scarf

Main (mc)	3
1st contrast (cc1)	1
2nd contrast (cc2)	1

Knitting needles: 3.75 mm (no. 9), 4.00 mm (no. 8) • crochet hook (for fringe) • wool sewing needle
● *Technique pages 323–7*

CHECKING THE GAUGE

Before you begin to knit, test your gauge to ensure that both the scarf and the hat will be as close as possible to the size specified. You should have 22 stitches to 10 cm in width over pattern, using 4.00 mm needles. If you have fewer stitches, you should use smaller needles; if you have more stitches, use larger needles.

❶ KNITTING THE SCARF

Using 4.00 mm knitting needles and mc, loosely cast on 46 sts.

NOTE
You will need only one ball of each of the contrasting colors to make both the scarf and the hat.

1st row: K2, ★ P2, K2, rep from ★ to the end.
2nd row: P2, ★ K2, P2, rep from ★ to the end.
3rd row: As for 2nd row.
4th row: As for 1st row.
(These 4 rows form pat.)
Cont in pat until work measures 140 cm from beg, working the last row on the wrong side.
Cast off in pat.

❷ FINISHING THE SCARF

Using mc, cc1 and cc2, make a fringe about 10 cm long at both ends.

❸ KNITTING THE HAT

Using 3.75 mm needles and mc, cast on 130 sts.
1st row: (right side of the brim) K2, ★ P2, K2, rep from ★ to end.
2nd row: P2, ★ K2, P2, rep from ★ to the end.
Rep 1st and 2nd rows 4 times, then 1st row once, in stripes of 2 rows cc1, 2 rows cc2, 2 rows cc1, then 3 rows in mc. Change to 4.00 mm needles. Beg pat.
1st row: (right side) K2, ★ P2, K2, rep from ★ to end.

2nd row: P2, ★ K2, P2, rep from ★ to end.
3rd row: As for 2nd row.
4th row: As for 1st row.
(These 4 rows form pat.)
Cont in pat until the work measures 19 cm from the beg, ending with a 4th row.

Shaping the top

1st row: K2, ★ P2 tog, K2, rep from ★ to end...98 sts.
2nd and 3rd rows: P2, ★ K1, P2, rep from ★ to end.
4th and 5th rows: K2, ★ P1, K2, rep from ★ to end.
6th row: As for 2nd row.
7th row: P2 tog, ★ K1, P2 tog, rep from ★ to end...65 sts.
8th and 9th rows: K1, ★ P1, K1, rep from ★ to end.
10th and 11th rows: P1, ★ K1, P1, rep from ★ to end.
12th row: As for 8th row.
13th row: K1, ★ work 3 tog, rep from ★ to last st, K1...23 sts.
Break off yarn. Run end of yarn through rem sts, draw it up tightly and fasten it off securely.

❹ MAKING UP THE HAT

1 Using the wool sewing needle, join the seam with backstitch, reversing the stitching for the ribbed section.
2 Turn back the ribbed edge to form a brim around the hat.

MAKING A FRINGE

1 Wind the yarn round a piece of cardboard as wide as the desired length of the finished fringe plus 2–3 cm, and cut along one edge.
2 Take three strands of yarn of one color and fold them in half.
3 With wrong side of the knitting facing, push the crochet hook

through the knitting and draw the folded loop through one stitch in the edge of the knitted piece.
4 Without removing the crochet hook from the loop, draw the cut ends through the loop and pull gently to form a knot. Adjust the knots so they are evenly tied.

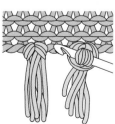

A calendar for all seasons

With its border of pressed flowers and foliage, this calendar is a beautiful reminder of the changes that come with the passing seasons.

Pressed flowers and foliage from different seasons: spring specimens, such as daffodils, yellow jonquils, hyacinths, crocus, scilla, violets, snowdrops, elderberry; summer specimens, such as delphiniums, hydrangeas, larkspur, candytuft, lavender, flowering sage, salvia, pansies, buttercups; autumn and winter specimens, such as seed cases, seeding grasses, seed heads from flowers such as poppies, colored leaves, berries • white or light-colored mounting board, 58 cm x 20 cm • A3 sheet of backing paper • one-year calendar • small glue-on hook (or short ribbon) • sharp craft knife • cocktail stick, toothpick or small paintbrush • ruler • pencil • dark green felt-tipped pen, 6 mm • craft glue • tweezers • water jar • paper tissues

● *Technique pages 332–3*

❶ PREPARING THE FLOWERS

1 Dismantle multi-petaled flowers such as roses and carnations before pressing. These will be reassembled when they are dry.

NOTE

Remember to tell the recipient that the calendar will retain its natural colors best if it is displayed away from direct sunlight or fluorescent lighting, and that it should not be hung in a steamy environment, which could cause the flowers to mildew. A hallway would be an ideal place to display it.

Use only bright-colored flowers, as pale flowers fade quickly. Avoid white jonquils – they often turn brown and will spoil the springtime grouping.

VARIATION

Instead of inserting a calendar into three holes in the mounting board, you could attach a flip-type month-by-month calendar to the bottom third of the mounting board and arrange the flowers above it.

2 Before pressing thick-throated flowers, such as daffodils, slice them in two down the middle.

3 Press flowers or petals individually, using the methods described in "Flower and foliage drying."

② PREPARING THE MOUNTING BOARD

1 Cut and assemble the calendar into three blocks of four months each (January to April, May to August, and September to December). Each block should measure 12 cm square, with a centered printed area of about 90 cm across by 60 cm down. If the blocks are too big or too small for the mount, reduce or enlarge them on a photocopier – or, for a charming handmade finish, write them out to the correct size by hand, using India ink.

2 Glue each calendar block to a larger piece of backing paper. Trim the backing paper so that it forms a border 1 cm wide around the block.

3 Using a pencil and ruler, rule three regularly spaced 10 cm squares on the mounting board. For a well balanced design, leave a slightly larger space at the bottom of the mounting board than at the top. Using a craft

knife, cut out the squares from the mounting board.

4 Take the January to April calendar block and, with the calendar side facing up, spread glue around the backing paper border. With the right side facing up, lower the mounting board so that the calendar block is accurately centered in the top frame in the mounting board, and press firmly down around the glued edges.

5 Repeat step 4 to insert the calendar block for May to August into the middle frame and the calendar block for September to December into the bottom frame.

6 With a light pencil and a ruler, measure and draw a border around the board, 1 cm from the edge. With the green felt-tipped pen, rule a line over the penciled border, wiping the ruler with a piece of tissue after each line to prevent smudging.

③ CREATING THE DESIGN

1 Reassemble any dried flowers that were dismantled for pressing. For tips on how to reassemble dried flowers, see *Reassembling the flowers* in "Framed wedding bouquet" (pages 188–9).

2 Sort the pressed flowers and foliage into three groups – spring, summer, and autumn/winter.

3 Beginning at the top, use the tweezers to arrange the blooms and foliage around the mounting board. Group the delicate spring flowers around the top third of the board, then the more robust summer blooms in the middle, followed by the dried grasses and autumn leaves of the cooler months at the bottom.

4 When you are satisfied with the arrangement, glue the specimens to the mounting board. Work from the top of the picture to the bottom so that you avoid brushing against glued specimens as you work. It may be necessary to hold some of the bulkier blooms flat with a heavy object (such as a book) until the glue dries.

④ FINISHING

Glue a small hook or a loop of ribbon to the back of the mounting board at the center of the top edge.

DESIGNING THE CALENDAR

Cut the frames in the mounting board following the measurements shown in the plan below. To balance the design, the space at the top should be smaller than the other spaces.

The calendar illustrated here is designed around the seasonal variations, however the flowers and foliage can be changed to suit a partner - just pick favorite blooms and arrange them decoratively around the three cut-out frames.

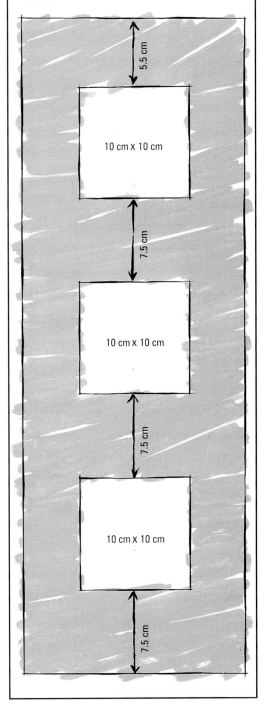

Folk art kitchen canisters

Decorate plain wooden canisters with this colorful design of fruit and grapevines, transforming them into a charming yet practical gift that will brighten any newlywed couple's kitchen.

WHAT YOU NEED

Master pattern 161(a–d) • 3 wooden rectangular kitchen canisters, the largest about 30 cm tall • FolkArt acrylic base coat: porcelain white • FolkArt pure pigment: alizarin crimson, ivory black, yellow light, phthalo green, Prussian blue • FolkArt acrylic color: Paisley blue, harvest gold, plum pudding, southern pine, raspberry wine, bayberry, calico red, persimmon, chocolate fudge, wicker white • drying retarder • water-based clear varnish • paint palette • paintbrushes: sponge brush (about 40 mm), no. 5 round, no. 12 flat, no. 00 liner • medium- and fine-grade sandpaper • lint-free cloth • tracing paper • transfer paper • fine-tipped marker • stylus (or empty ballpoint pen) • masking tape • palette • paper towels
● *Technique pages 334–5, 343–4*

❶ PREPARING THE CANISTERS

1 Lightly sand all the outside surfaces of the canisters with medium-grade sandpaper and wipe away all residue with a lint-free cloth.
2 Using the sponge brush, apply two coats of porcelain white base coat to the outsides of the canisters and lids, sanding between coats with fine-grade sandpaper. Be careful not to get paint on the insides of the canisters or on the surfaces where the canisters and the lids meet.
3 Allow the paint to dry thoroughly.

4 With the flat brush, paint a thin coat of drying retarder on the lower third of each canister and then a coat of porcelain white over the retarder.
5 Side-load the flat brush with phthalo green and float a band of color 2–3 cm wide around the base of each canister.

❷ TRANSFERRING THE DESIGN

1 Using tracing paper and the fine-tipped marker, trace the designs from the master pattern.

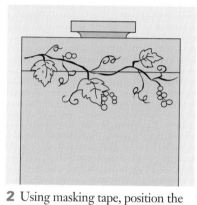

2 Using masking tape, position the vine leaf design on the front of the large canister, near the top. If the canister is the type with a lid extending over the side of the canister (as used in this project), place the design so it falls over both lid and canister.
3 Using transfer paper and stylus, transfer the design to the canister.
4 Remove the design carefully and attach it to the adjoining side of the canister, making sure that the beginning of the second design matches the end of the first design to form a continuous vine pattern.

HINTS

● *When painting the designs, use a round brush to apply two coats of the specified base color.*
● *Do all further work using a "wet-on-wet" technique, so that shading and highlights are blended with the central color.*
● *Use a round brush when blending the shading on the small fruit. Change to a flat brush for the larger plums, apples and pears, using short, patting strokes to give the fruit a rounded appearance.*

5 Repeat step 4 until the design appears right around the upper edge of the canister. Then repeat steps 2 to 5 on the other two canisters.

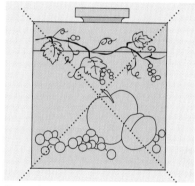

6 Find the center of the front of each canister by lightly ruling two diagonal lines from opposite corners. Where the lines cross is the center of the canister. Fix the relevant fruit design to each

GRAPEVINE BORDER

Build up the design gradually, starting with the larger elements, such as the leaves, and adding shading, highlights and details.

BLUEBERRIES

Over the Paisley blue base coats, apply darker shading to the lower sides and lighter shading to the upper sides.

PEARS

Use persimmon and chocolate fudge to shade the darker areas and yellow light and harvest gold for the lighter areas.

canister in turn, using masking tape and aligning the center mark on the design with the center mark on the canister. The bottom of the design should be about 3.5 cm from the bottom of the canister, just above the phthalo green band. The design may extend around the corners. Then transfer the design onto the front and sides of each canister.

3 PAINTING THE DESIGNS
Grapevine border
1 Base-coat the leaves with southern pine and allow them to dry.
2 Apply a coat of phthalo green to the center of each leaf, then shade with southern pine along the lower edge and bayberry along the upper.
3 Paint the grapes with Paisley blue. Shade them with Prussian blue and raspberry wine, then add highlights of phthalo green and wicker white. Using the liner brush and wicker white, paint in the veins of the grapevine leaves.
4 Using the liner brush, paint the grapevine stems in ivory black and chocolate fudge and the vine tendrils in chocolate fudge.

String bag
1 Base-coat the string bag with phthalo green.
2 Using rough comma strokes, paint the first and fourth stripes in harvest gold, the second in raspberry wine and the third in southern pine. Highlight each stripe by mixing wicker white into paint of the appropriate color.
3 Paint the strap in bands of southern pine and yellow light commas, highlighted in the same way as the stripes.

Blueberries
1 Base-coat the blueberries with Paisley blue.
2 Shade one side with Prussian blue mixed with a touch of raspberry wine, and shade the other side with Paisley blue mixed with wicker white. Add wicker white highlights.
3 Paint the blossom ends with ivory black highlighted with wicker white, and the leaves with southern pine highlighted with bayberry.

Oranges
1 Base-coat the oranges with harvest gold. Shade them with chocolate fudge and persimmon, then brush-mix

harvest gold, yellow light and wicker white to paint the highlights.
2 Paint in the stem ends using ivory black, bayberry and a mixture of ivory black and bayberry.

Plums
Base-coat the plums with plum pudding. Shade them with a mixture of plum pudding and Prussian blue and highlight them with raspberry wine, plum pudding and wicker white.

Apples
1 Base-coat the apples in calico red.
2 Shade the dark sides and the bases of the stems with chocolate fudge and raspberry wine.
3 Add a rosy glow to the centers using alizarin crimson, and then highlight the other sides with persimmon and harvest gold. Dry-brush light wicker white highlights.
4 Paint the stems in ivory black, with chocolate fudge and wicker white highlights.

Pears
1 Base-coat the pears with two coats of harvest gold.
2 Blend chocolate fudge and persimmon in the darker areas of the fruit, and blend yellow light and harvest gold in the lighter areas. Dry-brush highlights with wicker white.
3 Paint the stems in ivory black and highlight them with chocolate fudge and wicker white.

4 FINISHING
1 When the paint is quite dry, erase all transfer lines.
2 Wipe all surfaces thoroughly with a lint-free cloth before applying three coats of varnish with a flat brush.

NOTE
The fruit folk art pattern has been designed so that it flows from one canister to the next. When the canisters are displayed, the tallest one should be on the left and the smallest one on the right.

Ribbon & lace bridal garter

A beautifully crafted white garter is a part of a traditional wedding outfit, and the bride is sure to treasure a garter you have lovingly made especially for her.

WHAT YOU NEED

1.6 m satin ribbon, 25 mm wide •
1.7 m entredeux, 10 mm wide •
1.7 m edging lace, 25 mm wide •
non-roll elastic, 20 mm wide, cut to
the leg measurement plus 1.5 cm •
20 cm satin ribbon, 5 mm wide •
fine sewing thread • sewing machine
• fine sewing needle • scissors •
dressmaking pins
● *Technique pages 292–301, 303–4*

❶ PREPARING THE RIBBON AND LACE

1 Cut the 1.6 m of satin ribbon into two equal pieces.
2 With right sides together, and using a 5 mm seam, stitch the ends of one piece of ribbon together to form a circle. Press the seam open. Set this piece aside.

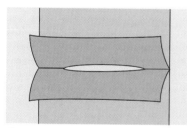

3 Join the second piece of ribbon into a circle in the same way, but on this piece, sew only a scant 5 mm in from each edge, leaving a 15 mm gap in the center of the seam to thread the elastic through. This piece forms the inside of the garter.
4 Cut the entredeux and edging lace in half and press all four pieces.

HINT
The satin ribbon that was used in this project has a floral motif embroidered on it. Look for a ribbon with a pretty variation like this to add that extra touch to the garter.

Carefully trim away one batiste edge of each piece of entredeux.
5 Butt the trimmed edge of one piece of entredeux to one piece of lace edging and, using a fine machine zigzag stitch, sew them together. Press well. Repeat this step with the second pieces of entredeux and lace.

❷ SEWING THE GARTER

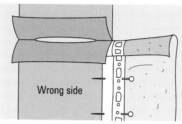

Wrong side

1 Pin the untrimmed edge of the entredeux to one edge of the wrong side of the inside piece of ribbon (the piece with the opening) so that the entredeux holes are just visible at the ribbon's edge. Fold the raw edges of the joined entredeux and lace under at the seam and trim away any excess.

2 Sew the joined entredeux and lace in place along the edge of the ribbon, using a straight machine stitch.
3 Repeat steps 1 and 2 on the other side of the ribbon.
4 With wrong sides facing, pin the two circles of ribbon together, making sure the seams on both pieces match.
5 Sew the pieces together along both edges of the ribbon using a straight machine stitch.
6 Handstitch the ends of the lace together at the seam, using a fine seam. Neaten the edges and trim any loose threads. Press well.
7 Thread the elastic through the opening, overlap the ends and handstitch the elastic firmly to secure it. Close the opening with slipstitch.
8 Tie the 5 mm ribbon in a small bow and sew it by hand to the center of the garter, opposite the seam.
9 Trim the ends of the ribbon at an angle to prevent fraying.

VARIATION
Use blue ribbon in the garter if you want to give the bride the traditional "something blue."

Coat-hanger for a wedding dress

A special dress requires special care when storing, and this padded coat-hanger covered with silk shantung is perfect for the purpose. The embroidery is adapted from a Brazilian pattern.

WHAT YOU NEED

Master pattern l66(a) • wire coat-hanger • 25 cm white silk shantung, 90 cm wide • 2 pieces polyester batting, 18 cm x 50 cm • needles: size 7 straw, size 7 embroidery • white silk embroidery thread • 30 cm white silk ribbon, 4 mm wide • tracing paper • dressmaker's carbon paper • fabric marking pen • pencil • dressmaking pins • scissors
For lace trimming: crochet cotton no. 50 • no. 3 cotton darning needle
● *Technique pages 292–301, 307–12, 328, 343–4*

❶ PREPARATION

Using tracing paper and scissors, trace and cut out the master pattern pieces. Trace the embroidery guidelines onto the larger piece.

Cover back

1 Pin the larger pattern piece to a single thickness of the silk shantung and cut carefully around it.
2 Fold the lower edge over 1 cm to the wrong side of the fabric and press. Put this piece to one side.

Cover front

1 Using a fabric marking pen, lightly trace the outline of the larger pattern piece onto the remaining shantung. Do not cut the fabric yet.
2 Using the dressmaker's carbon paper, transfer the embroidery guidelines onto the right side of the fabric.

VARIATION

Instead of working the knotted lace trimming, buy 50 cm of edging lace and trim and slipstitch the lace to the turned lower edge of the front hanger cover before sewing the back and front together.

Padding

1 Pin the smaller pattern piece to a double thickness of batting and cut out the two pieces.
2 Place the two batting pieces on either side of the wire coat-hanger, leaving the hook sticking out at the top. Use a double thread to oversew the pieces together.

Hook cover

1 From the silk shantung, cut a bias strip 14 cm long and 3 cm wide.

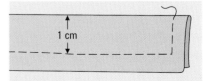

1 cm

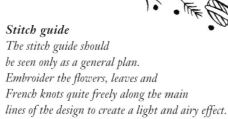

- French knot
- Stem stitch
- Couching stitch
- Bullion stitch flower
- Bullion stitch bud
- Satin leaf stitch

Stitch guide

*The stitch guide should
be seen only as a general plan.
Embroider the flowers, leaves and
French knots quite freely along the main
lines of the design to create a light and airy effect.*

2 EMBROIDERING THE DESIGN

1 Using the embroidery needle and the embroidery thread, work the main lines of the design in stem stitch.

2 Following the stitch guide, work the rest of the design, using the straw needle for bullion stitches and the embroidery needle for all other stitches. The flowers are worked in bullion stitch, the leaves in satin stitch and the tendrils in couching stitch.

3 Cut out the embroidered fabric, following the previously traced outline. Fold the lower edge 1 cm to the wrong side and press.

3 MAKING THE LACE

1 With the wrong side of the front cover facing, work a foundation row of a multiple of 12 basic loops plus 11 extra basic loops along the folded lower edge, leaving a 1 cm seam allowance at both ends. Turn.

2 Work a turning loop into the first loop. Work a basic loop into the next four loops. Miss one loop and work a large loop into the next loop. ★ Work 10 basic loops. Miss one loop and work a large loop into the next loop. ★ Repeat from ★ to ★ until four loops remain. Work four basic loops. Turn.

3 Work a turning loop into the first

2 With right sides together, fold the bias strip in half lengthwise. Sew a line of stitching 1 cm from the folded edge and across one end.

3 Turn the strip right side out. Thread the fabric tube over the wire hook and handstitch the hook cover firmly to the batting. The wire hanger is now completely covered.

loop. Work two basic loops. ★ Miss one basic loop and work a large loop into the next large loop. Close this loop with a closed loop knot. Work three more closed loops into the same large loop. ★ † Miss one basic loop and work seven basic loops. Repeat from ★ to ★ once.† Repeat from † to † until three loops remain. Work three basic loops. Turn.

4 Work a turning loop into the first loop and a basic loop into the next two basic loops. Work a bridging loop and three small picots into the next large loop. Bridge into the next loop and work a basic loop. Close this loop with a closed loop knot. Work another loop into the same loop. (You have thus made a side stitch.)

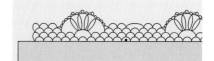

5 Work a bridging loop and a side stitch into the next two loops. Bridge into the large loop and work three

• small picots. ★ Bridge into the next loop and work a basic loop into the next two basic loops. Miss one loop and work a large loop into the next basic loop. Work a basic loop into the next two basic loops. Work a bridging loop and three small picots into the next large loop. Work a bridging loop and a side stitch into the next three loops. Bridge into the next loop and work three small picots. ★ Repeat from ★ to ★ until two loops remain. Work two basic loops. Turn.

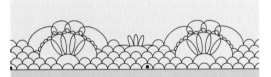

6 Work a turning loop into the first basic loop. ★ Work one basic loop. Miss the small picots and work a large loop into the top of the first side stitch. Work a loop into the next two side stitches. Miss the small picots and work a large loop into the next basic loop. Work one basic loop. Bridge into the next large loop and work three long picots. Bridge into the next loop. ★ Repeat from ★ to ★ until two loops remain. Work two basic loops. Turn.

7 Work a turning loop into the first basic loop, then work one basic loop. ★ Bridge into first large loop and work three small, one long and a

small picot. Into the next two loops work a bridging loop, one small, one long and a small picot. Work a bridging loop, and then one small picot, one long picot and three small picots into the next loop. Bridge into the next loop. Work a loop into the next three long picots, and a loop into the next basic loop. ★ Repeat from ★ to ★ to the end of the row. Work one basic loop. Turn.

8 Work a turning loop into the first basic loop. ★ Work a large loop into the next four long picots. Miss the small picots and the next large loop and work another large loop. Work one basic loop. ★ Repeat from ★ to ★ to the end of the row. Turn.

9 Work a small turning loop. ★ (Bridge into the next loop and work one small picot, three long picots and one small picot) four times. Work a bridging loop and three small picots into the next large loop. Work a

bridging loop and three long picots into the next basic loop and a bridging loop and three small picots into the next loop. ★ Repeat from ★ to ★ to the end of the row. Work a knot into the next loop. Pull it very tight and trim the thread close to the knot.

④ SEWING THE COVER

1 With right sides facing, stitch the back and front covers together following the stitching lines on the master pattern and remembering to leave the bottom edge open. The seam allowance is 1 cm. Turn the cover right side out and press.
2 Turn the raw edges at the small, top opening to the inside along a 1 cm seam allowance and press.
3 Slip the fabric cover over the padded wire hanger, making sure that the raw edges at the hook opening are tucked in neatly. Using ladder stitch, handsew the turned raw edges together at the base of the hook.
4 Slipstitch the back and front covers together along the bottom edge, keeping the stitches close to the lace.
5 Tie the satin ribbon in a bow around the base of the hook.

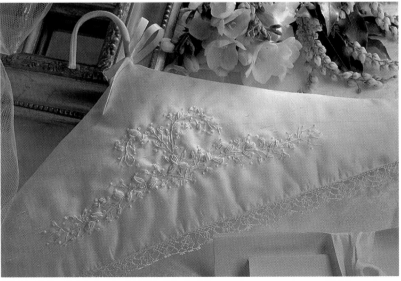

Satin bridal horseshoe

Put all your best wishes into making this beautiful satin-covered good-luck horseshoe trimmed with ribbon roses—it is a unique addition to a bridal bouquet.

WHAT YOU NEED

Master pattern 167(a) • 2 pieces thin craft batting, 18 cm x 16 cm • thick cardboard, 17 cm x 17 cm • 2.6 m plain white satin ribbon, 19 mm wide (to cover the horseshoe) • 1.5 m embossed white satin ribbon, 9 mm wide (for the loops) • 60 cm satin-striped sheer white ribbon, 39 mm wide (for 2 large roses) • 60 cm white waterwave taffeta ribbon, 39 mm wide (for 2 large roses) • 60 cm white satin ribbon, 23 mm wide (for 2 medium roses) • 1.2 m white satin ribbon, 15 mm wide (for 4 small roses and 2 small rosebuds) • white sewing thread • fine sewing needle • tracing paper • pencil • scissors • white glue
● *Technique pages 292–301, 343–4*

① PREPARING THE SHAPE

1 Using tracing paper, pencil and scissors, trace and cut out a working pattern from the master pattern.
2 Place the pattern piece on the batting and cut out two shapes slightly larger than the pattern.
3 Place the pattern on the cardboard, trace around it with the pencil and then cut it out.
4 Coat one side of the cardboard with glue. Glue one batting shape

> ### HINT
>
> *Give your horseshoe a touch of color by making some of the roses in colors to match the bridesmaids' dresses or the main flowers in the bridal bouquet.*

to the cardboard, making sure that the batting extends around the sides of the cardboard. Glue the remaining piece of batting to the other side of the cardboard in the same way.

② COVERING THE HORSESHOE

1 Lay one end of the 19 mm ribbon around one end of the horseshoe and secure it with a few small stitches.
2 Wind the ribbon firmly and evenly around the horseshoe, overlapping and splaying the ribbon as you go so that the batting is completely and smoothly covered.
3 Cut off any excess ribbon, tuck the raw end under the ribbon that is wound around the horseshoe shape, and secure with small slipstitches.

③ DECORATING THE HORSESHOE

1 Cut the 9 mm-wide embossed ribbon in half. Put one half aside. Fold the other piece in half and stitch it to the top of the horseshoe, 17 cm from the fold, to make a loop to slip over the bride's wrist. Leave the ends hanging free and trim at an angle.
2 Take the remaining length of embossed ribbon and cut it in half. Make each piece into three even loops and secure with two or three stitches. These loops will be placed among the roses as an additional trim.
3 Following the method given in the techniques section for making a silk rose (page 314), make two large roses from the satin-striped ribbon; two large roses from the waterwave ribbon; two medium roses from the 23 mm white ribbon; and four small roses and two rosebuds from the 15 mm white ribbon.
4 Glue the roses and the loops on either side of the arch of the horseshoe in the positions shown.

Chrysanthemum tablecloth

If the newlyweds have a small round table (about 70 cm across), this cutwork tablecloth will be an ideal gift for them. The flower head design is worked four times.

WHAT YOU NEED

Master pattern 162(a–b) • 1 m fine white linen, 115 cm wide • 10 skeins of white stranded embroidery cotton • needle: size 7 crewel • colored sewing thread • tracing paper • dressmaker's carbon paper • pencil • piece of string at least 50 cm long • scrap of stiff cardboard at least 4 cm square • dressmaking pins • dressmaking scissors • tape measure • embroidery hoop (optional) • sharp, pointed scissors
● *Technique pages 307–13, 343–4*

① PREPARING THE FABRIC

1 Fold and quarter the fabric along the grain. Using colored thread, baste along the folds to mark the center horizontal and vertical lines.
2 Spread the fabric out on a clean carpet, smooth it out carefully and secure it with pins. Tie one end of the string around the pin and the other end around the pencil so that the distance from the pin to the point of the pencil is 45 cm.

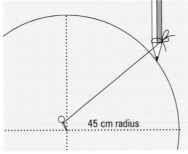

3 Push the pin through the center of the fabric where the basted lines intersect and secure it in the carpet pile. Hold the pin firm and use the string and pencil as a compass to draw the circumference of a circle on the fabric, keeping the string taut. This will create a circle 90 cm in diameter.

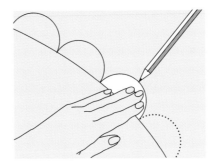

4 Using tracing paper and pencil, trace the outline of the scallop from the master pattern. Transfer the outline to the cardboard and cut it out to make a template.
5 Starting at the beginning of one quadrant, place the straight side of the template on the outside edge of the circle and trace carefully around it.
6 Continue to trace scallops around the circle until the entire circumference is scalloped. You should be able to fit 50 scallops around the circle (12½ to each quadrant).

② TRANSFERRING THE MAIN DESIGN

1 Using tracing paper and pencil, trace the working design from the master pattern.
2 Match the center of the fabric with the center of the working design and, using dressmaker's carbon and a stylus or empty ballpoint pen, transfer the design to the fabric one quadrant at a time, using the colored basting threads as a guide.
3 Remove the basting threads.

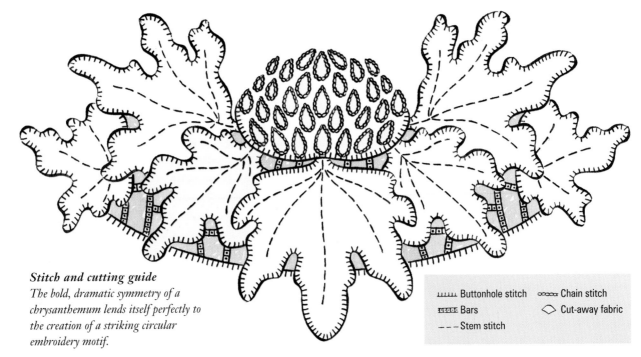

Stitch and cutting guide
The bold, dramatic symmetry of a chrysanthemum lends itself perfectly to the creation of a striking circular embroidery motif.

⊥⊥⊥⊥⊥ Buttonhole stitch		∞∞∞∞ Chain stitch	
▦▦▦▦ Bars		◇ Cut-away fabric	
- - - Stem stitch			

NOTE
Work all the embroidery with three strands of stranded cotton.

❸ EMBROIDERING THE DESIGN

1 Sew a line of running stitch around the edges of the scallops.

2 Embroider the scallops in buttonhole stitch, making sure that the ridge of the stitches lies toward the outer edge of the cloth.

3 Establish the floral design with running stitch, working the buttonhole stitch bars as you go.

4 Following the embroidery details given on the stitch and cutting guide, work the outlines of the leaves and the edge of the circular design in buttonhole stitch. Remember that the ridge of the stitches must lie against any area that is to be cut away.

5 Work the blossoms in chain stitch, and the leaf veins in stem stitch.

6 Using a small pair of sharp, pointed scissors, carefully cut away the fabric from around the outside edges of the scallops and from the shaded areas shown on the stitch and cutting guide opposite. Be very careful to trim under the linking bars and as close as possible to the buttonhole stitches without actually nicking them.

CARING FOR LINENS

- Wash linens in mild soap by hand or on the gentlest cycle in your washing machine.
- Treat stains immediately, then launder as soon as possible.
- Try to identify stains before you attempt to remove them.
- Always remove stains before washing the tablecloth.
- Dry linens away from strong sunlight, and do not allow them to get too dry.
- Roll linens loosely (do not fold) and store them wrapped in clean muslin in a well-ventilated area.

Photocopy these hints and mount them on a card to accompany your gift – or you may prefer to write them out by hand.

Needlepoint cushion

The contemporary needlepoint design on this cushion cover is satisfying to work, and the young couple are sure to treasure it for years. The cushion measures about 38 cm square.

WHAT YOU NEED

Master pattern J79(a) • 50 cm x 50 cm 10 gauge mono canvas • fabric, 60 cm x 50 cm • tapestry wool, DMC colors: 1 skein 7796 (blue), 6 skeins 7219 (dark maroon), 4 skeins 7139 (maroon), 5 skeins 7138 (light maroon), 3 skeins 7640 (dark pink), 4 skeins 7136 (very light pink), 4 skeins 7135 (pink) • no. 3 perle cotton, DMC colors: 4 skeins 796 (blue), 3 skeins 783 (golden yellow), 3 skeins 815 (maroon) • sewing thread • needles: size 20 tapestry, general sewing • scissors • dressmaker's chalk • ruler • canvas embroidery frame
● *Technique pages 292–5, 315–9*

❶ PREPARING THE CANVAS

1 Find and mark the center of the canvas, and then measure and mark a 38 cm square around the center.
2 From the top right-hand corner of the marked square, count six canvas threads in from the top and six from the right-hand edge. Mark the spot.

3 Insert the canvas into the frame. The canvas should be quite taut but not stretched out of shape.

❷ STITCHING THE DESIGN

To identify the areas, follow the stitch diagram on the master pattern.

Rhodes stitch (area A)

1 Using 7139 and working over three-thread squares, work 35 Rhodes stitches from right to left across the top, and 34 down the right side.
2 Starting from the right, work 10 Rhodes stitches and a half Rhodes stitch along the bottom edge. Starting from the top left, repeat this step along the left-hand edge.
3 Using perle 796, work a half cross-stitch through the center of each Rhodes stitch.

Six-step herringbone stitch (B)

1 Work herringbone stitch in 7796 over six lengthwise threads and four crosswise threads.
2 Over the same area, and working successively into the empty holes, repeat step 1 using 7219, 7138, 7640, 7136 and perle 783.

Mini-leaf stitch (C)

Work mini-leaf stitch over six-thread squares, working nine fanned stitches and a central straight stitch. This design uses three color combinations of three colors each. For each stitch, use the lighter pink or maroon at the top, the darker pink or maroon at the sides and the blue at the base.
1 Starting from the top right corner, inside the Rhodes area, work half a mini-leaf and then a diagonal row of 28 mini-leaf stitches, using 7135/7136 and perle 796. Work six diagonal rows of mini-leaf in the same colors below and to the right of the first row.
2 Work seven diagonal rows of mini-leaf in 7136/7138 and perle 796.

3 Work the rest of area C (the bottom right corner) in diagonal rows, using 7138/7219 and perle 796.

Diamond ray stitch (D)

1 Starting from the bottom, work up beside the first row of mini-leaf to the top right corner. Work five diagonal rows in each color, in the following sequence: 7135, 7136, 7640, 7138, 7139. For all colors, stitch the outside rays in perle 815.
2 Work the rest of area D (the top left corner) in 7219 and perle 815.
3 Along the top edge, work compensating stitches to fill the area.

Jacquard stitch (E and F)

1 For area E, start at the mid-point, below the junction of the mini-leaf rows and the diamond ray rows. Using 7138, work five-stepped Byzantine stitches down to the bottom edge. (There will be small triangles of unworked canvas between areas C/D and area E.)
2 Return to the mid-point and work up to the left edge. Leaving one row of canvas holes between rows, work two more rows of Byzantine stitch, using 7138, below the first one.
3 Work continental stitch between the Byzantine rows with two strands of perle 783. To fill the small triangles between area C/D and area E, work the edges in continental stitch with two strands of perle 796 and the centers in straight stitch with 7219.
4 Fill area F (the lower left corner) with jacquard stitch, working the Byzantine rows with 7219 and the continental rows with two strands of perle 796.

❸ MAKING UP

1 Block the worked canvas and trim it to within 2.5 cm of the worked area.
2 From the fabric, cut two pieces measuring 41 cm x 28 cm. Hem one 41 cm edge of each piece.
3 With right sides together, backstitch the two fabric pieces to the canvas through the outer worked holes to make an overlapped back.

Old-fashioned botanical picture

Traditionally, pressed flowers and leaves have been used for the identification of plants. This old-fashioned botanical picture is an unusual wedding gift that will be very handy for reference.

WHAT YOU NEED

This is a large picture. To fill the framed area you will need to collect quite a number of plants.

A selection of flowers and leaves of medicinal and culinary herbs, cultivated and wild, such as achillea, basil, bellflower, catmint, chives, coriander, daffodil, dandelion, delphinium, dill, dogwood, fern, feverfew, geranium, hyssop, jonquil, lavender, love-in-a-mist, nasturtium, parsley, pennywort, rose, rosemary, snowdrop, violet • picture frame with glass (inside measurement 56 cm x 76 cm) • A1 sheet of white handmade textured paper • A1 sheet of 5 mm white mounting board • scissors • spray adhesive • clear craft glue • craft knife • steel ruler • tweezers • cocktail stick or paintbrush • eraser • soft pencil • ruler • India (permanent) ink
● *Technique pages 332–3*

❶ PREPARATION

1 Press the flowers and foliage using the methods described in "Flower and foliage drying." Note that drying treatments vary for different plants.
2 Trim the mounting board and paper to fit snugly into the frame.
3 Decide which side of the textured paper to display and apply spray adhesive to the edges of the other side. Position it on the mounting board and leave it to dry completely.

NOTE
Remember to tell the recipient of this gift that the picture will retain its natural colors better if it is displayed away from direct sunlight or fluorescent lighting.

4 With a ruler and pencil, measure and lightly draw a margin around all sides, 2 cm in from the edges.
5 Divide the margin into three vertically and into four horizontally. Lightly mark this three-by-four grid on the paper with the soft pencil.

❷ ASSEMBLING THE PICTURE

1 Arrange the pressed plants evenly over the display area, using the penciled grid as a guide to help you to space them. Group flowers and leaves of each specimen together and try to place related families of plants next to each other.
2 Some flowers have to be pulled apart for pressing. To put them back together, refer to the guidelines for *Reassembling the flowers* in "Framed wedding bouquet" (pages 188–9).
3 When you are satisfied with the layout, apply a small amount of craft glue to the back of each flower or herb using the tweezers and a cocktail stick

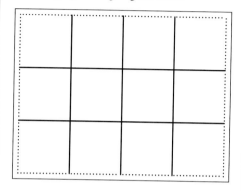

DRAWING UP A GRID
A grid drawn on the backing acts as a guide for arranging and aligning the herbs.

or small paintbrush, and lightly press into place. Allow the glue to dry.
4 Lightly label each specimen with a sharpened pencil. When you are satisfied with the lettering, go over the penciled labels with India ink.
5 Carefully erase any penciled guidelines that are still showing.
6 Insert the picture into the frame and secure the back according to the frame manufacturer's instructions.

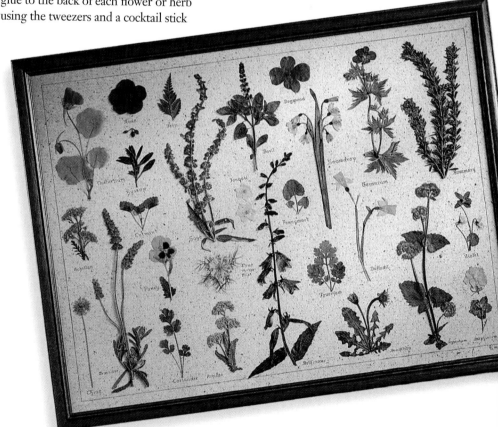

Monogrammed towels

Embroidered roses add a touch of romance to the monogrammed initials on these bath towels, hand towels and washcloths. Either embroider the initials of the bride and groom separately, or intertwine them to create personalized bathroom linen for the newly married pair.

WHAT YOU NEED

Master pattern **E35(a)** • bath towels, hand towels and washcloths – preferably with woven bands at each end • stranded embroidery cotton in green and a shade to blend with the towels (second color) • needle: size 3 straw • colored basting thread • scissors • tracing paper • pencil
● *Technique pages 307–12, 343–4*

❶ PREPARING THE MONOGRAMS

1 Using a photocopier, enlarge the initials on the master pattern to the right size for the item to be monogrammed. A letter 10 cm high is appropriate for a bath towel, and a letter 8 cm high for a hand towel. The washcloth has one flower spray and no initial.

VARIATION

Intertwine the monogrammed initials of the bride and groom to make a very romantic gift. Trace one initial onto tracing paper, then place this letter on top of the other initial. Move the tracing paper around until you are satisfied with the inter-twining effect. Trace the second initial over the first.

2 Making one tracing for each towel, trace the initials that you need onto tracing paper.
3 Center the initials on the end of the towel, placing the bottom of the initial on the woven band.
4 Using running stitch and colored basting thread, sew through the paper to mark the initials on the towel. Tear away the paper.

❷ EMBROIDERING THE BATH TOWEL

All the embroidery is worked with six threads. Before you use each piece of embroidery cotton, separate the strands and then put them back together again. This gives the work a textured appearance.

1 Study the lines of the initial you are using on your towel and decide where to place the rose design. As a general rule, the best position will be along the principal line of the letter.
2 Following the bath towel stitch guide, embroider the roses first, leaving enough space between the roses to insert the buds.
3 Work stems and foliage in green to form the rest of the initial.

Roses

Working in the second color, make three bullion knots of 12 turns each for the center of the rose. Around these knots work five more bullion knots of 16 turns each.

Buds

Still working in the second color, embroider two straight stitches, one on top of the other, to form a bud. On either side of these stitches, and using green embroidery cotton, work two straight stitches, one on top of the other, to form the calyx (the green outer part of the bud).

Hand towel stitch guide
The flower sprays for the hand towels are worked with straight stitch and finished with a French knot in the center of the spray.

Rose
Bud
Stems and leaves

Bath towel stitch guide

Make the roses by working three bullion knots for the centers and five longer, curving ones for the petals. Use straight stitch for the buds and leaves. Work a rose as the center of the separate flower spray.

2 To embroider the flower spray, follow the hand towel stitch guide (bottom left), embroidering the buds and leaves in straight stitch in the same way as for the bath towel and placing a French knot in the center of the design.

Stems and leaves

Using green cotton, work the stems in stem stitch and then embroider the leaves in straight stitch, placing one stitch on top of the other.

4 Following the bath towel stitch guide (top right), embroider a rose spray on each side of the initial. For a standard bath towel, place the rose spray about 10 cm from the letter.

❸ EMBROIDERING THE HAND TOWEL AND WASHCLOTH

1 The hand towel is worked in the same way as the bath towel, except that the flower sprays on either side of the initial are smaller.

3 Following the bath towel stitch guide for the separate flower spray, embroider a single flower spray in one corner of the washcloth.

Faux finish bedside table

Applying a faux finish to new or second-hand furniture gives it a stylish look of classic opulence that is sure to appeal to a young newly married couple. This bedside table has been treated to look like granite, but many other effects are possible.

WHAT YOU NEED

Bedside table, new or second-hand • artist's acrylic paints: black (for base color), dark gray, mid-gray, light gray • artist's paint medium (sealer) • water-based clear varnish • paintbrush: 50 mm decorating • paint palette • small natural sponge • paint stripper (for old furniture) • medium-grade sandpaper • parchment paper • lint-free cloth • rubber gloves

● *Technique pages 334–5*

❶ PREPARING THE SURFACES

1 For a new piece of furniture, sand down any rough patches or edges. For a second-hand piece, use stripper to remove old paint or varnish, following the manufacturer's instructions.
2 Using the medium sandpaper, sand all surfaces to a smooth finish and wipe them with a lint-free cloth.
3 Mix the black acrylic paint with an equal quantity of sealer and cover all surfaces, using the 50 mm paintbrush. Allow to dry, then sand lightly and apply another coat of black paint. Lightly sand again and wipe over with a lint-free cloth.

❷ CREATING THE MARBLED GRANITE EFFECT

1 First, rinse the sponge in water and wring it out thoroughly to soften it.
2 Thin the dark gray paint with paint

HINT

Choose your color combinations carefully. For the best effect, select colors and tones that are close to each other on the color spectrum. Using colors from opposite ends of the spectrum produces a garish effect.

medium. Wearing rubber gloves, dip the sponge lightly into the thinned paint and squeeze out the excess. Take off most of the paint by dabbing the sponge on parchment paper until there are no large globules of paint in the holes of the sponge.
3 Pounce the sponge at random over the surface of the furniture to create a light, speckled effect. Repeat this procedure until you have covered all the surfaces, aiming for an even coverage with some black base coat showing through. If you find you have sponged too much paint onto any area, sponge lightly over the top with the base coat color. Allow the paint to dry thoroughly.

4 Repeat step 3 using the mid-gray paint, covering less of the area than you did with the dark gray.
5 Allow to dry, and then sponge on the light gray paint in light, drifting strokes. The base coat should still show through in some areas.

❸ FINISHING

Allow the paint to dry, and then apply several coats of varnish. Let the varnish dry thoroughly between coats.

NOTE

Use a natural sponge for this project; synthetic sponges do not give the same softly mottled result. If you have not tried sponging before, experiment with the colors and techniques on an old board or heavy cardboard before painting the furniture.

ALTERNATIVE EFFECTS

Different marbled effects can be achieved with different colors. Study the colors in a piece of marble and then choose similar paint colors. Marble comes in many colors, including white, green, purple and black, so there is plenty of scope. A very attractive finish can be achieved by using a base coat of off-white and then sponging with pink, beige and reddish tones.

There are many other attractive ways to decorate furniture. Outlined below are two simple methods.

Crackle finish
Choose two different colors of water-based paint. Apply a base coat in the darker shade and allow to dry. Apply commercially prepared crackle medium over the base coat and leave to dry. Apply the second, lighter shade of paint in straight, even strokes. The paint will crack as it dries.

Dragging
Mix equal parts of paint, commercially prepared scumbling medium and mineral turpentine. Paint the glaze on with straight even strokes in one direction. Create a textured look by dragging a lint-free cloth in the opposite direction, then dragging a stiff paintbrush in the first direction.

Table centerpiece of dried flowers

For busy newlyweds, this floral centerpiece will ensure that there is always an attractive arrangement of flowers on the table.
To keep it looking fresh and colorful, do not stand the arrangement in direct sunlight and keep it dust-free by gently blowing over it with a cool hair dryer once a month.

WHAT YOU NEED

Low, round basket or vase • foliage, such as carthamus, nigella, nigella sativa, nigella orientalis or alchemilla • flat-headed flowers in tones of yellow, such as achillea filipendulina, achillea verticor, marigolds and sunflowers • approximately 20 yellow roses • dry foam bricks (available from florist's suppliers) • florist's spike • adhesive clay • pruning shears • craft knife
● *Technique pages 332–3*

❶ PREPARING THE FLOWERS AND FOLIAGE

1 Dry the flowers and foliage using the various methods described in the techniques section "Flower and foliage drying."
2 When working with the flowers and foliage you will achieve a more balanced and professional looking arrangement if you use groups of one type of flower or foliage rather than individual flowers or stems. Prepare your materials beforehand and have separate piles of each type of flower or foliage ready trimmed and within reach.

❷ ESTABLISHING THE BASE

1 Use a craft knife to cut a piece of florist's foam to fit the basket or vase. The foam should extend about 3 cm above the rim of the container.

Begin covering the foam base with a group of flowers positioned vertically in the center, then gradually angle the rest downward to form a semi-spherical arrangement.

2 Fix the florist's spike to the bottom of the vase with the adhesive clay. Push the foam firmly onto the spike.
3 With the knife, cut off the sharp corners of the foam, and round the top and sides to fit the container.
4 The flowers will be densely arranged and will overlap the container so that the foam will be invisible

HINTS
● *Dried roses, whether dried at home or commercially, have a tendency to close up as they dry. To achieve a "full-blown" appearance, hold the rose over the spout of a steaming kettle until you see the petals begin to soften and go limp. Using a hairpin or a piece of florist's wire, gently open out the petals, returning the rose to the steam as necessary. Use the steam moderately or the rose may begin to drop some of its petals. This technique may also be used for peonies.*

once the arrangement is complete.

❸ ESTABLISHING THE CENTER AND OUTLINE

1 The finished shape of the arrangement will echo the shape of the container and this is achieved by working with flowers and foliage with comparatively short stems (approximately 15 cm). This will allow you to control the outline of the arrangement more accurately than is possible with longer stems and will also make it possible to pack the flowers very closely together.
2 In the center of the container, place a group of foliage such as carthamus to establish the maximum height. The finished arrangement should be twice the height and width of the container.
3 Working from the center add groups of achillea, roses and foliage tightly around the central group of

carthamus. As you work outward begin to gently angle the stems so that the flowers begin to slope outward.

4 While you work, keep turning the arrangement to ensure that you are creating a balanced shape, and also bend down and look at it from table-top level. Remember this arrangement will be viewed from a sitting position as well as from above and sometimes an arrangement which looks wonder-ful viewed from above reveals flaws when viewed from the side.

5 Work systematically from the center point allowing the groups of flowers and foliage to flow curvingly into one another and avoid making straight lines. Imagine an herbaceous border as you work and picture how the flowers gently blend together.

6 As you reach the outer edges of the arrangement begin to angle the flowers and foliage more and more acutely until the stems are pushed horizontally into the foam. Then con-tinue the outline of the arrangement by angling the stems upward into the foam to break the line of the edge of the container. The arrangement will look more natural if the bottom edge of the flowers and the foliage curves softly and partially conceals the container.

Handmade writing paper

Handmade paper is an original gift that is bound to appeal to a conservation-minded couple. Paper-making requires no great experience or dexterity and, with a little help, this would be an ideal wedding gift for a child to make.

WHAT YOU NEED

Mold and deckle, A4 size or smaller • scrap paper (tissues, envelopes, writing paper) • plastic bucket • kitchen sieve • rectangular tub, big enough for you to submerge the mold and deckle and still be able to maneuver it • old blanket • about 10 couching cloths (pieces of hemmed felt or flannel), a little larger all round than the mold and deckle • 2 pressing boards, larger than the mold and deckle (large breadboards are ideal) • 4 G-clamps • masking tape • kitchen blender • spray fabric starch

❶ OBTAINING A MOLD AND DECKLE

To make paper, you need a mold (a wooden frame covered with wire mesh) to strain the pulp and a deckle (a frame without mesh that fits on top of the mold) to define the edges of the paper. You can buy molds and deckles in various sizes from paper-making suppliers. Alternatively, you can make your own by constructing two frames of a suitable size and stretching fine non-rusting mesh over one of them. Fix the mesh firmly to the wooden frame with staples and make sure it is quite taut.

❷ MAKING THE PULP

1 Tear the paper into pieces the size of postage stamps and put them in the bucket. Cover the pieces with warm water to which you have added a little dishwashing detergent. Allow the mixture to stand overnight.
2 Scoop about half a cup of the soaked paper into a sieve, drain it, and put it into the blender with three cups of water. Blend the mixture on high speed until the paper particles are very small, adding more water if necessary.

The resulting liquid should be cloudy, and you should be able to see tiny particles of paper floating in it when you hold it up to the light. Tip the mixture into the tub.
3 Repeat step 2 until the tub is about half full. It does not matter if you have to add more water to bring the level up to half full, as the water will be drained off later anyway.

❸ PREPARING A SIMPLE COUCHING PAD

1 Wet the blanket and wring it out as dry as possible. Then fold it so that it is larger than the mold and deckle by at least 5 cm all round.

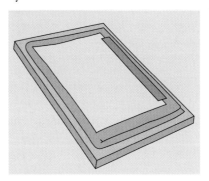

HINTS

• *When choosing paper for pulping, look for good-quality paper that was meant to be enduring in its original form. Shredded office paper is ideal. For best results, sort paper in color groups and use one group at a time. Do not use glossy paper, newspaper, paper that has been glued, or paper with a plastic, synthetic feel.*
• *To begin with, do not try to make paper larger than A4. For beginners, A5 is a manageable size, and it is practical for invitations and thank you notes.*

2 Place the blanket on one board. Wet a couching cloth and lay it on the blanket, smoothing out any wrinkles.
3 Press a piece of masking tape onto the cloth close to one edge; this will be a marker for aligning the sheets of paper neatly on top of each other.

❹ PULLING SHEETS OF PAPER

1 Place the deckle on top of the mold, with the mesh between them and all the edges aligned.

2 Stir the paper pulp mixture with your hand to distribute the paper particles evenly. Holding the mold and deckle by the sides, dip them into the tub vertically, then scoop them smoothly through the paper mixture and then upward, holding the mold and deckle horizontal so that the water drains through the mesh. (The scooping action spreads the paper pulp over the mesh and the draining action draws the particles together to form a sheet of paper.)
3 Remove the deckle, being careful not to spatter drops of water on the paper. Holding the mold on opposite sides, place its lower edge flat onto the prepared couching pad, over the top of the masking tape. Pause for a moment, then flip the mold over and

VARIATIONS

• *On a corner of each sheet of paper, stencil a simple motif or inscribe the intertwined initials of the newlyweds with a gold or silver pen. Use master pattern* **E**35(a) *for the alphabet, and follow the procedure described in "Monogrammed towels" (pages 180–1) for sizing and positioning the initials.*

• *Decorate a box to package and protect the paper, or use a transparent envelope file.*

one below, until you have made eight to 10 sheets. Finish with a layer of couching cloth.

5 Place the second board on top of the stacked paper. Clamp the two boards together with the G-clamps until the pressure is evenly distributed.

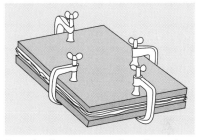

6 Take the press outside and stand it on edge so that as much water as possible drains off. Leave it for 15 minutes and then remove the top board. Lay the stack of paper flat. Leave to dry out overnight if possible.

7 Peel off the couching cloths, to which the sheets of paper will still be attached. Pin the cloths to a line and leave them to dry completely.

8 When they are dry, gently peel the cloths from the sheets of paper (not the other way around).

⑤ FINISHING

1 Spray the paper with fabric starch and iron it between two sheets of clean paper or fabric. (The starch will make the paper smoother and easier to write on.)

2 Tie a wedding gift ribbon and a silk flower around a sheaf of paper, ready to give to the bride and groom.

down to deposit the sheet of paper on the couching pad and cloth. Press the mold down to push the paper onto the fabric, and then carefully lift the mold away. Place a damp couching cloth on top of the sheet of paper.

4 Repeat steps 2 and 3, carefully aligning each piece of paper on top of the previous one so that the new sheet does not press ridges into the

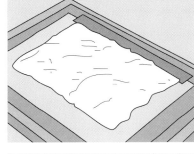

Framed wedding bouquet

Catch the bride's bouquet and return it to her in the form of a pressed flower picture that she can treasure for ever as a reminder of her special day.

WHAT YOU NEED

Wedding bouquet • oval wood frame, about 40 cm **x** 50 cm • fabric, 55 cm **x** 65 cm (similar to the fabric of the bridal gown) • spray adhesive • clear craft glue • adhesive tape • swizzle stick, toothpick or small paintbrush • pliers • tweezers • scissors
● *Technique pages 332–3*

1 PREPARING THE FLOWERS

1 Photograph or sketch the bouquet to record its shape and the position of the flowers. On the photo or sketch, number the flowers by species and make a numbered key listing each one. This will help you to recreate the bouquet after the plant material has been pressed.

2 Dismantle the bouquet, removing the most fragile flowers first to avoid unnecessary damage. If the flowers have been wired, carefully remove the wire with a small pair of pliers, taking care not to tear the foliage.

3 Dismantle multi-petaled flowers such as roses and carnations before pressing them. These are reassembled when dry. Orchids are best pressed with the throat separated from the other petals and the thick growth

NOTE
The fresher the flowers when you start, the more vibrant the result, so keep the day after the wedding free to make your sketch and begin drying the flowers.

in the center cut away. Thin out sprays of multi-headed blooms.
4 Press the flowers or petals individually, using the methods described in "Flower and foliage drying."

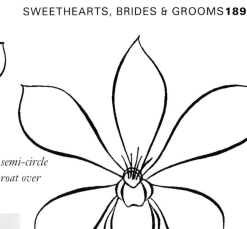

❷ PREPARING THE FRAME
1 Press the fabric and remove the backing from the picture frame.
2 Cut the fabric slightly larger than the picture frame backing.
3 Coat the surface and edges of the backing board with spray adhesive and carefully press the fabric onto it, smoothing the fabric out from the center to make sure there are no wrinkles or air bubbles.
4 Trim the excess fabric away.

❸ REASSEMBLING THE FLOWERS
Reassemble any dried flowers that were dismantled for pressing. The following steps show how to reassemble flowers commonly found in bridal bouquets. You should be able to apply similar techniques to other flowers.

Rosebuds

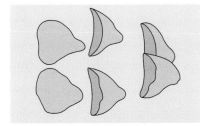

1 Starting with two small rose petals of similar size, fold the upper edge of each petal over and glue down using clear craft glue and a swizzle stick. Glue the two petals together, overlapping them at the center.

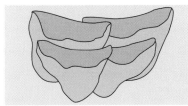

2 Repeat step 1 with two larger petals. Glue these larger petals behind the two smaller petals.
3 Form the center of the rosebud by folding a large petal in half and gluing it along the inside of the fold. Then

For orchids, reassemble the petals in a semi-circle using clear craft glue, then glue the throat over the center of the arrangement.

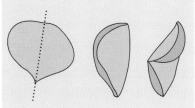

apply a little glue to the outside along the folded edge and fold the upper part to the right at an angle.

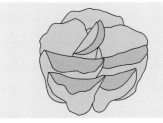

4 Glue the folded petal into the center, behind the assembled petals, with the top protruding and then glue three more petals behind the folded central petal.

5 Finish by gluing three sepals (the green, outer covering of the flower) over the assembled rosebud.

Carnations

1 Arrange the petals in a circle on a piece of adhesive tape, working inward until the tape is covered.

2 Apply a little clear craft glue to the back of a small petal and place it in the middle to form the center of the carnation.

❹ RECREATING THE BOUQUET
1 Using the sketch or photograph of the bouquet as a guide, lay the outermost foliage or flowers on the fabric backing. This will form an outline for the rest of the bouquet.
2 Fill in the rest of the bouquet, placing the outer flowers and foliage first and working toward the center, experimenting with the design. Do not lay out the central, focal-point flowers yet.
3 If the bouquet has trailing pieces, place the flowers so they face outward, in the direction of the trail.
4 When you are happy with the arrangement, use a swizzle stick or small brush to apply a thin coat of glue to the back of the foliage and flowers and press them gently into place on the fabric.
5 Now add the focal-point flowers and glue them into place. Fill any remaining spaces with small, light foliage or flowers.
6 When the glue is thoroughly dry, turn the picture on its side and gently tap it to dislodge any loose plant material. Mount the finished arrangement in the frame.

HINT
Remember to tell the bride that the framed bouquet will retain its natural colors better if it is displayed away from direct sunlight or fluorescent lighting.

Country-style dish rack

A pine dish rack is an original gift for a couple who are setting up house. Mounted on a wall above a drain board, the rack can be used for draining dishes or for storage.

WHAT YOU NEED

Pine: 1500 mm x 240 mm x 18 mm (finished size), 2100 mm x 290 mm x 18 mm (finished size) • 3600 mm wooden dowel, 12 mm diameter • scrap wood • 30 mm nails • white woodworking glue • clear varnish • paintbrush • wood filler • sandpaper: coarse, medium and fine • pencil • ruler • square • handsaw • jigsaw • clamps • wood rasp • drill, 12 mm drill bit • hammer • nail punch
● *Technique pages 338–42*

❶ PREPARING THE WOOD

1 Using a pencil, ruler and square, and following the cutting guide, measure and mark out the following pieces on the 290 mm wood: **A** one lower rear panel, 622 mm x 290 mm; **B** one upper rear panel, 622 mm x 280 mm; **C** one bottom front rail, 586 mm x 50 mm; **D** one rear support rail, 586 mm x 20 mm; **E** one top shelf, 586 mm x 210 mm.

2 Still following the cutting guide, measure and mark out the following pieces on the 240 mm wood: **F** two side panels, 430 mm x 210 mm; **G** two dividers, 270 mm x 210 mm; **H** two draining rails, 218 mm x 30 mm; **I** two draining rails, 186 mm x 30 mm.

3 Mark the curves on the rear and side panels (A, B and F). On the side panels, make sure the front edge between the curves is straight for 270 mm. Mark the front edge of the bottom front rail (C).

4 Using the handsaw, and the jigsaw for the curved edges of the rear and side panels, cut out all the pieces.

5 Cut the dowel into eight 295 mm lengths and five 186 mm lengths.

6 Clamp the dividers together with all edges aligned. Referring to "Constructing the dish rack" (opposite), drill the dowel holes through both dividers. Remove the clamps.

7 Clamp the bottom front rail over the top shelf, with the front and side edges aligned. Drill the dowel holes as described in "Constructing the dish rack," drilling right through the rail but only 9 mm into the shelf.

8 Remove the clamps. Smooth all cut edges with medium sandpaper.

❷ ASSEMBLING THE RACK

Refer to the box "Constructing the dish rack" while you are putting the dish rack together.

1 Glue the lower rear panel to the upper rear panel. Clamp the panels together and leave them to dry.

2 Glue one end of each of the 186 mm dowels. With a hammer, tap the glued ends into the holes in one of the dividers until the ends of the dowels are flush. Glue the other ends of the dowels.

3 Lay the divider flat on the bench and position the second divider over the dowel ends, maneuvering it until the drill holes are aligned with the dowels. Gently tap the second divider onto the dowels, hammering evenly until the ends of the dowels are flush with the surface of the divider.

4 Check that the dividers are square, then glue and nail them to the top shelf in the positions shown in the diagram, ensuring that the partially drilled holes are at the front of the top shelf and on its underside.

5 Glue the ends of the 295 mm dowels and tap them into the holes in the bottom front rail until they are flush.

6 Glue the other ends of the dowels. Glue and nail the bottom front rail to the bottom of the dividers, at the same time pushing the dowels into the holes in the underside of the top shelf.

7 Glue and nail the four draining rails to the bottom of the dividers, and the side panels to the partially completed shelf unit. Make sure that all sections of the completed shelf unit are square and then glue and nail it to the rear panels.

CUTTING GUIDE

Label all pieces as you work. Using a pencil, ruler and square, measure and mark the pieces as described in "Preparing the wood." Then mark the curves on the lower rear panel (A), the upper rear panel (B) and the two side panels (F). Use a handsaw to cut out the pieces and a jigsaw to cut the curves. To drill the dowel holes in the dividers, the top shelf and the bottom front rail, refer to the box on the opposite page.

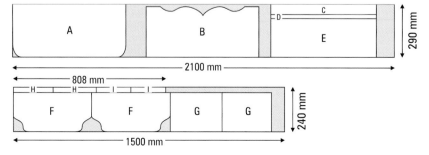

NOTES

● *Keep the distance between the dividers equal to 150 mm, the distance between the dividers and the outside edges of the top shelf and the front rail equal to 200 mm, and the inside height between the top shelf and the bottom front rail equal to 270 mm at both ends.*

● *The dish rack should be fixed firmly to the wall above the drain board, using a method suitable for the type of wall surface to which it will be fixed.*

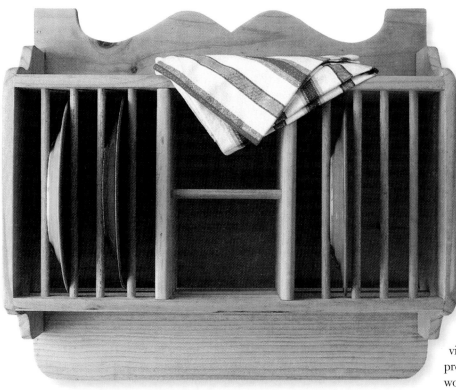

8 Using the rasp, file the front edges of the top shelf and the bottom front rail to match the curves on the side panels. Sand these edges smooth with coarse and then medium sandpaper.

❸ FINISHING

1 Punch all nail holes and fill them with wood filler. Sand all surfaces smooth. Using coarse and then fine sandpaper, round off the outside edges of all exposed surfaces, paying particular attention to the front edges of the dividers, the side panels and the rear panel.

2 Varnish the dish rack, being careful to coat all surfaces to provide a waterproof finish that will prevent dishwater from rotting the wood. You may need several coats.

CONSTRUCTING THE DISH RACK

Drilling the dividers

Clamp the dividers together, one on top of the other, and mark five holes on the top piece in a horizontally centered row. Mark the centers of the outside holes 25 mm in from the edges and allow 40 mm between the centers of the other holes. With a 12 mm drill bit, drill right through both dividers into a piece of scrap wood.

Drilling the top shelf and the bottom front rail

Clamp the bottom front rail to the underside of the top shelf. Mark four holes in a horizontally centered row 30 mm from the front edges with the center of the first hole 40 mm from the side edge and the centers of the other holes 40 mm apart. With a 12 mm drill bit, drill right through the bottom front rail and halfway through the top shelf. Repeat the procedure at the other end of the shelf and rail.

Draining rails (underside view)

The shorter draining rails are fixed across the dividers and the longer ones extend from the dividers to the side panels. The side panels (shown in cross section) and the rear panel are attached when the inner parts of the dish rack have been assembled.

Side and rear panels (front view)

The side panels and the rear panel (made by joining pieces A and B) are glued and nailed to the assembled inner components of the dish rack.

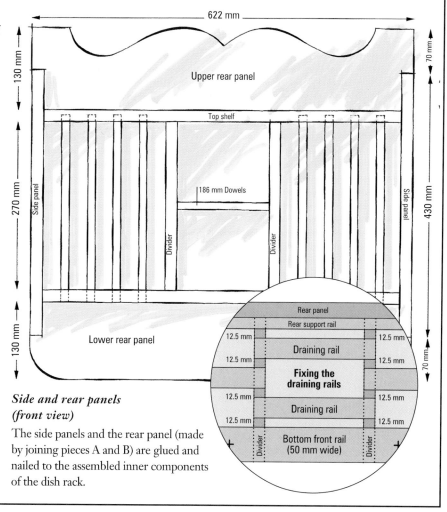

Fast-food station for birds

A bird feeding table is one way of attracting birds to a new or existing garden until suitable plants are established to provide a permanent food source for the birds. It can be secured to any pole or post, as long as it is out of the reach of cats.

WHAT YOU NEED

Master pattern 163(a) • marine plywood, 1500 mm x 500 mm x 10 mm • 600 mm wooden dowel, 19 mm diameter • 2 rounded wooden drawer handles, about 100 mm long (for perches) • 25 plated or galvanized brads, 12 mm long • white woodworking glue • exterior paint • wood filler or putty • paintbrush • medium-grade sandpaper • hard pencil (or empty ballpoint pen) • about 400 mm string • square • handsaw or power saw • jigsaw or coping saw • drill, 4 mm and 19 mm drill bits • scrap wood • clamp • screwdriver • nail punch • ruler • tracing paper • transfer paper • pencil
● *Technique pages 338–42, 343–4*

❶ PREPARING THE WOOD

1 Tie one end of the string around the pencil. Anchor the other end to the plywood with a brad so that the length of the string from nail to pencil point (when pulled taut) is 230 mm.

Holding the string taut, draw a circle on the plywood. Remove the nail and mark the center point clearly. The diameter of the circle you have just drawn (which will form the base of the feeder) should be 460 mm.

2 Using tracing paper and a pencil, trace a working pattern of the side panels from the master pattern. Using transfer paper and a hard pencil, transfer the pattern twice onto the plywood. Neaten the lines with pencil and ruler.

3 With a ruler, pencil and square, mark out two rectangles on the plywood, one 310 mm x 200 mm, and one 310 mm x 190 mm. These will form the roof panels.

4 Using a handsaw, power saw or jigsaw, cut around the outlines of all pattern pieces. Within the large circular shapes to be cut from the side panels, drill an access hole wider than the blade of the jigsaw. Place the blade of the jigsaw in the access hole and carefully cut out the circular shapes.

5 Clamp the side panels together with the edges aligned. Into scrap

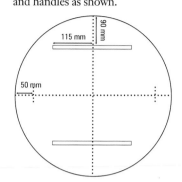

MARKING THE BASE
Mark the positions for the walls and handles as shown.

90 mm
115 mm
50 mm

wood, drill a 19 mm hole through both pieces in the position marked, making the hole big enough so that only light pressure is required to insert the dowel. Remove the clamp.

6 Using the pencil and ruler, carefully draw a diameter line through the center of the circular base. Using the square for accuracy, draw another diameter line at right angles to the first. The circle is now divided into four equal segments. Mark the diameter lines on the edges of the plywood, turn the base over and rule the diameter lines on the underside, making sure lines on both sides are aligned.

7 Measure and mark the positions of the walls on both the upper and lower surfaces of the base, as shown in "Marking the base" in the box above.

CUTTING GUIDE

Using string and a pencil, draw a circle 460 mm in diameter for the base. Trace the side panels from the master pattern, and then measure and mark out a left roof panel measuring 310 mm x 200 mm and a right roof panel measuring 310 mm x 190 mm. Cut the pieces with a handsaw or power saw and jigsaw or coping saw.

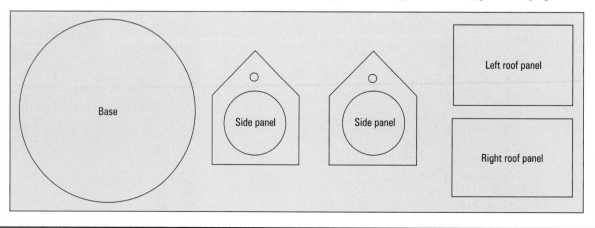

Base

Side panel

Side panel

Left roof panel

Right roof panel

8 Mark the position of the handles on one surface of the base only. Place the handles on the base and mark the position of the screws. Using the 4 mm drill bit (or a bit to match the diameter of the fixing screws), drill holes for the metal thread screws right through the base into scrap wood.

9 Round the ends of the dowel with sandpaper. Lightly sand the edges of all other pieces.

2 ASSEMBLING THE FEEDER

1 Apply glue to the bottom edges of the walls. Holding them steady in the positions marked on the top surface of the base, nail them in place from the underside, using the previously drawn lines as a guide. Glue and nail the roof panels together, making sure that the

long edge of the smaller piece is butted against the long side of the larger one, as shown in the diagram.

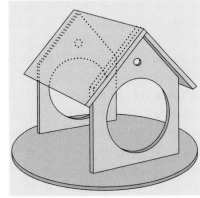

2 Center the roof on the walls so that the overlapping eaves are equal at both sides, and the back and front of the roof protrude equally over the

back and front walls. Glue and nail the roof into place.

3 Tap the dowel gently through both holes until the excess protrudes evenly at both ends. Squeeze glue around the holes to secure the dowel in place. Wipe off any excess glue.

3 FINISHING

1 Sink the nails with the nail punch and then fill all nail holes with putty.

2 Sand all surfaces until they are smooth and paint or stain inside and out. Allow the paint to dry.

3 From the underside, screw the perching handles into position on the upper surface of the base through the pre-drilled holes, as shown in the box "Marking the base." Use the screws supplied with the handles.

Wedding day sampler

Commemorate this special day in the bride and groom's lives with a traditional cross-stitch sampler; it will be a gift for the couple to treasure throughout the years to come.

WHAT YOU NEED

Master patterns **J71(a–b)** • 47 cm **x** 51 cm 14 gauge aida cloth • stranded cotton: Anchor colors 1 (white), 24 (pink), 38 (dark pink), 214 (light green), 216 (dark green), 343 (light blue), 891 (gold), 921 (dark blue) • colored basting thread and needle • needle: size 24 tapestry • picture frame, with an inside measurement of 41 cm **x** 36.5 cm • A2 white backing board • A2 mounting board • linen carpet thread or fine, strong string (for mounting) • craft knife • steel ruler • tracing paper • scissors • pencil • tape measure • spray glue
● *Technique pages 309, 343–4*

❶ MAKING THE SAMPLER

1 Iron the cloth and hand oversew or machine zigzag the raw edges.

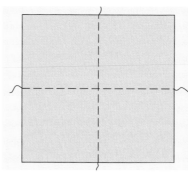

2 Fold the cloth in half and then in quarters, and mark the vertical and horizontal center lines with basting.
3 Following the stitch and color guide in the master pattern, first embroider the border design. This then becomes a point of reference for the remainder of the design.
4 Complete the design, working one small area at a time and following the stitch and color guide carefully.

❷ PERSONALIZING THE SAMPLER

1 On tracing paper, rule a straight line to act as a guide. Then, using the master pattern piece for cross-stitch letters, trace the letters of the bride and groom's names and the date of their marriage. Leave two empty stitches between letters and four between words. You will probably be able to fit only about 12 characters across the sampler, so abbreviate the names to initials if necessary and use an ampersand (&). Mark the mid-point of the tracings.
2 Match the mid-point of the name to the center point of the sampler in the space provided at the top of the sampler. Embroider the letters using

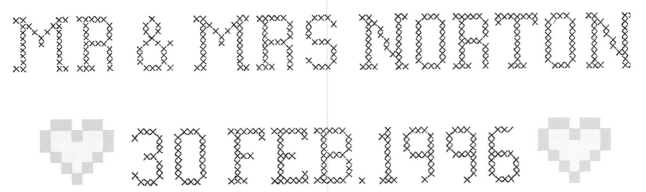

colors of your choice, starting from the middle and working out.

3 Repeat step 2 for the date, embroidering in the space provided at the bottom of the sampler.

❸ FRAMING THE SAMPLER

1 Ensure that the backing board and the mounting board both fit snugly into the back of the frame. If you need to trim them to the correct size, do so by placing the board on an appropriate cutting surface and using the craft knife and a steel ruler.

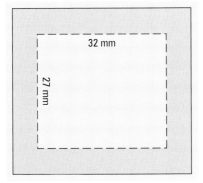

2 Using the pencil and ruler, mark a rectangle measuring 32 cm x 27 cm on the back of the mounting board. Take care to make the facing margins equal. Using the craft knife and the steel ruler, cut along the pencil lines to create a hole in the middle of the mounting board.

3 Press the sampler on the wrong side through a damp cloth, being very careful not to stretch the fabric or the stitching.

4 Lay the sampler right side up on the backing board, ensuring that it is centered on the board.

5 Fold one edge of the canvas back and secure it to the edge of the board with pins, and then do the same with

the opposite edge. Place the cut mounting board over the sampler to check that you have positioned the sampler correctly.

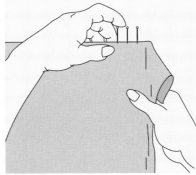

6 Turn the work over and, using linen carpet thread, sew the folded-over edges of canvas together with large herringbone stitches. With each stitch, go back to the beginning and tighten all the stitches to stretch the canvas firmly over the board.

7 Secure the thread at the start and take out the pins. Once again, tighten each stitch in succession. When the canvas is stretched tight, tie off the thread firmly.

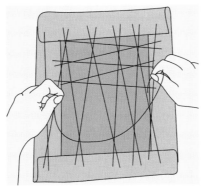

8 Stretch the canvas in the other direction by securing and sewing the other two edges in the same way. Fold the corners flat – do not miter them.

Mark the center points on your tracings of the text and match them up with the vertical center lines on the canvas, and then work the lines of text from the center toward the borders. Leave two empty stitches between letters and four empty stitches between words.

Check constantly that the stitches are progressively tightened and that the canvas is evenly stretched.

9 Place the mount over the sampler and insert mount and sampler into the frame. Close the back according to the manufacturer's instructions.

CROSS-STITCH TIPS

• *Match each color with its symbol on the stitch and color guide and fix a small piece of thread against each symbol on the guide before you begin work.*

• *Use an embroidery hoop to keep the tension even.*

• *Count outward from the center to the border and begin the embroidery by stitching the border design. Use the border as a reference to locate other stitches. Stitch in any other lines of reference.*

• *Divide the design into small areas and complete one area before moving on to the next.*

• *Always use two strands of embroidery cotton.*

• *Work each cross-stitch so that the top stitch lies in the same direction throughout your work.*

• *Never use knots to finish off a color. Always fasten your work off by passing the end of the thread under several stitches on the reverse side of the work.*

Broderie anglaise nightshirt

An heirloom nightshirt with pin-tucked inserts is a lovely contribution to a bride's trousseau. The finished nightshirt is 98 cm long and has three-quarter length sleeves.

WHAT YOU NEED

Master pattern 160(a–f) • 2.3 m batiste, 115 cm wide • 10 m fabric insertion lace, 33 mm wide • 10 m fabric insertion lace with entredeux, 18 mm wide • 10.5 m fabric edging lace, 30 mm wide • 15 cm lightweight iron-on woven interfacing, 115 cm wide • 7 decorative buttons, 10 mm diameter • fine machine thread • fine sewing needle • tracing paper • pencil • lace pins • scissors • tape measure • sewing machine, with fine needle, double needle and pin-tucking foot
● *Technique pages 292–301, 303–4, 343–4*

❶ CUTTING OUT THE FABRIC

1 Using the tracing paper and pencil, trace the pattern pieces, including all markings, and cut them out.
2 Following the cutting guide, fold the batiste in half lengthwise and cut the back skirt and the front bands. Open out the batiste and cut the right sleeve, the left front skirt and the neck bias strips. Then cut a rectangular

piece 115 cm x 80 cm, which will be machine pin-tucked before you cut a right front skirt, a left front yoke and a left sleeve from it.
3 Cut out two front bands from the iron-on woven interfacing.

❷ MAKING THE LACE FABRIC

1 Cut 23 pieces 40 cm long from both the insertion lace and the insertion lace with entredeux. Use method 2 to join the laces alternately, forming a piece measuring 112 cm x 40 cm. Trim away the excess fabric close to the zigzag stitching.

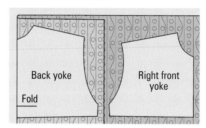

2 Fold the lace fabric along the center of one strip of insertion lace to form a double layer the width of the back yoke pattern piece, ensuring that the laces are symmetrical on either side of the fold. Lay the center back of the back yoke pattern piece along the

fold. Place the right yoke pattern piece on the remaining lace fabric with the grain parallel to a lace join.
3 Make sure that the laces will match at the shoulder seams, and then cut out the pieces.

❸ PIN-TUCKING

1 Following the settings for your sewing machine, pin-tuck the 115 cm x 80 cm rectangle of batiste along the lengthwise grain of the fabric.
2 Lay the pattern pieces for the left sleeve, the left front yoke and the right front skirt on the right side of the pin-tucked fabric, as shown in the cutting guide, and cut out.

❹ ASSEMBLING THE FRONT AND BACK

1 Staystitch the necklines of all the yoke pieces along the seamlines. With right sides together, and matching the insertion laces, join the shoulder seams, using method 1.
2 Cut two 55 cm lengths of edging lace for the front yokes and one 110 cm length for the back yoke.
3 Machine a row of gathering stitches on either side of the seamline on each piece (the seam allowance is 5 mm). Gather up the lace.
4 With the right sides together, machine staystitch the edging lace to the front and back yokes, adjusting

---

CUTTING GUIDES

Fold the batiste lengthwise to cut the back skirt and the front bands, and then open it out to cut the left front skirt, the right sleeve and the bias strips for the neck. Trim a straight edge on the remaining fabric and machine pin-tuck it along the lengthwise grain. From this pin-tucked fabric, cut out the right front skirt, the left front yoke and the left sleeve.

The back yoke and the right front yoke will be cut from the completed lace fabric.

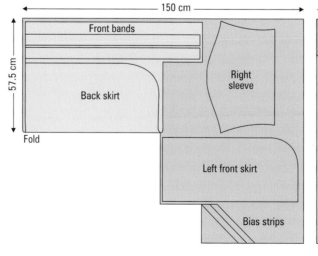

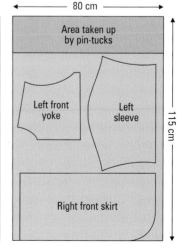

NOTES

• *Except for the edging lace, the seam allowances for this garment are 1 cm. When you are attaching the edging lace, leave a 5 mm seam allowance on the lace and a 1 cm seam allowance on the fabric to which you are stitching it.*

• *Methods 1 and 2 are the heirloom sewing techniques that you will need to make the nightshirt. For these methods, refer to the box "Heirloom sewing techniques" on page 14 of "Classic christening gown."*

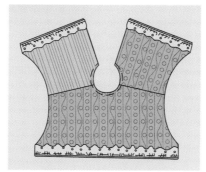

the gathers evenly and matching the 5 mm seam line on the lace to the 1 cm seam line on the yokes.

5 With right sides together, machine stitch the skirts to the yokes, sandwiching the edging lace. Trim the seams, zigzag to neaten, and press the turnings toward the yokes.

6 Cut a 140 cm length of edging lace. Repeat steps 3 and 4 to staystitch the lace to the right front opening of the nightshirt.

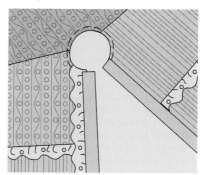

7 Iron the interfacings to the wrong sides of two of the front bands. With right sides together and raw edges aligned, machine stitch the interfaced bands to the front openings, sandwiching the edging lace along the right front opening. Press the turnings toward the bands.

❺ ATTACHING THE EDGING LACE

1 Cut 310 cm of edging lace and slipstitch one end to neaten. Gather the lace as before. With right sides together, place the neatened end of the lace on the seam joining the left front band and the neckline. Adjusting the gathers evenly, machine staystitch the lace to the nightshirt in a continuous seam around the neckline, down the right front band and round the right front hemline to the dot.
2 Cut 90 cm of edging lace for the left front hemline and slipstitch one end to neaten. Gather the lace as before. With right sides together and the neatened end aligned with the seamline on the outside long edge of the left front band, machine staystitch the lace around the left front hem to the dot, adjusting the gathers evenly.
3 Cut 140 cm of edging lace. Gather the lace as before, and machine staystitch it around the back hemline between the dots.

❻ ATTACHING THE FACINGS AND NECK BINDING

1 On the remaining two front band pieces, press a 1 cm seam allowance along one long edge. These pieces are the facings for the front bands.

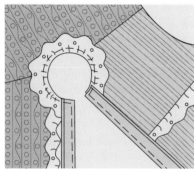

2 With right sides together, lay the band facings along the front bands, sandwiching the edging lace along the right front opening. Starting from the folded seam allowance on the facing at the neckline, machine stitch the facings to the band ends and the front

---

PIN-TUCKING WITH A SEWING MACHINE

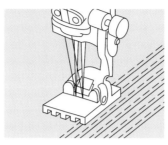

Machine pin-tucks are made using a pin-tucking foot and a double machine needle.

Double machine needles are threaded with two threads from the top and are available in various spacings; to make the pin-tucked fabric for the nightgown, use a fine, narrow-spaced double needle. Tucks must be stitched on the straight grain, otherwise they will twist.

The nightgown illustrated is pin-tucked in groups of one tuck, three tucks and five tucks. Try various effects on scraps of batiste to find one that you like.

---

openings. On the left front, take care not to catch the neatened ends of the edging lace at the neck and hem.
3 Join the bias strips for the neck edge, press the seams open and then press the strips in half lengthwise.
4 Trim the seam allowance of the neckline to 5 mm. With all raw edges aligned and right sides together, machine stitch the bias strip to the neckline, sandwiching the edging lace and extending the bias strip slightly into the front bands. Clip the neckline and the corners of the bands.

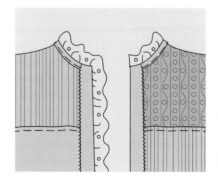

---

5 Turn the folded edge of the bias strip over to the wrong side and machine stitch it to the nightshirt close to the neckline. Turn the band facings over to the inside of the nightshirt and press. Slipstitch the folded edges of the facings to the seams joining the front bands to the nightshirt.
6 Trim the front and back hem edges to 5 mm and zigzag to neaten.

❼ SEWING THE SLEEVES AND SIDE SEAMS

1 Cut two 30 cm lengths of the 18 mm wide insertion lace with entredeux and two 45 cm lengths of edging lace. Machine two rows of gathering stitches around the lower edges of the sleeves and along the two pieces of edging lace. Gather up.

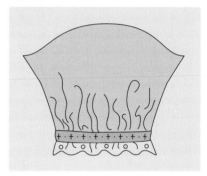

2 Join the insertion lace to the lower edge of the sleeves and the edging lace to the insertion lace, adjusting the gathers evenly. Roll and whip the seams to neaten (method 1).
3 With right sides together, machine stitch the sleeves into the armholes, matching notches and dots and easing the fabric to fit. Trim seams and zigzag to neaten.
4 With right sides together, machine stitch the sleeve and side seams from wrist edge to hem, taking care to match the sleeve lace trims, the underarm seams and the lace at the hems. Trim seams and zigzag to neaten.

❽ FINISHING

1 Machine stitch seven vertical buttonholes in the right front band in the positions marked.
2 Sew the buttons to the left front band along the center front line, in positions to correspond with the buttonholes.

PARENTS

Parents usually have
everything they need,
so it can be difficult to select
gifts for them. The perfect
solution is something
you have made yourself
that they can proudly
display or use.

Space-saving kitchen dish-towel rack

This is a miniature version of the large drying rack found hanging in many a Victorian kitchen. It is raised and lowered by a simple pulley system. The dish-towel rack can also be used for drying bunches of herbs or flowers.

WHAT YOU NEED

Master pattern E37(a) • surfaced lumber (e.g. pine), 1000 mm x 100 mm x 25 mm • 2400–4000 mm dowel (depending on length of rack), 19 mm diameter • 4 brass screw eyes, 15 mm diameter • brass cup hooks: 4 of 15 mm diameter, 2 of 20 mm diameter with long threads • 5 m light sash cord • 1 single and 1 double pulley, to match diameter of sash cord • 1 rope hook with wall mounting screws • strong thread • varnish • paintbrush • fine-grade sandpaper • white glue • tracing paper • transfer paper • pencil • scrap wood • fretsaw or coping saw • clamp • drill, 19 mm drill bit

● *Technique pages 338–42, 343–4*

❶ PREPARING THE WOOD

1 Trace and transfer the pattern for the end piece from the master pattern twice onto the wood, taking care to transfer all markings.

2 Cut out the two end pieces using the fretsaw or coping saw. Clamp the pieces together firmly and sand all the edges completely smooth.

3 Cut the dowel into four pieces of uniform length.

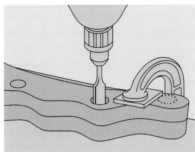

4 Keeping the end pieces clamped together, drill four 19 mm holes in the positions marked on the master pattern. Drill right through both end pieces into a piece of scrap wood.

5 Sand all the dowels. If necessary, sand the ends down to fit snugly into the holes in the end pieces.

❷ CONSTRUCTING THE RACK

1 Apply white glue to the insides of the dowel holes.

2 Insert one end of a dowel into the first hole of one end piece. With a block of scrap wood, tap the end piece gently until the end of the dowel is flush with the outer face of the end piece. Insert the other three dowels in the same way.

3 Insert the other ends of the dowels into the second end piece and tap into place until the dowel ends are flush.

4 Sand back any protruding dowel.

5 Apply a coat of varnish to the rack. Allow to dry. Sand gently, and apply a second coat. Leave to dry thoroughly.

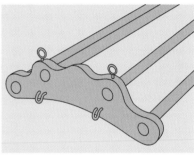

6 Screw two screw eyes and two 15 mm cup hooks into each end piece.

❸ SETTING THE SASH CORDS

1 Cut the sash cord into two pieces of equal length.

2 Thread one end of one piece of cord through the two screw eyes on one end of the rack. Fashion a triangle by joining the rope to itself

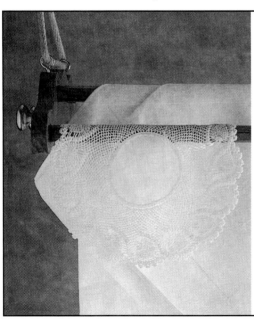

ANTIQUE LINEN RACK

Make this charming variation of the dish-towel rack for someone who has a taste for old-style elegance.

As well as the basic requirements, you will need walnut wood stain, golden shellac and methylated spirits. Instead of the 15 mm cup hooks, use four small drawer handles made of ceramic, brass or pewter-look metal.

1 When you have assembled the rack, sand it smooth and remove dust and wood particles with a tack cloth.

2 Use a rag to apply walnut stain to the rack, following the manufacturer's instructions. Let the stain soak more deeply into the end pieces and

the ends of the dowels than into the parts where the linen will hang. Apply stain until you achieve the effect you want.

3 Dissolve the shellac in methylated spirits following the manufacturer's instructions, and apply one or two coats to the rack using a good-quality paintbrush. Allow to dry.

4 Fit the drawer handles to the end pieces in place of the cup hooks.

5 To give the rack that authentic "antique" look, use off-white cord and a wooden rope hook finished in the same way as the rack. Bind the cord with gold picture wire.

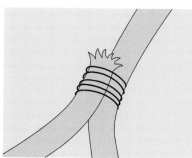

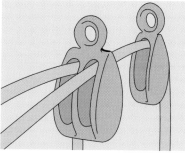

and binding the join tightly with strong thread. Apply white glue to the binding thread to strengthen the join.

3 Repeat step 2 with the other piece of cord and the other end of the rack.

4 Thread one piece of cord through the single pulley, then through the double pulley. Thread the other piece through the double pulley only.

5 Bind the ends of the cords with strong thread and strengthen the binding with white glue.

④ INSTALLING THE RACK

1 Find a cross-beam or joist in the ceiling that will support the weight of the rack. Drill one pilot hole fairly close to the wall end of the beam or

joist. Drill another pilot hole further along the beam. The holes should be the length of the rack apart.

2 Screw the two 20 mm cup hooks into the pilot holes and test that they will bear the weight of the rack. Hook the pulleys onto the cup hooks.

3 Screw the rope hook to the near wall about a meter below the ceiling.

NOTE

If it is not possible for you to install this gift yourself, copy out the installation instructions and include them with the rack, with the 20 mm cup hooks, the rope hook and the screws.

Rosebud nightgown

This old-time nightgown, made from fine woven wool fabric and batiste using heirloom sewing techniques, would be the perfect gift for your mother or grandmother. The nightgown is designed to fit sizes 10 to 12.

WHAT YOU NEED

Master pattern **F42(a–e)** • 2.5 m
wool challis, 150 cm wide • 1 m
batiste, 115 cm wide • 17.5 m
woven insertion lace, 15 mm wide •
3.8 m beading with entredeux,
12 mm wide • 8 m satin ribbon,
5 mm wide • 3 flat buttons, 10 mm
diameter • sewing threads: white,
a color to match the wool challis •
stranded embroidery thread, in a
color to match the wool challis •
needles: general sewing, fine
machine, fine embroidery • tracing
paper • pencil • lace pins • scissors •
tape measure • sewing machine
● *Technique pages 292–301, 303–4,
307–12, 343–4*

❶ CUTTING OUT THE FABRICS
1 Trace a working pattern from the
master pattern, using a pencil and
tracing paper and making sure you
include all markings. Cut out the
traced pattern pieces.
2 Following the cutting guide for the
wool challis, cut out all the pattern
pieces except the yoke and the back
facing. Still following the wool challis
cutting guide, cut two skirt hem frills
measuring 10 cm x 140 cm, two wrist

frills measuring 10 cm x 70 cm, and
a neck frill measuring 6 cm x 80 cm.
3 Following the cutting guide for
the batiste, cut a straight grain square
measuring 63 cm x 63 cm. Pull a
thread along all edges to ensure that
the square is on the straight grain.
(This square will be used to make
the heirloom fabric for the yoke.)
4 Still following the batiste cutting
guide, use the master pattern piece to
cut the back facings, and then cut two
skirt hem inserts measuring 11 cm x
90 cm and two wrist inserts measuring
6 cm x 45 cm.

❷ MAKING THE YOKE
1 On the square of batiste, pull
threads at 7 cm intervals across the
width of the square (eight threads in

> **HINT**
> *To stabilize the fabric when
> you are machining scallops, place
> strips of tissue paper between the
> fabric and the feed dog and
> stitch through both fabric and
> tissue paper. After machining,
> tear away the tissue paper and
> trim off the excess fabric.*

all). Turn the square through 90°
and pull eight more threads, at 7 cm
intervals, at right angles to the first
eight pulled threads.
2 Following the method for mock
lace insertion (page 204), sew insertion lace along all the pulled threads
for the full width of the square.

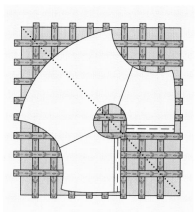

3 Fold the yoke square diagonally in
half and press lightly to mark the true
bias. Place the center front line of the
yoke pattern on the bias crease. Move
the pattern along the diagonal until
the lace inserts are identical on either
side of the center front and do not run
directly along the center back, the
center back seamline or the stitching
lines of the back neck.

CUTTING GUIDE

Wool challis: Cut the front and back
skirts in one piece along the fold, and
then cut the sleeves separately. Open
out the remaining fabric and cut out
the hem, neck and wrist frills.

Batiste: Cut all the pieces from a
single layer. Cut the yoke square
first, ensuring that it is cut on the
straight grain of the fabric by pulling
threads along all edges. The insertion

lace will be sewn into place on this
piece before the yolk is cut from it.
From the batiste, also cut the back
facing, two skirt hem inserts and two
wrist inserts.

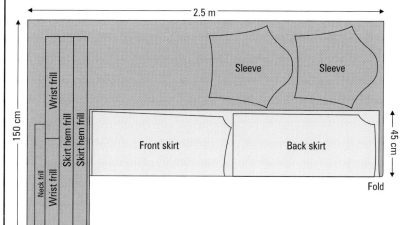

Wool challis

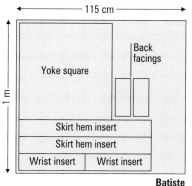

Batiste

4 Pin and cut out the yoke. Machine staystitch around the neckline, the armholes and the yoke curves to prevent stretching.

5 Cut 50 cm of beading with entredeux. Do not trim the fabric from the edges. With right sides together and raw edges aligned, machine stitch the entredeux to the front yoke curve, with a seam allowance the width of the fabric edging of the entredeux. To neaten the edge, machine a fine zigzag over the straight stitching and trim close to the zigzag.

6 Press the back facings in half lengthwise with wrong sides together. Lay the raw edges along the center backs of the yoke, on the right side of the fabric, and machine stitch along the seam lines through all layers. Trim and zigzag or overlock the seams and press the facings to the wrong side of the yoke along the seamlines. Slipstitch the facings to the wrong side of the yoke.

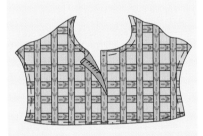

7 Overlap the left back yoke over the right back yoke, making sure the center back lines are aligned. Staystitch along the seamline at the yoke curve to hold it in place.

❸ SEWING THE YOKE TO THE SKIRTS

1 Machine two rows of gathering stitches along the upper edges of the front and back skirts.

2 With right sides together and raw edges aligned, match the armhole edges and center backs of the yoke and the back skirt. Pull up the gathering threads, adjust them evenly and machine stitch the seam. Neaten the raw edges with a fine zigzag stitch and trim.

3 With right sides together and raw edges aligned, match the armholes

and center fronts of the yoke and the front skirt. Pull up the gathering threads, adjust them evenly and machine stitch the seam, using a seam allowance the width of the entredeux fabric edge. Neaten the edges with a fine zigzag and trim.

4 Cut two 115 cm lengths of ribbon and thread them through the beading around the front yoke, so that the long ends emerge at the center front. Machine staystitch the ends of the ribbons at the armholes. Roll up the long ends and tie them loosely with thread to keep them out of the way.

5 Join one side seam only. Neaten the seam with a fine zigzag stitch, and then trim.

❹ ATTACHING THE SKIRT AND SLEEVE TRIMS

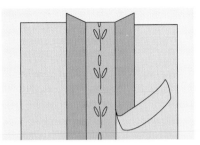

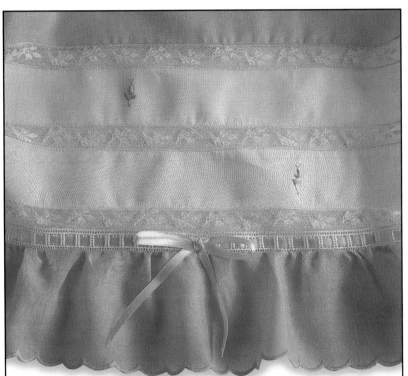

MAKING THE HEIRLOOM FABRIC

Methods 2, 3 and 4 are the heirloom sewing techniques that you need to make the rosebud nightgown. For these methods, refer to the box "Heirloom sewing techniques" on page 14 of "Classic christening gown." To make the rosebud nightgown, you will also need the method for mock lace insertion.

Mock lace insertion: Pull threads, or use a pencil, to mark the center of the lace placement lines. With the wrong side of the lace facing the right side of the fabric,

center the lace over the marked lines. Machine the lace headings to the fabric on either side. Using small sharp scissors and working from the wrong side, cut the fabric only along the marked lines. Press the cut edges back to expose the back of the lace. From the right side, zigzag over the lace headings. Trim the excess fabric from the wrong side close to the zigzag stitching.

To make laces easier to handle when machine stitching, spray them with a commercial fabric stiffener.

1 Join the batiste skirt hem inserts together along one short end. Neaten the seam with a fine zigzag and trim. Fold the joined strip in half lengthwise and press, and then unfold the strip. Center the insertion lace along the fold and sew it to the batiste, using the method for mock lace insertion.

2 Lay a row of insertion lace along each long edge of the skirt hem insert, matching the center of the lace with the raw edge of the batiste. Stitch the lace to the batiste, using the method for mock lace insertion.

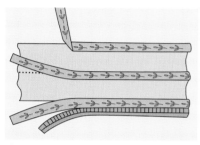

3 Cut 180 cm of beading with entredeux and trim the fabric mounting from one edge. Sew the trimmed edge of the beading to the insertion lace along one edge of the batiste, using method 3.

4 Match the center of the insertion lace along the other edge of the batiste strip with the lower edge of the skirt. Join the lace and the fabric, using the method for mock lace insertion.

5 Repeat steps 2 to 4 to make and attach the wrist trims.

5 MAKING THE FRILLS

1 Machine stitch the wool challis skirt hem frills together at one short end and neaten the seam.

2 Using thread to match the wool challis, and following your machine settings for making scalloped edges, machine scallop along one long edge of the frill, being careful to form a closed satin stitch.

3 Roll, whip and gather the raw edge of the frill, using method 4.

4 Trim the fabric from the lower edge of the entredeux on the skirt and use method 2 to attach the frill to the entredeux, adjusting the gathers evenly as you work.

5 Repeat steps 2 to 4 to make and attach the wrist frills.

VARIATIONS

• *The nightgown would be very attractive made with white or cream trimmings and embroidery and white or cream wool challis. It could also be made with coffee-colored fabric and trimmings.*

• *You can omit the embroidered rosebuds if you wish without spoiling the overall effect.*

6 Repeat steps 2 and 3 to make the neck frill, machining the scallops in a curve around both corners. Put the neck frill aside to be attached later.

6 ASSEMBLING THE NIGHTGOWN

1 Join the second side seam, taking care to match up the skirt trim and frill. Neaten the seam with a fine zigzag and trim.

2 Join and neaten the sleeve underarm seams in the same way as the side seam, again taking care to match up the trims and frills.

3 Sew two rows of gathering stitches in the space between the dots on the heads of the sleeves. With right sides together and raw edges aligned, set the sleeves into the armholes, matching the dots, notches and seams. Pull up the gathering stitches, adjust the gathers evenly, and join and neaten the sleeve seams.

4 With right sides together and leaving the entredeux untrimmed, align the raw edges of the entredeux and the neckline of the nightgown. Machine stitch the entredeux to the neckline, with a seam allowance the width of the fabric edging of the entredeux. Neaten the seam with a fine zigzag stitch and trim.

5 To neaten the ends of the entredeux, fold a small hem to the wrong

side, aligning the beading so that the ribbon can be threaded through.

6 Adjust the gathers of the neck frill evenly and trim the fabric from the other edge of the entredeux. Join the frill to the entredeux, using method 2.

7 FINISHING

1 Machine stitch three horizontal buttonholes on the left back yoke in the positions marked on the pattern. Sew three buttons to the right back yoke in the corresponding positions.

2 Cut 220 cm of ribbon. Starting at the center front of the skirt, thread the ribbon through the beading in the skirt trim and tie in a bow.

3 Repeat step 2 for each sleeve, using 110 cm of ribbon and starting opposite the underarm seams.

4 Cut a 50 cm length of ribbon and thread it through the beading at the neckline, trimming the ends and securing them with slipstitch. Make a small bow from the remaining ribbon and handstitch it to the center front of the neckline.

5 Using a single strand of embroidery cotton, work the rosebud design in the center of each batiste panel of the yoke. Repeat the design at regular intervals on the skirt and sleeve trims.

6 Undo the rolled long ribbons at the center front of the yoke and tie a bow.

With a single strand of embroidery cotton, work the rosebuds in satin stitch or bullion stitch. Use chain stitch to embroider the leaves and stem stitch for the stems.

Connoisseur's wine rack

For a parent who is a wine buff, this sturdy wine rack would be the ideal gift. Made of solid pine, it can hold up to 18 full-sized bottles.

WHAT YOU NEED

Master pattern **F40(a–b)** • surfaced lumber (e.g. pine): 2 lengths, 600 mm **x** 260 mm **x** 18 mm (for the end panels); 6 lengths, 580 mm **x** 65 mm **x** 18 mm (for the racks) • 24 flat-head wood screws, 38 mm, 8 gauge • stain, paint or clear varnish • 2 paintbrushes • tracing paper • transfer paper • hard pencil (or empty ballpoint pen) • pencil • jigsaw or coping saw • coarse and medium sandpaper • sanding block • ruler • drill and 2.5 mm, 4 mm and countersink drill bits • screwdriver

● *Technique pages 338–42, 343–4*

❶ PREPARING THE WOOD

1 Using tracing paper and a pencil, trace the patterns of the scallop-edged racks and the heart-shaped cut-out from the master pattern.

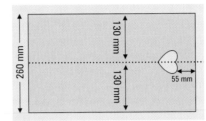

2 Using transfer paper and hard pencil, transfer the scallop shape onto the six racks. Then transfer the heart shapes to the end panels, placing them in the positions shown.
3 Using the jigsaw, cut out the scalloped edges.
4 Within the heart shape to be cut out, drill an access hole greater than the width of the jigsaw blade. Place the blade of the jigsaw in this hole and carefully cut out the heart shape.

5 Wrap coarse sandpaper around the sanding block and sand the edges of the end panels so that the square outside edges are slightly beveled.
6 Sand all surfaces completely smooth with medium sandpaper.

❷ ASSEMBLING THE WINE RACK

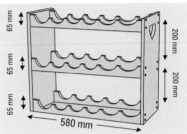

1 Following the dimensions shown, mark the positions of the racks on the end panels, noting that the racks are spaced 200 mm apart vertically and the top of the upper rack is positioned 5 mm from the top edge of the end panel. The outer faces of all racks should be flush with the vertical edges of the end panels.
2 Mark the positions of the screws on both the end panels and the ends of the racks. The center of each screw should be 10 mm from the outer edge and 10 mm from the top and bottom edges of each rack.
3 Using the 2.5 mm drill bit, drill holes for the screws right through the end panels and about 1.5 cm into the ends of the racks. Use a vise or a clamping system to help you to hold the panels and racks in position each time you drill through.
4 Using the 4 mm drill bit, redrill all the holes in the two end panels.
5 With the countersink bit, countersink the outside face of each hole in the two end panels.
6 Screw the racks to one end panel. Place the other end panel in position and screw it to the racks.

❸ FINISHING

1 Lightly sand all surfaces with the medium sandpaper.
2 Apply stain, clear varnish or paint to all the surfaces.

Strawberry garden chair

Personalize a director's chair for a parent who enjoys relaxing in the garden. The design is attractive, yet easy to paint – it would take very little time to decorate a pair.

WHAT YOU NEED

Master pattern **F41(a–b)** • plain canvas director's chair • Jo Sonja's (or Liquitex) artist's colors: green oxide, teal green, naphthol red light, burgundy, black, titanium white, Turner's yellow • textile medium • paintbrushes: no. 5 round, no. 00 liner • tracing paper • pencil • dressmaker's carbon • hard pencil
● *Technique pages 334–5, 343–4*

❶ TRANSFERRING THE DESIGN

1 Mark the center of the backrest. Using tracing paper and pencil, trace the designs from the master pattern.
2 Using dressmaker's carbon and a hard pencil, transfer the single strawberry design onto the front left-hand corner of the seat and the large design onto the backrest, matching centers.

❷ PAINTING THE DESIGN
Leaves

1 Using the round brush, paint all the large leaves with green oxide.

HINT

For a very special gift – perhaps for a wedding anniversary – why not team a pair of these chairs with the Iris garden apron (pages 210–11)?

Apply only one coat, allowing the plain canvas background to show through.
2 Using teal green, dry-brush a dark area on the backs of the large leaves, extending down the center vein.

Strawberries

1 Paint the strawberries in naphthol red light, using as many coats as necessary to completely cover the fabric. Allow to dry.
2 Dry-brush a little burgundy onto the underside of each strawberry. Blend the shading across the fruit so that some of the base color shows through.
3 Using Turner's yellow, dry-brush some highlights onto the upper side of each strawberry.
4 Load the liner brush with black and paint the seeds, using tiny comma strokes spaced slightly wider apart at the bulge of the fruit than at the tip.
5 Reverting to the round brush, dry-brush titanium white highlights in the center of the yellow highlights and over some of the seeds.

Painting guide
The larger design (shown below) goes on the backrest, and the complementary smaller version (above right) is for the front left-hand corner of the seat.

Flowers

1 Paint the flowers with titanium white, using two joined comma strokes for each flower petal. Using the end of the paintbrush handle, dot the centers of the flowers with Turner's yellow.
2 Load the liner brush with teal green and paint the sepals on the stem ends of the strawberries. With the same paint and brush, outline each leaf, paint in the tendrils, and then loosely outline the blossoms.

❸ FINISHING
1 Allow the paint to dry thoroughly.
2 Fix the painting on the canvas by following the manufacturer's instructions.

Breakfast tea cozy

Crochet this tea cozy to keep a parent's breakfast tea piping hot.

WHAT YOU NEED

2 balls cream wool • crochet hook: 5.00 mm (no. 6) • stranded embroidery cotton: gold, leaf green • needles: size 10 crewel, size 6 self-threader • 1 button
The tea cozy fits a 6-cup teapot.
● *Technique pages 320–2, 327*

CHECKING THE GAUGE

For the best results, check your gauge before you begin crocheting the tea cozy, so that the measurements of the finished article will be as close as possible to the size specified. You should have 18 double crochets and 22 rows to a 10 cm square over double crochet fabric, using a 5.00 mm crochet hook and 8 ply wool. If you have fewer stitches, use a smaller hook; if you have more stitches, use a larger hook. To achieve the effect illustrated, the tea cozy is designed to be worked on a bigger hook and at a looser gauge than is usually recommended in crochet patterns.

❶ WORKING THE CROCHET

Make two of these pieces.
Make 41 ch.
1st row: Miss 1 ch, 1 dc in each ch to end...40 dc.
2nd row: 1 ch, 1 dc in each dc to end. Rep 2nd row 26 times.

Shaping the top

29th row: 1 ch, 1 dc in next dc, ★ "Dec,"1 dc in each of next 2 dc, rep from ★ to last 3 dc, "Dec," 1 dc in last dc...30 sts.
Work 2 rows in pat.
32nd row: 1 ch, ★ "Dec," 1 dc in next dc, rep from ★ to end...20 sts.
Work 2 rows in pat.
35th row: 1 ch, ★ "Dec," rep from ★ to end...10 sts.
Work 1 row in pat.
37th row: As for 35th row...5 sts.
Fasten off.

❷ EMBROIDERING THE DESIGN

1 Fold one crochet piece in half lengthwise to find the center. Along the center line, count up 12 rows from the bottom. Match this point with the location point on the stitch guide.
2 Following the stitch guide, work the design in cross-stitch. If you wish, repeat the design on the other piece.

SPECIAL ABBREVIATION

"Dec": draw up a loop in each of next 2 sts, yo and draw through all 3 loops on hook.

---

❸ MAKING UP THE TEA COZY

1 Do not press. Using a flat seam, join the pieces on both sides, from the beginning of the decreasing row (row 29) to the top row of five stitches.
2 To make the loop at the top, join yarn with a slst in the top edge, make 15 ch for the loop, slst in opposite edge, turn, work 24 dc in loop, slst in the base of 15 ch. Fasten off.
3 Run a thread through the top edge and draw it up tightly.
4 Work a ch to make a button loop at lower edge below the handle and sew on the button. Sew the sides opposite the button together from the bottom, up 4 cm, leaving a hole for the spout.

STITCH GUIDE

Work the design in gold and leaf green, treating the rows and stitches of the crochet fabric as the cross-stitch grid. Because the crochet fabric is thick and soft, use the full hank of embroidery cotton.

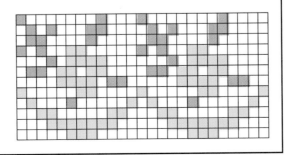

Old-time lavender bags

Lavender bags are always a welcome gift. They can be placed in lingerie drawers or linen cupboards or hung from coat-hangers so that their fragrance mingles with the clothes in a wardrobe. Work one lavender bag with a simple beaded fish design, and, for a more traditional look, embroider the other with rosebuds.

HINT

You can use any sheer fabric for making lavender bags – voile, Swiss cotton, or even very fine handkerchief linen, are all suitable. For the beaded lavender bag, use fine aida cloth, which provides a guide for positioning the beads.

WHAT YOU NEED

30 cm x 12 cm organza for each bag • sewing thread to match • seed beads: light blue, gold glass, 2 black (for the eyes) • embroidery cotton in salmon and green • needles: beading, embroidery, general sewing • sewing machine (optional) • 30 cm ribbons, 3 mm wide: gold lamé, salmon • dried lavender or lavender potpourri (see "Fragrant potpourri," pages 214–15)
● *Technique pages 292–301, 307–12*

❶ WORKING THE BEADING AND THE EMBROIDERY

Position the designs fairly close to the bottom fold lines, as the tops of the bags will be folded over in a wide hem to make the ribbon casing.

1 Fold the pieces of organza in half widthwise and press the folds – these will be the bottom edges of the bags. Unfold the pieces of fabric.
2 Following the beading guide, work beading for the fish design on one side of one piece of fabric.
3 On one side of the other fabric piece, embroider four roses in salmon embroidery thread. Make the rose-buds with three bullion knots of 12 turns each. Work the calyxes with two lazy daisy stitches in the green embroidery thread.

❷ MAKING UP THE BAGS

1 On the right side of each piece of organza, work a small buttonhole at the center of the fabric above the worked area, 8 cm from the fold.
2 With wrong sides facing, fold the

organza in half widthwise and join the sides with a narrow French seam, by hand or with a sewing machine.
3 With wrong sides together, turn down 5 mm at the top edge, and then turn down a wide hem so that the folded edge sits over the buttonhole. Sew a row of stitching on either side of the buttonhole to form a casing.

❸ FINISHING

1 Thread the gold lamé ribbon through the casing of the beaded bag and the salmon ribbon through the casing of the embroidered bag.
2 Fill the bags with dried lavender or lavender potpourri, pull up the ribbons and tie them in a bow.

BEADING GUIDE

The beaded fish is a simple but effective design. The tail is sewn using gold beads and the body is made from rows of alternating light blue and gold beads. One black bead is used at the appropriate spot for an eye.

Stitch the beads horizontally across the design, threading up to four beads on one stitch. Stitch all rows in the same direction, from the right to the left.

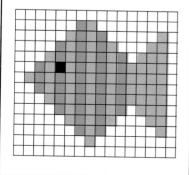

Iris garden apron

A gift painted by hand is a perfect way to say "I love you."
This iris-patterned apron is both pretty and practical, and
is equally at home in either the garden or the kitchen.

WHAT YOU NEED

Master pattern G47(a) • plain, light
colored cotton apron • 6 m dark
blue silk bias binding (optional) •
Matisse background paints: Ritz
blue, antique green, burgundy •
Jo Sonja's (or Liquitex) artist's
colors: Turner's yellow, warm
white, red earth, salmon pink,
burnt sienna, brown earth • textile
medium • paintbrushes: no. 5
round, no. 0 liner • fine-tipped
marker pen • dressmaker's carbon •
tracing paper • hard pencil • palette
● *Technique pages 299, 334–5, 343–4*

❶ TRANSFERRING THE DESIGN

1 Using the tracing paper and the
fine marker pen, trace the design
from the master pattern, ensuring
that you include the markings for
the center points.
2 Fold the apron in half lengthwise
and mark the center line.
3 Open out the apron, smooth it
out, and position the iris design on
it. Match the center line of the apron
with the center line of the design,
and pin the design carefully into place.
4 Use dressmaker's carbon and a
hard pencil to transfer the iris design
onto the apron.

❷ PAINTING THE DESIGN
Leaves

1 On the palette, mix three shades
of green. Use pure antique green for
the darkest shade, and then create the
two lighter shades by mixing various
quantities of warm white with antique
green. To each shade add equal parts
of textile medium.
2 Using a round brush, paint the
leaves with the three shades of
green. Paint the leaves farthest from
the front with the deepest green, and
also use the deepest green at the
bases of the leaves where they converge to join the roots. Use the lighter
shades for the closer leaves. Where
the leaves touch each other, side-load
the brush with warm white to accentuate the edges of the leaves.
3 Shade the edges of some of the
lighter leaves by dry-brushing a
darker shade along one side.

Stems

1 Load the tip of the round brush with medium green and dry-brush the stems. Using the darkest green, dry-brush over parts of the stems to create an effect of light and shade.
2 Loosely outline the stems up to the bud sheaths with the liner brush loaded with dark green.
3 On the paint palette, add a little Turner's yellow and warm white to some of the lightest green, and partially mix the paints. With the tip of the round brush, dry-brush in the bud sheaths. Let the color mix a little on the fabric.

Red iris

1 Load the round brush with a mixture of equal parts of burgundy and textile medium. Pick up a side-load of red earth and, keeping the side-load on the outside edge of the design, stroke in the buds and the lower petals of the flowers on the right-hand stem.
2 Mix salmon pink with warm white and burnt sienna, and add textile medium. Using the round brush, paint in the central petals of the two red irises. Add more warm white to the pink mixture, and dry-brush in from the edges of the pink petals.
3 Wipe the color out of the brush (do not wash it), and pick up some Turner's yellow with the tip. Paint some small comma strokes at the "flag" on the burgundy petals, keeping the brush on its tip. (You could use a liner brush for these strokes.)

Blue iris

1 On the paint palette, use textile medium, warm white and various quantities of Ritz blue to mix three shades of blue.
2 Paint the large outer petals on the left-hand side stem in medium blue, then overstroke them with deepest blue so that they are mostly dark.
3 Paint the buds in deepest blue and the remaining central petals in medium blue.
4 Dry-brush lightest blue from the edges inward, blending it into the medium blue.

Painting guide
Blue irises and dark red irises with pink throats rise from a clump of gray-green leaves. Below the leaves sit the roots and the root hairs, which are painted in brown earth brightened with warm white and burnt sienna.

5 Add touches of darkest blue at the base of the petals and at the points where the petals overlap.

Roots

1 On the palette, partially mix brown earth with warm white, a touch of burnt sienna and the textile medium.
2 Paint the roots with brushstrokes following the root shapes. Add more brown earth for the roots at the back.
3 Use the same mixture to stroke in the root hairs with a liner brush.

❸ FINISHING

1 Allow the painted design to dry, and heat-set the paints following the manufacturer's instructions.
2 For an optional touch of elegance, trim off the ties and hems. Bind the top edge and the lower curve from corner to corner with the bias binding. Bind one arm curve, leaving about 50 cm for the tie. Leave a loop of binding at the top for the neck, bind the other arm curve, and leave about 50 cm for the other tie.

Fine woolen summer shawl

Elegant enough for evening wear, this attractive shawl will also provide warmth on cool summer nights. The drawn threadwork on the fine wool is worked in embroidery cotton that matches the fabric to create a subtle effect.

WHAT YOU NEED

140 cm x 140 cm wool challis • 1 skein stranded embroidery cotton to match fabric • needle: size 20 tapestry • contrasting thread (for basting) • dressmaker's pencil • ruler • sharp embroidery scissors

① DRAWING THE THREADS

1 In order to make sure that the fabric is square, carefully pull threads along each side close to the edge and trim away the fringe of counter threads with sharp scissors.
2 Fold the fabric in four to find the center. Measure 20 cm from the center, along the folds, and mark the points with the dressmaker's pencil. With the ruler and dressmaker's pencil, rule lines through these points to form a square with 40 cm sides.

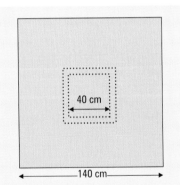

3 Baste around the ruled square, following one thread in each direction. Count 12 threads out from the first square and baste another square. The basting lines form the border from which the threads will be drawn.
4 Locate the middle of one side of the border and carefully cut through the 12 threads between the basting lines with a pair of sharp scissors.
5 Draw out the cut threads with a tapestry needle. Draw each thread as far as 3 cm from the corners of the basted square. Draw the threads in sections so that you do not pull

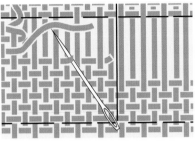

the threads in the body of the shawl.
6 Repeat steps 4 and 5 on each side of the square. Remove the basting.

② WORKING THE EMBROIDERY

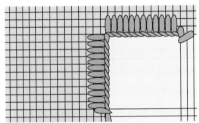

1 At the outside edges of the corners, overstitch the threads and work buttonhole stitch closely over the overstitching, using the tapestry needle and two strands of embroidery cotton. Draw the threads left at each corner of the square and trim them close to the buttonhole stitching. (You will have an empty square at each corner.)

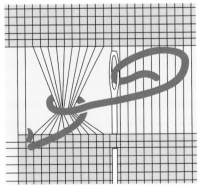

2 Secure the embroidery cotton with a few backstitches at one inside corner of the drawn thread square. Working from left to right, hemstitch around the inside of the drawn thread square, gathering 10 threads at a time.

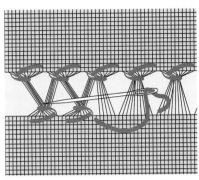

3 Now working from the outside edge of the square, create a herringbone pattern by gathering five threads from one bundle and five threads from the next bundle and hemstitching around the square.

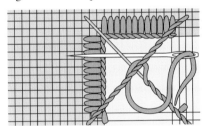

4 Fill each corner with two woven diagonal bars in the following manner. Starting in one corner, take the cotton over to the diagonally opposite corner and stitch into the corner, carefully tensioning the diagonal thread. Now wrap the cotton around the diagonal thread, ending back in the corner you started from. Repeat this procedure to make the other diagonal bar.

③ MAKING THE OUTSIDE SQUARE

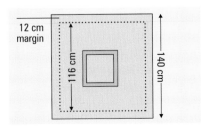

1 Measure and mark a square 12 cm from the outside edges of the fabric. Baste along this line, and then pull

three threads along the basting lines, carefully pulling the threads right to the edges of the fabric.

2 Hemstitch around the inside edge of this square, catching bundles of 10 threads as you go. (The outside edge of this drawn thread square is not stitched.)

④ FINISHING

1 Measure outward 10 cm from the outer square of drawn threads, and pull threads from this point, parallel to the sides of the shawl and right to the edge, to create a fringe.

2 Carefully press the shawl, paying particular attention to the embroidery.

NOTE

In drawn threadwork, always work hemstitch, which is used to secure the bundles of threads, from the back of the fabric.

Fragrant potpourri

Fill pillows and sachets with your own potpourri mixtures, in combinations to suit a particular recipient's likes and dislikes, to give an added personal touch to this gift.

WHAT YOU NEED

Fragrant flowers and leaves, spices, orange peel (see individual recipes in section 3) • scissors • sheets of newspaper • shoe-box with lid, or large paper bag

❶ PREPARING THE DRIED FLOWERS AND LEAVES

1 Gather flowers and leaves from the garden early in the morning (but after the overnight dew has dried, because damp plant material may rot). Pick flowers when they are fully open and before they begin to decay. Pick herbs just as they come into flower.

2 As soon as possible after picking, spread the flowers and leaves on several sheets of newspaper. Leave small flowers, such as tiny rosebuds, daisies or lavender, intact. To prepare larger flowers, remove the petals from the sepals (the green part at the base of the flower). Snip large leaves into several pieces with scissors.

3 Place the newspaper in a dry, airy place, away from wind and direct sunlight. Each day, toss the flowers with your fingertips to make sure that they dry out evenly. The material should be ready in three or four days.

4 When they are leathery to the touch, store the dried flowers and leaves in a lidded shoe-box or closed paper bag until you are ready to make the potpourri. This protects the plant material from dust and prevents it from becoming moldy.

❷ MAKING THE POTPOURRI

1 Put the ingredients for the recipe you want to make in a box or paper bag and shake them together lightly.

2 Fill sachets or pillows with the mixture as soon as possible, and stitch or tie the receptacle shut.

❸ RECIPES

Mixed flowers

½ cup mixed heavily scented dried flower petals
¼ cup dried lavender
¼ cup dried lemon verbena leaves
¼ cup dried rosemary
Peel of one orange, cut into slivers and dried

Sweet rose

1 cup dried scented rose petals
Peel of half an orange, cut into slivers and dried
¼ cup crushed cloves and cinnamon sticks
¼ teaspoon nutmeg

Rose and herb

¼ cup dried scented rose petals
¼ cup dried mint
¼ cup dried lemon balm
¼ cup dried lemon verbena

Lemon verbena

1 cup dried lemon verbena

HINTS

• To crush cloves, place them in a plastic bag and roll gently with a rolling pin.
• Crush leaves with your fingers to release the scent before placing them in the sachet.
• Unless the dried material you have chosen is heavily scented, (such as scented varieties of lavender, orange blossom, lemon verbena, rosemary, and some of the old-fashioned roses), you will need to add spices, herbs or citrus peel to intensify the fragrance.
• You can buy scented oils to boost the fragrance, but this type of potpourri is not suitable for clothing and linen sachets or for sleep pillows, as the oil will seep through and stain the fabric.
• Other suitable ingredients for potpourri are mimosa, jasmine, apple blossom, chamomile, sweet pea, narcissus, honeysuckle, and peel of lemon or lime.

Old English lavender

1 cup dried very fragrant lavender
5 or 6 crushed cloves

Lavender and rose

½ cup dried fragrant lavender
½ cup dried rose petals
¼ cup dried lemon verbena leaves or dried thyme
10 crushed cloves, or a small stick of crushed cinnamon

Lavender and rosemary

½ cup dried rosemary
½ cup dried lavender
Some slivers of dried orange peel
8 whole cloves

Herb

1 cup dried rosemary
1 cup dried fragrant pine needles

Citrus potpourri

½ cup lemon verbena leaves
½ cup rose geranium leaves
slivers of orange and lemon peel
10 crushed coriander seeds

SPICY POMANDER

For a deliciously perfumed room or wardrobe, you can substitute pomanders for potpourri sachets.

1 Stud a few oranges or apples (or both) with whole cloves.

2 In a bowl, mix together ground spices – for example, cloves, cinnamon, nutmeg and orrisroot.

3 Roll the fruits in the ground spices until they are well covered.

4 Place the fruits in individual paper bags for several weeks to dry out.

5 When the fruits are dry, dust them off. Thread a ribbon through them for hanging in a wardrobe, or arrange them in a decorative bowl.

Embroidered table linen

A round tablecloth lovingly embroidered in traditional cross-stitch is a timeless gift that a parent will be thrilled to receive. The rose motif on the tablecloth is repeated on the napkins.

WHAT YOU NEED

Master pattern J69(a) • 175 cm
x 110 cm cream aida cloth
(11 gauge) • 3.5 m cream
cotton edging lace • stranded
cotton: Anchor colors 78
(crimson), 77 (mid-pink), 73
(palest pink), 842 (pale yellow-green), 308 (deep old gold), 890
(old gold), 306 (yellow), 891 (deep
cream), 111 (purple), 109 (mauve),
108 (pale mauve), 103 (old rose
pink); 2 skeins each of 76 (rose
pink), 74 (pink), 261 (grass green);
3 skeins each of 262 (dark green),
215 (mid-green) • needle: size 24
crewel • sewing thread to match the
fabric • scissors • tape measure •
sewing machine (for zigzagging
the lace edge) • dressmaker's pencil
• 60 cm string
● *Technique pages 304, 309*

❶ PREPARING THE FABRIC
1 Cut a 110 cm square from the
fabric for the tablecloth. From the
remaining fabric cut four or six
31.5 cm squares for the napkins.
2 Iron all pieces and oversew
or zigzag the raw edges.
3 Fold the fabric for the tablecloth
in half and then in half again to find

Cutting guide
*Cut a 110 cm square for the tablecloth,
and up to six 31.5 cm squares, depending
on how many napkins you want to make.*

the center. Using colored thread,
baste along the fold lines to mark the
vertical and horizontal center lines.

**❷ EMBROIDERING
THE TABLECLOTH**
1 To start the embroidery, find the
center of the design on the master
pattern and count the number of

squares from the center to the start
of the cross-stitch design. Count the
same number of squares from the
center of the aida cloth, along one
line of basting. This will give you the
starting point for the embroidery.
2 Following the stitch and color
guide on the master pattern, and using
five strands of embroidery cotton,
embroider the design onto the table-cloth, completing it four times to
form a circle.

❸ FINISHING THE TABLECLOTH
1 Press the tablecloth piece and
spread it out flat on a clean carpet.

← 110 cm →	←31.5 cm→	31.5 cm

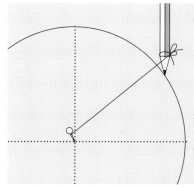

2 Attach the dressmaker's pencil to the end of the piece of string and measure 54 cm from the tip of the pencil along the string. Secure the string at this point to the center of the fabric.

3 Keeping the string taut, swing the pencil to inscribe a circle on the fabric. Cut along the pencil line to create a circle with a diameter of 108 cm.

4 Attach the lace by machine zigzagging it to the edge of the circle on the right side of the fabric.

④ EMBROIDERING THE NAPKINS

1 To find the starting point for the embroidery, match the edge of the grid on the master pattern with the edge of the cloth and count squares.

2 Using five strands of embroidery cotton, and following the stitch and color guide on the master pattern, embroider the rose design in one corner of each napkin.

⑤ FINISHING THE NAPKINS

Turn down all the edges 5 mm and then 1 cm and hemstitch around the napkins, mitering the corners neatly.

> **HINT**
> *For some helpful tips on counted cross-stitch, see "Wedding day sampler" (pages 194–5).*

Sunflower wall hanging

Lighten your parents' kitchen or breakfast room with this gold and yellow wall hanging.

WHAT YOU NEED

Master pattern **G77(a–c)** • 3 pieces fabric, 25 cm **x** 16 cm, in shades of gold (for the flowers) • extra piece of one gold shade, 50 cm **x** 30 cm (for the border and loops) • 2 rectangles cream-colored fabric, 48 cm **x** 35 cm (for background and backing) • fabric scraps (for flower centers) • 20 cm **x** 40 cm green fabric (for stems and leaves) • 48 cm **x** 35 cm batting, plus a few scraps • 30 cm **x** 25 cm double-sided iron-on webbing • scrap of iron-on non-woven interfacing • sewing thread to match flower centers, stems and leaves • quilting cotton: cream, gold • embroidery cottons: yellow, brown, gold, green • 75 cm gold cord • embroidery hoop (optional) • needles: sewing, quilting, embroidery • 50 cm dowel • tracing paper • pencil • compass • dressmaker's pencil • sharp-pointed scissors • dressmaking pins • sewing machine • iron

● *Technique pages 292–301, 302, 305–6, 307–12, 343–4*

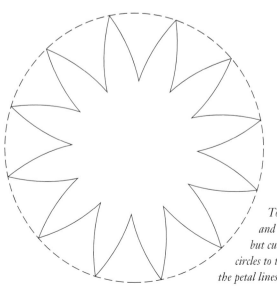

❶ PREPARING THE SUNFLOWERS

1 On the paper side of the webbing, use the compass and pencil to draw nine circles, three with a radius of 4.5 cm, three with a radius of 3.75 cm, and three with a radius of 3.25 cm. Cut out the nine circles.
2 Place one webbing circle of each size, paper side up, on the wrong side

To make the sunflower petals, trace the circles and the petal outlines from the master pattern, but cut out only the circles. Pin the tracing paper circles to the right-sized fabric circles, and cut along the petal lines through the pattern piece and the fabric.

of one of the gold fabrics. Fuse the webbing to the fabric by ironing over the paper. Peel the paper away and cut out the fabric circles.
3 Place the three webbing and fabric circles, fabric side up, on the wrong side of the remaining fabric. Fuse the fabric to the webbing with a hot iron and cut out the shapes.
4 Repeat steps 2 and 3 on the other two gold fabrics. You should now have nine double-thickness circles, one of each size from each fabric.
5 From the master pattern, trace the three circles with the petal design. Cut out the circles and pin them to the

fabric circles with the tips of the petals touching the edges of the circles. Cut out the flower shapes.

6 Draw three circles with a radius of 1.3 cm on the interfacing and three on the scraps of batting, using the compass and pencil. Draw one circle with a radius of 1.7 cm on each of the three pieces of scrap material. Cut out all the circles. (They will be used to make the centers of the three sunflowers.)

7 Center the interfacing circles on the wrong side of the fabric circles and fuse them to the fabric with a hot iron.

8 Separate the layers of batting to make thinner pads and place them on the top of the interfacing. Clip the edges of the fabric circles and fold them in over the batting.

❷ PREPARING THE STEMS AND LEAVES

1 Cut three slightly curving 1.5 cm strips of green fabric 22 cm, 16 cm and 14 cm long for the stems. Fold under and press the long edges of the strips so that the stems are about 6 mm wide.

2 On a piece of tracing paper, draw three leaf shapes, two about 7.5 cm long and one about 6 cm long. Cut out the shapes and use them as templates to mark and cut leaf shapes from the interfacing.

3 Iron the three leaf-shaped interfacings to the wrong side of the green fabric. Cut the fabric around the interfacing, leaving a 3 mm border. Fold the border back over the interfacing and press.

❸ ASSEMBLING THE DESIGN

Each sunflower is made up of three petal circles, each of which is a different shade and size.

1 Lay down the largest circle of petals, place the next largest circle on top and the smallest circle on top of that. Arrange the circles so that the petal tips are alternating.

2 Slipstitch the flower center into position, sewing through all thicknesses. Make sure the edges of the flower center are neatly turned under.

3 Ensure that the edges of the rectangle of background fabric are square.

4 Position and pin the stems, leaves and flowers in place on the background fabric. When you are satisfied with the arrangement, slipstitch each piece into place.

5 Using six strands of green embroidery cotton, work the stems of the embroidered daisies in stem stitch and the leaves in lazy daisy stitch.

6 Using six strands of yellow cotton, embroider the daisy petals in lazy daisy stitches. Fill the center of each daisy with French knots, using brown cotton.

7 Work the other flowers in a mixture of yellow, gold and brown, using six strands of cotton.

❹ ADDING THE QUILTING DETAILS

1 To make the backing, press and trim the other rectangle of cream-colored fabric.

2 Place the backing, wrong side up, flat on the table. Lay the batting over it and the appliquéd fabric, right side up, on top of that. Smooth out any wrinkles. Baste all three layers firmly together around the edges.

3 Following the dotted lines on the appliqué and stitch guide, use small, even running stitches to quilt the details through all layers.

4 When the quilting is complete, machine stitch all layers together around the edge. Remove the basting.

❺ SEWING THE BORDER

1 Cut four strips 5 cm wide from the border fabric, two 48 cm long and two 37 cm long.

2 Fold each strip in half lengthwise and press the fold. On the long sides of each strip, fold and press down a 1.25 cm hem to the wrong side.

3 Open out the strips. With right sides facing, place the raw edges of the long strips and the sides of the hanging together. Stitch the border to the hanging along the fold lines.

4 Turn the remaining raw edges of the borders to the back of the hanging

Cut-out fabric	• French knot
----- Cream quilting	⌒ Stem stitch
- - - Gold quilting	⬭ Lazy daisy stitch

Appliqué and stitch guide
The flowers and foliage are appliquéd first, then the details are embroidered, and finally the quilting lines are sewn.

and fold the seam allowances under. Hem the borders into place on the back by hand.

5 Repeat steps 3 and 4 to sew the shorter strips to the top and bottom edges of the hanging. Make sure that the corners are folded under neatly.

6 Press the wall hanging through a damp cloth, front and back.

❻ FINISHING

1 Cut three strips of the border material, 5.5 cm x 13 cm. Fold down 1 cm around all four edges of each strip and machine sew the hems.

2 Fold the strips in half to form loops and slipstitch them, evenly spaced, to the back of the hanging along the top edge. Thread the dowel through.

3 Attach gold cord to the ends of the dowel to form a hanging loop.

Flowery watering can

Redolent of summer meadows, this folk art design transforms a plain watering can into an attractive ornament. To complete the gift, slip a glass jar inside to hold water for cut flowers.

WHAT YOU NEED

Master pattern **F43(a)** • small galvanized metal watering can about 22 cm high • Matisse Folk Art background color: lichen gray • Jo Sonja's (or Liquitex) artist's colors: rich gold, yellow oxide, warm white, naphthol red light, Turner's yellow, red earth, Norwegian orange, pine green, raw sienna, brown earth, raw umber • metal primer • water-based flat or semigloss varnish • paintbrushes: 25 mm decorating, no. 2 round, nos. 12 and 8 flat, no. 00 liner • tracing paper • fine-tipped marker pen • masking tape • transfer paper • paint palette • old toothbrush • hard pencil (or empty ballpoint pen)
● *Technique pages 334–5, 343–4*

❶ PREPARING THE SURFACE

1 Follow the methods described in the folk art techniques section to prepare the metal surface for painting.
2 Using the decorating brush, apply three smooth coats of lichen gray, allowing each coat to dry thoroughly before applying the next.

❷ SPATTERING

1 Mix rich gold paint with a little water to a smooth, light consistency.
2 Dip the ends of the toothbrush bristles in the paint. Spatter gold lightly and evenly over the entire exposed surface of the watering can by holding the brush in one hand and drawing the thumb of your other hand toward you, across the bristles.
3 Allow the paint to dry thoroughly.

HINT
Practice spattering paint onto a sheet of scrap paper until you are confident of your technique.

❸ TRANSFERRING THE DESIGN

1 Trace the design from the master pattern using the tracing paper and the fine-tipped marker pen.
2 Place the traced design on the surface of the watering can so that it is centered between the handle and the spout, and secure it in position with masking tape.
3 Slip a sheet of transfer paper under the tracing paper and transfer the design to the can using the hard pencil or the empty ballpoint pen.
4 Repeat steps 2 and 3 to transfer the design to the other side.
5 Trace or photocopy the verse of Shakespeare from the master pattern onto a strip of tracing paper. Secure the tracing paper in position around the base of the watering can with small pieces of masking tape.

6 Slip a strip of transfer paper under the tracing paper and transfer the lettering to the watering can. Repeat or shorten the verse, as space permits.

❹ PAINTING THE DESIGN
Background wash

1 Using the no. 8 flat brush, paint a soft wash of Turner's yellow around the bases of the plants, in some places allowing it to reach about a third of the way up the can. The wash should be very transparent.
2 Allow the paint wash to dry.

Red anemones

1 Mix red earth, naphthol red light, Norwegian orange and Turner's

---

RED ANEMONES

Paint the petals first, then the centers. Float a shadow around the petal bases and detail the centers. Lastly, paint the buds and leaves.

PRIMROSES

Use two strokes for each petal and lightly shade the bases. Fill and detail the centers and then paint and highlight the leaves.

Make each petal with two strokes and allow them to dry.

2 Using a side-loaded no. 8 flat brush, float brown earth around the bases of the petals, butting up against the centers of the primroses.

3 Paint the centers in pine green. When they are dry, outline them with yellow oxide and paint a warm white dot in the middle of each one.

4 Paint the leaves with a round brush triple-loaded with pine green, yellow oxide and brown earth. When they are dry, side-load the flat brush with Turner's yellow and float highlights on the edges.

Floated shading

1 When all the flowers are dry, float a shadow around the base of the design using the no. 12 flat brush side-loaded with raw umber. Keep the loaded side of the brush on the outer edge of the design.

2 Using raw umber and the no. 12 flat brush, float another shadow at the top of the design, keeping the loaded side on the top outer edge.

3 Repeat steps 1 and 2 on the lower rim of the watering can, above and below where you plan to paint the Shakespearean verse.

Lettering

1 Mix some brown earth to an inky consistency with water and, using the liner brush, paint the words of the Shakespearean verse around the base of the watering can:

When daisies pied and violets blue
And lily-smocks all silver-white,
And cuckoo-buds of yellow hue
Do paint the meadows with delight…

2 When the lettering is dry, use rich gold to paint a shadow line under each letter.

5 FINISHING

1 Paint bands of rich gold around the top and bottom of the can, along the edges of the handles and around the spout. Apply at least two coats.

2 Using the decorating brush, cover all exposed surfaces with four to six coats of water-based varnish.

---

yellow on the round brush and paint the petals. Allow them to dry, then paint them again for greater depth and coverage.

2 When the petals are dry, paint the centers of the anemones with Turner's yellow.

3 Allow the centers to dry, and then add circles of pine green.

4 Side-load the no. 8 flat brush with brown earth and float a shadow around the bases of the petals, butting up against the centers.

5 Paint tiny dots of double-loaded warm white and Turner's yellow on and near the centers.

6 Paint the leaves and buds with a double-loaded round brush, using pine green and yellow oxide. When they are dry, repeat.

7 Apply the same color to the stems, using the liner brush.

Daisies

1 Mix warm white and yellow oxide to make cream and, using the round brush, paint the petals.

2 Base-coat the centers in Turner's yellow. When they are dry, add Norwegian orange detailing.

3 Side-load the no. 8 flat brush with raw sienna and float a shadow around the bases of the petals.

4 Outline the lower edge of the center of each daisy with brown earth.

5 Brush-mix pine green, warm white and yellow oxide and use this mixture to paint the leaves and stems. Use the round brush for the leaves and the liner brush for the stems.

Primroses

1 Using the round brush, paint the primrose petals with double-loaded yellow oxide and Norwegian orange.

Beaded butterfly evening bag

The fine beadwork on this evening bag is complemented by the cross-stitch butterfly design, which is sewn in metallic thread. This gift is the perfect accessory for any formal occasion, and it will draw admiring glances whenever it is used.

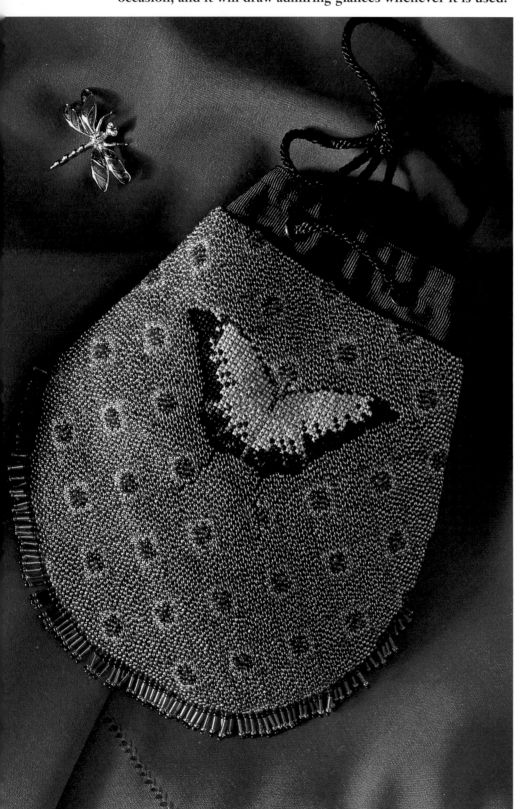

WHAT YOU NEED

Master pattern **J72(a)** • 30 cm **x** 30 cm black aida cloth (14 gauge) • 30 cm **x** 30 cm backing fabric (silk dupion or similar) • 60 cm **x** 30 cm medium-weight iron-on interfacing • 60 cm **x** 30 cm lining fabric • 40 cm black grosgrain ribbon, 40 mm wide • 2 m black silk cord • sewing threads (black and to match lining) • needles: size 24 crewel, size 10 beading • 8 medium black eyelets • eyelet punch • scissors • sewing machine • dressmaking pins

Stranded cotton: DMC colors 310 (black), 333 (purple), 959 (pale aqua), 995 (dark turquoise), 996 (turquoise), 3021 (brown)
Metallic thread: DMC Fils métallisés Art 271 black; Art 278 purple 4012, pale aqua 4052, dark turquoise 4065, turquoise 4033, brown 4251
Glass seed beads: Mill Hill colors 020 (bright blue) – 1 packet, 024 (antique rose) – 9 packets, 217 (ice blue) – 3 packets, 252 (purple) – 3 packets, 332 (green) – 1 packet.
Frosted glass beads: Mill Hill color 60020 (bright blue) – 1 packet
Small bugle beads: Mill Hill color 70020 (bright blue) – 1 packet
● *Technique pages 292–301, 309*

❶ PREPARING THE FABRIC

1 Oversew or zigzag the raw edges of the black aida cloth to prevent fraying.
2 Fold the fabric in half and in half again to locate the center vertical and horizontal lines, and mark them with colored basting. The intersection of these lines is the center of the fabric.

❷ EMBROIDERING THE BUTTERFLY DESIGN

1 Locate the center of the master pattern by joining the opposite arrows

at the mid-point of each side of the pattern. Count from this center line to locate the base line of the butterfly.
2 Using two strands of DMC stranded cotton with one strand of the Fils métallisés metallic thread, embroider the butterfly in cross-stitch, following the master pattern and the associated color key.

❸ ATTACHING THE BEADS

1 Following the master pattern and color guide, work one small section of beading at a time. Begin with the sections around the butterfly to give you a reference point.

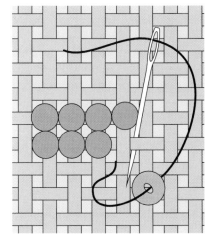

2 Using the beading needle, secure one strand of black thread at the back of the work. Bring the needle up in the bottom left-hand corner of the first square, thread on a bead and finish the stitch in the upper right-hand corner of the square.
3 Selecting beads according to the color guide, continue to stitch from left to right, keeping a regular tension on the thread. The beads will lie correctly when stitched in this way.
4 Stitch the beaded design with single beads, except where the symbol ▪▪ is marked on the master pattern. In this case, pick up two beads on the needle but stitch the thread over only one square, as elsewhere. This will create a raised effect.

❹ CONSTRUCTING THE BAG

1 Cut around the work, leaving seam allowances of 1.5 cm around the curved part and 3 cm along the straight edge at the top.

2 Using the trimmed beaded piece as a pattern, cut out an identical shape from the backing fabric, two identical shapes from the interfacing and two from the lining fabric.

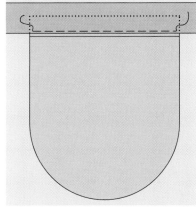

3 Cut the grosgrain ribbon in half. Place one piece along the top edge of the beaded section and stitch it in place as close to the beads as possible.
4 Iron one piece of interfacing onto the wrong side of the backing fabric, and then iron the second piece over the first piece.
5 Lay the other piece of grosgrain ribbon on the right side of this stiffened backing piece, 3 cm down from the straight edge, and stitch it in place.
6 Placing right sides together, sew the beaded section and the prepared backing fabric around the curved edge, leaving the top open. Stitch as close to the beaded area as possible. Turn to the right side.
7 With right sides facing, sew the two lining pieces together around the curved edge.
8 Place the lining bag inside the beaded bag, matching the side seams.

Trim the raw edges at the top of the bag so that the grosgrain ribbon stands above the other fabrics.
9 Fold the ribbon over the raw edges, pin, and stitch as close to the edge of the ribbon as possible. Then topstitch the ribbon close to the folded edge.

❺ FINISHING THE BAG

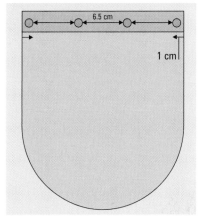

1 Position the eyelets 6.5 cm apart, starting 1 cm in from the seams. If you do not have an eyelet punch, your local shoe repairer may be able to do this for you.
2 Thread the black silk cord through the eyelet holes, starting and finishing at the back of the bag. Close the bag by pulling up the cord.

❻ MAKING THE FRINGE

1 At the point where the lighter backing fabric begins to fold in on itself (about 9 cm from the top of the beading), start to make the beaded fringe that goes around the bottom.
2 Work the fringe around the lower curve of the bag following the instructions in "Making the bead fringe."

MAKING THE BEAD FRINGE

Secure a double strand of black thread at the point where the fringe is to begin. Thread six beads onto the needle, following the color guide (right). Take the thread round the last bead and back up through the other five beads to the starting point. Continue around the bag to the other side, butting each stitch up to the preceding stitch.

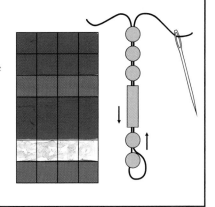

Painted apple plate

Make this beautiful and decorative plate for your parents to display with pride. It can be hung on the wall or used as a practical platter for serving fruit, nuts or chocolates.

VARIATION
You could paint this design on a flat plain-wood platter or bread-board with a diameter of at least 30 cm, or on any flat surface large enough to take the design.

WHAT YOU NEED

Master pattern **G46(a–b)** • plain-wood plate, diameter 30 cm, rim about 5 cm wide • artist's acrylic paint: green, olive green, forest green, avocado, jade green, medium green, cream, moon yellow, titanium white, cadmium yellow, naphthol red, oxblood, black, burgundy wine, deep burgundy, country red, cadmium red, russet, orange, red • water-based semigloss varnish • palette • paintbrushes: no. 5 round, no. 8 flat, no. 00 liner • fine sandpaper • tracing paper • transfer paper • pencil • hard pencil • plate hanger (optional)
● *Technique pages 334–5, 343–4*

❶ PREPARING THE PLATE

1 Prepare the wooden surface of the plate for painting, following the methods described in the folk art techniques section.
2 Using the flat brush, apply two coats of green to the plate, sanding lightly between coats.
3 Make a tracing of master pattern **G**46(a). Center the design carefully and transfer it onto the rim and inner

circle of the plate.
4 Using the round brush loaded with black paint, outline the design and fill in the leaves. Use the flat brush to fill in the rest of the area. Allow to dry thoroughly.
5 Trace and transfer master pattern **G**46(b) onto the plate, centering the apples on the rim. Note that pattern b covers almost all of pattern a.

❷ PAINTING THE DESIGN
The leaves

1 Load the round brush with avocado and stroke in the leaves that lie under the apples and over the previously painted black leaves. To create a more realistic effect, paint complete leaves, allowing the paint to extend over the apple designs rather than trying to paint around them. Allow to dry.
2 With the liner brush loaded with jade green paint, roughly outline each leaf, using a loose and curvy line to put some movement into the design.

Preparing the apples

1 Unless otherwise stated, use the round brush to paint the apples.
2 Apply enough coats of white to all the apples to make them completely opaque. Allow to dry.

Green apples

1 Paint a base coat of olive green over the titanium white.
2 *First shade:* Create a medium green shade by mixing equal amounts of olive green and medium green. Use this mixture to shade the lower two-thirds of each apple, and then dry-brush the edge of the color out into the base coat.
3 *Second shade:* Using medium green, dry-brush the lower third of each apple.
4 To create the stalk depression, place an open comma stroke of the medium green (first shade) at the top

of each apple, blending the outer edge of the stroke into the base coat. Then apply a smaller stroke of medium green (second shade) and blend the outer edge.
5 *First highlight:* Using cadmium yellow, dry-brush several shape-following strokes onto the shoulder of the apple.
6 *Second highlight:* Dry-brush a small white highlight in the center of the yellow area.
7 *Floated shade:* Using a flat brush, float forest green on the shaded outer edge and the inside of the stalk depression of each apple.

Red apples

1 For the dark red apples, follow steps 1 to 7 for "Green apples," substituting the following colors:
base coat – naphthol red;
first shade – burgundy wine (transparent);
second shade – deep burgundy;
first highlight – cadmium red;
second highlight – white;
floated shade – russet.
2 For the light red apples, follow steps 1 to 7 for "Green apples," substituting the following colors:
base coat – cadmium red;
first shade – country red;
second shade – burgundy wine (transparent);
first highlight – orange;
second highlight – olive green;
floated shade – red.

Cut apples

1 Paint all the cut apples with a base coat of cream. If necessary, re-trace the core pattern.
2 With the liner brush, paint a thin cadmium red line around the outside edge to represent the skin. It is more realistic if this line is a little uneven.

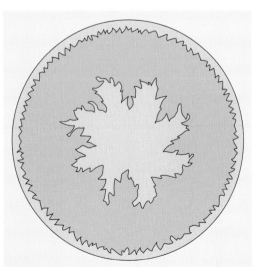

3 Using olive green thinned with water, paint the outer core lines and the seed pods. Allow to dry.
4 Mix together a small amount of burgundy wine and olive green and stroke in the seed cases. Mix in more burgundy wine to produce a dark brown shade and paint the apple seeds, leaving a tiny highlight on each middle seed.
5 Paint the stalks the same dark brown, then add a highlight to each stalk with the original mixture of burgundy wine and olive green.
6 Dry-brush some moon yellow shadows onto the cut surfaces.

Flowers

1 Using the round brush, paint the petals in titanium white.
2 Paint the centers with a double load of cadmium yellow and oxblood mixed with a touch of white.

❸ FINISHING

1 Allow all the paint to become completely dry.
2 Apply several coats of varnish.
3 If the plate is for display, attach a commercial hanger to the back.

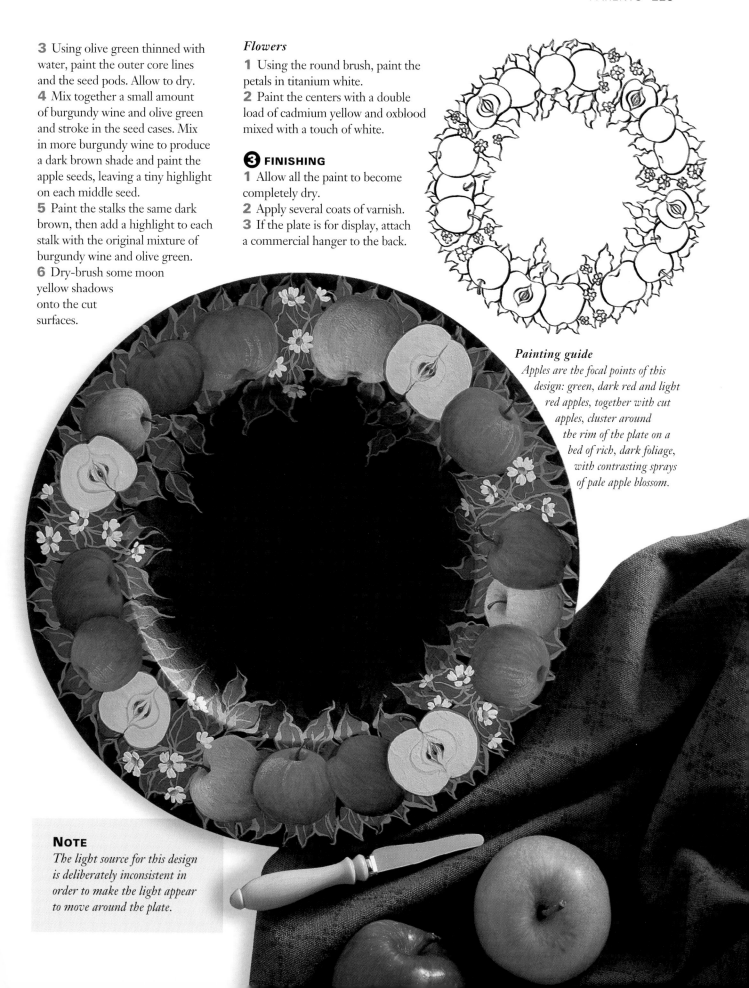

Painting guide
Apples are the focal points of this design: green, dark red and light red apples, together with cut apples, cluster around the rim of the plate on a bed of rich, dark foliage, with contrasting sprays of pale apple blossom.

NOTE
The light source for this design is deliberately inconsistent in order to make the light appear to move around the plate.

Log cabin quilt

Show your parents how much you care by making them this country-style quilt, based on a traditional design. They'll be proud to display your handiwork in a guest bedroom, as a wall hanging, or thrown over a favorite sofa.

WHAT YOU NEED

70 cm x 110 cm fabric (for the center squares and binding) • 6 light-colored fabrics, each 60 cm x 75 cm • 6 dark-colored fabrics, each 90 cm x 90 cm • 5.2 m backing fabric, 90 cm or 110 cm wide • 180 cm x 260 cm batting • sewing threads to match or tone with the fabrics • dressmaking pins • about 30 large safety pins • sewing needles • tape measure • ruler • rotary cutter and cutting surface (or sharp scissors) • sewing machine • masking tape
● *Technique pages 292–301, 305–6*

SIZE

Finished measurement (after binding): about 170 cm x 250 cm
Number of pattern blocks: 96
Pattern block measurement (after joining): 20.5 cm x 20.5 cm

❶ PREPARING THE FABRIC

1 Prewash all fabrics to check for shrinkage and colorfastness.
2 From each of the six light-colored fabrics, cut 16 strips, 3.5 cm x 75 cm.
3 From each of the dark-colored fabrics, cut 16 strips, 5 cm x 90 cm.
4 From the fabric for the center squares, cut a strip 45 cm x 110 cm and set it aside for the binding. From

the remaining piece of fabric, cut 96 squares, 5.5 cm x 5.5 cm. These will form the centers of the 96 blocks.

❷ CUTTING THE STRIPS

1 Take one strip of each of the six light fabrics and place them one on top of the other. Do the same with each of the six dark fabrics, keeping the two stacks separate.

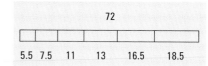

2 Using the rotary cutter, carefully cut through all six layers of light fabric to make strips measuring 5.5 cm, 7.5 cm, 11 cm, 13 cm, 16.5 cm and 18.5 cm. Keep the strips in six same-size stacks.

3 Carefully cut through all six dark fabrics to make strips measuring 7.5 cm, 11 cm, 13 cm, 16.5 cm, 18.5 cm and 22 cm, keeping these in same-size stacks also.
4 Repeat steps 1 to 3 for the remaining 15 light and 15 dark strips.

❸ SORTING THE STRIPS

A block is made from 12 strips of fabric, each a different color and size, together with one center square. The quilt is formed by joining 96 blocks together, eight blocks wide and 12 blocks long. The blocks are worked in groups of six so that even amounts of each fabric are used. To make sure that each block is formed in a different order, sort your piles as follows.
1 Arrange the six stacks of light-colored fabric in a row from largest to

COMBINING THE STRIPS

Altogether, there are 96 blocks in the quilt, and 13 different fabrics in each block. The strips are sewn to the central square in the order shown by the numbers in the diagram below. The fabrics are carefully cut and sorted so that no two blocks are pieced together in the same way.

HINT

Accumulate the fabrics and cut the strips over a period of time. Store strips of the same color in separate plastic bags until you are ready to use them.

smallest. Arrange the six stacks of dark fabric in the same way.

2 Leave the first stack of light strips and the first stack of dark strips as they are. Move one strip from the top of the second light stack to the bottom of that stack. Do the same thing with the second dark stack.

3 Move two strips from the top of the third light stack to the bottom of the stack. Do the same thing with the third dark stack.

4 Continue in this way along the rows of stacks, each time increasing by one the number of strips you move to the bottom of the piles. When you have finished, you will have 12 stacks

NOTE
A 7.5 mm seam allowance is used throughout.

of fabric, each with a different color on top of each stack.

5 Take one strip from the top of each stack, plus one square center piece. These 13 pieces form one block. Continue to take one strip from each stack plus a square piece until you have six groups of 13 pieces.

④ MAKING THE BLOCKS

1 Working with one group of 13 pieces at a time, sew the smallest light-colored strip to one edge of the center square, right sides facing. Finger press the seam away from the square.

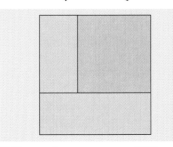

2 Rotate the center square 90° in a counterclockwise direction. Sew the second smallest light strip to the edge formed by the second side of the square and the end of the first strip.

3 Rotate the center square twice more, sewing the first and second smallest dark strips to the remaining sides of the square in the same manner as the light strips on the other sides of the square. You should now have a square enclosed by two light-colored and two dark-colored strips.
4 Continue in this way until you have sewn 12 strips (six light and six dark) around the center square. The completed block should make a square measuring 22 cm x 22 cm.
5 Repeat steps 1 to 4 to make five more blocks.
6 Complete all 96 blocks, cutting out fabric strips and assembling six blocks at a time. Make sure you vary the order of the strips in the stacks so that each block is different.

5 LAYING OUT THE DESIGN
1 Arrange the blocks in a rectangle, eight blocks wide and 12 blocks long. The quilt illustrated has been worked

HINT
If you lose track of which strip you sewed last and don't know where to sew the next one, look for the edge with two seams. This is the edge to which to sew your next strip.

in a "barn raising" pattern, but if you prefer, you can create your own design by laying out the blocks in a different pattern. Pin and then sew the blocks together in rows, right sides facing. Press the seams flat.
2 With right sides facing, pin and sew the rows together. Press all the seams flat.

6 ASSEMBLING THE QUILT
1 Cut the backing fabric into two equal lengths of 2.6 m. With right sides facing, sew the lengths together along the selvages with a flat seam.
2 Place the quilt front on the backing fabric and, keeping the seam in the center, trim the backing fabric so it is 5 cm larger all around than the front.
3 Trim the batting to the same size as the front fabric.
4 On a hard surface, lay out the backing, with the wrong side facing up, smoothing out any wrinkles. Pull the fabric taut and fix it to the surface with masking tape. Place the batting on top and then the quilted front, right side up, smoothing out any wrinkles as you work.
5 Using large safety pins, pin through the three thicknesses of fabric, right around the fabric, leaving about 15 cm between safety pins.
6 Starting from the center of the quilt, baste the three layers together in a sun-ray pattern to prevent the layers moving as you work. Remove tape.
7 Set a long machine stitch and sew along the seam lines between the blocks, feeding the quilt under the foot with the printed fabric uppermost. Maneuver the quilt as you go so that you can stitch right along a seam line to the other side without a break in the stitching.

8 Remove the basting and trim the edges, leaving about 1.5 cm of batting showing. This excess filling will be covered by the binding.

7 BINDING THE QUILT
1 From the reserved piece of centre square fabric, cut eight strips 5.5 cm wide, across the width of the fabric. With right sides facing, stitch the short ends of the strips together to make two strips 8 cm longer than the long sides of the quilt, and two strips 8 cm longer than the short sides of the quilt.
2 Turn both edges of the bindings 7.5 mm to the wrong side and press.

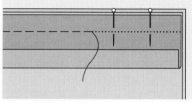

3 Unfold one of the pressed hems. With right sides facing and raw edges together, sew one edge of each side binding to the front of the quilt, through all thicknesses, 7.5 mm from the edge. Use the crease in the binding as a guide.

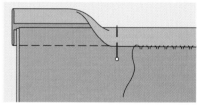

4 Turn the side bindings to the back of the quilt. Turn under along the crease and slipstitch the binding along the line of machine stitching.
5 Sew the remaining strips of binding to the top and bottom of the quilt, following step 3 above. At each end, extend the binding about 1 cm.

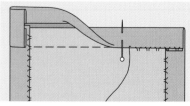

6 Turn the raw edges under at the ends of the bindings and slipstitch the binding to the back of the quilt.

HOMEMAKERS,
HOSTS & HOSTESSES

Every home needs
a multiplicity of things,
both useful and decorative.
A handmade gift for
a new home or to show
your appreciation to
your host or hostess will
be especially treasured.

Tulip cushion

Any homemaker will appreciate the elegance of this Art Deco–inspired cushion cover. The tulip design is worked in cutwork embroidery.

WHAT YOU NEED

Master pattern H54(a) • 50 cm white linen, 115 cm wide • cushion pad, 45 cm x 45 cm • 3 skeins white stranded embroidery cotton • needle: size 7 crewel • colored sewing thread • tracing paper • pencil • dressmaker's carbon paper • sharp scissors • sewing machine
● *Technique pages 292–301, 313, 343–4*

❶ PREPARATION

1 Cut two pieces of white linen 45 cm x 45 cm, and machine stitch the edges carefully with zigzag stitch to prevent them from fraying.
2 Fold one square in half and then in quarters to find the vertical and horizontal center lines. Baste along the lines with colored thread.
3 Trace the design from the master pattern onto tracing paper.
4 Pin the traced design to the fabric square with the basted center lines, matching the center lines of the fabric and the design. Place the fabric on a firm working surface.
5 Slip the dressmaker's carbon paper between the fabric and the design and transfer the design onto the fabric with a stylus or the pointed end of a knitting needle.

HINTS

● *To make the cushion larger or smaller, enlarge or reduce the design with a photocopier.*
● *Cover the cushion pad with a colored fabric to suit the home-maker's decor.*

❷ EMBROIDERING THE DESIGN

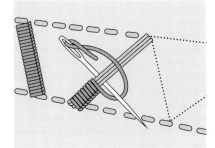

1 Use three strands of cotton throughout. Establish the design with stranded cotton and running stitch, working the buttonhole stitch bars as you go.

2 Following the stitch guide, work buttonhole stitch, making sure that the ridge of the stitches lies against the area to be cut away.

3 Carefully cut away the fabric where indicated, making sure that you cut under the linking bars and as close as possible to the buttonhole stitches without actually nicking them.

❸ MAKING THE CUSHION

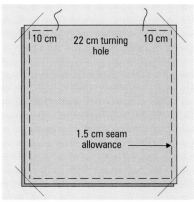

1 Place the two squares together, with right sides facing and all edges even. Pin, baste and stitch the front of the cushion to the back, leaving a 1.5 cm seam allowance and an opening at one side. Trim the corners and the seam. If the fabric has become soiled with handling, hand wash it in warm water using a good detergent, and dry flat.

2 Press the seams flat through a damp cloth. Turn the cushion through to the right side and press it carefully through a damp cloth.

3 Insert the cushion pad and close the opening with slipstitch.

Stitch and cutting guide
Establish the design with running stitch, working the button-hole stitch bars as you go. Complete the embroidery following the stitch guide at the right, then carefully cut away the fabric where indicated. Remember that the ridge of the buttonhole stitches must lie against any area that is to be cut away.

- - - Stem stitch
ⵑⵑⵑⵑ Buttonhole stitch
▦▦▦ Bars
▭ Cut-away fabric

Sweet home sampler

This sampler is a delightful way to mark the acquisition or completion of a new home. It will remind the homemaker in future years of a very special and happy occasion.

WHAT YOU NEED

Master patterns J70(a–b) • 45 cm **x** 50 cm aida cloth (14 gauge) • stranded cotton: Anchor color nos. 1 (white), 10 (pink), 95 (lilac), 262 (dark green), 264 (light green), 301 (yellow), 371 (brown), 382 (dark brown), 890 (gold) • colored basting thread and needle • needle: size 24 tapestry • embroidery hoop • picture frame, 40 cm **x** 45 cm • A2 white backing board • A2 mounting board • linen carpet thread or fine, strong string (for mounting) • craft knife • steel ruler or straight edge • tracing paper • scissors • pencil • tape measure • spray glue
● *Technique pages 309, 343–4*

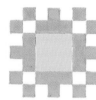

❶ MAKING THE SAMPLER

1 Iron the aida cloth and hand over-sew, or machine zigzag, the raw edges.
2 Mark the vertical and horizontal center lines with basting stitches.
3 Following the stitch and color guide on the master pattern, first embroider the border design. This then becomes a point of reference for the remainder of the design.

Choose one or two complementary colors for the names and dates – more colors will make the lettering hard to read.

4 Complete the design, working a small area at a time and following the stitch and color guide carefully.

❷ PERSONALIZING THE SAMPLER

1 On tracing paper, rule a straight line as a guide. From the master pattern for cross-stitch letters, trace the letters of the homemaker's name or names, and the date of moving in or completing work on the house. Leave spaces the width of two cross-stitches between letters and four cross-stitches between words. You will be able to fit only about 10 characters across the sampler, so abbreviate the names and use an ampersand (&) if necessary. Mark the mid-point of your tracings.

2 Match the mid-point of the names to the center point of the sampler in the space provided at the top of the sampler. Embroider the letters using colors of your choice, starting from the middle and working outward to the sides.
3 Repeat step 2 for the date, working in the space provided at the bottom of the sampler.

❸ FRAMING THE SAMPLER

1 Press the sampler on the wrong side through a damp cloth, making sure that you do not stretch the fabric or the stitching.
2 To frame the sampler, follow the steps described in "Wedding day sampler" (pages 194–5).

NOTE
On the sampler illustrated, the spaces for names and dates are filled in with extra embroidery to balance the design. Omit as much of the pattern as is necessary to fit in the information.

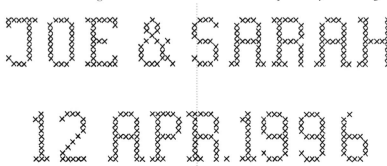

Country lace curtain

Long-wearing and easy to launder, this white cotton curtain will make a kitchen, bathroom or laundry window into a pretty feature. You can make the curtain to any width you like by repeating the pattern.

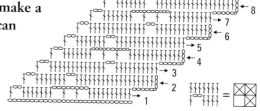

WHAT YOU NEED

For a curtain 55 cm wide and 47 cm long
Coats Mercer crochet cotton no. 10, 5 balls (20 g) • 1.50 mm (no. 7) steel crochet hook
● *Technique pages 320–2*

CHECKING THE TENSION

Before you begin crocheting the curtain, check your tension so that the measurements of the finished curtain will be as close as possible to the specified size. You should have 44 stitches and 16 rows to 10 cm over 1 tr, 2 ch mesh. Check carefully. If you have fewer stitches, use a smaller hook; if more, use a bigger hook.

❶ CROCHETING THE CURTAIN

(worked sideways)
Using crochet hook and cotton, make 171 ch loosely.

1st row: (wrong side) miss 5 ch, 1 tr in next ch, 2 ch, miss 2 ch, 1 tr in each of next 4 ch, (5 ch, miss 5 ch, 1 tr in each of next 4 ch) twice, (2 ch, miss 2 ch, 1 tr in next ch) 10 times, 1 tr in each of next 12 ch, 2 ch, miss 2 ch, 1 tr in each of next 13 ch, (2 ch, miss 2 ch, 1 tr in next ch) 20 times, 1 tr in each of next 6 ch, (2 ch, miss 2 ch, 1 tr in next ch) 3 times, 1 tr in each of last 9 ch.

2nd row: 9 ch, miss 4 of these ch, 1 tr in each of next 5 ch, 1 tr in each of next 10 tr, 2 tr in next sp, 1 tr in next tr, 2 ch, 1 tr in next tr, 2 tr in next sp, 1 tr in each of next 4 tr, 2 ch, miss 2 tr, 1 tr in next tr, 2 ch, 1 tr in next tr, 2 tr in next sp, 1 tr in next tr, (2 ch, 1 tr in next tr) 18 times, 2 ch, miss 2 tr, 1 tr in each of next 7 tr, 2 ch, miss 2 tr, 1 tr in next tr, 2 tr in next sp, 1 tr in next tr, 2 ch, miss 2 tr, 1 tr in each of next 7 tr, 2 ch, miss 2 tr, 1 tr in next tr, (2 ch, 1 tr in next tr) 10 times, 1 tr in each of next 3 tr, 2 ch, 3 tr in next

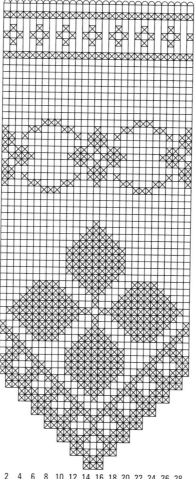

2 4 6 8 10 12 14 16 18 20 22 24 26 28

sp, 1 tr in next tr, 2 ch, miss 2 tr, 1 tr in next tr, 3 tr in next sp, 2 ch, 1 tr in each of next 4 tr, 2 ch, 1 tr in next tr, turn.

3rd row: 5 ch, 1 tr in first tr, 2 ch, 1 tr in each of next 4 tr, 5 ch, miss 3 tr, 1 tr in next tr, 2 tr in next sp, 1 tr in next tr, 5 ch, miss 3 tr, 1 tr in each of next 4 tr, (2 ch, 1 tr in next tr) 11 times, (2 ch, miss 2 tr, 1 tr in next tr) twice, 2 tr in next sp, 1 tr in each of next 4 tr, 2 ch, 1 tr in next sp, 1 tr in next tr, (2 ch, miss 2 tr, 1 tr in next tr) twice, (2 ch, 1 tr in next tr) 18 times, 2 tr in next sp, 1 tr in each of next 4 tr, 2 tr in next sp, (1 tr in next tr, 2 ch) twice, miss 2 tr, 1 tr in each of next 4 tr, 2 tr in next sp, 1 tr in each of next 7 tr,

Left: One pattern section, as the curtain will hang.
Top: Border pattern, as the curtain is worked.
Top right: Detail of stitches that make up pattern.

2 ch, miss 2 tr, 1 tr in each of next 9 tr, 1 tr in top of turning ch.
Working in pat from graph.

4th row: pat to last 24 sts and 5 ch, 1 tr in each of next 3 tr, 14 ch, miss 4 tr, 1 tr in each of next 4 tr, 2 ch, 1 tr in next tr, turn.

5th row: 5 ch, 1 tr in first tr, 2 ch, 1 tr in each of next 4 tr, 5 ch, 4 tr in 14 ch sp, 5 ch, 1 tr in each of next 4 tr, pat to end.

Cont in pat from graph until row 29 is complete, noting that rows 2 to 5 incl form pat for border on straight edge.
Rep rows 2 to 29 incl twice, or, for a wider curtain, rep these rows until you reach the desired measurement, ending with a 29th row.
Fasten off.

❷ MAKING UP

Press very lightly with a warm iron through a slightly damp cloth.

Painted planter

Reminiscent of a romantic bygone era, this painted aluminum planter features a design of violets in a traditional folk art style. Filled with an appropriate flowering plant, it makes an attractive gift to delight any homemaker.

WHAT YOU NEED

Master pattern H55(a) • aluminum container, about 18 cm high • FolkArt acrylic colors: taffy base coat, raspberry wine, thicket, wicker white • FolkArt metallic paints: pure gold, silver sterling, blue sapphire, regal red • FolkArt pure pigment: dioxazine purple • water-based clear flat varnish spray • paint palette • paintbrushes: no. 8 flat, no. 8 round, no. 00 liner, 40 mm decorating • medium sandpaper • lint-free cloth • tracing paper • transfer paper • masking tape • hard pencil (or empty ballpoint pen) • fine-tipped marker pen • soft artist's eraser

● *Technique pages 334–5, 343–4*

❶ PREPARING THE CONTAINER

1 Prepare the surface of the planter for painting, following the methods described in the folk art techniques section.

2 Using the decorating brush, apply two or three even coats of taffy base coat, allowing the paint to dry well between coats.

3 With tracing paper and a fine marker pen, trace the design from the master pattern.

4 Center the working pattern on the side of the container and secure it with masking tape. Using transfer paper and the hard pencil, transfer the design to the container.

VARIATION

This charming old-fashioned flower design could easily be adapted for painting onto any object – a jewelry box or a silk scarf, for example. Simply enlarge or reduce the design as required and use suitable paints.

HINT
*For a container of a different size,
use a photocopier to enlarge or reduce
the design to the right size.*

② PAINTING THE FLOWERS
Border
Using the flat brush side-loaded with
gold, float a border around the top
edge and the base of the container.

Purple violets
1 Mix a soft purple by adding a touch
of dioxazine purple to a little wicker
white. Using a flat brush and the soft
purple paint, fill in the lower portions
of the flowers. Use a round brush and
the same soft purple to paint comma
strokes on the upper petals.
2 Add shadows to the centers and
sides of the flowers using a flat brush
side-loaded with dioxazine purple.
3 Highlight the opposite sides of
the petals with blue sapphire. Brush
floats of silver sterling over the blue
to intensify the highlights.

Red violets
1 Using the flat brush, base-coat the
red violets in raspberry wine.
2 Pick up a sliver of dioxazine purple
on the side of the brush, blend well
across the brush and add shadows to
the centers and sides of the flowers.
3 Add highlights in regal red, silver
sterling and wicker white.

Faded violets
1 Use the color guide to identify
the faded red and faded purple violets
in the background.

Painting guide
*The two basic color combinations are
purple and blue for the purple violets
and raspberry and red for the red violets.
Two subsidiary color combinations for the
faded violets are created by diluting the
colors for the basic combinations.*

2 Paint the faded violets in the same
color combinations as the red and
purple violets, but add water to the
paints to give a softer, faded effect.

Violet buds, stems and ribbons
1 Following the painting guide,
and using the main color in each
of the four color combinations,
paint the buds with a round brush
using comma strokes.
2 Paint the stems using the liner
brush loaded with thicket. Add a
touch of faded red or purple to
some of the stems in the background.
3 Paint the ribbons in thin-thick-
thin strokes and loops using a round
brush loaded with gold and side-
loaded with raspberry wine.

③ FINISHING
1 Allow the paint to dry thoroughly,
then carefully erase any transfer lines
that are still visible.
2 Spray the surfaces inside and
out with a clear flat varnish to give
a protective coating and to enhance
the soft, romantic look.

Director's chair cover

With this loosely tailored cover, a homemaker can transform a humble canvas director's chair into a stylish piece of furniture that will look equally good in the garden or indoors. Choose a light furnishing fabric for a casual look, or a heavier fabric to dress the chair more formally.

WHAT YOU NEED

Master pattern H51(a–b) • canvas director's chair • 3.3 m strong woven furnishing fabric, 140 cm wide • sewing thread to match the fabric • about 2 m narrow cotton tape • dressmaking pins • tracing paper • pencil • tape measure • scissors • sewing machine
● *Technique pages 292–301, 343–4*

① TRACING THE PATTERN

1 Using tracing paper, pencil and scissors, trace a working pattern from the master pattern and cut it out. Make sure you have transferred all markings and details.
2 Pin the pattern pieces to the fabric, as shown in the cutting guide opposite, and cut them out.
3 From the remaining fabric, cut four 12 cm x 90 cm strips for the ties.

② PREPARING THE FABRIC

1 Using the sewing machine, neaten all the raw edges of the fabric pieces by zigzagging or overlocking.
2 On the side pieces, and with right sides together, match the dots at B and stitch from A to B. Clip the seam allowance at A.
3 Working on a clean floor or table surface, drape the pieces of fabric over the director's chair, with the wrong sides facing out. The main piece runs up from the floor at the back of the chair, over the top of the backrest, down to the seat, across the seat, and then down to the floor at the front. The side pieces run up from the floor at the sides of the chair and over the armrest to meet the main piece at the seat and back of the armrest.

CUTTING GUIDE

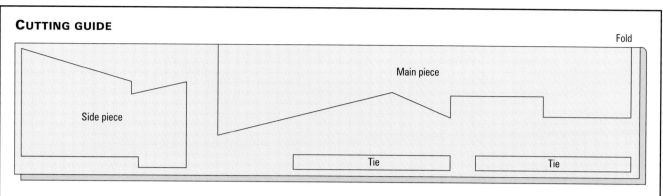

Fold

Main piece

Side piece

Tie

Tie

Fold the fabric in half, selvage to selvage, and pin the main pattern piece along the fold. Lay the side pieces away from the fold. Cut the pieces out. You may wish to transfer the pattern markings to the fabric using a fabric marker or colored thread. From the remaining fabric, cut four strips measuring 12 cm x 90 cm along the straight grain. These will be the ties.

❸ ASSEMBLING THE CHAIR COVER

Sew the chair cover together in the order given below. As you work, keep draping the cover over the chair to test the fit and to see how to ease the fabric around the corners. Pin each seam while the fabric is on the chair, using a seam allowance of 1.5 cm, and then sew the seam, clipping the seam allowances as necessary.

Sew the armrest seams first, then the side front seams, then the inner sides of the seat, then the inner back armrest. Finally, stitch the upper backrest seams and the side back seams down to the hem of the skirt.

1 On the side pieces, match the dots marked C. Join the front side seams from B to C.

HINT

The cover is designed to fit a chair about 55 cm wide, 38 cm deep and 85 cm high. The fabric should be able to withstand repeated laundering. Suitable materials include muslin, mattress ticking, printed cottons and washable furnishing fabrics, as well as more formal materials such as damask.

Unless you are an experienced sewer, it is best to avoid fabrics that will require a definite pattern match, such as tartans and plaids.

2 Join the main piece to the side pieces along the side front seams.
3 Pin and then sew the inner sides of the seat together, easing the fabric to fit around the corners and clipping the seam allowances where necessary.
4 Pin and then sew the main piece to the side pieces along the inner back armrest, again easing the fabric at the corners and clipping the seam allowances where necessary.
5 Pin the backrest seams together on the main piece, then continue down to the floor, pinning the main piece to the side pieces along the side back seams. Pin both sides to check the fit, stitch one side, and drape the cover over the chair to check the fit again before stitching the second side.
6 When all the seams have been stitched, put the chair cover over the chair again, wrong side out, and check that you have clipped the seam allowances where necessary.

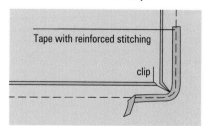

Tape with reinforced stitching

clip

7 Remove the cover from the chair and reinforce all corners by stitching about 10 cm of narrow cotton tape around them along the seam lines.
8 Turn the cover right side out and press it. Put the cover on the chair, right side out, and adjust the fabric.

❹ FINISHING

1 First making sure that the fabric cover is resting squarely on the chair, pin up the hem so that the fabric skirt of the chair cover just clears the floor. Remove the cover from the chair and machine stitch a double hem right around the skirt.
2 Fold the four 12 cm x 90 cm strips of fabric in half lengthwise, with right sides together. On each strip, stitch the long side together and then one of the short sides, using a 1 cm seam allowance on both seams.
3 Turn the strips right side out. Neatly fold the raw edges 1 cm to the inside and press.

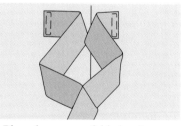

4 Place the unsewn folded and pressed ends of the ties on the right side of the cover in the positions shown on the master pattern, so that each tie crosses the side back seam at right angles. Machine stitch a rectangle of topstitching across the folded edges to secure the ties to the cover.
5 If you are intending to include the chair as part of the gift, press the cover well and fit it over the chair. Join the ties with a bow over the seam at each back corner to take up the fullness of the skirt.

Potted plant with bow

A bow-trimmed terra-cotta pot planted with seasonal flowers makes a delightfully different gift to please a homemaker.

WHAT YOU NEED

Terra-cotta flowerpot, treated on the outside with clear sealer • fabric suitable for tying in a bow • sewing thread to match fabric • potting soil to fill pot • flowering plants to suit size of pot • white glue • small mixing bowl • clear plastic food wrap or small plastic bags • rubber gloves • newspaper • sewing needle • sewing machine • scissors • tape measure
● *Technique pages 292–301*

❶ SEWING THE FABRIC

1 To calculate the width of fabric you need, measure the depth of the upper rim of the pot, double this measurement and add 2 cm. To determine the length, tie the tape measure in a bow the size you require, note the measurement and add 10 cm. Cut a fabric strip to these measurements.
2 Fold the fabric in half lengthwise, right sides facing.
3 To shape the tails of the bow, cut the fabric at each end of the strip at a slight angle.
4 Allowing a 1 cm seam, stitch along the raw edges, leaving an opening in the middle of the long side.
5 Turn the fabric right side out through the opening. Press the fabric and close the opening by hand using slipstitch, or by machine.

❷ MAKING THE BOW

1 Fold the fabric into a generous bow, ensuring that both sides and tails are equal. Hold the bow against the pot to check whether you need to make any adjustments.
2 Wet the bow thoroughly and squeeze out any excess water so that the fabric is damp.
3 Wearing rubber gloves, pour the glue into a small bowl, then immerse the bow in the bowl of glue until it is saturated. Soak and squeeze out the bow several times to make sure that the glue has completely penetrated the fabric. Gently squeeze out the excess glue.
4 Lay the pot on its side, placing a wad of crumpled newspaper along each side to keep it steady.
5 Push the back of the wet, glue-soaked bow firmly onto the rim of the pot. Fluff out or flatten the loops as required, smooth out any excess wrinkles, and arrange the tails in the shape and direction you wish them to go.
6 Tuck wads of plastic wrap into the loops to support the shape, and leave the bow to dry. To speed up the drying process, place the bow in the sun or use a hair dryer.
7 When the bow is completely dry, check that it is firmly glued to the pot. Apply more glue if necessary.

❸ FILLING THE POT

Fill the pot with potting soil and a plant that is just coming into flower. If you buy the plant from a nursery or flower shop, it should come with instructions for caring for the plant. Don't forget to include these, or write your own.

HINT
To seal a terra-cotta pot yourself, sand the outside surface lightly and then apply a coat of artist's gesso. Let the gesso dry, sand the surface again and seal it with artist's acrylic medium.

Decorative hat & coat rack

Made from solid wood with oval mirror and metal hooks, this hat and coat rack is sure to please a new home owner.

WHAT YOU NEED

Master pattern H52(a) • 1000 mm **x** 250 mm **x** 15 mm (nominal size) lumber, e.g. pine • mirror (cut 2 cm larger than the oval on the master pattern) • 4 metal double coat and hat hooks, with screws • 2 smaller metal double hooks, with screws • wood stain or varnish • clear silicone sealer • tracing paper • transfer paper • pencil • scissors • jigsaw or coping saw • drill and drill bits • sandpaper • paintbrushes • screwdriver

● *Technique pages 338–42, 343–4*

❶ PREPARING THE WOOD

1 Trace the half-pattern piece from the master pattern onto the tracing paper. Fold the tracing paper on the dotted line and complete the pattern. Transfer the shape to the wood.
2 Cut out the traced shape from the wood using a jigsaw or coping saw.
3 Inside the mirror area, drill a hole wider than the jigsaw blade. Insert the blade of the jigsaw or coping saw and cut out the oval for the mirror.
4 Sand all surfaces completely smooth and wipe them free of dust.

HINT
Before fixing the mirror in place, seal the edges with mirror edge sealer or lacquer to protect the silvering from moisture.

5 Stain or varnish the rack and allow it to dry thoroughly.

❷ MAKING THE RACK

1 Center the mirror over the hole and fix it to the back of the rack with silicone sealer; use just enough to provide good adhesion without oozing out onto the exposed mirror surface. If silicone appears on exposed surface, allow it to dry, then remove it with a single-edged razor blade.
2 When the silicone is dry, drill holes for the hooks. Screw the hooks into place, with the smaller ones in the two inner positions below the mirror.
3 To attach the rack to the wall, either drill access holes for wall screws right through the rack or attach small metal plates to the back, so that they protrude over the top edge of the rack to take wall fixing screws.

Wooden towel rail

Here is a handsome and very useful addition to a bathroom. It can also be used for drying small articles of laundry.

WHAT YOU NEED

Master pattern **G50(a)** • lumber (e.g. pine), 3000 mm **x** 300 mm **x** 20 mm • 3000 mm dowel, 19 mm diameter • 2000 mm dowel, 25 mm diameter • 4 rubber screw-in feet • 6 wooden knobs (with metal thread screws) • 4 wooden buttons, 30 mm diameter • white glue • epoxy resin glue • fine-grade sandpaper • tracing paper • transfer paper • scissors • pencil • jigsaw • hacksaw • drill and drill bits • scrap wood • clamps • sealer • paint or stain • varnish

● *Technique pages 338–42, 343–4*

❶ PREPARING THE WOOD

1 Trace the pattern from the master pattern onto tracing paper. Transfer it to the wood, marking all details.
2 Using a jigsaw, cut two end pieces from the wood. Within the area that is to be cut out, drill an access hole greater than the width of the jigsaw blade. Place the blade of the jigsaw in this hole and carefully cut out the inside pattern. Sand all edges smooth.
3 Using the jigsaw, cut the 19 mm dowel into three 1000 mm lengths and the 25 mm dowel into two 1000 mm lengths.

❷ MAKING THE TOWEL RAIL

1 Clamp the end pieces together, with the edges carefully aligned.
2 Using a 19 mm drill bit, drill three holes through the end pieces into the scrap wood, in the positions shown on the master pattern. These holes will take the 19 mm diameter dowels.
3 In the positions marked, and with a 25 mm bit, drill two holes through the foot of each end piece into the scrap wood to take the 25 mm dowels.
4 Unclamp the end pieces. Apply white glue to the dowel ends. Using a block of scrap wood as a hammer, tap the pre-glued dowel ends into the holes in one of the end pieces until the ends of the dowels are flush with the outer surface of the end piece.
5 Repeat this process with the other end piece, so that the two end pieces are joined by the five dowels.
6 Using a hacksaw, cut the heads from the metal thread screws for the cupboard knobs, taking care not to damage the threads while cutting.
7 Drill a hole corresponding to the diameter of the metal thread screw in the center of each end of the three 19 mm dowels. Pre-glue the cut ends of the screws with epoxy glue and tap them into the holes with a piece of scrap wood, leaving about 15 mm exposed. Allow to dry.
8 Apply glue to the backs of the knobs and screw the knobs onto the exposed screw ends. Tighten until the knobs fit flush.
9 Glue the wooden buttons in place to cover up the exposed ends of the lower dowels.

❸ FINISHING

1 Screw the rubber feet into place on the undersides of the end pieces.
2 Sand all surfaces before sealing, staining or painting to suit the wood and the decor of the bathroom.
3 Finish the towel rail with two coats of polyurethane varnish to protect fabrics from stains.

VARIATION
As an alternative to wooden knobs and buttons, you could use porcelain or metal ones for an old-world look, or bright plastic ones to suit a modern decor.

Découpage desk set

Découpage techniques can transform inexpensive office items such as a letter rack, an in-tray, a pen holder and a blotter pad into an elegant desk set to dress up a home study.

NOTE
This project is satisfying and not difficult, but you need time and space to produce a good result. The découpage techniques section describes the method fully.

WHAT YOU NEED

Desk items suitable for painting • selection of suitable images • artist's acrylic paint, in a color to suit the images • artist's acrylic gloss medium (sealer) • polyurethane gloss varnish • 3 small paintbrushes (for sealing, gluing and painting) • 20 mm imitation sable brush (for varnishing) • wet-and-dry sandpaper in various grades • sanding block • wallpaper paste • white glue • roller • clear beeswax • cabinetmaker's (or French furniture) polish • lint-free cloth • Blu-Tack • small sponge • fine, curved scissors • craft knife
● *Technique pages 329–31*

❶ PREPARATION
1 Seal the images with artist's acrylic medium and allow to dry.

2 Prepare the surfaces of all objects following the methods described in the découpage techniques section.
3 Paint all objects with artist's acrylic paint. Allow them to dry, then sand lightly with medium sandpaper.
4 Wipe the surfaces with a lint-free cloth and apply a further coat of paint, brushing in the opposite direction to get a good coverage. Allow all the objects to dry thoroughly.

❷ FIXING THE IMAGES
1 Lay out all the objects and arrange your images on them until you are satisfied. Try to see each item as part of a total design and arrange your images accordingly. Keep the images in place with Blu-Tack until you are ready to glue them down.
2 Working on only one object at a time, apply a mixture of three parts wallpaper paste and one part white glue to the surface where the image is to go, and a small amount of the mixture to the right side of the image.
3 Massage and mold the image onto the surface, adding more glue if necessary. With gentle pressure, use the roller over the image to distribute the glue evenly.
4 Remove all the excess glue with a wet sponge and allow to dry.
5 Apply two coats of artist's acrylic medium to the surface, allowing each coat to dry thoroughly before applying the next.
6 Follow steps 2 to 5 until all the images are in place.

❸ VARNISHING AND SANDING
1 Varnish the entire surface of each object, allowing at least 24 hours between coats and sanding each layer after the tenth coat, as described in the découpage techniques section.
2 When the surfaces are completely smooth and you cannot feel the edges of the images (about 20 coats), apply three more coats of varnish, sanding between coats with fine sandpaper.

❹ FINISHING
1 Taking one object at a time, mix equal parts of beeswax and cabinetmaker's polish and warm the mixture. Using a lint-free cloth, apply the wax to the surface a little at a time.
2 Wipe vigorously with a damp cloth. Polish with a soft, dry cloth.

Fuchsia cushion

The delicate tonality of the shadow appliqué design makes this cushion the perfect finishing touch for a newly decorated bedroom. The fuchsia design is overlaid with sheer fabric and the detail is picked out with fine embroidery.

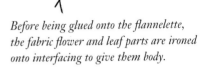

WHAT YOU NEED

Master pattern H56(a) • 75 cm white cotton voile or similar sheer fabric, 115 cm wide • 40 cm white flannelette, 90 cm wide • 20 cm **x** 20 cm bright pink homespun cotton • 20 cm **x** 20 cm green homespun cotton • 10 cm **x** 10 cm purple homespun cotton • 10 cm lightweight iron-on interfacing • 4 m pink organza ribbon, 20 mm wide • 2 m purple organza ribbon, 15 mm wide • round cushion insert, 30 cm diameter • 2 buttons, 12 mm diameter • sewing threads: purple, pink, green, white • stranded embroidery cotton: green • needle: crewel no. 8 • dressmaking pins • compass • 25 cm embroidery hoop • scissors • fabric glue • tracing paper • dressmaker's transfer pencil • pencil • sewing machine

● *Technique pages 292–301, 302, 307–12, 343–4*

❶ CUTTING OUT

1 Using a pencil and tracing paper, trace all the pattern pieces for the fuchsia appliqué design from the master pattern.

2 With the transfer pencil, transfer the traced pattern shapes onto the wrong side of the iron-on interfacing. Roughly cut around the shapes, leaving about 2 mm of interfacing outside the cutting lines.

3 Place the interfacing shapes for the bud and outer petals of the flowers on the wrong side of the pink fabric and press with a hot iron to fuse the interfacing to the fabric. Similarly, iron the interfacing shapes for the inner petals onto the wrong side of the purple fabric and those for the leaves onto the wrong side of the green fabric.

4 Cut out the interfaced shapes along the cutting lines, taking care with the

parts of the design that butt against each other.

5 With a compass, mark out a circle with a radius of 17 cm on the tracing paper and cut it out. Use this circle as a pattern to cut out a circle of flannelette and a circle of voile.

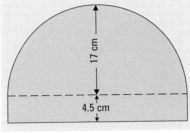

6 Fold the paper circle in half and trace the semicircle onto another piece of tracing paper. Elongate each end of the semicircle by 4.5 cm to make a squat arch shape. Cut out this shape and use it as a pattern to cut two pieces of flannelette and two pieces of voile. These pieces will become the back of the cushion, overlapping in the center to form a flap though which to slip the cushion insert.

❷ ASSEMBLING THE DESIGN

1 Referring to the photograph for color and position, arrange the various flower parts on the right side of the flannelette circle.

2 When you are happy with the arrangement, place a small amount of fabric glue on the wrong side of each of the appliqué pieces and fix them to the flannelette circle.

3 Place the voile circle on top of the flannelette so that the appliqué pieces are sandwiched between the voile and the flannelette. Baste lightly around the edge of the circle to hold the two pieces in position.

4 Place both layers of fabric in an embroidery hoop and tighten the hoop so that both fabrics are taut.

Before being glued onto the flannelette, the fabric flower and leaf parts are ironed onto interfacing to give them body.

5 Stitch around each piece of appliqué in a small, even running stitch, using single sewing threads in colors that match the different parts of the appliqué design. (The stitches should not pierce the colored fabric; rather, they should sit right on the edges of the various pieces.) Also use running stitch to define the details shown as dotted lines on the pattern.

6 With purple sewing thread, work the stamens in backstitch and the ends of the stamens in either French knots or satin stitch.

7 Use two strands of green embroidery cotton to work along the stems in backstitch.

❸ MAKING UP THE CUSHION COVER

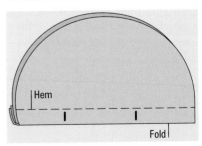

1 Assemble the pieces for the back, placing the voile over the flannelette. Neaten the straight edges with zigzag stitch and then fold them over to the

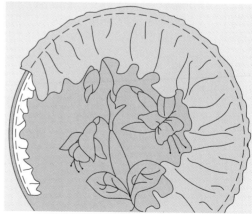

flannelette side to make a 3 cm hem. Machine stitch the hem in place.

2 On the hem of one piece, 10 cm in from each unstitched edge, make two buttonholes to fit the buttons.

3 From the remaining voile, cut two 17 cm strips the width of the fabric. At both ends, join the two strips together with a narrow seam to form a large loop. Fold the voile in half lengthwise and press.

4 Machine a row of gathering stitches through both thicknesses 1.5 cm from the raw edges. Draw up the gathering thread until the frill fits exactly around the outer edges of the appliquéd fabric circle. Spread the gathers evenly.

5 Cut the pink organza ribbon in half and lay the two lengths one on top of the other. Place the purple ribbon on top with one long edge aligned with a long edge of the pink ribbons. Join and gather the ribbons as for the frill.

6 With right sides facing, pin and then baste the gathered ribbons to the edge of the cushion front, easing the gathers to fit.

7 Pin and then baste the gathered edge of the voile frill over the top of the ribbon. Machine stitch the frills in place, working carefully to ensure that you catch in both the voile and the organza frills.

8 Pin the back pieces to the front, right sides facing, pinning the button-hole piece first. The hemmed edges of the two back pieces should overlap exactly. The frills will be sandwiched between the front and back. Machine stitch the front and the back together.

④ FINISHING

Trim the seams, turn the work to the right side and press. Sew the two pearl buttons to the back in positions corresponding with the buttonholes, and push in the cushion insert.

Traditional rag rug

An old-fashioned rag rug is a colorful addition to a kitchen or a sunroom. If you use bright fabric scraps left over from craft projects or dressmaking, this gift can be made for little more than the time and love you invest.

HINT

If the rag rug has been pulled out of shape while being worked, take a spray bottle filled with water and thoroughly spray the back of the canvas. Then place the rug on a wooden board or work bench, with the wrong side facing up, and push and pull the rug with your hands until it is restored to its proper shape. Use thumbtacks to fasten the rug onto the board, and allow it to dry completely.

WHAT YOU NEED

100 cm x 100 cm rug canvas • 1.25 m each of 12 different fabrics (or a mixture of scraps), sorted into 3 color families, with 4 shades to each family • pinking shears • 12 clear plastic bags • rug latch hook • ball of wool, 8 or 12 ply, in a color to complement the rug • needles: large darning or tapestry
● *Technique pages 292–3*

❶ PREPARING THE RAGS

1 The rug has nine blocks of pattern. Each block is made up of 16 squares.

Each square takes about 80 to 100 ties, depending on the thickness of the fabric. Since each shade covers 12 squares overall, you will need at least 960 ties for each shade. With 12 shades to prepare, this is a large number to cut, so save and cut the strips over a period of time.

2 Using pinking shears, cut the fabrics into strips 10 cm long and 1.5 cm wide.

3 Store strips of different shades in separate plastic bags until you have enough of each kind (between 960 and 1200 strips, depending on the thickness of the fabric).

4 Sort these 12 shades into three families of four shades each.

❷ COLOR: PLANNING AND ORGANIZATION

1 Before you start your rug, study the color guide and plan how you will

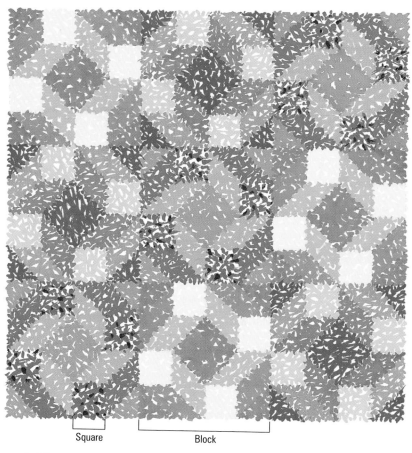

Square | Block

This close-up of the back of the rug shows how the squares are worked. Notice that some squares have rags of only one shade, and the others are filled with two shades.

work. The rug used in the illustration has been designed using three color families. Each family is made up of four different shades (12 shades in all). Each block on the rug contains four shades from the same family. Decide which block to start with and which color family. Assign one shade to each color on the chart.

2 Most squares contain two shades of fabric, but four squares in each block contain only one shade. Decide which color you will use for the single-shade boxes. Always work one square at a time, making sure it is full before you move on to the next square.

3 When a block is completed, put aside that family of fabrics and, using four shades from a different family, work the next complete block.

❸ WORKING THE RUG

1 Rug canvas is marked into squares by blue threads woven into the mesh. These squares are usually 10 x 10 meshes, and they are used as the unit square of the rag rug design. Mark out a grid of 12 x 12 squares and trim the

canvas five meshes outside these squares for a turnover.

2 Start at the top left-hand corner of the first block, and select the desired shade of rags.

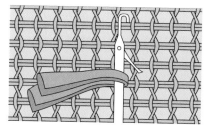

3 Fold a strip of fabric in half lengthwise, right sides facing out, and fold it round the shank of the latch hook.

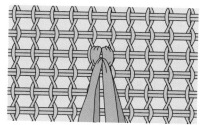

4 Holding the folded strip of fabric between thumb and forefinger, slip the tip of the latch hook under a crosswise mesh of the canvas. Still

holding the ends of the fabric strip, bring the fabric up and around into the open latch hook.

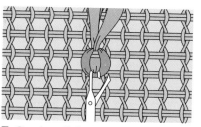

5 Gently pull the hook back through, under the canvas thread. When the bar of the hook closes, release the ends of the rag and pull them under and through, forming a knot.

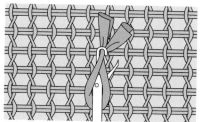

6 Tug on the rag strip ends to tighten the knot around the canvas threads and bring the ends even with each other.

7 Repeat steps 3 to 6, moving to adjacent fabric holes, until one shade area is full.

8 Move to the next square and repeat the method with the next shade.

❹ FINISHING

1 Fold the raw edges of the canvas under, keeping the corners neat.

2 Using a darning needle and wool, blanket stitch around all sides.

Leafy lemon jug

The old-fashioned craft of papier-mâché is used to make this lively cottage-style jug – a perfect ornament to any new home. It can be used to hold dried flowers and foliage or silk flowers, or put a glass jar inside it to hold water for fresh flowers.

VARIATION
This is a free-form project, and the shape and design shown are only suggestions. Experiment with different jug shapes and create your own design based on flowers, fruits or animals, or use abstract geometric shapes.

WHAT YOU NEED

About 120 cm fine chicken wire • 1 m flexible fine-medium gauge wire • wire cutters • newspaper • white paper • tissue paper: lemon yellow, orange, dark green, blue • wallpaper paste • bowl • masking tape • artist's acrylic paints: dark yellow, light lime green, lime green, dark green • clear acrylic varnish • pencil • paintbrushes
● *Technique page 336*

❶ MOLDING THE BASE

1 Using the wire cutters, cut a rectangle of fine chicken wire about 40 cm x 80 cm. Form the wire into a cylinder and join the sides by linking the cut ends of wire and pressing the loops closed.
2 Measure the diameter of the cylinder and cut a circular base with a diameter about 6 cm larger from the remainder of the chicken wire. Turn up the edge of the base about 2.5 cm.
3 Attach the base to the bottom of the cylinder by weaving in the cut ends of wire tightly enough to hold

the base in place. Mold the base and the cylinder with your fingers so that they fit smoothly together.
4 Take a length of chicken wire 20 cm wide and about two-thirds the height of the jug. Roll the wire into a long, thin cylinder and bend it into the shape of a handle.
5 Attach the handle to the jug by looping the cut ends of wire around the mesh and pressing the loops closed. Make sure the handle is attached firmly by "sewing" the handle to the main shape with wire.
6 Mold the lip by pushing out the wire at the open end of the jug, on the side opposite the handle. With your fingers, shape the wire just below the pushed-out area so that the lip blends in with the main part of the jug.
7 At the top of the jug, turn the cut edges of the wire over to the inside and press the loops closed.
8 Mold and adjust the wire jug until you are satisfied with the shape. Flatten the top and bottom of the handle, leaving the middle section tubular to form a hand grip.

❷ APPLYING THE PAPER

1 Half-fill a bowl with wallpaper paste and tear the newspaper into pieces roughly 5 cm square. Thoroughly saturate the squares of newspaper in the wallpaper paste.
2 Working on one half of the surface at a time, and leaving the handle until last, cover the wire frame with the

Shape and color guide
The lemons and leaves are made by gluing lemon yellow and dark green tissue shapes to the paper-covered wire jug and painting in the highlights and borders when the glue is dry. The blue tissue paper background goes on next, followed by the lemon yellow tissue paper handle.

squares of newspaper, following the method described in the technique pages for papier-mâché. Allow the paper on one half of the jug to dry before covering the other half.
3 Cover the handle, using smaller squares where the handle meets the jug to achieve a neat join. Allow the paper to dry, then reinforce and smooth the joins with masking tape.
4 Repeat steps 1 and 2 to cover the inside of the jug.
5 Apply a layer of white paper all over the jug. Follow the procedures described in steps 1 to 4, but do not use masking tape on the handle joins. The final surface should be uniform, without the wire armature showing through, but not completely smooth.

❸ CREATING THE DESIGN

1 Following the design in the shape and color guide, cut out as many lemons as you would like from lemon yellow tissue paper. Cut the shapes a little larger than those in the guide so that you can adjust their size when you add the lime green borders.
2 Arrange the cut-out tissue paper around the jug, placing the lemons evenly and allowing room for the borders and leaves. Lightly mark the positions of the lemons with pencil, and then glue them in place.
3 Paint dark yellow and light lime highlights on to the glued lemon shapes. Paint borders around the lemons in lime and light lime.
4 Cut out the leaf shapes from the dark green tissue paper. Glue them into position and highlight the centers with lime green paint.
5 Glue small pieces of blue tissue paper all around the lemons and leaves and right to the top and

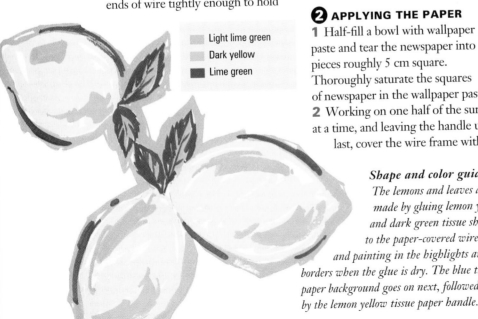

Light lime green
Dark yellow
Lime green

bottom edges of the jug, overlapping the pieces at random and being especially careful around the lemon motifs.

6 Let all the work dry completely and then paint dark green swirls all over the blue tissue paper.

7 Add texture by scrunching up small pieces of lemon yellow and orange tissue paper and sticking them randomly over the outer surface.

4 FINISHING

1 Paint the inside of the jug dark yellow. Cover the handle with a layer of lemon yellow tissue paper and the base with a layer of blue tissue paper.

2 Outline the edges of the handle with stripes of dark green paint.

3 Cut a number of small rectangles (about 3 cm x 1.5 cm) from the white paper. Paste these over the rim at intervals to make a checkered pattern, and allow them to dry thoroughly.

4 Apply two coats of clear acrylic varnish, allowing the first coat to dry thoroughly before applying the second. If the jug is to be used for fresh flowers, fit a glass jar inside.

NOTE

It is impossible to make the jug symmetrical, so do not try to do so – a rustic, handmade look is much more interesting and effective. However, as the final step in molding the wire, take care to make the circular base as even as you can around the rim and slightly concave, so that the finished jug will sit firmly.

Home bulletin board

A handy bulletin board on which to keep messages, postcards, photographs, appointment cards and all the other pieces of household paperwork is an appropriate gift for a homeowner. It would look equally good in the kitchen or in the home office.

WHAT YOU NEED

Master pattern **H57(a)** • **5 mm thick polyboard, 594 mm x 447 mm** • **red felt, 674 mm x 527 mm** • **6 m black ribbon, 10 mm wide** • **17 black thumbtacks** • **frame molding, 20 mm x 12.5 mm x 2445 mm** • **stapler with 5 mm max. staples** • **white wood glue** • **clear gloss varnish** • **varnish brush** • **tracing paper, about 620 mm x 470 mm** • **pencil** • **cross-cut saw** • **miter box** • **corner clamps (if available)** • **brads** • **ruler** • **2 mirror clips and screws**
● *Technique pages 338–342*

❶ PREPARING THE BOARD

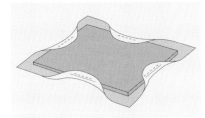

1 Lay the felt on a firm surface. Place the polyboard on top so that there is an equal amount of felt showing on each side.

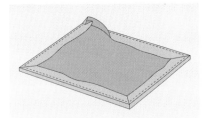

2 Fold the excess to the back of the board, then attach the felt to the back of the board by first stapling it at the approximate center of each side as shown. Gently stretching the felt as you go, gradually work toward the corners, finishing with a neat fold. Keep the staples about 25 mm apart and approximately 5 mm from the edge of the board. Trim the surplus felt with the craft knife and ruler taking care not to cut into the board.
3 With tracing paper and a pencil, trace off a template for the complete board using the quarter template supplied (turning the tracing paper over for two of the quarters).

4 Turn the board over so that the felt side is uppermost, and use the template as a guide to fix the ribbons in position ensuring that all the staples are within the rabbeted area marked on the template, and that the ribbons are fairly taut. Trim the ends of the ribbons after fixing.
5 Fix the thumbtacks to the crossed ribbons but not to those around the edges of the board.

❷ MAKING THE FRAME

1 Using the saw and miter box, cut the frame sides and ends from the molding to the following dimensions, but before cutting, check the board's dimensions in case the felt has made the board slightly thicker: two pieces 620 mm long and two pieces 475 mm long.
2 Make sure both pairs are the same length. Glue and, if possible, clamp the frame together making sure that the corners are square before the glue sets. Leave to dry.
3 Paint the frame with two coats of clear gloss varnish, leaving it to dry between coats.

❸ FINISHING

1 Fit the board inside the frame and hold at the back with three or four

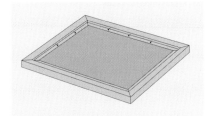

brads along each side.
2 Finally attach mirror clips to the top of the board.

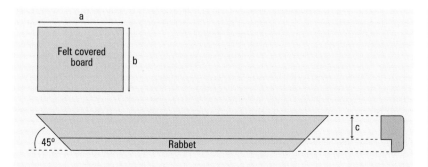

NOTE

To check on the exact cutting size for the molding to frame the board, add together measurement "a" and twice "c" plus 2 mm, for one side and "b," twice "c" plus 2 mm for the other. Cut two of each.

Parchment window tracery

The art of paper cutting, which originated in China, is not difficult; with a little practice, anyone can make interesting items like this window decoration. The tracery is designed to hang in a window so that it will cast intricate shadows as the light shines through it.

WHAT YOU NEED

Parchment (or calligraphy paper), A4 size • pencil • fine black marker pen • tracing paper • masking tape • small sharp-pointed scissors • scalpel or craft knife • cutting board • stapler • white eraser • ruler • pin • corrugated cardboard • sewing thread or nylon fishing line • needle
● *Technique pages 343–4*

❶ TRANSFERRING THE PATTERN

1 Using the marker pen, carefully trace the master pattern (below) onto the tracing paper.
2 Fold the sheet of parchment in half widthwise and use a ruler to

HINT
Entertain children by helping them to make a simple paper-cut gift for a teacher. Trace the three flowers from the middle of the design and enlarge and simplify them so that they can be cut out with blunt-nosed safety scissors.

make a sharp crease along the fold. Open the paper out.
3 Place the tracing paper under one side of the creased parchment, matching the fold in the parchment with the fold line on the master pattern, and lightly trace the design onto the parchment with a pencil.

4 Referring to the photograph, lightly shade the areas to be cut out. Refold the parchment along the crease line and staple it around the outer

edge to hold the two halves firmly together. Trim excess parchment to about 2 cm from the staples.

❷ CUTTING OUT THE DESIGN

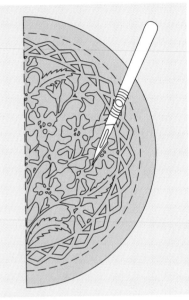

1 With the points of the scissors, puncture a shaded area of the paper near the center, away from the cutting line. This is your starting point for cutting. Cut the pattern out, removing the smaller areas in the center first and the outer edge of the pattern last.

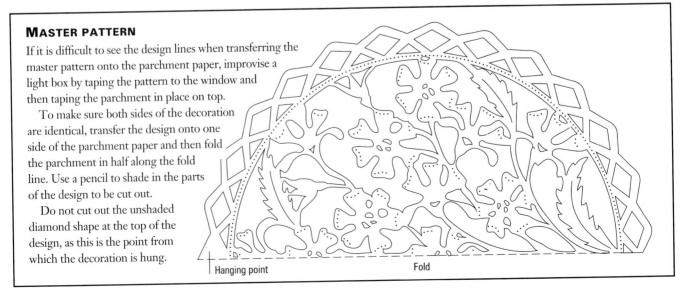

MASTER PATTERN

If it is difficult to see the design lines when transferring the master pattern onto the parchment paper, improvise a light box by taping the pattern to the window and then taping the parchment in place on top.

To make sure both sides of the decoration are identical, transfer the design onto one side of the parchment paper and then fold the parchment in half along the fold line. Use a pencil to shade in the parts of the design to be cut out.

Do not cut out the unshaded diamond shape at the top of the design, as this is the point from which the decoration is hung.

Hanging point   Fold

It is best to cut the center of each flower with the scalpel or craft knife, which should always be used over a cutting board.

2 Unfold the parchment and erase the pencil lines, being very careful not to tear the parchment. Place the cutting on a piece of corrugated cardboard or any firm but porous surface and, with a pin, prick around the top of each petal and along the circular border around the edge of the design.
3 Using the scalpel or craft knife, slit each leaf down the center, as indicated on the master pattern.

❸ FINISHING

1 Place the cutting between two sheets of clean paper and then between heavy books, and leave it until it is totally flattened.

CAUTION
You may find that a scalpel will give you much crisper cutting lines than scissors or a craft knife. However, remember that a scalpel is extremely sharp. Keep scalpels well out of reach of small children. Buy a scalpel with a sheath or a retractable blade, and sheathe or retract the blade after each use.

2 Thread the needle with the thread or fishing line and push it through the top, uncut diamond from the back to the front. Knot the thread several times at the back of the parchment to prevent it from slipping through.

Rose bouquet blanket box

Extra storage space is always welcome – convert a plain pine box into a pretty and practical blanket box.

WHAT YOU NEED

Master pattern **F38(a–b)** • pine blanket box, at least **850 mm x 450 mm x 450 mm** • wood filler • tannin blocking sealer • Jo Sonja's traditional European background color: blush (or Liquitex blush) • Jo Sonja's artist's colors (or Liquitex acrylic): rose pink, pine green, raw sienna, brown earth, Norwegian orange, warm white, red earth, burgundy, yellow oxide, rich gold • water-based varnish • brushes: 50 mm decorating, no. 2 round, no. 00 liner, nos. 6 and 10 flat • palette • natural sponge • medium- and fine-grade sandpaper • tracing paper • transfer paper • hard pencil • masking tape • furniture wax
● *Technique pages 334–5, 343–4*

❶ PREPARING THE SURFACE

1 Fill all nail holes and knots with the wood filler. Thoroughly sand the box along the grain and wipe it clean.
2 Apply the blocking sealer to both sides of any knots with the decorating brush. Allow it to dry.
3 Using a decorating brush, apply two coats of blush background color. Let the first coat dry thoroughly before applying the second.
4 When the paint is dry, mix a slightly darker version of the base color by combining blush with a touch of rose pink. Dip a damp sponge into the paint and practice sponging on a sheet of paper until you can produce a subtle, open effect.

NOTE
If you overdo the sponged color, tone it down by mixing blush with water to produce a transparent, milky glaze. Apply the glaze with the decorating brush. Allow to dry.

5 Lightly sponge all the surfaces of the box to create a soft, mottled background. Sponge the inside of the box as well as the outside. Allow to dry.

❷ TRANSFERRING THE PATTERN

1 Trace the designs from the master pattern onto tracing paper, marking the center points of the design and the colors of the roses. The large flower swag motif will be painted on the lid and front of the box and the small bouquets will be painted on the ends. If desired, a section of the pattern can be used on the inside of the box lid.
2 Mark the exact center of the lid by ruling diagonal lines lightly in pencil from each corner. The point at which the diagonals cross is the center.
3 Position the design, matching the center point with the center point of the lid. Secure it with masking tape and, using transfer paper and a hard pencil, transfer the design to the box. Keep your lines faint or they will be difficult to cover with paint.
4 Repeat steps 2 and 3 to transfer the appropriate designs to the front and ends of the box, and to the inside of the lid if desired.

❸ PAINTING THE DESIGN
Background washes
1 Using a flat brush, float a soft, watery shadow of pine green mixed with raw sienna around the bouquets and under the ribbons. If the shadow looks too strong, blot it with a soft cloth, working from the outside edge of the shadow. If it is too light, let the first wash dry and then repeat.
2 Using the mixture of blush and rose pink, apply additional sponging close to the floral bouquets.
3 Refer to the master pattern to identify which roses are to be painted coral and which pink.

Coral roses
1 Brush-mix rose pink, Norwegian orange and yellow oxide on one corner of the brush and pick up some warm white on another corner. Blend

the colors on the brush and paint the outer petals of the coral roses.
2 When the petals are dry, use a flat brush and a double loading of burgundy and red earth to float the dark throat area of each rose.
3 Add a touch of brown earth to the corner of the brush and deepen the darkest areas of the throats. Allow all the paint to dry.
4 With a liner brush and a mixture of warm white and yellow oxide, paint several dots in the center of each rose.

Pink roses
1 Paint the outer petals of the pink roses with a double-loaded brush of rose pink and warm white.
2 Proceed as for painting the coral roses, following steps 2 to 4.

Leaves
1 Using a small flat brush double-loaded with pine green and raw sienna, start painting from the base of each leaf and work up one side. Work at an angle, jiggling the brush as you go. Decrease the angle of the brush as you move up so that when you reach the tip of the leaf your brush is vertical.
2 When you reach the tip, turn the brush over and proceed to paint down the other side, jiggling the brush and increasing the angle as you move toward the base of the leaf.

RIBBONS
Over a rose pink base, highlight the broad parts and shade the narrow ones to give the illusion of depth and movement.

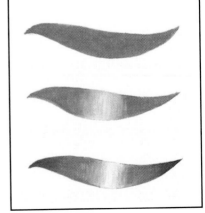

CORAL ROSES

Paint the outer petals first and then work in toward the centers, deepening the colors as you go.

Small cream flowers

1 Using a round brush, apply a base coat of warm white. Leave to dry.
2 Paint the centers of the flowers with yellow oxide. When the yellow oxide is dry, use a round brush to float brown earth around the centers. Float raw sienna around the outside edges of the petals.
3 With a liner brush, add a circle of Norwegian orange dots in the centers.

Ribbons

1 Using the medium flat brush, paint the ribbons with two smooth coats of rose pink. Allow to dry between coats.
2 Fully load the small flat brush with rose pink, then on one corner pick up some warm white. Blend the paints together on the palette. Working vertically, make a back-to-back float at the widest part of the ribbon to create a highlight.
3 Load the brush again with rose pink, but this time corner-load with burgundy. Shade the narrow parts of the ribbons with this color.

Edges of the box

1 Side-load a medium flat brush with brown earth.
2 Float a shadow of brown earth around the edges of each surface

HINT

To make sure your box has a truly professional finish, take the time to perfect the brush strokes by painting the separate parts of the design on paper first, until you are completely confident about your technique.

of the box, keeping the loaded corner of the brush toward the outside edges of the box.

Antiquing the flowers

If any of the flowers appear too bright, tone them down by antiquing.
1 Paint a very watery wash of brown earth over the flowers and blot it immediately with a soft cloth.
2 To deepen the antiquing, repeat this process as frequently as you wish.

④ FINISHING

1 When all the paint is dry, erase any guide lines that may still be showing.
2 Apply six coats of flat or semigloss varnish to the box, allowing each coat to dry between applications.
3 Let the varnish cure for at least a week, and then apply furniture wax to produce a rich sheen.

Open yellow flowers

1 Using a round brush and plenty of double-loaded warm white and yellow oxide, apply the paint in thick strokes. Allow the flowers to dry, and paint over them again if more texture is required.
2 With a small flat brush, float warm white around the edges of each flower. Float a crescent of burgundy mixed with red earth in the centers and leave to dry. Float raw sienna around the centers at the base of the petals.
3 With a liner brush, make several dots of yellow oxide in the center of each flower.

Rose-trimmed bed linen

Stencil this delicate rose border on pure cotton bed linen to create a beautiful and practical gift for a new home. The design is stenciled on the top sheet and the pillowcases.

WHAT YOU NEED

Master pattern H75(a–d) • pair
of sheets and pillowcases in pure
cotton • fabric paints: dusty green,
olive green, pastel pink, deep pink •
stenciling paintbrushes: 2 large,
2 medium • stencil film or treated
manila cardboard: 1 piece about
45 cm x 20 cm, 1 piece about
30 cm x 15 cm • spray adhesive •
tracing paper • dressmaker's carbon
paper • craft knife • ballpoint pen •
cutting mat or board • rag
● *Technique pages 337, 343–4*

❶ PREPARING THE LINEN

1 Wash and iron the bed linen.
Put the bottom sheet aside.
2 Fold the top sheet in half lengthwise and mark the center of the top
edge, where the stenciling is to go.
(The design goes on the part of the
sheet that is turned back on the bed.)
Fold the pillowcases widthwise and
mark the centers of the long sides.

❷ MAKING THE STENCILS

1 Trace the master patterns onto
tracing paper and, using dressmaker's
carbon paper and ballpoint pen, transfer the rose designs onto the stencil
film or treated manila cardboard.
2 Using the craft knife and the cutting board, cut out the designs.

❸ STENCILING

1 Open the top sheet out and place
the part to be stenciled on a hard
surface, smoothing out any wrinkles.
2 Spray the back of the stencil with
adhesive and center the design on the
sheet, about 10 cm from the top edge.
Position it so that the rose design is
nearest the edge of the sheet and the
scroll faces into the sheet.
3 Using pastel pink fabric paint and a
large stencil brush, stencil in the roses,

NOTE

*When stenciling the pillowcases,
slip a sheet of cardboard inside
each one to ensure that no paint
seeps through to the back.*

the scrolls and the circles. Using a
medium stencil brush and deep pink
fabric paint, add shading to the roses.
4 Wipe the stencil with a clean rag
and spray it again with adhesive.
Apply the stencil to the next part of
the sheet, making sure that the second
design is level and aligned with the
first design. Repeat step 3.
5 Continue applying the stencil and
stenciling the pink parts until you are
near the side of the sheet. When you
can no longer fit a complete motif
onto the sheet, turn your sheet and
arrange the stencil down the side.
Continue stenciling down the sides
as far as you think is appropriate for
a turnback (about two stencil lengths).

6 Position the large corner stencil to
stencil a rose in each corner. When

HINT

*To make this gift for a really
special person, look for linen that
has lace inserts, like that used in
the set illustrated. This type of
linen is more expensive, but it is
a beautiful way to show someone
how much you care.*

you have stenciled all the pink parts of
the design, allow the paint to become
completely dry.
7 Make sure the stencil is quite clean,
then spray it with adhesive again.
Reapply it to your design, aligning
the parts already painted under the
corresponding parts of the stencil.
With a large stencil brush and olive
green fabric paint, stencil the leaves.
8 When you have stenciled all the
leaves, use a medium stencil brush to
apply dusty green shading randomly
to some of the leaves, and then use
the deep pink fabric paint to "bronze"
some of the leaf tips.
9 Repeat the stenciling procedure
with the pillowcases, using the smaller
stencil designs.

❹ FINISHING

When the paint has completely dried,
seal it following the instructions given
by the manufacturer.

STENCILING THE DESIGNS

The same stenciling method is used for both the top
sheet and the pillowcases, but the layouts differ.
In the linen illustrated here, the design
is repeated three times across the top
of the pillow and twice down the
sides; on the sheet, the stencil is
repeated six times across the top and
twice down the sides. The rose stencil
is used in the corners.

Découpage memorabilia box

Most of us collect small mementoes, and they often become lost among our everyday objects. This colorful memorabilia box is a great place to store those precious bits and pieces, and it makes an attractive display item as well.

WHAT YOU NEED

Old wooden or craft wood box • suitable images • beeswax stick • artist's gesso • artist's acrylic paint in a color to tone with images • artist's acrylic gloss medium (sealer) • polyurethane gloss varnish • 3 small paintbrushes (for sealing, gluing and painting) • 25 mm imitation sable brush (for varnishing) • wet-and-dry sandpaper: fine and coarse • rubber sanding block • wallpaper paste • white glue • Blu-Tack • rubber roller • clear beeswax • cabinetmaker's or French polish • pieces of thick kitchen sponge • lint-free cloth • fine curved scissors • scalpel or craft knife • screwdriver

● *Technique pages 329–31*

❶ PREPARATION

1 Before you begin, mark the top, bottom and front of the box on the inside so that you can reassemble the box accurately. Then remove any hinges and brass corners.
2 Check all surfaces and fill in any crevices with the beeswax stick.
3 If you are using a craft wood box, seal all the surfaces with artist's acrylic medium before sanding to prevent the release of formaldehyde.
4 Sand all surfaces lightly with wet-and-dry sandpaper. Apply a coat of artist's gesso and allow to dry.
5 Seal the surfaces of the box and the images with artist's acrylic medium. Allow them to dry thoroughly.

❷ FIXING THE IMAGES

1 Make paper templates of all surfaces and arrange the images on them. Attach the images with Blu-Tack and rearrange them until you are happy with the design. The focus of the design should appear on the top and front of the box. With the curved scissors,

carefully cut the images to the required size and shape.
2 Mix three parts wallpaper paste and one part white glue. Working on one side at a time, apply plenty of the mixture to the surface of the box and a small amount to the right side of the images.
3 Massage and mold the images into the surface, adding more glue if necessary. Where images are placed on the corners of the box, miter the corners and trim away any excess paper so that the edges fit together flush. (You need not be so careful if metal corners are to be replaced on top.) Use the rubber roller to spread the glue evenly. Remove excess glue from the surface with a wet sponge.
4 Repeat this procedure until images have been applied to all surfaces.
5 Before the glue has dried, gently run your fingernail along all the edges of the box to lightly score the paper. Using extreme care, peel back the top layer of paper and run a sharp scalpel blade down the score line to remove the excess paper, at the same time ensuring that the paper abuts neatly and that there are no gaps.
6 When the glue is dry, apply two coats of artist's acrylic medium to the surface, allowing each coat to dry thoroughly before applying the next.

❸ VARNISHING AND SANDING

Varnish the entire surface of the box, following the instructions in the découpage techniques section.

❹ FINISHING

1 Paint the inside of the box with artist's acrylic paint. Allow the paint to dry, then seal it with two coats of artist's acrylic medium.
2 Screw the hinges and brass corners (if any) back into place.
3 Apply French polish following directions, or mix equal parts beeswax and cabinetmaker's polish and warm the mixture. Apply the mixture to the surface of the box, a little at a time.
4 Wipe over vigorously with a damp cloth and polish with a soft, dry cloth.

Place mats for a country kitchen

Mix and match odd fabric remnants to make these unusual padded and quilted patchwork place mats. Perfect for breakfast or an informal lunch, they are easy to sew. The amounts of fabric specified will make one place mat.

WHAT YOU NEED

20 squares assorted cotton fabric prints, 8 cm x 8 cm (for the patchwork) • 38 cm x 44 cm plain cotton fabric (for the backing) • 30 cm x 36 cm craft batting • sewing thread • dressmaking pins • tape measure • pencil • scissors • sewing machine
● *Technique pages 292–301, 305–6*

❶ SEWING THE PATCHWORK

1 Check that all the patterned pieces are cut squarely along the straight grain of the fabric, and that they are all the same size (8 cm x 8 cm).
2 Lay out the fabric squares in four rows of five to decide how you want the patchwork to look. Number the squares lightly with a pencil on the wrong side of the fabric to guide you when you are sewing them together.
3 With right sides facing, and following your numbered sequence, stitch together the five squares that make up each row, using a 1 cm seam allowance. Press the seams open.
4 Again following the numbers, and with right sides facing, stitch the four rows together using a 1 cm seam allowance. Press the seams open.

❷ QUILTING THE PATCHWORK

1 Center the patchwork right side up on the batting and pin it in place. There should be a 2 cm margin of

HINT

Be adventurous when you are choosing fabrics for making the patchwork. In the place mats illustrated, bold stripes and checks are combined with small floral prints to produce an unorthodox but colorful effect.

batting all around the patchwork. If necessary, trim the batting to this measurement.

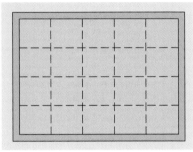

2 Quilt the patchwork fabric to the batting by machine stitching along the patchwork joins.

❸ ATTACHING THE BACKING

The corners of the backing are mitered over to the front of the place mat to form a border around the patchwork.
1 Trim the backing fabric to make a rectangle 38 cm x 44 cm. Press

the edges under 1 cm all round to the wrong side. Turn over another 3 cm all round and press.

2 Unfold the fabric. Using the press lines as guides, miter each corner neatly to form a border 3 cm wide. Stitch the diagonal mitering seams from the corners to the 1 cm press lines, leaving 1 cm to be folded under to make the inner edge of the border.
3 Turn the backing right side out, push the corners out, and press flat. Press down the 1 cm seam allowance around the inner edge of the border.
4 Insert the quilted patchwork, right side up, into the backing piece and tuck the edges under the border.
5 Pin and topstitch around the inner edge of the border, sewing through all layers of fabric.

European Easter eggs

There are many ways to paint and decorate eggs, so you can please everybody with these seasonal gifts. Children will be able to make some of the eggs for a host or hostess.

WHAT YOU NEED

Eggs • egg cup or egg carton • dye or artist's acrylic paints and gesso • white glue • clear polyurethane gloss varnish • small paintbrushes (for painting, gluing and varnishing) • tweezers
Blown eggs: needles: medium and large straw • small bowl • white vinegar • warm water
Red glitter egg: red paint • red glitter • 20 cm gold braid or ribbon, about 12 mm wide
Dried flower egg: small dried pressed flowers • pale green paint • 20 cm ribbon, 12 mm wide
Découpage-style egg: pale pink paint • small pictures from wrapping paper • fine, curved nail scissors
Beaded egg: small colored beads and sequins • paint in a color to suit the decorations
Icing flower egg: pink paint • small icing flowers and leaves (from a cake-decorating supplier)
Stenciled egg: small flowers, leaves or grasses, or fabric cut-outs • dye • bowl for dye solution • egg white • linseed oil or varnish • stocking • strong thread • rubber gloves
● *Technique pages 329–31, 334–5*

❶ PREPARING THE EGGS

If you intend to spend a great deal of time creating a design and you want it to last, it is best to use blown eggs (eggs from which the yolks and whites have been removed). Blown eggs will keep indefinitely, if they are completely clean and dry on the inside.
1 Use an egg at room temperature and shake it vigorously so the yolk becomes detached.

2 With a darning needle, make a hole at each end of the egg. Carefully enlarge the hole at the blunt end by breaking off tiny pieces of shell with the point of the needle until the hole is big enough to insert the blunt end of a wooden skewer.
3 Insert the needle through the larger hole and move it about to break up the yolk further. Lean over a bowl and place your lips firmly over the smaller hole. Blow the contents of the egg through the larger hole – once they start to move, they will flow easily.
4 Mix a solution of one cup of warm water and one teaspoon of vinegar in a bowl, and immerse the egg until the shell contains one or two tablespoons of the liquid. Hold your finger and thumb over the holes and shake the

egg to wash the inside thoroughly. Then gently blow the solution out of the large hole.
5 With the blunt end facing down, place the egg shell in an egg cup or carton to drain. Do not start decorating the egg shell until the inside of the egg is completely dry.

❷ COLORING THE EGGS

Most of the eggs in this project have been given a base coat of color before the design is added. Eggs can be colored with various mediums.
1 Dyeing with commercial dyes is one of the easiest ways. Dyes requiring boiling should not be used on blown eggs. Cold water dyes are suitable for dyeing both blown and hard-boiled eggs. To dye your eggs, follow

the manufacturer's instructions. Allow the eggs to dry completely before you begin decorating them.

2 Eggs can also be painted with artist's acrylic paints. Before you start, it is best to paint your egg with artist's gesso to give a smooth, clean surface on which to paint. Apply two coats of paint, allowing the paint to dry thoroughly between coats.

3 You can also experiment with dyes made from vegetable matter, such as onion skins (which produce a yellow dye), beets or spinach. Different teas also produce interesting hues. The amount of organic matter used determines the intensity of the color. Cover the organic material with water and add a small amount of malt vinegar to "set" the color. Bring the mixture to

the boil and simmer for about 15 minutes. Strain the mixture and allow to cool thoroughly before adding blown or hard-boiled eggs.

❸ DECORATING THE EGGS

The methods of producing the designs in the photograph are described below. These are only some of the possible ways to decorate eggs. With a little imagination, you can easily create your own designs.

Red glitter egg

1 Apply two coats of red paint to the egg and allow the paint to dry.
2 Coat the blunt half of the egg with glue and sprinkle it with red glitter. Carefully balance the egg in the dimple of an egg carton or in an egg cup and allow it to dry.
3 Repeat step 2 with the other half of the egg, making sure you leave a 5 mm band around the middle of the egg free from glue.
4 Brush the center strip with glue. Place the ribbon or braid around the egg and press it gently but firmly into position. Allow it to dry.

Dried flower egg

1 Apply two coats of pale green paint to the egg and allow it to dry.
2 Using a fine brush, carefully dab a little glue on to the backs of the dried flowers.
3 Using tweezers to pick up the flowers, arrange them on the egg and gently press them into place.
4 Tie the ribbon in a bow and glue it in position. Coat the entire surface with the clear varnish.

Découpage-style egg

1 Apply two coats of pink paint to the egg and allow it to dry.
2 Cut out a selection of small pictures from wrapping paper or books. Choose images printed on thin paper – they are easier to mold around the egg, and will give a smoother surface.
3 Apply glue liberally to the wrong sides of the shapes and press them onto the egg, smoothing out any air bubbles or lumps of glue. Wipe away any excess glue. Allow the glue to dry.

VARIATION
You can decorate eggs very simply using a batik technique. Draw a design in crayon or candle wax on the egg before immersing it in the dye. The area covered with crayon or wax will resist the dye.

4 Seal the egg by applying two or three coats of clear varnish.

Beaded egg

1 Apply two coats of paint to the egg and allow it to dry thoroughly.
2 With a very fine paintbrush, dab glue onto beads and sequins. Arrange the beads and sequins on the egg with tweezers. Allow the glue to dry.
3 Seal the the egg with two or three coats of clear varnish.

Icing flower egg

Follow the steps for decorating the beaded egg, but use cake decorations instead of beads.

Stenciled egg

1 Brush the undersides of small flowers, leaves, grasses or fabric cutouts with egg white and arrange them on the egg, pressing the coated sides on to the surface of the egg.
2 Carefully slip the egg into a stocking and tie up the stocking tightly enough to hold the decorations in place.
3 Immerse the egg in a dye bath for the time stated in the manufacturer's instructions.
4 Leave the egg in the stocking and hang it up to dry. Remove the egg just before the stocking is quite dry, and carefully peel off the decorations.
5 When the egg is completely dry, rub it with linseed oil or coat it with varnish to give a shiny effect.

Autumn wreath

This softly colored wreath is studded with cones, seedpods and nuts to evoke autumn.

WHAT YOU NEED

Vine wreath base (from florist's suppliers) • dried oak leaves on small branches • dried salal leaves (from florist's suppliers) or bay leaves • poppy seedheads, cedar roses or small cones • hazelnuts on wires • hot glue gun and glue sticks • 20 cm thin pliable wire
● *Technique pages 332–3*

❶ DRYING THE FOLIAGE

Air dry the oak and bay leaves following the methods described in "Flower and foliage drying."

❷ MAKING THE WREATH

1 Make a hanger across the back of the wreath with wire.
2 Build up the background by pushing small branches of salal leaves into the base. Intersperse with oak or bay leaves. Make sure that the top and sides are covered and that the base is

HINT

To wire nuts: stand the nuts in Plasticine and drill a small hole using a fine drill. Push a short length of florist's wire into the hole and glue in place using a hot glue gun.

concealed. Allow some branches to hang into the center of the circle and some to overhang the outside edge. Once you are happy with the arrangement, glue the leaves into place using the hot glue gun.
3 Glue small groups of cedar roses or cones randomly around the wreath ensuring that some of the groups are toward the inner side, some on top and some toward the outer edge. Be sure to glue the cedar roses or cones

to the base, not to the leaves, or they will not be secure. Turn the wreath as you work to ensure a balanced result.
4 Place groups of wired hazelnuts close to the cedar roses or cones and fix in place by pushing the wires through the vine base and twisting the wire round the vine at the back. Arrange the poppy seedheads fanning them out around the cedar roses or cones and when you are pleased with the result glue them in place.

Simple wooden tray

Even a beginner at woodwork can make this sturdy tray as a practical and appropriate gift for a host or hostess.

WHAT YOU NEED

Master pattern H58(a) • plywood, 450 mm x 330 mm x 9 mm • plywood, 450 mm x 310 mm x 3 mm • white woodworking glue • brads • wood filler • wood primer • paint, in a shade of your choice • paintbrush • medium- and fine-grade sandpaper • ruler • pencil • tracing paper • transfer paper • hard pencil • handsaw • jigsaw • drill and 20 mm drill bit • scrap wood • nail punch • hammer • clamp
● Technique pages 338–42, 343–4

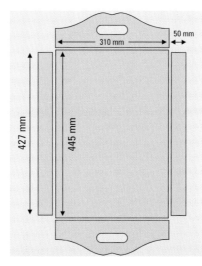

① PREPARING THE PLYWOOD

1 Using a handsaw, cut the plywood into the following pieces: **A** two 310 mm x 110 mm strips of 9 mm plywood (for the ends); **B** two 427 mm x 50 mm strips of 9 mm plywood (for the sides); **C** one 445 mm x 310 mm piece of 3 mm plywood (for the base).
2 Using tracing paper and pencil, trace the pattern piece for the ends of the tray from the master pattern and transfer all details, including the handle hole and drill points, onto the two 310 mm x 110 mm pieces of plywood. Cut out with a jigsaw.

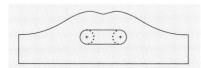

3 Clamp the ends together and drill two 20 mm holes through both ends into scrap wood. Keeping the pieces clamped, insert the jigsaw blade into one hole and cut out the wood between the drill holes, as shown on the pattern, to make the handle holes.

② ASSEMBLING THE TRAY

1 Butt the side pieces to the ends and attach them with brads and glue.
2 Turn the frame of the tray upside down. Position the base over the frame and nail and glue it in place, using three or four brads on each side. Leave to dry.
3 Sink all nails with the nail punch and fill the holes with wood filler. Allow the wood filler to dry.

③ FINISHING

1 Sand all edges and surfaces completely smooth and wipe the tray down with a damp cloth.
2 Paint the tray with the primer and allow it to dry thoroughly.
3 Paint a top coat in the color of your choice. Repeat if necessary.

Trimmed hand towels

With a little imagination and a few scraps of material, inexpensive hand towels can be transformed into attractive, individualized gifts with these simple trims.

WHAT YOU NEED

Selection of hand towels • for lace-trimmed towel: about 1.75 m of gathered lace (or edging lace) and two strips of fabric 6 cm wide and slightly longer than the width of the towel • for ribbon-trimmed towel: about 1.25 m of patterned ribbon • sewing thread to match the trim • tape measure • dressmaking pins • sewing machine • scissors
● *Technique pages 292–301*

Prewash towels, fabrics and ribbons in case of shrinkage. Towels are often washed in very hot water, so ensure that you use fabrics and ribbons that are sturdy and colorfast.

❶ LACE-TRIMMED TOWEL

1 On the straight grain, cut two strips of fabric 6 cm wide and 2 cm longer than the width of the towel. Cut four pieces of gathered lace 2 cm longer than the width of the towel.

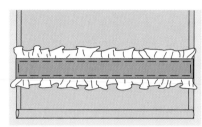

2 On either side of the woven band on the towel (or about 7 cm from the bottom if there is no band), stitch two rows of gathered lace, 3 cm apart, turning the ends of the lace under at the edge of the towel.
3 Turn down a 1 cm hem all round the fabric strip and iron it down. Place the fabric strip on top of the lace and stitch it around the edges.
4 Repeat steps 2 and 3 at the other end of the towel.

❷ RIBBON-TRIMMED TOWEL

1 Cut four pieces of patterned ribbon: two pieces 2 cm longer than the width of the towel, one piece 26 cm long, and one piece 6 cm long.

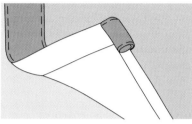

2 Pin one long piece of ribbon along the hem of the towel and stitch along both edges. Fold the free ends of the ribbon under and stitch them firmly to the wrong side of the towel.

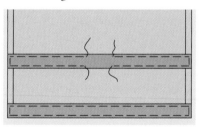

3 In the same way, sew another long piece of ribbon about 10 cm above the first, leaving a 5 cm unstitched section in the center of the ribbon.

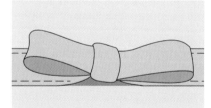

4 Join the ends of the 26 cm ribbon together, and place the join on top of the unstitched section of ribbon trim. Loop the 6 cm strip around the ribbon trim and the folded "bow" and handstitch it in place at the back. Iron the "bow" flat.

> ### EDGING LACE TRIM
> When you are using edging lace, place the fabric strip on the towel, position the lace on top of the fabric, along each edge, then pin and sew the trim to the towel.

Plastic bag dispenser

More and more people are aware of the need to protect our planet from indestructible litter. This handy dispenser for plastic bags intended for recycling would be a thoughtful gift for an environmentally conscious host or hostess.

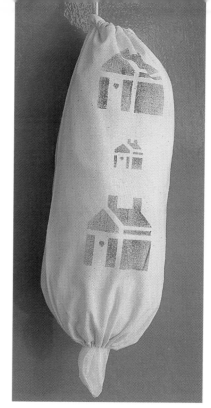

WHAT YOU NEED

45 cm x 45 cm muslin • 50 cm cotton tape, 20 mm wide • 20 cm elastic, 6 mm wide • sewing thread • bodkin • tape measure • dressmaker's pencil • scissors • sewing machine • fabric paints (your choice of colors) • stencil film or treated manila cardboard • spray adhesive • natural sponge • paper towels • cutting board • craft knife • tracing paper • dressmaker's carbon • black felt-tipped pen • hard pencil
● *Technique pages 292–301, 337, 343–4*

❶ PREPARING THE FABRIC

1 Press the muslin and lay it out flat, smoothing out any wrinkles.

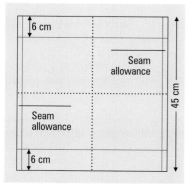

2 To position the designs, fold the muslin in half and then in half again to find the center point. Mark it with a dressmaker's pencil, and then mark off 6 cm at the top and bottom and 1.5 cm at each side. Stencil the designs inside the marked area.

❷ STENCILING THE FABRIC

1 If you are using cardboard, trace the design from the stencil pattern (bottom right) and transfer it onto the cardboard using dressmaker's carbon paper. If you are using stencil film, trace the design straight onto the plastic with a black felt-tipped pen.

NOTE
The plastic bags are stuffed into the dispenser through the top opening and pulled out as required through the elasticized opening at the bottom. The loop of tape that is left when the top is closed is used to hang the dispenser on the back of the kitchen or laundry door.

Cut the stencil with the craft knife.
2 Spread the muslin out and decide where to place the design and how often to repeat it.
3 Spray the back of the stencil with adhesive and place it on the fabric. Dip a dampened sponge into the fabric paint. Remove excess paint by dabbing the sponge on paper towels. Stencil the design onto the fabric. Allow the paint to dry.
4 Follow the paint manufacturer's instructions to fix the paint and make the bag washable.

❸ SEWING THE BAG
1 With the painted sides facing, sew the sides of the bag together using a 1.5 cm seam allowance.
2 Turn the top and bottom edges 1 cm to the wrong side and press.
3 Turn over and pin a 2.5 cm hem to the wrong side at the top and bottom. Machine stitch, leaving a 1.5 cm opening in both hems to thread the tape and elastic through. Backstitch

HINT
Instead of using the house motif provided here, try designing your own. For the best results, use only two or three colors and keep the design elements simple.

on each side of the openings to give extra strength.
4 Turn the bag right side out, smooth out the fabric and press.

❹ FINISHING
1 Thread the tape through the top hem with the bodkin to make a draw-string top. Handstitch the ends of the tape firmly together.
2 Thread the elastic through the bottom hem. Pull the elastic tight, until there is only a small opening in the bottom of the bag, then tie the ends of the elastic together and trim.

Stencil pattern
Make your stencil by tracing this pattern. If you wish, use a photocopier to enlarge the image before you trace it.

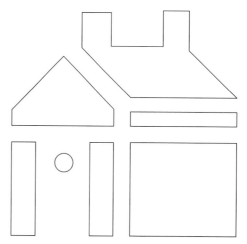

Découpage key chain

Select an image that will appeal to the recipient and use the découpage technique to transform a simple key chain into a charming gift for a host or hostess.

WHAT YOU NEED

Key chain with flat wooden medallion • suitable printed image • artist's acrylic paint: color to tone with image • artist's acrylic gloss medium (sealer) • polyurethane gloss varnish • 3 small paintbrushes (for sealing, gluing and painting) • 20 mm imitation sable brush (for varnishing) • wet-and-dry sandpaper: nos. 60 and 120 • rubber sanding block • wallpaper paste • white glue • small sponge • lint-free cloth • scalpel • clear beeswax • cabinetmaker's or French polish

● *Technique pages 329–31*

❶ PREPARATION

1 Using no. 60 sandpaper, sand the surface of the medallion until it is smooth and wipe it quite clean with a lint-free cloth.

NOTE

If you are unfamiliar with découpage techniques, study the craft techniques section for découpage before starting work on this project.

2 Paint the front of the medallion with artist's acrylic gloss medium (sealer) and the back with a mixture of sealer and artist's acrylic paint.
3 Place the medallion over the image and, using the scalpel, cut the image out, making it a little larger all around than the medallion.
4 Seal the image with artist's acrylic medium. Be careful not to coat the image too heavily – this may make it less pliable and more difficult to mold around the medallion. Allow it to dry thoroughly.

❷ FIXING THE IMAGE

1 Apply a mixture of three parts wallpaper paste and one part white glue to the surface of the medallion, and a small amount of the same mixture to the right side of the image.
2 Massage and mold the image into the surface of the medallion, adding more glue if necessary.
3 Remove all the excess glue with a wet sponge. Allow to dry before trimming the image to fit tidily around the edges of the medallion. If there is creasing around the edges, disguise this by painting a border.
4 Apply two coats of sealer to the surface, allowing each coat to dry thoroughly before applying the next.

❸ VARNISHING AND SANDING

1 Wipe the medallion with a lint-free cloth and use the imitation sable brush to apply a coat of varnish.
2 Leaving at least 24 hours between coats, apply at least 10 coats of varnish to make sure the image will not be damaged by sanding.
3 Continue applying varnish, sanding with no. 60 wet-and-dry sandpaper between coats. Make sure that the sandpaper is wet and that you sand in one direction only. Allow 24 hours between applications, and wipe the medallion with a lint-free cloth before applying the next coat.
4 When satisfied that the varnish is evenly applied and the surface has no shiny patches, sand the medallion lightly with no. 120 sandpaper and wipe with a lint-free cloth.
5 Apply three more coats of varnish, sanding with no. 120 sandpaper between coats to achieve a very smooth, dull finish.

❹ FINISHING

1 Apply French polish following directions, or mix equal parts of beeswax and cabinetmaker's polish and warm the mixture. Apply the wax to the surface a little at a time.
2 Wipe the medallion over vigorously with a damp cloth, and polish with a soft, dry cloth.

Stenciled writing paper & envelopes

Writing paper is always a welcome gift, and plain paper and envelopes take on a customized look when you apply this simple stenciled ribbon pattern. The stenciling looks particularly effective on handmade or recycled paper.

and stencil as much of the design as will fit onto the envelope. Stencil and paint the design in the same way as for the writing paper. Remember to leave enough of the surface plain to write an address and apply a stamp.

2 Add further interest by stenciling the bow onto the lower section of the envelope flap.

Stencil pattern
Trace the design onto tracing paper and transfer it to the stencil film. Carefully cut the design from the stencil film with a craft knife.

WHAT YOU NEED

Writing paper and envelopes • artist's acrylic paints: gold and black • paintbrushes: 1 medium, 1 small stenciling • stencil film or treated manila cardboard, at least 25 cm x 5 cm • spray adhesive • tracing paper • pencil • transfer paper • craft knife • ballpoint pen • cutting mat or board • rag
● *Technique pages 337, 343–4*

❶ MAKING THE STENCILS

1 Trace the design onto tracing paper and, using transfer paper and ballpoint pen, transfer the design onto the sheet of stencil film.
2 Using the craft knife and cutting board, cut out the ribbon design.

❷ STENCILING THE DESIGN ONTO THE NOTEPAPER

1 Spray the back of the stencil very lightly with adhesive.
2 Place the stencil about 2 cm from the top or bottom of the notepaper. Using the medium paintbrush and black paint, stencil the design.
3 Lift the stencil off the notepaper very carefully to prevent smudging, and wipe it with a clean rag before applying it to the next sheet of paper.
4 Stencil each sheet of writing paper with the black paint. Allow the paint to dry thoroughly.

5 Using the small paintbrush and gold paint, shade in the center of the bow and the spaces between each piece of the ribbon.

❸ STENCILING DESIGN ONTO THE ENVELOPES

1 Place the stencil at an angle across the left-hand corner of the envelopes

HINT

When applying adhesive, make sure you spray very lightly to prevent the surface of the paper from lifting when you remove the stencil. Alternatively, you could use "lift-off" sticky tape, being extra careful to avoid smudging the stenciled images.

Seashell picture frame

A picture frame decorated with seashells and containing a favorite print is an original way to thank a host or hostess who has a special affinity for the beach.

them evenly in the center of each side. In the project illustrated here, the largest shells were placed along the bottom edge to create a single focal point.

3 Heat the glue gun and glue the large shells to the frame.

4 Continue gluing the rest of the shells in place, overlapping or butting them together, until the entire frame is covered. Remember that the more irregular the shells appear, the better the effect is.

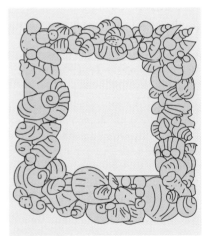

5 Glue the smallest shells on top of larger ones, tucking some of them into crevices to fill any gaps.

WHAT YOU NEED

Sturdy picture frame with a wide border • shells of varying sizes and shapes to suit the size of the frame • hot glue gun and glue sticks • strong picture-frame hook • clear gloss varnish • small paintbrush

❶ PREPARATION

1 Scrub the seashells thoroughly in a bucket of soapy water. Then rinse them several times in clear water, and leave them to dry.

2 Sort the shells into three sizes: small, medium and large.

❷ DECORATING THE FRAME

1 Remove the backing and the glass from the frame.

2 Arrange the large shells around the frame. As these large shells are the basis of your design, take time to plan their position. You could arrange the largest shells in the corners, or space

VARIATION

Say thank you for the use of a holiday cottage by buying a mirror and gluing shells around the edges to give it a frame.

❸ FINISHING

1 Using a small paintbrush, coat the shells with clear gloss varnish to seal them and to produce a shiny finish.

2 Reassemble the frame and attach a hook, making sure that it is adequate for the additional weight of the shells.

Marquetry bookmark

Contrasting wood veneers incorporating an inlaid motif are used to make this unusual bookmark – a perfect gift for someone who loves reading and dislikes dog-eared pages.

WHAT YOU NEED

Master pattern G76(a) • 2 wood veneers, contrasting in both color and grain: 10 cm x 20 cm (for the panels), about 5 cm x 20 cm (for the inlay) • 35 cm ribbon, 5 mm wide • pencil • square • cutting board • steel ruler • scalpel • tracing paper • transfer or carbon paper • white woodworking glue • old, coarse hacksaw blade • 2 sheets plastic, about 20 cm x 40 cm, cut from a plastic bag (do not use plastic food wrap) • rolling pin • damp sponge • heavy books • fine sandpaper • soft cloth • clear gloss varnish • paintbrush (for varnishing) • cut and polish compound
● *Technique pages 342, 343–4*

❶ CUTTING AND INLAYING THE VENEER

1 On the larger piece of veneer, mark two 5 cm x 20 cm rectangles with a pencil. Use a square to make sure the corners are right-angled. Cut out the panels on the cutting board, holding the ruler firmly and pressing the scalpel against it. Place the panels together to make sure that they are exactly the same. Trim if necessary.
2 Trace and transfer the cat motif from the master pattern onto the back of one of the panels and carefully cut around the design with the scalpel. Press the scalpel firmly but do not drag it, as this will chip the veneer. You may need to make several cuts before the design is cut through.
3 Tape the panel with the cut-out to the right side of the veneer for the inlay, arranging it so that the grain complements the motif shape.
4 Cut out the cat motif from the veneer for the inlay. Trim any wood slivers from the cat shape and from the space in the panel. Be careful not

to alter either the shape or the space, as the motif has to fit exactly into the space in the panel.

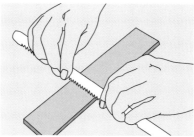

5 Using the teeth of the hacksaw blade, spread the glue evenly over the insides of the front and back panels. Press them together, making sure that they are square. Spread the glue carefully over the back of the motif and fit it into the space in the front panel.
6 Cover the work with a piece of plastic bag and roll the rolling pin firmly over it in one direction. Remove the plastic and wipe away excess glue with a damp sponge.
7 Cover the bookmark with a piece of clean plastic and place it under several heavy books for about four days.

❷ FINISHING

1 Using fine sandpaper, sand all surfaces and edges, and any glue spots. Wipe the dust away frequently with a soft cloth.
2 Sand the front panel until the inset motif is level with the surrounding veneer and smooth to the touch.

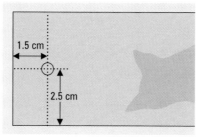

3 Make a pencil mark 2.5 cm in from each side and 1.5 cm down from the top edge. With the point of the

scalpel, cut a small round hole through both layers of veneer.
4 Varnish each side of the bookmark four times, allowing it to dry thoroughly between coats.
5 Lightly sand all surfaces and edges, and wipe away all traces of dust before continuing with the varnishing.
6 Apply six more coats of varnish, and then wait 48 hours before rubbing the surfaces gently with a cut and polish compound. The longer you rub, the better the finish will be.
7 Fold the ribbon in half, thread the looped end through the hole and then thread the cut ends through the loop and pull tight.

HINT
The bookmark needs 10 coats of varnish, and you need to leave at least 24 hours between coats. The most efficient method is to coat one side in the morning, prop it against a jar to dry, and then turn it over and coat the other side in the evening. Do not apply varnish too thickly, and watch carefully for any runs. If a run goes unnoticed, just sand the bookmark back until the surface is smooth and resume the varnishing.

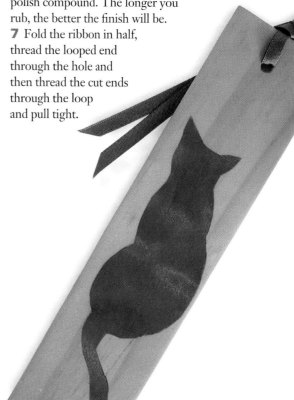

Lacework jug cover

This white crocheted jug cover would make a charming and useful gift for a host or hostess. The jug cover pictured is 16 cm wide and is trimmed with beads and looped tassels.

SPECIAL TERM
Thread bead: Draw the loop up on the hook, remove the hook from the work and slide a bead up to the chain. Insert the hook through the bead and into the loop, then pull the loop through the bead, thus threading the bead onto the chain.

WHAT YOU NEED

One 20 g ball Coats Mercer crochet cotton no. 40 • 1.00 mm (no. 10) steel crochet hook • 10 ceramic beads, with large holes • sewing needle • thick cardboard, 15 cm x 4 cm • scissors • tape measure
● *Technique pages 320–2*

CHECKING THE TENSION

Before you begin to make the jug cover, check your tension carefully. Using the no. 40 cotton and 1.00 mm crochet hook, the first four rounds should measure 3.5 cm in diameter. If your work measures more than 3.5 cm, change to a smaller hook; if it measures less, use a bigger hook.

❶ MAKING THE COVER

Thread the beads onto the cotton. Using crochet cotton and hook, make 10 ch, join with a slst to form a ring.
1st round: 3 ch, 23 tr in ring, slst in 3rd ch at beg...24 tr, counting turning ch as 1 tr.
2nd round: 5 ch, miss 1 tr, ★ 1 tr in next tr, 2 ch, miss 1 tr, rep from ★ 10 times, slst in 3rd ch at beg...12 sps.
3rd round: slst in first sp, (3 ch, 2 tr) in same sp as slst, 1 ch, ★ 3 tr in next sp, 1 ch, rep from ★ 10 times, slst in 3rd ch at beg.
4th round: 3 ch, (1 tr in sp before next tr) twice, 1 tr in next tr, 1 ch, ★ 1 tr in next tr, (1 tr in sp before next tr) twice, 1 tr in next tr, 1 ch, rep from ★ 10 times, slst in 3rd ch at beg.
5th round: 3 ch, (1 tr in sp before next tr) 3 times, 1 tr in next tr, 1 ch, ★ 1 tr in next tr, (1 tr in sp before next tr) 3 times, 1 tr in next tr, 1 ch, rep from ★ 10 times, slst in 3rd ch at beg.
6th round: 3 ch, (1 tr in sp before next tr) 4 times, 1 tr in next tr, 2 ch, ★ 1 tr in next tr, (1 tr in sp before next tr) 4 times, 1 tr in next tr, 2 ch, rep from ★ 10 times, slst in 3rd ch at beg.
7th round: 3 ch, 1 tr in each of next 5 tr, 3 ch, ★ 1 tr in each of next 6 tr, 3 ch, rep from ★ 10 times, slst in 3rd ch at beg.
8th round: slst in sp before next tr, 3 ch, (1 tr in sp before next tr) 4 times, 2 ch, 1 tr in 3 ch sp, 2 ch, ★ miss 1 tr, (1 tr in sp before next tr) 5 times, 2 ch, 1 tr in 3 ch sp, 2 ch, rep from ★ 10 times, slst in 3rd ch at beg.
9th round: slst in sp before next tr, 3 ch, (1 tr in sp before next tr) 3 times,

NOTE
Thread the beads onto the crochet cotton before you begin. They will slide along as you work until you are ready to pick them up in the 17th round.

2 ch, (1 tr in next 2 ch sp, 2 ch) twice, ★ miss 1 tr, (1 tr in sp before next tr) 4 times, 2 ch, (1 tr in next 2 ch sp, 2 ch) twice, rep from ★ 10 times, slst in 3rd ch at beg.
10th round: slst in sp before next tr, 3 ch, (1 tr in sp before next tr) twice, 2 ch, (1 tr in next 2 ch sp, 2 ch) 3 times, ★ miss 1 tr, (1 tr in sp before next tr) 3 times, 2 ch, (1 tr in next 2 ch sp, 2 ch) 3 times, rep from ★ 10 times, slst in 3rd ch at beg.
11th round: slst in sp before next tr, 3 ch, 1 tr in sp before next tr, 2 ch, (1 tr in next 2 ch sp, 2 ch) 4 times, ★ miss 1 tr, (1 tr in sp before next tr) twice, 2 ch, (1 tr in next 2 ch sp, 2 ch) 4 times, rep from ★ 10 times, slst in 3rd ch at beg.
12th round: slst in sp before next tr, 5 ch, (1 tr in next 2 ch sp, 2 ch) 5 times, ★ miss 1 tr, 1 tr in sp before next tr, 2 ch, (1 tr in next 2 ch sp, 2 ch) 5 times, rep from ★ 10 times, slst in 3rd ch at beg.
13th round: slst in first sp, 5 ch, ★ 1 tr in next sp, 2 ch, rep from ★ to end, slst in 3rd ch at beg...72 sps.
14th round: 3 ch, 1 tr in same place as slst, ★ (2 tr in next sp, 1 tr in next

---

MAKING A TASSEL

1 Cut a template measuring 15 cm x 4 cm from thick cardboard.
2 Wrap crochet cotton around the cardboard 50 times, using a continuous thread. Cut a 15 cm length of crochet cotton and use a needle to thread it through the wrapped cotton on the cardboard. Slide the wrapped cotton off the cardboard and tie the 15 cm length in a tight double knot to make a holding cord.

3 Cut a 40 cm length of crochet cotton and thread it through a needle. Wrap the cotton firmly several times round the neck of the tassel beneath the holding cord. Then thread the tail down through the neck into the skirt, and pull it tight.
4 Thread the holding cord onto a needle and stitch the tassels to the edge of the cover. You can cut and trim the bottoms of the tassels, or leave them looped.

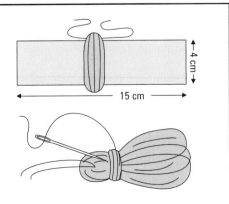

tr) 17 times, 2 tr in next sp, 2 tr in next tr, rep from ★ 3 times, omitting 2 tr at end of last rep, slst in 3rd ch at beg...220 tr.

15th round: 11 ch, miss 4 tr, 1 tr in next tr, 8 ch, ★ miss 5 tr, 1 tr in next tr, 8 ch, miss 4 tr, 1 tr in next tr, 8 ch, rep from ★ 18 times, slst in 3rd ch at beg...40 sps.

16th round: slst across first 4 sts, 11 ch, ★ 1 tr in next sp, 8 ch, rep from ★ to end, slst in 3rd ch at beg.

17th round: slst across first 4 sts, 12 ch, (1 tr in next sp, 9 ch) 3 times, thread bead, ★ (1 tr in next sp, 9 ch) 4 times, thread bead, rep from ★ 8 times, slst in 3rd ch at beg. Fasten off.

2 FINISHING THE COVER

1 Lay the cover flat and press it very lightly with a warm iron through a slightly damp cloth.

2 Following the instructions in "Making a tassel," make five looped tassels. Sew them to the doily at every eighth space, so that each tassel falls between a pair of beads.

VARIATIONS

● *To make a larger jug cover, simply continue working the pattern until you have made the size you want.*

● *For a quick and easy gift, buy a lace doily, some crochet cotton to match and some beads. Make the tassels, and then sew the beads and tassels to the doily in any sequence you like.*

Candles with pressed flowers

Using pressed flowers from the garden and a little imagination, you can create beautiful candles to present to your host or hostess. Several candles grouped together make an ideal table centerpiece, especially for dinner on a balmy summer evening.

WHAT YOU NEED

Flowers and foliage • beeswax candles • white glue • white paraffin wax • heat-proof container, deep enough to submerge the candles in • saucepan, large enough to stand the container in • cooking thermometer • tweezers • swizzle stick or small paintbrush
● *Technique pages 332–3*

❶ DECORATING THE CANDLES

1 Press the flowers and foliage, following the methods described in the techniques section for "Flower and foliage drying."
2 Using a swizzle stick or small paintbrush, apply a spot of glue to the back of the pressed flower that is to be the focal point of your decoration.
3 Carefully pick up the flower with the tweezers and position it on the candle. Press it gently into place with your fingers.

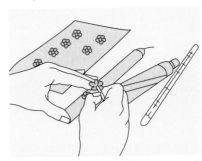

4 Add more flowers or leaves around the focal point until you are satisfied with the design. You can slip some of

HINTS
● *Before you place your plant material on the candle, draw an outline of the candle on paper and place the plant material on this, rearranging the design until you are happy with it.*
● *It is a good idea to keep a main part of your design near the bottom of the candle, so that it is not lost so quickly when the lighted candle melts down.*
● *Don't throw away unused paraffin wax; let it solidify and put it aside to use later.*

the plant material behind the focal flower so that it remains at the front of the design.

❷ SEALING THE FLOWERS ONTO THE CANDLES

1 Put the paraffin wax in the heat-proof container. Place the container in a saucepan of water and heat the water until the paraffin wax melts.

2 Put the thermometer into the paraffin wax and, when it reaches 82°–93°C, hold the candle by the wick and submerge it in the molten wax. Wait five seconds before you lift the candle out.
3 Allow the excess wax to drip off, then stand the candle upright. Leave the paraffin wax to cool and harden.

CAUTION
Do not apply direct heat to the paraffin wax, as it is extremely flammable if overheated.

EDIBLE GIFTS

Whether it be a spicy chutney or a traditional cake, a homemade delicacy is a gift for any occasion. There's a tasty treat here to suit every palate, from the conservative to the adventurous.

Nibbles & appetizers

Everybody likes to nibble on something before dinner. Here is a selection of recipes you can prepare at home for gifts. Most are perishable and should be stored in the refrigerator.

Marinated olives (left) look very attractive when the layers are built up carefully inside ornamental glass jars. Glazed chili nuts (right) are the perfect accompaniment for tall, cool drinks – present them to a host instead of wine or after-dinner mints.

Glazed chili nuts

Make sure you have the baking sheets and the ingredients before you start, as you will have to work quickly once the caramel is cooked.

WHAT YOU NEED

200 g toasted almonds
250 g granulated sugar
½ teaspoon chili powder
60 ml water

1 Preheat the oven to 180°C (350°F) and toast the almonds for approximately 8–10 minutes, or until golden.
2 Lightly grease two baking sheets.

3 In a heavy-based saucepan or frying pan, dissolve sugar and chili powder in the water over low heat, stirring constantly. Bring to the boil and simmer until the mixture is golden.
4 Stir in the toasted almonds and continue stirring for 2–3 minutes until they are well coated in the caramel.
5 Pour immediately onto one of the sheets and quickly separate the nuts with greased tongs. Using a greased knife, push the nuts off the sheet onto another lightly greased sheet, keeping the nuts well separated.
6 Allow the caramel to set before storing the nuts in screwtop jars.
● Makes 200 g.

Marinated olives

The following recipe is only a guide. The quantities will vary depending on the size and number of your jars.

WHAT YOU NEED

Oranges
Assorted medium-sized olives
(Kalamata, green, stuffed)
Fresh bay leaves
Fresh sprigs of thyme
or rosemary
Peeled cloves of garlic
Medium-sized green chilies
Virgin olive oil

1 Wash the oranges thoroughly to remove any waxy coating. Do not remove the rinds. Slice thinly and remove any seeds.

2 Put a layer of one type of olives along the bottom of a glass jar, then cover with a layer of one of the herbs. Add a layer of orange slices and a garlic clove. Continue layering in this way until you reach the top of the jar. Insert one chili, slit lengthwise, into each jar.

3 Pour in the oil until all the layers are completely covered. Tap the jar on a counter top to remove bubbles.

4 Seal and store in the refrigerator.

Savory cheeses

A delicious combination of taste and texture that reaches full potential at room temperature.

WHAT YOU NEED

Small to medium Camembert
or Brie cheeses
Sun-dried tomatoes
in oil, slivered
Kalamata olives,
stoned and slivered
Basil, coriander
or flat-leafed parsley,
freshly chopped

1 Halve each cheese horizontally. Drain tomatoes on paper towels, then scatter them over half of the cheese, together with the other ingredients.

Look for cheeses packaged in attractive wooden boxes and repack your savory cheeses neatly into the boxes.

2 Put the two halves of each cheese together, wrap in foil, and store in the refrigerator until ready to use.

Duck liver pâté

A rich, smooth, creamy pâté of mixed duck and chicken livers flavored with garlic, bay leaves and Grand Marnier or brandy.

WHAT YOU NEED

60 g butter
1 small onion, finely chopped
2 cloves garlic, finely chopped
125 g duck livers,
trimmed of sinew
125 g chicken livers,
trimmed of sinew
50 ml Grand Marnier
or brandy
20 ml cream
Salt and pepper
4–8 fresh bay leaves
About 100 g clarified butter

1 Melt the butter in a frying pan and sauté the onion and garlic until softened. Roughly chop the livers and add them to the onions. Cook for 4–5 minutes, tossing occasionally.

2 Flambé livers with Grand Marnier or brandy, add cream, and season to taste. Cook for a few more minutes over a gentle heat. Put into a food processor and process until smooth.

3 Spoon pâté into four 125 ml ramekin dishes and leave to set.

4 Place a fresh bay leaf on the top and spoon the clarified butter over the whole surface. Refrigerate for at least a day to allow flavors to develop.

HINT

Clarified butter forms a natural seal for pâtés. Melt 150 grams of butter over a low heat (do not let it burn) or in the top of a double boiler. Let it stand briefly to allow the solids to settle, and then pour off the clear liquid butterfat or strain through a filter. Cover the pâté with a layer of the liquid butter.

A loaf of walnut or olive bread would make a very thoughtful finishing touch to a gift of duck liver pâté (top right) or smoked fish pâté (left and front).

Smoked fish pâté

The strong, salty tang of smoked fish is accentuated with lemon and creamed horseradish.

WHAT YOU NEED

750 g smoked fish
(trout or mackerel)
125 g butter, softened
3 teaspoons lemon juice
1½ teaspoons creamed
horseradish
Black pepper
Pink or green peppercorns
About 150 g clarified butter

1 Remove any skin from the fish and put the flesh in a bowl. Pick through it to make sure that all bones have been removed. Put the fish into a food processor with the softened butter, lemon juice, horseradish and black pepper to taste, and process until smooth. Check seasoning.

2 Spoon into six 125 ml ramekin dishes and smooth the surface.

3 Scatter a few peppercorns on the top, then spoon the clarified butter over the surface. Store the pâté in the refrigerator.

Invited to a picnic? Take along a Thermos of Thai chicken soup (right back), a jar of spicy yogurt balls (left back) and some crusty bread.

Clear Thai chicken soup

A tasty variation on a classic gift for an elderly person or a convalescent.

WHAT YOU NEED

1 liter fresh
chicken stock
3 stalks lemongrass, cut
from root end and slit open
2 fresh chilies
400 g finely sliced
chicken breast
A few slices fresh
galangal, peeled
2 cloves garlic, crushed
3 kaffir lime leaves
8–10 oyster mushrooms
1 carrot, cut into a fine julienne
Fresh coriander (cilantro) leaves

1 Bring half the stock to the boil and add the lemongrass, the chilies, sliced lengthwise, and the sliced chicken breast. Gently poach the chicken for 6–8 minutes. Remove the lemongrass and the chilies, and discard.
2 Add the remaining stock, galangal, garlic and kaffir lime leaves and bring to the boil. Add the oyster mushrooms and simmer for 1–2 minutes. Add the carrot and coriander leaves and simmer another 1–2 minutes.
● Makes 1 liter.

Spicy yogurt balls

Friends who love to sample unusual foods will enjoy this snack.

WHAT YOU NEED

1 liter natural yogurt
1 teaspoon salt
2 tablespoons garam masala
Light olive oil

1 Mix the yogurt, salt and garam masala together. Pour into a sieve lined with cheesecloth and set over a bowl. Tie the top of the cloth and let the curds drain overnight.
2 The following day, roll the mixture into balls about the size of a walnut and arrange them on a tray lined with paper towels. Place the yogurt balls in the refrigerator until firm.
3 Put the balls carefully into a sterile jar, cover with oil and seal.
● Fills a 1-liter jar.

Marbled tea eggs

Marbled eggs make a pretty and nutritious Easter gift for a child.

WHAT YOU NEED

6 eggs
2 tablespoons tea leaves
2 tablespoons soy sauce
2 cloves
1 star anise
Orange or mandarin peel

1 Put the eggs into a saucepan, cover with cold water and bring to the boil.
2 Simmer for 10 minutes. Drain and leave to cool.
3 Crack the eggs gently all over with the back of a spoon without removing the shells.
4 Boil the tea leaves in approximately a liter of water and then add the remaining ingredients. Boil for a further 5–6 minutes, remove from the heat and add the eggs.
5 Let the eggs steep in this mixture until cool. Drain and shell the eggs.
● Makes 6 eggs.

Arrange the marbled eggs in a Chinese bamboo steamer or a porcelain bowl.

Candies, cakes & cookies

Candies, cakes and cookies make marvelous gifts for any occasion. Present them in a decorative container that will be a reminder of your gift long after the edible part has disappeared.

Truffles are the perfect luxury gift for special occasions like anniversaries.

Chocolate truffles

Dark chocolate, cream and rum or Grand Marnier combine to create a mouthwatering taste sensation.

WHAT YOU NEED

**200 ml cream
250 g dark chocolate, chopped roughly
20 g unsalted butter, softened
2 teaspoons dark rum or Grand Marnier
Cocoa**

1 Bring the cream to the boil and remove it immediately from the heat.
2 Put the chopped chocolate into a bowl and pour the hot cream over it, stirring until the chocolate has melted and is smooth and glossy.
3 Stir in the butter and when cool add the rum or Grand Marnier. Allow to set in the refrigerator.
4 When the mixture is almost set, roll it into bite-size balls.
5 Put the cocoa onto a plate and roll each ball lightly in cocoa, shaking off the excess.
6 Place the balls on a tray lined with wax paper and return to the refrigerator to set.
● Makes about 28 truffles.

Membrillo

This quince paste is an excellent addition to the cheese board.

WHAT YOU NEED

**1 kg quinces, washed
Granulated sugar
Juice of 1 lemon
Superfine sugar
Blanched almonds or pistachio nuts, chopped (optional)**

1 Preheat the oven to about 150°C (300°F) and cook the whole quinces for approximately 2 hours, or until soft when pierced with a skewer.
2 When cool, peel and cut the quinces into quarters, removing the seeds. Rub the flesh through a sieve or purée in a food processor.
3 Weigh the pulp, and weigh out an equal amount of granulated sugar.
4 Put the sugar and lemon juice into a large, heavy-based saucepan with about 150 ml of water. Bring to the boil, then gently simmer, stirring constantly until sugar has dissolved.
5 Add the quince pulp and cook over very low heat for 45–60 minutes, stirring occasionally with a wooden spoon, until the paste thickens and leaves the sides of the saucepan.
6 Spread the mixture evenly onto a shallow baking sheet lined with wax paper or edible rice paper. Dry the paste for 1–2 hours in a low oven (50°C/125°F).
7 Cut the paste into small squares, dredge in superfine sugar and scatter with the chopped nuts. Store between sheets of foil in an airtight container.
● Makes 25–30 pieces.

Quinces need to be cooked to reduce the bitterness of the raw fruit and bring out its fragrance. This is a version of an old Spanish recipe, dulce de membrillo.

HINTS

- *When making candies, always dissolve the sugar in water or liquid before bringing it to the boil. Do not stir the mixture once it has come to the boil.*
- *To minimize stickiness, cook candies on cool, dry days and pack them in individual truffle cases, available from cake stores and good supermarkets.*

Chocolate roughs

Chocolate roughs are an ideal festive gift. Combine them with chocolate truffles (page 275) for a doubly delicious offering.

WHAT YOU NEED

125 g dark chocolate, broken roughly into pieces
30 g unsalted butter
150 g shredded coconut

1 Melt the chocolate and butter in a bowl over gently steaming water.
2 Remove from the heat, add the coconut, and mix until all ingredients are well blended.
3 Drop teaspoonfuls of the mixture onto a sheet of aluminum foil or into fluted paper cups. Allow the chocolate roughs to set in the refrigerator.
● Makes about 20 pieces.

Chocolate roughs are easy to make. The combination of chocolate and coconut is not too rich and appeals to all ages.

Candied citrus peel looks pretty in a blue-and-white bowl. For a professional finish to the gift, wrap the bowl in cellophane and tie it with a bow to match the blue of the bowl.

Candied citrus peel

Someone who enjoys cooking will be delighted with a gift of candied peel. It can be added to cakes, cookies and puddings, or it can be eaten as is.

WHAT YOU NEED

Peel of 6 oranges, lemons, limes or grapefruit (or a mixture)
900 g sugar
500 ml water
Superfine sugar for coating

1 Wash the fruit well. Peel the fruit, including the white pith, which turns translucent during cooking.
2 Boil the peel in plenty of water until tender. Drain and boil again in fresh water for 20 minutes.
3 Bring the sugar and water to the boil, stirring constantly. Add the peel and simmer over a low heat until the syrup begins to thicken, stirring to prevent burning. Use a simmer pad if you have one.
4 Remove the peel from the saucepan with a pair of tongs and spread it on a tray lined with wax paper. Leave the peel to cool and then dry it in a low oven (50°C/125°F).
5 Roll the dry peel in superfine sugar. Store in airtight jars in a cool place.
● Makes a generous gift for a keen cook, or enough for six little packages for friends or coworkers at Christmas.

Chocolate, date & almond torte

This scrumptious mixture will fill three 12.5 cm x 6.5 cm pans – give two away and keep one for yourself.

WHAT YOU NEED

For the cake
200 g toasted almonds
200 g dark cooking chocolate
250 g seedless dates
6 egg whites,
at room temperature
150 g superfine sugar
For the chocolate coating
500 ml heavy cream
500 g dark chocolate,
chopped roughly

1 Preheat the oven to 180°C (350°F). Lightly grease and line the three cake pans with three layers of wax paper, bringing the paper up above the sides of the pans.
2 Chop the almonds, chocolate and dates, using a large, sharp knife.
3 In a large mixing bowl, whisk the egg whites with a pinch of salt until stiff. Fold in the sugar gradually.
4 Fold in the chopped almonds, chocolate and dates and spoon the mixture evenly into the prepared pans.
5 Bake in the oven for 45 minutes. Leave to cool in the oven, with the door open. Don't worry if the cake's surface looks cracked when you turn it out – the chocolate coating will cover these imperfections.
6 *To make the coating:* Bring the cream to the boil and pour over the chopped chocolate in a large saucepan or bowl, stirring until the chocolate has melted and the mixture is smooth and glossy.
7 Coat the tops and sides of the cakes with the chocolate mixture. Place on a rack over a plate in the refrigerator until the chocolate has set.
8 Recoat each cake with the coating mixture – which may need to be reheated over a pan of hot water – and smooth the sides for a glossy effect.
● You can make variations of the torte by substituting walnuts for almonds and dried figs for dates.

Place the torte on a broad satin ribbon. Bring the ribbon up to the top, loop it around itself and secure underneath with tape. Nest the torte in foil, tissue or rice paper.

Many Indian candies are linked to religious festivals and other special days.

Barfi

Barfi are Indian candies that are traditionally decorated with edible silver paper and given to friends and relatives during Divali, one of India's most colorful festivals.

WHAT YOU NEED

600 g raw sugar
250 ml water
375 g whole powdered milk
1 teaspoon cardamom seeds, lightly pounded
½ teaspoon ground nutmeg
550 ml heavy cream
50 g pistachio nuts, chopped

1 Make a sugar syrup by putting the sugar and water into a heavy-based saucepan and bringing it to the boil, stirring to dissolve the sugar.
2 Simmer the mixture over medium heat, stirring constantly, for 25–30 minutes until the syrup is sticky and forms a thick thread.
3 Meanwhile, put the powdered milk, cardamom seeds and nutmeg into a bowl. Add the cream and combine the ingredients with your hands until the mixture resembles breadcrumbs.
4 When the syrup is ready, pour it into the milk mixture, mixing it in quickly with a wooden spoon.
5 Pour onto a baking sheet lined with wax paper. Allow to cool. Scatter with chopped pistachios and then refrigerate until set.
6 Cut the barfi into squares or diamonds and decorate.
● Makes about 30 pieces.

Remove the fruit cakes from the pans when they are almost cool and decorate them with glazed fruits and nuts.

Festive fruit cake

Bake this cake as a gift to celebrate any festive occasion.

WHAT YOU NEED

250 g dried figs or pitted dates
250 g candied pineapple
125 g dried apricots
125 g whole green candied cherries
125 g whole red candied cherries
2 teaspoons grated orange zest
200 ml ginger ale
250 g macadamia nuts
2 eggs
100 g brown sugar
90 g melted butter
1 teaspoon vanilla extract
75 g all-purpose flour
1 teaspoon cardamom powder
½ teaspoon baking powder
Pinch salt
2–3 tablespoons dark rum

1 Preheat the oven to 150°C (300°F). If using figs, chop them roughly, but leave dates whole. Chop the pineapple and apricots roughly. Put fruits into a bowl with the cherries and orange zest. Soak overnight in the ginger ale.
2 The following day, drain the ale from the fruit and mix in the nuts.
3 Lightly grease three 12.5 cm cake pans and line the sides and bottoms with three layers of wax paper.
4 Beat the eggs in a bowl until they are light and foamy.

5 Add the sugar, butter and vanilla. Continue beating until the ingredients are well combined.
6 Sift the dry ingredients and fold them into the creamed mixture, then fold in the fruit and nuts. Spoon the mixture into the prepared pans.
7 Bake for 1¼ hours, or until a skewer inserted into the center of the cake comes out clean.
8 Remove the cakes from the oven and spoon the rum over the tops.

Boiled pineapple fruit cake

Crushed pineapple and spices liven up a favorite old recipe.

WHAT YOU NEED

450 g crushed pineapple
375 g mixed dried fruit
100 g raw sugar
125 g butter
1 teaspoon cinnamon
½ teaspoon allspice
1 teaspoon baking soda
150 g self-raising flour
175 g whole wheat flour
Pinch salt
75 g sunflower kernels
3 eggs, beaten

1 Preheat the oven to 150°C (300°F). Put the pineapple, dried fruit, sugar, butter, cinnamon, allspice and baking soda into a saucepan and stir over a medium heat until the sugar has dissolved and the butter melted. Bring to the boil, then simmer gently for 10 minutes. Remove the mixture from the heat and allow to cool.
2 Grease two 15 cm cake pans and line them with three layers of wax paper.
3 Sift together the flours and salt. Stir into the fruit mixture with a wooden spoon, along with the sunflower kernels and beaten eggs.
4 Spoon into the prepared pans and bake for 1½ hours or until a skewer inserted into the center comes out clean. Allow to cool in the pan, then turn out and decorate with glazed fruits and nuts.

Panforte

This nougat-like cake, originally a Christmas treat, has been a Sienese specialty since medieval times. It is now exported all over the world.

WHAT YOU NEED

50 g walnuts
50 g hazelnuts
200 g blanched almonds
200 g mixed candied fruit
25 g mixed candied peel
15 g candied ginger
200 g all-purpose flour
1 tablespoon cocoa
½ teaspoon ground coriander
½ teaspoon ground cinnamon
¼ teaspoon mixed spice
4 tablespoons honey
150 g icing sugar
1 tablespoon water
Rice paper

1 Preheat the oven to 150°C (300°F) and line two 20 cm shallow cake pans with rice paper. If you cannot find rice paper, line the pans with aluminum foil lightly brushed with oil.

Arrange wedges of panforte neatly in a flat basket lined with a paper doily, wrap in cellophane and tie with a bow.

2 Roast the nuts on a baking sheet in the oven until they are golden brown. Remove from the oven, allow to cool and then chop roughly.

3 Cut up the fruit and mix together in a bowl with the nuts, peel, ginger, flour, cocoa and spices.

4 In a small saucepan, combine the honey, icing sugar and water. Bring to the boil and cook until the syrup reaches 112–116°C (234–240°F) on a candy thermometer, or until a small drop of syrup hardens when dropped into a cup of cold water.

5 Add the syrup to the fruit and nut mixture and combine well – the mixture should be stiff and sticky.

6 Spoon the mixture evenly into the lined pans and top with more rice paper, pressing down with your hands to even the mixture. Place the pans in the oven and bake for 30 minutes.

7 Remove the panforte from the pans and allow to cool.

8 When cool, cut into thin wedges and dust thickly with icing sugar.

Tsoureki

Delight your host and hostess at Easter with this spectacular traditional Greek Easter bread.

WHAT YOU NEED

3 eggs
1 tablespoon vinegar
Red food coloring
700 g all-purpose flour
2 packets (14 g) dry yeast
½ teaspoon salt
75 g superfine sugar
1 teaspoon cinnamon
200–250 ml warm milk
125 g melted butter
2 eggs, beaten
50 g almonds, chopped
50 g golden raisins
50 g chopped mixed peel
confectioners' sugar

Eggs have always symbolized the renewal of life, and the Church has adopted the symbol to represent the Resurrection. Red eggs feature importantly in Greek Easter celebrations.

1 *To color the eggs:* Put the raw eggs into a saucepan and cover with cold water. Add the vinegar and the red food coloring. Bring gently to the boil, simmer for 10 minutes, then remove pan from heat. Leave the eggs in the steeping mixture for about 2 hours, and then drain.

2 To make the dough, put all the dry ingredients into a large mixing bowl. Make a hole in the center and pour in the warm milk, the melted butter and the eggs. Mix well, adding more milk if necessary.

3 Turn the dough out onto a floured board and knead it until it is quite smooth and shiny.

4 Put the dough in a lightly greased bowl and let it rise in a warm place for about an hour, or until it has doubled in bulk. Press two fingers into the dough. If the depression made by your fingers remains, the dough is ready.

5 Knead the dough again and turn out onto a floured surface. Gently knead the almonds, raisins and mixed peel into the dough, then divide it into three pieces and roll each piece into a long rope.

6 Braid the three ropes together and shape them into a circle on a greased baking sheet. Place the prepared colored eggs, unpeeled, at evenly spaced intervals in the hollows of the braid.

7 Cover the dough and leave it to rise again for about an hour.

8 Preheat the oven to 190°C (375°F). Bake the bread for 30–35 minutes. Remove the tsoureki from the oven and leave it to cool on a wire rack.

9 When cool, drizzle the bread with glacé icing, made from sifted icing sugar and a little water.

Biscotti

Italian biscotti are a delicious accompaniment for morning coffee.

WHAT YOU NEED

50 g pine nuts
275 g all-purpose flour
100 g superfine sugar
½ teaspoon baking soda
Pinch of salt
2 sprigs rosemary
Zest of 1 orange, finely grated
80 g unskinned almonds
2 eggs, beaten
1 egg, beaten with
a little water

1 Preheat the oven to 180°C (350°F). Spread pine nuts on a baking sheet and toast them for 8–10 minutes.
2 Put the flour, sugar, baking soda and salt into a bowl. Finely chop the rosemary leaves and add to the dry ingredients along with the grated orange zest, almonds and toasted pine nuts. Combine the ingredients well.
3 Add the eggs and mix to a dough.
4 Divide the dough into four and roll into thickish "sausages" on a lightly floured surface.
5 Place on a greased baking sheet, brush with egg wash and bake for 20 minutes. Leave on sheet to cool. Cut at an angle into 1 cm wide slices.
6 Brush the slices with the egg wash once again and bake at 150°C (300°F) for a further 10 minutes.
● Makes about 48 biscotti.

Brownies

This melt-in-your-mouth chocolate desert is always a hit.

WHAT YOU NEED

125 g butter
125 g dark chocolate
4 eggs
350 g sugar
1 teaspoon vanilla extract
150 g all-purpose flour
75 g walnuts
Icing
150 g dark chocolate, chopped
45 g butter

Yummy Italian biscotti (top left) and almond bread (bottom center) are classic twice-cooked breads. Brownies (bottom left) and gingerbread men (top right) are just as tempting, as are stuffed dates (top center) and Jaffa fudge (center).

1 Preheat the oven to 180°C (350°F). Line a 27 cm x 17 cm pan with wax paper.
2 Melt the butter and chocolate in a bowl over steaming water. Remove from the heat and allow to cool.
3 Beat the eggs with a pinch of salt until light and foamy. Gradually beat in the sugar and vanilla extract.
4 Quickly combine the cooled chocolate mixture and the eggs, using a wooden spoon. Fold in the flour, then the nuts.
5 Spoon this mixture into the prepared pan and bake in the oven for 35–40 minutes. Remove the brownies from the oven and allow them to cool in the pan.
6 *To make the icing:* Melt the chocolate and butter in a small bowl over boiling water. Mix well, and then leave to cool a little. Spread icing over the top of the brownies with a spatula and allow to set.
7 Cut into squares and place the brownies in a box between layers of greaseproof paper.
● Makes about 24 brownies.

Stuffed dates

Tasty and unusual tidbits to accompany after-dinner coffee.

WHAT YOU NEED

20 fresh dates
Candied pineapple or dried apricots
Toasted slivered almonds
Grated zest of 2 oranges
100 g granulated sugar

1 Remove the pits from the dates, being careful to keep the fruit whole.
2 Neatly fill each date with thick slivers of pineapple or apricots and a few slivered almonds.
3 Mix the grated orange zest and the sugar. Roll the dates in this mixture until they are well covered.
4 Pack the dates in miniature fluted paper cups in a flat box.

Jaffa fudge

A mouthwatering variation of the classic fudge recipe.

WHAT YOU NEED

2 cups granulated sugar
125 ml milk
125 g dark chocolate,
roughly broken
125 g unsalted butter
Juice and grated zest
of 1 orange

1 Put all the ingredients in a large, heavy-based saucepan and stir over low heat until the sugar has dissolved. Brush down any crystals that form on the side of the saucepan with a brush dipped in warm water.
2 Bring the mixture to the boil. Cook over a moderate heat, stirring occasionally, until the mixture reaches 112–116°C (234–240°F) measured with a candy thermometer, or until a small drop forms a firm, soft ball when dropped into a cup of cold water.
3 Remove the mixture from the heat and allow it to cool for 5 minutes, then beat rapidly with a wooden spoon until it is thick and creamy.
4 Pour into a 17.5 cm or 20 cm square buttered pan. As the mixture begins to set, cut it into squares.
5 Wrap up the squares of fudge individually in cellophane or package between sheets of greaseproof paper in a box. Keep in the refrigerator.
● Makes about 20 pieces.

Almond bread

These melting mouthfuls are light, crisp and not too sweet.

WHAT YOU NEED

6 egg whites
125 g superfine sugar
½ teaspoon almond extract
100 g all-purpose flour
100 g unskinned almonds

1 Preheat the oven to 180°C (350°F). Beat egg whites until stiff, then slowly add the sugar and almond extract.
2 Fold the flour and almonds into the meringue mixture, and then spoon the mixture into a lightly greased non-stick loaf pan, or a loaf pan lined with wax paper. The pan should be 25 cm x 10 cm x 9 cm.
3 Bake the bread in the oven for 30–40 minutes. Remove from the oven and allow to cool on a rack.
4 When the bread has cooled completely, cut it into the thinnest possible slices. You will find the bread very much easier to slice if you put it in the freezer for about 20 minutes before slicing.

5 Place the slices on a rack and dry them out in a cool oven (100°C/ 212°F) until they are crisp like toast.
● Makes about 36 pieces.

Gingerbread men

Give a child gingerbread men and remember your own childhood.

WHAT YOU NEED

125 g softened butter
150 g brown sugar
50 g granulated sugar
1 tablespoon fresh
ginger, grated
2 large eggs, beaten
500 g all-purpose flour
¼ teaspoon salt
½ teaspoon cinnamon
¼ teaspoon allspice
¾ teaspoon baking soda
60 ml hot water
Currants

1 Cream the butter with the sugars and ginger, then add the beaten eggs and mix well. Sift together the flour, salt and spices and dissolve the soda in the hot water.
2 Stir the sifted ingredients and the soda mixture alternately into the butter mixture and blend well.
3 Remove the dough from the bowl and knead on a floured board. If the dough is not firm, add a little more flour. Wrap the dough in plastic wrap and refrigerate for a couple of hours.
4 Preheat the oven to 180°C (350°F). Roll out the dough, on a floured table top, to a 5 mm thickness. Stamp out your chosen shapes with a cookie cutter and use currants for eyes and buttons.
5 Arrange the ginger-bread men on greased baking sheets and bake for 15–20 minutes. Remove from the oven and allow to cool.
● Makes about 30 gingerbreads.

As a children's party gift, dress up gingerbread men with eyes, mouth and buttons of colored glacé icing.

Jams & marmalades

Homemade jams and marmalades are an excellent way of preserving fruit, and they make wonderful gifts all year round. Present them in attractive jars from kitchenware stores, and make your own decorative labels and covers.

Banana jam

Banana jam is equally good as a spread or as a topping for yogurt or ice cream.

WHAT YOU NEED

500 g peeled weight, slightly under-ripe bananas
Juice of 2 small lemons
1 kg sugar, warmed

1 Slice the bananas into a large saucepan. Add the lemon juice and stir well to coat the banana slices in juice.
2 Add sugar to the pan, bring to the boil stirring gently to dissolve the sugar.
3 Reduce heat and simmer until setting point is reached.
4 Cool the jam, stirring to distribute the bananas.
5 Spoon into warm, sterilized jars. Seal the jars when the jam is cold.
● Makes about 500 ml.

Raspberry jam

This breakfast favorite keeps best stored in the refrigerator.

WHAT YOU NEED

750 g raspberries
750 g sugar, warmed
Juice of 2 lemons

1 Wash the raspberries, remove any stalks and dry the fruit carefully. Place in a large bowl. Add the warmed sugar to the fruit and cover. Leave for 12 hours or overnight.
2 Next day put the fruit, sugar and juices into a large saucepan. Bring to the boil, stirring to dissolve the sugar.
3 Add the lemon juice and boil quickly until jam reaches setting point. Pour into warm sterilized jars and seal.
● Makes about 750 ml.

Dried apricot jam

The almonds are optional, but they give the jam an interesting appearance and texture.

WHAT YOU NEED

500 g dried apricots
1 kg sugar, warmed
3 tablespoons lemon juice
60 g slivered almonds (optional)

1 Cover the apricots with water and soak them for 24 hours.
2 Place the apricots in a saucepan with the water and simmer until soft.
3 Add the sugar and lemon juice to the apricots. Simmer the jam until it reaches setting point. Stir in the almonds if using.
4 Spoon the jam into warm, sterilized jars. When the jam is cold and set, seal the jars.
● Makes 1.25 liters.

Apple & ginger conserve

A delicious conserve that can be made all year round. Experiment with different varieties of apple.

WHAT YOU NEED

1 kg tart dessert apples
250 ml of water
Grated rind and juice of
1 small lemon
750 g preserving sugar
100 g candied ginger, chopped
1 tablespoon ginger
syrup from jar

1 Peel and core apples and cut into chunks. Put into a large saucepan then add water, lemon rind and juice.
2 Bring to the boil and simmer for about 20 minutes. Add the sugar to the pan, stir well until sugar has dissolved then add ginger and syrup.
3 Bring back to the boil and simmer until the setting point is reached, stirring occasionally.
4 Cool slightly. Pour into warm sterilized jars. Leave until cold and set. Seal the jars.
● Makes about 1½ liters.

Kumquats in syrup

The kumquat is a citrus too bitter to eat fresh but is delicious preserved in a flavored syrup.

WHAT YOU NEED

1 kg kumquats
450 g sugar
250 ml water (for the syrup)
250 ml brandy, gin or vodka

1 Put the kumquats into a large saucepan and cover with water. Bring to the boil, remove from the heat and drain well. Cover with fresh water, bring to the boil and drain again.
2 Cover the kumquats with water a third time, bring to the boil and simmer for a few minutes until soft but not mushy. Drain well and tip into sterilized jars.
3 Dissolve the sugar in the cup of water, bring to the boil and simmer for 10 minutes. Remove the syrup from the heat, allow to cool a little, and then pour over the kumquats.
4 Top each jar with a few tablespoons of your chosen spirit.
5 Seal the jars and leave the mixture to mature for 6 weeks.
● Makes 1.5 liters.

HINT

Most jams and marmalades take a day or two to prepare. Setting point is reached when the jam "wrinkles" when dropped onto a saucer that has been chilled in the freezer, or when the jam's temperature reaches 104–107°C (219–224°F) measured on a candy thermometer.

Orange marmalade

Full flavored Seville oranges, originally from Spain, make the best marmalade.

WHAT YOU NEED

1.5 kg Seville oranges
3 liters water
Juice of 2 lemons
2.5 kg white granulated sugar
50 g candied ginger,
very finely chopped (optional)

1 Wash the oranges in hot water to remove any wax.
2 Using a vegetable peeler, remove the orange zest as thinly as possible and cut it into thin shreds. Place in a sauce pan with half the water and the lemon juice. Bring to the boil, then cover and simmer for 1½–2 hours or until the peel is soft.
3 Meanwhile, roughly cut the oranges and place them in another saucepan with the remaining water.

It is important to include both pith and pips. Bring to the boil, then cover and simmer gently for 1½ hours.
4 Strain the boiled orange pulp through a fine sieve into the pan with the softened peel. Bring to the boil and reduce slightly before adding the sugar. Boil rapidly until the marmalade reaches setting point. Stir in the ginger (optional).
5 Ladle the marmalade into warm, sterilized jars and seal well.
● Makes 4 liters.

Sliced oranges in caramel syrup

Serve these orange slices topped with crème fraîche or thick Greek yogurt.

WHAT YOU NEED

1 kg skinned seedless oranges
Water
225 g sugar
250 ml orange liqueur

1 Put the oranges into a large saucepan. Cover with water, bring to the boil, cover pan and simmer for about 20 minutes until the orange peel is soft.
2 Strain the oranges and discard the water. Leave the oranges until cool enough to handle, then slice thickly discarding the ends. Pack the orange slices into a sterilized jar.
3 Put the sugar into a pan with 250 ml of water. Stir gently until sugar has dissolved. Bring to a boil and boil rapidly until syrup caramelizes.
4 Remove the pan from the heat. Carefully stir in 225 ml of boiling water, stir well; cool. Pour into jar.
5 Pour on the orange liqueur. Seal jar and leave for about 6 weeks to mature.
● Makes about 750 ml.

HINT
Warmed sugar added to jams dissolves more quickly. To warm sugar, spread it on a large tray and place in a moderate oven (180°C/350°F) for 10 minutes.

Making jams and marmalades takes time, but the result is a wonderful selection of gifts for that unexpected occasion when you haven't time to make or buy anything.

Pastes, vinegars & spices

These make unusual and very welcome gifts, especially for friends who enjoy cooking but are busy and have to rely on shortcuts. After all, in these hectic days who really has time to make their own curry paste or garam masala?

Pastes, vinegars and spices can be presented in attractive bottles and jars bought from kitchenware stores.

Thai green curry paste

An innocuous-looking mixture that makes a very hot curry!

WHAT YOU NEED

3 teaspoons fermented
shrimp paste (gapi)
½ teaspoon white peppercorns
½ teaspoon coriander seeds
½ teaspoon seeds
3 cloves
225 g fresh green
chilies, chopped
Zest of 4 limes, finely grated
50 g lemongrass, cut from
the root end and finely sliced
25 g red shallots, finely diced
25 g galangal, peeled and diced
2 tablespoons finely diced garlic
2 tablespoons finely sliced
coriander root
3 teaspoons salt

Left to right: Vinaigrette, herb vinegar, Thai green curry paste, herbed oil, red chili vinegar – flavorsome cooking aids from all over the world.

1 Wrap shrimp paste in aluminum foil. Heat a heavy-based frying pan and dry roast the package for 2–3 minutes on each side. When cool, unwrap the foil and place the paste in a large bowl.
2 Roast the peppercorns, coriander, cumin seeds and cloves in the frying pan for 2–3 minutes, then grind in a coffee grinder or a pestle and mortar. Add to the shrimp paste with the remaining ingredients, and combine.
3 Put a third of the mixture into a blender and purée with enough water to make a smooth paste. Put the paste into a very fine sieve and press firmly with a wooden spoon, collecting any liquid obtained.
4 Reserve the paste and reuse the water to purée the next batch of dried ingredients. Continue sieving, reusing the strained liquid, until all the mixture is puréed.
5 Spoon the paste into sterilized jars or containers and seal. Keep refrigerated once seal is broken.
● Makes 600 ml.

Herbed oil

This makes an excellent base for a vinaigrette or salad dressing.

WHAT YOU NEED

3 cups virgin olive oil
25 g fresh herbs
Extra sprig fresh herbs

1 Pour the olive oil into a saucepan. Warm the oil gently, then pour it into a large, clean jar.

2 Lightly bruise the herbs with a pestle and mortar and add to the oil. Seal and leave to steep for two weeks.
3 Strain the oil through muslin or cheesecloth into sterilized bottles.
4 Add a sprig of fresh herb to each bottle, then seal and label the bottles. Keep in a cool, dark place.
● Makes 750 ml.

Herb vinegar

Use the finest vinegar to enhance the delicate flavor of the herbs.

WHAT YOU NEED

25 g fresh herbs
750 ml white wine or champagne vinegar
1–2 sprigs fresh herbs

1 Lightly bruise the herbs with a pestle and mortar, or with the back of a spoon on a wooden board.
2 Combine the herbs with the vinegar in a non-metallic container. Cover the mixture and leave it to infuse for two weeks.
3 Strain through double cheesecloth into clean sterilized bottles.
4 Add a fresh sprig or two of the herb you have used for the infusion to each bottle. Cork and label the bottles.
● Makes 750 ml.

Vinaigrette

A classic vinaigrette to accompany avocados, artichokes or asparagus.

WHAT YOU NEED

500 ml virgin olive oil
or light olive oil
100 ml red or white
wine vinegar
2 teaspoons Dijon mustard
Coarse sea salt to taste
6 whole peppercorns
1 bay leaf
Fresh thyme
1 whole head of garlic

1 Put the oil, vinegar, mustard and salt into a sterilized screwtop or clip-top jar. Shake well. Add peppercorns, bay leaf and thyme.

2 Slice the head of garlic lengthwise in half, removing any excess papery coating. Float one half in the jar. Use the other for another vinaigrette.
● Makes 600 ml.

Fruit vinegars

Fruit adds an appealing flavor and color to vingear, making it perfect for light salad dressings.

WHAT YOU NEED

500 g soft fresh fruits
(raspberries, strawberries,
blueberries)
750 ml white vinegar

1 Combine the fruit and vinegar in a bowl and stir well to lightly bruise the fruit. Cover the mixture and leave it to infuse for a few days.
2 Put the mixture into a saucepan. Bring it to boiling point, and then remove immediately from the heat and allow to cool.
3 Strain the mixture through double muslin or cheesecloth into sterilized jars. Seal the jars and label them.
● Makes 750 ml.

Variation

Peaches, plums and pears can also be used to make fruit vinegars. Slice the fruit in half, leaving a few of the pits attached. After a few months, filter off the vinegar. The fruit may be eaten as a pickle with cold meats and the vinegar used traditionally.

Red chili vinegar

Flavored vinegars add piquancy to vinaigrettes and sauces.

WHAT YOU NEED

2–3 long red chilies,
washed and dried
750 ml white wine vinegar

1 Cut one of the chilies in half lengthwise and place in a 750 ml bottle with the other two chilies.
2 Pour in the vinegar and then cork the bottles firmly and label them.
● Makes 750 ml.

Garam masala

Grind spices in a coffee grinder. Clean out before and after using.

WHAT YOU NEED

3 tablespoons coriander seeds
3 tablespoons cumin seeds
3 teaspoons cardamom seeds
1 tablespoon black peppercorns
3 cinnamon sticks
10 cloves
½ teaspoon grated
nutmeg (optional)

1 Dry roast the seeds separately in a hot frying pan, shaking constantly. Remove from the heat just as they begin to smoke. Place in a bowl and leave to cool.
2 Blend the seeds and the remaining ingredients (except the nutmeg) to a fine powder in a coffee grinder, adding the nutmeg if desired.
3 Store the garam masala in sterilized screwtop jars.
● Makes about 50 g.

Garam masala (front) will be a welcome addition to your hostess's kitchen.

Pickles

A gift of homemade pickles is a nostalgic reminder of the days when every housewife pickled and preserved garden produce.

Preserved peppers in oil

Preserved peppers with a hint of garlic make a colorful addition to any meat dish.

WHAT YOU NEED

3 large green peppers
3 large red peppers
Salt
1¾ liters white vinegar
1 or 2 cloves garlic,
cut in slivers
30 g fresh parsley
1 cup olive oil

1 Cut the peppers into five or six segments, removing the membrane and seeds. Wash and dry well. Place the segments in a bowl and sprinkle liberally with salt. Put a plate on the top and weigh down with a heavy weight. Allow to stand overnight.
2 The following day, drain the peppers well and return them to the bowl. Cover them with the vinegar and put a plate on top to ensure that the pepper segments are submerged in the vinegar. Allow to stand for about 8 hours or overnight.
3 Drain the peppers and pack them into sterilized jars, distributing the garlic slivers and parsley evenly throughout. Cover with oil and seal.
4 The following day, check the oil level and top up if necessary. Cover tightly and store in the refrigerator for a month before giving as a gift.
● Makes about 1.5 liters.

HINT
Pickles need to mature for at least four weeks to allow their full flavor to develop before you present them as gifts.

Preserved lemons

In the Middle East, this is a common way of preserving lemons. Both the skins and the juice add a unique flavor to salads and fish.

WHAT YOU NEED

Fresh lemons
Coarse sea salt

1 Wash and scrub the lemons to remove any wax.
2 Put them in a bowl of salted water and allow to stand for 24 hours. Drain well and dry.
3 Make two cuts, at right angles to each other, through each lemon from

Left to right: Pickled oranges with a hint of honey, preserved lemons from the Middle East, giardiniera from Italy, garlic-flavored preserved peppers and piquant pickled eggplant – marvelous presents to give your weekend host.

the stem end – do not cut them all the way through.

4 Put a teaspoon of salt into the center of each lemon.

5 Push three or four lemons into a sterilized ½-liter jar with a wooden spoon. Cover with water and seal.

6 After a couple of days, the lemons will have softened slightly; at this stage you can pack in another lemon or two.

7 When the jar is well packed, set it aside for a month. Don't worry if a film forms over the lemons; it can easily be washed off.

● You can also use this method to preserve very ripe limes.

Giardiniera

Fresh vegetables are pickled to make this colorful, delicately flavored antipasto from Italy.

WHAT YOU NEED

350 g cauliflower florets
200 g green beans
200 g Lebanese cucumbers
3 large carrots, peeled
3 peppers (1 green,
1 yellow, 1 red)
150 g small onions
125 ml olive oil
125 ml water
250 ml white wine
1¼ liters white vinegar
3 tablespoons sugar
3 tablespoons salt
4–5 bay leaves
½ tablespoon peppercorns

1 Wash and dry the cauliflower florets. Top and tail the beans and cut into halves. Halve the cucumbers lengthwise and then slice each half into thirds. Cut the carrots into thin strips. Remove the membrane and seeds from the peppers and cut into strips about 5 mm wide. Cut the onions into quarters.

2 Put the oil, water, wine, vinegar, sugar, salt, bay leaves and peppercorns into a large pot and bring to the boil. Simmer until the sugar and salt have dissolved. Remove from the heat and leave to cool for 5 minutes.

3 Drop the prepared cauliflower,

carrots, beans and onions into the pickling solution and place a plate on top to ensure that the vegetables are fully submerged.

4 When completely cool, add the cucumbers and peppers. Leave for 3–4 hours with the plate on top.

5 Pack into sterilized jars and cover completely with the pickling solution.

● Makes about 2.25 liters.

Pickled oranges

These oranges are delicious with ham, roast duck or pork.

WHAT YOU NEED

8 oranges, unpeeled
1 teaspoon salt
250 ml water
450 g sugar
250 ml malt vinegar
90 g honey
1 small knob fresh ginger,
peeled and chopped
1 teaspoon ground cinnamon
½ teaspoon five-spice powder
8 whole black peppercorns
8 cardamom pods
2 star anise
12 cloves

1 Wash the oranges thoroughly and put them into a large pot or saucepan together with the salt. Cover with water and bring to the boil. Reduce the heat and leave the fruit to simmer for about 40 minutes.

2 Drain the oranges, allow them to cool, and then cut them into slices about 5 mm thick.

3 Put the remaining ingredients into a saucepan and bring to the boil. Reduce the heat and simmer gently for 10 minutes.

4 Add the orange slices and bring the mixture back to the boil, stirring occasionally. Reduce the heat and simmer gently for another 15 minutes.

5 Remove the saucepan from the heat and allow the mixture to stand for approximately 10 minutes.

6 Ladle the oranges into warmed sterilized jars. Seal and label the jars. Keep refrigerated once seal is broken.

● Makes about 1.5 liters.

Piquant pickled eggplant in oil

A scrumptious taste with sun-dried tomatoes on Italian bread.

WHAT YOU NEED

2 kg eggplants, peeled
200 g coarse salt
750 ml white vinegar
1 tablespoon sugar
1 tablespoon salt
15 whole black peppercorns
Olive oil
4 small red chilies
4–6 cloves garlic, peeled
6 sprigs fresh oregano

1 Cut the eggplants into lengthwise slices about 5 mm thick. Place them in layers in a large earthenware dish, sprinkling salt on every slice. Finish off with a layer of salt. Place a flat plate on top of the eggplants, weigh it down with a heavy weight, such as a bag of potatoes, and leave for several hours. Take out the slices and squeeze them to remove excess liquid.

2 Mix the vinegar, sugar, salt and peppercorns in a saucepan and bring the mixture to the boil.

3 Drop a quarter of the eggplant slices into the boiling vinegar and simmer for 30 seconds. Remove and place on paper towels. Repeat until all the slices have been blanched. Make sure that they are well dried. Put them in a bowl and dress with olive oil.

4 Place the eggplant slices in layers in sterilized jars, adding the chilies, garlic cloves and oregano as you go.

5 Fill the jars with olive oil, pressing down to remove any air bubbles. Use a skewer to release any remaining trapped air.

6 Check the oil level the following day and top with more oil if necessary. Seal and store in a cool dark place.

● Makes about 1.2 liters.

HINT
When you are making pickles, remember to use only stainless steel equipment.

Preserves & chutneys

What nicer contribution to a picnic or special dinner than a spicy chutney, an unusual mixture of dried fruits preserved in mustard, a continental treat like olive paste or tapenade of figs, or a jar of tomatoes that you have dried and bottled yourself?

Red pepper marmalade

Red pepper marmalade is a tasty addition to pork, ham or chicken.

WHAT YOU NEED

12 large red peppers
2 tablespoons salt
675 g sugar
375 ml white vinegar

1 Wash the peppers, remove the seeds and the membrane and chop finely. Sprinkle with the salt and allow to stand for 2–3 hours in a colander.
2 Put the drained pepper in a heavy-based saucepan with the sugar and vinegar. Cook for about an hour, stirring occasionally, until thick.
3 Spoon into warm sterilized jars and seal. Refrigerate once seal is broken.
● Makes about 1 liter.

Apricot chutney

Apricots, garlic, chilies and ginger mingle to stimulate the taste buds.

WHAT YOU NEED

500 g dried apricots
8 large cloves garlic, peeled
4 medium chilies, chopped
1 medium-sized knob
fresh ginger, peeled
and chopped
400 g brown sugar
500 ml red or white
wine vinegar
½ teaspoon salt
150 g golden raisins

1 Cover the apricots with water and soak the fruit overnight.
2 The following day, put the garlic, chilies and ginger in the blender together with some of the soaking water and blend until smooth.

3 Put this mixture in a large saucepan, together with the apricots and their soaking liquid.
4 Add the sugar, vinegar and salt. Bring to the boil and simmer over the lowest heat for about ½ hour.
5 Add the raisins and cook for a further ½ hour or until the chutney is thick and glossy. Allow to cool.
6 Place in sterilized jars and store in the refrigerator.
● Makes about 850 ml.

Tomato chutney

Try this fiery South-East Asian variation of a familiar condiment.

WHAT YOU NEED

2 tablespoons black
mustard seeds
625 ml malt vinegar
4–6 kg ripe tomatoes, peeled
300 ml olive oil
4 tablespoons cumin seeds
200 g fresh ginger, peeled
and chopped
20 cloves garlic, peeled
10 fresh red chilies, chopped
2 tablespoons
turmeric powder
2 tablespoons sambal oelek
250 g palm sugar
100 ml fish sauce

1 Soak the black mustard seeds overnight in the malt vinegar. Drain the seeds and discard the vinegar.
2 Preheat the oven to 180°C (350°F), and roast the tomatoes in some of the oil for about 1½ hours.
3 Toast the cumin seeds in a hot frying pan for a few minutes. Shake the pan occasionally and watch that the seeds do not burn.
4 Put the cumin and mustard seeds and all the other ingredients except the oil into a blender and purée.

5 Simmer in a saucepan for about 45 minutes, stirring frequently.
6 Add the roasted tomatoes with their juices and the remaining oil.
7 Cook the chutney for a further hour, stirring frequently and adding more oil if necessary.
8 Spoon into sterilized, screwtop jars.
● Makes about 3 liters.

Olive paste

Anchovy-flavored olive paste can be spread on bread or tossed through a salad or hot pasta.

WHAT YOU NEED

300 g pitted black olives
18 anchovy fillets
130 g capers
4 cloves garlic, roughly chopped
1 teaspoon freshly
ground black pepper
½ teaspoon salt
125 ml olive oil

1 Put the black olives, anchovy fillets, capers, chopped garlic, pepper and salt into a food processor.
2 Process until smooth, drizzling in the olive oil gradually as you go.
3 Spoon into sterilized, screwtop jars.
● Makes about 500 ml.

Fig tapenade

This Provençale condiment goes well with barbecued lamb chops.

WHAT YOU NEED

125 g dried figs
175 g pitted Kalamata olives
Juice of 1 lemon
2 tablespoons olive oil
45 g anchovies
50 g capers

1 Put the figs into a bowl, cover with boiling water and leave to soak until soft. Remove the figs and chop them into small pieces with a sharp knife.
2 Put the figs in a food processor with the remaining ingredients and process to a fine pulp. Spoon the fig tapenade into a sterilized jar.
● Makes about 220 ml.

Left to right: Apricot chutney, tomato chutney, tomatoes in olive oil, olive paste, red pepper marmalade (top), mustard fruits (bottom), and fig tapenade – there's something here to suit every friend's palate and taste buds.

Mustard fruits

Mustard fruits are delicious with game, ham or roast pork.

WHAT YOU NEED

500 g sugar
375 ml water
250 g dried apricots
250 g dried peaches
250 g dried figs
250 g dried mango
1 cinnamon stick
4 cloves
6 black peppercorns
6 coriander seeds
125 ml white wine vinegar
50 g hot mustard powder

1 Put 400 g of the sugar with the water into a saucepan and gently heat until the sugar has dissolved. Add the fruit and spices, and cook over a low heat for 15–20 minutes.
2 In another saucepan, dissolve the remaining sugar with the vinegar and cook for about 10 minutes, until it forms a thick syrup. Allow to cool.

3 Mix the mustard powder with enough of the syrup to form a paste. Stir in the remaining syrup and then combine it with the cooked fruit compote. Mix well.
4 Return to the boil, allow to cool, then pour into warm, sterilized jars.
● Makes about 1.5 liters.

Dried tomatoes in olive oil

Use either plum or cherry tomatoes – the cherry tomatoes don't take as long to dry. Red and yellow cherry tomatoes look very attractive mixed together.

WHAT YOU NEED

2 kg vine-ripened tomatoes
10 g fresh thyme or oregano
10 g coarse sea salt
1 tablespoon sugar
8 cloves garlic, peeled
1–2 bay leaves
Capers (optional)
Olive oil

1 Preheat the oven (preferably a convection or fan-assisted oven) to 50°C (120°F).
2 Wash and dry the tomatoes, halve them lengthwise and arrange them cut-side-up on cake racks.
3 Finely chop the fresh herbs and sprinkle them over the tomatoes, together with sparing quantities of salt and sugar.
4 Put the racks into the oven. Remember to put a tray underneath to catch any liquid.
5 Leave to dry for 24–36 hours. The time will vary depending on your oven and the moisture content of the tomatoes. The tomatoes should be dry but still fleshy. Do not let them become too withered.
6 Remove and allow to cool, then place in sterilized glass jars with the garlic and a bay leaf or two. Add the capers if desired.
7 Cover the tomatoes with oil, tapping the jar on a counter top to remove any air bubbles. Seal the jars tightly and store in the refrigerator.
● Makes about 750 ml.

Drinks

A bottle of homemade cordial is a refreshing gift, especially at the height of summer. A tablespoon or two of cordial added to iced water makes a delicious cool drink.

HINTS
Label the bottle with the name of the drink and a list of ingredients. To make it a lasting gift include two tall glasses for adults or plastic beakers for children.

Blackcurrant liqueur (second from left) makes a luxurious gift. Ginger syrup (left), Earl Grey tea & lemon syrup (center) and Fifty-fifty cordial are great for family parties.

Earl Grey tea & lemon syrup

Dilute with water and lots of ice for an instant iced tea drink.

WHAT YOU NEED

2 Earl Grey tea bags
600 ml boiling water
700 g sugar
25 g citric acid
4 large unwaxed lemons

1 Put the tea bags and water into a saucepan. Allow to stand for 10 minutes, then remove and discard the tea bags.
2 Add the sugar to the pan, heat gently until the sugar has disolved.
3 Transfer to a sterilized bowl and stir in the citric acid.
4 Pare the rind from the lemons, squeeze juice and add both to bowl.

5 Cover the bowl with a clean cloth to prevent evaporation and leave for 8 hours or overnight.
6 Strain into sterilized bottles and seal.
● Makes about 1 liter.

Blackcurrant liqueur

Blackcurrant liqueur is the basis of the aperitif known as Kir. To make Kir, pour a teaspoonful of the liqueur into a wine glass and top with white wine or champagne.

WHAT YOU NEED

2 cups blackcurrants
Small cinnamon stick
2 cups brandy
½ cup sugar

1 Put all the ingredients into a sterilized jar and mix well. Seal and shake well. Store in a dark, cool place

for a month or two, shaking the jar well every other day.
2 Strain the mixture through a muslin cloth into sterilized bottles and seal.
● Makes about 1 liter.

Ginger syrup

Here is a soft drink that will please the most discriminating taste.

WHAT YOU NEED

900 g sugar
Juice of 3 lemons
1 dessertspoon ground ginger
1 teaspoon tartaric acid
4.5 liters water

1 Mix together all the ingredients in a very large bowl, stirring until all the sugar has dissolved.
2 Strain into sterilized bottles. The syrup will be ready in 2–3 days.
● Makes six 750 ml bottles.

Fifty-fifty cordial

Mix with fizzy mineral water and ice for a refreshing summer drink.

WHAT YOU NEED

4 oranges
4 lemons
2 kg sugar
30 g Epsom salts
75 g tartaric or citric acid
2 liters boiling water

1 Grate the citrus zest and squeeze the juice into a large bowl. Add sugar, salts, acid and zest. Add the boiling water and allow to stand overnight.
2 The following day, pour into sterilized bottles and seal.
● Makes five 750 ml bottles.

TECHNIQUES

Refer to this chapter
for the basic skills you
need to make the projects in
this book. Step-by-step
diagrams and instructions
will refresh your memory of
familiar craft techniques and
start you off in new ones.

Sewing

Sewing is a craft that everyone can become proficient in. You can make many of the simple projects in this book by hand while you sit in a comfortable armchair, but for the larger and more complicated projects a sewing machine is recommended.

Needles & threads

CHOOSING A NEEDLE

It is important to select a needle that is suitable for the fabric and thread that you are using. For both hand-sewing and machine sewing, the finer the weight of the fabric and thread, the finer the needle should be.

Many types of needles are available for handsewing (see the box at the bottom of this page). The size of a needle relates to its diameter, and the length varies in relation to the size.

CHOOSING A THREAD

Threads come in a variety of sizes and a wide range of colors. The most commonly used threads are 100% polyester and polyester/cotton, and these are suitable for both machine sewing and handsewing. A wide range of specialty threads is also available. If

you cannot match thread and fabric accurately, choose a thread that is darker than the fabric rather than lighter. For prints and plaids, choose a thread color that will blend well.

• *Thread size* is a measurement of the thickness or coarseness of the thread. Metric thread sizes are 120 – general-purpose; 140 – very fine (limited supply); 75 – thicker or coarser. The corresponding denier sizes are 50, 60 (limited supply) and 30.

• *Polyester/cotton* (size 120 metric) is a combination of synthetic and cotton threads. A core spun thread has a synthetic inside covered with cotton, which produces a strong thread with a good resistance to abrasion.

• *Polyester 100%* (size 120 metric) is a strong thread consisting of synthetic fibers spun together.

• *Cotton 100%* (mercerized or soft cotton) is not as strong as threads that contain synthetic components. Mercerizing is a finishing process that makes the thread smooth and

lustrous, and slightly stronger than soft cotton thread. Cotton thread is used for specialized sewing, such as heirloom sewing, to create a pure natural fiber article. The range of colors available is limited.

• *Heavy-duty polyester* (size 30) is a very strong thread that is available in a variety of colors. It is used for heavy-duty or decorative sewing.

• *Nylon thread* is a strong, monofila-ment thread, referred to as invisible thread, for both handsewing and machine sewing. It is most commonly used for sewing hems.

Handsewing

SECURING THE THREAD
Knotting the thread to begin
This is one method of securing the thread when you begin. For basting stitches the knot can be visible, but for permanent stitching it must be concealed at the wrong side of the work.

Backstitching to begin and end
This method is better than knotting the thread, as it leaves less indentation after pressing. Take a small running stitch through both layers a short distance from the edge. Take one or two stitches back over the first and pull

---

NEEDLES FOR HANDSEWING

Sharps (sizes 1–12) are general-purpose needles. They are of medium length and have round eyes.
Ball-points (sizes 5–10) resemble sharps, except that their points are rounded so as to penetrate knit fabrics without splitting the yarn.
Betweens or quilting needles (sizes 1–12) are short, which makes them ideal for fine stitches in heavy fabrics.
Self-threaders (sizes 4–8) are like sharps, but they have slots instead of eyes, which makes them easier to thread.
Straws or milliners (sizes 1–10) are long needles useful for basting.
Crewels (sizes 1–10) are sharp needles of medium length. Their long eyes

allow several strands of thread to be threaded at once. Crewels are usually used for embroidery.
Chenilles or couching needles (sizes 13–24) are sharp and heavy. They are normally used to embroider with woolen yarn or silk ribbon.
Beading needles (sizes 10–15) are long and thin. They are primarily used for beading and sequin work.
Tapestry needles (sizes 13–26) are heavy and have blunt ends. They are used mainly for tapestry work, and can also be used for silk ribbon embroidery.
Darning needles are used mainly for darning. Cotton darners (sizes 1–9) and double longs (sizes 1–9) resemble

each other, but double longs are longer so as to span larger holes.
Yarn or wool darners (sizes 14–18) are used to sew knitted garments together.
Glovers (sizes 1–8) have triangular points that will pierce leather, vinyl or plastic without tearing the fabric.
Sailmakers (sizes 14–17) are like glovers, except that the points extend further up the shaft. They are used to sew canvas and heavy leather.
Upholstery needles (sizes 5–20) are curved. They are used when a straight needle would be awkward.
Sack or packing needles have curved, wedge-shaped points for weaving, upholstery and stitching burlap.

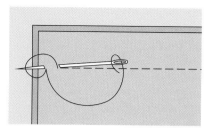

the thread through, making sure it is secure. Repeat at the end of the work.

BASIC STITCHES
Backstitch

A strong, general-purpose stitch for joining and repairing seams, topstitching, understitching and zipper hand-picking (a variation of backstitch).

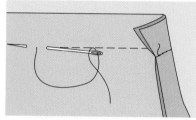

1 Secure thread at beginning of work through all layers, bringing thread out 2–4 mm in front of secured stitch.
2 For first and succeeding stitches, take needle into hole of previous stitch (i.e. 2–4 mm behind emerged thread), then bring needle and thread out the same distance in front of that point. Continue in this way, keeping stitches even, and secure thread at end.

Blanket stitch

Blanket stitch is used to neaten the raw edges of thick fabrics. Work blanket stitch from left to right, with the point of the needle and the edge of the work toward you.

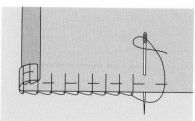

1 Fold back the edge of the fabric and secure with basting stitches.
2 Secure the thread within the fold and bring it out below the edge.
3 For the first and each succeeding stitch, insert the needle through the

fabric from the right side and bring it down below the edge of the hem.
4 Keeping the thread from previous stitch under the point of the needle, draw the needle and thread through to form a stitch over the edge.

Buttonhole stitch

Buttonhole stitch is used as a decorative finish and to make handsewn buttonholes. It is like blanket stitch, but the stitches are worked close together, forming a twist along the cut fabric edge for added reinforcement.

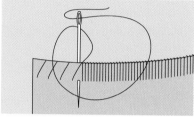

1 Overcast the raw edge. Working from right to left, with raw edge away from you, secure the thread and then bring the needle out above the edge.
2 For the first and each succeeding stitch, loop thread from previous stitch first over to the left and then down and across to the right.
3 Take the needle to the back and bring the point to the right side for the depth of the stitch, keeping the looped thread under both the point and the eye of the needle.
4 Pull the needle through the fabric and away from you to form the twist of the stitch on the fabric edge.

Ladder stitch

Ladder stitch is used for invisibly joining two folded edges by slipstitching them together. The stitches are made inside the fold on each side and pulled tight to close the opening. This stitch is often used for closing the seams in soft toys after they have been stuffed.

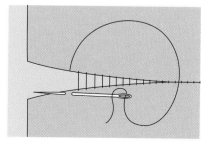

1 Secure thread under one edge of fabric and bring needle out to right side. Carry needle and thread to opposite folded fabric edge and take a small stitch along inside of fold.
2 Take needle back over to first folded edge. Insert needle into first folded edge, directly opposite where thread emerged from second folded edge, and take another small stitch.
3 Continue to end of seam.

Overcasting

Overcasting is a slanting stitch that is used to prevent raw edges from fraying. It can be worked either from right to left or from left to right. Overcasting is often used to neaten the seams on handsewn articles.

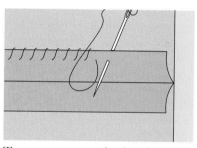

To overcast, secure the thread using backstitch. Take diagonal stitches over the raw edge, spacing them evenly and keeping the depth uniform.

Overhand stitch

Overhand stitch is used to topsew two finished edges – for example, to attach edging lace or ribbon to a garment. It is worked from right to left.

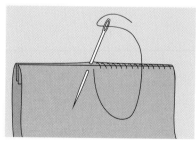

1 Place the two edges together. Insert needle diagonally from back edge through to front edge, picking up only one or two fabric threads each time. Insert needle directly behind thread from previous stitch and bring it out one stitch length away.
2 Keep stitches as uniform as possible in their size and spacing.

Running stitch

Running stitch is a very short, even stitch used for delicate sewing, such as tucking and gathering. Running stitch is like even basting, but the stitches are smaller and usually permanent.

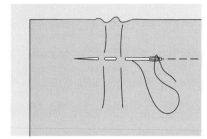

1 Working from right to left, weave the point of the needle in and out of the fabric several times before pulling the needle through.
2 Keep the stitches and the spaces between them small and even.

Basting

Basting is a temporary stitch used to hold edges together before joining them permanently by machine stitching or handstitching.

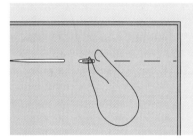

1 Working from right to left, sew along the seamline, taking several evenly spaced stitches onto the needle before pulling it through.
2 Keep the stitches and the spaces between them equal in length.

Whipstitch

This is a variation of overhand stitch, the main difference being the angle at which the needle is held. Whipstitch is generally used to topsew two finished edges together, but it can also hold a raw edge neatly against a flat surface. It is often used in heirloom sewing to join two edges or to roll and whip a raw edge by hand.
1 Insert the needle at right angles to the fabric and close to the edge, picking up only a few threads.

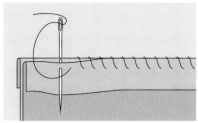

2 Slanted threads will be produced between tiny stitches.

HEM STITCHES

There are several stitches suitable for securing a hem to a garment.

Blind hemming

This is a very neat and almost invisible method of finishing a hem.

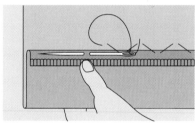

1 Neaten the raw edge of the fabric by overlocking or zigzagging.
2 Press the hem up for the desired width (normally 4 cm).
3 Secure the thread, concealing the end behind the hem. Work stitches with the hem edge temporarily folded back about 5 mm.
4 For first and succeeding stitches, catch one or two threads, then catch folded-back hem with a small stitch along the crease. The width and size of stitches will change according to weight of fabric. Stitches should be small enough to hold hem securely, but not too small or tight.
5 Press neatened hem edge back up, concealing stitches.

Hemming stitch

This is a small slanting stitch. It is a variation of slipstitch.

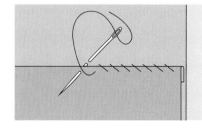

1 Fold the hem over 3 mm to the wrong side, and then fold the fabric over again to the depth you want to make your finished hem.
2 Secure the thread on the inside of the hem. Working from right to left, take the first and each succeeding stitch about 6–10 mm to the left, catching only one thread of the garment fabric and bringing the needle through the edge of the hem.

Herringbone or catch stitch

This is a strong stitch, particularly useful for single-fold hems. Neaten raw edges with an appropriate finish, and work from left to right, with the needle pointing to the left.

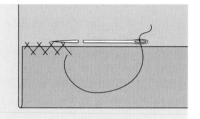

1 Fasten the thread on the inside of the hem. Take a small stitch in the garment fabric directly above the hem edge and about 6–10 mm to the right.
2 Take the next stitch on the hem edge, 6–10 mm to the right.
3 Continue to alternate stitches on garment fabric and hem edge, spacing them evenly. The cross-thread of each stitch crosses the previous one.

Slipstitch

Slipstitch can be used for hemming, attaching trims, stitching down coat and jacket linings, and so on. It joins a folded edge to a flat surface.

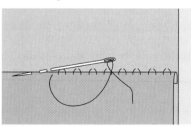

1 Fold fabric over to wrong side for 3–5 mm, and then press fabric over to wrong side again for width of hem.
2 Secure thread, concealing it behind hem, and bring needle and thread out through fold of hem. Take a small

stitch into garment fabric, catching one or two threads. Insert needle back into fold of hem. Slide needle along inside of fold for about 6 mm. Bring needle and thread out through fold.
3 Continue alternating stitches from garment to fold, keeping stitches even and ensuring that thread is not pulled too tight, so that stitches on right side are as invisible as possible.

Cutting out

PINNING THE PATTERN TO THE FABRIC

Press the pattern and the fabric and fold the fabric according to the cutting guide (the layout plan). Place the pattern pieces on the fabric as shown in the cutting guide. Pin the foldline or grainline first, measuring the grainline to ensure that it is parallel to the selvage. Then pin the corners and finally the edges, smoothing out the pattern pieces as you work.

When you are working with directional fabrics, the pattern pieces must all be laid in the same direction for cutting. Directional fabrics include napped fabrics (fabrics with pile or brushed surfaces), one-way fabrics (fabrics with designs that cannot be reversed), and fabrics with surfaces that reflect light in varying ways, such as satins and iridescent fabrics.

To test a fabric for the direction of the nap, run a hand over it. It will feel smooth with the nap running down and rough with the nap running up.

If you are sewing with plaid or striped fabric, lay the pattern on the fabric as follows.
1 Decide which lengthwise bar or space is to be in the center of the garment. Fold the fabric in half at this point if the pattern piece is to be cut on a fold. For other pattern pieces, align this point with the center seamline (or the center line for a piece with an extended facing). Ensure that centers are matching for all main sections.
2 Place dominant crosswise bars directly on, or as close as possible to, garment edges, such as the hemline and the sleeve edges.

PATTERN MARKINGS

Pattern markings are guidelines marked on the pattern to help you to cut out and make up the garment correctly.
The cutting line is a continuous line around the edge of a pattern piece indicating where the fabric should be cut.
The seamline or stitching line is a broken line indicating where the garment should be basted and sewn. It is usually 1.5 cm inside the cutting line, but this measurement may vary.
Notches may be single or double. Matching pairs of notches are sometimes numbered to make identification easier if there are several marked on the pattern. They indicate exactly where the edges of garment pieces are to be matched up.
Dots or circles, squares and triangles help you to match up adjoining pieces of material. They can also indicate special details such as darts, tucks or the position of a zipper.
The lengthen or shorten line is a heavy line or a double line provided on pattern pieces where either type of alteration may be required.
The grainline is a line with an arrow at each end to be placed on the straight grain of the fabric. Pin the patterns to the fabric

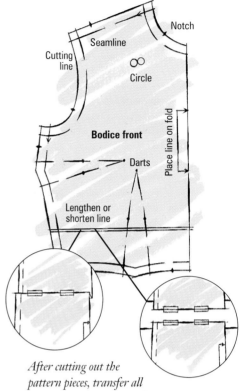

After cutting out the pattern pieces, transfer all relevant markings to the fabric to help you to assemble the garment.

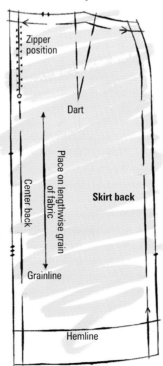

with the grainline parallel to the selvage to ensure that the finished garment hangs correctly. A bracketed grainline, indicating "Place on fold," shows that the pattern edge must be placed on the fold of the fabric. This may also be indicated by the written instruction "Place line on fold."
Darts are shown as broken lines (stitching lines) that meet at a point toward the center of the pattern.
The zipper position is often marked with a line of small triangles along the opening for the neck, waist or back, indicating the placement of the zipper on the seamline. Top and bottom markings show the precise length of a zipper.
Buttons and buttonholes are indicated by a circle and a horizontal line, showing button position and buttonhole size.
The hemline is the recommended finished edge, and marks the length of the finished garment. Check the length required against the pattern length before cutting out, and adjust the length, if necessary, at the lengthen or shorten line.

MARKING TECHNIQUES

Markings are your guides for effortless sewing. When you have cut out the pattern pieces from fabric, transfer the relevant symbols onto the fabric to help you to assemble the article neatly and accurately. Test your chosen method of marking on a scrap to ensure that it is suitable for the fabric.

Clips and notches

These are simple ways of marking symbols on the cutting line of the fabric. Clips are slits cut a short way into the seam allowance. Notches are V-shapes cut outward or inward from the cutting line. Shown below are ways of marking clips and notches.

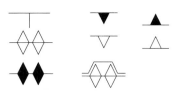

Marking tools

The tools listed below are quick and easy methods of marking the design symbols on the pattern pieces – for example, dart points, pocket positions, tucks, buttons and buttonholes.

- Tailor's chalk (brush out)
- Dressmaker's pencil (brush or wash out)
- Fade-out marking pen
- Wash-out marking pen
- Quilting pencil/water-soluble dressmaker's pencil

1 At each symbol, scratch a small hole in the paper pattern and stick a pin through both layers of fabric.
2 Remove paper pattern and mark the wrong sides of the fabric.

Tailor's tacks

Tailor's tacks are a good all-purpose way of marking design symbols. They involve more handling than marking tools but carry less risk of spoiling expensive fabrics. Tailor's tacks are generally used on sheer, multi-colored, bulky or spongy fabrics.

1 At each relevant symbol, scratch a small hole in the pattern. At this point, take a small stitch with double thread through both layers of fabric, leaving a 3 cm end. Take a second stitch over the first, leaving a 3–5 cm loop. Cut the thread, leaving a 3 cm end.
2 When all symbols are marked, remove the pattern with care to avoid pulling out the threads. Separate the fabric layers to the limits of the loops.

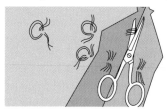

3 Cut the threads between the fabric layers, leaving thread markings on both layers. (Remove the threads after you have assembled the garment.)

Thread-marking

Thread-marking is often used for marking design lines on tailored garments or expensive garments (couture sewing). It is time-consuming, but should be used when very accurate marking is necessary. It is a basting stitch through a single layer of fabric, and is removed after assembly.

1 Remove lower layer of fabric so as not to catch it while thread-marking.

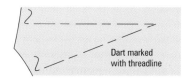

Dart marked with threadline

2 Fold pattern back along line to be marked (e.g. center front, seamlines, tucklines). Handstitch along all necessary lines within pattern piece with a single thread, alternating large basting stitches with small running stitches.
3 Remove pattern and pin to opposite layer of fabric. Repeat step 2, making sure that a left and a right side are formed.

Dressmaker's carbon paper

When using this method, take great care not to make markings other than those required. The method is not recommended for sheers or light-colored fabrics, as markings will show on the right side, or for couture sewing (expensive articles).

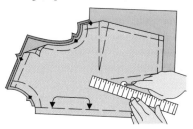

Place carbon against wrong side of fabric with waxed side facing fabric. With a tracing wheel or stylus, trace pattern markings from right side, using a ruler as a guide for straight lines. To mark two layers of fabric at once, place wrong sides together with double-sided carbon paper between them (or two pieces of single-sided carbon paper back to back).

3 To match major garment sections crosswise, place corresponding notches on identical crosswise bars. For example, to match the front and sleeve of a garment, place armhole notches of sleeve and front on the same cross-bars. Do all matching at seamlines, not at cutting lines. It may or may not be possible to match such diagonals as darts and shoulder seams.

CUTTING THE FABRIC
Scissors and shears

For accurate results when cutting fabric, always keep it flat on the cutting surface. Dressmaker's shears with a bent handle help to keep the fabric flat. You can use shears with either plain or serrated blades; serrated blades are best for gripping knits and slippery fabrics. Make sure that the blades of shears and scissors are sharp; dull blades will chew the fabric.

Rotary cutters

A rotary cutter can be used either right-handed or left-handed, regardless of application. Used correctly, a rotary cutter cuts fabric quickly and cleanly. It can also cut several layers at once to make pieces of uniform size. It is especially useful for cutting fabric for patchwork, appliqué and quilting. However, remember that rotary cutters are very sharp and can cause deep cuts in hands or furniture.

• Always use a cutting mat under the fabric. A self-healing mat with a rough surface that prevents the fabric from slipping is best.

• Always use a ruler (plastic or steel) to guide the cutting wheel.

• Iron the fabric before cutting and smooth it out over the cutting mat so that there are no wrinkles to cause uneven cutting lines.

• Holding the ruler down firmly with one hand, push the cutter blade away from you in one movement, pressing into the cutting mat and keeping the blade tight against the ruler.

• Retract the blade after each cut.

Scalloped edges

1 To calculate scallop size, measure the edge to be scalloped, excluding seam allowances. Keeping the size proportionate, work out how many scallops will fit along the edge. Scallops should be about a third as high as they are wide. Make a cardboard template of the scallop shape.

2 Baste tissue paper or tear-away fabric stabilizer to the wrong side of the fabric edge.

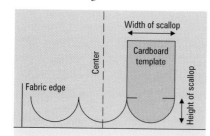

3 Center the template on the fabric edge and mark around it on the right side of the fabric. Then mark scallops right along the edge on either side of the center scallop.

4 Machine finishing: Zigzag along the scalloped edge with a small open zigzag stitch. Trim away excess fabric, and then machine a second row of zigzag stitches over the first to give a close satin stitch finish.

5 Hand finishing: Staystitch by hand or machine about 3 mm inside the

marked scallops. Cut around the scalloped edge and finish the raw edges with closely worked buttonhole stitch.

Machine sewing

STAYSTITCHING

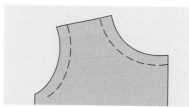

Staystitching is a reinforcing stitch, usually made through a single layer of fabric, to prevent stretching during assembly of a garment. It is generally placed just inside the seamline on curved or angled seams, and is done as soon as the pattern has been removed and before any further handling.

SEAMS

Seams are the basic structural elements of a garment, and must be formed with care. For most seams the right sides of the fabric are placed together, but occasionally the wrong sides are facing. The standard seam width is 1.5 cm (15 mm), but always check the pattern in case a seam requires a special width. Seams should be backstitched at the beginning and end for reinforcement.

Seam assembly

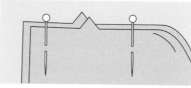

1 Pin the seam, matching notches and other markings along the seamline. Place pins perpendicular to seamline, with tips just beyond the seamline and heads toward seam edge.

2 If necessary, sew a row of basting stitches close to the seamline, removing the pins as you baste. (Note that with most seams, only pinning and machining are necessary.)

3 Backstitch (make a few reverse stitches) to secure the thread, then

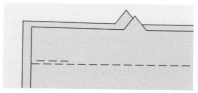

stitch forward along the seamline. Backstitch at the end of the seam for a few stitches. Clip off the threads close to the stitching.

4 If you used basting stitches, remove them. Either press the seam open or press it closed in one direction.

Corner seams

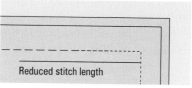

To reinforce a corner seam, reduce the stitch length for about 2 cm on each side of the corner.

Trimming a seam

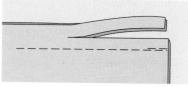

To trim a seam, cut away some of the seam allowance. Trim a seam in this way when the full seam allowance would interfere with the fit of the garment or with further assembly.

Grading a seam

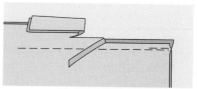

When a seam forms a garment edge or is to be enclosed, grade it so that the seam lies flat and does not make a bulky ridge. Trim the seam allowance (see above), and then cut a little more from the seam allowance that will fall farthest from the garment side.

Trimming a corner

1 When you reach the point, pivot the machine needle and take one stitch across to the next edge. Pivot the needle again and continue the seam along the other edge.

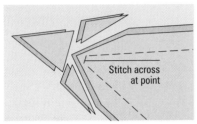

Stitch across at point

2 Trim the seam allowance across the point, close to the stitching, then taper it on each side. The more elongated the point, the further back the seam allowance should be trimmed, so that when the point is turned right side out the allowance will not overlap and create bulk.

Clipping and notching

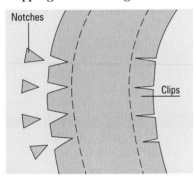

Notches

Clips

Clip and notch curved seams before pressing so that they lie flat. Clips are slits cut into the seam allowances of convex curves so that the edges can spread. Notches are wedges cut from the seam allowances of concave curves to allow the edges to draw in.

Understitching

Understitching keeps a facing and its seamline from rolling to the garment's right side. It is done after the seam allowances have been trimmed and

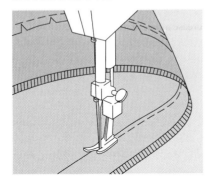

graded, and clipped or notched. Working close to the seamline on the right side, straight stitch through the facing and the seam allowances.

Finishing seams

Seam finishes are techniques used to neaten the raw edges of seams and prevent fraying. Depending on the assembly procedures used, seams may be pressed before or after neatening.

The most commonly used seam finishes are overlocking and zigzagging, both of which may be used on either open or closed seams.

Seam finishing techniques not as widely used are turned and stitched, hand overcasting, machine overedging, bias binding and pinking; these are special decorative finishes.

French seams

French seams are self-enclosed seams that do not need a separate seam finish. They are especially appropriate for sheer fabrics, in which the seams are visible from the right side of the finished garment. They look best if the finished width is 5 mm or less.

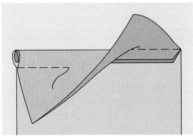

1 With wrong sides of fabric together and a 1.5 cm seam allowance, stitch 1 cm from edge. Trim seam allowance to 3 mm.
2 Press the seam open. Fold right sides together, with the stitched line exactly on the edge of the fold, then press again.
3 Stitch on the seamline, which is now 5 mm from the fold.
4 Press the seam to one side.

Bias bound seams

Binding produces a neat, well-finished seam. It is sometimes used to finish seams in unlined jackets or coats.
1 Trim any notches from seam edge and wrap binding around it. Press.

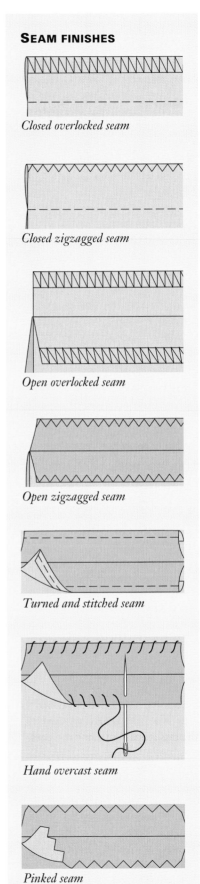

SEAM FINISHES

Closed overlocked seam

Closed zigzagged seam

Open overlocked seam

Open zigzagged seam

Turned and stitched seam

Hand overcast seam

Pinked seam

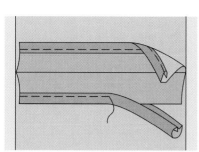

2 Stitch close to the edge of the top fold, catching the underneath fold in the stitching.

BIAS STRIPS

Bias strips are strips of fabric cut on the true bias (i.e. at a 45° angle to the crosswise and lengthwise grains). Bias strips are used for such things as hem facings, piping, corded piping and binding raw edges. Commercial bias binding is available in a variety of colors and widths.

Cutting bias strips

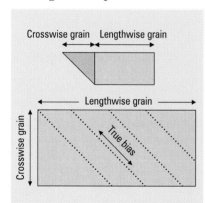

1 Find the true bias by folding the fabric diagonally so that an edge on the crosswise grain aligns with the selvage (lengthwise grain).
2 Press the fold and then open it out. With a ruler and fabric marker, mark lines on the fabric parallel to the crease for the required width of the bias strips. Cut along the lines.

Joining bias strips

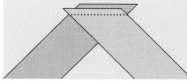

1 Right sides together, pin two strips at right angles with a 6 mm seam

allowance. Stitch the seam, starting and finishing at junctions of seamline.

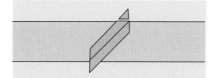

2 Press seam open. Trim away the protruding corners of seam allowances to align with edge of strip.
3 Repeat steps 1 and 2 to join as many strips as you need.

Binding a raw edge

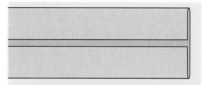

1 Cut a bias strip four times finished width of required bind and about 8 cm longer than the edge to be bound (join strips if necessary). Press strip lengthwise in half, wrong sides together. Open out, then fold edges in to meet center line and press.

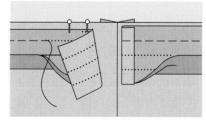

2 Unfold one edge of bias strip. With right sides together, pin bias strip to fabric, aligning raw edges. Turn back starting end 1 cm. Stitch binding to fabric along fold closest to edge until you are within 8 cm of starting point.

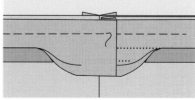

3 Trim away excess binding at this end, leaving a 1 cm overlap at starting point. With bind ends overlapped, continue stitching through all layers to complete.
4 Press seam allowances into binding. Bring remaining folded edge of bind-

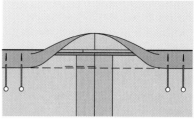

ing to wrong side of garment, enclosing raw edges. Place fold on stitching line. Pin in place, taking care not to stretch bias binding.

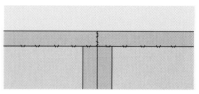

5 Slipstitch folded edge of binding into stitching. Slipstitch binding ends together where they overlap.

MITERING

The key to successful mitering is accurate pressing of the folds at the corner.

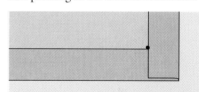

1 Press fabric to wrong side on seamlines of crosswise and lengthwise edges, forming corner. With a fabric marker, mark both raw edges at the point where they cross.

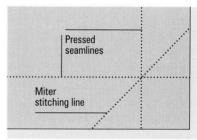

2 Unfold fabric and lightly mark or crease a diagonal line from junction points through corner of pressed seamline to form miter stitching line.

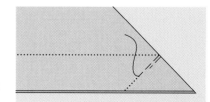

3 Fold fabric diagonally (on bias), right sides together, aligning edges. Stitch miter along diagonal line, back-stitching at beginning and end.

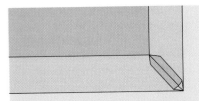

4 Trim miter, leaving a 6 mm seam allowance. Press seam open, then turn to right side and press.

Mitering a bias facing

A bias facing may be formed either by cutting bias strips of fabric or by using commercial hem facing (bias). Cut fabric bias strip 60 mm wide, joining strips if necessary. Press both cut edges to wrong side for 6 mm.

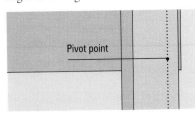

1 Trim fabric seam allowance to 6 mm along edges to be faced. Unfold one edge of bias facing. With right sides together, pin facing to edge of fabric, marking a pivot point on facing seamline at corner.

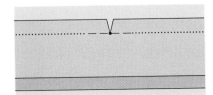

2 Remove facing and staystitch for a short distance along foldline at marked point to reinforce. Clip seam allowance to point, being careful not to cut stitching.

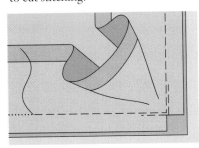

3 With right sides of fabric and facing together, pin and stitch along foldline of facing, pivoting around corner at clipped point.

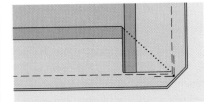

4 Trim seam allowances at corner. Carefully fold facing so it is at right angles to itself. Press lightly.

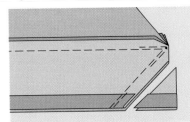

5 Fold garment, with right sides together, so facing edges are even. Stitch along the diagonal press line. Trim off the point leaving a 6 mm seam allowance.

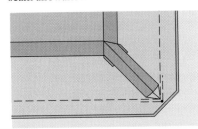

6 Press open the the seam allowances at the edges. Turn the facing to the wrong side and press.

PIPING AND CORDED PIPING

Piping and corded piping are often used as decorative inserts or trims – for example, around hemlines. Both can be purchased, but the range of colors and fabrics is limited, so it is often preferable to make your own.

Piping

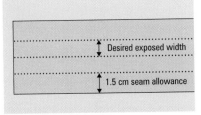

1 Cut a bias strip twice the desired exposed width, plus twice the seam allowance (i.e. 3 cm).

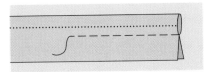

2 Fold strip in half lengthwise, with wrong sides together. Stitch in 1 cm from raw edges to hold.

Corded piping

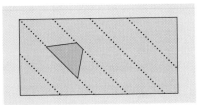

1 Fold a corner of fabric or paper over cord and pin, encasing the cord snugly. Measure 1.5 cm out from pin and cut.

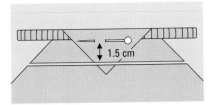

2 Use the cut piece as a gauge for measuring width of bias strips.

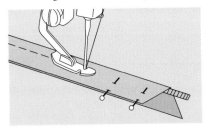

3 Wrap the cut bias strip around the cord, with right side of fabric out and edges together. Using a zipper foot, stitch close to the cord.

Attaching piping and corded piping

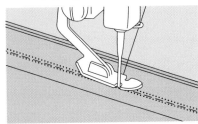

1 Mark hemline and trim hem allowance to 1.5 cm. Attach piping to right side of hem, aligning raw edges. Stitch in place. (For attaching corded piping, use zipper foot.)

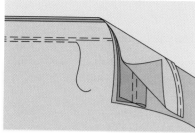

2 Cut facing (fabric) for required width and shape of hemline. Sandwich piping between hem and facing, aligning cut edges. Stitch a seam 1.5 cm from edges. (For corded piping, stitch as close as possible to cording.)
3 Trim, grade and clip turnings where required. Understitch facing if necessary.

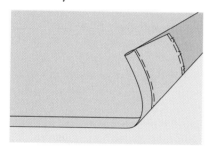

4 Press facing to inside of garment so that piping forms trim at hem. Hem facing in place along neatened edge.

TUCKS

A tuck is a stitched fold of fabric. Tucks are usually decorative, but they can also be used as shaping devices.

Marking tucks

Mark either the stitching lines or the foldline of each tuck with thread (tailor's tacks or threadline), or use a suitable marking tool. Ensure that markings are indicated on the side of fabric where tucks are to be formed.

Stitching tucks

When you have marked the tucks appropriately, press them to the inside or the outside of the garment, as required by the design. Matching the stitching lines, pin the tucks in place and then stitch.

Marking tucks by pulling threads

Tucks can also be marked by pulling a thread of the fabric to mark tuck foldline. This is an accurate method when tucks are on straight grain of fabric. Use this method when tucks are to be formed across the width or length of fabric or tucked insert.
1 Pull a single thread from edge to edge of fabric and press along each pulled threadline.
2 Stitch desired finished width of tuck from foldline, and press tucks according to the design effect that is required.

Marking tucks with a cardboard gauge

A cardboard marking gauge can eliminate the need for marking the stitching lines of tucks.
1 Cut a cardboard strip the desired width of tuck plus space between stitching lines. From one end of gauge, mark down finished width of tuck and cut a notch.

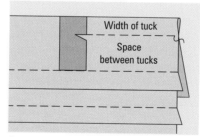

2 Place the unnotched end of the gauge on the stitching line of the previous tuck. The upper edge will then lie along the next tuck foldline and the notch will indicate the stitching line.

Making pin-tucks with a sewing machine

You can make very fine pin-tucks with a sewing machine. They are formed by using a twin needle (needles vary in size) with two top threads and a pin-tucking foot (these come with varying numbers of grooves). Consult your sewing machine manual for the correct settings.

BUTTONHOLES

Buttonholes can be either machine stitched or sewn by hand.

Machine buttonholes

Mark buttonhole. Consult your sewing machine manual for the correct settings. Machine using buttonhole foot and cut buttonhole opening with sharp, pointed scissors or seam ripper.

Handworked buttonhole

1 Mark buttonhole. Use sharp scissors or a seam ripper to cut along buttonhole through all fabric layers.
2 Baste around outline of buttonhole with a small running stitch to reinforce. Hand overcast raw edges through all layers to prevent fraying.

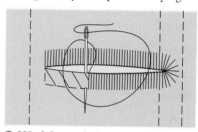

3 Work buttonhole using buttonhole stitch along straight edge, turning work and fanning stitches around end of buttonhole facing opening (i.e. where button pulls).

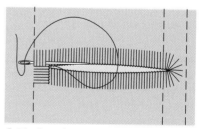

4 To form bar baste, make several straight stitches across remaining end of buttonhole. Work small horizontal buttonhole stitches over these stitches.

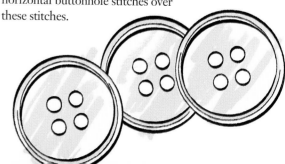

Appliqué

Appliqué is a great way of using up scraps of fabric left over from other sewing projects. You can produce beautiful appliqué work either by hand or with a sewing machine.

FABRICS

Smooth-surfaced fabrics of light or medium weight are best for appliqué work. Do not use loosely woven or extremely bulky fabrics. Press out all wrinkles and creases before using, and make sure that the appliqué fabric has the same washing requirements as the background fabric.

SCISSORS

You need two pairs of sharp scissors: a pair of medium-sized dress-maker's scissors for general cutting, and a pair of small, pointed embroidery scissors for close trimming.

CUTTING

Before cutting, assemble the fabric pieces and decide which piece will be used for each appliqué.

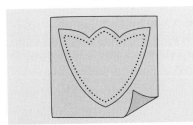

1 Pin the cutting template to the right side of the fabric and trace a dotted line around it. Remove the template and mark a 5 mm seam allowance outside the dotted line.
2 Cut out the appliqué piece outside this outer seam allowance line, leaving a generous margin all round.

3 Staystitch just outside the inner seamline (the dotted line), using 2 mm stitches. Trim the appliqué by cutting out along the outer marked lines. Clip and notch the seam allowances around the curves and corners.

SEWING BY HAND

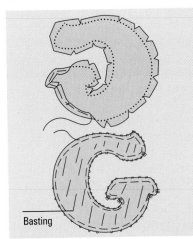

1 Finger press the seam allowance to the wrong side along the marked seamline of the appliqué and baste the folded edge as you go, keeping the stitching within the seam allowance.
2 Pin the appliqué to the background fabric and hold it in place with vertical basting. Secure the appliqué with a fine slipstitch along the folded edges. Alternatively, use a decorative embroidery stitch, such as running stitch or cross-stitch, to secure the appliqué. Remove the basting.

SEWING WITH A MACHINE

Appliqués may be sewn down with straight or zigzag stitch. First adjust the stitch tension and foot pressure to suit the fabric you are using.

Straight stitch method

1 Fold the seam allowance to the wrong side and baste in place.
2 Position and pin the appliqué on-to the right side of the background fabric. Hold the appliqué in place with vertical basting to prevent it from shifting while you stitch.

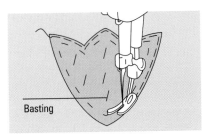

3 Using a stitch length of 2–2.5 mm, straight stitch along the folded edges of the appliqué. Use a handsewing needle to take the top thread ends through to the wrong side, and fasten them off together with the bottom threads. Remove the basting.

Zigzag method

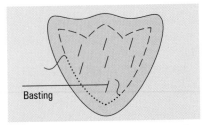

1 With the seam allowance exposed, position, pin and baste the appliqué in place on the right side of the background fabric. Straight stitch directly over the marked seamline.

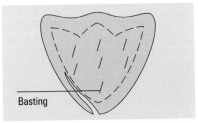

2 Using embroidery scissors, trim away the seam allowance, cutting as close to the stitching line as possible.

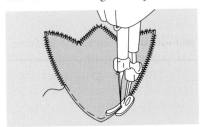

3 Sew short, narrow zigzag stitches over the raw edges and the straight stitching. Take the top threads to the wrong side and fasten off with the bottom threads. Remove basting.

Heirloom sewing

Around the turn of the century the techniques we now call heirloom sewing were practiced widely, even on everyday garments and household linen.

PREPARING THE FABRICS

As the items you make will have to be laundered and ironed, it is advisable to pre-shrink the fabric and lace before starting work.

Most fabrics used in the projects in this book can be gently handwashed in warm water using quality soap flakes. Rinse the fabric well and hang it out to dry, without distorting the fabric.

Iron the fabric while it is still damp, so that it is easier to press out any creases. Lightly spray fine fabrics with starch before final pressing.

ROLL AND WHIP

This technique is used to neaten the raw edges of fabric laces and to provide a firmer edge for joining two lace edges together. This ensures that the joined laces do not pull apart.

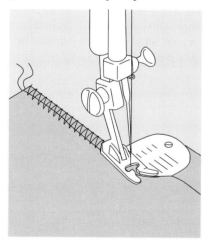

1 Using the zigzag setting on your sewing machine (stitch width at 3) and with the wrong side of the fabric facing up, stitch along the raw edge of the fabric, stitching no more than 3 mm on to the fabric and completely off the fabric on the right-hand side.
2 As you begin to work, the edge of the fabric will roll over to form a firm edge. You may not be able to control the way the fabric rolls, but do not worry, as this edge will be covered by additional trims.

ROLL, WHIP AND GATHER

This technique is the same as rolling and whipping, except that a quilting thread is enclosed in the rolled edge of the fabric.
1 Lay the fabric with the wrong side facing up.
2 Place a quilting thread along the edge of the fabric and under the presser foot of your machine.
3 Zigzag carefully over, but not through, the quilting thread and over the raw edge of the fabric, as for roll and whip. The thread will be encased by the rolled fabric edge.

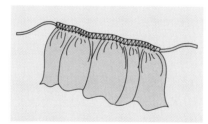

4 Gather the fabric by gently moving it along the quilting thread, spreading the gathers evenly.

ATTACHING FABRIC TO FABRIC

1 Take two pieces of fabric, both with edges rolled and whipped.
2 Place the two rolled and whipped edges together with right sides facing, so that the upper edge is just to the left of the lower one. (The pieces are

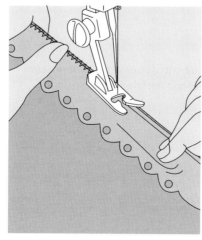

sewn in this way so that the rolled edges are not sitting right on top of each other, thus creating bulk.)
3 Zigzag over the two edges, making sure the stitching goes off the edge of the fabric to the right.

ATTACHING ENTREDEUX TO FABRIC
Stitching in the holes

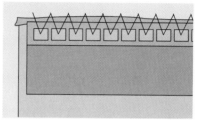

1 Before you begin, check the length of the zigzag stitch by placing the entredeux under the presser foot of the machine and moving the needle by hand. Adjust the stitch length so that the needle points accurately into each successive entredeux hole.
2 Cut away the batiste (fabric edging) along one side of the entredeux. Roll and whip the edges of the fabric piece.
3 With right sides together, place the trimmed edge of the entredeux on the fabric, with the entredeux just to the left of the fabric edge. Start sewing by positioning the needle in one of the entredeux holes, then zigzag along the edge, always sewing off the right-hand edge of the fabric.

Stitching on the selvage edge

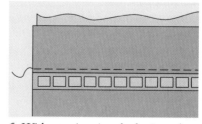

1 Without trimming the batiste edge, lay the entredeux on the fabric, right sides together.
2 Stitch right beside the entredeux holes, using a straight stitch.
3 To finish the raw edge, trim the batiste and fabric to 3 mm and zigzag along the edge.

ATTACHING LACE TO FABRIC

Widen your zigzag stitch to cover the entire lace heading. If it is not covered, the lace can change shape.

1 With right sides together, place the lace just inside the rolled and whipped edge of the fabric.
2 Zigzag along the edge, making sure that the stitch covers the whole width of the lace heading and goes off the edge of the fabric on the right-hand side.

ATTACHING LACE TO ENTREDEUX

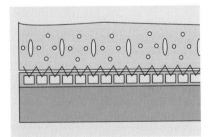

1 Trim away one of the batiste edges from the entredeux.
2 Butt the trimmed side of the entredeux to the edge of the lace and zigzag along, sewing into the holes of the entredeux and making sure that the stitch covers the lace heading.

GATHERING LACE

Laces with a straight woven edge have a strong, straight thread along the edge (the heading). Pick this thread out of the lace near one end with a pin and pull it up, spreading the gathers evenly as you go. To keep the heading as flat as possible, take a thread from the top and the bottom.

JOINING TWO STRAIGHT LACE EDGES TOGETHER

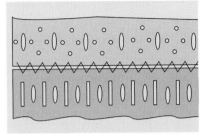

1 Butt the two lace edges together, but do not overlap. Place the laces under the machine presser foot so that the join is right in the middle.
2 Begin zigzagging, adjusting the stitch width and length to suit the laces you are sewing. Aim for a stitch that is not too noticeable, but that still secures the laces together firmly. Do not make the stitches too close together or the seam will be bulky.

HEIRLOOM LACES

As the name heirloom sewing suggests, an article produced by these methods is intended to last through generations and represents a big investment of love, care and patience. To achieve the best result, we recommend that you use laces made from natural fibers.

Two types of insertion and edging laces have been used to make the heirloom sewing projects in this book – woven lace and fabric lace (also called Swiss embroidery), which has a recognizable fabric background. Broderie anglaise lace is a type of eyelet lace.

Entredeux

Fagoting

Beading

Fabric lace

Edging lace

Edging lace

Insertion lace

Quilting

Quilting is an enduringly popular craft that can be as simple or as elaborate as your level of skill permits. Start with small, easily manageable projects and work up to larger ones.

A quilted effect is obtained by hand or machine stitching two layers of fabric together with a soft filling between them, which makes the finished article warm. The anchor stitching is usually worked in a regular pattern to create a subtly textured surface.

Although quilting is usually associated with making bed quilts, it can also be used to make garments, such as dressing gowns and vests, and home accessories, such as oven cloths, cushions and wall hangings.

FABRICS
Fabrics used for the top layer of a quilt should be smooth, light-weight to medium-weight, and opaque (not see-through). Heavy or stiff fabrics will not take up the contours of the quilting. The backing fabric can be decorative like the top layer, or it can be a solid color. For a bed quilt it should not be too smooth or the quilt will slip off. Fabrics should be pre-shrunk and checked for color-fastness.

FILLING
The most common quilt filling is cotton or polyester fiber batting, both of which are light-weight, warm and easy to quilt. Polyester batting is more stable than cotton batting, requiring less quilting to hold it in place, and gives a more puffy quilted surface. Thicker batting requires less stitching, but it is much more difficult to hand quilt. If you are not sure, seek the advice of your supplier.

Loose filling is also available, both in cotton and polyester, or you can use shredded foam.

NEEDLES
For hand quilting, use quilting needles or betweens. Use as small a needle as you can work with on your fabric; the smaller the needle, the smaller your stitching will be. For machine quilt-

ing, use a fine, sharp needle (a 60 or 70 denim needle) and a walking foot so the layers feed evenly through the machine without puckering.

THREADS
Use a strong thread. Quilting thread is cotton thread coated with a glaze, but you can use an all-purpose cotton or polyester thread instead. For a richer look, use a lustrous silk twist.

CUTTING THE FABRIC
Make the quilt top 10 cm longer and wider than the finished quilt to allow for "shrinkage" caused by the quilting. The more quilting you do, the more the quilt will "shrink."

The backing fabric should be 5 cm larger all round than the front. With thicker batting and more extensive quilting, cut the fabric with a larger allowance than specified above, since the take-up will be greater.

PREPARING THE BATTING
1 Cut the batting to the same size as the quilt top.

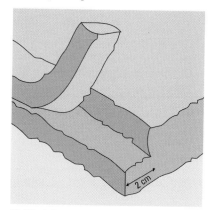

2 To join sections of batting, split one edge of one of the batting pieces to be joined and cut back a 2 cm strip from the upper side.
3 Repeat step 2 on one edge of the second piece, but this time remove the strip from the lower side. Overlap the edges and join the sections together

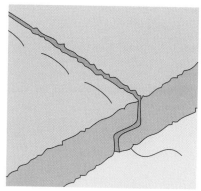

by machining through both thicknesses with a long, lightly tensioned straight stitch.

ASSEMBLING THE QUILT
The success of a quilting project depends on the accuracy and care with which you work these early construction stages.
1 Lay the backing material, wrong side up, on a hard, flat surface. Pull it taut and fix the corners of the backing to the working surface with masking tape. Spread the batting on top, stroking it with the edge of a ruler to get rid of wrinkles. Lay the top layer, right side up, over the batting.
2 Pin through all three layers, starting at the center and moving out toward the edges.

3 Using large basting stitches, baste the three layers together in a sunburst pattern or a rectangular grid. Start in the center and work toward the edges. Make sure that you use enough basting stitches so that the layers remain smooth and do not shift. Remove the masking tape and pins.

4 Fold the excess backing up and over so that the raw edge of the backing butts against the raw edge of the top layer. Fold it again about 10 mm over the edge of the top layer. Pin the folded material in place.

5 Baste the folded edge through all three layers. This very important step helps to prevent the edge of the quilt from stretching out of shape.

HAND QUILTING

Always place the layered fabric in a quilting hoop before stitching. Wear a thimble on your middle finger and use a fine, even running stitch.

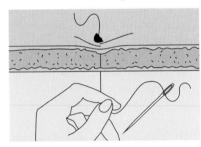

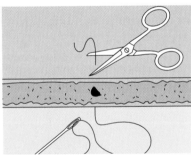

1 To secure the thread at the start, knot the end of the thread and insert the needle from the top through all three layers. Pull the thread from underneath so that the knot slips through the top layer and lodges in the batting. Trim any thread that is visible at the surface.

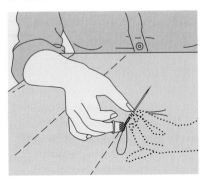

2 Start at the center of the quilt and work outward, adjusting the layers to remove puckers as you go. Take a few stitches at a time, pushing the needle through with your middle finger. To be sure the needle penetrates all layers, hold your other hand under the layers so that you can feel the tip of the needle each time a stitch is taken. Remove the basting as you go.

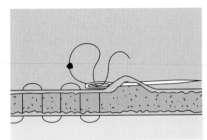

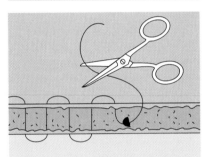

3 To end a line of quilting, make a knot on top of the quilting surface. Insert the needle one stitch length away and run the needle through the batting for a short distance. Bring the needle up and gently pull the thread so that the knot slips through the top layer. Trim the thread as close to the surface of the fabric as possible.

MACHINE QUILTING

Quilting by machine gives a durable and evenly worked result. It also takes only a fraction of the time that hand quilting does. Machine quilting is especially suitable for small projects because they are easy to maneuver.

For a large piece of quilting, you will need to modify your sewing area and plan the sequence and direction of your quilting carefully.

To modify the sewing area

Move your sewing machine to an open area. Raise a large piece of board or wood on two sawhorses or chairs to the same level as the sewing machine.

Place this surface flush with and to the left of the machine and use it to support large, heavy quilted pieces.

Quilting direction

Plan machine quilting so that the bulk of the piece always lies to the left of the needle. Roll up the bulk to the right of the needle tightly enough to fit under the sewing machine arm as it becomes necessary.

General instructions

1 When you are constructing the quilt, make sure you have basted the layers generously so that they do not shift as they are being fed through the machine. Around the area where you are quilting, use safety pins to secure the layers even more firmly. To avoid unsightly puckers, keep the stitch tension and the foot pressure low. Set the stitch length to about 2 mm.

2 Feed the quilt through the machine as evenly as possible. Smooth the quilt in front of the needle as you sew. When you need to stop stitching to rearrange the quilt, stop the machine with the needle in the down position to avoid jumps in the line of stitching.

Securing thread ends

1 Try to avoid starting a new thread in the middle of a line, starting always from an outside edge if possible. However, if you do need to secure thread ends in the middle of the work, leave long thread ends on both top and bottom of the quilted surface. Thread one end through a needle and run the needle through the batting for a short distance. Bring the needle out and cut off the thread end close to the quilted surface.

2 Run the other thread end through the batting in the same way. Thread ends that finish on the edges of the quilt do not need to be secured, as the edge finish will keep them in place.

FINISHING

Quilted pieces are usually finished and the loose threads around the edges secured with a fabric binding, which may be cut on the straight or the bias.

Embroidery

Embroidery is a craft you can do almost anywhere – in an armchair, on the bus, or during work breaks. Most stitches are easy, and you will rapidly be able to develop your own designs.

PREPARING THREADS

Use threads no longer than about 50 cm, because long threads can be damaged by stretching and knotting as you pull them through the fabric.

Stranded cotton

Stranded cotton comes with several strands (usually six) loosely twisted together. Many projects specify how many strands are to be used for the stitches, and you need to separate this number from the rest.

To detach the number of strands you need, cut a length of stranded yarn and at one end separate out the required number of strands. Hold the separated strands in your mouth and the rest of the strands in one hand. Hold the rest of the cotton length in your free hand and gently pull the divided strands apart, moving your free hand slowly down the thread length to control the twisting action.

Doubling single-strand cotton

If you need to double strands of perle cotton, do not fold the length in half. Instead, cut two separate lengths and insert them side by side into the eye of the needle.

SECURING THE THREAD

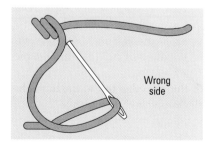

1 To start working with a new embroidery thread, hold the end of the thread against the wrong side of the fabric and work embroidery stitches over about 4 cm of this end.
2 To secure the embroidery when you come to the end of a thread, take

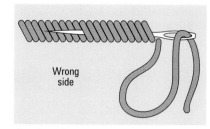

the thread to the wrong side and work it back under about 4 cm of worked stitches. Trim with sharp scissors.

USING AN EMBROIDERY HOOP

An embroidery hoop holds the fabric taut, reducing distortion and helping you to keep your stitch tension even. Hoops are made of wood, plastic or metal in a range of diameters.
1 To put the fabric in the hoop, place it over the inner ring of the hoop. Adjust the screw on the outer ring so that it fits snugly over the inner ring and the fabric. Place fabric in the hoop so that the fabric threads run straight in both directions. To protect delicate fabrics, place tissue paper on either side of the fabric before securing the frame, then tear the paper away from the working area.
2 To avoid marking the fabric, take it out of the hoop when finishing work for the day. Release the screw and press down the fabric at the edges of the hoop, at the same time easing up the outer ring.

HOLDING THE NEEDLE

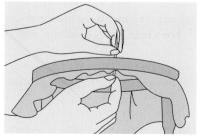

1 Insert the needle using a stabbing motion when possible – this will help you to keep an even stitch tension.

Push the needle straight down and pull the thread through, then bring the needle straight up again.

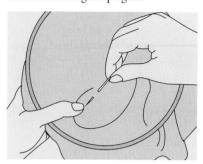

2 To work looped stitches, such as chain stitch or fly stitch, bring the needle up, and, before you pull the thread through, use your free hand to guide it around the needle.

EMBROIDERY STITCHES

This section contains instructions for working the stitches you will need to make the projects in this book.

Backstitch

This stitch can be used as a straight outline stitch or as the baseline for other decorative stitches.

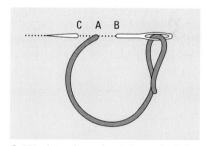

1 Working from the right to the left, bring the needle out at A, insert it at B, and exit at C. The distance between points C and A and points A and B should be equal.

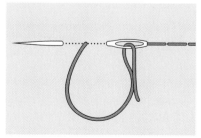

2 Repeat this sequence to form next stitch, entering at A of previous stitch. Keep all stitches the same length.

Bullion knot

This stitch can be used as a filling stitch or for outlining. It is also used to form grub roses.

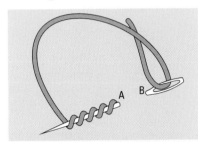

1 Bring the needle up at A. Insert it at B and exit again at A, but do not pull the thread through. Twist the thread around the point of the needle the number of times specified in the instructions for the project.

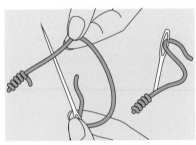

2 Carefully pull the needle through both the fabric and the twists.
3 Without distorting the twists, pull the thread toward point B so the coil lies flat. Pull the working thread tight and use the point of the needle to pack the threads in the coil together evenly. Reinsert the needle at B.

Buttonhole stitch wheel

This stitch is often used for embroidering flower motifs.

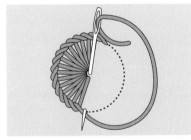

Work basic buttonhole stitch in a circle, inserting the needle into the same hole at the center for each stitch.

Chain stitch

This stitch is used for outlining. It is also occasionally used for filling areas.

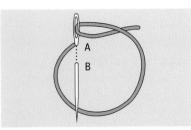

1 Bring the needle out at A, insert it back into the same hole at A and bring it out at B, carrying the thread under the needle point, before pulling it through. To work the next stitch, insert the needle at B.

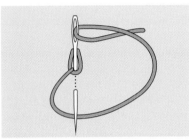

2 Continue stitching in this manner, always inserting the needle into the hole made by the emerging thread.

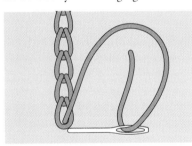

3 To end the row, take a small stitch through the last loop.

Colonial knot

A colonial knot is similar to a French knot. Colonial knots can be worked closely together to fill an area, or can be scattered more freely.

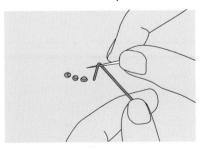

1 Bring the needle up at A. Holding the needle in one hand, take the thread in the other and wind it around the needle in a figure of eight.

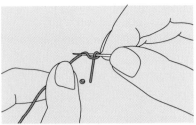

2 Pull on the thread to tighten the loops and take the thread down to the back of the fabric by inserting the needle into the fabric close to point A. Pull the thread through.

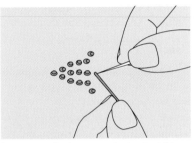

3 Scatter the knots as desired within the design area. The knots can be made larger by increasing the number of figures of eight that are wound around the needle.

Coral stitch

This is a simple outline stitch punctuated with small knots along the row.

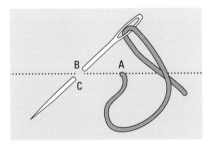

1 Working from the right to the left, bring the needle up at A. Insert the needle at B and then, taking up a few threads of the fabric, slant the needle out at C.

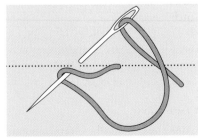

2 Loop the thread over and around the point of the needle, and then pull the needle through to secure the stitch and form the knot.

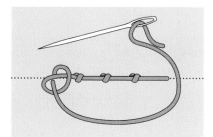

3 Continue in this way until the end of the row, spacing the knots evenly or in a more random fashion, as the design dictates.

Couching

This stitch is used to outline a design or to give more weight to a single line. It is worked with two threads: the laid thread and the couching thread. The couching thread is stitched over the laid thread to attach it to the fabric.

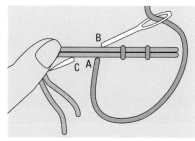

1 Securing them on the wrong side, bring up the desired number of laid threads at the right end of the design. Use your left thumb to hold and guide these threads as you couch over them.
2 Bring the couching thread up at A, just below the laid threads. Insert it at B, directly above the laid threads, and bring it up at C, further along the line. Point C now becomes point A of the next stitch.
3 Repeat steps 1 and 2 until the laid threads are completely anchored. Ensure that the distance between each stitch is equal.
4 To finish, bring the ends of the laid threads to the back of the work and secure by taking them back under the last few couching stitches.

Cross-stitch

Cross-stitch is usually worked in rows of even, slanted stitches, moving first from right to left to work part of each

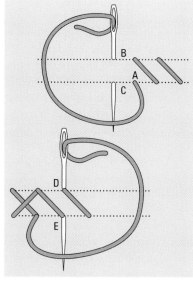

stitch, and then from left to right to complete the stitches.

Cross-stitch can also be worked as a single stitch by working right to left and left to right stitches alternately. Take care that the top stitches all slant the same way.

Feather stitch

This is a looped stitch that is worked alternately to the left and then to the right of a center line.

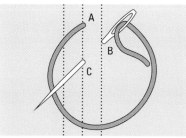

1 Working from top to bottom, bring the needle up in the center at A. Insert the needle at B, slightly lower and to the right. Angle the needle out at C on the center line, carrying the working thread under the needle point, and pull through.

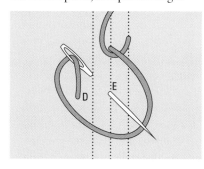

2 Insert the needle at D, slightly below and to the left of point C. Angle it out at E along the center line. Carry the thread under the needle point and pull it through.

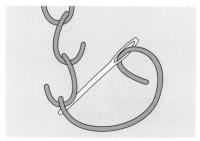

3 Continue in this way, alternating the looped stitches to the left and the right of the center line.
4 To end the row, take a small stitch over the last loop.

Long-armed feather stitch

This stitch is worked in a similar way to basic feather stitch.

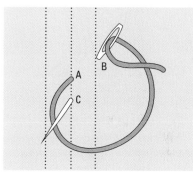

1 Bring the needle up in the center, at A. Insert it at B, slightly higher and to the right, then angle the needle out at C along the center line. Carry the thread under the needle point and pull through. The distance between all points should be the same.

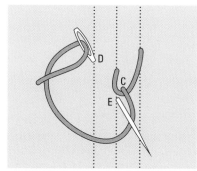

2 Insert the needle at D, slightly higher and to the left of point C, and then angle it out at E on the center line below point C.

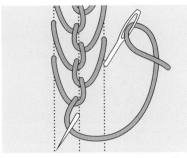

3 Carry the thread under the needle and pull it through. Continue in this way to the end of the row.
4 To finish off the row, take a small stitch over the last loop.

Fly stitch

Fly stitch is a single looped stitch, similar to feather stitch. It can be scattered about or used as a border.

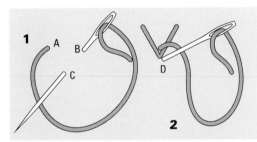

1 Bring the needle up at A, then insert it directly across at B and angle it out again at C. The distance between the points should be equal. Carry the thread under the needle point and pull through.
2 Complete the stitch by inserting the needle at D, over the loop.
3 Continue forming the stitches in this way, placing the stitches in a random manner or in a row, depending on your design.

French knot

This stitch is used like seeding stitch, but it is more raised and textured.

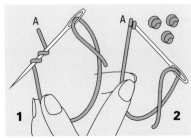

1 Bring the needle up at A. Holding the thread taut with one hand, wrap

the thread around the needle twice. Gently pull the thread so the twists are tightened against the needle.
2 Insert the needle near point A and pull it through, making sure that the thread end is still held taut.
3 Scatter the knots as you wish within the design area. You can make French knots larger by increasing the number of twists around the needle.

Herringbone stitch

This stitch, which is a form of cross-stitch, is often used as a border. You can work a second row of herringbone stitch in another color over the first, in the spaces between the stitches.

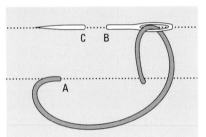

1 Working from left to right, bring the needle up at A. Make a slanting stitch toward the top right, inserting the needle at B. Bring the needle out a short distance back, at C.

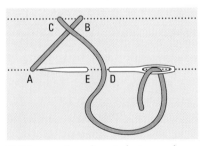

2 To complete the stitch, insert the needle at D, below and to the right of B, then bring the needle up at E to start a new stitch.
3 Repeat steps 1 and 2, keeping the the length of the stitches, and the spacing between them, even.

Lazy daisy stitch

Lazy daisy stitch is a single looped stitch, normally worked in a circle to give the appearance of petals.
1 Bring the needle out at A, insert it back into the same point, and bring it out at B. Carry the thread under the needle point, then pull it through.

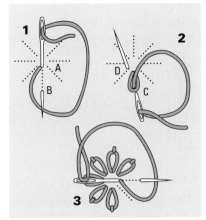

2 Insert the needle at C over the chain loop, then bring the needle out at D to begin the next stitch.
3 Repeat steps 1 and 2 until you have completed all of the "petals."

Pistil stitch

A variation of the French knot, this stitch looks like the pistil of a flower.

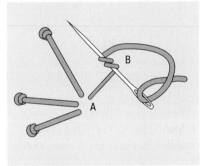

1 Bring the needle out at A. Then pick up the thread and wind it twice around the needle.
2 Return the needle to the back of the work at B, the required distance from point A, pulling the thread taut around the needle as you pass it through the fabric.

Running stitch

This is an easy-to-work outline stitch. It can be the same length on both sides or longer on the right side.

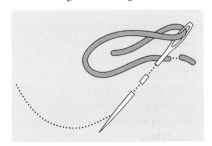

Satin stitch

This is a solid filling stitch.

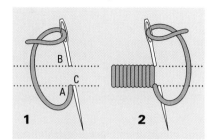

1 Working from left to right, bring the needle up at A and insert it directly above at B. Bring the needle out again at C, close to point A.
2 Continue in this way until the whole area is filled. Keep the stitches smooth and even.

Slanted satin stitch

This stitch is worked in a similar way to basic satin stitch.

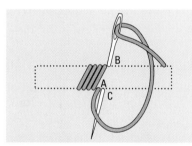

1 Start in the center of the shape to establish the angle of the slant. Work across to fill one side of the shape, taking shorter stitches to fill in any corners. Then start again at the center and work the other way to fill the other side.
2 When the shape you are filling is a large one, slanting satin stitches may straighten out as you work. To prevent this, take great care to insert and bring out the needle at precisely the same distance, both top and bottom, from the previous stitch.

Padded satin stitch

This stitch gives the same effect as basic satin stitch, except that the stitched area is slightly raised. The padded area is made up of an outline of split stitches and then of two layers of satin stitches, the second worked diagonally over the first.
1 Work a row of split stitches right around the area to be filled.

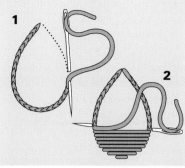

2 Work horizontal satin stitch to fill the outlined area, making sure that you cover the split stitches.

3 Work a second satin stitch layer at an angle to the first. Take special care to keep the outline edges even.

Seeding stitch

This is one of the simplest filling stitches. It can be scattered around the design area or worked in clusters.

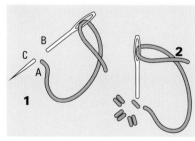

1 Bring the needle up at A, make a tiny stitch down at B and bring the needle up at C.
2 Make another small stitch, the same size and parallel to the first. Scatter seeding stitches as desired, changing the direction of the stitches.

Shadow stitch

This is one of the few embroidery stitches that are worked from the wrong side. Fine, sheer fabric is used so that the work will show through to the right side. Because only one strand of thread is used, stitches must be small to create the shadow effect.

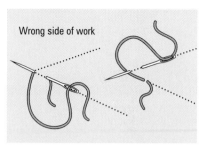

1 Using only one strand of thread, secure the thread by working a few running stitches on the wrong side along one of the design lines.

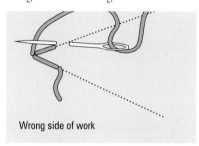

2 Continuing to work on the wrong side of the fabric, make a small backstitch on one line. Keeping the thread lying down the center of the design, carry it over to the opposite line and make another small backstitch.

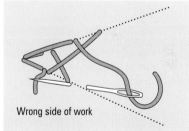

3 Continue working the design in this manner, checking the right side of the work as you stitch to make sure there are no gaps between stitches. Adjust the length of stitches where necessary to accommodate varying shapes of the design, but always keep them as small as possible. A herringbone stitch will be formed on the wrong side of the work and a backstitch outline on the front.
4 To finish off, weave the thread back along a side edge of a few completed shadow stitches.

Spider's web stitch

This circular motif can be used to represent flowers. Before you start, divide the circle into nine equal parts.

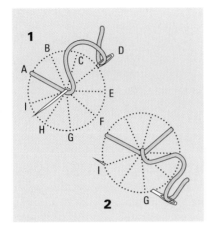

1 Bring the needle out at A and insert it at D. Then bring it out at the center over the working thread and pull it through.
2 Insert the needle at G and bring it out at I.

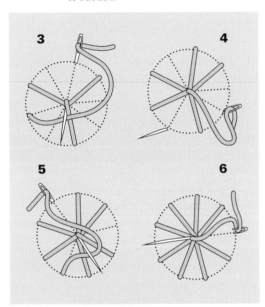

3 Insert the needle at C. Bring it out at the center, over the working thread, and pull it through.
4 Insert the needle at F and bring it out at H.
5 Insert the needle at B. Bring it out at the center over the working thread and pull it through.
6 To make the last spoke, insert the needle at E and exit at the center.
7 Weave or whip to finish.
• *Weaving:* Start from the center and pass the needle over and under the spokes in a counterclockwise direction until all the spokes are covered.
• *Whipping:* Carry the needle under and back over a spoke, then under that

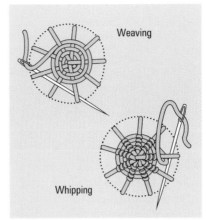

spoke and the next one ahead. Work around the web, always moving the needle back over one spoke and forward under two until all of the spokes are covered.

Split stitch

This stitch is worked in the same way as stem stitch, except that when the needle emerges it splits the working thread. The final effect resembles a thin chain stitch. Although outlining is its most common use, split stitch can also be used in solid runs.

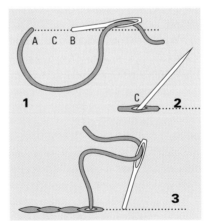

1 Working from left to right, bring the needle up at A and then take it down at B.
2 Bring the needle back up at C, through the laid thread, so that it splits the center of the laid thread.
3 Continue, keeping the stitch length even except around curves, where it should be shortened slightly.

Stem stitch

Primarily an outlining stitch, this stitch is often used to work plant stems in floral designs as well.

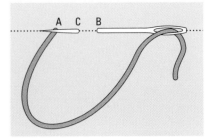

1 Working from left to right, bring the needle out at A. Insert it at B and bring it out at C, half a stitch length back.

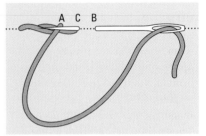

2 Repeat this sequence, keeping the thread below the needle and to the left. Keep stitches even in length.

Straight stitch

This is a single satin stitch that can be of any length and worked in any direction. It can be used to cover straight design lines, or scattered to make an open filling. Be sure that the thread is not carried too far on the wrong side between the stitches.

Worked in a circle, a cluster of straight stitches resembles a stylized flower, the center of which can be filled in with French knots.

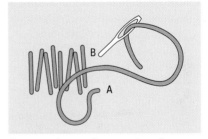

1 Bring the needle up at A and take it to the back at B.
2 Work as many straight stitches as needed for the desired design.

Whipped stitch

Whipped stitch is a simple, decorative variation of running stitch. A second thread (often in a contrasting color) is

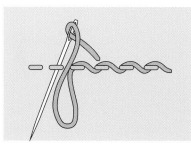

woven under the running stitch without picking up any of the fabric. It is very effective when several rows are worked under each other.

CUTWORK EMBROIDERY

In cutwork embroidery, the design is outlined with buttonhole stitch and then portions of fabric are cut away from the inside of the design.

Cutwork embroidery uses two main stitches – running stitch and buttonhole stitch – both of which are easy. However, great care and precision are needed, particularly when working bars and cutting the fabric. Fine, sharp needlework scissors are essential.

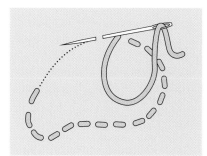

1 Using either embroidery floss or perle cotton, establish the design with running stitches.

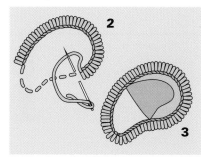

2 Work over the running stitch with a fine, close buttonhole stitch. Make sure that the ridge of the stitching lies against the line that is to be cut away.
3 Working from the wrong side, use fine needlework scissors to cut away the enclosed area close to the base of

the stitches. Be very careful not to cut into any of the stitching.

Working a bar

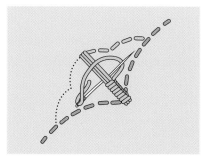

1 Mark the design with running stitches until you come to a bar position. Carry thread across design area and take a small stitch. Bring thread back and take another stitch. Take thread across design area again.

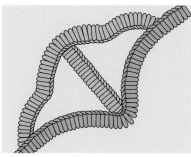

2 Work buttonhole stitch over these three laid threads, without catching the fabric underneath, then continue working running stitch around the rest of the motif.
3 Outline the whole design with fine buttonhole stitch, as for basic cutwork. Cut away the enclosed area close to the ridge of the stitches, being careful not to cut the worked bar.

SILK RIBBON EMBROIDERY

Silk ribbon embroidery is worked like thread embroidery, but because the ribbon is flat and wide, some special techniques are needed.

Work the stitches with about 30 cm of ribbon at a time. You can increase this length slightly as you become more experienced, but remember that overworked and worn ribbon is much harder to manipulate.

Two basic types of needles are used in silk ribbon embroidery: chenilles and tapestry needles. Both types have large eyes to accommodate the rib-

bon. For the most successful results with ribbon embroidery, use good-quality silk ribbon. Synthetic ribbons tend to twist and do not lie smoothly.

Threading the needle

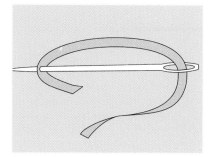

1 Pass the end of the ribbon through the eye of the needle.
2 Thread this end onto the point of the needle, piercing the ribbon about 1 cm from the end.
3 Pull back on the long end of the ribbon until the ribbon locks firmly onto the head of the needle.

Securing the ribbon

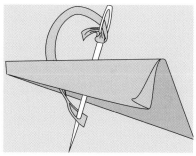

1 At the start of the embroidery, bring the ribbon through to the front of the work, leaving a small tail on the wrong side. To secure the ribbon, pierce this tail with the needle as you work the first stitch or two.
2 At the end of the work, weave the ribbon in behind the stitching if possible. If not, cut it off, leaving a tail that can be caught up when you begin the next part of the embroidery.

Flat straight stitch

The following technique ensures that the silk ribbon stitches will lie flat and untwisted against the fabric.
1 Bring the needle up at A. Hold the ribbon flat against the fabric, under your thumb, directly opposite the required position of the stitch.

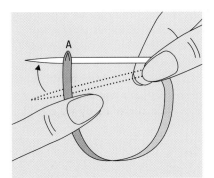

2 Spread the ribbon by placing the needle under the ribbon and then sliding it back along the ribbon with an upward pressure to the point where the ribbon emerges from the fabric.

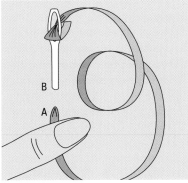

3 Make the stitch the required length, and then pass the needle back down through the fabric at B.

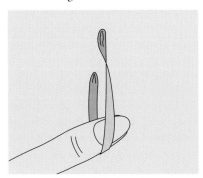

4 Keeping your left thumb in position as long as possible, form the ribbon loop over it. Pulling the ribbon firmly at this point should remove any twists in it. Slide your thumb from the loop and gently tighten the stitch.

Making a silk rose

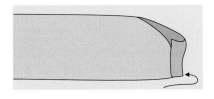

1 Take about 50 cm of 25 mm wide silk ribbon and fold over the corner. Roll the end of the ribbon several times to cover the folded edge.

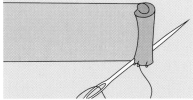

2 Stitch the side of the roll firmly to the inside of the ribbon, about one-third of the way up the roll, and then stitch right through the bottom of the roll several times to hold it firm.

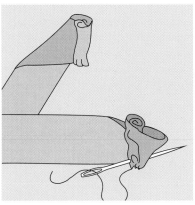

3 Turn the free end of the ribbon away from the roll, then roll the rolled up ribbon to the left, toward the turned away ribbon. Stitch through the side and the base several times.

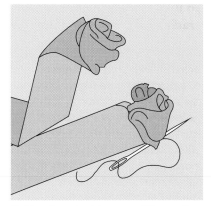

4 Continue in this way, rolling and stitching the ribbon, until the rose is the desired size.

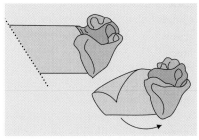

5 To finish, cut the end of the ribbon at an angle, tuck in the corner and raw edges, and stitch it in at the base.

BLOCKING

When you have finished your embroidery, check whether the fabric has stretched out of shape. This is likely to happen on loose-weave fabrics and on canvas, or where your stitching tension is tight. If there is little or no distortion of the fabric, you need only give your work a light steam-press from the back, using a damp cloth to stabilize the shape and even out the stitching surface.

Canvas and other fabrics that have become badly distorted should be blocked to restore the original shape. Cover a board larger than the embroidery with polyethylene. If your work has a selvage, cut clips along it to ensure that it stretches evenly. Dampen the fabric and place it face down on the board. Hammer a tack into the unworked area at the top of the fabric, near the center. Stretch the fabric gently down, keeping the threads vertically aligned, and hammer in a second tack at the center of the bottom edge. Do the same in the center of the two sides. Then, working outward from the center, hammer in tacks along all four edges, gently stretching the fabric as you go. Check the straightness of the threads and adjust if necessary. Let the fabric dry before removing.

Needlepoint

Needlepoint is rather like painting – once you have learned to make the stitches, you can create pictures in any style, from traditional to contemporary, from delicate to bold.

Needlepoint is the name usually given to embroidery worked on canvas. As the stitches must be worked into the holes between the woven threads, they can be worked only diagonally or parallel to the horizontal and vertical woven threads of the canvas. Despite this restriction, many different stitches can be formed. The stitches used to make the projects in this book are described in the following pages.

CANVAS

Canvas is made up of lengthwise and crosswise threads woven to produce precisely spaced holes between threads. The intersections of these threads are known as meshes. The thickness of the woven threads and the size of the holes vary with different sorts of canvases. This difference is called the gauge; a fine-gauge canvas has more threads to the centimeter than a large-gauge canvas.

Canvas is usually made from cotton, but can also be made in various synthetic materials. There are very fine-gauge canvases made from silk. Some canvases are woven from single threads, and some from double threads. Double-thread canvas is stronger than single-thread canvas, and stitches of different sizes can be worked on the same piece.

HINT

If you are unfamiliar with any of the stitches described here, it is a good idea to practice them on scrap canvas until you have learned the "rhythm" of the stitches. This is especially important for the more complicated stitches where you have to insert the needle into the back of the canvas and out at the front following a sequence of numbers.

Binding the edges

As canvas has a tendency to unravel, selvages should be trimmed off and edges bound with masking tape or bias binding. Attach bias binding with a medium zigzag machine stitch.

YARN

Needlepoint can be worked with various yarns. The most commonly used are tapestry wool, viscose and cotton. Use thick yarns for large-gauge canvas and finer yarns for fine-gauge canvas. The yarn should slide through the canvas without distorting the fabric or damaging the yarn, but should be thick enough to cover the canvas when the stitches are formed.

Securing the yarn

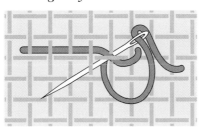

To secure the yarn at the start of your work, allow 5–6 cm of yarn to remain at the back of the canvas. Hold this yarn end against the canvas and catch it in with the first few stitches. When the end is secured, clip off the excess and continue to work the rest of the stitches.

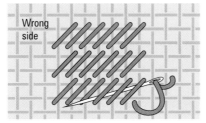

To secure the yarn at the end of the work, bring the needle and yarn to the back of the canvas. Weave the yarn through the underside of the last few stitches, and then trim off the excess.

STITCHES

Binding stitch

Binding stitch is used for finishing edges and for sewing seams together. It must be worked neatly and evenly.

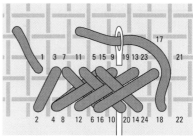

To form binding stitch, follow the sequence of numbers in the diagram, taking your needle to the back of the work at the odd numbers and through to the front at the even numbers. After you have made the starting stitches (nos. 1–8), a "rhythm" will be established of crossing three threads diagonally forward and two threads diagonally back.

Byzantine stitch

Byzantine stitch is worked in steps moving across the work area. The steps are usually made up of rows of four, five or six long, slanted stitches.

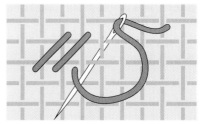

1 Starting at the upper left corner of the area to be covered, work a row of four to six long, slanting stitches horizontally across the canvas.

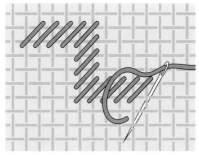

2 Under the last stitch, work the same number of stitches vertically.

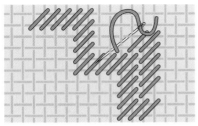

3 Continue to work in this manner, creating "steps," until you reach the bottom of the area to be worked. Begin a new row by fitting the steps of the new row into the steps of the preceding row.

Herringbone stitch

Herringbone stitch forms a tightly woven texture. It is like cross-stitch, except that the stitches cross off-center. All rows are worked left to right.

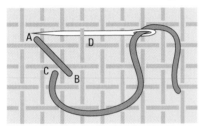

1 Starting at the upper left of the area to be worked, bring the needle out at A, down over two canvas meshes, and in at B. Take the needle under one lengthwise thread, out at C, up over two meshes, and in at D.

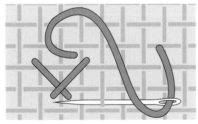

2 Pass the needle back under one lengthwise thread and start working the next stitch.

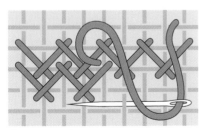

3 Begin each new row of stitches in the canvas hole directly below the start of the stitches in the row above.

Leaf or fir stitch

Leaf or fir stitch can be worked singly, or in groups or rows. Turned sideways or upside down, it makes a feather.

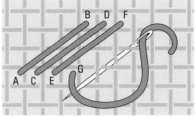

1 Work the side stitches first, as in the example illustrated, starting at A and working through to G.

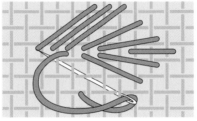

2 Work five top stitches, fanning them out to form the top of the leaf. Then complete the leaf by working the side stitches on the opposite side.

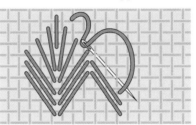

3 Start a new leaf six holes away from the start of the previous leaf, and repeat steps 1 and 2 above.

4 With each new row, reverse the working direction, positioning the new row so that the tops of the leaves fit into the base leaves of the row above. When working from left to right, form the leaves in a clockwise direction, as described in steps 1 and 2 above. When working from right to left, reverse the working order and form the leaf counterclockwise.

JACQUARD STITCH

This stitch is worked diagonally from the top left to the bottom right. It is made up of rows of spaced Byzantine stitch with rows of continental stitch filling the spaces between.

1 Starting at the top left, work steps of Byzantine stitches across the work (normally four to six stitches per step).

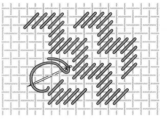

2 Work more steps of Byzantine stitch, leaving a stepped row of blank canvas between each row.

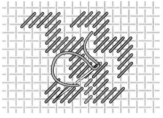

3 On each row of exposed mesh, work continental stitch (see instructions under "Tent stitch" later in this section). Work the rows from the bottom up, turning the canvas around the other way for each row so you are always working in the same direction.

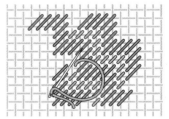

4 On horizontal steps, form the stitches in the usual way, bringing yarn out at the base (point A) and in at the top (point B). On the vertical rows, reverse the direction, bringing the yarn out at the top (point C) and in at the base (point D).

Long-armed cross-stitch

Long-armed cross-stitch (sometimes called Greek stitch) is made up of short and long stitches. The long stitches are usually worked over twice the number of canvas meshes as the short stitches.

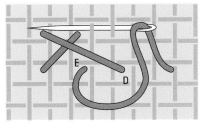

1 Bring the needle out at A and up over two meshes, and insert it at B. Bring the needle out again, two meshes to the left, at C.

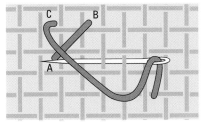

2 Insert the needle at D, which is four canvas holes away from point A. Pass the needle back under two canvas threads and out at E to start the next stitch. Always end a row with a short stitch (as stitch A–B).

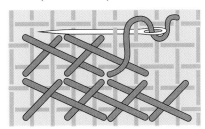

3 To begin a new row, turn the work upside down. Working from left to right, begin with a short (A–B) stitch.

Mosaic stitch

Mosaic stitch produces a block-like pattern through repetition of the same three stitches. Rows of these stitches can be worked either horizontally or diagonally across the canvas.

Worked horizontally

1 Working from right to left and starting at the upper right of the area to be covered, work one tent stitch

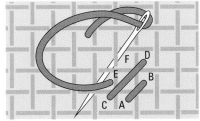

(points A to B), then a longer stitch across two canvas meshes (points C to D), and then another tent stitch (points E to F). This forms one block.

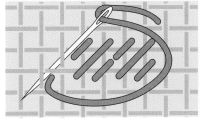

2 Begin the next block one canvas hole to the left. Continue to end of row, leaving needle at back of canvas at the end of each row.

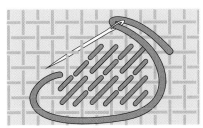

3 Turn the canvas upside down. Align the blocks of the new row with the blocks of the previous row, as shown in the diagram.

Worked diagonally

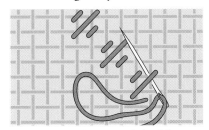

1 Starting at the upper left of the area to be worked, work the first row of blocks diagonally across the canvas, skipping one canvas hole between each block.
2 At the end of the row, leave the needle at the right side of the canvas and work the second row in the reverse direction. Work successive rows up and down the canvas, fitting

the new mosaic blocks into the spaces left between the blocks of the preceding row.

Reverse mosaic stitch

This stitch can be worked in one color or two.

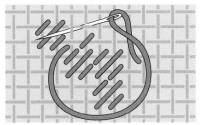

1 Work rows of mosaic stitch diagonally, missing every second row.

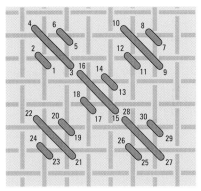

2 Turn the work 90° so that the upper right is now the upper left. Repeat step 1 to fill in the spaces.

Norwich stitch

This stitch can be worked in various sized squares, as long as the square always has an uneven number of threads. The diagram shows how to work Norwich stitch over a nine-thread square. If you intend working the stitch over a different number of threads, plan it on graph paper first.
1 Bring the needle up at 1 and down at 2. Continue in this way, following

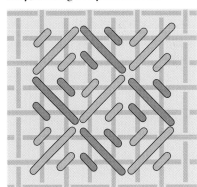

NINE PATCH

Nine patch is a square design consisting of five triple cross-stitches worked in one color and four clusters of diagonal stitch worked in another color (making nine components all together). The design is worked over a nine-thread square.

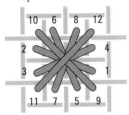

1 Working over a three-thread square, stitch a triple cross-stitch following the sequence of numbers in the diagram above. Bring the needle to the front of the work at the odd numbers and to the back at the even numbers.

2 Work the other four triple cross-stitches in the same manner, being careful to position them in the right holes so that the diagonal stitches will fit exactly between them.

3 Using a different colored yarn, work the diagonal stitches between the triple cross-stitches, as shown in the diagram. Take care to cross over the correct number of canvas threads, and make sure all stitches are slanted in the same direction.

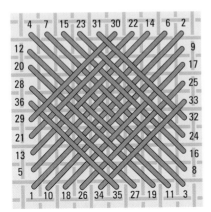

the sequence of numbers exactly until point 34. Ensure that you bring the needle to the front of the canvas at the odd numbers and down to the back at the even numbers.

2 Bring the needle up at point 35, weave the needle under stitch 29–30, and insert the needle at point 36. Secure the yarn.

Ray stitch

Ray stitch consists of seven stitches radiating from a common canvas hole and forming a square. Expanded ray stitch is made up of thirteen stitches, forming a rectangle. The color of the yarn can be alternated with each square or row of squares.

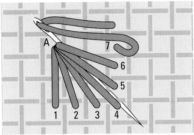

1 Begin at the upper left-hand corner of the area to be covered and work rows from left to right and from right to left alternately. Work each ray stitch in a counterclockwise direction, following the numbers from 1 to 7; each stitch begins at a number and ends in the canvas hole, A, that is common to all stitches. Fan each ray stitch as shown in the diagram.

2 Point 7 of the first ray stitch now becomes the common hole, A, of the new stitch. At the end of each row, reverse the working direction and place the new stitch units below those just completed.

Diamond ray stitch

This is a variation on ray stitch. The outer stitches can be worked in a dif-

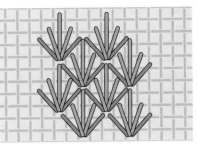

ferent color to achieve the distinctive diamond pattern when several rows are worked in a block.

Rhodes stitch

Rhodes stitch is used for large areas and to fill in backgrounds. Diagonal stitches are superimposed to make a pattern of raised square blocks. Each block consists of straight stitches across the square, following each other counterclockwise so that they all cross the same central point.

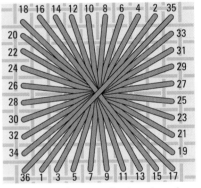

1 Begin each square (a nine-thread square in this example) at the bottom left-hand corner (point 1). Insert the needle at 2, carrying the needle under the square and out at 3.

2 Fill every hole around the square in this way, following the sequence indicated by the numbers 1 to 36.

Tent stitch

A tent stitch is a diagonal stitch formed over one canvas mesh. There are three kinds of tent stitches, each with its own stitch name – the half cross-stitch, the continental stitch, and the basketweave stitch. The basketweave and continental stitches are more durable than the half cross-stitch and give more coverage on the back of the canvas. The half cross-stitch is more economical of yarn and distorts the canvas less.

Half cross-stitch

Half cross-stitch is worked from left to right. The needle is carried horizontally across the back of the work, forming horizontal stitches on the back of the canvas.

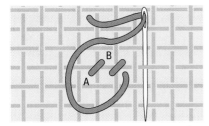

1 Starting at the upper left, bring the needle out at point A and in at point B. Continue to work the stitches in this way to the end of the row.
2 Work the last stitch and leave the needle at the back of the canvas.

3 Turn the canvas upside down and form the new row in line with the stitches of the row just completed.

Continental stitch

Continental stitch is a form of tent stitch that can be worked horizontally from right to left or vertically from top to bottom. In both methods of working, a diagonal stitch is formed on the back of the canvas.

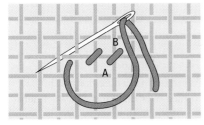

1 To work continental stitch horizontally, start at the upper right-hand corner of the area to be worked. Form each stitch by bringing the needle out at A and inserting it at B. When you come to the end of each row, finish the last stitch and leave the needle at the back of the canvas.
2 Turn the canvas upside down and

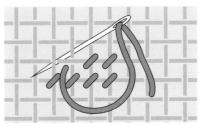

work the stitches of the new row directly in line with those in the row you have just completed.

1 To work continental stitch vertically, start at the top corner of the area to be covered and work a row of stitches down the canvas. When you come to the end of the row, leave the needle at the back of the work.

2 Turn the canvas upside down to reverse the working direction, and form the new row of stitches beside the first. Repeat until the area is filled.

Basketweave stitch

Basketweave stitch is worked in rows alternately down and up the canvas.

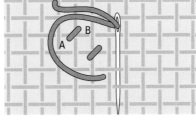

1 Starting from the top left-hand corner of the area to be worked, bring the needle out at A and insert it again at B. Work stitches in a diagonal row, skipping one canvas hole between stitches. To work down, hold the needle vertically, as shown.

2 Form the first stitch of an up row by bringing the needle out through the hole directly below the beginning of the previous stitch.

3 To work an up row, hold the needle horizontally between stitches. Form the first stitch of the next down row beside the last stitch of the previous down row.

Window eyelet stitch

A window eyelet is made up of four ray stitches radiating from a central cross-stitch (worked last). The stitches are worked in the numerical sequence shown, so that each ray finishes with a corner stitch on top. The window eyelet illustrated here has been worked over a nine-thread square.

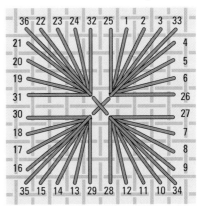

1 Over a nine-thread square, work the stitches in the sequence shown, coming up to the front of the work at the numbered points and taking the needle back down at the common hole of the individual ray stitches.
2 Finish the pattern by working a cross-stitch in the center.

Crochet

Crochet uses a small number of simple stitches to create a variety of patterns and textures. It can be worked with threads and yarns ranging from very fine to quite coarse.

These instructions are for right-handers; if you are left-handed, substitute right hand for left and vice versa. As a left-hander, you will find the diagrams easier to follow if you look at them through a mirror, which will give you the correct position for the left hand.

BEGINNING THE WORK
Holding the hook
There are many different ways of holding a crochet hook, and most people develop a style of their own as they become more experienced. The following is a common method.

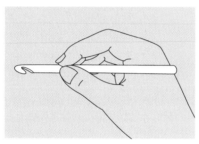

Hold the hook like a pencil, with the thumb and index finger on either side of the flat portion of the hook and the middle finger resting against the thumb.

Holding the yarn

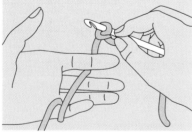

Wrap the ball end of the yarn around the little finger of your left hand. Take it under the fourth and third fingers, then over the top of the index finger, leaving about 5 cm of yarn between finger and hook. Use your index finger to keep the yarn taut so that you can manipulate the yarn easily and with an even tension around the hook.

Slip knot
Most crochet begins with a slip knot, which secures the yarn to the hook. Make the knot about 15 cm from the yarn end.

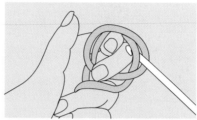

1 Wind the yarn once around two fingers and over the fingers again to the left of the first thread. Using the hook, pick up the second thread through the first one.

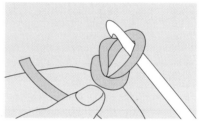

2 Pull the second thread through the first one to form a loop.
3 Keeping the hook inside the loop, pull both yarn ends and draw in the loop until it is close to the hook, but not too tight.

WORKING A CHAIN
Chain stitch is used to form the foundation row in crochet work, and is also an integral part of many crochet pattern stitches.

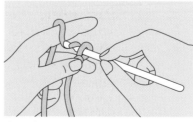

1 Hold the slip knot between the thumb and middle finger of the left hand. Keeping the yarn taut over the

BASIC CROCHET RULES
- Always insert the hook into a chain or stitch from the front to the back, unless the directions clearly specify otherwise.
- Always insert the crochet hook under the top two loops of a chain or other stitch.
- At the completion of a stitch or sequence, you should have only one loop remaining on the hook.

index finger, pass the hook under the yarn. Draw the yarn through the loop on the hook to form a new loop. The new loop should be loose enough for you to draw the next chain through.

2 Repeat step 1 until the required number of chains are completed. When counting chains, remember that the loop still on the hook is not counted as a chain.

Turning chains
At the beginning of each row, a certain number of chains must be added to bring the work level with the first stitch of the new row. The exact number of chains to be added depends on the height of the stitch you are using. (See the instructions that follow for working basic stitches.)

BASIC STITCHES
Slipstitch (slst)
Slipstitch is a short stitch, used for joining and shaping. It is sometimes worked along an edge to strengthen it and minimize stretching.

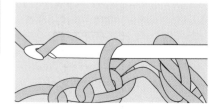

Insert hook in chain or stitch. Wrap yarn over hook and draw a loop through both chain and yarn loop on hook.

Double crochet (dc)

Double crochet is often used to finish edges, and sometimes to join crochet pieces together. When turning double crochet use one chain.

Insert hook into stitch or chain, yarn over hook, and draw yarn through stitch or chain. Draw yarn through both stitches on hook. Double crochet complete.

Half treble (htr)

Half treble is not often used. It makes a firm, attractive fabric with a pronounced ridge. When turning half treble, use two chains.

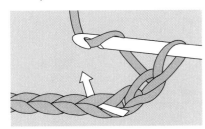

1 Wrap yarn over hook, and then insert hook into stitch or chain.

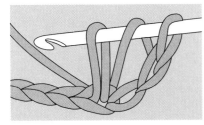

2 Draw loop through stitch or chain. You should now have three loops on the hook.

3 Wrap yarn over hook and draw through all three loops on hook. Half treble complete.

Treble (tr)

Treble is a compact stitch and is the most commonly used. When turning treble, three chains are used.

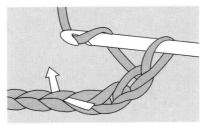

1 Wrap yarn over hook and then insert hook into stitch or chain from front to back.

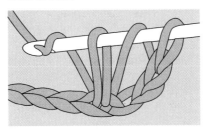

2 Draw loop through. You should have three loops on the hook.

HINTS

• *To keep edges straight, never work into last stitch of previous row, as the turning chain counts as the first stitch of each row.*
• *Count the stitches after each row to make sure you have worked the correct number.*

CHECKING THE GAUGE

Before starting to make a crochet project, it is important to check the gauge. Make a test swatch, as instructed in the pattern. Place the swatch on a flat surface, insert two pins, 10 cm apart, into the swatch, and count the stitches between. Place the pins vertically to count rows and horizontally to count stitches.

After checking your gauge, if you find your work is too loose, change to a smaller hook. If it is too tight, change to a larger hook. With practice, you will be able to achieve the correct gauge.

3 Wrap yarn over hook. Draw loop through first two loops only, leaving two loops on hook.

4 Wrap yarn over hook and draw it through last two loops on hook. Treble complete.

WORKING A ROUND

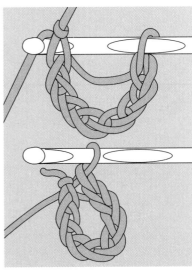

1 Chain required number of stitches and join them into a ring by slipstitching into the first chain.

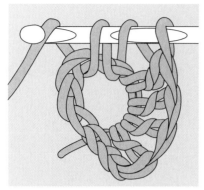

2 If working first round in double crochet, begin round with one chain. If working first round in treble, begin round with three chains. Work number of stitches required into ring.

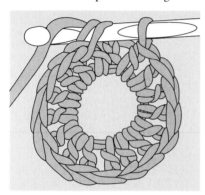

3 When round is complete, close with a slipstitch in top of beginning chain, unless otherwise directed.

INCREASING

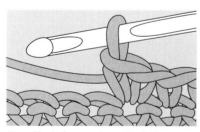

For all stitches, make a single increase by working two stitches into one. The illustration shows double crochet.

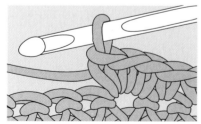

For all stitches, double increase by working three stitches into one. The illustration shows double crochet.

DECREASING

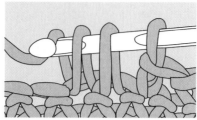

1 To decrease one stitch in double or half treble, insert hook into next stitch. Wrap yarn over hook and draw yarn through.
2 Insert hook into next stitch. Wrap yarn over hook and draw yarn through three loops on hook.

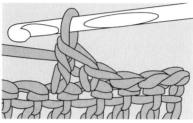

To decrease several stitches at the beginning of a row, omit turning chain and work slipstitches for required number of decreases. Work one double crochet into next stitch and continue in pattern. Do not work the slipstitches on the return row.

JOINING YARN

Yarns should never be joined by knotting them together. Instead, use the following method.

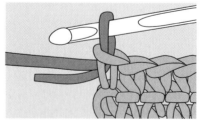

1 Work to final two loops of last stitch at the end of a row with first yarn, and then draw new yarn through these two loops to complete stitch.

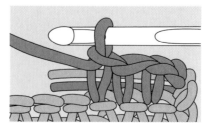

CROCHET ABBREVIATIONS

alt	alternate
beg	begin, beginning
ch	chain
cont	continue
dc	double crochet
dec	decrease, decreasing
dtr	double treble
htr	half treble
inc	increase, increasing
pat	pattern
rem	remain/ing
rep	repeat
rnd	round
sk	skip
sp	space
slst	slipstitch
tog	together
tr	treble
ttr	triple treble
yo	yarn over hook
★	Repeat the stitch instructions between the asterisks as many times as there are stitches to accommodate them.
( )	Work the series of steps within parentheses according to the instructions that follow the parentheses.

2 Trim first yarn to 5 cm. Make a chain and turn. Lay the ends of the new and old yarn together over the work and crochet over the top of them for four or five stitches.

FINISHING

1 Trim off the yarn to 10 cm. Pull this end through the last loop and tighten the loop.

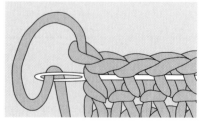

2 Using a tapestry needle, weave the yarn into the back of the work below the top row of stitches for 3–5 cm. Trim off the remaining yarn.

Knitting

Knitting is a relaxing pastime, and a wonderful way of creating handmade garments with a touch of individuality. It is also a good first craft for children, as it is safe and simple.

NEEDLES

Whether you use plastic, metal or wooden needles depends on personal preference and availability. Stitches slide well along metal needles, but they tend to be noisy and their rigidity may cause problems for arthritic knitters. Plastic needles are quieter than metal ones and easier to handle. Bamboo and wooden needles are more expensive, but their ease of handling and superior performance make the extra cost worthwhile if you intend doing a lot of knitting.

Needle thickness is expressed in millimeters (mm). The size of the stitch increases with the thickness of the needle. In general, work thicker yarns with large needles and thinner yarns with smaller ones. If the needles are too large for the yarn, the knitted fabric will be loosely structured; if the needles are too small, the stitches will be too compact and rigid.

Needle length depends on the size of the project. Needles should be long enough to hold all stitches comfortably. Very large projects may be easier to work on circular needles.

CASTING ON OR BINDING ON

Casting on forms the first row of stitches and one selvage of the finished article. Three common methods of casting on are described here.

For all methods, form the first stitch by making a slip knot. To form a slip knot, make a loop 15 cm from the end of the yarn. Insert the needle into the loop, draw the yarn from the ball end of the wool through the loop and tighten the knot.

Knitting on

This method forms a versatile selvage that is soft when worked through the front of the loops and firm when worked through the back.

1 Hold the needle with the slip

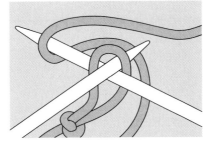

knot in the left hand. Insert the right needle through the front of the loop and take the yarn around the needle.

2 Draw the yarn through to form a second loop. Transfer the new loop to the left needle and knit into it to form the next new stitch. Continue forming new stitches in this way until you have made the required number.

Cable cast-on

This is worked in the same way as knitting on, but each new loop is made by inserting the needle between the two previous stitches instead of into the last loop. This gives an edge that is both elastic and decorative.

1 Make the first two stitches as for knitting on. For each new stitch after that, insert the right needle between the two previous stitches.

> ### HINT
> *With practice you will develop your own way of holding the needles and handling the yarn. The methods described here can be adapted to suit what feels most comfortable for you.*

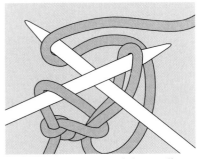

2 Take the yarn around the needle as for knitting on, draw through a new loop and transfer it to the left needle.

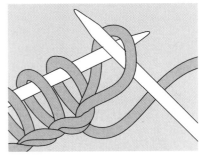

3 Continue forming new stitches between loops until you have made the required number.

Single cast-on

This method uses only one needle. It forms a loose selvage that is particularly good for hem edges, for buttonholes or for lacy knitting patterns.

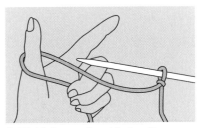

1 Hold the needle with the slip knot on it in your right hand. Wrap the yarn from the ball end around your left thumb, then grasp the yarn firmly between the palm of your hand and the tips of your fingers.

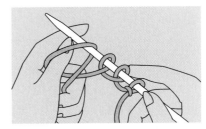

2 Turn your hand so that the back of your thumb is facing you. Insert the needle from front to back through the loose loop that is formed.

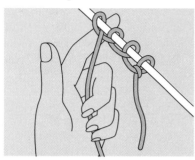

3 Slip your thumb out of the loop and at the same time pull the yarn downward to close the loop around the needle. Continue making stitches in this way until you have made the required number.

BASIC STITCHES
There are only two basic stitches in knitting – the knit stitch and the purl stitch. All other stitch patterns are made by combining and varying these two stitches. For some examples, see "Basic stitch patterns" on page 326. Knitting methods vary from place to place, and people generally develop a style of their own. One of the more common methods follows.

Knit stitch

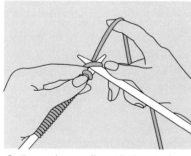

1 Grasp the needle with the stitches in your left hand. The first stitch should be about 2 cm from the tip. Take the yarn around the little finger of your right hand, under the next two fingers and over the top of the index finger, extending it about 5 cm from the first stitch on the needle.
2 Holding the yarn behind the work, insert the right needle into the front of the first stitch from left to right (the needle tip pointing toward the back).

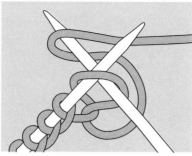

With your right index finger, loop the yarn around the right needle and over the top in a counterclockwise direction.

3 Draw the loop on the right needle forward through the stitch, at the same time pushing the stitch on the left needle toward the tip. With practice you will be able to coordinate these two movements smoothly and increase your speed.

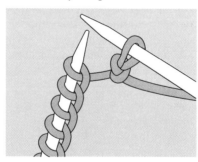

4 Allow the stitch on the left needle to slip off, while the new stitch (the loop you have just made) remains on the right needle.
5 Repeat steps 1 to 4, pushing the stitches forward on the left needle with your thumb, index and middle fingers, and moving the stitches back on the right needle with your thumb.

Purl stitch
1 Grasp the needle holding the stitches in the left hand, as described in step 1 for knit stitch.
2 Holding the yarn in front of the work, insert the right needle into the

front of the first stitch, from right to left (the needle tip pointing slightly upward). With your right index finger take the yarn backward over the right needle, then forward and under it.

3 Draw the loop on the right needle backward through the stitch and at the same time push the stitch on the left needle toward the tip. With practice you will be able to coordinate these two movements smoothly and increase your speed.

4 Allow the stitch on the left needle to slide off the needle. The new stitch (the loop you just made) remains on the right needle.
5 Repeat steps 1 to 4, pushing the stitches forward on the left needle with your thumb, index and middle fingers, and moving the stitches back on the right needle with your thumb.

CASTING OFF OR BINDING OFF
Plain cast-off is the easiest and most versatile method of casting off.
1 Knit the first two stitches at the

beginning of the row in the stitch pattern you have been working.

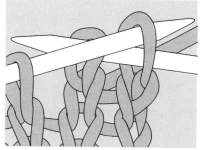

2 With yarn behind the work, insert the left needle into the first stitch.

3 Pull the first stitch over the second stitch with the left needle and then let it slip from the needle. Knit the next stitch on the left needle in pattern.

4 Repeat steps 2 and 3 until you have cast off the desired number of stitches.

INCREASING, OR ADDING STITCHES
Knit increase

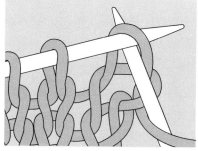

Bring the yarn forward, in front of the right needle. Insert the needle knitwise in the first stitch and knit a new stitch through the first stitch. Put the new stitch back onto the left needle and knit it in the normal way, placing it, at this stage, on the right needle as usual.

Purl increase

Holding the yarn behind the right needle, insert the needle purlwise

in the first stitch and purl a new stitch through it. Place the new stitch back onto the left needle and purl it, placing it on the right needle as usual.

DECREASING, OR REDUCING STITCHES
Knit decrease

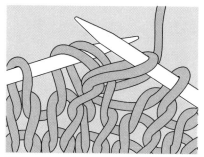

Knit two stitches together (K2 tog) through the front of both loops.

Purl decrease

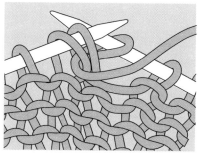

Purl two stitches together (P2 tog) through the front of both loops.

JOINING WITH A SEAM ALLOWANCE

Joining pieces with a seam allowance is ideal where the edges of the knitted piece are uneven, such as shoulder seams that have been cast off in steps. It is also suitable for taking in a garment or for shaping curved seams because the stitches can be formed at any distance from the edge.

CHECKING THE GAUGE

Knitting instructions always specify a gauge; that is, the exact number of stitches (and sometimes rows) per 10 cm using the specified needles, yarn and stitch pattern. The size of the finished article is based on the specified gauge, so it is important to make sure you knit at the gauge specified.

1 Before beginning any new project, make a test swatch at least 15 cm square, using the recommended yarn and needles and working in the specified stitch.

2 Place the completed swatch right side up on a flat surface (the ironing board is a good place to work) and pin the edges, taking care not to stretch the sample.

3 To check the horizontal gauge, insert two pins 10 cm apart on a row and count the stitches between them. It is easier to count stitches on the knit side of stockinette stitch, where each loop represents one stitch. When counting stitches for garter stitch, count the loops in one row only.

4 To check the vertical gauge, insert two pins 10 cm apart vertically and count the rows between them. It is easier to count rows on the purl side of stockinette stitch, where each two ridges equals one row. In counting rows for garter stitch, every ridge equals one row and every furrow equals another.

5 If there are too many stitches or rows in your gauge square, knit another sample using needles one size larger; if there are too few stitches, try using needles one size smaller. The time taken to get the gauge right will be well spent, because an error of even one stitch per 10 cm multiplies to a substantial size difference over a wide area. However, do not use needles more than one size away from that specified. If you cannot match the stated gauge, choose another pattern.

Backstitched seam

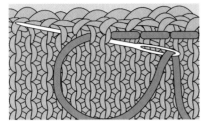

Hold the two pieces together with right sides facing. Using a knitter's needle and a length of the yarn used in the knitting, backstitch the seam, taking in two knitting stitches at a time.

Slipstitched seam

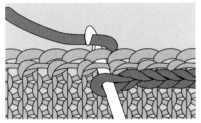

1 Using a crochet hook of appropriate size and a length of the yarn used in the knitting, draw a loop through a corresponding stitch on each section.
2 Insert the hook through the next two stitches and draw a loop through both stitches and the loop on the hook. Repeat steps 1 and 2 along the length of the seam.

JOINING EDGE TO EDGE
Joining knitted sections edge to edge makes a smooth, bulkless seam that is almost invisible.

Flat seam on garter stitch

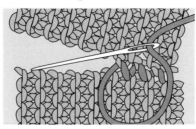

1 With right sides facing up, lay the two knitted pieces side by side with corresponding stitches aligned.
2 Sew stitch by stitch, placing the needle under the horizontal loop next to the edge stitch on one section, then under the corresponding loop on the other.

Flat seam on rib

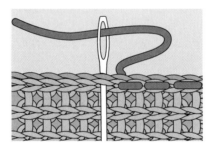

1 Place the knitted pieces together with right sides facing and corresponding stitches aligned.
2 Attach the yarn at the right-hand end. Bring the needle up through the center of the next two corresponding edge stitches and down through the next two. Continue stitching in this way to the end of the seam.

EMBROIDERY ON KNITTING
Duplicate stitch
Duplicate stitch is best worked with yarn of the same thickness as the knitted garment. Take care not to pull the embroidery yarn too tightly.

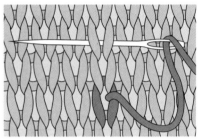

1 Bring the needle from the back through the center of the stitch below the one to be covered. Then take the needle from right to left under both strands of the stitch above the one to be covered. Bring the needle back to the start of the stitch and take the needle behind the two strands in the

---

BASIC STITCH PATTERNS
The following knitting stitch patterns are the easiest to create and are ideal for beginners.
Garter stitch is the simplest stitch pattern, and is normally produced by knitting every stitch of every row. It has a pebbly surface, identical on both sides, and a loose structure that stretches equally in both directions.
Stockinette stitch is the most versatile stitch pattern, and is produced by knitting one row and purling the next. It is smooth on the knitted side (which

is usually considered to be the right side) and pebbly on the purled side. The fabric stretches more crosswise than lengthwise. Stockinette stitch is used for jumpers and dresses, and for knitted accessories such as hats, gloves and socks.

Stockinette stitch – knitted side

Rib stitch is produced by alternating one or more knit stitches with one or more purl stitches in one row, then purling the knit stitches and knitting the purl stitches on the return row. This produces a pattern of vertical ridges that is identical on both sides when knit and purl stitches are knitted in equal numbers. Rib stitch has considerable crosswise elasticity and is especially suitable for welts (cuffs and waists) of garments, where the ribbing ensures a snug fit.

Garter stitch

Stockinette stitch – purled side

Rib stitch

row below. Take the needle across into the center of the next stitch.

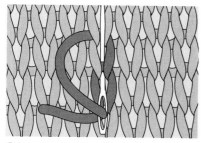

2 Repeat step 1 until you have made the required number of stitches.

3 To finish, bring the needle back to the start of the stitch and through to the back of the work.

Cross-stitch embroidery

Cross-stitch embroidery on knitting should be worked with a finer yarn than that with which the garment is knitted. Be careful not to pull the embroidery yarn too tightly.

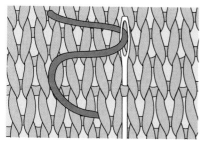

1 Bring the needle up under a purl strand connecting two knit stitches. Cross diagonally into the stitch one above and one to the right. Take the needle down behind the purl strand into the stitch below.

2 Cross to the left diagonally to complete the cross, and then take the needle through to the back. Pass the needle diagonally behind the next knit stitch on the left and bring it out again under the next purl stitch.

POMPOMS

1 To make a pompom, you need two identical circles of cardboard with holes cut out of the middle. To determine the size of the cardboard circles, estimate the desired diameter of the finished pompom; add 1.5 cm to this measurement to allow for trimming, and add the diameter of the center hole. (The diameter of the center hole is a quarter of the finished diameter of the pompom.) For example, to make a pompom with a finished diameter of 8 cm, you will need two cardboard circles with diameters of 8 cm + 1.25 cm + 2 cm (11.25 cm), with center holes of 2 cm diameter.

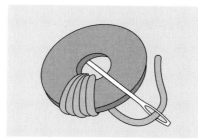

2 With the two circles flat together, wind the yarn round and round the cardboard until the center hole is filled up and you can no longer push the yarn through.

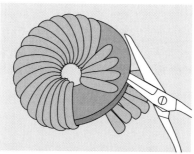

3 Place the point of a pair of scissors between the two circles of cardboard and cut around, keeping the scissors between the cardboard circles.

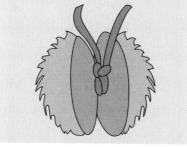

4 Wrap a double strand of yarn round between the two circles of cardboard, knot it firmly and cut away the cardboard. Trim the pompom.

KNITTING ABBREVIATIONS

alt	alternate
beg	beginning
cc	contrasting color
cont	continue
dec	decrease
foll	following
gst	garter stitch
inc	increase
incl	including, inclusive
K	knit
K-wise	knitwise (insert needle as though to knit)
K2 (3) tog	knit two (or three) stitches together
l	left
mc	main color
P	purl
P-wise	purlwise (insert needle as though to purl)
P2(3) tog	purl two (or three) stitches together
pat	pattern
psso	pass the slipped stitch over
r	right
rem	remain/remaining/remainder
rep	repeat
rs	right side facing
sl	slip a stitch, without working it, from left needle to right needle
st	stitch
stst	stockinette stitch
tbl	through back of loop (enter stitch from the back instead of the front)
ws	wrong side facing
ybk	yarn back (take yarn to back of work)
yfwd	yarn forward (take yarn to front of work)
work even	continue work without increasing or decreasing
★ ★	Repeat the instructions between the asterisks as many times as there are stitches to accommodate them.
( )	Repeat instructions enclosed in parentheses the number of times indicated after the parentheses.
[ ]	Instructions within square brackets explain the method of working a particular stitch or technique.

Knotted lace

Knotted lace looks complex, but it is based on a very few simple stitches. It is important that loops be of an even size, so practice the stitches before attempting a project.

BASIC LOOP

You must form a row of basic loops along the edge of the fabric before beginning to make the pattern (rather like casting on in knitting). Always work from left to right when working on a straight edge. Basic loops should be uniformly small and evenly spaced.

1 Thread the needle with a thread about 60 cm long. Holding the end of the thread between the thumb and forefinger of your left hand (right hand if left-handed), place the thread behind the fabric. Insert the needle into the fabric from the front, 2 mm from the edge and under the thread. Do not pull the needle through.

2 Hold the doubled-over thread near the eye of the needle. Loop the threads under the point of the needle from right to left, and down toward the eye of the needle.

3 Pull the needle through in an upward direction. Pull the knot tight. You have now made a basic knot.

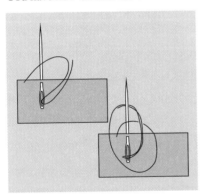

4 To make the first basic loop, insert the needle from the front of the work, 2 mm along from the first knot, and repeat the basic knot, this time leaving a loop about 2 mm high. Continue in this way until you have completed a row. Do not cut the thread.

5 Turn the work over and work a turning loop into the first loop. Then work the second and subsequent rows by inserting the needle through the loops of the previous row.

CLOSED LOOP AND BOW

1 Work a foundation row in an even number of basic loops and turn the work over.

2 Work a small turning loop into first loop. Into the same loop work a long loop, one and a half times higher than the basic loop. Place the needle through the front of the loop. Do not pull it through.

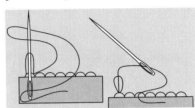

3 Taking the thread from the knot end, pass it over the point of the needle from left to right. Pull the thread through and pull it tight. You have now made a closed loop.

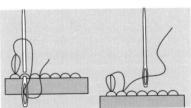

4 Make another loop of the same height into the next basic loop.

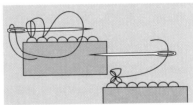

5 Place the needle behind all the long loops and pass the thread over the needle from front to back. Pull all the threads tight together in the middle.

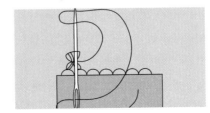

6 Put the needle through the top of the last long loop and work another closed loop.

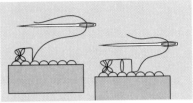

7 Work another loop of the same height into the next loop and close it with a closed loop knot.

8 Repeat steps 4 to 7 until the end.

SMALL TURNING LOOP

This is a small loop made like a basic loop and worked into the first loop when turning. It is not part of a row.

BRIDGING LOOP

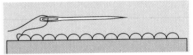

This is a small loop made like a basic loop and worked into a large loop. It is not worked on the next round.

PICOT

A picot is made by working a number of loops into the same large loop. Small picots produce a scalloped effect and large picots make a fan shape.

INCREASING AND DECREASING

If the foundation rows are correct, you should not need to increase or decrease. If you do need more loops, increase by working two knots into one loop. To decrease, miss a loop or make one knot through two loops.

JOINING THREADS

1 Cut the thread about 5 cm from the last knot worked. Over this knot make another with a new thread.

2 Work into next loop, catching the cut end of previous thread with the knot. This will make a double loop.

3 Keep the thread ends at the back of the work. On the next round, work into the double loop before trimming the thread.

Découpage

Découpage is a time-consuming but satisfying craft. Take great care at every stage of the work, and the result will look as though the images are floating in translucent porcelain.

Découpage is the art of decorating hard surfaces with cut-out paper images. It originated in eighteenth century Venice, and enjoyed a popular revival a hundred years later in the England of Queen Victoria.

The printed images are glued onto the surface of the object, and then many coats of varnish (often 30 or more) are applied until the images are completely submerged and their edges cannot be felt.

Anything with a hard, smooth surface can be ornamented with découpage. Boxes, old suitcases, violin cases, wooden screens, trays, wooden bowls, chairs and tables are all suitable. Small objects like blown eggs can also be découpaged.

EQUIPMENT AND SUPPLIES
Preparing the surface
You will need sandpaper, wood putty (filler) or beeswax, gesso, rust guard for protecting metal surfaces, sealer, and inexpensive paintbrushes.

Preparing the images
You will need fine, sharp scissors (long-bladed and curved cuticle), a scalpel or craft knife, a cutting board or mat, artist's acrylic gloss medium (for sealing), and Blu-Tack.

Fixing the images
You will need wallpaper paste, white glue, a brush, sponges, and a small rubber roller with rounded edges.

Varnishing
You will need a chiseled imitation sable paintbrush (or any other good-quality brush that does not shed its bristles), about 25 mm wide, good-quality polyurethane gloss varnish, wet-and-dry sandpaper of several grades of fineness, a sanding block (rubber or cork), lint-free cloths, and mineral turpentine.

Waxing
You will need cabinetmaker's polish, clear beeswax, French polish or liquid car wax, and soft cloths. Alternatively, use a micromesh kit, available from craft suppliers.

CHOOSING IMAGES
The images are a major part of découpage, so choose carefully. Make sure the images are clear and consistently colored. Ideally, images should be on thin, nonporous paper because thicker surfaces will need many more coats of varnish to submerge them and therefore will make a raised, uneven surface, which will spoil the overall effect.

Books are an excellent source of images. You can also use magazine pictures, as long as they are well sealed so that the printing on the other side will not show through. If you use wrapping paper, avoid the folded kind, as the creases will show, and seal the paper well before applying.

PREPARING THE SURFACE
Before applying découpage, ensure that surfaces are nonporous and extremely smooth. If you do not take the time to prepare surfaces well, the result is likely to be less than perfect.

Wood

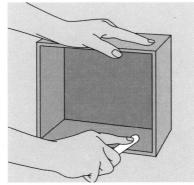

1 Remove old paint or varnish with paint stripper. Wash with dishwashing

liquid to remove all dirt, grease and wax. Fill cracks or indentations with wood filler or a beeswax stick.

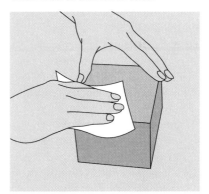

2 Sand all surfaces thoroughly to ensure a smooth working surface. If the surface is not smooth enough, apply several coats of artist's gesso, allowing coats to dry completely between applications. Sand until the surface feels like smooth ivory.
3 Apply wood sealer to all surfaces.

Metal
1 Remove any rust with a wire brush or sandpaper. Clean the surface with methylated spirits. For larger objects, you can save hours of preparation and achieve a better finish by taking the object to a professional sandblaster to have it sandblasted and sealed.
2 Apply a coat of rust-inhibiting metal primer. Lightly sand the surface and apply a coat of sealer or rust-resistant paint.

Porous surfaces
Apply several coats of gesso to any surface that will soak up varnish. Polystyrene foam is eroded by varnish, so ensure that the surface is well finished with gesso and sealer.

SEALING THE IMAGES
Before they are fixed in place, images must be sealed to prevent varnish from seeping under the paper. Sealing also preserves the color and prevents the image from stretching and wrinkling when it is glued down. Always seal images before cutting them to exact size. Photographs with non-porous backs do not require sealing.

1 Apply artist's acrylic gloss medium sparingly to the back of the image and allow to dry.

2 Apply a similar coat to the front and allow it to dry thoroughly.

LAYING OUT THE DESIGN

Do not cut away the background from the images until you are completely happy with the design, as you may want to use some of the background images elsewhere in your design.

1 Before you fix the images to the prepared surface, take time to arrange the pictures on paper templates or on the object itself. Fix the images with Blu-Tack and rearrange them until you are satisfied with the design.

2 Before trimming the outside edge of an image, remove any enclosed background areas by first cutting a hole through the top then cutting the background from under the paper. This ensures you have enough paper to grasp without damaging the image.

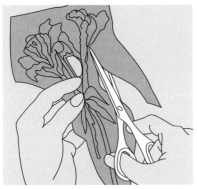

3 Cut away the excess background, feeding the paper smoothly through the scissors to produce a crisp edge. If the image does not have too many curves, you can use a scalpel instead.

CAUTION

To achieve good results, the printed images must be neatly and accurately cut out, so use sharp, good-quality instruments. However, be careful – especially with scalpels, which are very sharp. To prevent the scalpel from slipping when cutting straight edges, hold it firm against the edge of a steel ruler.

RULES FOR VARNISHING

- Always wear a mask or respirator to avoid breathing in fumes.
- Use goggles to protect your eyes.
- Work in a well-ventilated, dust-free area where you can leave your découpage to dry, and work in good light to ensure even coverage.
- Varnish away from direct sunlight.
- Varnish in dry weather, as dampness and humidity can cause a misty effect in the varnish.
- Keep the brush clean and free of excess varnish as you work by washing it in turpentine. Clean the brush thoroughly after each application.

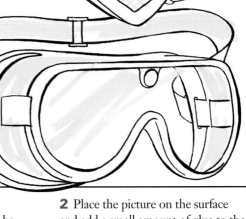

GLUING

It is essential that the pictures be glued securely to prevent varnish from seeping under the image and lifting it. It is also essential to remove every trace of glue from the surface before you begin varnishing.

1 Mix three parts wallpaper paste and one part white glue. Unless the images are very small, apply the glue to the hard surface rather than the image, as the glue can make the paper stretch and tear. Be generous with the

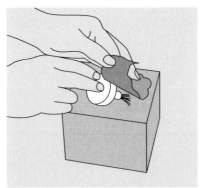

glue and work with only one image at a time. On curved surfaces use wallpaper glue only, mixed to a thick, jelly-like consistency. This mixture will give you more time to work on the image and mold it onto the shape.

2 Place the picture on the surface and add a small amount of glue to the upper side of the image. Massage the picture carefully to smooth out any lumps of glue and air bubbles from under the paper.

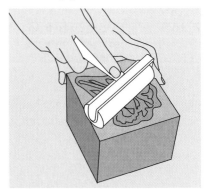

3 With gentle pressure, run the roller over the picture to distribute the glue evenly. Always roll from the center of the image out toward the edges, and roll in one direction only, not backward and forward.

4 Wipe excess glue from the top of the image with a well-wrung-out sponge. Difficult glue smears can be removed with a solution of water and a little vinegar or lemon juice.

5 When all the images are in place and the glue is thoroughly dry, use

colored pencils to conceal any white edges that appear around the images. This ensures that the images will blend together in the finished piece.
6 Apply a coat of sealer over the images and the surface of the object.

VARNISHING

The aim of varnishing is to build up the background to the level of the images, so that the images appear to be inlaid in the surface.

Initial coats

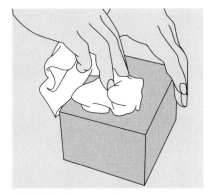

1 With a lint-free cloth, remove surface dust before varnishing. Using an imitation sable brush, apply a generous coat of varnish to the surface, brushing out from the center in one direction only.
2 Remove any excess varnish from the brush and then lightly apply the tip of the brush to the work in order to remove air bubbles and excess varnish. Allow the varnish to dry for at least 24 hours.
3 When dry, rub lightly with a lint-free cloth to remove surface dust particles. Apply another coat of varnish, brushing at right angles to the first coat to ensure good coverage.
4 Repeat steps 1 to 3 until a good depth of varnish has built up and you are sure that a light sanding will not damage the paper images. This will take at least 10 coats. Leave to dry for 24–48 hours.

Upper coats

Sanding between coats will remedy the lumps and bumps that start to appear after varnishing.
1 Using no. 60 wet-and-dry sandpaper wrapped around a sanding block,

and a little water, sand the varnished surfaces lightly in one direction. Do not use a circular motion, as this will scratch the surface. Concentrate on the images, sanding back the varnish on top of the image at each sanding and allowing the background varnish to continue building up.
2 Remove all residue with a sponge and a lint-free cloth and then varnish again, allowing each coat to dry thoroughly. Change the direction of sanding between coats and keep the sandpaper moist.

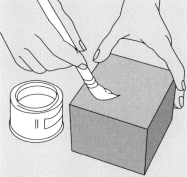

3 Repeat steps 1 and 2 as often as necessary to achieve a uniform thickness of varnish. The varnish must be built up until you can no longer feel the edges of the images. The number of coats needed will vary, depending on how thickly the varnish is applied and how thick the image is. All crevices must be filled with varnish; this can take anywhere between 10 and 30 coats of varnish. Pay particular attention to any areas of the design where many images are superimposed. Perseverance and patience are required at this stage.
4 When you are satisfied that the surface is absolutely flat, apply three further coats of varnish, polishing the surface with no. 120 wet-and-dry sandpaper between applications to produce a very smooth, dull finish.

WAXING

1 Mix together equal amounts of beeswax and cabinetmaker's polish and warm the mixture (microwaving on high for 20 seconds is an ideal method). Spread the wax evenly over the surface with a soft, lint-free cloth, working on a small area at a time.

> **NOTE**
> *The varnishing techniques described apply to polyurethane varnish only. Traditional varnishes need a slightly different technique and much longer curing times between coats.*

2 Before the wax dries too hard, wipe the surface with a damp cloth, using a brisk, circular motion. Polish with a soft, dry cloth.
3 If necessary, apply a second coat of wax to achieve a hard, glossy appearance. Wax the object again from time to time to maintain the smooth, silky finish.

MICROMESHING

If you intend your project to last a long time – and perhaps be handed down through generations – you may wish to finish the project using micromesh techniques, rather than waxing. Micromesh kits contain products to cut and polish the varnish, creating the effect of fine porcelain. This glow will last indefinitely, whereas ordinary polishes need to be reapplied every six months or so. Micromesh kits are available from craft shops.

PROBLEMS AND SOLUTIONS
Air bubbles

Using a scalpel, carefully make a small slit, preferably on a design line or any other unobtrusive place. Lift each edge of the cut and insert a little glue beneath the image. Press the glue further under the image and then press it toward the slit to expel air and excess glue. Allow the glue to dry, and camouflage the area if necessary with an oil-based pencil.

Build-ups and drips

Do not sand these off, as sanding will leave dark marks. Slice off the excess varnish with a scalpel and allow the underneath varnish to dry thoroughly. Then carry on varnishing.

Sanding through varnish

Stop sanding immediately. Color with an appropriate oil-based pencil, smudge, seal, and continue varnishing.

Flower & foliage drying

Flower drying is a perfect way of preserving nature's beauty. Handle plant material gently, and let your imagination run riot when you are arranging flowers in a bouquet or picture.

Foliage and flowers suitable for dried floral arrangements can be prepared in a number of ways. Most of the floral art projects in this book use flowers and leaves that have been pressed, air dried or silica gel dried.

PICKING THE FLOWERS
The early morning of a dry day is the best time to pick flowers for drying. Pick only blooms in perfect, blemish-free condition, and make sure that they are free of moisture.

PRESSING
This method is used to preserve foliage and flowers that are fairly flat when in their natural state – such as maidenhair fern, pansies, freesias, anemones and simple daisies – and that are to be used in flat arrangements, such as pictures, and on objects like candles and book covers. Most leaves retain their color while they are being pressed, but the chlorophyll that gives leaves their green color disintegrates when exposed to light. You can preserve the color of leaves by spraying them with light-fast natural dyes, which are available from most florists and florists' suppliers.
1 Spread out the plant material evenly on several sheets of absorbent paper (newspaper will do). Make sure the sprays do not overlap, otherwise they will stick together.
2 Place several layers of absorbent paper over the flowers and foliage. Cover the entire surface with something fairly heavy, such as a sheet of thick glass or large books.
3 Leave in a well-ventilated place, checking occasionally to make sure

the leaves and flowers are not sticking to the surface of the paper. The length of time plant material takes to dry depends on humidity and the thickness of the material, but check after about 10 days, and then every few days after that. Two to three weeks is a normal drying time in summer, but it may take up to six weeks in winter.

AIR DRYING
This is the simplest and most common method of preserving plant material, but it should be used only for foliage and flowers that do not wilt easily, such as straw flowers, paper daisies, baby's breath, globe amaranth, statice, delphinium, lavender and hydrangeas. Do not use this method for flowers that are very fleshy or have long stems or large heads, because shrinkage will alter their shape.

1 Sort the leaves and flowers into small bunches and remove any excess foliage from the lower stems.
2 In a dry, warm, dark and airy place, either stand the bunches upright in an empty container or secure the ends of the stems with string and suspend them upside down. The plant material will take a week or so to dry, depending on the size of the individual pieces and their moisture content.

SILICA GEL DRYING
Silica gel is a chemical compound that absorbs moisture. When dry, it takes the form of fine blue crystals, which gradually turn pink as they absorb moisture. The crystals can be used over and over again if you dry them in a warm oven after each use and store them in an airtight container.

Plant material dried with silica gel retains its form and color very well. Suitable flowers for silica gel drying include roses, zinnias, anemones, poppies, shasta daisies, gerberas and Canterbury bells. Only flowers of the same or similar varieties, which will dry in the same time, should be placed in the same container of gel.
1 Cover the bottom of a plastic airtight container with a layer of silica gel 2 cm deep.

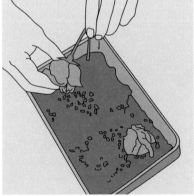

2 Study the shape and bulk of the flowers and decide which way they should lie. Some will dry best when laid upright, some face down, and others when laid sideways. If you want to preserve long flower heads (such as delphiniums) that are likely to be squashed by the weight of the gel, support them from below with notched pieces of cardboard.

3 Use a small scoop to cover each bloom carefully with the gel crystals. As you work, separate the petals to make sure that all surfaces are well covered. Use a small artist's brush to work the crystals into any small, multi-petaled blooms.

4 When the blooms are completely covered with the silica gel, seal the box and put it aside.

5 After two days, carefully pour off enough silica gel to expose the tips of one or two flowers. If the petals are papery to the touch, remove them from the gel immediately, otherwise they will dry out too much and become extremely brittle. If the blooms are still soft, replace the gel and wait one or two more days before checking again.

6 If the petals are dry but the base of the flower (calyx) is not, brush or shake the gel from the dry petals and leave only the calyx covered with the gel. Check again in one or two days, and remove when the calyx has dried.

7 When the blooms are ready, remove them from the gel and brush them gently, making sure that you remove all traces of the crystals. If you are not using the flowers immediately, store them in an airtight container with a small amount of the gel to keep the atmosphere dry.

CAUTION
Always wear a mask and gloves while working with silica gel, as it gives off a hazardous dust when it is handled.

ATTACHING FALSE STEMS
Silica-dried foliage and flowers can rarely be dried with their natural stems. You will need to attach artificial stems to the blooms before you can use them in most arrangements.

Using a hot glue gun, put a small dab of glue in the hollow of the residual stem of the flower. Insert 0.7 or 0.9 gauge wire into the hollow and hold it in place until the glue hardens. Then mask the join with green florist's tape.

Alternatively, hold a length of 0.7 or 0.9 gauge wire firmly against the stem and bind it in place with green tape. Continue winding the tape down the wire until it is covered.

Gluing
Silica-dried flowers must be glued to give them stability and to prevent the petals from falling off.

Hold a single bloom upside down. Run a thin ribbon of fast-drying, transparent glue around the petals where they join the calyx. If any petals have broken off during the drying process, glue them back into place.

Waxing
The backs of silica-dried flowers should be waxed to stop them wilting in hot, humid weather. Use the following method.

1 Place pieces of paraffin wax in a small heat-proof bowl or container. (You can use white household candles for this.)

2 Melt the wax by placing the container in a small saucepan of boiling water and heating until the wax resembles clear water. Do not heat the wax in a pot placed directly on the stove, as it is extremely flammable when overheated.

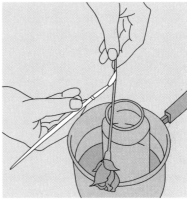

3 Using a small artist's paintbrush, carefully coat the backs of the flowers with the melted wax, starting at the ends of the stems and working toward the tips of the petals.

4 Wax the blooms one at a time, holding them upside down until the wax hardens. Repeat this process two or three times if necessary, taking care that you do not get any wax on the front of the blooms.

Sealing
To complete the preservation, seal silica-dried flowers with a flat (matte) plastic spray sealer, available from florists' suppliers. The spray protects the flowers from moisture and humidity, and prevents them from wilting. As the sealer fumes are very volatile, always wear a face mask and spray outdoors on a sunny, windless day.

1 Ensure that the flowers are completely free of silica gel.

2 Hold the spray can upright, about 12–14 cm from the surface of the flower, and apply a light coat, using a gentle, side-to-side motion.

3 Wait 30 minutes and apply a second coat. Allow to dry.

Folk art

Folk art is the traditional craft of painting the surfaces of common household items with decorative natural forms.

Folk art techniques are very simple. All you need are artist's acrylic paints and brushes, sponges and rags.

EQUIPMENT AND SUPPLIES
Paints
In this book we have cited specific brand names and colors for some projects. However, you can use any good-quality artist's acrylic paints. Most arts and crafts supply outlets have paint charts that you can use to match colors from different brands.

For most projects, you must apply a base coat first to give a smooth, even colored surface on which to build the design. Use an opaque enamel paint mixed with sealer. Folk art paints designed specifically for use as a base coat are ready mixed with sealer.

To produce an antique effect, you will need oil paint (usually burnt umber, which is available in small tubes) and commercially prepared antiquing medium. Alternatively, make your own antiquing medium by mixing three parts gum arabic turpentine and two parts boiled linseed oil.

Brushes
You will need round and flat paintbrushes, which are available in many sizes, and several liner brushes. To apply the base coat, you will need a small decorating brush.

Brush sizes are specified in all projects. However, these are suggestions only, because sizes can vary between manufacturers and because brush size is a matter of individual preference and experience. Practice the basic painting techniques on paper before you begin your project, and experiment with different-sized brushes to find which suits you best.

For the best results, it is important to wash the paint completely out of your brushes between colors and after a painting session.

Palette
Any smooth, flat surface, about the size of a dinner plate, can be used as a palette. Cover the palette with plastic wrap and discard the wrap after use. In this way you can use the palette many times and store it easily.

PREPARING SURFACES
Old metal
1 Remove all rust with a wire brush or sandpaper, clean the surface with methylated spirits, and coat the object with a rust-inhibiting metal primer. Alternatively, you can save hours of work on a large project if you have the article professionally sandblasted and primed. (This is not an expensive procedure, and all cities and most towns have sandblasting companies.)
2 When the surface is thoroughly dry and clean, apply a base coat of flat enamel paint.

New metal
1 Clean the surface thoroughly with vinegar to remove any greasy residue left by the galvanizing process.
2 Apply a sealer and dry according to the manufacturer's instructions.
3 When thoroughly dry and clean, apply a base coat of flat enamel paint.

Terra-cotta
Coat both the inside and the outside of the container with sealer to stop water from seeping through the porous terra-cotta and lifting the design. Sealing also reduces brush drag when you apply the paint.

Wood
Remove any peeling or bubbled paint with paint stripper, and sand surfaces smooth. On both new and old wood, mix sealer with the base color and apply two coats, sanding lightly between coats. (Folk art base-coat paints are already mixed with sealer.)

PAINTING TECHNIQUES
Let each coat of paint dry thoroughly before applying the next coat – the previous coat will pull up or streak if you apply another coat too soon. For the best results, leave the piece to cure for several days before varnishing.

There are certain brush techniques common to folk art. If you are new to the craft, it is a good idea to practice these strokes on paper before you attempt any projects.

Comma stroke
The comma stroke consists of a downward stroke with a blunt head and a tapering tail. It is the most important stroke in folk art painting.

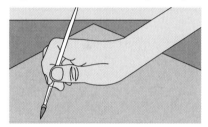

1 Load a round brush with paint. Touch the tip of the brush to the painting surface.

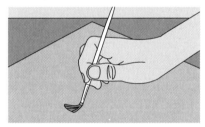

2 Press the brush down onto the ferrule (the metal portion of the brush between the bristles and the handle). At the same time, bring the handle to a completely upright position. This will make the bristles flare out.

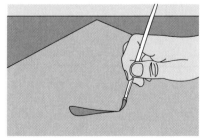

3 Pull the brush toward you, at the same time taking the pressure off the bristles to allow the brush to return to its normal pointed shape.

Side-loading

Flatten a brush, which you have already loaded with the first color, to a wedge shape, and swipe one edge of the brush through the second color. When painting, keep the side-loaded color uppermost if you want it to appear at the beginning of the stroke and underneath if you want it to appear at the end of the stroke.

Double-loading: method 1

Load the brush with one color. Then pick up a second color on the tip of the brush and paint the stroke. The second color will dominate at first, but will blend into the main color at the end of the stroke.

Double-loading: method 2

1 Side-load one corner of a flat brush generously with one color, then load the other corner with a second color.
2 With the tip of the brush on the palette, move the brush from side to side. The two colors will merge toward the center of the brush.

Dry-brushing

Dry-brushing is used to highlight or to shade, and to create fuzzy, roughly defined areas of color.
1 Squeeze the color you want to use onto the palette and leave the paint to thicken.
2 Clean the brush and wipe it dry with paper towels. Flatten the brush in the thickened paint, and then wipe most of the paint from the brush with a paper towel.
3 Lightly stroke on the color, using just the tip of the brush to make soft, fuzzy lines.

Floating a color

This technique is used to create a blended wash of color.
1 Wet a flat brush and wipe off the excess water so that the bristles are damp but not dripping.
2 Dip one corner of the brush into the paint and then, on the palette, move the brush from side to side in the one spot until the paint blends across the bristles.
3 Place the edge of the brush

with the most paint onto the line to be shaded or highlighted. Apply the paint, following the shape of the line, to form a light ribbon of color.
4 Before you reload with further color, rinse the brush thoroughly.

Back-to-back floating

This technique involves floating a color with the brush facing one way, then turning the brush over and floating the same color so that it butts against the first float.

Sponging

This technique produces a textured surface. Use two or more colors to create a textured blend of colors.
1 Dip a section of a small natural sponge, or a scrunched-up rag, into one color.
2 If more than one color is being used, turn the sponge and dip a clean section into another color. Repeat this procedure for a third color.
3 Press the sponge onto the palette to get rid of any excess paint.
4 Lightly bounce the sponge across the surface of the article being painted, turning the sponge frequently so that a variety of colors appear next to one another. The base coat can be covered completely with the sponging, or it can be left to show through.

Wet-on-wet technique

In this method of highlighting and shading, the colors are made to blend into each other. The technique is especially useful on large areas of background.
1 Load a brush with the base color and dip it into drying retarder. Then apply the final layer of the base coat.
2 Before the base coat dries, stroke in the shading and highlighting colors, blending the inner edges of the strokes into the base coat.

ANTIQUING

Antiquing is done after painting to give an aged effect to a piece of work by mellowing the colors.
1 Allow all paint to dry completely, and then rub a light coat of antiquing medium onto the painted area with a

soft cloth. This prevents too much color being absorbed into your painted design.
2 Squeeze a touch of burnt umber artist's oil paint onto another cloth and rub it on to the areas to be darkened. For a darker effect, rub the whole piece lightly with the oil paint and then, in the areas to be highlighted, rub it off with the turpentine and oil mixture.
3 Leave the paint to dry for a few days before varnishing.

CRACKLING

This technique causes paint to crack, giving an old, weathered appearance to the work. It is achieved with crackling medium, which is available from craft shops. Apply crackling medium according to the manufacturer's instructions.

VARNISHING

Varnishing helps to protect your project. If you have used acrylic paints, you can apply a water-based varnish, which is much easier to use than oil-based products. However, they cannot generally be used over oil-based paints. Read the manufacturer's instructions carefully.

Varnish is available with a variety of finishes, including flat, semigloss and gloss, depending on what type of effect you want. Some varnishes can also be bought in spray cans.

ART TERMS

Load the brush: Put paint onto the paintbrush.
Base coat: A coat of paint that is applied to an object in smooth, even strokes to give an opaque, single-colored background for the design.
Highlight: A color lighter than the main color of an object, applied to produce a three-dimensional effect.
Shading: A dark tint, applied on the opposite side of an object from the highlight to produce a three-dimensional effect.

Papier-mâché

All you need to make papier-mâché is scrap paper, white glue or wallpaper paste, paints – and a lively imagination. It is an ideal craft for children, as it is inexpensive and enjoyably messy.

Papier-mâché is a method of using torn paper or paper pulp and glue to create light but sturdy objects in a variety of shapes and finishes. The appearance varies according to the type of paper used, the shape of the mold, and the way the paper is torn.

SELECTING THE PAPER

The best types of paper to use are newspaper, used photocopy paper, brown paper, wrapping paper, colored paper, computer printout, telephone directories and tissue paper. The lighter and thinner the paper, the smoother the finish. Do not use shiny, waxed or waterproof paper – they do not absorb glue or paint very well.

Tissue paper will give the project a soft texture and an attractive color. However, it can be difficult to work with, as it pulls apart easily.

Newspaper and sturdy paper towels are the best papers for building up shapes, particularly the initial layers around a wire mold. Once you have made the basic shape, you can use a finer paper on the outer layers.

Paper has a grain, just as fabric does. Find the grain by tearing in several directions until you find the easiest, smoothest direction. Tear all the strips in this direction. Always tear the paper rather than cutting it, because the rough ends will mesh together more smoothly.

The length and width of the strips you tear depend on the object to be covered. You can use pieces up to 3" wide to cover big, flat surfaces, but you will need smaller, thinner pieces (some as small as postage stamps) when you are making small pieces or working on fine details.

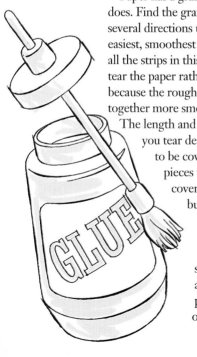

MOLDS

You can use bowls, plates and blown-up balloons as molds. Cover the mold with petroleum jelly before you begin gluing, so that it is easy to remove when the papier-mâché is dry. Fine-gauge chicken wire can also be used to make basic shapes. Cut the wire and mold it into shape, and then twist the wire ends together so that they are secure and the join is smooth with no jagged edges protruding.

GLUE

The best glues to use are nontoxic white glue or wallpaper paste. Mix wallpaper glue using 10 parts water and one part glue. Mix white glue with an equal amount of water to thin it to a milky consistency. White glue dries quickly, so complete all preparations before starting work. As white glue can stain, ensure that both you and your work area are well protected.

COVERING THE MOLD

1 Make sure all surfaces in your work area are well covered, then mix the glue and prepare the mold. Tear the paper into strips of the right size and soak them in the glue or paste until they are completely saturated.
2 Smooth a layer of glued paper strips onto the mold, laying them all in the same direction and smoothing out any wrinkles so that the paper does not dry ridged. If ridges do develop, you can sand the object back when it is dry.
3 To strengthen an object, let the first layer of paper dry, then stick strips of masking tape over the top. Place the second layer of strips at right angles to the first layer to strengthen the piece and to make it easier to see which areas are not totally covered.
4 Go on adding layers of paper until you are satisfied that the paper is thick enough to hold its shape and strong

enough to withstand wear and tear. If you are using white paper, reserve it for the last layer.

DRYING

Drying time depends on the size of the papier-mâché piece and the number of paper layers. For a large object with several layers of paper, leave it in a warm place for approximately 12 hours per layer. Smaller objects with fewer layers will take less time.

Do not leave the object to dry in direct sunlight as this may make it warp or crack. For quicker drying, place the object in a very cool oven or an airing cupboard for several hours. Whatever drying method you use, the object will shrink slightly when dry.

PAINTING AND FINISHING

1 When dry, sand any rough edges or wrinkles back with fine sandpaper. If you did not use white paper in your final layer, apply two coats of white acrylic paint as a base. This covers up the newsprint and provides a light, smooth background to paint on. It has the additional advantage of making the finished colors more luminous.
2 Over the base of white paper or paint, apply the final colors. Thin the paint slightly so that it spreads easily, and then apply two coats to give a good strong color.
3 Make sure each coat of paint is dry before adding the next. If the paint is not allowed to dry completely, it may crack. If this happens, sand the object back with fine sandpaper and repaint.
4 Add any fine details to the painted article with black India ink.
5 As an alternative to painting your papier-mâché, you can create different finishes by using such materials as colored paper or tissue paper for the last layer. If you use foil or shiny paper, you will need a suitable glue.
6 Although not essential, an acrylic sealer brushed over the paint will strengthen the object and enhance its colors. Apply several coats of clear acrylic sealer, allowing each coat to dry before applying the next.

Stenciling

Stenciled motifs can add an individual touch to any number of simple household items.

MAKING STENCILS

Cut stencils from sheets of semi-transparent acetate film or treated manila cardboard. Transparent film is easier to use, because you can trace the design straight onto it and can see what is happening through the film. If you use cardboard, you will need to waterproof it first by saturating it in a mixture of equal parts of linseed oil and turpentine. Leave it to dry for about 30 minutes, then remove excess linseed oil with a paper towel.

1 If you are using clear film, trace the design directly onto the material, using a fine-tipped permanent marker pen. If you are using cardboard, trace the design onto tracing paper and then, using transfer (graphite) paper and a stylus or empty ballpoint pen, transfer the design onto the cardboard. (See page 343 of "Tracing, transferring & scaling.")

2 Place the stencil material with the traced design on a cutting mat or any other suitable surface. Using a craft knife, cut along the lines of the traced design. Work from the center of the design outward. Always cut toward your body and away from the hand you are using to steady the stencil.

3 When cutting around curved edges, swivel the plastic or cardboard around the knife to create flowing edges, rather than trying to maneuver the knife around the curve.

4 If you accidentally cut beyond the guideline, repair both sides of the stencil with strips of masking tape.

POSITIONING THE STENCIL

Apply a light mist of spray adhesive to the back of the stencil and attach it to the surface to be decorated. The adhesive will hold the stencil in place and help to prevent paint from bleeding under the edges of the stencil and ruining the crisp outline. When the stencil starts to unstick, apply another light coat of adhesive. Alternatively, secure the edges of the stencil with masking tape.

APPLYING THE PAINT

The paint is applied to the surface of the object through the holes in the stencil material. The idea is to build up the color on the object gradually. Colors can be blended and textures controlled by a range of methods.

Stippling or pouncing

This is the traditional method of stenciling. A stiff stenciling brush is used to stipple paint onto the surface. If you do not have a stenciling brush, trim the bristles of an ordinary, wide, round paintbrush.

1 Dip the brush into the paint, and remove the excess paint by tapping the brush onto scrap paper.

2 Holding the brush vertically, apply the paint to the stencil cut-out with a light, up-and-down pouncing movement. Begin lightly and do not overload the brush with paint. If you apply too much paint it may bleed under the outline of the stencil.

Rolling

This is an alternative method of applying paint that produces a smooth, flat finish. Dip a small foam roller into the paint and roll it backward and forward on some scrap paper until it is nearly dry. Apply the roller to the stencil cut-out.

Sponging

This method allows you to control the texture of the paint. Use a fine, uniformly textured, synthetic sponge for a smooth finish, and a natural sponge for a more textured finish.

1 Fold the sponge to make a small pad. Dip it lightly into the paint and then force out any excess paint by dabbing the sponge on a paper towel.

2 Using either an up-and-down pouncing motion or a light swirling motion, fill in the stencil cut-out.

Soft brushing

Using a softer stencil brush allows you to blend several colors in a gentle, controlled way.

1 Dip the brush into the paint and remove any excess by moving the brush backward, forward and in a circular motion on a paper towel. Make sure that the paint is evenly distributed on the bristles to a depth of a few millimeters.

2 Holding the brush upright, apply the color using a soft circular motion, as if you were dusting the surface of a table.

3 Repeat steps 1 and 2 with other colors, allowing the colors to blend into each other in some places.

AEROSOL SPRAY PAINTS

These paints can be applied in thin, even coats, giving a smooth, regular finish. Always use aerosol sprays in a well-ventilated area.

1 Attach newspaper or lightweight cardboard to the outside edges of the stencil with masking tape to protect the area immediately surrounding the stencil from paint drift.

2 For the best results, release the paint in short, sharp bursts using a pumping action, while holding the can directly in front of the stencil and about 15 cm away from it.

CARING FOR STENCILS

- Wipe off any excess paint as soon as you remove the stencil from the work. Make sure any remaining paint is dry before you apply the stencil again.
- Store stencils in plastic envelopes for using again.

Woodworking

Learn basic woodworking skills, and you will be able to make toys and household articles. Make sure your working area is large enough to work comfortably and store tools neatly.

LUMBER

Lumber is generally either softwood or hardwood. There are also a number of sheet materials made from wood or wood pulp. These include plywood, particle board or chipboard, medium density fiberboard (MDF) and hardboard. All these materials have their own special characteristics and limitations, so the type of lumber to be used has been specified in each project. If you wish to substitute one wood for another, make sure that it is suitable for the job.

WORKBENCH

Any firm working surface, such as a bench in the garage or an old, sturdy table, can be used as a workbench.

MEASURING TOOLS

To ensure your work is accurate, you will need the following tools.
• A retractable tape for measuring
• A steel ruler for measuring, for using as a straight edge when cutting with a knife, and for determining whether a surface is even
• A try-square for marking and testing right angles

> #### CAUTION
> *Working with wood can be dangerous, as tools are sharp and wood can splinter and chip. It is important to wear suitable clothes and use the appropriate safety equipment.*
> • *Wear sturdy shoes that cover your feet completely.*
> • *Wear safety goggles whenever flying debris or dust might be hazardous to your eyes.*
> • *Always clamp wood firmly so that you are confident that it cannot shift while you are working on it.*

• A spirit level for testing whether surfaces are level or "plumb." If the air bubble in the glass indicator on the spirit level is dead center, the surface you are testing is level.

VISES AND CLAMPS

Portable vises, which are attached to the bench with thumb screws, and C-clamps (sometimes known as G-clamps), are very useful for holding wood steady and for clamping glued sections together until they are dry.

HANDSAWS

There are various types of handsaws. Each type is suitable for performing specific tasks.

Coping saw

Designed for cutting curves and holes close to the edge of a piece of wood, a coping saw has a fine, removable blade that is held taut in a U-shaped frame. (A hacksaw is similar in design, but is used for cutting metal.)

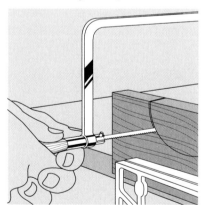

1 With the wood clamped firmly in a vise, grip the handle of the saw with both hands. Following the marked guide line carefully, aim to make one continuous cut if possible.
2 The blade of a coping saw can be rotated around its axis. As you progress around the curve, periodically rotate the blade to follow the direction of the cut.

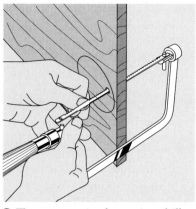

3 To cut out a circular section, drill a hole inside the circle large enough to accommodate the width of the blade. Unclamp the blade from one end of the frame, thread the blade through the hole and reclamp the blade. Proceed as outlined in steps 1 and 2.

Crosscut saw

This saw is used to cut large blocks of lumber, as well as sheet materials such as plywood, chipboard and fiberboard. It has a long, flexible blade designed to cut across the grain of the wood. The flexible blade allows you to adjust the cutting line if it begins to wander. The saw leaves a rough cutting edge, which must be sanded smooth.

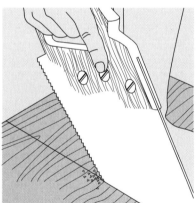

1 Grip the handle with your index finger pointing down along the handle to stabilize and guide while you cut. Place the saw at the beginning of the cutting line.
2 Cut a starting groove by making a few short cuts back toward your body. Use the thumb of your free hand to guide and steady the blade.
3 Hold the saw in the starting groove at an angle of 45° to the cutting surface (this is the angle at which the

POWER SAW SAFETY

- Keep the electric cord well away from the blade. Plug the cord into a circuit breaker so that the current will be cut off if the saw cuts into the cord.
- Check that the blade is the right way round when fitting it.
- Do not remove the saw from the wood until it has stopped.
- Switch off the power and pull the plug from the socket whenever the saw is not in use, even for short spells.
- Keep children out of the room while you are using the saw.
- Wear safety goggles when cutting, as flying dust can injure your eyes.
- Make sure the blade will not cut anything underneath the piece you are working on.
- Never use blades that are damaged, blunt or bent.
- Replace the cord if the sheathing is damaged. Check that the outer sheathing runs right into the saw housing and the plug.

teeth of the saw are designed to cut) and saw backward and forward in

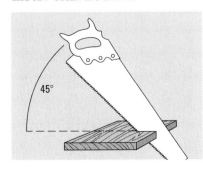

long, easy strokes, allowing the weight of the saw to do the work.

Fretsaw

This saw is used for detailed work. It is similar to the coping saw, except that it has a finer, more flexible blade.

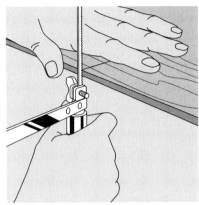

1 Sit in front of the work and hold the saw upright in one hand.
2 Use your free hand to hold the wood, and cut on the downstroke.

Keyhole saw

A keyhole saw is used to cut out shapes that are too far from the edges of the wood to be cut with a coping saw. A keyhole saw has a narrow replaceable blade that is clamped into a wooden or metal handle. It is gripped like a screwdriver.

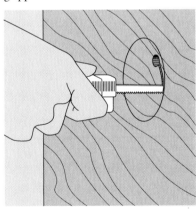

1 Within the shape to be removed, drill a hole large enough to accommodate the saw blade.
2 Insert the blade into the hole and cut with a back and forth motion.

Ripsaw

A ripsaw is designed to cut along the wood grain. It is similar to the crosscut saw, but has coarser teeth. It is

unsuitable for cutting across the grain, as the teeth leave a jagged edge. Grip the ripsaw in the same way as the panel saw, but hold it at an angle of 60° to the cutting surface.

Backsaw (tenon saw)

This is an excellent, general-purpose saw. It is a short, fine-toothed crosscut saw with a reinforced metal spine to hold the blade rigid. It cuts accurately and smoothly, and is especially good for cutting joints.

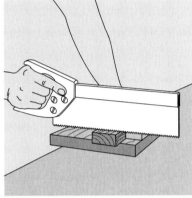

1 Grip the handle with your index finger lying alongside the handle.
2 Saw using a back and forth motion, applying light pressure on the forward stroke. To keep the backsaw level so that you cut square to the wood, make sure that your forearm is in line with the spine of the saw.

POWER SAWS

Power saws take the physical effort out of sawing and get the job done in a fraction of the time that it would take using a handsaw.

Hole saw

These are sold as attachments for power drills. They come in a range of diameters and will cut perfect holes up to 6 cm in diameter. Holes can be cut to greater depth if you stop from time to time and clear out waste wood before proceeding.

Jigsaw

Jigsaws are speedy, powerful and highly maneuverable. A jigsaw fitted with the right blade can cut straight lines and intricate curves in wood, laminate or metal.

MITER BOX

A miter box is a saw guide used for cutting the precise 45° angles required for making mitered right-angled joints. It consists of a simple wooden frame with two raised sides, in which there are pre-cut slots to guide the blade of the saw.

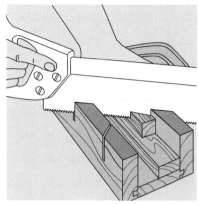

1 Clamp the wood firmly against the far side of the miter box and use a backsaw to cut it. If you are miter-cutting molding, ensure that it is clamped the right way around.
2 Make sure that you hold the saw horizontally to avoid cutting into the sides of the guide slots.

DRILLS

Wheelbrace drill

This type of drill is used to make holes up to 6 mm in diameter. Grip the straight handle with one hand and use the other hand to turn the drive wheel.

Brace

A brace is used to drill holes with a diameter greater than 6 mm and a depth of more than 38 mm. Grip the rounded handle with one hand to hold the brace steady and turn the offset handle with your other hand.

Power drill

With a power drill you can drill holes in almost any surface in a fraction of the time taken by a hand drill.

Drill bit

A bit is the detachable drilling tool that fits into the end of the drill. Drill bits come in various thicknesses, depending on the size of the hole you

want to make. The bit is inserted into the jagged jaws of the drill (called the chuck). The jaws are then tightened by means of a chuck key inserted in the barrel of the drill.

Drilling holes for screws

When drilling holes for screws, always use a drill bit smaller than the diameter of the solid core of the screw. For softwoods use a smaller bit than for hardwoods, so that the screw has to bite deeper into the wood and thus will hold the work securely.

Countersinking screws

Drill a hole in the usual way. Change to a drill bit 1 mm larger in diameter than the screw head, and drill a shallow depression at the top of the screw hole. The head of the screw will now lie flush with the surface. Alternatively, use a countersink bit.

SCREWDRIVERS

Screwdrivers have either flat blades for screwing conventional, single-slot screws, or special heads for cross-slotted screws (Phillips screwdrivers).

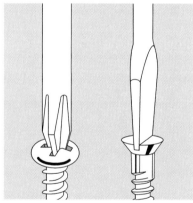

1 Choose a screwdriver that is the right size for the screw. If the blade is too narrow, it will distort the screw head; if it is too wide, the blade will tend to slip, damaging the wood.
2 When using a screwdriver, always hold it so that the blade is squarely in the slot of the screw.

PLANES

A plane is used to finish wood to an exact size. Planing is always done in a forward direction away from the body and following the grain of the wood.

Make sure that the wood is clamped firmly and that the plane blade is not set too deep, otherwise it will dig into the surface.

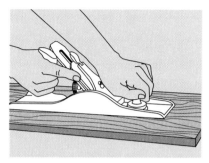

1 Hold the plane by the handle and the small knob at the front.
2 As you make each stroke, smoothly transfer downward pressure from the front to the back of the plane.

Planing the end grain

1 Clamp the end firmly in the vise to avoid vibration.
2 Plane from each end, toward the center of the wood to prevent the wood from splitting.
3 Check frequently that the planed end is square and level, using a try-square and a straight edge.

CHISELS

A chisel is used for cutting joints, rabbets and shallow recesses, or for shaping work. If your chisel is kept sharp, hand pressure should be sufficient for most jobs. If a great deal of wood is to be removed and more pressure is required, use a wooden mallet to tap the end of the chisel. When using

---

CAUTION

The sharpness of a chisel and the force applied to it make it one of the most dangerous tools to use.
* *Take considerable care to clamp the wood firmly so that it will not slip as you work and so that you have both hands free.*
* *Always work away from your hands and your body.*
* *Never place a chisel where it might be knocked to the floor, as the sharp blade could cause serious injury to feet.*

NAILS AND SCREWS

Nails

Nail length depends on the type of wood you are using. For hardwoods, use a nail length that is twice the thickness of the wood; for softwoods, select a nail length three times the thickness of the wood.

Finishing nails are round nails with heads shaped like a bullet. These heads can be punched below the surface of the wood.

Oval finishing nails have heads that are hammered flush with the surface of the wood. They should be inserted so that the longer axis of the head aligns with the grain of the wood.

Wire brads are very fine nails that are used for most of the light projects in this book.

Screws

Flat-head wood screws are used most often in woodwork because they can be tightened to "set" flush with the surface of the wood.

Oval-head wood screws are usually made from shiny plated metals, and are used when appearance is important. They are screwed only down to the countersunk rim, leaving the rounded head exposed and raised.

Round-head screws are most often used with hardware fittings that are not countersunk. If a washer is placed under the head, these screws can also be used for toy wheels or other moving parts.

Self-tapping screws are used for fixing thin metal whenever it is not practicable to use a nut-and-bolt. First drill a hole in the metal slightly smaller than the thread of the screw so that the screw will fit in firmly.

---

a chisel to pare or trim wood to shape, work at a slight angle to the vertical, using both hands in the same way as for cutting across the grain. Shave away a thin slice of wood with each stroke.

1 Clamp the wood firmly, so that you have both hands free.

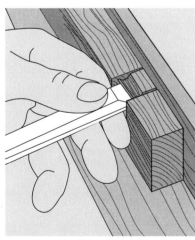

2 To cut with the grain, keep the beveled side of the chisel facing up. Use one hand to guide the blade and the other to apply pressure. Work away from your body and your hands.
3 When cutting across the grain, work from directly above the wood surface. Hold the chisel with your thumb on top of the handle to provide

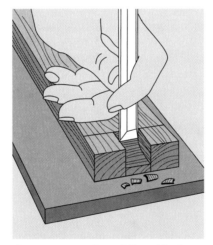

the pressure, and carefully guide the blade with the index finger of your other hand.

HAMMERS

A cross-peen hammer has a flat, tapered end (the peen) opposite the striking head, and is used for light work. A claw hammer has a heavier head and a "claw" for pulling out old or crooked nails.

When you use a hammer, grip it so that the end of the handle extends about 4 cm behind your hand. First tap the nail gently to embed it in the wood, and then swing from the elbow, keeping your wrist straight

and allowing the weight of the hammer to do the work. If the nail is hit at any appreciable angle, it will bend.

To avoid bruising the wood with the hammer when you are driving home a nail, lay a small piece of scrap wood over the head of the nail and hammer it flat against the working wood. Alternatively, use a nail set. Choose one with a point slightly smaller than the head of the nail. Center the point of the nail set on the nail and tap the set with the hammer until the nail head is flush with the surface of the wood.

Removing nails

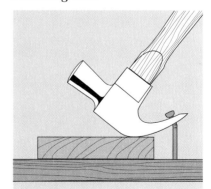

Place a small block of scrap wood under the hammer head to avoid bruising the wood. Slide the claw of the hammer under the head of the nail until the nail is held tight, then pull the handle back.

Hammering a small nail or tack

1 Hold the nail or tack steady between your thumb and index finger, and tap it gently with a cross-peen hammer until the nail stands upright. Drive the nail below the surface.
2 If the nail is too short to hold, push it through a piece of stiff paper. Drive the nail partway below the surface. When the nail is nearly in, tear away the paper.

NAIL SETS

Nail sets are used for driving wire brads or finishing nails below the surface of the wood, or to finish driving in nails where you do not want to mark the surface with a hammer head.

RASPS

Rasps are steel rods covered with raised abrasive metal teeth. They are useful for shaping wood, but are not suitable for finishing, as the metal teeth do not produce a smooth surface. A good general-purpose rasp for woodworking is one about 25 cm long with one flat and one convex side.

FILES

Files are like rasps, except that they have much finer teeth. They produce a smooth finish but will not remove large quantities of wood.

SANDPAPER

Also known as abrasive paper, sandpaper is heavy-duty paper covered with granules of abrasive material. It is generally sold in sheets, which can easily be torn into more manageable pieces. Used for smoothing wood, sandpaper is available in various grades, from coarse (50-60 grade) to very fine (160 to 240 grade).

When sanding wood, first use a coarse paper, and then progressively finer papers, until the wood surface is smooth to the touch. Always work along the grain. To sand flat surfaces, wrap the sandpaper around a block of cork or light wood.

COMPLEX CUTTING WITH BASIC TOOLS

For some projects in this book, you can cut curved edges or holes using only a backsaw (tenon saw) or crosscut saw, a drill, a chisel, a rasp and a file.

Convex curves

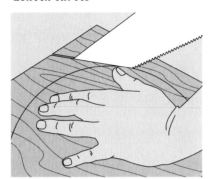

1 Cut the curves roughly to shape, cutting across the corners of the wood and close to the drawn curve.

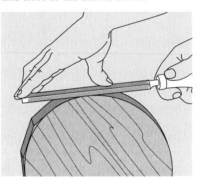

2 Go on cutting off corners until you are as close to the curve line as you can get without cutting into it. Finish the curve with a rasp and a file.

Concave curves

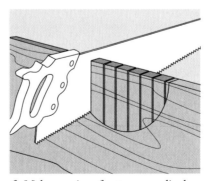

1 Make a series of cuts perpendicular to the edge of the wood, passing through the waste area as far as the marked curve.
2 Cut away the waste between the saw cuts with a chisel.

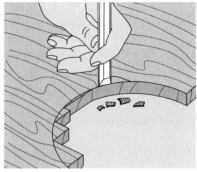

3 Use a chisel to pare the curve close to the marked line. Finish off with a curved rasp and a file.

Small circular holes

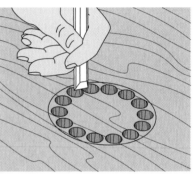

1 Drill a series of adjacent holes just inside the marked circumference.
2 Cut the wood between the holes with a chisel and remove the center.
3 Using the chisel, pare the wood back to the circumference and finish off with a curved rasp and a file.

Large circular holes

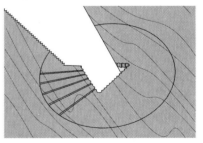

1 Drill a series of adjacent holes within the waste area, in a triangular pattern large enough to take the blade of a backsaw or crosscut saw. Remove the resultant rough triangular shape.
2 Saw radial cuts to the marked circumference. Cut away the waste between the saw cuts with a chisel.
3 Use a chisel to pare the curve close to the marked line. Finish off with a curved rasp and a file.

Tracing, transferring & scaling

If you take the time and trouble to transfer patterns accurately and neatly, it will be much easier to assemble and finish your project to a professional standard.

There are several ways of transferring an outline or a design from a master pattern to the material you are going to work with. The method you use depends on what material you are transferring the pattern to. If the material is transparent or semi-transparent, the best method is to trace the design directly onto the material using an appropriate marker.

If you cannot see through the material, first trace the pattern onto tracing paper and then transfer this working pattern to the material using one of the methods described below.

DIRECT TRACING

To trace a pattern directly onto transparent plastic (as when making stencils), use marker pens especially designed for the purpose, such as the pens used on overhead transparencies.

To trace onto transparent or semi-transparent fabric, place the design under the fabric and trace the lines with a marker. You may find it easier to see the design lines if you use a light box or tape the fabric and working pattern to a window. To trace onto fabric, choose the most suitable marker from the following.

• A water-soluble marker pen washes out in cold water after use.
• A fade-out pen can be used when you cannot wash out the fabric. Marks last up to 48 hours. You should, however, check by marking a piece of scrap fabric and leaving it for two days. Examine the fabric in different lights, including fluorescent, to make sure the marks have disappeared.
• A silver or white marker pencil (or quilter's pencil) can be sharpened to a fine point. Marks can be removed with a fabric eraser.
• A hard lead pencil gives a fine line, but the marks may prove difficult to remove completely.

• A chalk-based dressmaker's pencil has the disadvantage that the marks can brush out, sometimes while you are still working.

TRANSFERRING FROM TRACING

First trace a working pattern from the master pattern onto tracing paper.

Wood, metal, paper and cardboard

Use transfer (or graphite) paper, available from artists' suppliers.
1 Using small pieces of masking tape at each corner, attach the tracing paper to the surface to be decorated.
2 Slip the transfer paper underneath the tracing paper and, using light pressure, trace over the design lines with the tip of a hard pencil or an empty ballpoint pen. You can remove transferred lines with a pencil eraser.

Fabric
Dressmaker's carbon paper
If you need to transfer detailed design lines, one of the easiest methods is to use dressmaker's carbon. Carbon paper comes in several colors, so choose a color that will show on the fabric. The marks made by dressmaker's carbon paper can sometimes

CAUTION
Before you mark your work, always test a fabric marker on a scrap of the fabric you are using to make sure the marks can be removed when you have finished the work. When using water-soluble markers, rinse the fabric under cold water until the marks have completely disappeared. Using hot water or an iron is likely to set the chemicals in the marker, making it impossible to remove the marks.

POSITIONING DESIGNS ON FABRIC

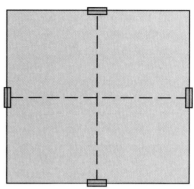

1 Fold and quarter the fabric and crease along the lines. If the crease line will not hold, baste along the fold lines. Pin or tape the fabric to a flat surface.

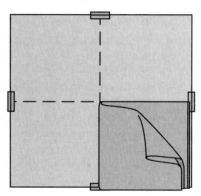

2 Find the center of the design and fold and quarter the traced pattern so that the folded mid-point corresponds with the mid-point of the design. Place the pattern on one quarter of the fabric, aligning center points.

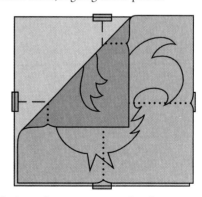

3 Open the pattern out so that the pattern fold lines correspond with the fabric fold lines. Fix the pattern down with masking tape, and then transfer the design to the fabric using the appropriate method.

be difficult to remove, so it is best used when the design lines are to be covered with stitching.

1 Place the pattern in position on the right side of the fabric and pin at the corners. Carefully slip the carbon paper, carbon side down, between the fabric and the pattern.

2 Draw over the design lines using a tracing wheel or a stylus.

Transfer pencil

Some transfer pencils are marketed as water-soluble, but test them on your fabric before you use them.

1 Trace the design onto tracing paper and then turn the paper over and trace over the design lines with the transfer pencil.

2 Place the tracing paper in position on the fabric with the transfer pencil lines against the fabric. Press down on the paper for a few minutes with a warm iron (not hot).

3 Lift the iron to the next area of the paper (do not slide). Without moving the tracing paper, lift a corner to make sure the transfer has taken.

Pricking out

An alternative method of marking simple design outlines is to prick out the design by hand or machine.

To prick out by hand, trace the design onto tracing paper using an ordinary pencil. Pin the tracing in position on the right side of the fabric. Lay the

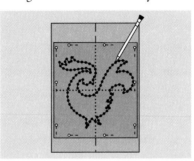

pattern and the fabric over a thick wad of fabric, such as a blanket. Prick holes with a needle through the tracing paper, along the lines of the design. Use a fabric marker to mark dots on the fabric through these holes. Remove the tracing paper and join up the dots on the fabric.

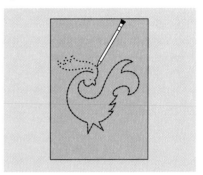

To prick out a simple design very quickly with a sewing machine, remove both the top thread and the bobbin thread from the machine, set the stitch length to about 3 mm and "stitch" along the design lines. Then trace over the outline of holes left by the needle with a suitable washable fabric marker.

SCALING

Sometimes you will want to enlarge or reduce a design – for example, to repeat a stencil design on various articles. The simplest way to do this is to use a photocopier with an enlarging function to copy a pattern or design to the size you want. However, if you do not have access to a photocopier, use the following method to make your design larger.

1 Decide how much bigger you want the design to be and make a note of the desired width. Draw a small grid over

the design and then rule a rectangle around the design.

2 Tape the design to the lower left-hand corner of a sheet of paper. Using a ruler, draw a diagonal line from the bottom left corner of the rectangle to the top right corner, extending the line past the top corner onto the paper. Extend the base of the rectangle to the desired width of your enlargement. Draw a line from this point at right angles to the base of the rectangle, extending it until it crosses the diagonal. Draw the remaining sides of the enlarged rectangle and remove the original design.

3 Onto the enlarged rectangle, measure and draw the same number of rows and columns as you drew over the original design, so that you have an identical grid, but with larger squares than the original.

4 Working square by square, copy the design lines from the original grid onto the corresponding squares on the larger grid. You may find that it is easier to transfer the lines if you first mark dots where the design lines intersect the squares and then connect the dots.

5 To make a design smaller, draw a grid smaller than the design and follow step 4.

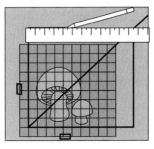

1

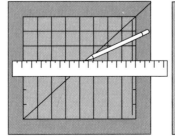

2

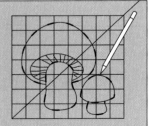

3

4

Gifts & crafts index

Gifts are listed alphabetically, with the principal crafts shown in italics and additional crafts shown in italics and parentheses. The symbol • denotes a gift that is "quick and easy" to make.

EDIBLE GIFTS 271–290

Techniques index

This index covers the techniques section (pages 292–344), which describes the principal crafts required to make the projects. Use it to quickly find the instructions for individual techniques.

General index

Go to "Garden gifts" to find something for a keen gardener, or look under "Clothing" if you want to make a gift for the fashion-conscious.

Key to master pattern pieces

A1 Daisy & bee baby's outfit: *a* Skirt back & front, *b* Front yoke, *c* Back yoke, *d* Sleeve, *e* Sleeve binding, *f* Collar front, *g* Collar back, *h* Bonnet crown, *i* Bonnet brim

A2 "B is for Baby" quilt: *a* Butterfly, *b* Bird, *c* Bear, *d* Bunny, *e* Heart, *f* Bow, *g* Top border, *h* Side & bottom border

A3 Classic christening gown: *a* Front panel, *b* Skirt, *c* Back yoke, *d* Side yoke, *e* Sleeve

A4 Rocking horse overalls: *a* Pants front, *b* Pants back, *c* Front yoke, *d* Back yoke, *e* Leg band

A6 Baby's bootees in soft leather: *a* Front, *b* Side/back, *c* Sole

A7 Jingle bears: *a* Bear shape

B8 Raggedy Anne doll: *a* Head, *b* Front body, *c* Back body, *d* Arm, *e* Leg

B9 Doll's dress: *a* Front, *b* Back

B10 Push-along duck: *a* Body, *b* Wing, *c* Foot, *d* Wheel

B12 Edward Bear suit: *a* Front, *b* Back, *c* Sleeve, *d* Hood front, *e* Hood back, *f* Ear, *g* Paw pad, *h* Mitten

B13 Soft animal toys: *a* Octopus, *b* Koala, *c* Pig, *d* Whale, *e* Frog

B14 Soft rattles for a baby: *a* Handle, *b* Sphere segment

C15 Toddler's table & chairs: *a* Table top, *b* Table leg, *c* Table leg support, *d* Chair back, *e* Chair seat, *f* Chair side/legs, *g* Chair cross bar supports

C16 A very special Christmas stocking: *a* Stocking, *b* Collar, *c* Appliqué design

C17 Mouse bookends: *a* Body, *b* Head, *c* Arm, *d* Foot, *e* Tail

C18 Cuddly cow sweatshirt: *a* Cow design

C19 Personalized name plates: *a* Painting design

C20 Mommy's little helper's apron: *a* Front & back, *b* Shoulder frills

C21 Rock-a-bye doll's cradle: *a* Head, *b* Foot, *c* Side

C22 Balloon shorts: *a* Front/back

C23 Benjamin Bear: *a* Side head, *b* Back head, *c* Front head, *d* Ear, *e* Front body, *f* Back body, *g* Legs, *h* Foot pad, *i* Arm, *j* Paws

D26 Crazy patchwork evening bag: *a* Patchwork design

D27 Stylish soft knapsack: *a* Base, *b* Bag flap, *c* Pocket flap

D28 Beach tote bag & towel: *a* Large seaweed, *b* Small seaweed, *c* Shells, *d* Clam

D29 Pastoral poppy tray: *a* Poppy design

E32 Cream-on-cream cushion: *a* Embroidery design

E35 Monogrammed linen handkerchief *and* Monogrammed towels: *a* Alphabet

E37 Space-saving kitchen dish-towel rack: *a* End piece

E74 Crinolined lady lampshade: *a* Crinolined lady, *b* Daisies, *c* Forget-me-not, *d* Hyacinth

F38 Man's summer nightshirt: *a* Front, *b* Back, *c* Sleeve, *d* Facing, *e* Collar

F39 Rose bouquet blanket box: *a* Large rose design, *b* Small rose design

F40 Connoisseur's wine rack: *a* Scallop pattern, *b* Heart shape

F41 Director's chair: *a* Large strawberry design, *b* Small strawberry design

F42 Rosebud nightgown: *a* Front skirt, *b* Back skirt, *c* Yoke, *d* Sleeve, *e* Yoke facing

F43 Flowery watering can: *a* Flower design & verse

G45 Sewing box: *a* Base, *b* Back panel, *c* Lid front, *d* Lid top, *e* Rear top, *f* Side, *g* Divider, *h* Shelf, *i* Shelf front, *j* Cotton reel holder

G46 Painted apple plate: *a* Background design, *b* Rim design

G47 Iris garden apron: *a* Iris design

G48 Quilted oven cloth & mitt: *a* Mitt pattern

G49 Oak & acorn shelf paper: *a* Oak & acorn design, *b* Bow design

G50 Wooden towel rail: *a* Side piece

G76 Marquetry bookmark: *a* Cat design

G77 Sunflower wall hanging: Circles – *a* 4.5 cm diameter, *b* 3.75 cm diameter, *c* 3.25 cm diameter

H51 Director's chair cover: *a* Main piece, *b* Side piece

H52 Decorative hat & coat rack: *a* Plaque shape with cut-out for mirror

H54 Tulip cushion: *a* Tulip design

H55 Painted planter: *a* Violet design

H56 Fuchsia cushion: *a* Fuchsia design

H58 Simple wooden tray: *a* End piece

H75 Rose-trimmed bed linen: *a* Rose design (sheet), *b* Corner design (sheet), *c* Rose design (pillowcase), *d* Corner design (pillowcase)

I60 Broderie anglaise nightshirt: *a* Front yoke, *b* Front skirt, *c* Back yoke, *d* Back skirt, *e* Sleeve, *f* Front band

I61 Folk art kitchen canisters: *a* Large canister design, *b* Medium canister design, *c* Small canister design, *d* Grapevine design

I62 Chrysanthemum tablecloth: *a* Chrysanthemum design, *b* Scallop pattern

I63 Fast-food station for birds: *a* Side panel

I65 Garden tote box: *a* Large strawberry design, *b* Small strawberry design

I66 Coat-hanger for a wedding dress: *a* Coat-hanger cover with embroidery pattern

I67 Satin bridal horseshoe: *a* Horseshoe shape

J68 New baby sampler: *a* Cross-stitch design, *b* Alphabet

J69 Embroidered table linen: *a* Cross-stitch design

J70 Sweet home sampler: *a* Cross-stitch design, *b* Alphabet

J71 Wedding day sampler: *a* Cross-stitch design, *b* Alphabet

J72 Beaded butterfly evening bag: *a* Butterfly design

J78 Ribbon & needlepoint pincushion: *a* Stitch guide

J79 Needlepoint cushion: *a* Stitch guide

Acknowledgments

Jean Alderton:
A calendar for all seasons

Penny Anderssen:
Découpage desk set

Diana Brandt:
Pastoral poppy tray

April Briscoe:
Folk art frames for baby photos

Ruby Brown:
European Easter eggs

Margaret Burch:
Dried flower wreath

Vicki Carr:
Log cabin quilt

Marilyn Carter:
Doll's dress

Margo Cavill:
Découpage memorabilia box

Coats Patons Crafts
(Coordinator Barbara Lennon):
*Balloon cardigan & striped sweater,
Breakfast tea cozy, Child's hat &
scarf, Crib blanket, Embroidered
table linen, Man's luxury sweater,
Man's scarf & hat, New baby
sampler, Rainbow sweater, Sweet
home sampler, Wedding day sampler*

Kate Coombe:
*Iris garden apron, Painted apple
plate, Personalized name plates,
Strawberry garden chair*

Chris Dawson:
*Beginner's flower press, Country-style
dish rack, Decorative hat & coat rack,
Elegant indoor planter box, Fast-food
station for birds, Marble kitchen
board, Mouse bookends, Push-along
duck, Rock-a-bye doll's cradle, Sewing
box, Space-saving kitchen dish-towel
rack, Toddler's table & chairs,
Wooden towel rail*

Edward Dew:
Home bulletin board

Elena Dickson:
*Coat-hanger for a wedding dress,
Delectable lace collar*

DMC (Coordinator
Effie Mitrofanis):
*Country lace curtain, Lacework
jug cover*

Stephanie Donaldson:
*Autumn wreath, Table centerpiece of
dried flowers*

Rachel Dulsom:
Beaded butterfly evening bag

Jan Eaton:
*Chrysanthemum tablecloth, Daisy &
bee baby's outfit, Tulip cushion*

Brigitte Eckardt:
*Candles with pressed flowers,
Framed wedding bouquet,
Old-fashioned botanical picture*

Rosemary Evans:
Marquetry bookmark

Kate Finnie:
Printed T-shirts

Kate Finnie & Paula McPhail:
Fairy wings & wand

Janet Grice:
"B is for Baby" quilt

Christine Harris:
*Cuddly cow sweatshirt, Fuchsia
cushion, Monogrammed towels,
Sunflower wallhanging*

Alan Hayes:
Sweet-scented solutions

Amanda Ho:
Raffia bag, Raffia sunhat

Colleen Hughes:
*Quilted oven cloth & mitt,
Traditional rag rug*

Mark Hunter:
Braided leather belt

Aristea Kaydos:
Cuddly rag doll

Elizabeth Kaydos:
*Découpage pencil box, Faux finish
bedside table*

Deborah Kneen:
*Flowery watering can,
Luxury handkerchief bag,
Rose bouquet blanket box*

Denise Lawson:
Stylish soft knapsack

Dianne Leeson:
*Balloon shorts, Edward Bear suit,
Fine woolen summer shawl,
Jingle bears*

Sandra Levy:
Parchment window tracery

Marion Loveridge:
Garden carry box

Jessica Maude:
Bead jewelry

Lyn McBride:
Découpage picture frame

Lorell McIntyre:
Painted planter

Paula McPhail:
*A very special Christmas stocking,
Director's chair cover, Easy mothball
bags, Hand-covered photograph
album, Herb-filled sleep pillow,
Man's summer nightshirt, Mommy's
little helper's apron, Old-time
lavender bags, Place mats for a
country kitchen, Rocking horse
overalls, Satin bridal horseshoe*

Beryl Miller:
Soft animal toys

Jennifer Newman:
*Monogrammed linen handkerchief,
Ribbon & lace bridal garter*

Judy Newman:
Handmade hatboxes

Diana Oakley:
*Broderie anglaise nightshirt,
Classic christening gown, Rosebud
nightgown*

Alison Park:
Needlepoint cushion

Marie Platt:
Cream-on-cream cushion

Judy Pullen:
Seagrass basket, Seagrass mat

Albert Richardson:
Basic window box

Susan Roach:
Sculpted floral hair comb

Frances Robinson:
*Connoisseur's wine rack, Dollhouse,
Miniature furniture, Simple wooden
tray, Treasure chest*

Sheridan Rogers &
Katharine Blakemore:
Edible gifts

Skye Rogers:
*Leafy lemon jug, Painted mat,
Snappy sneakers*

Lyn Silver:
*Aromatic beeswax candles,
Birdseed rings, cakes & bells,
Fragrant potpourri*

Nerida Singleton:
*Découpage key chain, Fabric hair
accessories, Fabric necklace*

Di Skarratt:
*Elegant Victorian bows, Flower seeds
in homemade packets, Fragrant herbs
in a terra-cotta pot, Kindergarten
carry bags, Plastic bag dispenser,
Potted plant with bow, Romantic
flowers in a pot, Soft rattles for a
baby, Trimmed hand towels, Wind
chimes*

Mike Spiller:
Sporty clothespin players

Ruth Stoneley:
Crazy patchwork evening bag

Madeleine Strongman:
*Beach tote bag & towel, Crinolined
lady lampshade, Garden sculpture,
Rose-trimmed bed linen, Stenciled
writing paper & envelopes*

Yvonne Theriault:
Folk art kitchen canisters

Tonia Todman:
*Baby's bootees in soft leather,
Handmade writing paper,
Hanging flower basket, Seashell
picture frame, Trinket box*

Gerry Warlow:
Benjamin Bear

Jenny Wilkinson:
*Embroidered baby's T-shirts, Party
pinafore dress*